THE

SHAKER

EXPERIENCE

IN

AMERICA

THE
SHAKER
EXPERIENCE
IN
AMERICA

A History of the

United Society

of Believers

Stephen J. Stein

Yale University Press

New Haven and London

Publication of this volume has been supported by a grant from the National
Endowment for the Humanities, an independent federal agency.

Published with assistance from the Kingsley Trust Association Publication Fund
established by the Scroll and Key Society of Yale College.

Designed by Sylvia Steiner.
Set in Primer type by G&S Typesetters, Inc., Austin, Texas.
Printed in the United States of America by Courier Westford, Inc.,
Westford, Massachusetts.

Library of Congress Cataloging-in-Publication Data

Stein, Stephen J., 1940–
The Shaker experience in America : a history of the United Society of
Believers / Stephen J. Stein.
p.   cm.
Includes bibliographical references and index.
ISBN 0-300-05139-5 (cloth)
      0-300-05933-7 (pbk.)
1. Shakers—United States—History.   I. Title.
BX9766.S74   1992
289'.8'0973—dc20   91-30836 CIP

The paper in this book meets the guidelines for permanence and durability of
the Committee on Production Guidelines for Book Longevity of the Council on
Library Resources.

⊗™

10 9 8 7 6

For

Irene Edith Stein,

my mother,

and

Devonia Sue Stein,

the mother of our children

CONTENTS

FIGURES

TABLES

PREFACE

In 1966 Thomas Merton wrote, "The peculiar grace of a Shaker chair is due to the fact that it was made by someone capable of believing that an angel might come and sit on it." Less than two decades later Mildred Barker, the octogenarian leader of the Believers at Sabbathday Lake, Maine, quipped, "I almost expect to be remembered as a chair or a table." These citations epitomize the dilemma confronting Shaker studies today: the fascination and the preoccupation with material culture have prevented a balanced recovery and interpretation of the past. The current popularity of the society's artifacts has overshadowed the fact that the Shakers chose to call themselves the United Society of Believers, not the United Society of Furniture Makers. This fixation on "things" has begun to block from view the primary reason for the existence of the United Society of Believers in Christ's Second Appearing. In Mildred Barker's words, "There's something special behind" those artifacts. "There's the religion."[1]

Ironically, one casualty of the contemporary surge of interest in the Shakers has been their religion. At times, especially in the popular literature, we look in vain for any mention of the religious dimension of Shakerism, or we find a mélange of sentimental spiritual values imposed on the material culture. We are more likely to be instructed on how to assemble an oval box or appraise a candle stand than we are to learn that the Shakers were once a radical religious sect despised, hated, harassed, and some times physically persecuted by fellow Americans. Even in much of the scholarly literature the image of the Shakers bears little resemblance to historical reality. Their prophetic message has been softened, if not muted, and the ethical implications of the Believers' condemnation of the "world" glossed over and often ignored. The result is a highly selective, idealized picture that perpetuates an uncritical perspective on the society. The Shakers have become icons for many.

This volume, surprisingly, is the first general history of the United Society. Numerous earlier accounts have dealt with local communities or limited time periods, but never has any book covered systematically the full range of Shaker experience. For example, the most influential study, Edward Deming Andrews's *The People Called Shakers,* provides a highly sympathetic account that focuses almost exclusively on antebellum Believers. Andrews pays scant attention to the twentieth century. Another important work, Priscilla J. Brewer's *Shaker Communities, Shaker Lives,* tells the story of eastern Shakerism to 1904. More specialized studies, such as Daniel W. Patterson's *The Shaker Spiritual* and Clarke Garrett's *Spirit Possession and Popular Religion,* treat particular issues and themes. These and many other volumes are useful, but none attempts a general history of the society.[2]

In this account I have brought the story of the Shakers, East and West, down to the present. I am concerned equally with developments in the community and within the larger cultural context. Those who attempt to explain the society's development from an esoteric perspective alone often fail to recognize fundamental parallels between the United Society and other religious groups. Although striking analogies do exist between the evolution of Shakerism and that of its cultural host, the American republic, those who focus exclusively on external forces in their interpretation of the Believers' history frequently appear blind to the distinctive dynamics of Shaker life and thought. Those who ignore the religious center of the society's experience are guilty of projecting their own fantasies on the historical record. Those who reduce Shaker religion to some other reality may possess a valid theoretical insight, but they stand in fundamental tension with *the* essential element of the tradition. Those who pay little or no attention to Shakerism after the Civil War or during the twentieth century miss the obvious continuities within the experience.

The contemporary schism between the last two Shaker villages, for example—a conflict that has been brewing for the better part of three decades—is not without precedent in the society's history. In fact, that controversy may be more understandable in terms of history than as an ecclesiastical debate, a personality conflict, or a struggle over financial assets—though it may also be all of those. Despite its name, the United Society of Believers has never been united in any simple way. The time has come to put an end to the fiction that the Believers achieved their utopian ideals. On the contrary, my reading of the extensive documentary records of the society and of those interacting with its members forces me to conclude that the Shakers were an extremely factious people. They faced the same problems that confront every community—religious or secular—as it seeks to build a sense of common purpose and to structure institutions congruent with its ideals. On balance, they were no more successful in solving those problems than many other groups. I find the Shakers no less interesting when they are viewed in this realistic way. On the contrary, the long history of the United Society is all the more remarkable when romantic notions are put aside and America's "favorite sect" is treated in an even-handed historical manner.

It is my intention in this work to address three identifiable audiences: the general reader who possesses relatively little knowledge of the Shakers, the growing number of persons with specialized interests in one or another aspect of the United Society, and members of the historical guild concerned with the relation between religion and American culture.

I accept the risks that come when writing for a divergent readership. The narrative may be sufficient for some who will find the critical issues of less interest; others knowledgeable about particulars may discover useful links with unfamiliar topics, though they may be frustrated by the limited attention paid to their areas of expertise; academics may focus on the interpretive issues while possibly wishing for more discussion of the theoretical implications of the Shaker experience. My hope is that all three audiences will profit from this account—that the general reader will find the story engaging and instructive, that Shaker aficionados will discover the larger context for their hobbies and commercial interests, and that academics will come to a new appreciation of the complexity of Shakerism.

Part I tells of the movement's beginnings and of the pivotal role played by the founders, especially Ann Lee, up to 1787. I have attempted to slice through the layers of tradition that surround this early period and, in doing so, have reduced the amount of historical detail that can be verified. At the same time I acknowledge the powerful role of oral discourse in shaping the image of the founders. Similarly, I have taken seriously the observations rendered by contemporaries who stood outside Shakerism, even though in many instances those critics were hostile to the society. The practical effect of this approach is to cast a skeptical eye on hagiographic reconstructions of the period. It also forces us to reevaluate the depictions of Ann Lee as a gentle matriarch who possessed a fully developed sense of messianic responsibility. For academics, this section raises the challenge of source criticism and sets forth the task of searching for the historical Ann Lee. This approach also shifts the critical moment in the history of Shakerism from the Age of the Founders to the subsequent Formative Period. For that reason my account of the beginnings is intentionally sparer than may be customary.

The establishment of the United Society as a national organization is the subject of Part II. I contend that the efforts of the second and third generations of the movement were more significant than those of the founders in shaping Shakerism as it has been known for more than two hundred years. Structures and forms are necessary for any movement to endure. Between 1787 and 1826 processes were set in motion that allowed the United Society to prosper in the short run and to endure over the longer period. Such leaders as Joseph Meacham, Lucy Wright, and David Darrow inspired hundreds of less prominent Shakers to invest heavily in the effort to establish and expand the society. These same years witnessed the development of communal structures, including social, economic, and religious institutions as well as rituals and patterns of thought. The Believ ers formulated their beliefs and supported them with elaborate historical and theological arguments. As they constructed their physical and mental world, they also created a past, furnishing it with figures bigger than life. For too long the myth of the founders has overshadowed the contributions of subsequent generations. Classic Shakerism was a product of this Formative Period.

Part III describes the United Society during the middle years of the nineteenth century, 1827 to 1875, a time when it became increasingly difficult for the Believers to maintain union and order. The Shakers were enjoying unprecedented economic prosperity and growing acceptance within the United States, and yet there were ominous signs that all was not well. The sectarian strategy of withdrawal from the world became nearly impossible to maintain. Recruitment of new members slacked off. Disobedience within the ranks proved a persistent problem for local and central ministries alike. The closing of a Shaker village in Indiana—a symbolic geographical retreat—was a forecast of things to come. In these circumstances, the society experienced a convulsive religious revival beginning in 1837. This outburst of spiritualistic energies preoccupied the Believers for more than a decade, and from it emanated some of the most creative but provocative theological and ritual innovations. During the Middle Period the authority of the ministry was challenged in new ways and established communal patterns were questioned. The Shakers debated among themselves the relative significance of the principles of gift and order. The conflict was resolved before the outbreak of the Civil War in favor of the ministry, or the party of order, and the society returned to less ecstatic patterns of spirituality and daily living. This attempt at revitalization, which manifested itself in complex religious phenomena and diverse gift "texts," presents a special interpretive dilemma for historical critics and students of religion. These years also saw a gradual change in the attitude of outsiders toward the Believers.

In Part IV I trace the accommodations made by the United Society to the rapidly changing circumstances of the late nineteenth century and the painful adjustments that followed during the first half of the twentieth century. Little has been written about this Time of Transformation, especially the latter half of the period. The Shakers were caught in the flow of events in post–Civil War America. Drawn into the world of big business and modernity, many Believers abandoned more traditional ways and conformed increasingly to the secular standards of American society in matters of religion and way of life. Less distance separated the Shakers from their counterparts in the world than ever before. Even the residents of Shaker villages felt the force of urbanization and industrialization. From 1876 to 1947 the society also literally aged. Declining numbers forced radical changes, and as a result all but three of the Shaker villages had been shut down by 1947. During the first half of the twentieth century talented female leaders emerged and began to dominate the society's affairs. Yet the forces of change in America were unrelenting, and the United Society proved unable to hold its own. Even the headquarters at Mount Lebanon was sold to outsiders. Nevertheless, individual Believers persisted in their religious commitment, displaying a resilience of spirit and a fortitude that momentarily put the lie to the realities confronting them. The principal interpretive issue during this period centers on the meaning of *decline*.

Part V charts the history of Shakerism since 1948. It has never before been written, in part because of the contemporary controversies and also because of severe limitations placed on access to documents that bear on the recent past. The story as told here is both heroic and pathetic, for the dwindling number of Shakers manifest extraordinary confidence in public about the future while privately they anguish over their circumstances. But the tale of the few remaining Believers is only part of the story of Shakerism since midcentury. An astonishing renaissance of interest in the society and its material culture has occurred. The complex of "Shaker" enterprises that developed outside the society has become a major factor in the Shaker story, affecting the Believers in manifold ways. This world of Shaker, as it is sometimes called, exists in symbiosis with the actual Believers. The dominant force in that relationship today is not the society but the mythic Shakers created by this wave of popular culture. The remarkable embrace of this sect by outsiders is without parallel in American religious history. Side by side with the popular movement is a groundswell of serious scholarship seeking to recover what has been hidden and to broaden our understanding of this tradition. It is my hope that this volume, as part of that effort, will open a new level of discourse among professional historians and among those who admire the Shakers and their artifacts.[3]

ACKNOWLEDGMENTS

This book has been more than seven years in the making, sufficiently long to incur numerous debts to individuals and institutions. I have met many people for whom the Shakers are a topic of special interest. These individuals and organizations have influenced this undertaking more than they will ever know.

My special thanks to Chuck Grench of Yale University Press for planting the idea that led to this project, and even more for his patience during the germination period and his willingness to allow me to rethink the enterprise.

I am delighted to acknowledge the support of a research fellowship from the National Endowment for the Humanities in 1984–1985 that made possible the initial immersion in Shaker manuscripts. That contact with the immense body of primary resources reshaped my thinking about the Shakers and clarified the magnitude of the project. At that point I determined not to parrot the same old story. Since then I have received generous support from the Lilly Endowment, Inc., as well as from the College of Arts and Sciences, the Office of Research and Graduate Development, the Department of Religious Studies, and my colleagues—all at Indiana University.

Over the past several years I have tested some of my judgments about the Shakers on various audiences. I thank the people who sat patiently through these lectures and especially those who reacted and offered valuable suggestions and encouragement. My thanks also to the sponsoring institutions.

This kind of research would be impossible without the direct assistance of many librarians and their associates. Some will remain unnamed here, but several must be acknowledged for their special help: Nancy Cridland, Diana Hanson, and Marty Sorury at the Indiana University Library; Jerry Grant and Ann Kelly at the Emma B. King Library at the Shaker Museum and Library in Old Chatham, New York; Sarah McFarland at the Williams College Library; Barbara Adams and E. Richard McKinstry at the Henry Francis du Pont Winterthur Museum; Anne Gilbert and Paige S. Lilly at the Shaker Library, The United Society of Shakers, Sabbathday Lake, Maine; Mary Ann Sanborn at the Shaker Library, Shaker Village, Inc., Canterbury, New Hampshire; Magda Gabor-Hotchkiss and Robert F. W. Meader at Hancock Shaker Village, Inc., Pittsfield, Massachusetts;

James J. Holmberg at the Filson Club in Louisville, Kentucky; and Gary J. Arnold at the Ohio Historical Society.

I have been privileged to share my interest in the Shakers with a number of students at Indiana University. Their research, in turn, has affected how I view the subject. These fellow researchers include Rainer Baumgaertner, Trent Hoffmann, Hilary Selby Polk, Cristy Ramage, Suzanne Thurman, Teresa Treat, and John Wolford. I also want to acknowledge the research assistance of Jennifer Bott, Helen Horton, and Laura Shulman. Three graduate assistants—Dawn Bakken, John Buggeln, and Sarah Pike—became eyes, ears, and legs for me at the last stage of the writing endeavor. My special thanks for help with every aspect of the project. Jennifer Mobley provided technical assistance with the manipulation of electronic files. John Michael Hollingsworth drew the maps in this volume, and Cynthia Carter Ayres improved my prose.

I have profited greatly from the scholarship of many who have written about Shakerism. I trust the notes are a clear indication of my scholarly debts. I have also had numerous conversations with others working on the Shakers; some are academics and others are professionals associated with Shakerism. Among those I must acknowledge are Leonard Brooks, Jane F. Crosthwaite, Clarke Garrett, Jean McMahon Humez, Richard Kathmann, Stephen A. Marini, Marjorie Procter-Smith, Sally M. Promey, Viki Sand, Diane Sasson, and James C. Thomas. I have enjoyed the hospitality and assistance of the Shakers and their staff members at the Canterbury and Sabbathday Lake villages. Colleagues in American religious history and in the Department of Religious Studies at Indiana University, often without knowing, have provided encouragement, advice, and support for this project. Among them are Catherine L. Albanese, Jon Butler, E. Brooks Holifield, J. Patrick Olivelle, Robert A. Orsi, J. Samuel Preus, Jan Shipps, Mary Jo Weaver, and Peter W. Williams. I alone, however, am responsible for what I have written.

My special thanks to Irene Edith Stein for faithfully clipping every magazine and newspaper article with the word *Shaker* in it for the past seven years. For Devonia, Beth, and Steve, thanks are not sufficient for putting up with me.

PART

ONE

A New

and Strange

Religion:

The Age

of the

Founders

1747–1787

It was an inauspicious beginning in America for the small band of English enthusiasts, known to some as Shaking Quakers, or Shakers, who landed at New York in early August 1774. Ann Lee, leader of the religious group, probably took employment as a domestic. Her companions, including her blacksmith husband, apparently did likewise. Several years would pass before Lee, a woman of nearly forty, resumed public leadership of the remaining handful of her followers.

These were turbulent times for the American colonies. The same New York newspaper that listed an opening for "a middle-aged woman of good character, well acquainted with cookery and the management of a small family," reported the debate in Parliament over the rebellious Americans. A rival publication in that port city celebrated in verse the insurgents who took part in the Boston Tea Party, pledging that

> Like them we are ready, as firm and as steady,
> To fight for our freedom with swords and with guns.

During the next two years, events in America moved inexorably toward revolution—the battles of Lexington and Concord, Bunker Hill, the publication of *Common Sense,* the Declaration of Independence. At that precise time the "passion for arms"—what the French called the *rage militaire*—enjoyed its widest vogue in the colonies. The arrival of Ann Lee and the small group of Shakers could hardly have been more untimely. Their pacifism was bound to be offensive to a populace increasingly disposed toward conflict with the mother country.[1]

Tradition has it that the Shaking Quakers came to America as the result of a vision Ann Lee had received. More likely their situation in England had deteriorated sufficiently to warrant a move, even migration to North America with its special difficulties. The time-honored Shaker explanation for the trip adds spiritual significance to a journey already reasonable on other grounds. It is the nature of religious communities to embellish the story of their past with tales of providential guidance and divine direction.[2]

To understand the story of the Shakers in America, we must recognize the existence of diverse and sometimes conflicting evidence bearing on the society's development. The task of the historian is to identify the strata and to distinguish the respective value of each. The critical appraisal of sources is especially necessary with the Shakers because many writers in recent years have adopted an overly sympathetic, if not romantic, perspective on this sect. Some seem uninterested in distinguishing the historical record from interpretations offered of it. Most seem unaware that a problem even exists. This is an exceptionally acute issue for the study of the earliest period of Shaker history because so little contemporary documentary evidence remains from the Age of the Founders. Yet this era has assumed increasing significance in the life of the community with the passage of time. Here we seek a reliable history of the sect's origins.[3]

Background

The world of religious sectarianism in eighteenth-century England was crowded with sometimes strange but always interesting groups. The Shaking Quakers were one among many manifestations of radical religion that arose in the land during and after the English Civil War. Many sects were "enthusiastic" in character, a designation used pejoratively on both sides of the Atlantic to condemn radical dissenters for heterodox beliefs and excessive emotionalism. Sectarians, by definition, live in tension with their host culture; they seek to turn the world upside down. "Enthusiasts," from the vantage point of the orthodox and established parties of that day, were "unconventional but religiously devout sectarians who would not, could not, contain their zeal within the organized limits of religious convention." Ann Lee and the Shakers fit well within both categories.[4]

Obscurity shrouds the details of Lee's life and activities in England. Manchester, a manufacturing town in the northwest, was her birthplace. The daughter of John Lees, a blacksmith who lived on Toad Lane, she was baptized in the cathedral on 1 June 1742. Ann Lee had little formal education; the workplace—probably textile shops—was her school. She married Abraham Standerin, also a blacksmith, on 5 January 1762. The wedding banns had been published the previous three Sundays in the local Anglican parish. Abraham and Ann signed the registry with their marks only. From this marriage came no surviving children. The death of one, "Elizabeth, daughter of Abraham Standley," appears in the burial records for 7 October 1766. These were trying years for the couple.[5]

The documentary evidence concerning Ann Lee's religious development in England is almost as sparse. At some point she began to associate with a small group of religious enthusiasts in Manchester led by James and Jane Wardley, tailors from nearby Bolton. According to a 1769 newspaper account, this group became known as Shakers because of their "uncommon mode of religious worship." The category Shaker was not new to England, having been used as early as the midseventeenth century for sectarians whose devotional activities produced a trembling or shaking of the body. The term had been applied derisively to the followers of George Fox, the Quakers, for the same reason—namely, a quaking caused by "Vapours in their Estatick Fits." The designation was apt for the members of the Wardley society because they trembled and shook when "the spirit" moved them in worship. It was reported that sometimes their heads jerked so rapidly that their facial features were "not distinguishable." They screeched "in the most dreadful manner," too, disturbing whole neighborhoods at some distance with the "commotions." Late in the meetings the frenzy of the "fits" gave way to "singing and dancing." These gatherings closed, it was reported, when the strength of the participants was "exhausted."[6]

The same contemporary source provides valuable clues about the beliefs and practices of this small society. Its members regarded the Wardleys as "prophet and prophetess." Their "ceremonies and tenets" were based on a "vision" received years earlier. The leaders made heavy demands on their followers, meeting with them "constantly three times a day." The society required no special building for its gatherings, assembling in the homes of members. In the meetings, members discussed passages from the Bible, their notions concerning "a future state," and the opinions of competing groups. The Shakers proclaimed themselves "the only true religion" and condemned all others.[7]

A series of local arrest records documents Ann Lee's heavy involvement with the small society in the early 1770s. On 14 July 1772 the Manchester constable paid twelve shillings to a group of twenty-four assistants who had apprehended five Shakers on the preceding Sunday. The next day the group appeared before Justice of the Peace Peter Mainwaring. Eight days later the record shows that "John Lee and his daughter Ann" were prosecuted before a jury, and both received a "sentence of commitment." Later that year the constable again acted against this group of enthusiasts, apprehending some on 3 October and "quelling a mob who were beginning to pull down the house of John Townly a Shaker." On the nineteenth of the month the constable's log reads: "To repairs making good the breaches at Lee's in Toadlane in order to apprehend a gang of Shakers lock't up there 5s 2d." By 1772 Ann Lee and members of her family were indisputably principals in the activities of the Manchester society.[8]

Conflict with the authorities began to increase. On 30 May 1773 "Ann Lees a shaker" was arrested "for disturbing the Congregation in the old Church." She was detained for two days in prison, where the constable provided "meat and drink" for Lee and "her attendant." Near the end of July she was apprehended again, this time in company with three other Shakers—John Townley, J. Jackson, and Betty Lees. The official account of the Quarter Sessions states that the group was placed in custody "for going into Christ Church, in this town, and there willfully and contemptuously in the time of divine service, disturbing the congregation then assembled at morning prayer." On this occasion Ann Lee again spent two days in prison. She and the others were each fined twenty pounds.[9]

The sectarian pattern is unmistakable. By 1772 the Shaking Quakers of Manchester, including Ann Lee and members of her family, were engaging in confrontational tactics. They intentionally incurred public censure and hostility in order to communicate their message to local residents. They flagrantly violated religious mores, forcing the hand of authorities responsible for keeping order. Most offensive, they adopted a tactic employed earlier by Quaker prophets, invading the sanctuaries of congregations assembled for worship. The Shakers denounced both clergy and laity, reflecting their negative judgment of other religions. The substantial fines levied in mid-1773 suggest that the patience of local officials was wearing thin. External pressure was mounting on the society.[10]

The Shaking Quakers of Manchester were religious fanatics, zealous in their enthusiasm and bold in their methods. In several respects they resembled the Quakers of the seventeenth century. Like them, the Shakers of the 1770s placed a primary accent on the direction of the spirit. For both, the process of religious inspiration was accessible to male and female alike. Members of these sects spoke with urgency about an impending apocalyptic judgment. With equal harshness they condemned the churches of the land, the clergy, and most established ecclesiastical practices. The two groups especially appealed to lower- and working-class segments of the population. These similarities between the Shakers and the Quakers are highly instructive, but they do not explain the origins of the Shaking Quakers, for by the mideighteenth century the members of the Society of Friends had entered an introspective and quietistic period, having largely abandoned their earlier radical prophetic behavior.[11]

The Wardley society more likely derived inspiration and nurture from the French Prophets. This celebrated group of enthusiasts emigrated from France in the early years of the eighteenth century after Louis XIV vigorously suppressed a revolt by radical Protestants known as Camisards in the Cévennes district. The small band of French refugees arrived in England at a time when one-fifth of the population of London—their principal location of activity was "composed of dissenters and Huguenot refugees." These newly arrived visionaries proclaimed impending judgment and an imminent millennium. They created a great stir within the churches of England as well as within the smaller sects.[12]

The French Prophets and their English converts appealed to the early Christian church as a sanction for their views on visions, miracles, and prophecy. Their worship was spirit directed and embraced various forms of ecstatic behavior, including "agitations" in a style "akin to dance." The actions and proclamations of these *inspires*—called "sacred theater" by Clarke Garrett—attracted large crowds as well as opposition from the established clergy. Women, thought to be more susceptible to inspiration, occupied a special place among the followers of the Prophets; they were revered in the community for their sacerdotal powers and castigated by critics for alleged promiscuity. The missionary activity of the Prophets and their followers spread quickly throughout the British Isles and even to the Continent, achieving success in a number of localities, including Manchester. Near the end of the first decade of the century, however, the movement suffered a loss of popular support and added notoriety when Thomas Emes, a deceased English convert, was not resurrected as had been predicted. The number of adherents declined rapidly as members sought religious answers in other sects. But some followers remained faithful and "gathered silently around inspired women, awaiting agitations and eager to hear prophecies that combined judgment, instruction and mercy."[13]

In spite of obvious similarities with the early Quakers and the French Prophets, there is little agreement concerning the formative influences on the Shaking Quakers. One of the most perceptive students of the period has been "unable to confirm any Wardley attachment to the Quakers or the French Prophets." Another scholar has argued for the widespread diffusion of the Camisard influence throughout Europe, the British Isles, and North America, but even he admits that the path of "the spark of divine possession" cannot be traced with certitude to the society in Manchester, although that industrial town had been the site of activity by the French Prophets and was later a center of operations for Methodist and Swedenborgian preachers. George Whitefield, the itinerant evangelical preacher, for example, visited the area frequently in the 1750s. Some scholars see Whitefield as the most likely influence on later Shaker doctrine, but his Methodism was only one of many elements in "the rich heritage of English popular religion" in the second half of the eighteenth century. The religious origins of the Shaking Quakers, therefore, remain an open issue, but that uncertainty does not obscure a more significant observation. The development of the Manchester society followed a pattern typical of scores of sectarian groups in eighteenth-century England.[14]

The Wardleys were charismatic leaders—gifted individuals—whose views attracted a following. They challenged their disciples to live by inspired principles in tension with the surrounding culture. Dissent is the essence of the sectarian spirit. The Shaking Quakers were pious radicals, and their religious dissent fueled hostility from the host culture, which in turn strengthened the sense of community within the beleaguered sect. Ann Lee emerged from the Wardley society as a devout and gifted disciple, displaying the marks of a true believer. Her expanding involvement led to her inevitable arrest, prosecution, and public persecution as well as to an increase in her esteem within the society. Lee's decision to leave England in the spring of 1774 with her husband and a few fellow Shakers was eminently prudent, based on limited success in Manchester, growing pressures on the sect, and the promise of different circumstances in North America.[15]

Contemporary sources from the 1770s reveal little about the arrival of the small group of religious sectarians in America. No extant account reports the appearance or presence of the group of Shaking Quakers in New York City. The date of their arrival—later fixed as 6 August and marked by special ceremonies—is uncertain. The entry in the log of the custom house in the port notes only "Snow Maria, Smith, Liverpool." This square-rigged vessel under a Captain Smith apparently carried the Shakers from Liverpool to America, but no passenger list remains. The record grows even slimmer for the next several years. The group scattered, no longer gathering in the manner previously documented in Manchester, and certainly not engaging in the same aggressive religious tactics. If they assembled for worship, they did so without attracting attention. If Ann Lee exercised any leadership role, she did it inconspicuously. The members of the group probably dispersed for practical reasons—to earn a living and to avoid provoking hostilities from their neighbors. In 1774 the Shaking Quakers dropped out of sight, apparently abandoning public witness to their beliefs and adjusting as best they could to the new environment.[16]

After several years the members of the small band, augmented by a few additional arrivals, reconstituted themselves as a society. The site they chose was a tract of land several miles northwest of Albany in the manor of Rensselaerwyck. Some may have arrived as early as 1776, but firm evidence for Shaker landholdings is not available until 1779. In that year the tax records for the northwest quarter of the "Manor of Ranselear District" in Albany County listed a real estate assessment of fifty pounds under the name of John Partington with taxes due totaling seventeen pounds, ten shillings. Adjacent acreage may have been leased in the name of John

Hocknell, but no contemporary record confirms the transaction. Partington and Hocknell had both followed Ann Lee to New York. Other members of the group settling in this district, known by its Indian name of Nisqueunia, later Niskeyuna, included Partington's wife, Mary, Hocknell's wife, Hannah, and their son Richard, Lee's younger brother William, her relative Nancy Lees, James Whittaker, and James Shepherd. Sometime before this move Ann Lee and Abraham Standerin had separated permanently. Only after 1779 do the activities of the Shakers begin to surface in contemporary records.[17]

This spare description of the English background and the first years in the colonies takes no account of the fuller narrative supplied by later Believers. This intentional omission on my part, however controversial, underscores the exceedingly slim documentary base on which the early history of the society rests. By contrast, the official Shaker history, nurtured in the memories of the Believers and harking back in published form to 1808 (and subsequently repeated in countless writings within the society as well as in scholarly and popular texts), amply fills in the documentary record in a manner complimentary to Ann Lee and the founding generation. This authorized narrative bears the characteristic marks of sacred story or myth and provides a foundation for the society's later claims regarding its origins and founders. The repetition of the narrative has confirmed the faith and commitment of the Believers.[18]

The official version provides more details concerning the earliest years of the society. It tells a story of persecution, miracles, and divine protection. Ann Lee's "inexpressible sufferings" in England are described as the product of her own "labor and travel," the opposition of enemies, and the "immediate revelation of God." Her agonies were such that she is said to have sweat blood on occasion; at other times she appeared "a mere skeleton." One celebrated account in this hagiography tells of Lee being confined in prison for two weeks without anything to eat or drink. Her cell was so small that she could not stand. She was miraculously sustained, according to the tale, when a faithful friend nourished her by pouring "wine and milk" through a pipe stem inserted into the keyhole. The official history also explains in detail one of the most puzzling episodes of the first years in America—Ann Lee's separation from her husband. After Ann nursed him through a prolonged sickness in New York, he repaid her "care and attention" with "very ungodly" behavior. According to Shaker tradition, threats and sexual intimidation ultimately forced a "final separation" from Abraham Standerin, justified by his guilt and her innocence.[19]

Much of the official narrative of this earliest period is the product of the Believers' later collective recollections of the past. Many years after the events in question had taken place, the Shaker ministry decided to compile "a faithful record of those precepts and examples and other contemporary events" reflecting the character of Ann Lee and other early leaders. They undertook this task to benefit those who had not known the founding generation and to defend the reputations of the first Believers, especially that of Ann Lee. This early history was carefully shaped by the leaders of the society, who solicited information from the Believers, coaxed and encouraged memories, and skillfully edited the oral testimonies. The compilers acknowledged that many of the statements from these witnesses, "and those too, the most important, have been brought to remembrance by a special gift of God, after having been, as it were, entirely forgotten, for many years." These testimonies, reportedly recovered with divine assistance, were then given "a suitable arrangement" in "short sketches of the lives, character and manners" of Ann Lee and the others. The resulting story — no less valuable for the process of collection and editing — has historical relevance more for the time of its collection and composition than for the earlier ages that it purports to describe.[20]

Reconstructing the Age of the Founders has been made more difficult by the early hostility of the society toward written creeds, statements of belief, and even written testimonies. This opposition stemmed in part from Ann Lee's illiteracy, a limitation that fueled her rejection of all writing. The sectarian mentality manifested among the Shaking Quakers in Manchester—their denunciation of established ecclesiastical patterns and practices—also fostered antipathy toward formal theological documents. On the positive side, the Shakers' early prohibition against writing was an affirmation of the value they perceived in verbal testimonies offered by "eye and ear witnesses" and a reflection of their view of revelation as dynamic and changing. For Ann Lee and her followers, the written word paled in veracity as well as efficacy when compared with the spoken word. This negative bias prevailed among the Shakers for many years after her death.[21]

But when the Shakers began to feel the sting of repeated written attacks, they changed their practice and began to write in their own defense. Similarly, they used the printed page for instructing members about principles and practices. The Believers also, ironically, inaugurated a program of systematic record keeping that eventually covered all aspects of the society's activities. As a result, the problem of scarce documentary resources is confined to the Age of the Founders. Even material culture items from this earliest period—scraps of dress cloth, apron fabric, a rocking chair, all purported to have belonged to Ann Lee—are so few and so undocumented that little can be established on the basis of such relics. Abundant sources exist for every other period of Shaker history. The critical interpretation of the earliest resources, therefore, remains a major challenge.[22]

Beginnings in America

Nearly all observers agree that 1780 marked the "opening" of the Shaker gospel in America, when events catapulted the Shaking Quakers into the public eye. Guided by charismatic leaders, the English immigrants had secured sufficient land for home sites and had reassembled as a religious society in the Albany area. Initially the distinctive beliefs and practices of the small group attracted little attention, perhaps because of the relative isolation of Niskeyuna. That same isolation from the outside world, according to Shaker tradition, allowed them to hold "solemn meetings" once again without interference. But the society did not escape all notice. One contemporary report of their "religious exercises," written in 1778, spoke of the members "dancing in extravagant postures" and whirling with "inconceivable rapidity" before falling "lifeless on the floor." A more hostile witness noted the presence in the area of a "sect" that engaged in "gross immoralities" and held heretical beliefs. As reports about the group spread, changes in the society's situation seemed almost inevitable.[23]

Ann Lee, William Lee, and James Whittaker emerged as the guiding leaders in the group at Niskeyuna. How responsibilities in practical matters were divided among them remains unclear. The Shaker acreage, forested and swampy, required intensive labor to yield food and shelter. Although skilled in other trades, few of the members had extensive experience in agriculture. Yet the society managed to provide for itself, even if at first the fare was meager and the dwellings primitive. The situation at Niskeyuna was far from ideal, but its isolation did allow the group to stabilize its temporal affairs. The circumstances in the wilderness taxed the Shakers, but their previous experiences with hardship had prepared them well for these challenges. They worked together to survive.[24]

External events soon put an end to the isolation at Niskeyuna and brought the Shakers both new problems and opportunities. The War of Independence was the dominant sociopolitical event of these years, a reality no one in the colonies could escape, even those remote from the battlefields. More regional in character but no less influential on the Shakers

was a religious revival among evangelicals in the border region between
New York and Massachusetts, an area east of the Hudson River one histo
rian has called "the Yankee zone." In the summer of 1779 a New Light
stir, centering on the towns of New Lebanon, New York, and Hancock and
Pittsfield, Massachusetts, fanned religious fervor and raised expectations
concerning an imminent millennium. The belief in an impending transformation of the earth had been a doctrine of widespread interest among
American Protestants since the founding of the colonies, but especially
after the Great Awakening of the 1740s.[25]

The events of 1780 now forced the Shakers out of their seclusion.
In April two travelers from the Yankee zone happened on the society at
Niskeyuna and carried news of the peculiar beliefs and practices of these
"strange and wonderful Christians" across the Hudson. No doubt a goodly
measure of skepticism and caution greeted their report in New Lebanon.
Outsiders were often viewed suspiciously, not simply because of the war
but also because of decades-old controversy over land and property rights.
In addition, no love was lost between the descendants of the Puritans
(Congregationalists or New Lights) and the Quakers or other radical sectarians. Joseph Meacham, an elder among the New Light Baptists at New
Lebanon, was sufficiently curious about the reported group to investigate
the strangers' religion further. He and others from the congregation went
to Niskeyuna, hoping perhaps to discover something of use. By this time
the extraordinary religious zeal manifested in New Lebanon the preceding
summer had subsided.[26]

According to later Shaker tradition, Ann Lee anticipated Joseph
Meacham's arrival at Niskeyuna. Prophesying that "the first man in America is coming," she directed the group to "prepare victuals for him & those
with him." It was the custom of the Shakers to extend hospitality to visi
tors, and this occasion was no exception. Meacham conferred with the
members of the society, questioning them and inquiring about the sect.
"At length," in the words of his Shaker biographer, "he was fully convinced that these strange people professed the spirit, kingdom, & work for
which he had so earnestly prayed, & sought, & of which he had prophesied. And that indeed their testimony was the voice of the son of God."
The delegation returned to New Lebanon and reported their judgments to
the congregation, urging them to visit the society and investigate for themselves. Many did travel to Niskeyuna, and they, too, became convinced of
the truthfulness of the sect's claims.[27]

Shaker historians date the first public testimony of the society in
America to 19 May 1780—the celebrated Dark Day in New England,

when the sun reputedly did not shine. (The ominous shadowing was apparently caused by smoke from fires used to clear farmlands). The perceived significance of the apparent conjunction of earthly and heavenly affairs was unnerving, especially among a people given to apocalyptic reflections. Religious activity, in general, quickened. The Shakers gained a substantial number of converts from New Lebanon and the surrounding area. Among the first to confess their sins were Joseph Meacham, Talmadge Bishop, Calvin Harlow, and David Darrow, as well as members of their families. One convert, Eleanor Vedder, had been "induced to open her life" to Ann Lee two years earlier.[28]

It is noteworthy that the opening of the Shaker gospel in America resulted from the inquiries of outsiders rather than from initiatives by members of the society. Before 1780 the Shakers were content to follow the logic of sectarianism by retreating from the "world," remaining in isolation, and not actively seeking converts. Their reluctance to proselytize may have been a lingering effect of the earlier English experience. When they did begin to represent their faith publicly, according to Shaker sources, they spoke with zeal in a language familiar to their visitors, proclaiming the spirit of Christ with an apocalyptic urgency. Ann Lee, for example, exhorted her followers: "If you will take up your crosses against the works of generation, and follow Christ in the regeneration, God will cleanse you from all unrighteousness."[29]

Some of the earliest converts no doubt found the Shaker and New Light traditions highly compatible. The case of Samuel Johnson is instructive. Educated at Yale College, he subsequently served as the minister of a Presbyterian congregation in New Lebanon. In that position, however, he did not find the "spiritual substance" he desired, and he resigned his pastorate. For several years he searched for a more satisfactory religious system, coming to the conviction that the "power of salvation" was not available in most churches. Johnson watched eagerly for the second coming of Christ, expecting the arrival of that kingdom to be heralded by visions, signs, and gifts. He also believed that the "spirit of Christianity" was inconsistent with warfare. Johnson learned of the Shakers in 1780 while living at West Stockbridge, and he immediately went to Niskeyuna to investigate. There he spent a week and spoke at length with Ann Lee and James Whittaker. Afterward, finding the promise of God fulfilled and his prayers answered, he confessed his sins to the leaders. He then received the gift of prophecy and began to see visions. His spiritual search—and that of many others like him—ended successfully with the Shakers.[30]

The revolutionary struggle was the second major factor bringing an end to Shaker isolation in America. The war had not been going well for the patriots since 1778. New York City, for example, had been occupied by British troops. The colonial armies were finding it difficult to secure sufficient enlistments. The glamor of military action had faded, and many Americans sought ways to avoid serving in the armed forces. Some areas, including the region around Albany, were notorious for their Tory leanings. Revolutionary officials were forced to administer oaths of allegiance as a test of commitment to the patriotic cause. They hoped thus to compel the allegiance of those who were lukewarm in support of the revolution and to discourage Tories from fighting on the British side by compromising their loyalty to the crown. The government of New York had established a body of "Commissioners for detecting and defeating Conspiracies," which was empowered to test and enforce loyalty to the revolutionary cause. By April 1778 members of this commission were active in the Albany area, but there is no evidence that the small band of Shakers immediately attracted any notice. By mid-1780, however, the commissioners in Albany were taking steps against members of the society whom they suspected of being British sympathizers, if not agents of the crown. This official action was, in part, a by-product of the growing number of conversions, which brought public attention to the sect.[31]

The initial provocation for the commissioners' actions occurred on 5 July 1780 when David Darrow attempted to drive a flock of sheep to Niskeyuna. The authorities feared that he and others, "from their disaffection to the American cause," intended to "convey them [the sheep] to the Enemy or at least bring them so near the Frontiers that the enemy may with safety take them." Two days later Darrow, John Hocknell, and Joseph Meacham (the other two having appeared before the commission on Darrow's behalf) were imprisoned because they acknowledged "that it was their determined Resolution never to take up arms and to dissuade others from doing the same." The commissioners regarded the peace-loving principles of this "set of people who call themselves shaking Quakers" as "highly pernicious and of destructive tendency to the Freedom & Independence of the United States of America." Other Shakers were soon apprehended on similar charges.[32]

On 24 July the commissioners issued a warrant for the arrest of "John Partherton, William Lees, and Ann Standerren." Frequent complaints had been lodged by inhabitants of the county, charging that these three "by their conduct and conversation disturb the publick peace and are daily dissuading the friends to the American cause from taking up

Arms in defence of their Liberties." Two days later the appointed officer reported to the commission that in addition to those mentioned in the warrant, he had also arrested "James Whiteacre, Calven Harlow, and Mary Parthington, whom he found in Company with them and it appearing that they have also been guilty of the like Practices." After interrogation, having acknowledged the correctness of the complaints, the Shakers were jailed. The society was clearly no longer following a strategy of retreat. Once again its members had taken to the streets, boldly proclaiming an unpopular message, ready and willing to incur public hostility.[33]

One month after the Shakers' incarceration, the commissioners ordered Ann Lee and Mary Partington to be transferred to Poughkeepsie "for the purpose of their being removed within the Enemies Lines"—a standard procedure established by the legislature. The removal, for some unknown reason, did not take place. The male Shakers remained in jail in Albany until mid-November, when they were set free on bail of one hundred pounds apiece, provided each did "his duty" and was of "good behavior" throughout the balance of the war. After gaining his freedom, William Lee sought the release of his sister through the agency of Gen. James Clinton at Albany and the commissioners. On 19 November the general wrote to George Clinton, governor of New York, asking that "Ann Standivin," a member of the "Denomination of shaking Quakers," be released. "You are better acquainted with the circumstances relating to her," he wrote, "than I can be; you can best determine what is to be done with her, and if nothing material has been proven against her, I shou'd suppose she may [be] released agreeable to their requisition."[34]

On 4 December the commissioners approved the application of William Lee and released Ann Lee from the prison, provided that she agree to maintain "good Behaviour" and not say or consent to "any Matters or Things inconsistant with the Peace and safety of this and the United States." William Lee and James Whittaker posted her bail at one hundred pounds. While noting that the Shakers had a "Tendency to alienate the minds of the People from their Allegiance to the State," the commissioners justified their release because, according to their report, "many of the Persons of the said Persuasion have been reformed and . . . no further Evil is to be apprehended from her Influence or Example." Ann Lee returned immediately to Niskeyuna. The events of 1780, however, had altered irrevocably the situation of the small society. Never again would the Shakers enjoy the isolation they had known during the first years in America. They had gained public attention and new converts as well as notoriety and some convinced enemies.[35]

An Apostate's View

One day after Ann Lee's release from prison, Valentine Rathbun, a Separate Baptist minister in Pittsfield, Massachusetts, signed the draft of a publication describing "the matter, form and manner, of a new and strange Religion, that has lately taken place among many people, in the States of Massachusetts and New York." His account of the Shakers, which appeared in print in 1781, is the first extensive published report dealing with the society in America. It is an extremely valuable contemporary description based in part on his personal contact with members of the society.[36]

Rathbun had embraced the Shaker gospel in 1780 after visiting Niskeyuna. Several members of his family had also converted. In time, however, according to his account, "inconsistencies and falsehoods" within Shakerism began to bother him, mention of which brought him "a clamour, hiss and uproar" from the Shakers. Turning to his Bible, he determined that the prophecies and signs associated with the society were false, "that the spirit which leads on this new scheme, is the spirit of witchcraft, and is the most powerful of any delusion I ever heard or read of." After leaving the group, he determined to expose and destroy the society by attacking its beliefs and practices and by discrediting its members, especially the leaders. Despite his destructive intent, Rathbun's account demands close scrutiny by the historian interested in the evolution of the sect.[37]

When Rathbun first visited Niskeyuna one week after the Dark Day, the resident Shakers numbered only twelve: five males and seven females. The inquirers from the Yankee zone had not yet taken up residence. He took special note of the political views of this small band: as "Europeans, a part of which came from England," they were not supportive of the revolutionary effort. Rathbun echoed the charges for which the Shakers were imprisoned, namely, their counsel that "it is contrary to the gospel to bear arms" or to give any support (by ballot or money) to the "defence of the country." Eager to identify the Shakers as dangerous enemies of the state, he reported: "I have heard some of them say, that all our authority, civil and military, is from hell, and would go there again." Near the end of his tract he urged "Ministers of the Gospel" to use every possible means to thwart the Shaker scheme. From his perspective as a Separate Baptist and a former Believer, the religious practices, doctrines, and rituals of the Shakers confirmed that they were radical enthusiasts and dangerous sectarians.[38]

Rathbun was angered by the way the Shakers treated visitors or those who inquired about their beliefs. They met such persons, he wrote, "with many smiles, and seeming great gladness." The society fed them and entertained them with songs—hospitality Rathbun deemed feigned and deceitful. If an individual agreed to instruction, the Shakers would gather round, "touch him with their fingers here and there, and give him a sly cross, and in a very loving way, put their hands on his head, and then begin to preach their doctrine to him." Sometimes they used "great severity" and other times "great flattery" with inquirers. If males wished to join the group, they were required to cut their hair short rather than wear it long or clubbed in a knot. By these practices, according to Rathbun, the Shakers hoped to cultivate "absolute dependence" among their adherents.[39]

Indoctrination followed initiation into the sect, Rathbun asserted. First came "a multitude of good words," such universal Christian injunctions as "we must hate sin, love God, take up our cross, &c." Then they would state that the millennial dispensation had begun in their society. Rathbun reported that "three of the males, and two females, profess to be perfect, or to have attained a state of perfection; the other seven not perfect yet, but very far advanced." The Shakers pointed to their "apostolic gifts" as proof of the society's claims. All other churches in the world were antichristian and false. In this new dispensation, they contended, the external ordinances of baptism and the Lord's Supper had no place.[40]

Only when potential converts were deemed ready, Rathbun declared, were they introduced to the more esoteric Shaker doctrines, such as the necessity for public confession to the leaders, the condemnation of marriage as sinful, the possibility of communication with angels and spirits, the notion that a judgment of the world was under way, the idea of progress through degrees of punishment, and the concepts of immortality and immunity to suffering and temptation. As offensive as these beliefs were to Rathbun, they paled in comparison to the scandal he associated with the woman whom the Shakers called "the mother." This one, "about forty years of age," they claimed "is the woman spoken of in the xiith chapter of the Revelations of John, who was clothed with the sun, having the moon under her feet, and on her head a crown of twelve stars; and that she has travail'd and brought forth the man child. Further, that she is the mother of all the elect; and that she travails for the whole world; and that no blessing can come to any person, but only by and through her; and that in the way of her being possessed of their sin; by their confessing of them, and repenting of the same, one by one, according to her direction." Some Shakers contended that Ann Lee had "the fullness of the God Head" within her and called her "the queen of heaven, Christ's wife."[41]

But doctrines were probably less significant in attracting early converts than certain symbolic acts that forged a strong sense of community within the society. Rathbun observed, for example, that the members of the sect shared food and lodging. They spoke in a similar manner, using "yea and nay" and without complimentary titles. Their close-cropped hair set them apart from outsiders. They enjoyed an intimacy and a camaraderie with one another. They joined in public testimony to their principles and suffered together as a result of that common endeavor. These shared activities bound the members of the society together.[42]

Equally attractive to new converts were the charismatic power and apostolic signs perceived to be in abundance among the Shaking Quakers. Much of their ritual was ecstatic in nature. "Their actions in worship," Rathbun reported, "is according to the dictates of the spirit that governs them." There was no public prayer or preaching and little reading. By contrast, of singing there was an abundance; some songs were with words and some without, some words known and some unknown. The gifts of this new "spiritual dispensation" included shaking and singing, hopping and turning, smoking and running, groaning and laughing. The Believers viewed all these actions as manifestations of divine power and union with God.[43]

Outsiders, including Rathbun, saw only commotion and "bedlam" in the spirit-directed activities of the Shakers. The noise of night meetings was heard two miles away, he reported. The members of the sect did strange things—hooting like owls, crowing like roosters, "hissing like a gander," following an outstretched arm, running naked through the woods. These actions, ridiculed by observers, provided some new converts with a unique sense of assurance. Rathbun confessed that these signs had initially made a deep impression on him. Similarly, "a very extraordinary and uncommon power" attended the instruction by Shaker leaders. A "strange infatuation of the mind to believe all their teachers say" exerts itself on inquirers. The body, he noted, gave expression to this power by "a twitching, as though his nerves were all in a convulsion." Rathbun compared this physical effect to "the operation of an electerising machine; the person believes it is the power of God, and therefore dare not resist, but wholly gives way to it."[44]

One ritual described by Rathbun is especially revealing of the mentality of the society at Niskeyuna. The Shakers taking part "lie down on the ground, make a round ring with their finger, among the dirt, puther about in it, then start up, double their fist at it, run away from it, come at it again, show the looks of vengeance at it, threaten it with postures, then run and jump into it, and stamp it all to pieces." Rathbun added, "This sign they interpret to be the old heavens, which are to pass away with a great noise." By these actions members dramatized their condemnation of the world and their determination to end its influence over their lives. This behavior embodied the sectarian spirit of the early Shakers, who believed that the destruction of worldly influences would prepare the way for a new dispensation.[45]

Ann Lee's Public Ministry: An Insider's View

Following Ann Lee's release from prison in 1780, the activities of the society again centered on Niskeyuna, the principal residence of the English Shaking Quakers. To that site came a growing number of Americans seeking nurture and instruction, counsel and advice, from the leaders of the sect. Converts and inquirers alike participated in the meetings and then returned to their homes throughout New England and adjacent areas of New York. Shaker tradition speaks of large numbers visiting and of remarkable religious manifestations among them. "Signs and operations, prophecies, visions and revelations of God greatly abounded," one recalled. Thus the word spread concerning this new faith, and the sect grew in numbers during the winter months of 1781.[46]

This pattern of resident evangelism changed dramatically in the spring when the three Shaker leaders—Ann Lee, her brother William, and James Whittaker—and several companions set out from Niskeyuna to visit those who had embraced the new gospel or were favorably disposed toward it. According to Shaker tradition, Ann Lee viewed the journey as fulfillment of a vision received in England. Several practical reasons more likely contributed to the decision to travel. The demands for hospitality at Niskeyuna had become burdensome. The return of warmer weather made it more difficult for converts who were farmers to leave their land for extended periods. The journey also momentarily relieved local concerns about the increasing number of Shakers assembling in the Niskeyuna area. The religious advantages of the trip were obvious: it provided an opportunity to strengthen bonds among scattered adherents and an occasion to carry the Shaker gospel into other areas. Perhaps for all these reasons the Shaker leaders found the new pattern of itinerant evangelism profitable enough to prolong this journey for more than two years.[47]

The Shaker entourage departed Niskeyuna in May 1781; it did not return until September 1783. This extended missionary tour took place during the closing years of the War of Independence. Lord Cornwallis surrendered to George Washington at Yorktown on 19 October 1781; a pre-

liminary peace treaty was signed in Paris on 30 November 1782; and the
British finally withdrew from New York City on 25 November 1783. These
were transitional moments for Americans, filled with turmoil as they ad-
justed to the winding down of the war and searched for ways to institu-
tionalize a republican government. Likewise, these years were critical
times for the young sect.[48]

The path of the missionary journey, as far as it is recoverable from
existing Shaker sources, had little geographical logic. After leaving Niskeyuna, the leaders visited the homes of converts, crisscrossing central Massachusetts and Connecticut, dipping occasionally into the southeastern
corners of these two areas. The founders and their entourage visited some
locations more than once. The itinerary seems to have been influenced by
the intuitions of the leaders, by invitations extended to them, by the reception accorded the group among those favorably disposed, and by the response of non-Shakers in each locale. What is most remarkable about the
journey is the wide range of locations where converts to Shakerism were
found in these early years. Individuals and families committed to the society lived in localities as scattered as Shelburne and Shirley in northern
Massachusetts, Norton and Rehoboth in the coastal lowlands south of
Boston, and Preston and Stonington in the southeastern corner of Connecticut (fig. 1). The widespread distribution of converts may have been a
result of the revolutionary struggle, which led people to move more than
under peacetime circumstances.[49]

The standard Shaker accounts of the missionary journey present a
highly stylized picture. In nearly every town, Ann Lee and her companions resided at the home of a convert and used that house as their base of
operations. A warm welcome always greeted the itinerants, who enjoyed
the fullest hospitality from their hosts. The traveling band had two major
objectives: "visiting and strengthening" converts and "bearing testimony
to the world." To achieve the first, they "labored" with the members of the
host family, teaching and instructing them as much as possible, given the
round of necessary daily chores and the religious excitement surrounding
the visit. For the second, the visitors held "public meetings" where they
opened "the testimony of the gospel" for both Shakers and non-Shakers.
On these occasions the missionaries explained the principles of the sect
through preaching and personal witness, the members of the society participated in songs and spirit-directed exercises, and those who had gathered
frequently ate together.[50]

The private laboring and the public testimony at these sites followed
no fixed order. The impulses of the charismatic leaders controlled the flow

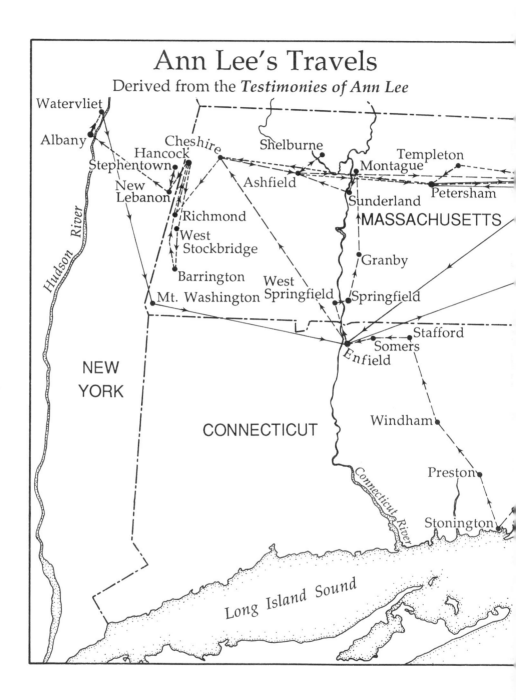

Ann Lee's Travels

Derived from the *Testimonies of Ann Lee*

Watervliet

Albany

Cheshire
Hancock
Stephentown
Shelburne
Templeton
Montague

New
Lebanon
Ashfield
Petersham

Richmond
Sunderland
MASSACHUSETTS

West
Stockbridge
Granby

Barrington
West
Springfield
Mt. Washington Springfield

Hudson River

Stafford
Somers
Enfield

NEW
YORK

CONNECTICUT
Windham

Preston

Connecticut River
Stonington

Long Island Sound

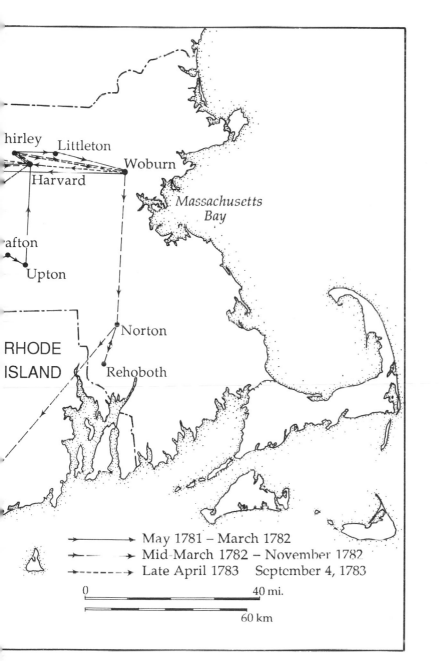

hirley
Littleton
Woburn
Harvard

Massachusetts Bay

afton
Upton

RHODE
ISLAND
Norton
Rehoboth

→ May 1781 – March 1782
→ Mid-March 1782 – November 1782
→ Late April 1783   September 4, 1783

0   40 mi.

60 km

1. Ann Lee's Travels
Drawn by John Michael Hollingsworth.

of events. Ann Lee, William Lee, and James Whittaker all counseled with individuals, praying and encouraging them in their quest for conviction. All three were bold in rebuking evil and denouncing the ways of the world. All spoke in the meetings, although some traditions suggest that Ann Lee was "a woman of few words" and that her brother—especially talented as a singer—was not "much gifted in public speaking." Whittaker, by contrast, was reputedly a skilled and able public spokesman. He, not Ann Lee, was probably the principal Shaker speaker in the meetings. This triad of Shaker leaders moved according to the inner direction they felt at the moment. Stephen A. Marini's characterization of their pattern of leadership as "a kind of ensemble improvisation" is useful as long as it is sufficiently recognized that the three played varied roles and that none of the three exercised any particular function exclusively.[51]

It is impossible, nonetheless, to deny Ann Lee's primacy in these activities. Yet describing her precise role in the society at this time is difficult. The early characterizations of her by apostates and outsiders as "the mother" provide one important clue to her functions both at Niskeyuna and on the missionary journey. According to Shaker traditions, too, Ann Lee embodied the highest ideals of motherhood. She was depicted as a concerned, loving, solicitous individual who developed deep personal relationships with her followers—her children. But tenderness was accompanied by a resolute firmness that she displayed when disciplining her disciples, rebuking them for mistakes, or encouraging them to strive for perfection. These two sides of the mother image, which depend on traditional conceptions of a woman's role, are leading features of Ann Lee's persona in the Shaker tradition. Lee is also described as a humble servant who waited on her followers, caring for their spiritual and physical needs, providing them with food and shelter, even giving her own bed to those who came to inquire about the Shakers. She was not aloof, but rather expressed affection for her followers in the most human and natural ways—taking them by the hand, touching them, loving them as a parent. This maternal image does nothing to diminish the power of Lee. On the contrary, it reflects her charisma in a distinctively feminine manner as measured by the standards of her time.[52]

The response to the Shaker leaders was mixed. Those favorably inclined toward the society were strengthened in their convictions and nurtured in the faith. New converts also were attracted who confessed their sins to the missionaries. Yet those opposed to the Shakers were likewise fortified in their resolve to oppose the group, and they frequently engaged in verbal abuse of and open hostility toward the traveling band. The public meetings of the Shakers often angered local residents. Physical attacks on the itinerants sometimes followed. Mobs formed in several towns, provoked occasionally by local clergy, other times by ruffians bent on mischief. Sometimes the opposition became so rabid that it drove the Shakers from the area.[53]

This scenario was repeated time after time, according to the society's accounts of the journey. The visit to Stonington, Connecticut, was typical. There the itinerants resided at the home of Joshua Birch for more than three weeks, while also visiting other families in the area that had "professed" the faith. Several public meetings were held, according to the record, where "the testimony of the gospel was opened" with its demand for confession and forsaking all sin, especially the "carnal gratifications of the flesh." But this doctrine displeased a number of "false professors, who wished to be Christians without the cross." Embarrassed by the exposure of their guilt, these opponents "maliciously stirred up persecution against these witnesses of the truth." Members of the Baptist society in Stonington, for example, were the ringleaders of the opposition; they harassed the visitors, "threatened and reviled them," and "beat and abused" some of their followers. Given an ultimatum to leave town within twenty-four hours or face the consequences, the Shaker leaders departed.[54]

Some of the local visitations were as short as three or four days; others extended to several weeks or, in a few cases, several months (the Shaker party spent the entire winter of 1782 at Asa Bacon's in Ashfield, Massachusetts). The only significant exception to this pattern of itinerant evangelism was the prolonged, recurrent residence of Ann Lee and the others at Harvard, Massachusetts. The Shakers first arrived at Harvard in June 1781. Initially they stayed at the home of Isaac Willard, an early convert to the new gospel. Later they took over the large house constructed by the followers of Shadrach Ireland, a charismatic Baptist elder from Charlestown who, upon becoming a communitarian, had attracted a substantial following after fleeing to the Harvard area. Ireland had called for an end to traditional marriage and the inauguration of a celibate society for everyone, that is, everyone but himself. The members of his sect hoped to achieve "physical and spiritual perfection." They adopted an apocalyptic perspective on events of their day, expecting the imminent arrival of Christ. Shortly before his death in 1778, Ireland spoke of his own immortality and instructed his followers not to bury him, a command they obeyed for ten months after his demise. Despite their eventual disappointment, many members of Ireland's sect continued together, centering their activities in Harvard at the Square House.[55]

The traveling band of Shaker missionaries found in Harvard a ready-made audience for their message. Some of the Irelandites quickly embraced the Shaker gospel and joined the new society. The Square House, in turn, was purchased for the Shaker leaders, who used it as the center for their activities in the eastern part of Massachusetts. From it they traveled to such surrounding towns as Shirley, Littleton, Woburn, and Petersham. They attracted large numbers of the faithful and the curious. Harvard became the most significant Shaker location in New England, the eastern center of the society's activity corresponding to Niskeyuna in the West. At Harvard the Shakers experienced their greatest missionary successes and, as a result, also some of the most violent opposition.[56]

In Harvard the Shakers attracted large crowds of people, many of them poor, who often received food at the Square House. But rumors again circulated widely about the Shakers' unwillingness to support the revolution. When local officials confronted the itinerants with these charges, they denied being enemies of the patriotic cause. Wartime circumstances in which food and grain were in short supply aggravated the situation. Local officials, unconvinced by the Shaker claim to legitimate residence, "warned them out"—a customary practice in New England whereby transients were kept from becoming a local burden. This formal warning, however, was ineffective. In January 1782 the local militia moved to enforce the expulsion order and drove the Shakers physically from the Square House and from the township of Harvard. According to Shaker tradition, these actions represented persecution and opposition to the gospel. From the perspective of the townfolks, the action was taken to rid the area of undesirable transients and the unworthy poor.[57]

The violence directed against the Shakers at Harvard was repeated at other locations. More than once on the journey Ann Lee was dragged from her bed, abused by mobs, and examined physically to see if she was a man, a woman, or a witch. William Lee and James Whittaker were whipped and beaten by opponents and driven out of town by rioters. The dwellings where they lodged were stoned. Pistol shots were fired at houses where worship was conducted. Their disciples were clubbed, caned, and beaten with "cudgels and large whips." These actions, similar to those of other early American mobs, were directed with all their fury against the Shakers in the 1780s.[58]

The missionary journey, according to Shaker tradition, came to a close when the party of itinerants was run out of Massachusetts by an angry mob that literally escorted them to the border, forcing them to return to New York. After nearly twenty-eight months on the road, the travelers arrived back at Niskeyuna at eleven o'clock at night on 4 September 1783, having "travelled many hundred miles, and suffered indescribable hardships, afflictions and persecutions, to establish the gospel in this land, and lay the foundation of Christ's Kingdom on earth." The New England journey was the high point of the public ministry of Ann Lee. It gained for her and the other leaders new stature and reputation among both the Shakers and those outside the society. Highly successful, the trip laid the groundwork for the subsequent numerical and geographical expansion of the sect. It also occupies an especially significant place in the annals of the society. The oral traditions surrounding this itinerancy later shaped the public image of Ann Lee as the founder of the Shakers.[59]

The journey came at a critical moment in the development of the young sect. Rapid growth in the number of converts presented both opportunities and problems. Ann Lee and the other leaders of the expanding society needed to establish their authority and control over the widely scattered members. The journey allowed them to do this and to strengthen new converts in their commitment to the Shaker gospel. The Shaker leaders exerted spiritual influence through their charismatic powers. They were able to identify likeminded persons in the scattered towns, thereby building local cells of disciples. Without such networks of support, the new converts would have faced unbearable pressures to give up their new faith and return to their former religious traditions. The persons who hosted the itinerants often became leaders in the young society, pivotal individuals around whom others subsequently gathered and identified themselves as Shakers. The missionary journey set the stage for the gathering of the Believers into local societies.[60]

The Teachings of the First Witnesses

The teachings of Ann Lee and the other early leaders were not written down during her lifetime. Therefore one of the most difficult tasks facing the historian who wishes to reconstruct the development of Shaker theology is identifying the original kerygma proclaimed by the founders. That proclamation must be distinguished from pronouncements ascribed to them by later traditions. Making this distinction is essentially the task of the source critic, for within the body of oral testimonies collected, edited, and printed by the Believers in the nineteenth century lie clues to the original Shaker gospel. The confidence of some scholars notwithstanding, recovering that religious message in its pristine form may be impossible.[61]

The sayings attributed to Ann Lee constitute a rich body of traditional lore preserved, in some cases, for more than two hundred years. These sayings, first published in substantial number in 1816 as part of the *Testimonies of the Life, Character, Revelations and Doctrines of Our Ever Blessed Mother Ann Lee, and the Elders with Her,* form the basis for the society's ongoing claims concerning her teachings. Although far less numerous, similar traditional materials exist in the same collection for both William Lee and James Whittaker. The critical question is to what extent the *Testimonies* accurately represents the teachings of the first witnesses.[62]

The published testimonies do not reveal directly the kerygma of Ann Lee. That original proclamation is buried under several layers of Shaker tradition, including the nineteenth-century *Testimonies* as arranged by the editors and the oral traditions from the "eye and ear witnesses" who knew her. Only the printed text is accessible with certainty. The oral traditions may be available, but only if the nineteenth-century editors have reproduced faithfully and without emendation or gloss the statements of the older Shakers. The actual sayings of Ann Lee remain unverifiable because few, if any, external independent sources exist for confirmation. The visions and revelations ascribed to Lee by the Believers are inaccessible by any means. The historical and religious implications of these judgments will become apparent as we proceed.[63]

The hand of the nineteenth-century Shaker editors is evident in the text of the *Testimonies.* The Believers who collected the statements acknowledged that their intention was to defend the reputation of the "first Witnesses"—a term used to designate the original English Believers—especially that of Ann Lee. The editors arranged the testimonies into a coherent narrative and grouped the evidences and teachings relating to the Shaker gospel. "Herein may be seen," they wrote, "as in a mirror, the lives, examples and sufferings, the precepts, doctrines, spiritual gifts and divine manifestations of our ever blessed parents in the gospel; by which it will readily be perceived, that we have received the gospel, not by precept only; but by example also." Rather than recording "every transaction" in the lives of the founders, the nineteenth-century editors sought to "prove" the truthfulness and authenticity of "the spiritual Zion, now established on earth." In other words, the *Testimonies* is first and foremost a collective confession of faith in narrative form.[64]

The editors chose to tell the story of the first witnesses in a fashion reminiscent of spiritual autobiography. The unifying theme in the narrative is the struggle between good and evil, the conflict between witnesses to the truth and opponents of the Shaker gospel. The text depicts the founders repeatedly suffering persecution at the hands of the wicked. Although evil appeared to prevail, the editors assured their readers that "the gospel would be kept; that the work of God would increase . . . and God's people would be protected . . . and that the power of God would yet overcome all things." Furthermore, they promised, the wicked would in time receive their due, for those who have "rejected the gospel" do not prosper but die uncommon deaths, "distinguished by judgments, beyond what falls to the ordinary lot of mortals."[65]

The editors used the recollections of older Shakers to fill in the story line and to sketch the teachings of the first witnesses. Numerous didactic statements are attributed to Ann Lee, sayings that subsequently have become sacrosanct by their repetition. The editors declared, for example, that the founders had taken "great pains" to "teach and instruct" concerning "temporal things" because such affairs impinged directly on spiritual development. One Shaker recalled, "At a certain time, on taking leave of some who had been at the Church, and were about to return home, Mother addressed them as follows; 'Go home, and put your hands to work and your hearts to God: for if you are not faithful in the unrighteous mammon, how can you expect the true riches?'" Lee's most celebrated epigram—"Hands to work and hearts to God"—is repeated elsewhere in the edited collection. These didactic formulas, although transmitted with "great accuracy" as fixed texts, have limited historical usefulness because it is impossible to establish the specific circumstances from which they originated.[66]

Other sayings ascribed to Ann Lee in the *Testimonies* reflect the same character. "A certain young man came to Mother," Lucy Wright remembered, "with some peach and plumb stones in his hand, and asked her if he might plant them. 'Yea; (answered Mother;) do all your work as though you had a thousand years to live, and as you would if you knew you must die tomorrow.'" Similarly, Hannah Cogswell recollected that Lee told her and other young women at Niskeyuna "to live together, every day, as though it was the last day you had to live in this world." The preservation of these sayings concerning industry and the value of time suggests that in the early *nineteenth* century Shakers placed a high priority on such virtues. Whether Ann Lee ever spoke these precise words is relatively unimportant. By associating these sayings with her, the Shaker editors provided the highest possible sanction for such principles and practices.[67]

The *Testimonies* contains ritual injunctions relating to specific religious practices, such as the necessity of public confession of sins. Ivory Wilds, for example, remembered that Ann Lee once said, "It is the heart which God looks at. The heart, with its hidden abominations, covered and concealed from the witnesses of Christ, becomes like a cage of unclean birds, and never can be cleansed short of a full and free confession." It is impossible to determine the original historical setting of this saying. From the standpoint of nineteenth-century Shakerism, however, the context was immaterial because the point of the tradition—the necessity of ritual confession—was extremely clear to all members of the society.[68]

Many of the stories recorded in the *Testimonies* are properly classified as "historical tales." Such recollections, perhaps based on real incidents in the life of the storyteller, become narrative creations when recounted. They often combine personal experience with other "traditional aspects of story-telling—predictable form, evidence of cultural and personal stylization, conventional functions." In such tales the historical dimension is secondary to the goal of instructing, edifying, giving pleasure, or defending certain positions. Students of oral traditions generally find such tales less historically trustworthy than other kinds of sources, and therefore these accounts must be used with great caution for reconstructing the basic story.[69]

The testimony of Samuel Ellis, an early convert, fits this pattern. According to the *Testimonies,* Ellis recalled an incident in the autumn of 1782 when Ann Lee entered a room full of followers at Ashfield. After singing for a time, she addressed those assembled and chided them for loving their lust, ease, and sloth instead of "the gospel." "You are a lazy idle people; you have set out in the way of God," she said, "and think you have travelled far enough." According to him, "the people all received from her a great gift of sorrow and repentance; and were sent away with a blessing." This account has the conventional marks of the genre. In this instance, Ellis himself profited from the instruction and from his acquaintance with Lee. He recognized something as "story worthy" in his tale. Furthermore, telling the story confirmed his place in the society as one who had known the founders. The tale itself, however, contains nothing to validate the authenticity of the particular saying attributed to Ann Lee.[70]

In sum, any attempt to recover the original proclamation of Ann Lee from the *Testimonies* is fraught with difficulties. The accounts of the "eye and ear witnesses," edited and arranged by the nineteenth-century editors, cannot be accepted uncritically as the basis for reconstructing the kerygma of the founders or the early history of the society. The principal historical value of the sayings in the *Testimonies* is that they underscore the norms, values, and practices prevailing in Shaker society at the time the oral traditions were collected, that is, during the second decade of the nineteenth century. Because of these difficulties, the earliest external sources reflecting on the teachings of Ann Lee, such as Valentine Rathbun's *Account*, although few in number and biased, become valuable resources in any effort to reconstruct and confirm the substance of the religious message of the founders.[71]

One such external source is Amos Taylor, an apostate whose experiences in the early 1780s included personal contact with five Shaker settlements. Like Valentine Rathbun, he denounced the sect and warned against falling prey to its devices. Taylor was explicitly concerned with the theological challenge posed by the Shakers. Like Rathbun, he believed that they intentionally concealed their more offensive beliefs from potential converts, and therefore he set out to expose their doctrinal scheme. According to Taylor, the Shakers believe in free will and human capacity; every individual is able "to choose or reject the truth of God." Through their society, however, God is reconciled with humans: sins are forgiven through confession to the first witnesses. Only in their church and not in any "single person" is Christ's "publick appearance," or second coming, fulfilled. No salvation exists outside their society. Those "assimilated into the character of Jesus Christ in his Church," according to the Shakers, are truly regenerate; those who accept this "gospel of the first resurrection" will not experience the "second death." The Shakers teach that a new dispensation has begun on earth and that the judgment of the world is now under way. The church in the new age has abandoned "the order of natural generation." Final redemption is also available for the "departed spirits" through "travel and labour." Through the perfection of "the Elect Mother of the Shakers" and the other leaders, the authority of the society is established.[72]

The private correspondence of William Plumer of Epping, New Hampshire, who visited several groups of Shakers in 1782 and 1783 and spoke with Ebenezer Cooley among others, is another important external source for the early teachings of the sect. Plumer's comments, less hostile and less systematic than Taylor's, were not intended for publication. He singled out Ann Lee as "the famous matron known as 'The Elect Lady'" whom the Shakers associate with the figure in the Book of Revelation, equating her flight to America with the biblical flight into the wilderness. He emphasized the society's belief in perfection and the power of "mighty works," such as miracles and healings, as well as in direct leadings from God. It was this ecstatic dimension of the sect that most bothered Plumer, whose own religious perspective was rationalistic. He criticized the Shakers for avoiding all "reasoning on the subject of religion" and for their condemnation of "vain philosophy." Like other "enthusiasts," he noted, they "use every method to stifle the voice of nature and prevent rational inquiry." Their religion rests "on the authority of Scripture [which they knew well, according to Plumer] and testimony of the Spirit." But, he added, they seem overly concerned with trifles, such as the length of their hair, cleanliness, and neatness in "houses, dress and food."[73]

Another valuable printed source appeared in 1783, the work of Benjamin West, who described himself as having been "deluded by them [the Shakers], to the great injury of himself and family." As a result of his own "sorrowful experience," he hoped to save others from "impending delusions" by publishing biblical cautions against these "false Christs and false prophets." West spared no words in his attack on "the strange Woman, or her Prosolites." He charged Ann Lee with witchcraft and deceit, with enticing converts through flattery and threats. The rules governing this "body of Europeans" violate the created order of God because men and women do not "lodge in one bed" and women do not remain in subjection to men. "Thus women become monsters, and men worse than infidels in this new and strange religion." Furthermore, they curse their own fathers and mothers and support the destruction of families. They explain their belief that Christ has come a second time by "the mistical numbers specified in the prophecies of Daniel, as well as by their signs and wonders." For a time West himself was persuaded "that a new dispensation had taken place" among them, and he became "deeply involved" with the group. At length, however, he became convinced that he had been deceived by "a papist system" and "false testimonies." He thus set out to warn others that the "cannons of God's word are loaded with heavy curses" against "all such miserable offenders."[74]

In the same year yet another hostile description was published as part of a general account of religious errors. Its unsigned author wrote,

> A new sect of religionists appeared, in the state of New York, in 1779, who have commonly gone by the name of Shakers, from the unnatural motions, and convulsive contorsions of the body which distinguished them from all other sectaries; these shocks of nature, were attended with so much violence, and pain, as to afford ground to conclude them the issue of some diabolical influence, yet, with them, they passed for acts of the most exalted devotion; sufficient to authorize them to overset the christian religion, and entitle them to

be regarded as the final judges of the quick and dead. These visionaries have dispersed themselves in New England; and given no
small trouble to sundry places in each of its States.

The implication was that satanic influences were producing unnatural
and wicked behavior among members of the sect.[75]

Using such outsider observations, Clarke Garrett argues that in the
two-year period ending with Ann Lee's death the Shakers experienced a
unique time of unrestrained spirit possession. During this period, the leaders encouraged a variety of extraordinary ecstatic and ascetic behavior that
subsequently became the object of sustained attacks by critics. Apostates,
for example, charged the Shakers with using alcohol excessively, dancing
naked, exorcising demons, burning books, and destroying other objects of
value. Apologists for the Believers have standardly dismissed these charges
as hateful inventions. Garrett, by contrast, takes seriously the logic of spirit
direction and explains how these actions demonstrate the fervor of sec
tarians. Nakedness became a testimony of commitment to purity, liquor a
means of fostering visions, exorcism a form of spiritual healing, and icono-
clasm a token of the full rejection of the material world. The Shaker obses-
sion with overcoming lust may have led the Believers to practice severe
forms of public mortification. In that context the charge that Ann Lee
pummeled the private parts of her followers as a frenzied act of ascetic
discipline cannot be dismissed. Garrett has measured the contemporary
accounts carefully and from them concludes that the Shaker proclamation
during the last years of Lee's public ministry fostered extreme behavior
that was later curbed within the society.[76]

The descriptions of the society by Taylor, Plumer, West, and others
also confirm that certain distinctive eschatological claims were being
made by the Shakers in the early 1780s. The members of the sect were
announcing the arrival of a new dispensation of regeneration and perfection. The demands they made on converts were consistent with this apocalyptic vision. Likewise, they were harsh in their condemnation of the
established churches and conventional social institutions. The sayings in
the *Testimonies* that underscore the eschatological vision of the early
Shakers may be among the oldest and most authentic of the recorded traditions. Those concerned with the details of communal living seem to be of
later origin. The outsider accounts of Ann Lee's role in the sect offer insights into her particular style of leadership and at the same time confirm
the standard cultural attack against all women who presumed to exercise
authority in religious matters.[77]

The Close of the Age of the Founders

Following the return of the itinerants to Niskeyuna in September 1783, the resident ministry of the Shaker leaders resumed much the same pattern as previously. The autumn and winter months were filled with counseling, spiritual labor, and preaching. Increasing numbers of converts and inquirers sought these services. The sect had profited greatly from the missionary effort to "lay the foundation of Christ's Kingdom on earth," even though the three leaders of the society had suffered physically from the hardship and fatigue attendant on the travel and from the persecution and hostility.[78]

Soon, however, the situation of the young society changed dramatically. William Lee died at Niskeyuna on 21 July 1784 and was buried two days later. According to Shaker tradition, he did not "appear to die by any natural infirmity; but he seemed to give up his life in sufferings." Shortly before his death, he reportedly "rose from his bed" and danced as a fellow Shaker sang for him. After the funeral, according to later reports, James Whittaker eulogized William Lee for "his faithfulness and zeal in the work of God." Whittaker declared that Lee was "the most violent man against sin that ever my eyes beheld."[79]

William Lee's death no doubt was a source of sadness to his sister. Whether it had other immediate effects on her is unclear. The *Testimonies* reports that she began to anticipate her own death and tried to prepare her followers for that departure. Less than two months later, early on the morning of 8 September, Ann Lee also expired. According to tradition, shortly before she died she told those around her, "I see Brother William coming, in a golden chariot, to take me home." Her death, it was reported, was "without a struggle or a groan." The *Albany Gazette* printed the following short obituary: "Departed this life, at Nisquenia, Sept. 7, Mrs. Lee, known by the appellation of the *Elect Lady*, or *Mother of Zion*, and head of that people called Shakers. Her funeral is to be attended this day." At the funeral, as described in the *Testimonies*, James Whittaker addressed separate comments to the Shakers and the non-Shakers. With the Shakers he shared his sorrow at the loss of "two friends" and his concern for the "gospel of Christ." "You have all got to feel so too—to be reconciled to do God's will," he said, "and to feel that the gospel is your only interest." To the non-Shakers he announced that the Shaker gospel was the only way of salvation, "the last display of God's grace to a lost world."[80]

The death of a charismatic leader is always threatening to the cohesion and stability of an infant sect. The Shakers were no exception, but they had an advantage over many groups. After William Lee and Ann Lee died, James Whittaker stepped forward and assumed full responsibility for directing the fortunes of the society. The tripartite pattern of leadership had given Whittaker the experience, a substantial measure of public recognition, and the widespread respect that enabled him to establish quickly a base of authority in the society. His actions, however, were not without opposition. Whittaker's natural rivals were the other remaining English Shakers. John Hocknell accepted his leadership; James Shepherd, Richard Hocknell, and John Partington did not, and they soon left the society.[81]

James Whittaker brought to his new position several special qualifications. He was one of the original English witnesses and had been a faithful disciple of Ann Lee from the beginning. According to the recollections of Mehetabel Farrington, he was the one who had supplied nourishment to Ann Lee through the keyhole of her jail cell in Manchester. In America, Whittaker emerged as the most able and forceful public spokesman for the sect. He had established his credentials within the society by playing a major role in the missionary journey through New England, by standing with Ann Lee and William Lee at the head of the sect, and by suffering with them in times of hardship. He possessed another advantage, too: he was literate—able to both read and write. According to tradition, he read the scriptural passages during worship meetings. Whittaker used these abilities to communicate with the scattered Shakers and to represent their cause to the outside world. As the most prominent remaining Shaker at the time, he was ideally situated to take over leadership.[82]

Whittaker had already used his skills on behalf of the young society. In 1782 he had written a letter to Josiah Talcott, a new convert at Pittsfield, urging him in the name of "truth, industry, honesty and faithfulness" to get busy and do what was necessary to be a good farmer. "Thou art idle and slothful whereby thy Land lay unimproved and pretty much waste; whence arises want and a great burden to the poor man who dwells in the house not far from thee." Whittaker minced no words; he called Talcott's inactivity "abominable in the Sight of God," sure to bring divine wrath in hell. He also condemned the women who lived with him as "idle hatchers of Cockatrice eggs and breeders of Lust and abominable filthiness as well as covenant Breakers." In the manner of an evangelical preacher, he challenged Talcott and the others to mend their ways. Whittaker was a strict disciplinarian; his style was harsh, judgmental, and direct.[83]

Whittaker was also a skillful manager and administrator. In his letter, he ordered Talcott to put his "whole place in order," both physically and spiritually. Get the farm ready for plowing and seeding, mend the fences, and haul the dung, he ordered. "Make your women turn out and mortify their lusts," he also commanded. According to Whittaker, Talcott had enough land to maintain three or more families. If he neglected his responsibilities, he warned, God's wrath would descend. Talcott would be cut off from the church and lose his land, too. "He that is slothful in business is Brother to him that is a great waster and such God hates," Whittaker proclaimed.[84]

In the months following the death of Ann Lee, Whittaker secured his position as leader of the society and took some new initiatives, too. He continued the effort to consolidate the families of Shakers scattered across New England by visiting them and encouraging them to share their possessions with one another. This "gathering" of the society required some to sell their homes and farms and live with others. In 1783 William Plumer had noted that the converts in the New Hampshire area were practicing the Shaker "doctrine of having all things in common," patterned after the New Testament apostles. The act of sharing also made it possible to marshal the necessary resources for construction of a meetinghouse for the society. The first such structure for worship was raised at New Lebanon on 15 October 1785, on land owned by George Darrow (fig. 2). At the dedication of that building, Whittaker reminded the members of the society about their covenant responsibilities. He also issued a series of orders concerning their behavior in the meetinghouse. They were to act there with "reverence and godly fear," men and women taking care to enter by separate doors and not to sit together. Idle chatter and laughter were prohibited as was all commercial activity, because the meetinghouse "was built to worship God in, and to repent in." It was always to be kept clean and orderly.[85]

The circumstances of the society during Whittaker's leadership are illustrated further by his correspondence with the non-Shaker Henry Van Schaack of Richmond, Massachusetts, who was active in the fight against the Congregational establishment in that state. Provoked by opposition from a man named Hezekiah Frailey, Whittaker declared to Van Schaack that Frailey was a person of questionable character. Van Schaack's reply provides details concerning the harassment of the Shakers and their apparent unwillingness to seek public redress. Van Schaack stepped forward to serve as an advocate for the sect; yet he questioned the Shakers' refusal to stand up for their own rights. "I find them to continue inflexible in absurdity," he wrote, "and that they would hear Gods name profaned on Sundays in their places of worship, themselves abused, their women treated with obscenity rather than make a complaint to a Magistrate." He feared that such behavior might lead to a general decline of respect for the law.

2. First Shaker Meetinghouse in New Lebanon
Watercolor by Benson John Lossing, dated 18 August 1856. By that year the building,
which served as the meetinghouse from 1785 to 1824, had been moved and converted
into a seed house. (Courtesy the Huntington Library, San Marino, California.)

Van Schaack also expressed "deep concern" about an "opinion" being
spread among the members that it was "for the Glory of God" that the
Shakers should "quit their present possessions and seek for an uncertain
residence elsewhere." That move, he hoped, would not take place. A friend
of all dissenters, Van Schaack tried to persuade Whittaker and his followers to be less radical so as to maintain peace and order in the region.[86]

Whittaker acquired a reputation for preaching the full severity of the
Shaker gospel, demanding complete withdrawal from the world. According to Shaker tradition, he emphasized "self-denial and the cross, and the
necessity of confessing and forsaking all sin," often couching his proclamation in eschatological language. "The judgment of God is coming," he
reportedly declared, "and it is nigh at hand." In a letter to his "natural relations" in England in 1785, he underscored the ascetic side of the Shaker
gospel, boasting that he had left behind all "earthly profits and pleasures,
all earthly generation, and propagation." He exhorted his relatives to do
the same by putting to death the "man of sin." Those who "obey the gospel
of Christ's second appearance," he wrote, will also renounce the "desire of
copulation with woman." The intensity of Whittaker's zeal became apparent in the condemnation of his relatives. "I hate your fleshly lives, and

your fleshly generation," he wrote, "as I hate the smoke of the bottomless pit." He warned that he would not assist them in any temporal way unless they would forsake their "wicked lives and serve the living and true God." Only if they embraced the pure gospel would he look on them with "charity and compassion." At present, he wrote, you are "a stink in my nostrils." Be forewarned, he cautioned, for "the day of God's final visitation" is at hand. Whittaker embodied the spirit of radical sectarianism that is characterized by the condemnation of the ways of the world.[87]

Whittaker's harsh denunciation of those outside the Shaker fold was matched by his liberal affection for those within the society. In a 1786 letter, for example, he expressed "tender Regard" for Joseph Meacham's "Prosperity in the Gospel" as well as "tender Love & feelings" of his soul. In all his actions Whittaker confessed to being led by Scripture and by the "Gift" of the "Great power of God." His reliance on the gift in particular placed him squarely within the camp of the enthusiasts. But the period of Whittaker's leadership did not last long. While visiting scattered Shaker residences in 1787, he became ill. On 20 July he died at the home of David Meacham in Enfield, Connecticut. According to later tradition, at the grave site Joseph Meacham was "taken under operations of the power of God" and spoke with great power—a sign subsequently assigned prophetic significance.[88]

Whittaker's last will and testament provides an instructive measure of his mature religious views. In it he used highly traditional language to request the burial of his body in a "Desent Christian Manner" and the commitment of his soul to God, by which "hopeing throw the Merits of Christ Jesus my Lord to Meet with Eternal Salvation." The absence of any mention of Ann Lee in the testament is striking. Whittaker willed the balance of his estate, after debts and funeral expenses, "towards the Help Support and furtherhence of the Gospel and the Support of the Poor the Widdows and the fatherless of the Church of my Communion and of others." In death, too, Whittaker gave himself completely to the cause of the Shaker gospel, although he did so in a manner that was surprisingly charitable toward non-Shakers.[89]

Five months before Whittaker's death a brief essay dealing with "the tenets and practice" of the Shakers was published in Philadelphia. This unsigned piece, identified as "Written in Massachusetts," consists of nineteen articles of belief attributed to the Shakers, including the notions that the term "Christ" refers to "the attributes of wisdom and power," that Jesus was a man, and that the Holy Ghost signifies a "power or influence" on believers. Other articles focused on the "mother" who was "to be revered, believed, and obeyed" because the blessings of heaven came through her. Her followers, the article stated, think of themselves as the true church through whom the gospel is preached and gifts, such as miracles, are imparted. Their particular practices include confession of sin, labor in worship (singing, dancing, turning), combating evil, expelling devils, and blowing "the mother's love into each other, by breathing in their faces." At the same time, they avoid all bodily contact between the sexes. While acknowledging the common charges of "obscenity, intemperance, and madness," the article noted that the Shakers denied these allegations. "But," the essay continued, "it is notorious that they call rum the Spirit of God!!! and account it a piece of devotion to be filled therewith."[90]

The Age of the Founders came to a close with the death of James Whittaker in mid-1787. The first witnesses, who had guided and shaped the initial expansion of the sect, now no longer controlled its fortunes, although traditions about the three founders proved increasingly influential in the life of the society with the passage of time. The historical development of Shakerism during this period embraces two discrete and separable stages with only tenuous links between them. The earliest activities of the sect in England are obscured behind a cloud of later traditions. The story of the American Shakers begins afresh at Niskeyuna, with a handful of the same personnel and some of the same ideas. The controlling circumstances in the two locations were radically different.[91]

The initial historical period was above all an age of ecstatic gifts and signs, a time of free-flowing religious energies. In both England and America the leaders—most notably, Ann Lee—felt themselves directed by the spirit in their thoughts and actions. They drew strength for public testimony from an inner sense of direct experience with God. That conviction created a dynamic that attracted and persuaded disciples, first members of their own families and later others who heard and saw them.[92]

The proclamation of the first Shakers was apocalyptic in tone and sectarian in intention. The founders condemned the churches of the day as antichristian, claiming to possess in their society the only way of life and salvation. They demanded that their followers withdraw from tainted institutions—both ecclesiastical and social—and join them in seeking a more perfect union with Christ. The Shakers regarded the works of the spirit in their midst and the persecution provoked by their testimony as primary evidence of the truthfulness of their claims, thereby completing the circle of their religious logic. The message of the Shakers struck a responsive chord, especially among Americans beginning in 1780. Converts were drawn to the sect from the ranks of committed evangelicals for whom religious experience was commonplace, eschatology a shared language, and dissent a way of life. The turmoil of the revolutionary period created a congenial context for the growth of radical religious societies.[93]

The early Shakers were people of action, not persons given to rational reflection. Their religious ideas were neither systematic nor necessarily internally consistent. It may even be a misnomer to speak of an early Shaker theology. The ideas of the founders—confession as a necessity, the authority of the spirit, condemnation of sin, perfection as a possibility, the spirit of Christ in their midst, a new dispensation, the alteration of traditional family relationships—were not yet fixed points in a well-defined theological constellation. In fact, the society manifested its creative and vital energies in the constant flux of ideas.[94]

Ann Lee, the acknowledged leader of the sect, was clearly not its sole founder, nor was she the only charismatic force in the young society. In England she was initially overshadowed by the Wardleys. In America she shared power, authority, and the public platform with others, especially James Whittaker. There is considerable ambiguity in the record about her status and role in the society. In some documents she is ignored, in others featured. The ambiguity surrounding Lee is perhaps a product of her personality and style of leadership as well as of the cultural patterns of the day in which males dominated the leadership of religious activities. Considering such societal constraints, it is all the more remarkable that Ann Lee emerged during her short public ministry as the most creative force in the sect.[95]

The opening period of Shaker history was a time of beginnings. The founders planted seeds that would take root in subsequent years. The members of the society ultimately would develop an integrated system of doctrines, laws, rituals, and institutions. As of 1787, however, their religious ideas were unsystematized, their social relations unorganized, their worship unstructured, and their activities together rather informal. In other words, later views from the nineteenth century should not obscure the nascent quality of the sect in 1787.[96]

PART

TWO

The Gathering

and Building

of the Church:

The Establishment

of the

United Society

1787–1826

In the years following the War of Independence, Americans struggled to find a satisfactory arrangement for guarding republican virtues and sustaining a national union. Near the end of the 1780s the Articles of Confederation was set aside for a new constitution that established the framework for a federal system of government. Yet the crisis was not over for the young nation. The decades surrounding the turn of the nineteenth century were times of continued turmoil. The growth of organized political parties solidified opposing interests and led to increasing social conflict. Fiscal instability threatened a shaky national economy. At the same time, many of the problems facing the United States were themselves the product of growth, success, and emerging prosperity.[1]

Similarly, after the deaths of the English founders the scattered Shakers struggled with questions of union and order. During the Formative Period of their history, 1787 to 1826, a number of critical questions confronted members of the young society. How would the sect survive these difficult times? Who would emerge as the new leaders? What religious principles would guide the group? How should life be structured for the members? How should the Believers relate to the institutions of the new nation? Sectarian societies universally confront a difficult transition following the passing of the founding generation.[2]

The quest for union and order dominated the Formative Period of Shaker history. During this stage the sect was transformed from a loose group of scattered followers spread across New England and eastern New York into an organized national society of Believers gathered in nineteen villages located in eight states, from Maine in the East to Kentucky in the West. By 1826 the unity of the Shakers was expressed not only in their new name—the United Society of Believers—but also in their doctrines, covenants, laws, and rituals.[3]

These forty years were a time of building. The men and women of the society established a communal framework that has endured in some form for more than two centuries—a remarkable accomplishment, especially compared with other religious communitarian experiments in America. This organizational transformation did not take place without a price. The Shakers paid dearly for their success with heavy investments of time, energy, and resources as well as with physical hardship, internal conflict, and external persecution. In my judgment, the four decades of this Formative Period have had a greater impact on Shaker history than any other era, including the Age of the Founders.[4]

The Beginnings of Communitarianism

Less than a month after the death of James Whittaker, two Shakers in the Pittsfield, Massachusetts, area were attacked while traveling to a public meeting. Summoned before a justice of the peace, the assailants confessed that without provocation they had assaulted and shamefully abused the two, both verbally and physically. This incident reveals only one of the problems facing the members of the society at the time. Scattered across the countryside, the Shakers were extremely vulnerable to harassment and attack. Without strong leadership, they also faced the prospect of quickly losing the sense of common purpose and commitment that bound them together.[5]

Because the Shakers were dispersed widely throughout New England and eastern New York it was difficult for them to settle on a new leader. The young society lacked a structured means for determining who should assume the lead. No provision for succession had been established by the founders. Three early converts in the New Lebanon area—Calvin Harlow, Joseph Meacham, and Meacham's brother David—each laid some claim to leadership. All had earned respect within the society by their close involvement with the first witnesses and by their experiences during the opening of the Shaker gospel. According to tradition, each had been singled out for special attention and affection by Ann Lee. All three had spoken at Whittaker's funeral.[6]

For several months the three shared leadership responsibilities, traveling to the scattered locations where the faithful lived and seeking to strengthen bonds among the Believers. They attempted to marshal the resources of the sect to meet the challenges of the moment. Of the three, Joseph Meacham proved the most effective. Forty-five years old, Meacham had acquired considerable experience as a Baptist elder and as a leader of the schismatic Separates. He possessed a reputation for "knowledge & proficiency in religious subjects" as well as for piety and fervor, gifts that contributed to his emergence as Whittaker's successor. By December 1787 his two rivals withdrew and "acknowledged him as their Elder."[7]

Meacham became a pivotal figure in the evolution of Shakerism, the leader at a critical moment in the society's history. Although possessing charismatic gifts similar to those of the English founders, he ultimately established a different basis for authority within the sect. Meacham defined and structured the office of the ministry as it was practiced for the next two hundred years of Shaker experience. After him, leadership was exercised by the officeholder without primary respect to the spiritual gifts of that person. Succession in the leadership was never again in question, for the ministry bore responsibility for choosing its own successors.[8]

Joseph Meacham's rise to authority within the young society parallels the increasing availability of written resources about the movement. The history of the society after 1787 is more accessible to scholarly investigation because, despite continuing strictures against written creeds, the Shakers began to produce a voluminous documentary record of their activities. Meacham himself was literate, and though he left relatively few writings, the period of his leadership was not marked by the strident anti-intellectualism of the Age of the Founders. Nonetheless, reconstructing the society's history during the last years of the eighteenth century remains a difficult task.[9]

A biography of Meacham written some thirty years after his death illustrates the nature of the problem. This memoir, composed by Calvin Green, himself a prominent Believer, was part of a Shaker effort to recover a past that was quickly disappearing. It provides an extended hagiographical account of Meacham's life, work, and thought. Green's biography reflects the veneration felt for that second-generation leader in the middle of the 1820s. Meacham is praised for his intellectual abilities, religious fervor, and practical wisdom. Likewise, he is depicted as a gifted visionary, the frequent recipient of revelations. On one occasion, for example, it was reported that at New Lebanon he "walked out as far as the lot called the north cow pasture . . . and was there taken in a prophetic trance, & was laid down on a rock." The memoir noted that even the cows stopped feeding and surrounded him in silence, attracted to his spirit "with a reverential awe." This account underscores the theme of providential guidance during the society's formative years.[10]

According to Shaker tradition, prophecy and revelation were abundantly evident in Meacham's life. His arrival at Niskeyuna in 1780 was allegedly anticipated in a vision received by Ann Lee. Later he was identified by her as the person who would gather the church into the gospel order. His eventual succession to leadership in the society was supported by prophetic statements attributed to both Lee and Whittaker. Similarly, it was reported that shortly after he accepted the Shaker gospel Meacham received a revelation predicting that someday he would lead the sect. The society later construed the reports of these prophecies and visions as divine confirmation of his leadership role. (Such interpretations are commonplace in sectarian communities.) Meacham's close association with revelations emphasizes the continuing value placed on such activity within the society in the midnineteenth century.[11]

Meacham was not, however, an otherworldly mystic. On the contrary, he was a man of affairs whose principal accomplishments as leader of the society were practical: gathering the scattered converts into settlements, building physical structures for their life together, arranging the system of government for the community, and establishing rules and regulations. He also played a role in the development of a distinctive Shaker religious outlook and worship pattern. He did not accomplish these things singlehandedly, however, for he had numerous able assistants. Initially he gathered about himself a group of the most respected and experienced male members of the sect. Then, in one of his most significant administrative decisions, Meacham reaffirmed the principle of female leadership in the society and introduced the principle of parallel female authority by choosing as his partner in the ministry Lucy Wright, another talented early convert in America. Wright, who had been a close associate of Ann Lee in charge of the Shaker household at Niskeyuna, according to tradition enjoyed a special preeminence among the Believers because of her experiences with the English founders. In the years that followed her selection, she and Meacham worked together closely.[12]

The "gathering" of the scattered Shakers began in earnest at the end of 1787. Although Whittaker had made a limited effort to cluster converts during his brief tenure as leader, it was not until Meacham assumed responsibility for the sect that a clear directive to join together was delivered to all members. Even then, many were unable to comply with the mandate and continued as outlivers apart from the gathered communities. The effort at clustering had several practical advantages. It provided a measure of physical security from external opponents, it promised increased economic stability for participating members, and it fostered a strong sense of unity and common purpose within the sect. This move toward communal living contrasted sharply with the strategy followed during Ann Lee's lifetime. Now geographical consolidation replaced itinerant evangelism. Even before 1787, Whittaker had halted efforts at gaining new converts. After 1787 the energies of the Shakers were directed inward as they combined resources and attempted to stabilize the internal situation of the society.[13]

Meacham centered his activities at New Lebanon, which soon replaced Niskeyuna as the hub of Shaker life. This new location possessed several advantages over the initial settlement near Albany, not least of which was its position east of the Hudson and the resulting greater ease of travel to other areas of New England where Shakers were congregated. The early success of the sect in the New Lebanon area had created a

strong base of support for the movement in that locale. The new meetinghouse, too, gave the site a certain public prominence. Nevertheless,
Niskeyuna—after 1795 increasingly referred to as Watervliet—always retained a special status among members of the society because of its close
association with the English founders.[14]

During the years of Meacham's leadership, the Shakers constructed
a village suited to their collective needs on the mountainside overlooking
New Lebanon. Land donated by early converts in that area provided the
nucleus for the settlement. At first the Shakers used the existing buildings
on the property, but they gradually erected additional structures. The
meetinghouse, for example, had been built in 1785 on a site that was part
of the Darrow farm. After 1787 the society began constructing other buildings designed specifically for communal living.[15]

The schedule of construction was dictated by the needs and circumstances of the Believers. Following the meetinghouse, the first major project at New Lebanon was the "Great House" built in 1788 to accommodate
the influx of gathering Shakers. In October of the following year a "little
brick house" was begun south of the Great House. In June 1790 the foundation was laid for a "bake house." On 16 October the boys of the settlement moved into the chamber of that building; on 11 December the
"Little Girls" moved into the Brick House. In June 1791 dwellings were
begun for the "Second Family" and the "Elderly Peoples," structures that
were completed and occupied in August and September respectively. In
December the Shakers constructed a "spinning house." A dwelling for the
youths and the children and a store to serve as the deacons' Office, where
business was conducted with outsiders, were erected in the summer of
1792. The next summer the Believers constructed a kitchen and carried
out extensive renovations on the meetinghouse. In 1795 a new shop was
built west of the Brick House, which the sisters began to use in the fall.[16]

The initial internal structuring of the young community also took
place under Meacham's direction. He devised a hierarchical system of
three "courts," or families, each with its own designated leaders and responsibilities reflecting different levels of membership. All were in union
with one another. Distinctions among the three hinged on age, spiritual
accomplishments, and the degree of separation from the world. An inner
circle of adult Shakers constituted the first court, younger members of
lesser spiritual ability the second, and elderly persons the third. Male and
female were distinguished throughout the system. In each court the responsibility for spiritual affairs was in the hands of elders and eldresses
who were to be obeyed by all in the family. Temporal matters were the

concern of the deacons and deaconesses. Ultimate authority in the village resided in the spiritual officers of the inner court—the Shaker elders. This system of government, probably in place in some form by the beginning of 1792, would change substantially in future years, but the principles of structured authority, supervised living, and separation of the sexes as well as the division between spiritual and temporal responsibilities were firmly established.[17]

The gathering and structuring of the community at New Lebanon provided a pattern for similar activity at other locations throughout New England. Shaker settlements developed where the missionary journeys of the first witnesses had been especially successful. Meacham and Wright devoted special attention to the Believers at these locations, appointing male and female leaders for these places from among the most respected Shakers at New Lebanon. In 1790, for example, Calvin Harlow and Sarah Harrison were put in charge of the converts at Hancock and Tyringham, Massachusetts, as well as at Enfield, Connecticut. Eleazar Rand and Hannah Kendal were chosen for leadership at the Harvard and Shirley villages in eastern Massachusetts in 1791. The next year Job Bishop and Hannah Goodrich were appointed to supervise the settlements at Canterbury and Enfield, New Hampshire, and David Darrow and Ruth Farrington were selected for leading roles at New Lebanon as Elder Brother and Elder Sister. In 1793 John Barnes and Sarah Kendal undertook the parental responsibilities at Alfred and Sabbathday Pond in Maine. With these appointments Meacham and Wright consolidated their authority and that of New Lebanon (and Niskeyuna) over the distant Shaker settlements. They also took a crucial step toward developing a structural bond and a common identity among the residents of the scattered villages.[18]

Meacham played the principal role in formulating the rules and regulations that governed membership in the society and the activities of the gathered Shakers. Beginning in 1788, those accepting the gospel order entered into an informal oral covenant, which was probably renewed annually by the participants. In 1795, however, when conflicts arose over persons leaving the society, the first written covenant was signed by members of the church at New Lebanon. It focused primarily on the possession and use of assets—real and personal. In the agreement the Shakers articulated the principle of "joint interest," whereby all members "have an Equal right and privilege, according to their Calling and needs, in things both Spiritual and temporal." Consistent with this principle, the covenant allowed full membership only to those adults who, free of debts or claims, willingly gave their substance to the church for the "mutual good" and for such "Charitable uses" as the officers of the society saw fit. Members pledged never to bring claims against the sect for "Interest or Services." The Shakers believed that the principle of joint interest was not merely a right, but a duty, given that they had "received the grace of God in Christ by the Gospel, and were Called to follow him in the Regeneration." Special provisions were made in the covenant for younger persons and children who were not yet responsible for their own actions.[19]

In addition to regulations controlling admission into the society, rules governing diverse aspects of life together developed during these years. By at least 1790, for example, daily routines were fixed: "Times of lying down and rising, of meal times and meetings, etc." Six hours were allotted for sleep, but the precise times for sleeping varied from season to season. One Shaker noted in 1791 that "we had order to eat breakfast at 6, and eat our supper before meeting at night." The ministry fixed standards for various manufactured products. Their instructions for the production of wool hats governed acceptable style, suitable quality, and fair pricing, all of which reflected on "the Honnor of the Testemony and the Real good of Mankind." Young people at New Lebanon were taught proper respect for their leaders, including "how to call the elders of the church." Other rules traditionally associated with Meacham include counsels for kindness to animals, injunctions against the hybridization of plants and animals, strictures against unnecessary adornment in the construction of buildings, and admonishments to pursue a healthy life.[20]

Meacham influenced the formulation of the theological views of the community, too. He was probably the unsigned author of the first public description of the faith and practice at New Lebanon that appeared under the sponsorship of the society. That tract, the *Concise Statement*, attempted to substantiate the claims of the sect to be "the only true church." Meacham cast his explanation of the "gospel of the present appearance of Christ" in a historical mode, contending that God had extended grace to sinners through four discrete dispensations. In each, obedience was the key to salvation. Collectively, the four underscored the role of continuing revelation and the progressive character of redemption.[21]

According to Meacham, the patriarchs received the "first light of salvation" through promise, and under that covenant circumcision was the "sign" of obedience and an anticipation of future redemption. In the second dispensation, a "further manifestation" was made through the law of Moses; blessings were promised to Israel for obedience to the divine commands. This, too, was but a "shadow" of things to come. The "first appearance" of Christ in the flesh constituted the third dispensation. The gospel was the power of God to those who obediently "took up a full cross" and struggled against all sin. But the "mystery of God" was not "finished," because the church had fallen under the influence of "anti-christ, or false religion." During the fourth dispensation, or "last display of God's grace to a lost world," Antichrist would be destroyed and God's kingdom established on earth. The last dispensation had begun, according to Meacham's calculations, in the year 1747. Its inauguration was signaled by "visions, and revelations, and prophecies" as well as by the outpouring of other pentecostal "gifts." Salvation, he wrote, is accessible to those who obey the truths revealed in the day of the "second appearing of Christ."[22]

The *Concise Statement* provided a theological framework for understanding the events that had transformed the handful of Shaking Quakers at Niskeyuna into a substantial society by 1790. The gathering of the society, according to the tract, was part of a larger scheme. The divine plan for history was rushing toward its culmination in the activities of the Shakers. The publication therefore accented the responsibility of avoiding all sin and obeying the gospel of Christ as the way of salvation. Notably absent from the tract are any mention by name of Ann Lee or the Shakers and any explicit reference to the practice of celibacy or communal living. Meacham may have downplayed these elements in his public statement for strategic reasons. It is also possible that these concerns had not yet become definitive elements within the Shaker gospel.[23]

The private writings attributed to Meacham, by contrast, are more explicit on some of these difficult issues. Meacham is said to have defined the relationship between male and female. "The order & relation of the man & woman, is established of God in the new covenant." The one inaugurates, the other completes "the restoration of all things." The priority of man in the new covenant was unquestioned, according to these writings: he is "head over all things to his church." Nevertheless, the "further dispensation" had begun in "the day & work of Christ in his second appearing. . . . The Lord is now shaking the kingdoms & powers of the earth" while he is "building & establishing his Church."[24]

Meacham's role in the development of worship patterns in the young society was significant. According to the most authoritative study, Meacham was responsible for adapting to the changing circumstances of the society the "solemn songs" of the English founders, which had first given voice to the ecstatic utterances of the early charismatics. The need for union and order led him to curb the spontaneous movement of the spirit in the meetings. Meacham regularized the times for such gatherings and the structure of activities. Solemn songs—the "mixture of words & unknown

sounds as of words"—were sung at regular intervals in the worship, drawing all together in their "solemn & melodious Tone." This pattern of singing prevailed in the society until 1807. Meacham is also credited with
introducing "laboring" or ritualized dancing into the meetings, thus largely
supplanting individualized exercises. Meacham taught the "Holy Order,"
also known as the "Square Order Shuffle," to the members, which remained a prominent worship practice among the Shakers for generations.
In music and dance alike, Meacham moved to curtail individual expression by cultivating more collective forms of worship.[25]

Shortly before his death Meacham wrote to Lucy Wright, reflecting
on several concerns, including the issue of succession. Aware that his life
was rapidly drawing to a close, he expressed admiration and respect for
her role in the church. The success of the community, he asserted, was
the product of our "union & mutual Labours." He took special delight that,
in their efforts "for the Good of the Whole," they had been kept "from all
sin With Each other." Their intimacy had been a "union of the spirit"
whereby "foundations" had been laid for the "Gathering & Building of the
Chh." In that task "the man & the woman have Equal Rights in order &
Lots & in the Lead & Government of the Church *according to their Sex*
[emphasis mine] in this Latter Day." That equality "according to their
Sex," which Meacham understood patriarchally, was about to change.
After my death, he wrote, you will become "the Elder or first born," a position he had occupied until that time. Only then would the principle of
equality include the prospect of a female assuming the first position in the
Shaker order. Meacham also promised that Wright would receive the
"Greatest measure of the wisdom & Knowledge of God For the Protection
of souls."[26]

In mid-July 1796 Meacham traveled to the Shaker settlement at
Harvard, where he met with leaders from other locations. Shortly afterward, he returned to New Lebanon, where his health declined rapidly.
Less than a month later, on 16 August, he died. According to Shaker tradition, Father Joseph, as he was called by that time, filled his last days with
counsel and encouragement for the members of the community. He spoke
often of "the glories & beautiful revelations of the heavens." Several hours
before his death he reported that he had heard "a heavenly trumpet" sum-
moning him home—a last sign of divine approval. The death of Meacham
did not mark the close of an era. On the contrary, his consolidation of the
Shaker community subsequently made possible a new age of expansion
under his successor. By 1796 the sect no longer comprised a roving band

of charismatics and their followers. The foundations had been laid for a full-blown communitarian society.[27]

The Ministration of Lucy Wright

"Your Mother will have the gifts of God for you after I am gone." With these words Joseph Meacham is said to have assured the smooth transfer of power to Lucy Wright after his death. She, in turn, was acknowledged to be first in the order of the ministry by consent of the elders and by union of the members. The change in leadership did not bring immediate alterations in the fortunes of the young society. Nor were there indications that the Shakers were about to enter their most creative and productive decades, or that this daughter of New England, who had given up financial security and a good marriage to "bear the cross," would have more influence over the next twenty-five years on the sect's development than perhaps even Ann Lee had.[28]

When Wright took over the leadership in 1796 she inherited a series of problems facing the society. Not least of these was the persistent difficulty with younger members. Meacham had earlier expressed his frustrations concerning these "troubles," which he blamed in part for his own "weakness and sufferings." During the 1790s a large number of younger members "forsook the Church and went to the world." In 1796 alone twenty young members of the Church Family at New Lebanon defected, according to statistics cited by Isaac N. Youngs. Such youths were unable, Meacham wrote, to receive the "planting of faith in their understandings." This loss, unlikely to diminish "unless the older [Shakers] who are established are able to protect them," was a source of consternation to the leadership, for with the "rising generation" lay the ultimate fortunes of the celibate society.[29]

The problem was doubly embarrassing because this "great fermentation" among the young had become apparent to outsiders. One critic in 1796 predicted "an approaching revolution" within the ranks of the Shakers because they would be unable to retain the young persons who labored in their "lucrative manufactories." Not only were the youths deserting, but they were also pressing for the recovery of wages. This development came as no surprise to the observer who detailed the restrictions placed on the young in matters of learning, leisure, personal liberties, and "natural affections." No wonder they throw off the "irksome and barbarizing bondage," he declared, even though by so doing they are threatened with pursuit, whipping, and possible imprisonment. The decline of "frantic enthusiasm" has forced the society to resort to "artful" devices to keep its members. The leaders, including the "Chief Elder, or Pontiff, and Mother, or Chief Matron," he thought added to the problem with their double standard, demanding greater austerity and sexual restrictions from their followers than they themselves observed.[30]

The status of young Shakers would remain a nagging issue for the community. From the perspective of the ministry, the members of the rising generation were bent on pleasing themselves "with every fancy" and having "their own ways." From the perspective of outsiders, they were victims of a system that prevented them from leaving the villages and assuming their rightful place in American society. The second charge was especially heated and anguishing when made by relatives. In 1800, for example, more than forty citizens from the New Lebanon area, including at least two clergymen, petitioned the New York legislature on behalf of young persons at the village. The group charged that the Shakers had threatened their young members with physical and psychological "terror" to prevent them from communicating with their parents, relatives, and friends. According to the petition, the young were kept in a state of ignorance and under the "influence of their superiors." The petitioners sought redress of these conditions in order to obtain "legal access" to those who "wish to leave them and are weary of labouring for them on the Condition of Common Slaves." The relatives and friends hoped to provide information not subject to the censure of the elders, and thereby allow the youths the opportunity to "freely choose whether to remain there or not." Opponents repeated similar charges against the Shakers many times during the following years.[31]

The youthful rebellion was only the most manifest expression of a persistent problem with apostasy. Apostates in this and every other period threatened the society by draining its membership, tarnishing its public image, and jeopardizing its economic base. Departures also shook the community's collective sense of well-being. No period of Shaker history was immune to this threat. Early "turn-offs," such as Valentine Rathbun and Amos Taylor, were but the first among many who sought to expose and destroy the society. Some were less vindictive than others, like Seth Watkins, who demanded pay for his labor on the construction of the meetinghouse at New Lebanon, a claim that Joseph Meacham refused in a firm but reasoned manner. Others acted with more deliberate malice. Benjamin Goodrich, a member of the New Lebanon community, for example, brought a compensation suit against the deacon for his services even though he had received a settlement when he left the village. He maintained that he had signed the discharge under duress. The case of Goodrich v. Walker was heard in the supreme court of the state of New York in 1799. The jury decided against the plaintiff, but the society suffered in the public eye.[32]

Some apostates sought redress by vilification. Such was the strategy of Reuben Rathbun, who had converted to Shakerism in 1780 and served as an elder at Hancock village. In July 1799 he left the society after a sustained period of doubt and conflict. The next year he published an account of his "life and experiences," featuring the "trials and tribulations" that led to his separation. The challenge of the Shaker "cross," Rathbun reported, had attracted him to the sect. After joining, he labored "to become an *Eunuch* for the kingdom of heaven's sake." He had become a true believer, zealous in his dedication and unquestioning in his loyalty to the leaders. In spite of the afflictions associated with gathering and building the church, he wrote, "my faith was unshaken," for we were "encouraged by her whom we called and esteemed to be our mother," Lucy Wright. In 1796, however, he began to question Shaker practices. At issue for him were the definition of "gifts" in the church at New Lebanon, the process of mortification, the matter of compensation for those leaving the society, and the theological interpretation of Christ's return. Following disclosure of his doubts, Rathbun was publicly discredited by the leaders. Physically and psychologically distressed, he left the society, determined to make "the spirit of the Lord Jesus" rather than devotion to Shakerism the motivating force in his life.[33]

After leaving, Rathbun judged that Shaker teachings were "repugnant to the Gospel" and their actions uninformed by the "principles of morality." He reported occasions when there had been "a gift for men and women to strip naked and go into the water together." He described ascetic practices so severe that many lost physical control and were subject to "involuntary evacuations" of the "seed of copulation." Rathbun wrote about drunken brawls between Ann and William Lee, blasphemous language used by the English founders ("there never was a sailor that stepped on board a ship that exceeded them"), and "whoredom" committed by James Whittaker. In sum, he claimed to have been misled by an "*ignis fatuus*" into "a dismal wilderness of darkness" before coming to his senses and discovering "the true light." The Shakers summarily dismissed Rathbun's publication as a false and scurrilous attack on their beliefs and practices.[34]

Not unrelated to the difficulties caused by apostates were the economic problems facing the society. Despite the industry and frugality of the members, the society teetered for years on the edge of insolvency. The economic successes of the Shakers were constantly tested by uncontrollable contingencies. Frost, pestilence, and drought affected crop yields, monetary values fluctuated, fire destroyed buildings, claims were pressed by departing members, and debts to the world mounted. Although in 1798 the Shakers in New Lebanon and Hancock were able to send twenty wagons "Loaded with Provisions" to New York "for the Relief of the Poor of that Cyty," they themselves were forced to balance carefully their own needs and assets as well as the demand for goods with the society's capacity to produce.[35]

The Shakers' consistent refusal to bear arms or to take part in local militia drills was another steady drain on their resources. Because of their pacifism, they suffered persecution and financial penalties. Petitions for exemption from military duty were drawn up by the society as early as 1788. In one instance in 1790, two members "averse to bearing arms" were excused as long as the elders in their village annually certified that they belonged to the society. Exemption, however, was accompanied by the responsibility of providing funds for an alternate. In 1793 the Shakers at New Lebanon paid more than one hundred pounds for their "neglect of duty in the militia." Similar penalties plagued the Shakers throughout the first decade of the new century as they annually paid fines for "Nonatandance," "nonapparince," and "delinquencies on Company training." In 1809 the Federalists in the Massachusetts legislature drafted a bill providing that "every Quaker & Shaker taking the usual oaths of exemption shall pay six dollars & produce a certificate to the Officers of the Company." These penalties increased the financial burdens of the society.[36]

To these problems inherited by Wright must be added one more, provoked by her appointment as first in the ministry, namely, the challenge she presented to the traditional principle of male dominance in religious matters. Despite the precedent of Ann Lee, the principle of female leadership was not uniformly accepted throughout the society. Joseph Meacham himself initially had been scandalized by the idea. Following Lee's death, males had dominated as leaders of the sect for more than twelve years. Even the selection of Wright as Meacham's partner in the ministry had not altered that pattern radically. "In the first stages of building & arranging the Order of this consecrated Community," noted one Shaker historian, "like the Primitive Church in its first rise, the leading influence & directive Power rested almost exclusively in the male line; the females had not a corresponding share." Only later was the "correspondent Order & relation of male & female" revealed, understood, and instituted in the church. According to Calvin Green, Wright was chosen because she had "gained" the "Order of spiritual Mother." But her selection—a radical step—caused "much labor & extreme tribulation." These difficulties within the society were compounded by the "universal sentiment & custom" in the larger culture that called for binding females under the rules for married women laid down by the apostle Paul. In 1799, for example, Angell Matthewson was expelled from the society because he thought that "wimmin are fools & that men that are willin to have a woman to rule over them are fools also." The issue of "petticoat government" would not go away during Wright's tenure in the ministry.[37]

A general hostility toward the Shakers in the decades surrounding the turn of the century aggravated many of these problems. The Believers did not fare well during these times of turmoil. Pacifism and a disinterest in the political process attracted negative comment in an age of aggressive republicanism. Critics charged that the society's pattern of government by the ministry was undemocratic. The joint-interest scheme drew condemnation on the grounds that it exploited the labor of the rank and file for the benefit of a few. Celibacy, offensive to many outsiders, invited censure on moral and familial grounds. The belief in continuing revelation affronted the Protestant principle of biblical authority. Small wonder that the society was the object of sustained attack throughout the period.[38]

The Shakers needed a strong leader to deal with these complex internal and external problems. Wright was such a person, prepared for the task by her background and previous experience. Before joining the Shakers, she had been married to Elizur Goodrich, a merchant in Richmond, Massachusetts. After her conversion, she became a companion of Ann Lee, who had reportedly said that if the Shakers converted Wright it would "be equal to gaining a Nation." According to tradition, it was Wright who cared for Lee during her last illness and for whom the English founder expressed special affection. Wright emerged as a leading figure among the sisters at Niskeyuna. In early 1788 she was one of an inner circle chosen by Meacham to live at the meetinghouse in New Lebanon. By 1796, therefore, she was accustomed to exercising responsibility and had gained the respect and confidence of her colleagues, both female and male.[39]

The Shaker traditions surrounding Wright feature the miraculous elements accompanying her selection as first in the ministry. There is little need for miracles, however, to explain her remarkable success as a leader. She was a person of great practical ability who possessed remarkable administrative and organizational skills. Although her rise to power may have been aided by the ineffectiveness of Elder Henry Clough, Meacham's colleague in the ministry who had been responsible for supervising the young, Wright nevertheless quickly seized the initiative and established her authority within the society by dealing with the problems at hand. Most important, she gathered about her a cadre of able and loyal associates who implemented her policies and plans. She was also successful in winning the confidence of the membership scattered throughout the villages.[40]

Wright correctly perceived that many of the society's problems were interrelated. Some had been exacerbated by Meacham's decision to turn the energies of the society inward, no longer seeking converts from the outside world. Reversing his policy, she recognized, would strengthen the position of the Shakers by adding to the membership and stopping the drain on resources. By the end of the century the general mood in the society was supportive of these changes. The Shakers had been watching with interest the outbreak of new religious stirrings in the region, events historians subsequently have called the Second Great Awakening. The experiences of the past were not lost on the Believers: their own earlier successes had followed in the wake of the evangelical revivals. In 1799 Wright reopened the testimony and set about equipping the society to take advantage of a new period of missionary activity.[41]

As part of her strategy, Wright established a special "gathering order" within the society "for the purpose of laboring with, & initiating those who were, or might be prepared to receive the Gospel." In 1800 the Shakers set aside for this purpose the North House at New Lebanon, as well as surrounding land and other buildings. Wright appointed Ebenezer Cooley, distinguished by his earlier evangelistic successes, as the first elder of this unit and made him responsible for attending to the needs and interests of new converts and those considering membership. The Gathering Order became the Shakers' chief agency for the religious nurture of new Believers. Among the first to be gathered were members of the Wells family of Long Island, many of whom eventually occupied positions of leadership within the society. The establishment of the new order was also a partial response to the problems with the youths, for this arrangement allowed more attention to their discipline and education.[42]

Thomas Brown, perhaps the most perceptive and informative apostate of the early nineteenth century, described the functions of the Gathering Order in its early years. A resident of Cornwall, New York, his contact with the society began with a visit to Watervliet in mid-1798. Brown believed that the millennium was fast approaching, and he hoped to find a people ready to greet Christ on his return. It was a thoughtful and reflective Brown who inquired about the Shakers' fundamental principles and practices. After several visits, he confessed his sins and identified with the society, although he did not yet move to the village. He was especially impressed by the kindness as well as the "order, neatness, peace, love, and union" of the Shakers. Persuaded that Christ was with these people, Brown became an active proselytizer for his new faith, pressing his family and friends to join with him. He held public meetings to speak about his discovery of this new dispensation. During these months he continued to confer with leaders from Watervliet and New Lebanon, raising questions about the society's beliefs and practices and also about the vicious rumors concerning promiscuity and scandal among the Believers.[43]

After 1800, once the Gathering Order was in place, the society at Watervliet began to supervise more closely Brown's activities. Members of his family accepted the Shaker gospel, and he moved to a location near the village. At Watervliet he met frequently with Ebenezer Cooley and other elders, who grew increasingly concerned about his inquiries and his religious views. Brown, in turn, was uneasy because he began to perceive disagreement among the testimonies of the leaders. The decisions of the hierarchy seemed to him at times arbitrary and unreasonable. Lucy Wright, he thought, had become isolated from the common members. It was the demand for unquestioning obedience, however, that drove him from the society. Brown sadly concluded that Shakerism "could not be that clear dispensation pointed out in the scriptures, in which God would pour out his spirit upon all flesh, and all should know the Lord." As a result of his change of heart, he was censured by the elders and ostracized by the society.[44]

Following his expulsion, Brown published "a full and impartial account" of the Shakers, drawing on his own experiences and additional research. Although the society condemned his volume without even reading it, his account is a valuable source of historical information. Brown provides a detailed narrative of his interaction with the Believers as well as extensive citation of conversations with them. By contrast with the judgments rendered by other early apostates, Brown's observations are not jaded or overtly biased. His relative impartiality is evident in a closing prophetic note. "I am not of the opinion of many," he wrote, "that they [the Shakers] will soon become extinct. Their general character of honesty in their temporal concerns, and their outward deportment and order being such, that many may be induced to join them; and as industry and frugality are two great points in their religion, it is likely they will become a rich people." Brown's prediction was to be fulfilled in the years ahead.[45]

Under Wright's direction and with the consent of other leaders, the Shakers launched a second opening of the gospel. They devoted new energy and resources to the task of spreading their proclamation to a world not particularly interested in hearing it. For this evangelistic purpose Wright handpicked several members to serve as missionaries. Among those chosen to preach the Shaker gospel were Benjamin Seth Youngs, a talented convert who had joined the society in 1794, and Issachar Bates, a former Baptist preacher and seeker who entered in 1803. Youngs and Bates both had risen quickly to positions of responsibility in the sect. Accompanied by one or more companions, these Shaker missionaries began traveling to widely scattered locations throughout New York and New England. Youngs spent months on the road, taking every opportunity to speak about Shakerism. His activities as a missionary, recorded in a series of daily journals, reveal the standard evangelistic procedures of the Believers and some of the reasons for their success.[46]

The Shaker missionaries resided at the homes of converts or sympathetic inquirers, attempting to nurture commitment and to persuade others to join. Youngs summarized a typical situation in one family: "it is trying times, & very hard to give up all, & the way that he [the husband] turns doubtless She will—This day we spent in labouring to hold, & gather them as much as we were able." Some visits provoked domestic strife when relatives disagreed about the Shakers. On one occasion, Youngs reported, a husband "was enraged because his wife believd in this way, and meant to keep her faith." When she came home wearing a Shaker cap as a sign of commitment, the man "immediately foull'd it off." Because this violence persisted, the Shakers prudently decided that "it did not appear like wisdom to carry water in a basket—therefore the poor woman must do as well as She knows how at present." In spite of this setback, the membership records of the society attest to the success of this strategy of family networking.[47]

In some locations the itinerant Believers sought out the religious meetings of evangelical denominations, most commonly the Baptists, Presbyterians, and Methodists. This tactic immediately gained them several advantages and avoided the charge that they were secretly infiltrating an area. Through these assemblies they attracted widespread attention and came into contact with the most religiously inclined portion of the population. Sometimes the ministers welcomed the Shakers and invited them to speak during the meetings. Other times, however, public conflict erupted with the clergy and with dedicated religious "professors." Frequently ministers used the occasion to launch a bitter attack on the missionaries. In

one meeting Youngs encountered a "Methodist preacher" who carried a
Rathbun anti-Shaker tract with him.[48]

Nonetheless, these journeys allowed the Shakers to disseminate
their beliefs, strengthen the commitment of isolated members in remote
areas, and add converts to the society. These activities also confirmed the
dedication and resolve of the missionaries themselves. "Riding along the
river," Youngs recorded, "we feel A Solemn Sence of the desolation of this
land—as respects any feeling after the Gospel." Another effect of reopening the testimony was the enhancement of Lucy Wright's authority and
influence within the society. "In all these arrangements & their attending
increase, Mother Lucy [as she was known to the members after 1792] was
the primary Counselor & guiding Star. And such was the wisdom of her
Counsel, & the evident blessing that attended obedience thereto, it plainly
showed her to be the 'Lord's Annointed,' to lead his People in the way they
should go. And she was revered in that character not only by the Sisters,
but also by the Brethren. The leading Elders & most faculized Brethren
sought her counsel as the best Oracle they could obtain on Earth." In
Wright the Shakers had found an aggressive and capable leader. She took
advantage of the moment, shaped a strategy for dealing with the problems
at hand, and moved the society toward the future. As first in the ministry,
her influence extended to every area of Shaker life.[49]

Expansion into the West

Lucy Wright's most significant decision during her twenty-five years
of leadership was the authorization of a missionary expedition into the
Ohio Valley at the beginning of 1805. According to Shaker tradition, Ann
Lee had anticipated this move many years earlier. It is reported that Lee
prophesied, "The next opening of the gospel will be in the southwest; it
will be at a great distance and there will be a great work of God." But
prophecy was hardly the determining factor in Wright's decision. Reports
concerning western revivals had been circulating throughout America for
years, filtering into the Shaker villages, too. One published account told of
thousands attending and many falling "before the word, like corn before a
storm of wind," only to rise with "divine glory shining in their countenances." The news of frontier camp meetings and the religious exercises
accompanying them quickened the spirit of the Believers and caused
them to reflect on the new opportunities offered by these circumstances.[50]

Shakerism was poised for expansion at that very moment, having
successfully come through the period of gathering and institutional con-

solidation. The necessary organizational structures were in place. Valuable experience had been gained by Shaker missionaries in the East and by the elders in the Gathering Order. This new western undertaking nonetheless involved considerable risks. The distance separating New Lebanon from the Ohio Valley, for example, created enormous problems of communication and logistics, difficulties plaguing the villages in the Northeast on a smaller scale. The frontier region into which the missionaries were venturing was notorious for its uncivilized population, reputed to be boisterous, violent, and irreligious. There were no guarantees that the mission would succeed.[51]

On 1 January 1805, John Meacham, Issachar Bates, and Benjamin Seth Youngs set out from New Lebanon, traveling through Pennsylvania, Maryland, Virginia, and Tennessee to Kentucky. Journeying most of the way on foot with only one horse to carry baggage, they moved into a "Wilderness of very tedious Mountains, lonesome rivers, & some disagreeable inhabitants," keeping a watchful eye for subjects of the religious awakenings whom some called "Jerkers" because of their paroxysms of the spirit. The missionaries carried instructions concerning their own behavior in the world, an epistle addressed to the inhabitants of the region, and funds to support the venture. In early March the three arrived at Paint Lick, Kentucky, where Matthew Houston, a so-called New Light minister, invited them to address his congregation. A few days later at Cane Ridge they met with Barton W. Stone, another leader of the emerging "Christian" movement. Then they crossed the Ohio River and traveled northeast of Cincinnati to Turtle Creek, Ohio, where they lodged at the home of Malcolm Worley. Their journey had covered more than twelve hundred miles.[52]

The congregations at Paint Lick, Cane Ridge, and Turtle Creek were part of a schismatic movement among New Light Presbyterians centering on northern Kentucky and southern Ohio. Reacting against the conservative Calvinism of the infant Synod of Kentucky, these factious liberals gave voice to a theological Arminianism based on the principle of biblical authority. In late 1803, led by Stone and Richard McNemar of Turtle Creek, they had formed the Springfield Presbytery, which they disbanded in mid-1804. These seceders combined a commitment to democracy with a fervent anti-institutionalism and a radical congregationalism. They believed that the indwelling spirit of Christ was the bond of religious unity. With the first-century Christian church as a model, they maintained a heightened eschatological expectation, a concern for sharing goods, and an acceptance of visions, prophecies, and bodily manifestations of the spirit. Above all, however, they rejected the notion of divine election, affirming that each individual was an actor in the work of regeneration and must press for additional spiritual light, even perfection. These schismatics were moving toward universalism.[53]

Five days after their arrival at Turtle Creek, the apostles from the East gained a first convert in the West, their host, the well-educated Malcolm Worley. His decision to join the Shakers was aided by a belief that God "had promised to send help from Zion," which he identified with the missionaries. Less than a month later Richard McNemar also confessed his sins and entered the sect. "For upwards of 15 years my soul has been on the wheel forming into union with professed followers of the Lamb," he wrote, "but never did I find my mate, until I found the spirit from New Lebanon." His conversion was accompanied by a vision of a guiding hand and a miraculous healing. As a leader of the New Lights, McNemar's decision to become a Shaker was especially significant. He subsequently emerged as a prominent spokesman and apologist for the Believers, playing a critical role in the expansion and consolidation of the society in the Ohio Valley. By 27 April the eastern missionaries reported that thirty persons had "opened their minds." A few weeks later the initial public meeting of the Believers was held in Warren County, Ohio. These were the first fruits of the Shaker harvest in the West.[54]

The evangelistic strategy of the western missionaries varied only slightly from the methods employed in the East. The Shakers continued to travel from house to house, relying on individual families for hospitality and entrance into local communities. Often they sought out camp meetings, where they were assured of large assemblies and a high level of religious excitement. There they became the center of attention for curious and hostile onlookers as well as for others in the audience. At the meetings, whenever possible, they took the preaching "stand" themselves and opened their testimony by reading the letter from the leadership at New Lebanon, which served as an introduction to the Shaker gospel. In it, the church at New Lebanon testified that Christ had made "his second appearing here on earth" in this "latter day" and that the witnesses to it, especially the "First Pillar"—an oblique reference to Ann Lee—had been given "the same gifts of the Holy Spirit" as the apostles of the first century. The gospel, the Shakers wrote, demands belief in the "manifestations of Christ," confession of all sins, and acceptance of the "cross against the flesh, the world, and all evil." This was the message that the eastern apostles proclaimed as "the way of life."[55]

The missionary strategy of the Believers proved successful throughout southern Ohio and Kentucky. Among the noteworthy converts were several New Light ministers, including Matthew Houston at Paint Lick, John Dunlavy (McNemar's brother-in-law) at Eagle Creek, and John Rankin of Logan County in Kentucky. In turn, these clergy frequently influenced members of their families and congregations to accept Shakerism. Their conversions legitimized the claims of the missionaries and thus fueled the hostility of the sect's opponents, especially those belonging to the Christian party. Barton W. Stone, splitting with his former colleagues, became an ardent enemy of the sect; he denounced the Shaker apostles as the "vortex of ruin."[56]

The conversions among schismatic congregations in the Ohio Valley followed the pattern established in the East. Stephen A. Marini has shown that the initial successes of the Shakers in New England occurred among groups on the western and northern frontiers who were rebelling against the tenets of Calvinism. The Shaker gospel—as well as the proclamation of the Universalists and the Freewill Baptists—was persuasive in those regions precisely because it addressed religious issues of concern to many involved in the evangelical revivals: "free grace, freedom from sin, and the coming end of the world." In the new settlements of the hill country where instability, fragmentation, and conflict were the order of the day, the "search for autonomy and identity" often involved religion. The conditions prevailing in the Ohio Valley during the first decade of the new century were not unlike those on the earlier New England frontier. The Shaker missionaries had arrived at a propitious moment.[57]

Malcolm Worley's house at Turtle Creek became the center of activity for the Shakers in the West. From this base the missionaries traveled, often in pairs, sometimes alone, to other locations throughout the region. On these journeys they commonly encountered physical danger and harassment, the wilderness and the "world" seemingly united against their efforts to plant the Shaker gospel. The apostles did not flag in dedication to the mission, but they did request more laborers from the East. A first contingent of reinforcements, three additional brethren, arrived near the end of July, led by David Darrow, formerly the Elder Brother at New Lebanon. Darrow, who played a prominent role among the early converts in the East, had been selected by Lucy Wright as the leader of the society in the West, a position he held for the next twenty years.[58]

Darrow immediately tried to bring some semblance of gospel order to Turtle Creek. He recognized the importance of securing sufficient land for the Shakers, an objective made more difficult by local speculators. Worley's farm and McNemar's adjacent acreage formed the likely nucleus for a settlement. One non-Shaker neighbor offered to sell his property at the inflated price of twelve dollars an acre, nine dollars above the market rate. The Believers seemingly had little choice in the matter, for Darrow recommended that funds be sent for the purchase. He also recognized the need for a "place of retreat" for the Shakers apart from the homes of converts. Plans were drawn for a substantial dwelling similar to those constructed in the eastern villages. For more than ten months, however, the six brethren from the East lived with nine members of the Worley family in a one-story house measuring eighteen by twenty feet with an attached eighteen-by-eight-foot lean to. The first sisters arrived in the spring of 1806 under the leadership of Ruth Farrington, formerly the Elder Sister at New Lebanon. They were housed for several months in a rough-hewn log cabin, so primitive that water streamed in from every side whenever it rained.[59]

Under Darrow's leadership the Shakers created a society at Turtle Creek patterned after the eastern villages. In doing so, they joined other Americans in the task of taming the wilderness. The men felled timber and grubbed roots and stumps to clear fields for planting. In the winter they cut planks, shakes, and clapboards for their construction projects. The women faced an equally exhausting daily routine, a continual round of cooking and domestic chores under adverse physical circumstances, including a shortage of water. Several months after their arrival in the West, the sisters reported to New Lebanon: "we have not had one day of rest sence we left you[. W]e work very hard." The settlement at Turtle Creek slowly took shape as the Shakers completed their building projects. The elders' house was finished in October 1807. Service and utility buildings, including a sawmill and a smith shop, were erected or adapted from existing structures. In 1812 a meetinghouse was completed as well as a dwelling for the Young Believers—a term used to distinguish the new western converts from the Old Believers, those from the East. These visible signs of progress became a source of great encouragement to all.[60]

The effort to establish a village at Turtle Creek was made more difficult, however, by repeated acts of violence against the Believers. The homes of converts, for example, were damaged by night raiders who threw stones through the windows. Horses owned by the Shakers had their ears cropped. In the fall of 1805 local ruffians burned the preaching stand erected for worship in the woods and the surrounding plank seats. A large barn containing substantial amounts of grain and feed was set on fire in late 1807 by the angry family of a young woman who had joined the sect. The most celebrated case of hostile action against Turtle Creek occurred in August 1810. Incited by the published charges leveled against the Shakers by James Smith, a mob composed of apostates, relatives of a Shaker con-

vert, New Light ministers, and local drunken rowdies stormed the settlement, demanding that the Believers leave the area and insisting on
interrogating the sisters. This incident, finally resolved without bloodshed,
was not the last attack on the village. The Shakers continued to face both
overt and covert violence.[61]

David Darrow also assumed reponsibility for supervising the activities of the missionaries, who frequently faced the threat of physical violence. On one occasion, Benjamin S. Youngs was stopped by a crowd,
accused of being a Quaker, and charged with being "the Benjamin of
whom there is So much talk,—who goes about to seduce the people and
ravish the weomen, acumulating property and making disturbance among
those who before lived happy." Despite such difficulties and organized opposition from anti-Shaker groups, the Believers made substantial numerical gains. Approximately one year after their arrival, Youngs reported the
presence of 160 "grown" Believers in the vicinity of Turtle Creek and
Eagle Creek in Ohio, 60 in Kentucky, and many children in both states.
Traveling preachers nurtured the scattered clusters of Young Believers.
Youngs and McNemar made a two-week trip in 1807 to spread the Shaker
gospel among Indians living in western Ohio, a dangerous effort that
yielded no appreciable long-term effects. For several years the Shakers
maintained this pattern of itinerant evangelism. The easterners resided at
Turtle Creek, but they traveled extensively, instructing converts in the society's gospel, the traditions concerning the first witnesses, and the discipline introduced by the second generation. The new Believers requested
frequent visitations, but the constraints of time and distance and the demands of the building program at Turtle Creek often made it impossible
for the missionaries from the East to comply.[62]

Nevertheless, substantial gains in membership continued. Early in
1812, the ministry at Turtle Creek (by then called Union Village) reported
that the "present situation stands thus—in the new house there is 56
young Believers—in the house we built 32. Cheifly the most aged & Some
young people—where Richard formerly lived half a mile east is 22—also
in about one quarter of a mile there is 13 brethren & Sisters that have the
care of 80 Children—these have all come into a joint Interest—besides
the hatter Robert Baxter that lives by the Saw Mill with a family of 6 in
number—the rest of the Society without there is 4 large families & 12
Small ones." That same year the Believers at Union Village signed their
first formal covenant. Simultaneously, four other villages were being gathered in the West: Beulah, five miles from Dayton in Ohio; Shawnee Run
in Mercer County, Kentucky; Gaspar in Logan County in the same state;

and Busro on the Wabash River at the western edge of the Indiana Territory. At each of these locations the dedication of land by early converts
made possible the beginnings of communal life. Other Believers then
moved to the sites and purchased or rented nearby land. Darrow, in consultation with Lucy Wright, eventually selected eastern Shakers as elders
and eldresses to govern each settlement.[62]

The gathering at Shawnee Run, just off the Kentucky River, illustrates the western pattern. Missionaries from Turtle Creek first visited
Mercer County in 1805. By January 1806 Youngs reported 21 grown Believers on Shawnee Run, where Elisha Thomas's farm of 140 acres, located in a "rich & fertile" area, became the center of activity. Intermittent
visits by itinerant Shaker preachers proved less than satisfactory for the
new converts, and in May 1807 a group of eight Kentuckians traveled to
Turtle Creek. They pleaded for additional instruction in their new faith
and support in the face of growing adversity. On one occasion a band of
"ruffians" had threatened the Kentucky Believers with "Guns, knives &
whips." Fences had been torn down and horses stolen. The Kentucky assembly had passed an act requiring military duty or a stiff penalty for
noncompliance. The Shakers of Mercer County needed strong leadership.
In desperation, they even tried to purchase the services of John Meacham.
Late in 1808 David Darrow appointed Meacham, Samuel Turner, Lucy
Smith, and Anna Cole as leaders of the village. Growth and prosperity followed, but not without hardship and "pinching times." By the end of 1809
a new stone dwelling for the ministry was in use. Several families, including a Gathering Order, had been established. Crowds of spectators, sometimes four or five hundred in number, regularly thronged the public
meetings. The "exercises" that engaged the new converts included "some
very mortifying scenes," including wallowing in the mud and pounding
"with their fists" the furniture they had formerly cherished. Despite efforts
by the legislature to limit Shaker growth and new hardships caused by the
War of 1812, 128 Believers signed a formal covenant in June 1814 at the
village, by then known as Pleasant Hill.[64]

At Busro the situation differed somewhat. Shaker missionaries first
visited Busseron Creek, sixteen miles north of Vincennes in the Indiana
Territory, in June 1808. Their stay and visits by other Old and Young Believers produced a number of confessions among local residents. By mid-
March the following year 110 new Shakers lived in the area. Land was
dedicated, a ministry appointed, families gathered, and soon agriculture
and industry were thriving. These favorable developments gave little warning, however, of impending problems. In 1810 rumors spread concerning

possible warfare with Indians. In the winter of 1811 eighty Young Believers from Eagle Creek in Adams County, Ohio, arrived in Busro—an influx that proved something of a mixed blessing. They had failed to form a viable communal society at Eagle Creek. By mid-1812 the situation at Busro had reached a crisis. Conflict did break out with the Indians, and fourteen hundred militiamen were quartered nearby. Earthquakes, malaria, and the war with Great Britain added to the problems at the settlement. Fear of attack and mounting deaths from the fever led to a decision to abandon the site. Three hundred Believers with their livestock and baggage left Busro and journeyed to Union Village by way of Kentucky through Gaspar (South Union) and Pleasant Hill. In the spring of 1814 these Shakers returned to Indiana, only to be ravaged further by dissension and illness, among them Eldress Ruth Darrow, David Darrow's natural daughter, who was a fever victim. With turmoil never far away, West Union, as the settlement was now called, lacked both effective leadership and a clear sense of collective purpose.[65]

On balance, however, the geographical expansion of the Shakers into the Ohio Valley was a remarkable success. The story reads like a frontier saga. Hundreds were converted, instructed in the faith, gathered into communal families, and settled into villages patterned after the societies in the East. Thanks to the industry, frugality, and dedication of both Old and Young Believers, as well as to the economic assistance and community support from the East, most of these settlements quickly moved toward economic stability and a measure of self-sufficiency. By 1815 five new western outposts were fixed on the Shaker map, and substantial pockets of Believers were located elsewhere.[66]

The negative aspects of this geographical expansion have been less frequently noted. In 1808 one contemporary correctly observed that the western converts, although nearly equal in number to the eastern Shakers, were at a distinct religious disadvantage. The eastern Shakers had thirty-five years of collective experience and traditions. They lived in the settings where the events of primary religious importance to the Believers had taken place. Their circumstances were stable because the gospel order was firmly established among them. By contrast, the new western converts lacked even an elementary knowledge of the history and ideas of the society. There was no observant community close at hand. Even the eastern Believers in their midst could not overcome this lack of religious context. The new converts needed additional instruction and discipline in order to progress in the gospel. "It would not be wisdom," wrote David Darrow, "for a man to go into the wilderness & Clear land & Sow it to

wheat & leave it with out fence, for the beasts to devour it, & then Go &
Clear & Sow more & leave it in like manner[;] he would lose his Labour."
During the height of the missionary successes, Shaker leaders—both East
and West—began to question the wisdom of converting those they were
unable to nurture in the faith.[67]

The westward expansion of the Shakers also had a draining effect on
the eastern societies. The mission effort required a large investment of resources, both human and financial. The eastern Believers chosen by Lucy
Wright to work in the West were some of the most talented and promising
younger members, who often occupied positions of responsibility. The
skills of these individuals were thus lost to the seaboard societies. Furthermore, the missionary enterprise preoccupied many Shakers remaining in
the East. The financial assistance, for example, took the form of agricultural and mechanical equipment, domestic supplies of all kinds, and
money—the last calculated by one source to be more than $26,000. The
burden of this support weighed heavily on the eastern villages, especially
New Lebanon. Requests for additional aid were almost continuous during
the first decade of expansion. The ministry in the East finally began to
refuse the petitions, explaining that the drain was adversely affecting the
morale and activities of the eastern Believers.[68]

One practical result of this expansion was the emergence of Union
Village as the leading center of western Shakerism. Not only was the
settlement at Turtle Creek first in time, but for a number of years, by Darrow's decision, it remained the permanent residence of the eastern Believers. They alone possessed full knowledge of the Shaker gospel and direct
authority from the central ministry at New Lebanon. Darrow and the Old
Believers represented the link between the Young Believers and their spiritual parent in the society, Lucy Wright. The village functioned as the
nerve center in the West through which flowed most of the communication with the East during the early years. Union Village served as the primary conduit for temporal assistance, too. Ultimate authority in the West
resided in David Darrow, who had held the position of First Elder since his
arrival at Turtle Creek in mid-1805. His leadership was accepted because
of his appointment by Lucy Wright. A farmer by background, not formally
educated, Darrow was a practical man who rose to the demands of the
frontier situation. But he was not above using his authority to favor or discipline individuals. Nor were his decisions always wise. On more than one
occasion he was reprimanded by Wright for his actions. Nevertheless, for
the first generation of western Believers, Darrow   Father David, as he

came to be called—symbolized the authority and sanctity of the ministry, and his achievements were substantial.[69]

Another result of the westward expansion was the development of an extensive communications network among the Shakers. The villages in the East previously had maintained close relations with one another through visitations and messengers. The ministry at New Lebanon made at least one annual circuit among the New England settlements. Couriers traveled even more frequently between locations. The same pattern continued during the years of the western mission. The distance to the Ohio Valley, however, forced the Believers to rely on the postal service of the young nation. Letters were exchanged with growing frequency—formal epistles from ministry to ministry, financial advisories to and from the deacons, testimonies, expressions of thanks from families and individuals to Lucy Wright and other leaders, personal greetings among friends. No topic of spiritual or temporal concern escaped comment in these communications. All earlier prohibitions attached to the written word were now forgotten; out of necessity, the Shakers began to produce a staggering volume of correspondence for which historians today remain grateful. These letters, more than any other source, carry us to the center of the western undertaking.[70]

There is little reason to believe that Lucy Wright understood the full implications of her actions when she commissioned the three missionaries in 1805. In later years the Believers interpreted her decision as "a gift in union with the zealous life movement & strength of the whole Church." Though Wright did not know it at the time, the western expansion was the most important step taken by the society in the nineteenth century, setting the stage for a series of subsequent critical developments.[71]

The Origins of Shaker Theology

One of the guiding assumptions of this study is the fundamental tension between "charism" and "institutions," to use the categories of sociologist Max Weber. Charism manifests itself in radical enthusiastic movements that express ideals of equality. Institutions give rise to established routines, rules, traditions, and rationalizations that confirm the principles of hierarchy and bureaucracy. Theological reflection is part of the process of building institutions. By contrast with religious experience or the direct encounter with the divine, theology represents "an intellectual *rationalization* of the possession of sacred values." Theology follows religious experience in both temporal and logical sequence in the evolution of sectarian societies. Experience and reflection, nonetheless, are not mutually exclusive and often stand in creative relation to one another.[72]

In the case of the Shakers, the beginnings of sustained systematic theological reflection lie in the period of western expansion. Neither the sayings ascribed to Ann Lee nor the published or unpublished writings of Joseph Meacham were theology in a technical sense, for they were not concerned with demonstrating the intellectual viability and coherence of the Shaker gospel. The task of "rationalization and intellectualization" remained unaddressed in Shakerism until the first decade of the nineteenth century, when practical realities forced Lucy Wright to consent to the writing and publication of the first major theological treatise by Believers. Her permission simultaneously created a class of Shaker theologians within the society who shed the earlier anti-intellectualism and consciously donned the mantle of intellectual respectability.[73]

The social circumstances of the Believers during the early decades of the nineteenth century gave birth to Shaker theology. Attacks in the public press were becoming an embarrassment to the society and a provocation to added harassment. Persons outside the community, even those inclined to be fair and impartial, were learning about the sect from its enemies rather than from its members. The "ignorance" and "prejudice" of the published accounts were complicating the Believers' mission to the world. One widely circulated description, for example, charged that Shakerism was "a species of Roman Catholicism" with popes, saints, oral confession, exorcisms, purgatory, and the like. According to this source, Shakers also forbade marriage, prayed to saints, and believed in miracles. They claim to be "the only true church upon earth," declared the anonymous writer. These accusations were guaranteed to incite a Protestant audience.[74]

Such attacks combined with other circumstances to break down the long-standing resistance of the ministry to written doctrinal statements. Shaker missionaries in the West desperately needed materials for instructing and nurturing converts in the fundamentals of the faith. The initiative for the society's first major publication came from leaders at Turtle Creek in the summer of 1806. In a letter to the ministry at New Lebanon, they stated: "We have for some time past from prevailing circumstances been greatly pressed in our minds to publish our faith to the world by letter." (Perhaps that concern explains their request five months earlier for a copy of Daniel Goodrich's manuscript history of "the rise & progress of the church.") In the same August letter they forwarded "a first piece of writing" to Lucy Wright, the draft of "a candid statement" of their principles, by which inquirers might judge for themselves the rumors concerning the Shakers.[75]

The "Candid Statement" comprises thirteen pages of miscellaneous theological observations, some focused on biblical texts and others related to contemporary religious issues. In this short document the western Believers justified a number of Shaker principles and practices. The manuscript sounds an eschatological note, drawing frequently on images from the Book of Revelation—the "awful trump," the beast, the Antichrist, Babylon versus Zion, the last judgment. A stark dualism informs the whole. The authors employ contrasting pairs to underscore the fundamental conflict between light and darkness, good and evil, tares and wheat, elect and reprobate. Their observations, set in a dispensational framework, appear as a gloss or commentary on the earlier *Concise Statement*. The "Candid Statement" affirms that salvation comes not through the law, but through Christ, who is "revealed more than in the man Jesus," namely, in the saints "transformed into his likeness." The judgment of the world comes not by a "visible appearance" of the Son, but by the elect, who, filled with his spirit, "love God & keep his commandments." They execute the final separation of good from evil by "opening their minds," forsaking all sin, and "gathering together" in unity. By contrast, carnal divisions prevail among the denominations that belong to the Antichrist, which cling to legal ordinances and live "after the flesh."[76]

The letter from Ohio in mid-1806 throws more light on the evolution of the Shaker gospel. "We also express our desires," the leaders at Turtle Creek wrote, "& we think we feel a gift in it, To request the privilege of opening to the world the first Foundation & Pillar of the present appearing of Christ." The foundation and pillar to which they referred was Ann Lee. They continued, "It truly feels to us that so long as the foundation of our faith in the present day is kept concealed, the testimony of the Gospel will ever be under weakness—Must it be hid from the world till the eye Witnesses of Her power & Majesty are all gone, & none left to strengthen the testimony of their children?" The Ohio Believers were persuaded that they were laboring under a severe handicap in their efforts to spread the Shaker gospel.[77]

Prior to the summer of 1806 the public testimony of Shaker missionaries apparently did not feature Ann Lee. The "Candid Statement" of the principles and practices of the Believers contains no allusion to her or to any special female principle. It refers only to the role of "living witnesses" in the proclamation of the "spirit of truth." The 1790 *Concise Statement* did not mention Lee either. Other Shaker documents up to 1806 are equally vague about her. The request by the Believers in Ohio, which confirms that the silence of the sources before 1806 was not accidental, marks a critical turning point in the development of the Shaker gospel.[78]

Lucy Wright responded promptly and positively to the brethren's request, declaring that what they had written was "the Gift of God." She went on to defend the society's earlier reluctance to publish a public theological statement. She wrote, "I have felt & experienced considerable with Father Joseph [Meacham] in relation to writing, & making more fully known to the world the foundation of our Faith—We always felt the time was not come." Now, however, the moment was appropriate and the western brethren possessed "the gift" to accomplish the task. (Here "gift" might refer to an intuition or leading, an ability or experience, or a sense of divine direction.) "I am sensible your Gift & calling that you are called to, in the present opening of the Gospel, brings every gift clear & plain that is necessary for the full accomplishment of this work." Wright closed her letter with a word of caution and a promise. She warned that "the wicked" would be aroused by the circulation of such a book. Therefore they should print only "what you are willing to Live by & die by." Nevertheless, she pledged, "I am with you, & the Church also; & can strengthen you in the work."[79]

The eastern ministry's permission to open the "foundation" of the faith to the world had an immediate effect on activities at Turtle Creek. The preachers began to speak at the stand about "the first Pillar of the Gospel in Christ['s] Second Appearance Even Anne Lee—the 2d part of the man Jesus—the two foundation pillars of the New Creation." Benjamin S. Youngs, for example, explained the "signification" of the Hebrew name "Anna—Gracious, & merciful," and that the "holiest of all" was manifested "in the latter days." Work on a new larger publication also started in earnest. Youngs "began the second time with the Public writings" on 9 December and continued "by spells" through much of the next two years, including one extended period of several months "without the intermission of scarce a day." Closeted in a garret of the newly constructed elders' dwelling, he wrote the text of the manuscript with the assistance of David Darrow and John Meacham. At least twice they requested additional historical information from the East. This collaboration drew on the personal experiences of Darrow, the theological interests of Meacham, and the literary talents of Youngs. The joint endeavor proved slow because the three did not always agree. From Darrow's perspective, Meacham was a "difficult man to agree with on Such matters" and Youngs had an inflated sense of his own abilities. Nevertheless, the manuscript was finally completed, printed, and bound into books.[80]

Late in December 1808 the leaders at Turtle Creek sent to New Lebanon several copies of "the first General Statement of the prensent [sic] faith & principles of the gospel that has ever appeared, on parchment or paper, in this day of Christs Second Appearing." They warned that special "care & attention"—maybe even a second and third reading—would be required by the Believers to understand fully "the truth of Some things in it." The authors were expecting hesitation and possible condemnation from their fellow Shakers. It will be difficult, they wrote, to leave behind all former ideas and notions planted by Antichrist and take "a Strict Speculative view" of the present work. Those in the first opening of the gospel in the East, the western Believers thought, had had an easier time initially because their faith was confirmed by "visible Signs & miracles"; they could follow the spirit and ignore the "letter." Old Believers might therefore have difficulty "when anything new is brought forward." Even more problems would be provoked by this publication for Young Believers and "the blind world of mankind." Despite these drawbacks, the Ohioans maintained, the volume was timely, for the "foundation of the City of God" had already been established as "a Safe refuge for Souls." It was the appropriate moment to destroy "the City & works of Babylon" with a clear demonstration of "the true nature of the work of Christ." This, rather than signs and miracles, was the preparatory work for the present.[81]

The authors of the *Testimony*—Darrow, Meacham, and Youngs, all of whom signed the preface—presented their "statement of the foundation principles, and reason of our faith and practice" as a corrective to misrepresentations concerning the Shakers, not as a "*creed* or *form of government*." With that disclaimer they tried to stand within the Shaker tradition of avoiding doctrinal statements. In fact, however, the *Testimony* soon functioned as a theological norm. It announced that the confirming evidence for the Believers' view of the "second appearing of Christ, commonly called the MILLENNIUM or *Latter day of glory*," was drawn from the Bible, ecclesiastical history, and "the testimony of living witnesses," the last being the highest possible authority. After a brief overview of the origins of the society and its early leaders, the authors set out on their primary task, to trace the history of the work of redemption from creation until the new creation.[82]

The body of the 602-page treatise is divided into eight parts, seven of which describe in sequence the creation and the fall, the beginnings of a new creation in Jesus the Christ and his apostles, the rise and progress of

Antichrist's kingdom, the division of that kingdom by the Reformation, the expansion of the Christian world, and the finished work in the second appearing of Christ. The final part of the volume is an exposition of particular doctrines associated with the second coming. In tone and style—despite disavowals in the preface—this treatise is erudite, reasoned, and intellectually demanding. Not even the concluding remarks addressed especially to Young Believers alter its formidable character.[83]

For the first time, Shaker theologians had constructed a scheme of salvation history that moved beyond the four dispensations identified by Joseph Meacham. Influenced by a variety of sources, including the work of the American Calvinist theologian Jonathan Edwards, whom they called "that eminent Protestant writer," the authors employed the historical mode for apologetic and theological purposes. The intended erudition of the work is obvious. The *Testimony* constituted "a full Survey of the darkness of this world," a detailed exposé of the forces of evil in all their variety and perversity. The established religious traditions bore the brunt of the attack; even the Reformation was not a "restitution" of the union and the order of creation, but merely a "change of form" for the kingdom of Antichrist.[84]

Only the "heretics" of ecclesiastical history escaped censure, for they—like the Shakers—suffered at the hands of the "orthodox." Heretics shared with the true church the marks of self-denial and mortification, holiness and purity, union and order. Though "branded" with the charge of enthusiasm, they testified that the second appearing of Christ was inward rather than outward. Identified with charismatic activity instead of institutional forms, these virtuous few were harbingers of the greater work expected in the latter days. At that time the new creation would be finished, the order destroyed in the fall restored to a higher degree, and the lost union recovered and made eternal.[85]

This theological defense cast in a historical mode appealed to contemporaries in the early nineteenth century because of its biblicism, millennialism, and common sense. The *Testimony* sanctioned the Shakers' peculiar way of life, rationalized the society's institutional structures, justified their belligerence against other Christian denominations, and supported the strategy of withdrawal from the world. According to the 1808 publication, the Shaker world view not only unlocked the secrets of history, but also tied the fortunes of the Believers to the finishing work. The biblical language in the text commended the volume to evangelical Protestants who were well acquainted with scriptural images. The millennial perspective added urgency to the collective enterprise and simplified identification of the parties in the conflict. This form of argument was convincing to persons accustomed to common sense reasoning, the use of the laws of cause and effect, and the testimony of eyewitnesses.[86]

The scandal of the *Testimony* lay elsewhere, namely, in its revelation of the Shaker beliefs concerning "the man who is called JESUS and the woman who is called MOTHER [Ann Lee]." They are "the two first foundation pillars of the Church of Christ—the two anointed ones—the two first *heirs* of promise," wrote the authors, "between whom the covenant of eternal life is established—the two first visible parents in the work of redemption—and the invisible joint parentage in the new creation." Contrary to expectations held by many in the world, that Christ's second appearing would be in "pomp and grandeur," the Ohio Believers declared that the Savior appeared as a woman, to the bedevilment of natural comprehension.[87]

Taking the offensive even further, the authors of the *Testimony* attacked as absurd the orthodox doctrine of Christ's divine and human nature. In its place they voiced the idea of Christ's dual adoption. They argued that as the natural creation was not completed until both man and woman were formed, so in parallel fashion there could be no "spiritual union and relation" in the work of redemption until a woman was appointed to "complete the order in the foundation of the new creation." Therefore the same Christ—signifying the "anointing"—that filled Jesus was "in the fullness of time revealed and given unto Mother [Ann Lee], by which she was anointed and chosen of God, to reveal the mystery of iniquity, and to stand as the first in her order, to accomplish the purposes of God, in the restoration of that which was lost by the transgression of the first woman, and to finish the work of man's final redemption." For this reason the western brethren urged that the testimony of Ann Lee's "power & Majesty" ought to be opened, for without it the necessary complementarity of redemption was destroyed and the Shaker gospel weakened.[88]

The *Testimony* contained an equally radical view of order in the deity, especially its understanding of the Holy Ghost. On the basis of the principles of cause and effect and because of the necessary "correspondence" of man and woman, the authors affirmed that the nature of God as Father was revealed through the Son in Christ's first appearance and that the nature of God as Mother, or the Holy Ghost, was made known through the Daughter in the second appearance. Thus was the "mystery of God" finished. Likewise, as man "cannot exist without woman" in the natural order, so perfection in the order of the deity requires a male and a female principle according to the rules of complementarity. Father and Mother, however, are attributes of God, not separate persons or personalities. Known respectively as Almighty God and Wisdom, they are one in "union and essence." These "hidden things" were not revealed sooner, wrote the authors, because the "fulness of times" had not come.[89]

The publication of the *Testimony* elicited a mixed response from the Shakers. Less than two months after copies were sent east, the ministry at New Lebanon thanked the western Believers for their "very trying labour" with the project and assured them that "Mother [Lucy Wright] together with the Church feels it came in a Gift & in the right time." Another letter from New Lebanon and Watervliet declared, however, that this "most consistant, beautiful & enlightening publication ever exhibited" was not above criticism or suggestions for improvement. Six weeks later Wright herself wrote to Darrow and Farrington at Turtle Creek, voicing her appreciation for their "heavy burden" relating to the volume. "But I can Say you have not been altogether alone in it," she continued, "for I have experienced the Same in my measure & do not expect to be released but in part until I can See the effect it has upon the believers, & also the world." Yet she expressed irritation that the authors had "varied" from her counsel in their discussion of "the Order of the Godhead," for she feared—despite the clarity of their logic and position—that uncovering these beliefs before the world was "too much like casting pearls before Swine." She also chided the western Believers for their open expression of "political sentiments," urging that such views be kept within the society because, she wrote, "our Kingdom is not of this world."[90]

Plans were made almost immediately for a revision, to be edited and printed in the East. When it was requested that Benjamin S. Youngs be sent to New Lebanon to assist, Darrow refused permission, at the same time carefully avoiding any hint or pretense of "teaching Mother." During the months that followed, a series of letters passed between Turtle Creek and New Lebanon, identifying issues for discussion and items in need of clarification or revision. Always diplomatic and collegial, this correspondence nonetheless revealed theological differences, tensions, and personality conflicts between the East and the West. The exchanges also identified the leading theological spokesmen for the factions, Seth Y. Wells in the East and Youngs in the West. These two managed at best a polite relationship. The theological discussion covered a variety of topics, including the nature of Christ's sufferings and the proper terminology for the Holy Ghost. A spirited exchange also took place concerning political attitudes, the eastern Believers being more conservative in outlook and the westerners more willing to celebrate the emergence of republicanism in North America. The most significant dimension of this correspondence was the revelation of the clear intention of the eastern leaders to regain control of spiritual matters within the society. The publication of the *Testimony* and the appearance one year earlier of Richard McNemar's account of the western revivals, together with the erudition and aggressive intellectual style of both Youngs and McNemar, seemed to threaten the eastern leadership. The appearance of the second edition of the *Testimony* in the summer of 1810, edited by Wells and Calvin Green (in "cooperation" with Youngs), did little to ease the growing tension.[91]

In subsequent years the increase in theological writing among the western Shakers continued to be of special concern to the ministry at New Lebanon and a potential irritant to East-West relations in the society. All parties took pains to obtain official consent and union for their intellectual undertakings. At the same time they attempted to retain some autonomy, which the great distances between villages made possible. One case illustrates this pattern and demonstrates the growing sophistication of theological writing among the Believers.[92]

In 1815 John Meacham—then the leading elder at Pleasant Hill— wrote to Lucy Wright, asking permission to publish some writings of his and John Dunlavy's, a former Presbyterian minister turned Shaker preacher, concerning the confession of sins, the "marks and signs" of the true church, and the resurrection and last judgment. He estimated that the publication would be no more than two hundred pages in length. Meacham explained that he had originally intended "to send the manuscript to the Ministry & Church [at New Lebanon] for perusal," but that no convenient means existed to do so. If Wright did not want anything published, he added, she was to inform them. More than two years later, when the proposed volume had not yet appeared, the eastern leaders became anxious. Wright invited Dunlavy to visit New Lebanon before the books were distributed, because they treated "subjects of weighty importance, both to believers and the world." That visit did not take place, however, for in June 1818 she wrote again, thanking Dunlavy for the gift of his "profitable" book and expressing the hope that it would "do much good."[93]

Dunlavy's *Manifesto* departed significantly from the *Concise Statement* and the *Testimony*. Rather than adopting a historical approach to the definition and defense of Shaker doctrines and practices, Dunlavy discussed a series of theological issues ranging from the existence of God to the final judgment. He took his organizational cues from the agenda of systematic theologians. He also employed their techniques for argumentation and proof. The most striking characteristic of his text is the relative absence of the distinctive language and rhetoric of the Believers. The

Manifesto recasts Shaker beliefs and practices in the mode of contemporary nineteenth-century Protestant apologetics. Dunlavy took pride in his mastery of the conventions of formal theology, in his ability to cite Greek and Hebrew biblical texts, and in his effort to address "the thinking part of mankind." His volume is far more abstract than the *Testimony* and intellectually more demanding. It was also, correspondingly, less accessible to Believers and outsiders alike.[94]

Dunlavy constructed his volume as a negative critique of classic Reformed dogma. Based on his understanding of Scripture and revelation, he rejected the conservative ideas of election and reprobation as well as the concepts of the imputation of original sin and the vicarious atonement of Christ. The *Manifesto* underscores the freedom and responsibility of individuals to accept the gospel, the role of Christ as an example for Believers, the function of obedience in the process of justification, and the goal of a sinless life for the Christian. In addition, Dunlavy provided a framework for understanding the peculiar Shaker practices of confession, celibacy, joint interest, and withdrawal from the world, designating these as marks of the true church of Christ. Finally, he distinguished the Believers' view of the resurrection, which he equated with regeneration, from that of contemporary evangelicals by emphasizing its spiritual and progressive character.[95]

The ministry at the parent church was again not completely satisfied with this newest exposition of the faith. Calvin Green, one of the leading eastern theologians, requested alterations in the *Manifesto*, but Dunlavy was unable to comply with all of them because of "too many difficulties in the way," including the fact that a number of the books had already been distributed. Nevertheless, he struck out some words in the remaining copies as an accommodation to the criticism. At the time of publication, the circumstances were even more complicated, for by 1818 Pleasant Hill was involved in conflict with both Union Village and New Lebanon. John Meacham had been recalled by the ministry to the East, where he later confessed to having lost his gift. Dunlavy subsequently gained respect and reputation as an able preacher and apologist for the Shaker cause, even though his publication increased pressure on the East to regain the theological initiative within the society.[96]

The beginnings of Shaker theology date from the publication of the *Testimony* and the *Manifesto*. Henceforth the most distinctive element in the Believers' proclamation was the female principle—both in the work of redemption and in the order of the deity. The Shaker gospel underwent a transformation and augmentation at the hands of the emergent group of theologians. Unlike earlier Believers, whose views had been based primarily on personal religious experience and the strength of individual testimony, they used intellectual resources—scriptural interpretation, logic, and reason—to establish and defend their religious positions. These theologians began to construct a Shaker system of thought in which all elements cohered and made sense. Ironically, this intellectualization moved the Shakers closer to the religious denominations that they so roundly condemned. The intellectuals among the Believers came to regard the products of their activity as an accurate representation of the community's faith and practice. The literature they produced began to take on a normative status within the society.[97]

The rise of Shaker theology had major social implications, too. The intellectuals emerged as a new elite within the society. Their special status challenged communal leaders who held authority on other grounds, and it conflicted with the principle of radical spiritual egalitarianism. The intellectuals were increasingly set apart as a class by their accomplishments. This development also had ramifications for relations between the sexes. At this point women had little opportunity to participate in the male-dominated world of theology. Finally, the knowledge that the earliest initiatives for the rationalization of the faith and the first publications themselves came from the western villages fueled the growing tension between eastern and western Believers.[98]

The Creation of a History

The anonymous author of the earliest effort to write the history of the Shakers compared himself to a traveler moving through an unmapped and "almost impervious wilderness, without a single way-mark to guide his steps." His task was all the more difficult in 1795 because this "wild sect" had written no accounts of its own "profession or practice." Drawing on limited public information, he traced the origins of the society to Jane Lees, a woman who "procured her living at the expence of her chastity." A person of "extraordinary pretensions" whose activities were "subversive," she had been declared a "public nuisance" in England. In America she became "the mighty power of God" for multitudes, although she was "ugly," uneducated, "lewd," intemperate, "vulgar," and often intoxicated. Her fanatical followers, according to this report, were driven like a wildfire by "a large number of enthusiastic spirits." Unfortunately, the half-life of rumors is often more enduring than that of truth. Shakerism suffered for years at the hands of opponents who relied on hearsay, the Believers themselves refusing to mount a public counteroffensive.[99]

The initial attempt by a Shaker to provide a written historical account was apologetic in tone. In his brief "history" of the beginnings of Shakerism in the West, Richard McNemar set out to refute "reports" and "conjectures" being circulated by the Christian party. Barton W. Stone had called the Believers wild enthusiasts who "made shipwreck of faith, and turned aside to an old woman's fables." More salacious reports suggested that the Shakers "castrated all their males, and consequently exposed their necks to the gallows; or divested of all modesty, [they] stripped and danced naked in their night meetings, blew out the candles, and went into a promiscuous debauch." According to McNemar, the opponents of the Believers were willing "to publish anything which a fruitful imagination was capable of composing." He met the charges in 1807 by countering a number of common objections against the Believers. His responses were brief and to the point, but they supplied little historical information beyond the scope of his own experiences with Shakerism in the West. In a postscript, however, he announced that another publication was being prepared by those more experienced in the faith, which would explain Shaker principles and doctrines "from their proper source and foundation."[100]

The work to which McNemar pointed was the *Testimony*, the first serious effort by the society to provide a "correct statement" about itself. Its authors at Turtle Creek defended the earlier silence of the sect in the face of false accusations by referring to Christ's sacrificial example and to the founders' animosity toward creeds and written confessions. Furthermore, they declared, the activities of the latter day were *"a marvellous work and a wonder,"* strange and inaccessible to "systems of human invention." Verbal affirmation had been sufficient for the first sixty years of the society, they contended, but now the time had come for "the first public testimony in writing" in order to establish the facts and the truth as derived from the firsthand knowledge of those well acquainted with the "eye and ear witnesses."[101]

The introduction to the 1808 *Testimony* contains a brief historical account of Ann Lee, the origins of the society, and its early development. Based in part on information from the East, the authors situated Lee in a line of "faithful witnesses" in England that included the Quakers, the French Prophets, and the Wardley society. Lee's story was for them a kind of miracle play, a tale in which humble origins contrasted with spiritual accomplishments. After joining the Wardley society, by her "perfect obedience" she advanced in "knowledge" and "spiritual light." She "laboured" continuously for nine years, subjecting her "soul & body" to an ascetic regimen of "deep mortification and suffering." In these circumstances (and following the death of four infants), by "special and immediate revelation" Ann Lee received insight into the root cause of human depravity, namely, *the flesh*." Her testimony was confirmed in the society by manifestation of the "gifts of the Holy Ghost" and by persecution from the world. Miraculous events were further proof of divine favor—nourishment provided through a keyhole in a prison door and deliverance from disaster at sea. In America she was charged with witchcraft, blasphemy, and treason; she was harassed, abused, and cast into prison once more; yet her testimony and that of the "Elders" flourished. She was "the *morning star* of Christ's second appearing." Following her death, the successors in the "visible administration"—Whittaker, Meacham, and Wright—presided over the consolidation and expansion of the testimony.[102]

The western Shakers portrayed the history of the society as a story of spiritual power, miraculous gifts, providential guidance, and the triumph of righteousness over evil. These themes meshed well with the theological message of the *Testimony*—the revelation of Christ's second appearance in Ann Lee. The parallels between the lives of Jesus and Lee were not lost on an audience familiar with the Bible; nor were they merely left to the imagination of the readers. The authors explicitly stated that "the same power over diseases, which Jesus and his apostles manifested, was given to Mother, with other apostolic gifts." As added proof, they published a number of personal testimonies by elderly Believers concerning healings. No one reading the *Testimony* could doubt the stature of Ann Lee in the minds of its authors.[103]

The eastern leaders shared this adulatory view of Ann Lee. Their only criticism of the biographical materials in the *Testimony* was related to the authors' suggestion that the death of Lee's four children had increased her religious "conviction." The ministry at New Lebanon thought that remark might give critics occasion to say that losing children "would naturally throw almost any woman into a religious turn of mind." They proposed striking the reference, lest Lee's religious judgments be ascribed to her misfortune as a natural mother. (That explanation has since become commonplace.) The editors of the second edition of the *Testimony* followed the ministerial recommendation.[104]

The publication of the *Testimony* influenced the society's subsequent efforts to write its own history. The western brethren pressed for inclusion of the sayings of Ann Lee in the second edition, a move resisted by the ministry at New Lebanon. After much "labour," the leadership in

the East decided that the *Testimony* was sufficient as it stood, for "who is
able to write the *sayings* of *Mother* more clear and plain to the understanding," they asked, "than what is now recorded in the publication of
Mother's Gospel?" The ministry was persuaded that the 1808 publication
contained the substance of her sayings—lust as the root sin, the responsibility of charity to the poor, the need for confession, the full cross of celibacy, the importance of justice, mercy, and humility, the corruption of
false religion. What was the point of repeating them? If Lee's sayings had
not been "planted" in the authors of the *Testimony*, "they could not have
wrote one page of the Book; so then in reality, the whole matter is *Mothers
sayings*."[105]

That conviction, nonetheless, did not stop the ministry in New Lebanon from collecting testimonies about Ann Lee and the English elders
from older members of the society, an undertaking that lacked universal
support in the East. Among those objecting to the effort was Elizur Goodrich, Lucy Wright's former husband, who thought nothing "could be
collected to profit." He had known the founders as well as anyone, he
thought, and possessed a "good memory for one of his age." But he was
unable to "recollect any particular speeches that would be of any use to
record," and he doubted others could either. In spite of his doubts, the collection went forward as "a matter of importance" under the direction of
Rufus Bishop.[106]

Elizur Goodrich's skepticism notwithstanding, a large body of testimonies was gathered. These, in turn, were edited, arranged, and published in 1816. The preface to the *Testimonies* (not to be confused with
the *Testimony* of 1808) underscores the unusual nature of the new publication. Much of the material was "given by those who were eye and ear
witnesses," thereby implying a high degree of historical reliability. Yet the
editors took "particular notice" that many of the testimonies, "and those
too, the most important, have been brought to remembrance by a special
gift of God, after having been, as it were, entirely forgotten, for many
years." In other words, the Believers regarded the process of recollection
as something of a miracle and truly extraordinary.[107]

The traditions forming the core of the *Testimonies* described personal relationships with Ann Lee and the elders. Sometimes these memories were firsthand; others had been passed through third parties who
remembered conversations and experiences or recollected visions and
prophecies. The editors organized the collection by clustering the materials chronologically and thematically. The first half of the volume comprises a narrative of the life and activities of Ann Lee and the elders, from

their English experiences through the conclusion of the missionary journey in 1783. The second half features the teachings and counsel of the first witnesses, including reflections on such topics as the status of Ann Lee, the necessity of confession, and the importance of industry. This half also contains additional sketches of the three founders, descriptions of their deaths, and accounts of divine judgment falling on "reprobates and persecutors." [108]

The primary purpose of the publication was instructional. The testimonies were "for the benefit of those who have honestly confessed and forsaken their sins, and have set out, once for all, to follow Christ in the regeneration." By this means, members of the society would "know and understand, more fully" the truth of the instruction they received and be strengthened by it. At the same time, with this book the Believers would be better protected against reports circulating in the world that "vilify and calumniate the characters of the first Witnesses, and especially that of Mother." The "honest" and "upright" would recognize that the testimonies were not "cunningly devised fables," but rather manifestations of "the spirit of ETERNAL TRUTH." [109]

The editors set out to "prove" that Christ made "his second Appearance in *Ann Lee,*" that she had inaugurated a "new dispensation" by revealing the true nature of the "flesh." According to the *Testimonies,* Lee became "the first spiritual Mother of all the children of the resurrection" and with the elders had laid a foundation for the "redemption of lost man" and for the establishment of "the spiritual Zion" on earth. Through their arrangement of the narrative and explicit references, the editors evoked parallels between Jesus of Nazareth and Ann Lee—an "extraordinary female whom God had chosen." [110]

The editors also employed anticipation as a literary device. Lee was depicted as a child, admonishing her parents against "fleshly cohabitation of the sexes"; during her own marriage she was shown to have refused intercourse with her husband. The editors interpreted both actions as prophetic of her subsequent testimony against lust. According to the *Testimonies,* at an early age Lee was the frequent recipient of "religious impressions and divine manifestations." She labored in anguish of body and soul, seeking spiritual knowledge and insight. "Well might her sufferings and trials be compared with those of the Lord Jesus," the editors wrote, "when he was in the wilderness, tempted of the Devil." She endured pain and travail because "she was ordained of God, to be the first Mother of all souls, in the work of regeneration." [111]

The editors of the *Testimonies* described the public ministry of Ann

Lee as accompanied by diverse wonders and miracles. "Signs and opera
tions, prophecies, visions and revelations of God greatly abounded." More
than once Lee told inquirers the deepest "secrets" of their hearts or all the
experiences of their lives. She fed large crowds that gathered around her
itinerant band, even when provisions were scarce. "Sometimes the people
were ordered, by Mother, to sit down upon the floor, or on the ground; and
a small quantity of bread and cheese, or some other kind of provision, was
served round to the multitude, much in the manner as Christ fed the multitude, with a few loaves and fishes: and the power and blessing of God
evidently attended them." Miraculous healings of "body and mind" were
reported in the *Testimonies,* the result of "a mere touch of the hand . . . or
the sound of her voice." [112]

According to the *Testimonies,* Ann Lee and the elders were repeatedly delivered from threatening situations by providential means—the appearance of an unexpected benefactor, warnings through a vision, or her
own unexplainable "great power and authority." Those who befriended
Lee and her followers experienced remarkable blessings. The editors reported at length, for instance, the case of Elijah Slosson of West Stockbridge, Massachusetts, whose pasture of white clover was eaten "bare" by
more than one hundred horses kept there for three days while the missionary band visited his home and preached in the area. Slosson's worldly
neighbors laughed at his apparent misfortune, but by the following Satur-
day the pasture was "fresh grown, and in blossom; and so abundant, that
Elijah took in cattle and horses to pasture for his neighbors." The cows
that fed there also produced a "miraculous" quantity of "butter and
cheese." These miracles confirmed the faith of the Believers. [113]

The editors compared Ann Lee's teachings, too, with those of Jesus.
Her "words were like flames of fire, and her voice like peals of thunder" to
those whom she reproved. When she spoke, according to the *Testimonies,*
it also had the effect of "confirming and establishing" the "young in the
faith." She drew encouragement for her followers from her own sufferings. Lee spoke of her intimacy with Christ, and thereby evoked the possibility of an equally close relationship between her followers and Christ as
well as between herself and her followers. [114]

Even the death of Ann Lee invited comparison with the conclusion
of Jesus' ministry. "And knowing that her work was nearly at a close," the
editors wrote, "she accordingly endeavored to prepare the minds of the Believers for it. She repeatedly warned them to be faithful; for she was about
to leave them." Death came to Lee, according to the *Testimonies,* "without
a struggle or a groan," seemingly a willful departure. [115]

The editors of the *Testimonies* were under no illusion that this collection of stories and sayings would placate their opponents. It was not intended for the eyes of the "world," but rather for the "benefit" of the Believers, to provide them with a fuller account of the origins of the society. The editors sought to "improve" the testimonies with glosses and homiletical comments that appeared throughout the text, especially near the end of sections. The account of Ann Lee's imprisonment in New York, for example, provided an occasion to underscore the providential direction that made a hostile situation the means for sounding the "gospel trumpet" and spreading news of the second appearance of Christ. The violent opposition to the itinerants at Petersham, Massachusetts, served to illustrate that no act or saying against the society and its founders was "too bad" for the opponents of the gospel, defined alliteratively as "priest and people, professor and profane." But the "evil designs" of these persons were ultimately "frustrated," and in time the wicked persecutors received their due reward. Many of the Harvard mob, as a case in point, reportedly came to "poverty and beggery." The final two chapters of the *Testimonies* close on an imprecatory note, declaring that those who have "rejected the gospel" and turned back to the world do not prosper but rather experience "judgments, beyond what falls to the ordinary lot of mortals."[116]

The *Testimonies* presents a special challenge for the historian. The traditions published in 1816 are not contemporary accounts, but rather products of a community of memory, confessional statements collected and edited more than thirty years after the events they describe. They combine religious testimony with the literary form of a personal narrative. Collectively, they reveal as much or more about the society in the Formative Period as about the Age of the Founders. The themes running through the *Testimonies* confirm the nineteenth-century context of the collection. All treat pressing contemporary matters—the status of Ann Lee, the authority of the elders, the lineage of the society, the historical precedents for communal patterns, the religious sanctions for ethical views, and the censure of apostates. These were fundamentally second-generation issues among the Believers and not the preoccupation or even the concern of the charismatic founders. The editors created the historical framework by which the Shakers understood the foundations of their society. In other words, the *Testimonies* reflects accurately the evolution of the society from its charismatic origins to its later consolidation under the leadership of Lucy Wright.[117]

Even in the eyes of the society, the *Testimonies* was no ordinary publication. The ministry at New Lebanon took special care not only with the editing and arrangement of the text, but also with its distribution to "believers only." They did not allow the testimonies to be copied before the collection was edited, even though the brethren at Union Village were eager to see them. Although the volume was printed at Hancock in 1816, it was not available to the western Believers, including David Darrow, until after mid-1818. "Mother [Lucy Wright] feels unwilling to send one of them to her beloved Son David," wrote the New Lebanon deacons, "until there can be a safe conveyance lest it should get to the world. She does not like to give that which is holy unto Dogs, nor cast her pearls before Swine." In the meantime, the copies distributed throughout the East were being "read once in a while in publick" with good results, especially among the young. Few, it was reported, were able to avoid weeping when they learned of Ann Lee's sufferings. According to the ministry, the collection proved a "peculiar gift and blessing" among the eastern Believers.[118]

A few months later, the *Testimonies* was generating a different kind of excitement and response. A cautionary letter from the ministry at New Lebanon to Benjamin S. Youngs at South Union indicated a rising fear about the general and "indiscriminate perusal" of the publication. Special concern was voiced for "young believers," lest they hear more than they could bear. The ministerial caution was rationalized by noting that many of Ann Lee's "labours were private, & peculiarly adapted to the time place & circumstances of the persons then present," and therefore of "no use to any other souls." The ministry connected these admonitions with the society's current distress at Canterbury, in part the product of slanderous reports being circulated there about the founders.[119]

But it was more than the welfare of the Young Believers that moved David Darrow to write Lucy Wright late in 1818. Although he was thankful to the church in the East for the *Testimonies* and had been moved to tears when he read it, Darrow urged that the publication be fully revised and corrected in order to eliminate contradictions. He was especially interested in underscoring the consistency between "the Gospel of Mother" and "the gospel of Jesus Christ." To that end he felt that several things should not have been included in the text, among them certain sayings attributed to Ann Lee and descriptions of her actions. Her declaration that she would be unable to help anyone after her work was done, for example, he found inconsistent with the promise of Jesus and with his own experience. Lee's visionary declaration that Benjamin Goodrich (a lustful man on earth) was a "fine angel" in heaven Darrow thought might discourage people from bearing the cross. Her apparent willingness to use force, to "wring noses," was also offensive and out of character, according to Darrow. In addition, he felt, it showed little wisdom to repeat the description of Lee as behaving like a "drunken squaw."[120]

Darrow feared that these and other problems in the *Testimonies* would cause Young Believers to stumble and that "Judases" in the society would use the text against the Shakers. Darrow's fears may have reflected a measure of personal skepticism about the collection itself. He wrote, "Whether the witnesses understood all the words that Mother Spake—I do not pretend to Say—it is rather Singular that Mother Should open the deepest misteries of the Gospel that mankind Stumble at the most to weak minds—instead of Such as Father Joseph Mother Lucy brother David Samuel Fitch &c that had the greatest opportunity with Mother." Nevertheless, he acknowledged, biblical precedent (Matthew 11:25) "partly" justified this unusual procedure.[121]

Events moved quickly after the receipt of Darrow's letter in the East. By late February 1819 the ministry at New Lebanon had recalled all copies of the *Testimonies* from the eastern societies. Seth Y. Wells, writing again for the ministry, in no uncertain terms directed Youngs at South Union to keep the book from public view. "Mother says it will be a much greater treasure to you to keep it close," he wrote, "than to expose it to your people; and that she would much rather you would commit it to the flames than to expose it to them." Wells justified this counsel in terms reminiscent of Darrow's criticisms of the volume, arguing that the time was not right, that "sacred records" should not be "shamefully polluted," and that portions of the account needed correction. At the same time, he defended the early release of the book in its "imperfect state," declaring that it had been printed in order to allow wider opportunity for reading and amendment—a weak rationalization at best.[122]

Little more than a month later, the ministry at New Lebanon justified the recall to the leaders at Union Village: "This treasure is, and must continue to be a sacred record for future ages; but it needs revising, and perhaps newmodelling before it can be made public." They repeated the demand that the publication be kept from the public and even from society members, concurring with Darrow's views and adding yet other problems to the list. In particular, they identified the chapter dealing with "the great manifestations of God in Mother" as "*too great*" to be understood "even among believers." In that section Ann Lee spoke of her intimacy with Christ in sexually explicit terms. He was her "husband" and "lover." She reportedly said, "I feel great union with him, and walk with him in union, as with a lover." The ministry now recognized from experience the liabilities of unguarded public statements, even if they were intended only for Believers.[123]

The effort of the eastern leaders to collect and publish the traditions concerning Ann Lee and the elders had backfired, creating new problems and fueling ongoing conflicts with apostates and opponents. This was an especially inopportune moment for additional embarrassing disclosures because a vigorous campaign was being waged against the Shakers in the press and in the political arena on behalf of Eunice Chapman, a woman who struggled for years to regain custody of her three children from the society. Claims concerning Ann Lee figured prominently in the public debate. Chapman's attacks on the society and her attempts to discredit it featured the *continuing* role of Lee in the life of the community. She cited Thomas Brown's *Account* and the society's own *Testimony* to prove Lee's "close communion" with the elders even after her death. Chapman went further, charging that the Shakers "considered Ann Lee as belonging to the Godhead and that she is co-equal and co-eternal with God and, (that is the character of the Holy Ghost) she sat with God and assisted him in the creation of the world." No wonder the ministry feared what might happen if the *Testimonies* fell into the hands of enemies![124]

The pressure on the society increased in the following years. Public attacks, in fact, gained in intensity. The *Western Star*, edited by Abram Van Vleet and published at Lebanon, Ohio, near Union Village, spearheaded the opposition in the West. In the East the appearance of *A Brief Statement of the Sufferings of Mary Dyer* and the much longer *A Portraiture of Shakerism*, both by Dyer, marked the culmination of more than forty years of sustained public opposition. Dyer, like Chapman, was seeking to reclaim her children from the Shakers. The *Portraiture*, in particular, carried the genre of apostate literature to new levels of sophistication by using sworn affidavits to claim innocence, impartiality, and incontestible truth. Dyer's ultimate objectives were clear despite the disclaimer she placed on the title page: "The author has endeavored, while exposing to the world the dark side of the picture, to give it no deeper shade than the light of truth will warrant. And although she has endured innumerable wrongs, she can say in conscious truth, that her only object in giving to the world this history, is, that the unsuspecting may not be entrapped by the apparent virtue and rectitude of the people called *Shakers*." In the preface she declared that the Shakers' "principles and conduct are in several respects, not only subversive of christian *morality*, but as far as their influence extends, operates peculiarly detrimental to the *well-being* of society."[125]

The *Portraiture* was not just one of many attacks by apostates. The work comprised a compendium of hostile materials and cited at length previous publications, including those of Daniel Rathbun, Thomas Brown, and Eunice Chapman. Dyer filled nearly 450 pages making her case for the recovery of her children, but her larger intention was to permanently discredit the society's founders, its beliefs and practices, and its present leadership. She released a barrage of charges, some echoing earlier attacks, others formulating new indictments. Most devastating, from the standpoint of the Shakers, was Dyer's use of affidavits sworn before duly constituted court officers. These documents supplied an apparent credibility for her claims that no previous apostate had managed. They reflected the political ambience of the new nation, which placed great value on sworn testimony. Dyer's strategy was an especially apt refutation of the *Testimonies*, which the society had published and then withdrawn from circulation. Her choice of documentation may have been influenced by the withdrawal of that publication. In any case, the irony could not have been lost on the members of the United Society who were familiar with the *Testimonies*.[126]

The Shaker leadership must have shuddered when they read the following observation by Dyer. "It appears that the life and conduct of Ann Lee and her disciples hath much need of a covering. Time will come, when you, Shakers, will see her in all the horribleness of her own deceivings." But the society did not sit idly by. In the West Richard McNemar almost immediately published *The Other Side of the Question*. In the East, following the recall of the *Testimonies*, the central ministry had commissioned Seth Y. Wells and Calvin Green, two of their most trusted intellectuals, to prepare "a plain and correct statement of facts relative to the history of the Society, in a concise form, containing its origin, progress and present state; with a fair view of the religious faith and practice of the Society, and the principles on which their peculiar tenets are founded." This was to serve as an answer to the charges and attacks by opponents of the society. In addition, it was designed to provide information for "candid enquirers."[127]

The *Summary View of the Millennial Church*, published in 1823, was the result of this commission. Green and Wells were quick to identify the Shaker cause with that of the "primitive" Christians, who had also suffered slander and persecution from unbelieving neighbors. The Virgin Mary and Ann Lee alike had been charged by "calumniators," one with adultery and the other with "lewdness and intoxication." The authors proposed to set the record straight on the origins and progress of the Shaker society.[128]

The *Summary View*, authorized by Lucy Wright but not completed until after her death, became the official statement of the history of the society. It bears a striking resemblance to Dyer's *Portraiture* in that it, too, is a compendium of materials drawn from earlier publications. The opening historical section, in particular, is a new version of the materials previously presented in the *Testimony* and the *Testimonies*. Portions of the early history are quoted verbatim from the *Testimonies*, which had been withdrawn from public usage. Other materials from that volume also are incorporated into the text, but in such a manner as to avoid the offense and scandal that had occurred earlier. By 1823, therefore, the framework of the Shaker story as formulated by the leadership of the society was firmly established. After this, individual elements of the early history might be emphasized or deemphasized as the needs of the society dictated, but the basic narrative was in place.[129]

The Consolidation of the Millennial Church

The appearance of the *Summary View* in 1823 signaled the completion of the establishment of the Shakers as a society, now formally called the United Society of Believers. In their publication Green and Wells provided not only carefully crafted historical and theological statements, but also information on the "progress" and "practical order" of the society. By the middle of the 1820s the Believers could point with pride to their success as a national communal society, stretching from Maine in the East to Kentucky and Indiana in the West. Not surprisingly, Shaker accounts accented the union and order prevailing in the society. Rather than accepting that depiction uncritically, however, twentieth-century historians need to measure it against contemporary evidence of internal dissent and conflict. Shaker achievements are no less remarkable when viewed honestly against the backdrop of stress and turmoil.[130]

One measure of Shaker success was statistical. Although the society had been reluctant to disclose membership figures to the "world," in 1823 Green and Wells reported that the number of Believers exceeded 4,000, two-thirds of whom had joined since 1800. The general reliability of these figures and other estimates remains an open question, for the demographic study of Shakerism is only now beginning. Priscilla J. Brewer attempted to determine the size of the eastern villages during the nineteenth century on the basis of United States census schedules. Her results suggest smaller numbers at several villages than those reported by Green and Wells, although with three exceptions the differences are not great (see table 1).[131]

Evaluating any set of figures necessitates caution because the records are not uniformly complete, and the categories of membership are at times ambiguous. William Sims Bainbridge has pointed out the limitations of the census schedules, especially for the period before 1850, when households rather than individuals were the basic datum. Membership lists drawn from Shaker sources, including church records, covenants, ministerial correspondence, indentures, deeds, and other incidental documents, may also be incomplete or inaccurate. The resident population of a village was rarely the equivalent of the membership of the society. In fact, it would be a mistake to assume a stable population during this period because large numbers of persons came and went, inquiring and joining, rejecting and leaving. Children present a special problem for membership calculations. By the 1820s Shaker villages accepted foundlings, orphans, displaced or impoverished youths, and those indentured to the society by their parents. According to Brewer's figures for 1820, an average of 20 percent of the populations of the ten eastern villages was under sixteen years of age. In Canterbury the figure was as high as 28 percent. But runaways and parents who changed their minds make these numbers especially fluid. Similarly, "outfamilies"—small groups not living in the villages— were likely to be missed in the counts, as were nonresident Believers who identified themselves as members by conviction, but whose circumstances did not permit them to live with the gathered Shakers.[132]

The Shakers recognized that they were "but a small people, and few in number" compared with other established denominations. But this was not grounds for discouragement because they counted themselves among the "chosen few." Growth in "the principles of peace and righteousness" was more important than statistical gain. (This sort of spiritual calculus has often been employed by small sects.) Nonetheless, the Believers found consolation in the biblical promise "I will multiply them and they shall not be few" (Jeremiah 30:19). Compared with other communitarian groups in America before the 1830s, the Shakers numerically were more successful. The eighteenth-century Ephrata colony founded by Johann Conrad Beissel, for example, numbered approximately 300 followers at its height, as did the Jerusalem colony of Jemima Wilkinson, the "Publick Universal Friend," who was a contemporary of Ann Lee. The Moravian community at Bethlehem, Pennsylvania, included more than 750 members in the 1760s before declining sharply. The Harmony Society of George Rapp

Table 1
Shaker Population in the 1820s

Location	1823 (Green & Wells)	1820 (Brewer)
New Lebanon, N.Y.	500–600	390
Watervliet, N.Y.	200+	193
Hancock, Mass.	About 300	317
Tyringham, Mass.	About 100	92
Enfield, Conn	About 200	190
Harvard, Mass.	About 200	173
Shirley, Mass.	About 150	84
Canterbury, N.H.	200+	218
Enfield, N.H.	200+	No data
Alfred, Maine	About 200	154
New Gloucester, Maine	About 150	139
Union Village, Ohio	About 600	—
Watervliet, Ohio	About 100	—
Pleasant Hill, Ky.	400–500	—
South Union, Ky.	300–400	—
West Union, Ind.	200+	—

numbered as many as 800 persons during the 1820s, whereas the Separatists of Zoar, followers of Joseph Bimeler, were never more than 150. Other smaller short-lived communities embraced only a few dedicated individuals or families.[133]

The Shakers also achieved a geographical expansion without parallel among religious communitarian groups. By 1826 the Believers spanned nearly "half" of the continent, drawn to distant places east and west by the pull of evangelical revivals. When the euphoria surrounding the missionary successes subsided, the practical implications of the distances separating the villages began to dawn on the leadership of the society. In 1805 the distance between New Gloucester, Maine, and New Lebanon was approximately 175 miles as the crow flies, but closer to 225 by land. These figures pale compared with the distance between New Lebanon and South Union, Kentucky—725 miles in a straight line and more than 1,000 by overland travel. Maine's Shakers, in turn, were separated from their most remote western colleagues by an additional 225 miles. The society invested large

amounts of time, energy, and money on travel, communication, and hauling between villages. Most communitarian groups in America did not face
an equivalent challenge, for with a few exceptions they were located in a
single settlement or area. Against these geographical odds, the achievement of a measure of union and order among the scattered Shakers was
an accomplishment.[134]

But distance was only the physical part of the problem. From the
standpoint of the ministry at New Lebanon, the gap at times also seemed
spiritual. The farther a village was from the "Mother Church," the more
likely it was to experience difficulties—religious, social, and economic.
The influence of the central ministry diminished with distance. Canterbury, Alfred, and New Gloucester exemplified this in the East; West
Union, the most remote though not the most distant village in the West,
was an unending source of difficulties for the society. Early in the century
both Lucy Wright and David Darrow had warned against extending missionary efforts farther than the society could sustain, for practical as well
as spiritual reasons. Some of the spirit of independence in the distant villages, branded by the leadership as a lack of union and order, was probably
the natural and necessary product of their relative isolation.[135]

Distance and difficulties aside, a distinctive sense of geography developed among the Believers, a mental map reflected even in the *Summary View* when Green and Wells enumerated the sixteen villages in
sequence. New Lebanon and Watervliet stood at the center of the Shaker
universe; from that fixed point the "branch churches" stretched out in two
directions, east and west, in that order. This fundamental orientation,
which originated before the western expansion, prevailed even after 1805.
In the West, however, a new dimension was added with Union Village,
which occupied the center point from which satellite settlements extended in three directions—north, south, and west. For the western
Shakers "east" always pointed back to the area of Shaker origins. Thus
the residents of the western villages viewed themselves as doubly subordinate, obedient to the leaders at Union Village and to the ministry at New
Lebanon. This geospatial perspective among the Shakers confirmed an
orderly sense of place with respect to both geography and authority.[136]

The Believers' numerical and geographical expansion was accompanied by a limited measure of demographic diversification. During the
eighteenth century the Shakers attracted "a representative cross section of
rural New England society," not just social misfits. In like manner, converts on the western frontier in the early nineteenth century reflected the
full range of social, economic, and educational levels. By the mid-1820s

the society included farmers and laborers, artisans and merchants, school-teachers and clergymen, as well as women of all backgrounds. With notable exceptions, the majority of the members, both East and West, hailed from areas of relatively new settlement, whether New England hill country or backwoods settlements in the Ohio Valley. More detailed judgments concerning the overall makeup of the society in this period await additional research by social historians.[137]

The trend toward demographic diversification was paralleled by the further consolidation of the government of the society in the hands of a relatively small number of self-perpetuating leaders. By the mid-1820s the theological justification for a hierarchical structure of visible authority among the Believers had been fully developed. Green and Wells pointed to biblical precedents for the selection of leaders "by the last preceding head or leading character," citing both the "Jewish dispensation," according to which God chose Moses, who picked Joshua, and so on, as well as the example of Jesus, who selected his disciples and they their successors. In this fashion the ministry at New Lebanon—"consisting of male and female, not less than three, and generally four in number, two of each sex"—appointed ministers, who supervised two or more villages constituting a "bishoprick," elders and eldresses, who handled the "spiritual administration" of individual villages or families, and deacons and deaconesses, who were responsible for the temporal concerns of these same units. The persons appointed by the ministry were confirmed in their positions "by the spontaneous union of the whole body."[138]

In practice the exercise of authority by the leaders of the society was often far more circuitous, frequently affected by local circumstances as well as by other concerns. Appointments were influenced by such factors as natural family ties, self-promotion, and the availability of candidates. Persons placed in positions of responsibility became difficult to remove, even on grounds of gross incompetence, insubordination, or self-aggrandizement. The local pattern of government varied frequently, especially early in the century. In 1801, for example, the Shakers at New Gloucester assembled to choose John Barnes as their "Elder and minister" and to select deacons. Five years later they met again, "att Sabathday pond (So Called)," to choose a successor to Nathan Merrill as deacon. Twenty-two individuals cast votes for John Anderson; the records of the meeting note that "Elder John Barnes Choice with the rest of the members is— John Anderson." Here an election was confirmed by the leadership. By 1823, however, the United Society was taking a strong stand against elections, declaring such worldly devices "contentious" and destructive of union and order, resulting potentially in the loss of relations and the members falling off "like withered branches."[139]

Local variations notwithstanding, during the opening decades of the nineteenth century a strong network developed among scattered Shaker leaders, based in part on personal relationships. The oldest among the leaders had known not only Joseph Meacham and Lucy Wright, but also the founders. As of 1815, most of the third generation of leaders had been appointed by Wright and were personally acquainted with her. A number of the chosen leaders were also biological relatives, even though in theory the Shakers had given up traditional blood relationships for the family of Believers. Members of the Meacham family, for example, served as deacons at New Lebanon and as elders at Union Village, Pleasant Hill, and West Union. At least two of these individuals were openly criticized for their failures, and yet they remained in responsible positions. Members of the Goodrich, Darrow, Bishop, Wells, and Youngs families—to name but a few—also occupied prominent positions of leadership in the society. It is difficult to avoid the conclusion that "natural relations," as the Shakers called them, still counted in the world of Believers.[140]

In spite of the bonds of friendship, shared authority, and blood relations, controversy and contention dogged the leaders of the society from its earliest days. When James Whittaker assumed the leadership, three of the English witnesses departed, refusing to accept his authority. Joseph Meacham succeeded Whittaker after vying for the position with Calvin Harlow and his brother David. When Lucy Wright became first in the ministry, there was widespread disgruntlement among male members who did not wish to submit to the authority of a woman. This male-female conflict recurred throughout the quarter-century of her leadership, surfacing in controversies over specific decisions as well as over the general issue of "petticoat government." The debates between eastern and western leaders over matters of theology and publications added to the tensions among the leaders. With the rise of yet another generation of Believers who did not know the founders or their successors, new grounds existed for contention—the conflict between generations. The society nevertheless retained its commitment to a hierarchical, centralized system of authority.[141]

The expansion and diversification of the society resulted in changes within the Shaker covenants. Public documents with the express purpose of establishing and protecting the principle of joint interest, the covenants dealt primarily with the temporal welfare of the society. When the collective security of the Believers was in jeopardy, the documents were revised.

A number of such changes during the early decades of the century served in general to strengthen the hold of the Believers on consecrated properties and to lessen the ability of departing persons to lay claim to community resources. These revisions frequently followed court actions taken against the society. The covenants also served another useful purpose, namely, to represent to outsiders, especially inquirers, the principles on which the joint interest rested. Shaker covenants initially contained little theology, but with the passage of time the religious grounds of community life entered the documents, making the texts increasingly similar to congregational covenants in Protestant America.[142]

The leadership at New Lebanon, for example, early in the second decade of the century, judged their covenant "deficient" for displaying "only the male part of our Parentage in Church relation." Therefore in 1814 an amended covenant was signed by the members of the Church Family, acknowledging "both Father and Mother in a Spiritual line of succession from the two first foundation pillars in the new creation." In the new document the Shakers affirmed the "foundation" of their faith; that is, the truth that our Lord and Saviour Jesus Christ did make his second appearance, by his Spirit, first in Ann Lee, whom we acknowledge to be the first Mother of all souls in the work of regeneration, and the first spiritual head of the Church of Christ then in the body: That the spiritual lead of the Church descended from her to James Whittaker. . . . That since the decease of the said Joseph Meacham, the ministration of the gifts of God, and the spiritual protection of souls, have rested with the said Lucy Wright, whom we still acknowledge, love and respect, as our spiritual Mother in the Church." This change, which followed the publication of the *Testimony*, appears to have been a by-product of the evolving status of Ann Lee. The covenant was no longer simply a document to protect the joint interest; it was also a theological and apologetic tool in the hands of the society.[143]

Sometimes the covenants reflected the internal politics of the villages. Calvin Green reported one change in the 1811 covenant at New Lebanon that Lucy Wright authorized on the basis of a night vision. In response to a local problem she reorganized all the families into two orders with clearly defined relationships. The 1815 covenant at West Union dealt with troublesome tensions in that village by strengthening the hand of the elders. The Indiana society had experienced very difficult times, especially during the War of 1812. In the new agreement the Indiana Believers pledged to accept "the spiritual care of our Elders Archibald Meacham and Isacher Bates appointed by the Gift of God to have the rule over us, and to

watch for our souls and admonish us." The covenanted members also
promised that "according to the rule and order of the Gospel it shall be our
duty at all times to reverence and respect them [the elders] in their Gift
and calling to be subject to them in the Lord to follow their faith, and to
esteem them very highly in love for their works sake." This covenant became a device for enforcing discipline within the society.[144]

The expansion and development of the Shaker society produced a
proliferation of rules and regulations governing all aspects of communal
life. Two contrasting processes affected this change. The ministry at New
Lebanon exercised its general supervisory role, and these leaders regularly
issued recommendations for all the villages. This hierarchical principle,
embodied in the notion of a parent or central ministry, was complemented
by local initiatives generating particular rules for specific villages. Initially
these regulations were not written down, but rather formed a part of the
instruction given by the leaders to the members and to inquirers. The earliest rules sought to strengthen the common life. The attitude of the Believers
toward such instruction is apparent in the following early statement from
Maine: "It is church order for all us who are the professing members of
christs church to be obediente to all instructions of the teaching members
of the church who teach us all the principles of the eternal Law of moral
rectitude and what ever else which proceeds from the heavenly kingdom
of Light from which proceeds all good." Order and obedience were, therefore, fundamental to the process.[145]

Among the earliest extant statutes are rules governing the seasonal
times of rising and retiring for residents of the villages, regulations concerning the instruction of youths, directions about the "use of books," and
recommendations dealing with the proper forms of address to be used
when speaking to other members or to the ministry. In 1802 the ministry
at New Lebanon enacted a moratorium on new building projects and on
inventions designed for convenience. They also established proper procedures for seeking approval from the deacons for construction projects. The
documentary record contains repeated counsel against the use of "spirits."
As early as 1800 specific injunctions limited liquor to medicinal use. Even
wine and cider were to be drunk sparingly, and then only in specified circumstances. (The frequency of these exhortations suggests that excessive
drinking may have been a persistent problem in the villages.) Several of
the rules that survive from the early period focus on distinctions between
the Believers and the inhabitants of the "world." The ministry at New
Lebanon in 1817 recorded strong disapproval of a hat worn by one of the
younger Believers, condemning it as a reflection of the "fassions of this

wicked world." The ministry reported that Lucy Wright had received a gift concerning other "wearing apparel," which had been received enthusiastically by the New Lebanon society.[146]

When a proposal was made to gather these scattered rules into one set of regulations for the United Society, Wright stubbornly refused permission. Although she believed "the orders of God were like a golden Chain that held the People of God together[;] that every order and every gift formed a link in this golden Chain," she feared the inflexible application of a written code. She also retained the founders' respect for the oral transmission of gospel truths. Near the end of her life, however, Wright relented and allowed Freegift Wells at Watervliet to assemble a group of existing regulations and arrange them into appropriate categories. But even then she refused to allow copies to be distributed or read in the meetings of the society, a prohibition quickly rescinded following her death. Less than six months after Wright died in 1821, the new ministry began circulating manuscript copies of the "Orders and Rules of the Church at New Lebanon."[147]

The Millennial Laws of 1821 represent the first systematic codification of regulations within Shakerism. They address a host of specific concerns, including confession of sins, worship, sabbath observance, contact between the sexes, business activities, travel in the world, fire safety, hygiene, dining etiquette, the care of animals and plants, hunting, and funerals. Some give voice to general principles, such as avoiding anger and offensive conversation; others detail particular injunctions, such as those forbidding brothers and sisters to "pass each other on the stairs" and prescribing that the right thumb and fingers should be above the left when one's hands are clasped. Although embracing more than 125 separate rules, the Millennial Laws did not cover all aspects of communitarian activity. The preludium explained the selective character of the collection, pointing to the Believers' unity as one body "governed and influenced by one spirit," namely, the law of Christ. The guiding principles for life in a Shaker village, according to the laws, were obedience to the ministry and love to others. These were deemed sufficiently encompassing for all cases not spelled out in the statutes.[148]

The Millennial Laws evolved out of the practical needs of the growing society, but they accomplished more than simply regulating daily activities. They also defined the boundaries between Shakerism and the world, establishing clear lines of demarcation between the sect and the larger American culture, both in a literal and in a symbolic fashion. The collection included specific restrictions on the liberty of Believers to leave the villages as well as regulations governing their physical, conversational, and financial relations with outsiders and strangers when they did travel abroad in the world. Detailed arrangements were described for handling necessary business affairs through the deacons and deaconesses. Contamination by the world was to be confessed to the leaders and ritual cleanliness restored before returning to normal activities within the society.[149]

But the world was not only physically external to the villages. The forces of evil threatened constantly to erupt within the community, too, and to contaminate the Believers. The Millennial Laws therefore provided elaborate counsel for maintaining purity inside the society. The central axiom of the "gospel of Christ's second appearing" was the strict prohibition of "all private union between the two sexes." To that end, the Shakers were to avoid situations where such contact was necessary or likely, whether in shops or at the meetinghouse, on a staircase or in the fields. Private conversations, group singing, and recreation involving both sexes were similarly cautioned against because such activities had "a tendency to naturalize" the Believers and to open "a door for disorder." The concern for personal cleanliness and community hygiene reflects in a different fashion the preoccupation with order. The prescriptions for cleaning were not designed simply to create a healthy environment in the village, for the pollution the Shakers feared was more than rotting apple parings or unsightly animal dung. By these efforts at collective purity, the Believers were creating "a total universe in which all experience is ordered," to use the language of anthropologist Mary Douglas, and in doing so they were strengthening the boundaries around their society by which they wished to avoid defilement. The Shakers' fixation on cleanliness mirrored their fears of disorder.[150]

New converts to Shakerism, according to the Millennial Laws, were required to leave behind the pollution of the world. Passage into the society of Believers was ritually effected by confessing one's sins—"opening the mind"—to an elder or eldress. At that threshold moment, the convert renounced the claims of the old life and submitted to the new realities of the Shaker order. The society signaled acceptance of the new Believer in various ways, including the gift of a distinctive cap and handkerchief to females and the close cropping of the hair of the men. By the 1820s entrance into the church was contingent on the confession of sins, the acceptance of celibacy, and the agreement to live according to the communal principles of the Shakers, including the joint interest. Confession, unlike baptism in other religious traditions, was a process Believers could repeat as often as necessary. Whenever a member crossed the established boundaries or violated the gospel statutes, that individual was required to seek purification through confession. In this manner the Shakers maintained an ongoing state of spiritual tension among the most devout members.[151]

The Millennial Laws were immensely useful during the closing years of the Formative Period. The written code established a new measure of uniform behavior among the scattered Shaker villages. It also created a sense of distinctive identity among the Believers by setting them off from individuals in the world. Furthermore, the statutes helped to discipline wayward members in the more remote villages by providing a constant reminder of the symbolic presence of the central ministry instead of depending only on intermittent contact through correspondence and occasional visits. As copies of the laws circulated throughout the villages, they were welcomed warmly. The ministry at Harvard, for example, expressed their thanks for the parental counsel and especially for "the Beautiful Gift to repeat the Rules & Orders given from time to time for our Protection & Increase." They viewed the statutes as gifts from New Lebanon and were confident that they would produce a "very Good Effect." Elsewhere, too, the Shakers pointed with pride to these regulations.[152]

By contrast, outsiders who regarded these controls as restricting the rights of individuals found the regulations in the Millennial Laws offensive. The statutes relating to the enforcement of celibacy and the rigid separation between the sexes were deemed particularly immoral and unnatural. Outsiders frequently charged that the society was holding individuals against their will, especially young females. Mob action against the Believers sometimes aimed to free such persons. At Harvard in 1825 the neighbors of the Shakers went to court in an effort to gain custody of Seth Babbit, a long-time member who was confined because of mental illness. Eight brethren were charged with "abusing" him physically. They were found innocent by a jury. Mutual misunderstanding, hatred, and wide spread paranoia about the Shakers fueled these hostilities.[153]

One account of such action illustrates the hatred and violence the Shakers engendered among some outsiders. At Pleasant Hill in 1825 a mob attempted to free Lucy Bryant, a teenage girl, from "bondage." She and her brother had been indentured to the society by their father. The actions against the Believers were instigated by Lucy's brother, who had run away from the village, and by her mother. On the evening of the sixth of June a group of forty to fifty men, "armed with clubs dirks or pistols," attacked the Center Family dwelling shortly after the meeting had been

dismissed. They broke open the door, forced their way into the building, and began randomly assaulting the Shakers. "The clubing went on
furiously considrable time, till a number of Brethren and Sisters were in-
humanly beaten, some of which were knocked Sensless." After considerable time the men agreed to interview Lucy Bryant, who persuaded them
that she was "stedfast and determind to stay." They then dispersed, but
one week later a mob of two to three hundred, similarly armed, returned to
Pleasant Hill, led this time by Bryant's mother. According to the ministry,
"A more savage looking set of human beings never traversd the wilderness
of the West." Their passions had been worked up by exaggerated stories,
by "artful insinuations," and by whiskey. Bryant's mother, "dressed in
black from head to foot," rode at the head of the yelling mob. To the Believers she appeared "like a fury from the lower regions." They "dragged the
girl off without mercy," the ministry wrote, "and it was a day of Sufferings
with us, and an awful sight to behold." The Shakers were powerless to
help Lucy Bryant, although one year later she was reportedly still resisting
the efforts of her relatives "to recreate her mind," for she did not desire to
live "in the world." [154]

The religious principle of separation from the world, given full expression in the Millennial Laws, also led to the society's quest for economic self-sufficiency. The Shakers attempted to establish their villages
on a sound financial basis. The consecration of property, real and personal,
made this possible. Hundreds of acres of land were signed over to the society
by converts. The Believers purchased additional tracts with community
resources. Farmlands were cleared, woodlots logged, orchards planted,
and gardens cultivated. The society built mills for grinding its own flour
and sawing lumber, which subsequently became a source of income from
non-Shaker neighbors. The Believers constructed barns and sheds for
storing crops and feed and housing animals. They built shops and offices,
dwellings and meetinghouses—some with distinguishing architectural
marks that reflected Shaker principles, others following the common patterns of the day. The Believers planted cash crops and "manufactured"
marketable items to be sold to the "world"; with that income they purchased the goods they could not produce on their own. Although the
Shakers aspired to economic independence, they never achieved absolute self-sufficiency. Their industry and dedication, however, eventually
brought substantial prosperity. [155]

Visitors to the villages frequently commented on the physical accomplishments of the Shakers. Timothy Dwight, the president of Yale College,
after visiting New Lebanon dismissed Shaker doctrines as harmless and

"silly," but he expressed admiration for their industry and neatness, complimenting them also on their ingenuity and "good reputation." On balance, he considered them productive members of society. Historians have sometimes exaggerated the picturesque character of Shaker villages while paying insufficient attention to the drudgery that confronted the Believers, especially during these formative years.[156]

The buildings constructed by the Shakers may be among their most lasting endeavors. Every village could point with pride to at least one edifice—a towering dwelling, a prize meetinghouse, or specialized barns. In most of the eastern villages the gambrel-roofed meetinghouses were built by Moses Johnson of Enfield, New Hampshire. At New Lebanon, however, the second meetinghouse, completed in 1824, was a distinctive structure whose rounded roof sharply contrasted with the surrounding buildings. Its cavernous interior provided sufficient space for the worship activities of more than five hundred Believers. The Great Stone House built in 1837 at Enfield, New Hampshire, overshadowed the surrounding shops and other buildings. It rose six stories from the ground, and from its windows the Believers obtained a commanding view of Lake Mascoma and the adjacent area. The sheer bulk of the Center Family dwelling at Pleasant Hill, designed by Micajah Burnett and completed in 1834, was impressive, its white stone walls, contrasting with the red brick of the other buildings within view, seemed to embody solidity and permanence (fig. 3). At Hancock, the Church Family round stone barn built by Daniel Goodrich in 1826 drew the most attention. Ingenious in design with many practical advantages, it stands as an exception to the Shakers' preference for linear living space. The huge barns at the North Family in New Lebanon and at the Church Family in Canterbury were more typical. Each of these edifices required enormous resources and commitment to complete.[157]

Shaker men and women, east and west, struggled to build and maintain their villages. Unending chores and backbreaking responsibilities were the daily lot of the Believers. Samuel Johnson, Jr., a resident at New Lebanon during the first decade of the century, was engaged almost daily in physically demanding labor. Although his tasks occasionally rotated, chopping and hauling wood was a regular responsibility. In a single year he transported two hundred loads of firewood. He once cut himself badly with an ax and also suffered frostbite in his foot, necessitating crutches for six months. Rachel Johnson's situation in Ohio was even more demanding. Daily she fed three or four sittings of people at mealtimes. She also took care of the laundry for a large number of people, pounding and rubbing their clothing in tubs of water. She lived in a half-completed dwelling

3. Center Family Dwelling, Pleasant Hill, Kentucky
This massive limestone dwelling, set on a 55 × 60 foot foundation with a 34 × 85 foot
dining and kitchen extension, required more than a decade to build. (From Charles
Edson Robinson, *A Concise History of the United Society of Believers*, 1893.)

where brethren and sisters were separated only by blankets hung between
their beds. Samuel Johnson voiced little complaint about his tasks. Rachel
expressed loneliness, the feeling of being "poor and needy," and a desire to
be remembered by her eastern friends.[158]

At times whole villages, even those established for several decades,
found themselves in difficult circumstances. The unprecedented cold of
the summer of 1816, affecting several Shaker locations in New England,
forced the inhabitants at New Lebanon to take extreme measures. Twice
in early June the village experienced snowfalls, and then a frost in July.
The brethren exerted every possible means to "protect plants from utter
destruction." A subsequent drought added to their problems. The ministry
dealt with the "approaching Scarcity of food" by calling for conservation in
both the preparation and the consumption of food. They also directed that
the number of livestock be reduced. In addition, they offered words of
encouragement, expressing confidence that these afflictions would ultimately "work for good" to true Believers. Faith aside, the Shakers remained
vulnerable to the forces of nature.[159]

The task of educating the young attracted increasing attention
from the society during the formative years. The earliest Shakers had
dismissed formal education as unnecessary and undesirable. But this anti-

intellectualism gradually moderated, and with the formation of the communal society the need for more education became apparent. Joseph Meacham emphasized the importance of practical subjects and the dangers of "unnecessary arts & sciences." The boys were taught the crafts and skills necessary to become productive members of the society, and girls the corresponding domestic arts. The first efforts at formal education, therefore, stressed the application of practical knowledge. As early as 1792 the village at Enfield, Connecticut, successfully secured a share of tax monies to educate their children. As the advantages of a more diverse education became evident to the Believers, instruction was undertaken in various villages, including Canterbury. The efforts were often uneven, however, and sporadic. Concerted attempts to provide formal education for Shaker children initially occurred in the West. By 1811 at the school in Union Village 110 students were being instructed in reading, spelling, speaking, and manners. Perhaps western successes had something to do with new initiatives in the East. Following a gift received by the ministry at New Lebanon, systematic efforts to improve the schools were begun. Seth Y. Wells, who had served as a teacher before joining the Shakers, was appointed to supervise the undertaking. Largely because of his initiative, a version of the Lancastrian system of instruction, employing the use of monitors, was introduced into the society's schools. In 1823 Wells spent several months traveling to the eastern villages to instruct them in the new teaching methods and additional subject areas. The Believers no longer dismissed education as unimportant; now they eagerly sought to improve their schools.[160]

The opening decades of the nineteenth century also witnessed changes in worship among the Believers. Shaker dance, the feature of the society's life "that most provoked curiosity and ridicule," sometimes attracted spectators by the hundreds (fig. 4). The case of Henry Bedinger is typical. At the urging of friends, this traveler from Virginia in 1810 attended a Sunday morning meeting of the "Dancing quakers Commonly Called Shakers" at South Union, Kentucky, to observe their "Exercises." There, as part of a crowd, he saw "42 women formed in a Solid Column ranging each way, but facing toward a body of about the Same number of Men formed in likemanner all Singing & Jumping with Very exact time & Step, or rather Jump and with much to the tune and words Sung, which words I could not distinctly understand but the Verse always ended with 'Heavenly Jubilee,' at the end of about a Minute every person on the floor Jumped quite round but without Moving out of Spot, & this exercise Continued at least 15 or 20 Minutes when they all Clapped hands for about

4. Shaker Worship
Lithograph titled "Shakers near Lebanon state of N York, their mode of Worship,"
probably first executed by New York City lithographer Anthony Imbert. It was subsequently copied many times. (Courtesy Shaker Museum and Library, Old Chatham,
New York.)

half a minute & then all Stood Still, & silence reigned for about 5 Minutes
when the Same exercise again Continued." After three such repetitions,
Bedinger noted, "the farce ended." This account confirms the centrality of
the dance throughout the society, even in the most remote western locations. Abundant energies were channeled into these exercises. The dancing in meetings gave expression to the society's values of union and order,
but at the same time allowed outsiders to deride and mock the Believers.[161]

Among the innovations in Shaker worship was the introduction of
words into the songs of the Believers. Western converts, acquainted with
the hymn traditions of the evangelical churches, began to compose verses
about their new faith and to sing them in meetings. These hymns, characterized by multiple stanzas using the same melody, often related events or
religious ideas in narrative form. The composition and use of such songs
spread quickly throughout the society. Before this, hymns had been only
"rarely used in services" in the East; by 1806 they had become integrated

into the worship, even at New Lebanon. In fact, they became so popular among Believers that it proved impossible to supply sufficient copies in manuscript. For this reason the society published *Millennial Praises* in 1813, a collection of 140 texts composed by Shakers at various locations. The Believers, without knowing it, were participating in the larger "hymnodic revolution" that was sweeping America during these years.[162]

Millennial Praises was presented to the society as a "gift of songs," having received the "general approbation" of the leadership of the church. The hymns reflected the "present faith and testimony of Believers," containing doctrinal statements, expressions of trust, thankfulness, love, and union—attitudes present among the Believers—and descriptions of the works of Antichrist in the world. Many echo the ideals of the Believers, but others sound fierce notes of condemnation, contrasting the truths of the gospel with false notions. The relationship between Jesus and Ann Lee as well as the nature of the heavenly parentage is described in the following stanza of a hymn titled "The Son and Daughter."

> The blessed Son and Daughter,
> Completely join'd in one,
> In a divine submission,
> Their heavenly Parents own:
> The Father and the Spirit,
> Have sent the blessed Two,
> To visit the creation,
> And teach us what to do.

The special affection directed to Ann Lee is confirmed by such lines as "My ever blessed *Mother*, Forever I'll adore." These same themes emerge in an invitation to unite in obedience and bear the cross.

> Come Brethren and Sisters, let's joyful unite,
> In Godly communion let all take delight;
> 'Tis joyful and pleasant in union to join,
> And praise our dear Saviour, and Mother divine.
> We now have our calling, in this blessed day,
> To follow our leaders in this holy way,
> To take up our crosses, live pure just and true,
> Be fully united in all that we do.

By contrast, another hymn depicts the inhabitants of the world as the illegitimate children of a carnal union.

This mark the deceivers do carry,
And all may their character view;
For when they wax wanton they marry,
As all carnal creatures will do:
And as they are led by old nature,
They prove their inferior birth,
By union with some fallen creature,
That binds them still down to the earth.

The preface to *Millennial Praises* warned the society against regarding these compositions as eternally useful, "for no gift or order of God can be binding on Believers for a longer term of time than it can be profitable to their travel in the gospel." It is ironic that these hymns, which contrasted the church and the antichristian world, were sung to tunes largely "plundered" from the world.[163]

New dance forms were also introduced during these years. Several were variations on the square shuffle, incorporating contrasting tempos and styles. The quick dance, for example, introduced in 1811, involved both singers and dancers, the singers often filling melodies with words, the dancers skipping, sometimes in a circle. This dance form celebrated spiritual "zeal and power" and thus was a favorite during times of religious stirring. It is significant that Shaker dance forms, although they bore some resemblance to secular dances, retained their distinctiveness by avoiding such elements as the unpredictable choices of a caller and the rotation of partners. Shorter songs composed by members of the society often accompanied these dances. Longer hymns, by contrast, usually were the work of the intellectual leaders. "Extra songs" were also sung. Sayings of Lucy Wright spoken in meeting, for example, were framed as short songs. Other occasions gave rise to songs of praise and thanksgiving, of greeting and farewell.[164]

Additional innovations took place in Shaker worship in the early part of the century. Toward the close of the first decade, for example, it became increasingly common for a member of the ministry or an elder to address the meetings. Although not called a sermon, it fulfilled the same function, providing an occasion for exhortation, instruction, and admonition. Often a biblical text or theme served as the starting point for these homilies. This pattern was especially pronounced in the West, where a number of the leaders had formerly been Protestant ministers. In 1815 Lucy Wright introduced the practice of using gestures with the song texts. This "motioning" added interpretive actions to the words, thereby strengthening the impact of the song. During the 1820s a gift of marching was received at

New Lebanon. Marches, by contrast with dances, allowed aged members to participate fully in the exercise, for marching employed a pacing step instead of a skip. In these same years Believers also experimented in the meetings with foot washing, a ritual act of humble service.[165]

Despite the steady growth of liturgical forms, the ecstatic impulses characteristic of the earliest period were never far below the surface and often burst into the ordered and structured meetings. In 1815, for example, the ministry in Ohio reported that both Union Village and Watervliet were experiencing the "Power of God" in an unprecedented fashion. Large numbers were "Speaking with tongues at once turning Stamping with their foot throw[n] down and tossed about So that it is Impossible for language to describe their Exercises." These manifestations were taking place not only in the meetinghouse, but also throughout the dwellings. At times the noise was so loud "that the Explosion of Cannon or heavy peals of thunder Could not be heard at a Small distance." This same warring and roaring was creating a tumult at West Union, too. Issachar Bates believed "this stamping business" was connected with "the marks of the Lord Jesus." He wrote in rhyming lines, "When I see one repeat his blows—Till the blood gushes from his nose—And others round all stomping too—With heels and ancles black and blue—this seems like bringing sometime to pass—Think what the serpents head must feel—Beneath a black and bruised heel—His hope of life is small indeed—Among the blessed womans seed." At Busro, religious energies found release in startling ways, somewhat reminiscent of the physical excesses of the Age of the Founders.[166]

Within Shakerism, ecstasy was never totally suppressed by structured worship forms. In 1820, for example, during a period filled with "harmonious Songs, and graceful exercises," the ministry at Pleasant Hill reported the extraordinary case of a young man who had not yet opened his mind. One night he was jerked about "mightily" in bed. Again the next night "he was taken with Such compelling power, that he was flung out of his bed" onto the floor and tossed back repeatedly. His feet, it was said, were flung "Some times as high as the pegboards." The next day he "desired a privilege" and confessed his sins. Other unusual gifts were received. The "smoking meeting," observed by the Believers in 1826 according to William Haskett, an ex-Shaker, was one of the more unusual. This ceremony, celebrated in several villages in honor of Ann Lee's arrival in America, united brethren, sisters, and children in billowing smoke as all puffed on their pipes. Haskett, who considered this "gift" as another evidence of Shaker "fanaticism," delighted in the humor of the scene, "the like of which stands unrecorded on sacred page, or history's broad scroll." The clouds of smoke rose quickly, but the hour passed slowly. When adjournment came, Haskett wrote, "we rushed for the doors, glad to breathe again in the pure air." Some reported feeling "Mother's spirit" among them. One sister "exclaimed, 'They may well say *spirit*, for if it was her *body*, they would have smoked her to death.'"[167]

Critics aside, by the 1820s the Shakers were solidly established in America. The members of the United Society of Believers were confident that the expansion and consolidation they had experienced were both the fulfillment of prophecy and the foretaste of greater things to come. The editors of the *Summary View* affirmed that "as the light of Divine truth is progressive in the Church, and as the preparatory work of salvation and redemption increases on earth; so the solemn and important truths of the gospel will continue, from time to time, to be more clearly manifested to mankind." The Believers also sang about the millennial vision.

> The kingdom now advances,
> The great Messiah reigns,
> And virgins join in dances,
> On Zion's blissful plains;
> How happy we, who live to see
> The glorious day increasing!
> Give thanks, give thanks, give thanks, give thanks,
> Be thankful without ceasing.[168]

The Close of the Formative Period

The history of the Shakers does not divide neatly into distinct, self-contained periods. Developments that began during the Age of the Founders continued into the era of their successors. The forces set in motion by Joseph Meacham and Lucy Wright, the second generation of leaders, lasted long after their deaths. The tendency of historians to draw sharp dividing lines within the story of Shakerism distorts our understanding of the society. The most egregious errors of this sort involve the selection of wars as turning points in Shaker history, an especially inept choice for a community committed to the principles of pacifism for more than two hundred years.[169]

This account of Shaker history assumes that sects commonly move through a series of identifiable stages in their evolution. In the case of the United Society of Believers, the second stage, involving the development and elaboration of community forms and structures, ended during the third decade of the nineteenth century. It did not terminate at one moment or with one event, but rather with a series of events. I have selected 1826, the year of the founding of the last major Shaker settlement, at Sodus Bay, New York, to mark the close of the Formative Period. This significant public event stands independent of subjective judgments about its advantages or disadvantages for the Believers. A number of other important events also occurred in the years immediately preceding 1826.[170]

The death of Lucy Wright in 1821 received more attention than any other occurrence within the society during these years. Her demise frequently has been interpreted as signaling the end of Shakerism's period of geographical expansion. That judgment is misleading, however, because the society did not immediately experience a marked change in goals or activities. In fact, Wright's decease was accompanied by a new determination on the part of the leaders—old and new—to carry forward in her spirit. Major initiatives in evangelism and settlement took place over the ensuing years.[171]

Wright's death at Watervliet on 7 February 1821 was not totally unexpected. She had been sick intermittently for years. Letters from New Lebanon regularly carried news of her illnesses, and in turn correspondence addressed to the central ministry standardly inquired about her health. Two days before her death, Rufus Bishop noted: "Mother having regained her health, in a small degree, walks out to the Office, & is there seized violently with a pain in her back side, & bowels which seemed to threaten the disolution of her mortal existence." This time her situation did not improve, and the following evening the society at Watervliet assembled to pray for her. Wright died the next afternoon about 2:45. News of her death was carried immediately to New Lebanon, and from there word was sent to the other villages. At the funeral held on the morning of 10 February, the elders from both New Lebanon and Watervliet addressed the assembly. According to Calvin Green, "many tears were shed." Only Shakers attended the service; "not one of the world made their appearance" until the grave site had been reached, which pleased the Believers.[172]

Formal notification of Wright's death went out in a circular letter to the eastern villages and in other letters to the West. The ministry announced that the "Cup of Affliction" had been poured out on the society. "God has Called home his Anointed," they wrote; "our *Ever Blessed Mother is no more!*" Although sorrow and tears were abundant, the ministry also affirmed that "Mother lives and her Remembrance will ever live in the hearts of all her faithful Children." The letters included a hymn composed for the occasion that served both as a eulogy for Wright and as an encouragement to the faithful in Zion. As the news spread to the scattered villages, expressions of grief circulated throughout the society. Statements of love and affection for Wright and for the central ministry were directed to New Lebanon.[173]

For some Shakers, Wright's presence seemed as powerful in death as in life. Lucy Smith, who had taken the name Lucy in honor of Wright when appointed to the ministry at Pleasant Hill, received several visions concerning her "Mother" after Wright's death. Shortly after retiring one night, Smith reported that "a bright light spread over me and I sensibly felt Mother placed right before me, and my soul felt refreshed." When she looked, she saw a sister wearing a white veil. On another occasion Smith saw the same sister lying face to face with her on her pillow. This sister was "very butiful, her handkerchief and Collar appeared very white pure and Angelic, and the folds that filled her handkerchief around her neck were exceeding neet and butiful." From her collar button streamed a "large blooming light" of a brightness too glittering to behold with "natural eyes." These visions comforted a grieving Smith and others at Pleasant Hill.[174]

The response of the ministry at Union Village, no less mournful, addressed a different issue. The ministry in Ohio had always felt themselves special companions to the leaders at New Lebanon. Wright had been their Mother and they her loyal and loving children, but in their minds David Darrow's role as Father paralleled her position, in terms of both parental status and endearment. With Wright's death Darrow's seniority in the western ministry raised a critical question for the future of the society. Would he accept the new leaders in the East as his gospel parents?[175]

In April 1821 Darrow wrote to the new ministry at New Lebanon, describing the reactions to Wright's death at Union Village and pledging his loyalty. He stated his determination not to let the church be divided: "union we must have with you," he wrote, "or we cannot live. [F]or the Church of Christ is one and cannot be devided. God is one and cannot alter, God is Love and they that gather into that Love, will be one, and cannot be devided." Darrow urged the ministry not to be reluctant or embarrassed to communicate candidly with him, "whether it is admonition or teaching or counsil or whatever the gift of God may direct." He promised to accept their directions "as tho Mother [Lucy] was their in body." Near the end of the year, when reporting the death of his colleague Eldress Ruth Farrington, Darrow fervently repeated the same pledge, vowing that he had no desire "to set up Independent Churches" in the West. Rather he intended to keep "Union & love," for the western villages were but branches of the church "first planted at Jerusalem—that is—New Lebanon." Scripture, he wrote, speaks of only one church of Christ, not many.[176]

Nevertheless, several initiatives by the leaders at Union Village during the next few years invite a different interpretation. Two new Shaker settlements were planted in Ohio as the result of successful missionary endeavors by western Believers. In 1822 at Warrensville, south of Cleveland some 240 miles from Union Village, a small settlement was organized and named North Union. Local residents led by Ralph Russell, who had become acquainted with the Shakers, provided a committed nucleus for this gathering. Members of the Russell family, relatives, and friends were instructed by missionaries sent from Union Village, including Richard W. Pelham, James Hodge, and Richard McNemar—all western converts themselves. Farms were dedicated to the joint interest, additional land was purchased by the trustees at Union Village, and the settlement was supervised by personnel assigned by the western Shaker leaders.[177]

Some of the same processes were involved with the beginnings of a settlement in 1824 at Whitewater, Ohio, about 35 miles west and a little south of Union Village. This settlement also included converts from Darby Plains, 70 miles north of Union Village, where Shaker missionaries had experienced success among the members of the Christian (New Light) church who had migrated to the area from Vermont. Contacts at Darby Plains had begun as early as 180 when Darrow sent McNemar and Calvin Morrell among them. Visitations back and forth produced results, and by the summer of 1823 a small group of Shakers had gathered and built a meetinghouse. But the society at Darby Plains was troubled by unfriendly neighbors, persistent illness, and questionable land claims. Therefore when Shaker efforts among Methodists in the Whitewater area were successful, the ministry at Union Village decided to relocate the group from Darby Plains there. Unfortunately, conditions did not at once improve for the settlers. Food was scarce, the land poor, and sickness continued to take its toll on the Believers. Assistance from Union Village became vital for survival.[178]

Unlike earlier settlements in the West, the new villages at North Union and Whitewater were almost totally the work of western Believers. The leaders in Ohio had taken the initiative for the missionary work, supplied the personnel for leadership and organization, and provided much of the necessary financial assistance. As a result, the members of these villages "acknowledged the Church at Union Village to be [their] Parent and

Mother Church, and Head of influence to council guide and direct and in every emergency [they] always found her true to her interests, and ready to extend the helping hand in every time of need." The steady flow of people and advice between Union Village and these new sites strengthened the bond among the western communities.[179]

New settlements, however, are not unmixed blessings, as the ministry at New Lebanon knew well from previous experience and as the leaders at Union Village were to discover. Reporting on the progress of the new colonies in mid-1824, the western leaders acknowledged that it was easier to convince people of sin and even to bring them to confession than "to protect & save them afterwards." The problems at Whitewater, in particular, showed no sign of abating, and the demands on the resources at Union Village were rising. Furthermore, the continuing difficulties at West Union, which was on the verge of breaking apart again, proved anguishing to the society's leaders. From the standpoint of the ministry at New Lebanon, the decision to form the two new settlements at this time was questionable, if not unwise. These undertakings also seemed to confirm the suspicions of some in the East that Darrow and other western leaders planned to establish Union Village as the new center of an expanding western Shakerism. That fear was fed in some measure by the continuing debates between eastern and western leaders on matters of theology, specifically on issues provoked by the latest revision of the *Testimony* and by criticism of the *Summary View*.[180]

These plans, real or imagined, suffered a major setback when, after a prolonged illness, David Darrow died on 27 June 1825 at the age of seventy-five. His funeral the next day was attended by five hundred Shakers. Richard McNemar spoke at the service, expressing the Believers' shock at the loss of this "foundation of the west." Darrow, according to McNemar, had established the western church in accord with "the pattern shone him in the mount, as it was given by the revelation of God." McNemar associated Father David with the "everlasting Father, the God that should rule in the Earth, the spirit of the Eternal parentage in whome his soul was anchored." Other eulogies recalled Darrow's relationship with the "first Mother," Ann Lee, and his willingness to suffer persecution for the gospel. An elaborate solemn procession of Believers arranged in orderly ranks accompanied the coffin to the grave site.[181]

Almost immediately, Darrow seems to have acquired a greater stature in death than he occupied in life. One speaker at the funeral reminded his hearers that Father David was "not gone," but could be of more assistance now than before as "the spiritual lead & protector of this people."

Even Darrow's corpse appeared "beautifull beyond discription" to his followers: the "brightness of heaven" seemed to rest upon it. Some said his corpse "surpassed any thing they ever saw of the kind," for it scarcely showed the signs of his age. Others marveled that it emitted no odors.[182]

The formal announcement of Darrow's death sent to New Lebanon extolled him as the father of Believers in the western country, universally loved and esteemed. "A miraculous work of God has been wrought in this western land under the administration & through the instrumentality of our much beloved & ever worthy Father David," wrote the Ohio ministry. "And he has been a faithful planter, supporter & defender of Mother's gospel in this western country from the beginning. . . . His soul was devoted for the honor of the gospel & the upbuilding of Christ's kingdom on earth." In the same letter, the western ministry announced that Issachar Bates, assigned to West Union, would now take up residence at Union Village as an elder.[183]

Little wonder that the eastern leaders searched for diplomatic ways to remind the western Believers of proper order in the society and to reassert their authority in the West. The letter from the East responding to the news of Darrow's death was unambiguous. "And we hope you have an understanding that the removal of the most important pillar does not alter the order of God, nor take away the birthright of a Society," the ministry wrote. "And that you will gather closer to the standard—strengthen your union by meekness & simplicity—fear God, & love one another, & God will surely bless you." Within a year the leaders at New Lebanon declared "obsolete" the titles of Mother and Father for the heads of villages or members of the living ministry. Several years earlier the central ministry had expressed regret that a uniform practice had not been established in the use of these terms; they expected such parental language to die out with the persons bearing those titles. From now on these honors were to be reserved for the founders and their immediate successors. The practical effect of this ruling was to reduce the possibility of any individual cultivating a local following and thereby drawing off the special affections of the Believers. In addition, the ministry at New Lebanon continued to solicit affirmations of loyalty by regularly discoursing on the importance of union and order.[184]

One year after Darrow's death, more than thirty leading members of the society at Union Village signed a letter addressed to the ministry at New Lebanon in which they pledged their loyalty and union in the gospel. Although they acknowledged the "cross" that Darrow's loss represented for them, they were determined not to allow that "grievous dispensation" to destroy their relation to the church in the East. The question was "whether the building has . . . sustained material damage in consequence of a change in its foundation pillars." They assured the eastern ministry that "the foundation of God stands sure" and confessed that they "considered it dangerous to have men's persons in admiration." The western Believers stated their intention "to promote a spirit of reconciliation to whatever may come in the order and gift of God" as it had been established by earlier leaders and was "now firmly supported by their successors." "In this order we have found salvation," they wrote, "and to it we are determined to cleave at the risk of all things."[185]

These were the circumstances surrounding the establishment of the settlement at Sodus Bay in 1826. This time the ministry at New Lebanon took the initiative in responding to a request for instruction. Joseph Pelham, the older brother of Richard, lived on a farm near Lyons, New York. Earlier he had visited Union Village and read the *Testimony*. In 1825 he wrote to the eastern ministry, requesting assistance in his spiritual quest. Believers from the East, including Calvin Green, conferred with him on several occasions. These visits attracted to Shakerism a small circle of persons in the center of the region that historians have branded the "burned-over district."[186]

The potential religious and physical advantages of this western New York location were not lost on the leadership of the society. The ferment provoked by the evangelical revivals in the district seemed a promising environment for possible Shaker gains. The area was yielding rich harvests for other religious societies. The region was also served by the Erie Canal, newly opened in 1825, connecting the Hudson River at Albany and Troy with Buffalo on Lake Erie. This internal improvement became the major waterway to the West, opening the areas through which it passed to new commerce and travel. Lyons, located on this new highway, stood approximately halfway between the eastern Shaker villages and the western settlements.[187]

For all these reasons and perhaps others, the ministry at New Lebanon wasted little time. They sent Proctor Sampson, Jeremiah Talcott, and Samuel Southwick to explore possible sites for a settlement. In February 1826 in cooperation with Joseph Pelham, these agents purchased a tract of land containing more than 1,330 acres on Great Sodus Bay, at the time thought to be one of the most promising natural harbors on the shores of Lake Ontario. The agreed upon price was $12,600, funds for which were later borrowed from several eastern villages. Within a few months Pelham and other Shakers in the area began to establish the institutions of the common life in western New York. The new outpost had the additional advantage for the eastern Shakers of reasserting symbolically the authority of the central ministry west of the Alleghenies.[188]

With the settlement at Sodus Bay, the period of the society's greatest geographical expansion came to a close (fig. 5). After this, efforts to establish new settlements were infrequent and generally unsuccessful. These same years had witnessed the deaths of the principal architects of that expansion—Lucy Wright and David Darrow—and the bridging of the geographical gap that separated the East from the West. The villages of North Union and Sodus Bay drew eastern and western Shakers together again by serving as convenient way stations for travelers heading either direction. From this time forward, the line of travel for Believers journeying between the Ohio Valley and the East Coast often shifted north to the Erie Canal and the Great Lakes. The ecclesiastical fissure within the society was not bridged so easily.[189]

The Formative Period of Shaker history was critical for the survival and subsequent development of the sect. During these forty years scattered bands of converts, committed to an apocalyptic faith and loosely drawn to one another by the charismatic gifts of their leaders, were transformed into a national communal society of Believers clustered in nineteen villages spread across a distance of more than fifteen hundred miles. Under the guidance of Joseph Meacham, Lucy Wright, and David Darrow, and with the assistance of countless elders and eldresses, deacons and deaconesses, the Shakers acquired the marks of institutional religion—a structured hierarchy, an intellectual elite, other specialized functionaries, a body of dogma, canonical writings, a written history, a reasoned apologetic, liturgical forms, a collection of hymns, and a distinctive way of life.[190]

Students of religion often describe the second stage in the evolution of sects as a time when charisma is routinized; that is, when "gifts" are organized in such a way that they can be handled in a routine manner. Some conclude that ecstasy disappears at this stage and that the extraordinary element in religion is destroyed by structures and ordered patterns. For these critics, religion is by implication less authentic when routines are introduced because forms lead to formalism. These conclusions smack of an "evangelical fallacy" that exalts the "spirit" over the "letter."[191]

I do not share the assumption that a dramatic vision is inherently more spiritual than the actions of an instructed conscience or that a frenzied dance in the spirit is more legitimately religious than reading and writing about the nature of good and evil. Forms and structures are the

Shaker Villages

1. Watervliet, N.Y.
2. New Lebanon, N.Y.
3. Hancock, Mass.
4. Enfield, Conn.
5. Harvard, Mass.
6. Tyringham, Mass.
7. Canterbury, N.H.
8. Enfield, N.H.
9. Shirley, Mass.
10. Alfred, Maine
11. Sabbathday Lake, Maine
12. Union Village, Ohio
13. Watervliet, Ohio
14. Pleasant Hill, Ky.
15. South Union, Ky.
16. West Union, Ind.
17. North Union, Ohio
18. Whitewater, Ohio
19. Sodus Bay, N.Y.
20. Narcoossee, Fla.
21. White Oak, Ga.

5. Shaker Villages, 1827, 1900, 1925
Drawn by John Michael Hollingsworth.

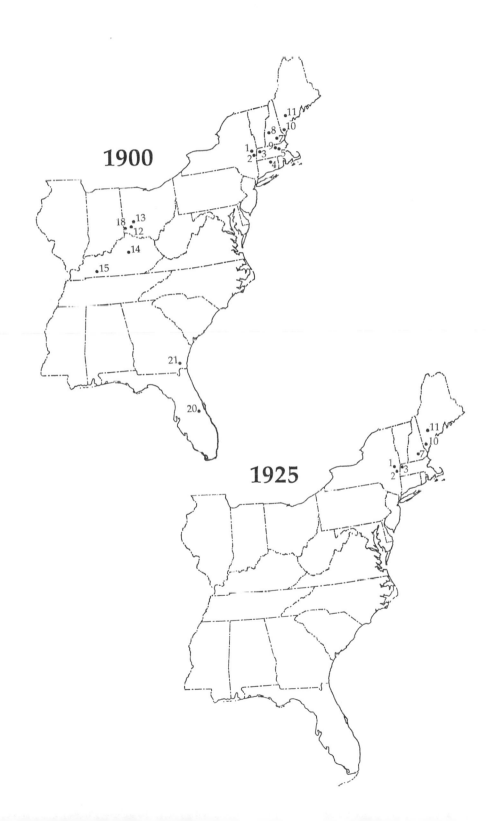

stuff of religious life. Repetition and patterns constitute the way men and women attempt to find meaning in something other than themselves. The religious quest motivated the Shakers to create a multitude of forms and structures for their life together, and these institutions reflect the fullness of the Believers' religion.[192]

The Shaker experience during this second period found appropriate expression in such emergent forms. A hierarchy of leaders, both spiritual and temporal, made decisions for the evolving society. Written covenants legalized and protected Shaker assets. Theological writings formulated, rationalized, and systematized beliefs. A written history made sense of the present by arranging and elaborating on the past, organizing oral traditions into a meaningful, coherent story. Millennial laws codified the rules governing the common life. Dances and marches gave ritual expression to the sense of union and order. Songs written and sung by the Believers echoed the society's ideals. Daily routines including chores and work, meetings and meditation, provided the life rhythms necessary for the communitarians. The second generation was struggling to retain and preserve the Shaker gospel. The forms they developed made it possible for themselves and others to share and to repeat their experience in its fullness.[193]

At the heart of Shaker religion was the concept of gift. In the earliest period gifts frequently took the form of charismatic powers exercised by the founders, accompanied by ecstatic activity. The concept of gift was no less pronounced during the second stage of development, although its manifestation among leaders and members was increasingly varied. Gifts were manifested in direct revelations and night visions (dreams) as well as in the instincts, wisdom, and practical experience that informed decisions of all kinds, whether matters of religion or everyday life. With this concept the Shakers sanctioned the initiatives and authority of their leaders as well as the choices and actions of individual members. In this manner they affirmed an underlying confidence in the providential guidance of the society's affairs as carried forward by the Believers.[194]

The strength of this notion of gift explains to some extent the success of Meacham, Wright, and Darrow. These three were builders, pragmatic leaders whose efforts resulted in the establishment of an institution that has weathered nearly two centuries of stress and strain. Meacham's genius lay in recognizing that the sect must move beyond the founders. Wright's vision of a united society guided the Believers toward an integrated community. Darrow's energies made possible geographical expansion into a national society. All three were driven by religious motives in pursuit of their goals. The successful institutionalization of Shakerism was one measure of the strength of the Believers' faith.[195]

Historians have traditionally singled out Joseph Meacham as the primary architect of the Shaker communal order. His contributions were substantial indeed. Nonetheless, Lucy Wright clearly played a far more instrumental role in the evolution of Shakerism. She was perhaps the most influential figure in all of Shaker history. Even Ann Lee may have had less direct impact on the society's development. Wright's administration shaped the United Society of Believers as we know it. There was virtually no significant change during the Formative Period that she did not influence, at least indirectly.[196]

The recovery of the role of David Darrow during these years adds a new dimension to the story of the society. His central position in the westward expansion is patently clear, but his contributions (and those of other western Believers) to the evolution of Shaker theology and history have been obscured. Darrow has been almost lost in the standard accounts of Shaker history because of a prevailing bias in favor of the eastern experience. The beginnings of the society in the East and the location of the central ministry at New Lebanon have blinded historians to the significance of the western experience and, in general, to the importance of local developments. The whole of Shaker life was not summarized at New Lebanon. In fact, the central ministry was repeatedly goaded into action by the requests or demands of western Believers. Shaker historians have resisted accepting the negative implication of this, namely, that conflict and competition within the society sometimes led to creative developments. In other words, union and order were high ideals that the Believers frequently failed to achieve.[197]

Lucy Wright's influential role in the development of the society was directly affected by another significant change. During these formative years the figure of Ann Lee emerged from the obscurity of the past, and she was confirmed in her special role as founder of the society—"Mother Ann Lee." Shaker theologians and historians alike contributed to this process. The theologians defined Ann Lee as an agent of redemption, of equal, if not greater, importance in salvation history than Jesus of Nazareth. The concept of the second appearance of Christ authenticated her position. Historians depicted Lee as a gifted individual whose life and sufferings were commensurate with this high calling. The power and authority of "Mother Ann" increased accordingly. The primary beneficiary of Lee's changing image was Lucy Wright, who emerged during these years as "Mother Lucy," empowered with some of the same authority and gifts as the "first mother," although motherhood was exercised by the two in very different ways. Wright's accomplishments are unthinkable apart from the shadow of Ann Lee. In other words, the social sources of Shaker theology and history are found in Wright's administrative tenure, and the ideological support accounting for her success as a leader is tied to the evolution of the image of Lee as the founder of the society.[198]

The Shakers evolved from an apocalyptic sect into a millennial church during the Formative Period. In the process the sectarian edge of the society was blunted somewhat, but never lost. The Believers retained their prophetic stance against the culture of the young republic, condemning it in word and deed. They engaged in "defensive structuring" by protecting themselves from the world. They set themselves apart in their own villages to pursue the regenerate life and to avoid the unregenerate patterns of the larger culture. Their union and order were defensive adaptations against the threat of a hostile environment. The Believers condemned marriage, private property, the established churches, democracy, and individual freedom by advocating celibacy, common property, the superiority of their own society, the authority of the ministry, and submissive obedience. In the minds of their contemporaries, the Shakers deserved the opposition and hostility directed toward them because of their scandalous views.[199]

At the same time, the institutionalization of the society muted its sectarian critique, for the Believers' success at constructing a national society confirmed their commitment, even indirectly, to the present world. The establishment of villages documented their belief in the possibility of a new and different order in the world. The millennial vision of the Shakers provided a blueprint—however offensive to non-Shakers—for a more perfect social order. The settlements, which attracted so much attention from visitors and outsiders, gave public notice that the Shakers had moved beyond the apocalyptic proclamations of their founders. In this respect the Believers were in tune with the larger culture of the day, for in the opening decades of the nineteenth century the youthful nation attempted to build a new society by taming a continent and constructing an indigenous American culture. The Shaker vision shared the optimistic mood, and thus the Believers participated in the making of America.[200]

PART THREE

Too Much

of the Wind,

Fire, and

Earthquake:

The Maturation

and Revitalization

of the Society

1827–1875

The middle of the nineteenth century presents a study in contrasts for the student of United States history. The nation was experiencing periods of growth and prosperity alternating with times of turmoil and upheaval. Geographical expansion, internal improvements, advances in agricultural technology, the influx of immigrants, the growth of a middle class, the beginnings of industrialization and urbanization—these and other changes were contributing to the modernization of America. Yet at the same time political, economic, and social conflict was the norm. The citizens of the United States marked fifty years of independence in 1826 with increasing debate over a host of issues. By the time the nation reached the eve of its centennial, Americans had passed through an internecine struggle provoked in great measure by competing conceptions of union and order. The catastrophe of the Civil War, in turn, created new possibilities and different problems for America.[1]

Religious activity in the United States reflected the same mixture of growth and controversy. In the late stages of the Second Great Awakening, evangelicals and their opponents debated the techniques and results of the revivalists. The spectacular success of Charles Grandison Finney and of the Methodist movement challenged the established centers of religious authority and intellectual leadership. New, more radical versions of Christianity were storming across the land. Some, such as the Latter-day Saints, offered fresh revelations. Others called for an end to social and ecclesiastical privilege. Most placed authority in the hands of the laity. A few established distinctive communal practices and ways of life. All, according to Nathan O. Hatch, were part of a "wave of popular religious movements that . . . did more to Christianize American society than anything before or since." But not all religious activity was taking place within the confines of the churches or in protracted revival meetings. Jon Butler has demonstrated the existence of another world of popular religion in America. Dreams and visions, witches and diviners, fortune-telling and spiritual healing, miracles and magic—these and other extraordinary phenomena were interacting with one another and with the established religious traditions, creating a "spiritual hothouse" in America.[2]

During these fifty years the United Society of Believers was experiencing prosperity in temporal and spiritual affairs as well as distress and confusion. The Shakers, too, began to mark anniversaries, a telltale sign of the society's maturation. Beginning in 1835 the Believers regularly commemorated the traditional birth date of Ann Lee—29 February or an adjacent day when it was not on the calendar. On that occasion, there was a "general gift for all the Societies far & near, who claim Mother as their leader, to unite upon a certain day & hour" for the purpose of "a general union and blessing." They sang two designated hymns, "Mother" and "Precious Way of God." It was reported at New Lebanon on that day that the Believers felt as though "the Saints on earth & angels in heaven had met together, & truly many of [their] departed friends were felt & seen in the meeting." The society also began noting other earlier events, thereby creating its own liturgical calendar.[3]

Although union and order remained the guiding principles of the Shakers during this Middle Period, the maintenance of these ideals proved increasingly difficult as boundaries between the church and the world blurred. The ministry at New Lebanon struggled to assert its authority over the scattered villages as centrifugal forces within the society sought to diminish that federal control. In the midst of these fifty years, an upheaval of unprecedented proportions, an outburst of spiritualistic manifestations, shook the society to its foundations. From this religious commotion, known among the Believers as Mother Ann's Work and the Era of Manifestations, Shakerism never fully recovered.[4]

The developmental parallels between the United States and the United Society of Believers are not surprising. No matter how large or small, social groups—like individuals—pass through stages: birth, infancy, adolescence, adulthood, old age, and death. Adulthood and maturity bring special challenges not previously experienced, and established patterns of thought and action are not always satisfactory. Some individuals are content to live in a state of chronic disjunction between ideals and reality, but others search for ways to reduce that stress. In antebellum America countless reformers sought to transform the culture, turning to political parties, economic proposals, social programs, and religious movements for solutions. A few called for radically new cultural systems.[5]

"Revitalization movements," one name given to these more revolutionary proposals, often emerge when established world views no longer make sense of daily experience. Individuals arise who propose alternative ways of conceiving reality, and conflict frequently follows. Sometimes the struggle results in the renewal of traditional perspectives, other times in the birth of genuinely new ways of thinking and behaving. Anthony F. C. Wallace has pointed out that revitalization movements are "recurrent" in history and have played an especially important role in the origin and development of sectarian religious groups.[6]

The years 1827 and 1875 mark significant moments in the history of the United Society of Believers. In 1827 the Believers permanently closed a major western village, the problem-plagued settlement at Busro, Indiana. In 1875 they shut down the first eastern village, the settlement at Tyringham, Massachusetts. During the half-century between these two events—the Middle Period of Shaker history—the society experienced changing patterns of leadership, increasingly complex financial dealings, growing social conflict, and alternate periods of religious vitality and stagnation. The outburst of spiritualistic frenzy among the Believers—Mother Ann's Work—was, at best, a mixed blessing. That surge of religious energy, which momentarily revitalized the society, exaggerated certain disruptive tendencies already present and, contrary to the opinions of many, worked to the general disadvantage of the Believers. It also set the stage for changes in subsequent decades.[7]

A New Generation of Leaders

During the 1820s responsibility for leadership in the society passed into the hands of the third generation of Shakers in America, for the most part members who had come to maturity after the deaths of the English founders. Some of these Believers had known only Lucy Wright's tenure in the central ministry. The transition to new leadership was accomplished with relative ease, for now the principle of a self-perpetuating hierarchy was established in practice and sanctioned by tradition. Following Wright's death in 1821 at the age of sixty-one, only one member of the parent ministry at New Lebanon continued to serve, Mary A. (Polly) Landon, known as Eldress Ruth, who advanced to the position of first eldress. It was she to whom Wright had "opened" a gift concerning succession in the ministry shortly before her death. On the strength of Wright's directions, Abiathar Babbit, an elder since 1790, was retired to Watervliet, ostensibly because of his advanced age. He was replaced by Ebenezer Bishop and Rufus Bishop, standing first and second, respectively, in the male leadership. Asenath Clark was selected to join Landon in the female lead, thereby completing the central ministry. These four jointly exercised leadership in the society from 1821 until 1848.[8]

The members of the new ministry at New Lebanon, whose average age in 1821 was forty-seven, brought to their collective task considerable experience in positions of responsibility. Landon had stood second in the female order since 1804, when Wright chose her as a companion. Her more than sixteen years in the meetinghouse provided direct continuity with the policies and practices of the preceding years. Ebenezer Bishop had served as first elder in the Gathering Order at New Lebanon since 1807. Rufus Bishop had been the second elder in the Church Family from

1808 until his selection. Clark had occupied the office of family deaconess in the First Order for six years. Wright's choices for the succession appear eminently sound: these individuals were esteemed for religious as well as practical achievements. By contrast with their predecessors, however, few stories told of miraculous selection. Only Rufus Bishop, according to later Shaker tradition, had been singled out prophetically. Henry Clough, Joseph Meacham's companion in the ministry, identified Bishop as "first of all the rising generation of Believers" based on a vision in which Clough saw Bishop "wearing a crown."[9]

None of the four in the newly formed central ministry emerged as a dominant figure. On the contrary, during the following decades they developed a pattern of collective leadership that became the norm for subsequent generations. Resting less on claims of spiritual authority, governance increasingly depended on structured relationships defined by explicit functions and responsibilities. Obedience and respect from the members were still required, but now these responses were motivated differently. Formerly, the personal influence of the charismatic leaders, friendship among the members, shared experiences, and the relative proximity of the villages to New Lebanon had cemented the bonds of community. By the third decade of the nineteenth century, however, these factors no longer operated in the same way. The members of the central ministry were individuals of a practical bent, increasingly preoccupied with temporal concerns. Greater physical distance and contrasting points of view made close personal relationships more difficult. New Lebanon had lost its commanding geographical position with the expansion into the West. Converts from diverse backgrounds brought conflicting experiences into the society. The challenge facing the leadership after 1821, therefore, was substantial.[10]

The new ministry recognized that its authority was more tenuous than that of earlier leaders. Their primary claim to honor and respect— selection by Wright—was not insignificant, but it was less weighty than the credentials held by the charismatic leaders. The traditional distinction between the ministry and the members still obtained, but the new leaders felt compelled to strengthen their hold on parental prerogatives in a way never before necessary. They desired respect based on love and affection, but often were forced to settle for obedience derived from discipline and regulations. The concept of the society as an extended family was undergoing subtle but important changes. As a result, the ministry at New Lebanon took several steps to secure their position.[11]

One such move by the leadership was the decision to limit the use of the designations Mother and Father within the society. These honorific titles had been employed by the Shakers for more than three decades, not only for the founders and members of the central ministry but also for local leaders, some of whom had held their positions since the 1790s. Often these leaders enjoyed considerable power and influence because they had founded the villages over which they presided. (Some years earlier there had been a debate about the use of these terms in the West.) The members of the ministry at New Lebanon found themselves in the awkward position of trying to assert their authority over scattered leaders who, in many instances, were their seniors in both age and tenure in office. Attempting this over a distance of many miles compounded the problem. The ministerial prohibition against the parental titles circulated throughout the society, but it did not receive a uniformly positive reception. At Pleasant Hill, for example, where Lucy Smith had been called Mother Lucy ever since her appointment, that pattern of reference continued as late as 1830. At other villages, too, the use of these terms of endearment and respect died out slowly.[12]

As part of the effort to consolidate authority, the central ministry continued its regular visitations to the eastern villages, a practice stemming from Ann Lee's extensive travels and those of subsequent leaders, including Lucy Wright. The ministry routinely kept written logs of their travels, including the destination, duration, and distance. In 1830, for example, members of the parent ministry spent 80 days on the road visiting eastern villages, in addition to 122 days at Watervliet. In other words, the ministry resided at New Lebanon less than half of that year These visitations enabled the leaders to become acquainted with the presiding elders and eldresses as well as with the members of the scattered villages. Ideally, every eastern village was to be visited annually, but in reality that schedule proved an impossibility. Constraints of time, energy, and distance as well as duties "at home" restricted the number and length of such journeys.[13]

When the members of the central ministry were unable to visit in person, they used other means at their disposal to cement bonds within the society. Sometimes they selected Believers to serve as messengers and couriers, carrying information, counsel, or greetings from New Lebanon. Even more frequently they resorted to written correspondence. The postal service became an essential link among the scattered villages. The ministry spent a great deal of time writing letters and, in turn, requested that the Believers, far and near, write to them with regularity. Before 1834, no member of the central ministry at New Lebanon had ever traveled to the Shaker settlements in the Ohio Valley. Initially, couriers and correspondence were the only means of direct communication with the more remote western settlements.[14]

Letter writing became a bureaucratic science among the Shakers. Members of the new central ministry, especially Rufus Bishop, wrote scores of official letters each year. Leaders at nearly every village did likewise. In 1836, for example, Bishop took note of thirty-eight official letters (three of which were packets) written and received by the central ministry at New Lebanon. Those numbers represent only a fraction of the total exchanged within the society during that year. Before the invention of modern communication devices, written correspondence was the principal means of interaction among the scattered villages and a primary contributor to the maintenance of a sense of community.[15]

The body of extant Shaker correspondence from these years requires special comment. The letters are remarkable not only for their number, but also for their diverse content. They reflect the full range of the Believers' activities. In general, a familial spirit pervades the exchanges; in many the language of love becomes highly stylized. The ministry at Harvard, for example, expressed their gratitude to New Lebanon as follows: "We feel it to be our duty & Privilege to return you our best Thanks for your very kind & Parental Letter. Expressing your Love, Prayers & Blessing together with your frequent Remembrance of us, Ministering to us much Consolation. We Could Sensibly feel Mother's Spirit breathe through every Sentence." By contrast, some letters are rather matter-of-fact, a few even distant, severe, and censorious. At times the central ministry resorted to "circular letters" when the message was to be shared with all the villages. They also used some Believers as clerks to assist with the tedious work of writing and copying letters. Those individuals were often the same people involved in the intellectual and theological enterprises.[16]

The limitations of this Shaker administrative system became increasingly apparent with time. The skills of the leadership at New Lebanon were tested sorely as they were forced to deal with a series of problems festering in the society. Among these difficulties perhaps none was more vexing than that posed by West Union. The geographical isolation of the Indiana village made communication and exchange with other Shaker settlements, even those in the West, extremely difficult. The physical circumstances of the frontier created hardship among the Believers as they struggled to build a community. Illness and death stalked the village population. To these difficulties was added spiritual distress, manifested in disorder and unfaithfulness. The focus of the problem at Busro was, in the words of a lament by Richard McNemar, the "rising generation," who had deserted their "station," thereby creating grief for the Believers. In one four-month period in 1825, for example, thirteen young people left the village and "went to the world." The local leadership, headed by Archibald Meacham and Issachar Bates, was ineffectual in dealing with the situation.[17]

By 1826 the United Society was in a general stir over West Union. A steady stream of leaders traveled to and from the village, seeking a solution. In June Archibald Meacham set out from Busro to consult with the ministries at both Union Village and New Lebanon. The leaders in the West made regular visits to West Union, offering advice and assistance; those in the East expressed "grief" over the wholesale apostasy among the young "who might have been beautiful ornaments in the kingdom of God" had they not degraded themselves through disobedience. In November a collective decision was reached calling "for all the people to rise once more and move away from Busro, and so abandon the place forever." The next three months were filled with preparations for the removal, which was carried out in March 1827 by steamboat, keelboat, and wagon with the help of Believers from South Union, Pleasant Hill, and Union Village. The members of the Indiana society were relocated at these three settlements.[18]

Among the one hundred or so Believers removed from Busro more than one celebrated the end of the settlement, but the closing represented a major defeat for the United Society's strategy of geographical expansion. Although West Union was not the first site to be abandoned by the Shakers, it was the largest and most significant. There was no attempt to rationalize the decision. The closing stood as a public retreat, an ominous sign that the period of expansion had ended and that the leadership had erred in its judgments concerning the Indiana village. It would be almost fifty years before another major settlement was closed, but the lesson of Busro was clear enough: the Shaker sites were not exempt from failure.[19]

The difficulties plaguing the Believers at Busro were not confined to that village. Dealing with the rising generation proved a challenge at every location. As Priscilla J. Brewer has shown, for years the younger members of the society had been a major drain on collective resources and energy. During the opening decades of the nineteenth century, the proportion of individuals within the society below age sixteen rose dramatically, from 2.8 percent in 1800 to 19.8 percent in 1820. But the long-term success rate of the Shakers with these youths was very low. On attaining maturity, many chose not to stay with the Believers. Others did not wait to reach legal age before deserting or running away. The problem of desertion was noted in nearly every family journal. In 1828, for example, the Pleasant Hill leadership reported, "There has been but little ingathering of Souls from the world for a long time, and the most that do come, are runaways from other societys, and they do not stay long."[20]

The case of the Wickes family at Watervliet, New York, may not be typical, but it is representative. Job Wickes arrived at Watervliet in the summer of 1824. Fifty years of age, he "Opened his mind" to the Believers and within a period of two months had returned home to gather his family. Although details concerning Wickes's religious background are lacking, he came from Reading in Steuben County, on the southern edge of the "burned-over district," a region of intense revivalistic activity. On 27 October he returned to Watervliet with his wife, Polly, who was thirty-eight, and ten children between the ages of seventeen and one, six girls and four boys, "expecting to live among Believers" at the South Family. That day Polly Wickes "confessed" to the leaders.[21]

Within a week the Wickes family had moved into the house formerly owned by Benjamin Youngs, Sr., on the South Family's east lot. A few days later three of the children were moved to the Church Family. Four more children were relocated during the first four months of 1825, at least one to New Lebanon. In the late summer and early fall of 1826 the two youngest children were sent to the Second Family, and their mother to the South House. By this time Job Wickes had left the society, his name appearing on a roster of "Turnoffs, or those who have gone away in their own gift." In 1829 Polly and eight of her children were still at the village. By 1835, however, only Polly and her oldest daughter, Nancy, were listed among the Shakers at Watervliet, although a younger daughter, Mary, was also there. Two children had died in the early 1830s; the others apparently left, either individually or in groups. It is impossible to discover the reasons for their departures; it is less difficult to speculate why Polly and her oldest daughter may have chosen to stay, given contemporary domestic realities.[22]

Problems with the rising generation frequently became entangled with other local issues in the scattered villages. One of the most complex struggles into which the central ministry was drawn surfaced at Pleasant Hill in the mid-1820s. At stake were the United Society's core commitments to union and order. Lucy Smith, known to the villagers as Mother Lucy, and Samuel Turner held the positions of leadership at the village. Both had journeyed to the Ohio Valley at Wright's direction. Smith, the dominant figure in the village after John Meacham was recalled to New Lebanon, had achieved a special reputation for "the purity of her life and conversation." She was less skilled as a practical administrator and lenient in matters of discipline. Turner stood in her shadow during their period of joint leadership.[23]

Trouble developed at Pleasant Hill as early as 1825, when a group of Believers headed by John Whitbey and several other young men called for reforms at the village. This faction was fed by the democratic spirit of the times as well as by the ideas of the Scottish philanthropist and social philosopher Robert Owen, who captured the imagination of many Americans with his utopian proposals for a new moral order. In 1824 Owen had purchased Harmony, Indiana, from the followers of the German communitarian George Rapp, the leader of the Harmonists. When Whitbey called for the selection of leaders by the people and for a different handling of community assets, he was forced to leave Pleasant Hill. With the help of the Owenites, he then published a spirited attack on the Shakers. Pressure mounted for changes within the village, and Lucy Smith agreed to a number of structural reforms.[24]

The leaders at New Lebanon refused to approve the changes, however, declaring the Kentucky village no longer in union with the rest of the society. Elders were sent to Pleasant Hill to admonish the residents and to seek confessions. Rather than bringing peace, these visits provoked greater conflict. A major defection resulted: perhaps a third of the village residents, including young and old members, apostatized. Several in high positions joined the rebellion and left the village. James Gass, who had served as Elder Brother of the First Order, and his former wife, Lucy, departed together, to the shock and dismay of many at Pleasant Hill. Confusion and dissension abounded. The central ministry removed Lucy Smith from office, replacing her with Samuel Turner. She was escorted to Union Village and subsequently recalled to the East, ostensibly for reasons of "age and infirmity." In fact, she was no longer in control of the village and was viewed as contributing to the problem.[25]

The turmoil in Kentucky revealed deep-seated tensions and animosity among the western villages. Benjamin S. Youngs, the leader at South Union, blamed the "deplorable" situation at Pleasant Hill on the residents there, whom he described as selfish and conceited, considering "themselves superior in gifts and talents; in order and arrangements to any order of believers in the Western country, if not to any order of believers any where." In his opinion, the problem in Mercer County was that they "applauded their Mother, as a being superior to all others on Earth. All the concerns spiritual and temporal, were almost solely in her hands, and under her personal counsel and direction." As a result, Young contended, "infidelity, pride, presumption, disorder and confusion" prevailed in the village. He believed that other leaders, too, were "contaminated, or as they now call it 'smoked'."[26]

Lucy Smith dutifully accepted her "retirement," but the central ministry faced a situation in Maine that proved far more difficult. John Barnes had served as First Elder at the Alfred settlement (fig. 6) and in the Maine bishopric from 1793 until 1815, when he was "released" from his responsibilities and ordered by Lucy Wright to reside in the Church Family at New Lebanon. The precise circumstances surrounding his removal remain unclear, but subsequent accounts leave little doubt that he was "high minded, contrary, wilful [and] quick tempered." After four months at New Lebanon, Barnes returned to Alfred, having requested permission to "take up his residence there." He was not, however, restored to his leadership position. In Maine he became the source of unending "tribulation" for the local ministry with his "warlike" testimony, eccentric public behavior, and spirit of dissension. On one occasion, for example, he threatened to break down the door of the meetinghouse with an ax. It was his contention that the female leadership of the United Society, that is, Lucy Wright, had brought "great distress upon the body" and had unfairly removed him from office. Letters from Alfred detailed the discord and distress he provoked. Barnes's challenge to the ministry was a direct affront to the basic principles of the Shakers. Wright's inaction in the case appears inexplicable. Local authorities appeared powerless to discipline him because of his loyal following among the Believers in Maine.[27]

Barnes exercised a detrimental influence in Maine as late as 1831, even though the leadership finally took extraordinary steps to limit his activities. He was forbidden to use writing materials in the hope of putting "a stop to his Spreding his trash." He managed, nevertheless, to secure ink and paper and to continue writing. The village leaders decided that if necessary they would "confine" him, that is, physically restrain him, because outsiders who hated the Shakers were taking advantage of him. Barnes, the ministry wrote, has "Jest reason or mental faculties sufficant to do evil." In other words, they concluded that he was mentally disturbed and needed firm but loving care. Meanwhile, the village at Alfred was experiencing difficulties caused by the "artfull insinuations" of several young women—"witches or female divels," as they were called.[28]

At last the central ministry acted decisively. After two visits to the Maine area in 1830, they placed the Believers at Alfred and New Gloucester under the supervision of the ministry at Canterbury, an administrative arrangement recommended many years earlier by Joseph Meacham and tried once by Wright. If this arrangement had been followed when originally proposed, the ministry reasoned, the situation might not have come to the "present condition." The leadership at New Lebanon made this

6. Shaker Village, Alfred, Maine
Engraving showing the buildings of the Church Family in the foreground, including
the meetinghouse and the ministry's shop on the right of the road opposite the large
dwelling house and adjacent shops. (From Charles Edson Robinson, *A Concise History of the United Society of Believers*, 1893.)

change after consulting with a number of local leaders. The turmoil at Alfred underscores the limitations confronting the society's leadership. Their
prolonged inaction perhaps demonstrates the more humane and charitable side of the Believers' decision-making processes.[29]

This mix of bureaucratic and collegial principles is even more evident in the ministry's resolution of continuing difficulties at Pleasant Hill,
a village with a long tradition of independence. Two early leaders had been
forced out of office. Yet a third removal was occasioned by the central ministry's decision to send Rufus Bishop to visit the western villages. This trip
represented another move to reassert the authority of New Lebanon. Bishop
was accompanied on his journey in 1834 by Isaac Newton Youngs, who
compiled a daily log describing their activities, observations, and impressions (fig. 7).[30]

The visitors' stay at Pleasant Hill lasted nearly three weeks, during
which Bishop and Youngs examined all aspects of village life, including
both the physical and the spiritual dimension. They walked fields, toured
buildings, and inspected shops and mills. They talked at length with the
ministry and with leaders in each unit as well as with members of the families. They ate, sang, played, and worshiped with the Believers. The trav-

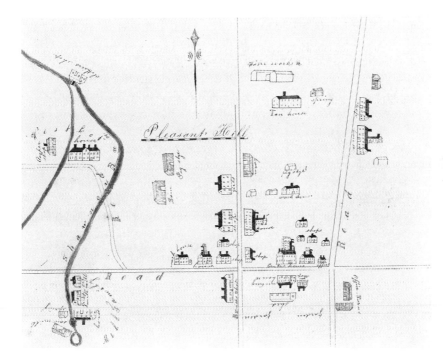

7. Shaker Village, Pleasant Hill, Kentucky
Map drawn in July 1835 by George Kendall, a member of the society at New Lebanon,
based on sketches made by Isaac N. Youngs on his trip to the West with Rufus Bishop.
(Courtesy Geography and Map Division of the Library of Congress, Washington, D.C.)

elers were duly impressed with the physical accomplishments of the
Kentuckians and with the hospitality they received. Yet the visit ultimately
led the central ministry to force Samuel Turner from his leadership position. While at Pleasant Hill, Bishop and Youngs received a number of complaints from residents who accused Turner of making arbitrary decisions.
Some members of the East Family resented his plan to combine their unit
with that of the Center Family upon completion of a large new dwelling.
Others at the Office, where business with the world was transacted, expressed discontent with their heavy work load. None of these negative
judgments appear in Youngs's public travel journal, which depicted life
and circumstances at Pleasant Hill in glowing terms.[31]

But all was not well at Pleasant Hill from the viewpoint of the central
ministry. Bishop himself took umbrage at the way Turner treated him,
suggesting in later correspondence that perhaps the Kentucky leader had
resented the official visit. He also accused Turner of claiming personal su-

periority on the basis of his natural family's position in the society—an old issue from the days of their youth. In other words, the complexities of the personal relationship between these two men, who had known each other for many years, became entangled with their administrative activities. The process of removing Turner was slow. After assessing reports from the trip, the central ministry deliberated about the best course of action and began to prepare Turner for his inevitable recall to the East. More than two years elapsed before this circuitous process led to his departure from Pleasant Hill. Such a roundabout approach allowed the leaders in Kentucky to retain face and the central ministry to maintain a public fiction concerning union and order at the village and throughout the society. Turner, a devout Believer, accepted the recall and returned to New Lebanon, where he, like his predecessors, faded into the ranks of the society.[32]

The pattern of governance that evolved at New Lebanon between 1821 and 1848 was demonstrably less autocratic and more bureaucratic than that of earlier times. Major decisions came only after consultation and extended discussions at the meetinghouse. This procedure has drawn criticism from historians who disparage these third-generation leaders because they depended less on charismatic intuition and more on rational processes in making decisions. Others have bemoaned the ministry's increasing preoccupation with temporal and institutional affairs. Both views fail to reckon sufficiently with the realities of the situation, namely, the growing demands on the leaders and the increasing complexity of the society.[33]

The members of the central ministry were confronting an almost impossible set of tasks and responsibilities. They were expected to embody Shaker values in their personal lives and at the same time to satisfy the religious and spiritual needs of the members of the society. The leaders were constantly engaged in private counseling and public exhortation, listening to individual confessions and preaching to the assembled society or to the general public. The ministry was called on to make important temporal decisions, including appointment of local leaders, approval of financial arrangements, representation of the society's interests in the world, and general supervision of the community's resources. In addition, they were expected to work at a trade and to perform daily chores, including maintaining their living quarters, preparing food, and chopping wood, as well as the special tasks associated with their office, such as writing letters, keeping journals, and recording documents.[34]

One unintended result of the change in leadership following Wright's death was the gradual but real subordination of women in the upper ranks of the society. Males increasingly dominated the central ministry as well as most of the local societies during this period. It is true that Shaker women had more opportunities for positions of responsibility than their counterparts in the world and that they filled those roles with distinction. On that the record is clear. But on the issue of power within the society the evidence is also unambiguous. In the public sector Shaker men exercised a dominant role in religious, economic, and political affairs. Women played a correspondingly significant function in domestic activities as well as in the governance of women within the society. This pattern of gender distinction mirrored arrangements that were then commonplace in American society. Women, especially those of the white middle class, presided over the domestic sphere. Even among the Shakers real equality of the sexes did not exist during this period of the society's history.[35]

It has been suggested that after Wright's death the leadership of the United Society did not measure up to the tasks at hand. Priscilla J. Brewer, for example, argues that the quality of the ministry declined, in part because of a shrinking pool of qualified candidates. Her judgment assumes a necessary correlation between the quantity of applicants and the quality of those chosen. In fact, the leadership from 1821 to 1848 was remarkably successful in dealing with a range of complex social, economic, and religious problems. Their administrative skills were responsible in considerable measure for holding the society together during very difficult times.[36]

The Economics of Community

By the mid-1820s the United Society of Believers was composed of a highly complex network of social and economic units tied together by religious commitments and a growing body of legal arrangements. The society was no simple utopia, nor did it resemble the primitive communism of the early Christian church. On the contrary, Shaker common life had become highly structured, involving multiple levels of subordination and established patterns for making decisions. Gone were the days of the early Believers, who shared their possessions out of a sense of spiritual affection and joined in the tasks at hand because it was the natural thing to do. That earlier sense of fellowship—what sociologists call *Gemeinschaft*—had given way to more ordered, rational, corporate arrangements.[37]

The society's federal structure embraced a four-tiered organizational scheme involving both local and central authorities. The primary group to which every Believer belonged was the family, a unit varying in size from a handful of persons to more than one hundred members. The leaders of a family were elders and eldresses, deacons and deaconesses. Typically, two or more families constituted a local society or village. For instance, in 1835 the settlement at Whitewater, Ohio, consisted of the Center Family and the South Family, numbering 48 and 28 Believers, respectively. By contrast, New Lebanon in 1839 included seven families totaling more than 480 members. A local ministry, usually made up of two men and two women, presided over each village. Two or more villages in relative proximity to one another formed a bishopric, an administrative unit designed to facilitate cooperation among villages and represent the central authority of the United Society. The local ministry of the largest village in an area was commonly designated overseer of the bishopric. The ministry at Union Village, for example, administered the affairs of the Whitewater settlement as well as those of the other Ohio societies. The central ministry at New Lebanon was the head of all the local societies that constituted the United Society of Believers. It also functioned as the ministry for the New Lebanon society and for the bishopric of which it was a part, including the Watervliet, New York, and Sodus Bay villages.[38]

The strength and vitality of the United Society during the antebellum period was in part a result of this multilevel organizational structure. In temporal matters, too, these arrangements were significant. In the earliest years of the western expansion, the deacons at New Lebanon, who served as the chief financial officers of the society, organized the massive support tendered to the new villages. But local initiative was also vital for the well-being of the separate sites, and this federal system encouraged decisions by leaders at each location and by subordinates within individual families. At the same time, coordination and a measure of uniformity among the scattered parts of the United Society were necessary for cooperation and effective interaction among the Believers.[39]

No centralized economic plan governed the separate villages, but responsible persons within the society frequently exchanged counsel and advice. That arrangement, however, did not prohibit local leaders from taking initiatives. The residents at each settlement attempted to establish their own financial base, drawing on resources and opportunities at hand. Each village adapted the structure of deacons and deaconesses to its particular circumstances. Early in the century, for example, the labor and business responsibilities at Sabbathday Lake were organized around specific tasks, such as coopering, wheelmaking, shoemaking, blacksmithing, gardening, farming, tanning, dairying, milling, and serving tables. By contrast, at South Union later in the century deacons supervised the farm, dooryard, and carpentry activities and deaconesses oversaw clothes, preserves, and the kitchen. At Sabbathday Lake the Believers developed a unique tradition of electing their deacons. As the years passed, the United Society clarified and regularized the procedures for appointment as well as the functions of deacons and trustees. The 1829 covenant at Union Village, for example, specified that the Office deacons, who were selected by the ministry, were to keep "regular books of account" that could be inspected by others. Business records abound from the middle years of the nineteenth century. Arrangements varied from village to village, but the basic division between temporal and spiritual concerns was accepted throughout the society.[40]

The religious logic of the Shakers called for strict separation from the world in temporal affairs and a radical form of self-sufficiency. Reality, however, pulled the society into the economic orbit of the young nation. The Believers aspired to independence, but in fact they became functioning members of the expanding market system in the United States. They sold or bartered a long list of products and, in turn, purchased a wide range of necessities. Goods "manufactured" in the villages provided currency with which the Believers bought products from the world. By the second decade of the nineteenth century the United Society was inextricably linked to American capitalism: radical separation from the larger system was out of the question. The sectarian strategy, therefore, became less and less viable during this period. Although the Believers struggled to maintain symbolic boundaries, the prosperity of the society brought increased economic interaction with the world.[41]

The Shakers developed a mixed economy, which rested predominantly on agricultural production but also included selected "small manufactures" and the provision of a few critical services. Farming varied between villages, but everywhere the Believers attempted to raise essential foodstuffs for their communal existence—grains, fruits, vegetables, meat, and dairy products. They were more successful in meeting this goal in some locations than in others. Family journals and account books record instances when staples were in short supply and had to be purchased. One year at South Union, for example, large amounts were expended for eggs, butter, coffee, sugar, bacon, oats, and cornmeal. The Shakers also raised such cash crops as fruit for preserves, flax for linseed oil, broomcorn, cotton, indigo, and tobacco.[42]

The reputation of the Shakers as excellent farmers has been deeply etched into the American mind. Numerous visitors during the nineteenth century expressed "nothing but admiration for Shaker agriculture." That reputation was no doubt well deserved, for in most villages the Believers were successful in their farming enterprises. They made effective use of their extensive communal landholdings and large supply of inexpensive labor. Those advantages undoubtedly fueled some of the opposition to the society from neighbors who could not compete on equal terms. The Believers controlled the distribution systems for their own produce and goods, giving them an edge over others. Their religious traditions sanctioned the value of manual labor and the necessity for everyone, including the leaders, to engage in such tasks. Shaker brothers attempted to stay abreast of scientific and technological changes. Some within their ranks were especially adept at such matters. But perhaps too much has been made of the Believers' work ethic and not enough of the real market advantages the society enjoyed. The agricultural accomplishments of the Shakers need to be considered within the context of the larger culture.[43]

The most significant subsidiary enterprise for the Shakers in the antebellum period was the seed industry. Inaugurated as early as the 1790s, selling seeds to farmers became a major source of income. New Lebanon and Watervliet, Canterbury and Sabbathday Lake, South Union and White-water—these villages and others eventually engaged in this business. They sold seeds in bulk and in small packets. Shaker peddlers distributed the "papers" throughout the country, often placing them on consignment with merchants (fig. 8). Seed agents, following established routes, normally traveled in the fall and winter months. Salesmen from Hancock, for example, covered a territory stretching from the Catskill Mountains to the Chesapeake Bay. Peddlers from South Union journeyed down the Ohio and Mississippi rivers to Louisiana, a trip requiring about three months, but well worth the time and expense. In 1832–1833, one such expedition, involving the sale of other produce as well as seeds, netted income of $3,025 for South Union. The seed business at New Lebanon recorded sales for 1832 and 1833 of $8,251 and $10,573, respectively, approximately half of which was profit. More than one-tenth of the Harvard Shakers' total income for 1847, $8,108, was from seed sales. A decade later, seed income was still significant, although it represented a smaller portion of that village's total income.[44]

Marketing seeds required an elaborate distribution system and a measure of coordination among the Believers at the scattered villages. It was commonplace for seed agents to be on the road for months. In 1838–1839, for example, F. J. Shannon and Spotswood Perkins spent more than three months on one trip, their two-horse wagon filled with seeds produced and packaged at South Union. Sometimes, however, the spirit of competition rather than that of cooperation prevailed among the Believers. In the 1820s and 1830s the Shakers at Canterbury disputed with those in Maine

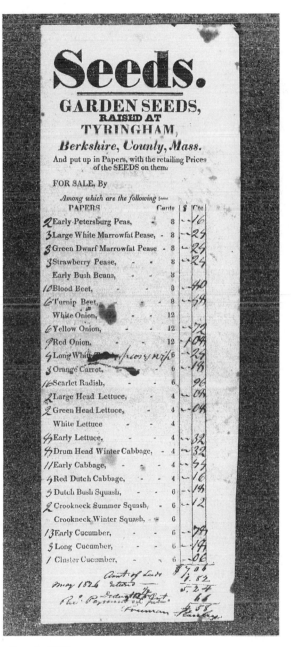

8. Garden Seed Bill

Bill from Tyringham, Massachusetts, documenting the prices of garden seed papers in May of 1824. Peas, for example, cost eight cents a paper, onions twelve cents, and lettuce only four cents. (Courtesy Shaker Museum and Library, Old Chatham, New York.)

about the proper boundaries of their sales districts. The deacons at Canterbury wrote, "We wish to come to some proper agreement . . . to promote the cause of union and leave no place for the *World* to say we are not united." A similar conflict broke out between agents from Hancock and Watervliet. Competition for sales divided villages in the West also. In 1836 the agents from South Union complained that "the P. H. brethren" had gone up "every river & bayou" on the Mississippi with their seeds, leaving "no hole" for them. "It makes us think," they wrote, "that the first and great commandment was allmost given in vain." The bonds of union among the Believers were not always strong enough to overcome the quest for profits.[45]

The selling of herbs in dried form and as extracts was another agricultural industry for which the society was well positioned. Among the many herbs raised were wormwood, sage, spikenard, catnip, boneset, mandrake, horehound, and skunk cabbage. Harvesting and stripping the plants was a labor-intensive effort that often involved many of the society's women and children. Drying, pressing, and packaging herbs for cooking and medicinal use required fewer laborers. Shakers both East and West engaged in this business by the 1830s, but herbs never assumed the same importance in the western economies as in the eastern. The Believers at Watervliet, New York, pressed 710 pounds of herbs in 1832. By 1860 the village had increased its output to more than 5,000 pounds. At New Lebanon the acquisition of new machinery, including power presses and a globular vacuum pan, allowed the Shakers to increase production dramatically. In 1853 they pressed "42,000 pounds of roots, herbs, and barks" and produced "7500 pounds of extracts." The rise of the patent medicine industry in the 1870s, however, undercut the economic viability of large portions of the herbal business among the Believers.[46]

In the West especially, raising and selling cattle was another major source of income for the Shakers, although not as profitable as the seed industry. The extensive acreage and excellent pasturage provided ideal grazing land for livestock. In the decade between 1827 and 1837, the Believers at South Union sold 64 head of cattle for $2,214, plus bartering several items, including three merino lambs. One calf brought a mere $8, whereas they received $160 for a bull. Their customers came from both Kentucky and Tennessee. Shaker sales records list the sire and the dam of each animal sold, thereby providing information about the pedigrees. The Kentucky Believers took special pride in their stud bull "Comet," which sired many of the cattle sold during this decade. At South Union the animals were often identified by such names as Daisy, Jewel, Pet, Celina, Pompey, Myrtle, Henry, and Duke, suggesting that the Shakers may have had difficulty observing the society's regulations concerning the care of animals. At nearly every village it was standard practice to give a full account of the livestock in the annual summary of assets recorded in family journals. In 1834, for example, the Pleasant Hill society owned 312 head of cattle, 62 horses, 611 sheep, and 495 hogs. During the 1850s the cattle industry became increasingly important in the western villages. Believers made large investments in imported breeds, most notably Durham cattle and premium varieties of hogs and sheep. By 1855 cattle sales soared to more than $10,000 at Union Village, but with these rising investments came a growing concern by the central ministry about the expanding scope of the enterprise.[47]

Agriculture led naturally to other economic activities. Blacksmithing, a service performed first for the Believers themselves, subsequently extended to neighboring residents. Almost every village had a blacksmith who shod horses and shaped metals into items essential for transportation and domestic life. Shaker smiths also produced income for the villages when they undertook these tasks for outsiders. In 1831 Solomon Stanley paid the blacksmith at South Union $11.60 for a variety of services, including constructing, repointing, and sharpening plows, shaping and nailing horseshoes, mending copper pots, chains, and bridle bits, and building a "cart box." Among the items listed in Stanley's account were a "new tress for Black man" and "one lag [sic] Chain link"—striking evidence of the nearby presence of slavery.[48]

More important to the village economies were the numerous mills the Shakers constructed, again, for their own use initially and only later to produce income from neighbors who brought grains to be ground, wood to be sawed, or seeds to be pressed into oil. In the order of village life, building gristmills and sawmills often preceded the construction of other permanent dwellings. These mills document the mechanical interests of the Shakers. Machines of all kinds became a preoccupation of the Believers, who were quick to accept technological changes and adapt them for their own use. The Shaker work ethic did not require that tasks be physically taxing or destructive. The Believers therefore eagerly embraced labor-saving devices—extracting, carding, and threshing machines as well as mechanized looms, pumps, and lathes.[49]

The extent of the industrial dimension of the society's economy is illustrated dramatically in the elaborate system of mills constructed at Canterbury, "one of the most industrialized of the Shaker communities." In 1800 a waterpowered gristmill and sawmill was constructed, replacing an earlier horse-drawn mill. Unfortunately, no natural source of water-

power was available at the site; the Shakers were forced to build what became a series of millponds and connecting ditches to bring water from a
distance of more than two miles. This system of man-made reservoirs,
dams, sluices, and spillways eventually embraced eight ponds. By 1850 it
powered nine operating mills, the majority of which were used in the manufacture of wood products. Collectively, these ponds and mills constituted a
significant industrial complex with a major impact on the Canterbury
economy, the life situation of the Believers at that site, and the landscape
and physical environment.[50]

Other Shaker villages, too, depended heavily on an industrial component in their economies. Watervliet, Ohio, responded to the rise of nearby
Dayton, the growing demand for textiles, and the decline in the number of
male members by investing in a textile mill in 1848. In this way they were
able to manufacture a variety of products for adjacent markets. Likewise,
because of poor soil and the growth of Cleveland, the North Union Believers erected several mills and produced salable goods for customers in that
region. Similar considerations were involved in a decision at midcentury
by the Shakers at Sabbathday Lake to enter into "large-scale manufacturing." In Ohio and elsewhere, F. Gerald Ham notes, the Shakers were "un-
remitting in their search for new markets." Yet these industrial activities
are often overshadowed by popular depictions of the Believers as a rural,
agrarian people.[51]

Many of the light manufacturing items produced by the Shakers
were handcrafted. The members first made these goods to supply their
own needs, and only later began to sell them to the world's people. By the
1830s the Believers were producing baskets, brooms, and brushes; buckets, churns, and tubs; carpet, cloth, and yarn; shoes and leather goods;
hats, socks, mittens, and "footens"; and similar products for sale to outsiders. The work of the sisters was central to these community industries.
They turned out prodigious amounts of handwork. In 1836 the sisters of
the Church Family at Watervliet, New York, produced 696 "runs" of tow
and linen yarn, 1,981 runs of worsted wool, 1,449 yards of cloth, 3,166
yards of woven tape, 150 pounds of worked wool, 6 jackets, and 63 pairs of
trousers. In addition, they made for sale 123 runs of stocking yarn and 7½
of worsted, 30 pairs of knit stockings, 60 dozen footings, 6 dozen footens,
115 palm leaf baskets, 48 dozen mops, 4 dozen small mops, 32 pairs of
gloves, 1,606 bonnets, and 43 dozen lashes. Their expenses were $249,
and they recorded profits of $1,252.[52]

Not all community industries were so "light." Building furniture and
manufacturing chairs, for example, required mills for cutting and turning

the wood. Having first produced these items for themselves, the Shakers began selling chairs to the world by the 1790s. Large-scale production did not come until later, especially after midcentury. The technical skills needed for the construction of chairs are itemized in the records kept by the society's furniture makers. These tasks included cutting and turning chair rounds, cutting, bending, and planing backs; cutting and tapering posts; boring and morticing, assembling and finishing the units. Both handwork and millwork were involved. Some Believers, such as David Rowley at New Lebanon, had been accomplished cabinetmakers before joining the society. Other Shakers learned these skills through an elaborate system of apprenticeships established early in the society's history. Thanks to the study of Shaker furniture, which has become something of a cottage industry, our knowledge of these matters has reached new levels of sophistication. We now know to look for local variations in design, style, and workmanship.[53]

The manufacturing of chairs by the Shakers, for example, perhaps has been studied more closely than the production of any other group of objects. According to Charles R. Muller and Timothy D. Rieman, the Believers borrowed the basic structure of the slat-back chair from the world and refined its form over a period of a hundred years. The "improvements" they made on the style included the omission of "superficial turnings" and other embellishments. The gradual standardization of style within the society resulted from travel and trade between villages. In 1831, for instance, Shirley purchased 102 chairs from New Lebanon. Master chairmakers, such as Freegift Wells, moved from one village to another. From time to time the leadership also sanctioned particular patterns. Yet the gracefulness, the harmony and proportion, the balance and beauty of the objects themselves were rarely the subject of conscious reflection by the makers. Refinements of style and design are more likely to evolve than to occur by fiat. Even though the principle of simplicity informed the community, its translation into material objects required time and expertise. Skilled Shaker artisans working together over many years constituted a craft guild possibly unmatched at the time. Shaker design—whether in a chair, a trestle table, or a candle stand—had as much to do with custom, purpose, and function as it did with ideology or theology.[54]

The production of baskets by the Believers has certain parallels to the manufacturing of chairs. In neither case did the Shakers set out to develop a commercial item. On the contrary, they did what was natural; that is, they made baskets for their own needs similar to those they had made for themselves before entering the community. They employed traditional tools and processes to produce baskets for a host of community needs. Each village made large numbers in different shapes and sizes. Only gradually did a Shaker basket evolve, thanks in part to new tools and the collective capacity of the gathered community. Shaker basketmakers at New Lebanon, led by John Farrington and subsequently Daniel Boler, refined the production process, using such innovations as the trip-hammer and the buzz saw to create ash stock for weaving. Refinements in such details as the handles left a unique Shaker signature, which as Martha Wetherbee and Nathan Taylor observe, derives "from an integrated effort, a collective expertise, and from advanced tooling." In time, the production and sale of baskets became a major source of income for the Believers. By the 1840s New Lebanon alone was producing between 300 and 700 annually. It is estimated that by the end of the nineteenth century the Church Family had sold 71,244 baskets. What began as a necessity developed into a major industry.[55]

In spite of this wide range of economic activities, the Shakers were never completely self-sufficient. From earliest times they depended on interaction and trading with the world. Daybooks and journals kept faithfully by deacons and deaconesses document that many villages not only were forced to buy staples from time to time, but regularly purchased from the world such domestic supplies as shirting, handkerchiefs, pins, sundries, plates, cups, bed ticking, muslin, and feathers. In Kentucky one list of purchases included less typical items—indigo, "rum for the sick," camphor, quicksilver, "rectified" whiskey, a shaving box, and almanacs.[56]

Prosperity came to the Shakers through their diverse enterprises, which actively expressed the principle of joint interest. Covenanted members pooled their resources and thus multiplied their return on investments of time and energy, whether in the field or shop, the garden or kitchen. When bad weather or other natural forces threatened, the Believers marshaled their collective resources to meet the emergencies. Society journals frequently tell of brothers being excused from meetings to harvest crops, bring in hay, or perform other necessary tasks. Sisters, too, varied their daily routines to deal with exigencies. The Shakers were not legalistic about such matters. Financial claims were another recurrent threat to the stability of the collective enterprise. Despite provisions in the covenant against such action, the society regularly compensated apostates and other claimants. In 1831, for example, Oliver Burt and Nathan Willard, the trustees at Shirley, paid $150 to Sheffield Haywood to satisfy his claims against his father's estate, which had been consecrated to the society.[57]

Yet the expanding financial success of the society also created new problems. As Shaker assets multiplied, the complexities of management increased. Greater skill and competence were required of the trustees; more opportunities for mismanagement and dishonesty existed. This expansion took place at a time when the national economy was in turmoil, especially after the panic of 1837, and when investment capitalism was beginning to take hold in America.[58]

In 1835, for example, major economic hardships dogged Union Village. That year natural disasters complicated matters further, testing the Shakers' will and the strength of their resolve. Caterpillars wreaked havoc on the forests in the spring. On 9 June a flood swept the settlement, destroying mill dams, damaging shops, and washing away a large amount of timber. The losses from the water were estimated at $25,000. Then on 9 September the principal trustee at Union Village since 1812, Nathan Sharp, left the society, "taking with him a valuable horse, saddle bridle & saddle bags, a large trunk, with cash & property" of an unknown value, subsequently estimated at $10,000. His brother William, Elder Brother of the Brick Family, had apostatized several days earlier. The immediate effect of these departures was "a heavy shock" to all concerned, new "labors & sufferings throughout the body," and a widespread feeling that the brothers were "traitors to God & Men." This was not, unfortunately, the first time the Ohio society had been victimized by its own officers. In 1818 John Wallace, also a trustee, had absconded with a large amount of cash. In 1835 the primary objective was recovery of the stolen funds, a task made more difficult because the village properties were legally vested in Sharp as trustee. Furthermore, he controlled undetermined assets that had not yet been liquidated after the closing of West Union.[59]

Extended debate among the leaders at Union Village and New Lebanon followed Sharp's departure as the Shakers searched for an appropriate plan of action. No consensus was forthcoming, and the inaction compounded the problem, leaving the society even fewer options for recovering their funds and prosecuting a recalcitrant Sharp. Correspondence passed back and forth between eastern and western leaders, but without effect. New Lebanon sent advisers to counsel with the Believers in Ohio, but judgments were mixed. Sharp's defection was not unrelated to other difficulties plaguing Union Village after the death of David Darrow. Solomon King, Darrow's successor in the ministry, had proved unable to maintain discipline and order—one reason for Rufus Bishop's 1834 visit to the western villages. Several years earlier Richard McNemar had warned of an impending crisis because of the lack of supervision over the trustees.

Pressure was mounting for a leadership change, and in October 1835 King departed for a visit to the East—a clear signal to all that his tenure was over. In the spring of 1836 the central ministry appointed Freegift Wells, one of their trusted eastern subordinates, first in the ministry at Union Village. He arrived in April and immediately set about reforming the society. Wells "bore a powerful and scathing testimony against hidden iniquity and all manner of sin." He also instituted new regulations concerning personal behavior.[60]

In the short run, the Sharp episode produced a flurry of activity both West and East as Shaker leaders attempted to do everything possible to protect Union Village from "the fangs of apostate tygers." Sharp himself was condemned as "deeper in iniquity" than Judas, who hanged himself after betraying his master. Seth Y. Wells wrote, "and if N. [Sharp] only had sight enough to see and feel that he would do much better to return all his money and papers, and go and hang himself, he might stand a chance to find some relation to Judas." The village sought legal counsel and prepared to enter the civil courts, though they recognized that it would be costly and lengthy with no guarantee of securing their objective. The central ministry tried to restore union and order by mandating changes at the village, tightening the legal procedures used to empower trustees and handle assets, and exhorting the Believers in Ohio to be humble, obedient, and faithful. "Remember," they wrote, echoing a saying ascribed to Lucy Wright, "that the orders, rules and regulations of the gospel are . . . like a golden chain encircling us around to protect us from evil; every order forms a link in this chain, & if one link is broke the chain is parted and we are exposed to evil." In the long run, Sharp's defection seems to have had little lasting effect other than the loss of funds. The United Society was destined to repeat this experience many times in the years ahead.[61]

Several villages experienced even more severe financial losses that threatened their well-being and the reputation of the entire society. In 1849 the Believers at Shirley (fig. 9) undertook the bold "venture" of constructing a large cotton mill, the Phoenix factory. Upon its completion, they leased the facility and four adjacent tenement houses to a firm from New Bedford that employed a large number of immigrant laborers. The mill quickly became a losing enterprise for the Shakers because they could not keep the dams, traces, and buildings in repair. Rents did not cover the costs of maintenance, and the Shirley society dropped deeper and deeper into debt. By 1858 the village owed a staggering $32,648, in part a result of unwise decisions by Jonas Nutting, the deacon. In response, the central ministry moved to strengthen the leadership of the bishopric by nominat-

9. Shaker Village, Shirley, Massachusetts
Engraving showing the modest size of the Shirley buildings compared with those at other locations. The third structure on the right, the meetinghouse designed by Moses Johnson, stood next to the ministry shop and across the road from the Church Family dwelling. (From Charles Edson Robinson, *A Concise History of the United Society of Believers*, 1893.)

ing William Leonard to assist Grove Blanchard, who had been a member of the ministry at Harvard since 1818. Rufus Bishop noted, "Harvard *needs the aid of Angels*." Cash assistance was sought from other societies, but only modest sums were received. Later in 1859 the central ministry observed, "The Shirley people are not making much headway out of debt, indeed, none at all this season." Less than two years later the Shirley factory was "about 50 thousand dollars in debt."[62]

At the same moment, the village at New Gloucester was locked in a desperate struggle for financial survival, the product of the village's experimentation with "large-scale manufacturing." In the mid-1850s their investment in a large new mill seemed to be paying handsome dividends until a combination of events—some controllable, some not—forced Ransom Gilman, the trustee in charge, to undertake a series of investments to cover operating losses. A drop in the price of wheat, a dramatic rise in interest rates, and the general loss of confidence accompanying the financial panic of 1857 caused Gilman, inadvisedly, to speculate—borrowing money to buy wheat in Chicago, shipping it to Maine to grind into flour, and hoping to sell at an advantage. The scheme did not work, and even after disclosure of the problem Gilman continued borrowing to buy more grain, hoping thereby to extricate the society. By 1859 the village debt had reached approximately $14,000, with some $9,000 falling due in early 1861. The central ministry's response to this "fraudulent management" was to transfer the Maine bishopric of New Gloucester and Alfred to its own immediate supervision, removing it from the care of Canterbury. They also took other steps to stabilize the situation, including the prohibition of all borrowing and the regulation of the mill. (Strangely enough, for a time Gilman remained in charge of daily operations.)[63]

When the situation worsened the following year, the ministry at New Lebanon issued a circular letter to all societies, explaining the "dilemma" confronting New Gloucester. What made this loss different was that the small family of fifty members had few assets that could be liquidated to repay the debts to banks and outside creditors without jeopardizing the existence of the village. Faced with the prospect of having property attached and exposed to a "sheriff's sale" and the village broken up, the central ministry called on the "main body of Believers" to rise in support of "one of the branches of Zion." In the circular letter they proposed a scheme whereby every village would be "taxed" to pay a portion of the note that was coming due and thus enable the Maine village to survive. The ministry assigned specific amounts to each village and urged that they accept the obligation. The levy amounted to about one dollar per person. The ministry at New Lebanon expressed the hope that their "gospel friends in all parts of Zion" would be moved to "open their arms of charity and extend some assistance" to the Believers in Maine. Accompanying this request for assistance was a stern admonition, repeated several times, against contracting any debts to the world, a practice that had repeatedly brought distress on the United Society.[64]

The society at Sabbathday Lake was not yet finished with its trustee problems. Gilman's successor, Charles Vining, began selling timber lands owned by the village without consulting the leadership. When his scheme for "quick profits" was exposed, Elder Otis Sawyer discovered that $5,000 had been embezzled and another $9,000 incurred in debts before Vining deserted. "Satan transformed himself into an Angel of Light, and fairly deceived the very elect," wrote Sawyer in 1870. Efforts to bring the dishonest trustee to justice were not successful. Meanwhile the conservative Sawyer was struggling on yet another front with Isaiah Wentworth, the trustee of the Poland Hill Family. Wentworth, who had served in that position since 1842, operated with complete disregard for established authority, buying and selling property "in his own name" in violation of standard Shaker practices, borrowing money from the world, and mortgaging society properties as collateral to finance lumber and barrel stave enterprises. Wentworth was a shrewd businessman. For years he was openly disdainful and defiant of Shaker regulations, to the consternation of many Believers. In September 1867, after repeated efforts to remove this "Prince of Evil," Sawyer finally succeeded in forcing Wentworth to leave his position. The village at Sabbathday Lake struggled for decades to recover from the combined effect of these losses. The situation became so desperate in the early 1870s that both societies in Maine contemplated selling out and moving to a new location in the South or the West.[65]

Alongside these financial disasters, other less controllable hardships frequently affected the economic well-being of the society. Fires, set by apostates or caused by the carelessness of Believers, ravaged dwellings and shops. A seed agent absconded with a year's receipts totaling $600 and had to be pursued and apprehended. The loss from a theft of items at the Hancock seed house was set at $3,325. Apostates leaving the society continued to bring lawsuits to recover wages or consecrated property, despite the legal prohibitions against such actions. Individual Believers were fined for not fulfilling military obligations and were required to pay for a substitute. These and other debts were a steady drain on the resources of the society.[66]

By midcentury, therefore, the villages were engaging in more complex, diversified economic enterprises for which their Shaker traditions had not equipped them well. The Believers were entering a new world in which it seemed that "hands to work" was no longer a sufficient operative principle. Often there were not even enough Shaker men to do the heavy chores, and as a result more and more hired hands were present in the villages. For other tasks, machines were replacing manual labor. The ministry seemingly had little relevant spiritual counsel to offer on many of these matters. The society's prohibition against debt to the world worked in opposition to the pursuit of more lucrative financial ventures. The trustees, ignoring that injunction, frequently took matters into their own hands, often with disastrous consequences. The principles of joint interest and mutual concern were breaking down.[67]

No Shaker location was immune to these problems. Even Mount Lebanon (the designation used for New Lebanon increasingly after 1861), under the immediate supervision of the central ministry, did not escape. In 1871 Edward Chase, the elder and business agent for the East, or Brick Yard, Family, went to the world after "being found many thousands of dollars in debt to individuals" outside the society. Upon investigation, it became clear that his records were insufficient to explain the indebtedness.

Chase had "intentionally" kept many of his transactions "entirely hidden from the authorities." When first discovered, he was reproved, but allowed to keep his position because he said that with a few thousand dollars he "could cancel all obligations." That money was given to him, but it covered only a small part of the debt. Later, when the full scope of Chase's financial dealings became known, the East Family was forced to sell real estate and other assets to meet the obligations. The Believers attempted to deal with this embarrassing incident with a public notice, stating their intention to pay the debt in full and no longer to authorize promissory notes on behalf of the society. They also repeated a cardinal principle of the society, "to owe no man anything but love and good will."[68]

The Shaker economic order produced mixed results during the Middle Period. Agriculture and household manufacturing initially provided a strong base for expanding prosperity. Subsequent departures into the world of finance capitalism and heavier industry frequently proved less sound. The Believers were not totally successful in diversifying their economy and keeping pace with the changing business world. In at least one village, Sabbathday Lake, the lack of success in these more risky ventures may have predisposed some of the members under the leadership of Otis Sawyer to return to the agrarian way of life and a more traditional, or conservative, way of thinking. One Believer of similar mind wrote, "It would be as consistent for a fish to attempt the majestic flight of the eagle . . . as for believers to attempt to become a manufacturing and commercial people, and keep their integrity, purity, & faith intact." In other locations, these early speculative undertakings only whetted the appetite of some. Shaker federalism was far from a perfect system. Maintaining the society's boundaries became more and more difficult as tension grew between the spiritual and temporal orders.[69]

The Social Situation

Reconstructing the social situation of ordinary Believers in the mid-nineteenth century requires a careful handling of historical evidence, whether written documents or material objects. The inherent biases of these sources frequently skew the picture of daily life in the villages. Shaker documents often reflect the official view of the society because they were penned by persons appointed or approved by the ministry. Physical artifacts can also be misleading because some "things" that have endured may have had little actual use. Worn-out items, by contrast, are frequently discarded. Material objects must be resituated in their proper historical context. Reconstruction of the Believer's life situation therefore demands both the trained eye of the ethnographer and the skill of the creative historian.[70]

Believers established their identity as Shakers in different ways—as individuals, as members of a particular family, as residents of a village, and as part of the larger society. Each of these levels had social significance, but all were not equally central to the daily experiences of an individual. Membership in the United Society, for example, identified a Believer with the 3,600 or so other Shakers who professed common beliefs, participated in distinctive practices, and accepted the leadership of New Lebanon, but that organizational bond did not always have daily impact. In fact, membership in the society may not have entered the Believer's consciousness on a daily basis. Residence in a village had greater social significance because it determined personal location—New England or New York, Ohio or Kentucky. Shaker sites differed not only culturally and geographically, but also topographically (figs. 10 and 11). Hills, mountains, and valleys, rivers and lakes, provided contrasting settings for the scattered Believers. Sometimes these natural features gave rise to village names—Sabbathday Pond, Pleasant Hill, Whitewater. Uniformity of village context was not a fact of life in the nineteenth century.[71]

It was as a member of a particular family within a specific village that the Believer established primary social identity as a Shaker. In this context individuals formed close personal relationships. Family members lived and worked together. They ate at the same tables, shared living quarters, slept in the same rooms (sometimes even in the same beds), and used the same sanitary facilities. They performed daily chores together, labored side by side in the shops and fields, attended union meetings, and worshiped with one another. In the families the elders and eldresses replaced biological fathers and mothers. Shaker brothers and sisters played critical roles in the socialization process. Relationships among family members were often very close and overtly emotional. The distinctive tone of domestic life among the Believers depended on a range of variables, including the personalities of the leaders, the pattern of family discipline, the sense of well-being and goodwill within the group, and the particular circumstances surrounding the unit. No two Shaker families were identical.[72]

The accent on union and order in Shakerism did not produce mindless conformity. Believers were able to establish a healthy individualism within the society. Countless family journals from the nineteenth century reveal that members of the society regularly asserted their independence. Believers established their own personalities precisely as they would in

10. Shaker Village, South Union, Kentucky
The Center Family dwelling on the right and the meetinghouse on the left bracket the
wide corridor of road between, leading to the Office complex in the distance. (From
Charles Edson Robinson, *A Concise History of the United Society of Believers,* 1893.)

11. Shaker Village, Hancock, Massachusetts
John Warner Barber's *Historical Collections . . . of Every Town in Massachusetts*
(1839) included this engraving, which features the meetinghouse built in 1786 (left),
the Church Family brick dwelling erected in 1830 (center), and the roof and cupola of
the round stone barn constructed in the mid-1820s (background).

biological families—by cultivating certain traits, learning special skills, nurturing particular friendships, making choices, asserting themselves in word and action, and resisting or defying parental expectations. It was not only the apostates, runaways, and rebels who emerged as individuals, but also the Believers in good standing. Shakerism frowned on selfishness and disobedience, but accepting communal principles did not automatically end the quest for individual identity and autonomy.[73]

The primary physical setting for social interaction among Believers was the village. The logic of sectarianism called for withdrawal from the world, but Shaker settlements provided only relative isolation from outside influences. Shaker villages varied in location, yet all sought to exploit topographical advantages. Often they occupied some prominent feature in the landscape from which the surrounding countryside could be viewed—a knoll, mountainside, or wide valley (fig. 12). Such a vantage point seemed to confirm the society's sense of superiority and distance from the world. But total isolation was never the objective. Shaker settlements commonly had easy access to nearby population centers or towns. Roads connected Believers to the outside world and served as arteries for trade and potential converts. As the nineteenth century progressed, the physical and psychological distance between the Believers and the world narrowed.[74]

The physical arrangement of Shaker villages followed no single plan. Yet in most cases the meetinghouse bulked large on the mental landscape, for it was the dwelling of the ministry and the central site for religious gatherings. Likewise, the Office assumed prominence because it was where the trustees lived and carried out their business transactions with the people of the world. The meetinghouse and the Office symbolized opposing forces in the ecology of village life. Neither, however, was the physical center of life for an ordinary Believer. The family dwelling was the focal point of an individual's existence and the primary locus of daily activities. The dwelling, whether a large dormitory specially designed for the Believers or a smaller building adapted to their needs, was the hub of a complex of buildings and outbuildings, including shops, mills, barns, and washhouses as well as sheds, pens, and stables and surrounding dooryards, gardens, fields, woodlots, walkways, and fences.[75]

The dwelling house was filled with chairs and tables, beds and bureaus, stoves and woodboxes, lamps and chests, tools and utensils, foodstuffs, and other supplies. The social space that remained was congested, if not crowded, with people and allowed little room for privacy. Such peculiar features of Shaker architecture as double entrances and parallel staircases did little to reduce the general congestion in the dwelling; others, includ-

12. Shaker Village, Canterbury, New Hampshire
This pastoral scene accompanied an essay in the *American Magazine of Useful and Entertaining Knowledge* (1835). The white building on the right is the meetinghouse and the large newly erected trustees' Office is in the center.

ing the large number of peg rails and built-in chests of drawers, were more helpful. Four or more Shakers often shared a "retiring room," which contained their personal possessions in addition to necessary furniture. Here intimacy with a few companions occurred daily. Within the confines of the retiring room Believers became familiar with the personalities and idiosyncracies, the body odors and sleeping patterns, and the personal habits of their roommates. Group activities took place in the larger confines of the dining area and the family meeting room. The dooryard, which served as an extension of the dwelling, was viewed as domestic space requiring special concern for its maintenance and cleanliness. From this fenced location walkways and roads carried Believers outside the immediate boundaries and shelter of the dwelling.[76]

The family complex was the scene of activity from dawn to dark. Brothers and sisters performed routine daily tasks. Sisters prepared meals, cleaned the dwelling, washed and mended clothing, and carried out other domestic responsibilities. Brothers cared for livestock, cut and hauled firewood, maintained the buildings, and performed heavier jobs. Children, if part of the family unit, participated in these chores and performed other lesser duties assigned to them. The greater part of the day for many members, however, was spent in the production side of family life. Sisters devoted long hours to spinning and weaving, knitting and sewing, gardening and processing produce; brothers toiled in the shops and mills, the stables and fields; children, serving as understudies and apprentices, learned skills and trades by working at all these tasks. On a normal day the family compound bustled with energy and purpose.[77]

Believers found order within this activity as they went about their work. Daily routines were dictated by the season and by the needs of the family. The sisters of the Second Family at Watervliet, New York, were never idle. In 1846 they recorded their "main employ" (except for the constant demands of kitchen work, washing, and ironing) month by month. In January and February, the sisters worked at spinning, braiding, and sewing; in March they "ketcheled" flax, carded tow, and spun mops. April was for housecleaning and making soap. In May they made starch, serviced the brethren's clothes, sheared sheep, and painted. June was devoted to the wool business, July to spinning, August and September to processing corn, pickles, and apples. In October the sisters boiled cider and completed work on the wool; in November they cleaned the dwelling and the shops and prepared for winter; and in December they butchered hogs and made applesauce. This cycle repeated itself year in and year out with only minor changes.[78]

The annual cycle for the boys at New Lebanon in 1846 was no less demanding. During school months they carried out such regular chores as milking, handling firewood, and working in a shop. After school was dismissed on 17 March, the spring days were filled with hauling wood, picking up stones, repairing fences, and planting corn, potatoes, and beets. When the planting was finished, the boys gathered manure, hoed the gardens, cut and burned brush, cleared meadows, cleaned the sheep hovels, and picked cherries. The last half of July was spent haying, hoeing again, and cleaning roads. In August they cut corn, herbs, and oats, and dug potatoes. They husked corn, gathered walnuts, and pulled beets in September. In October they gleaned corn, cleaned shops, spread manure, prepared the orchard for winter, and hauled more wood. In November, before they started schoolwork for the day, the boys made brushes. Life was ordered and disciplined by these routines, although not all the youths took kindly to the structured life.[79]

Shaker men also worked at more than one task, using skills they had employed in the outside world or acquired in the society. The need for skilled laborers was constant among the Believers, and as a result individuals were forced to learn new trades. This pressure was especially severe when the number of male members began to decline sharply near midcentury. The apprentice system was designed to produce trained workers, but as the years passed, few young men remained within the society. The villages were forced to rely increasingly on hired help, a practice in fundamental tension with the sectarian principles of the society. One youth who did stay was Henry Blinn of Canterbury, who became a Believer at the age of fourteen and spent nearly sixty years as a Shaker. Most of his skills were acquired within the society. He worked for prolonged periods at a number of tasks, including sawing pail staves, carding wool, teaching school, braiding whiplashes, typesetting, bookbinding, beekeeping, dentistry, writing, and editing, and at the same time he served in various leadership positions. Among the Shakers, occupational categories did not mean a great deal because individuals contributed in many ways. Even members of the New Lebanon ministry practiced trades. Ebenezer Bishop was an accomplished basket weaver, and Rufus Bishop a skilled tailor. Ruth Landon and Asenath Clark joined other female leaders in the production of carpets. When the situation demanded, everyone in the family, including the skilled artisans, pitched in.[80]

Job rotation was never an end in itself among the Shakers, nor was it a consistent practice in all families. On occasion it was used to release persons from especially taxing situations or as a form of community discipline. In general Believers remained in positions where they were productive. No attempt was made to force skilled artisans into other trades. Productivity was enhanced by job satisfaction, skill, and experience rather than by an artificial principle of rotation for the sake of fairness. Watervliet records show, for example, that the production of bonnets was the province of a small number of skilled women. During the twelve months of 1836, one sister individually made 730 bonnets. Four others produced 341, 270, 192, and 90, respectively. The records give no indication that these sisters wished for different responsibilities. On the contrary, they took great pride in their productivity.[81]

Shakers who worked together often became close personal friends. Deep and abiding relationships between members of the same sex were one result of these friendships. Anna Dodgson described Mariah Lapsley, her coworker in the dye house at New Lebanon, as a "long loved companion" with whom she had "happily" spent a decade "without being disturbed by strife jar or contention." According to Dodgson, they had been more concerned "for each other's comfort" than for their own. This friendship parallels the pattern of female bonding observed in American society throughout the nineteenth century. Close relationships also developed among men in the society, sometimes between older Shaker brothers and youths who served as apprentices or helpers. Such was the case with Isaac N. Youngs and Benjamin Gates, who shared long hours in the tailor shop at New Lebanon. In 1826 a youthful Gates expressed the hope that Youngs, who was absent, might "Come home and see me so that I can stroke your head and kiss you once more as I used to." He promised to "be a good Boy" so that Youngs would love him and "take care of" him when he returned. More than ten years later Gates wrote to Youngs again, expressing the great "pleasure" and "satisfaction" he derived from spending time with him in the shop. "But the lonely lonesome hours that I have pass'd thro' in your absence," he confided, "have not been verry few I assure you." Gates reconciled himself to the separation, however, by recognizing that duty called and by hoping that the time would be "short" before they were again "face to face." The language of these letters suggests that there may have been a sexual dimension to this relationship, but there is no direct evidence to support this. Overt expressions of love and affection were commonplace among male Shakers. (There were, however, strong prohibitions against homosexuality among the Believers.)[82]

Family life reflected the spirit of community and the principles of union and order. Daily labor was religious confession in the fullest sense of that term; that is, witness to the values that motivated the Shakers. Perhaps no single testimony ever put this more simply than the following undated statement: "To No my order and place and Ceep it and Seek my union Aright is my Desire for my union is my Strength as we Are Joined together in order So the Body is Complet for thare is one Body and one Spiret." Another Believer described the family situation of the Shakers at Enfield, New Hampshire, in 1868: "Here in this lovely valley you will find Fathers and mothers to caress you as all Mothers know how to, and Brothers and sisters that it fairly makes your heart beat with unusual velosity to even think of parting with [those] who appea[r] to be much engaged in their efforts to come up into a higher life." In daily exchanges and personal relationships among Believers, theology took on flesh and the Millennial Laws came alive. Shaker religion was essentially a lived experience.[83]

Daily routines ordered the Believers' experience even more than the Millennial Laws. Although the written statutes were read with some regularity in most villages, the regulations never replaced the instructional role of Old Believers in the socialization of new or young Shakers. The written rules addressed a wide range of social concerns, but local customs varied substantially among the villages. The ordinances of 1821, even with the supplementary orders and regulations issued in 1839, 1840, and 1841, did not deal with all aspects of communal existence. The central ministry often addressed itself to other matters in both formal and informal exchanges; local leaders also improvised and formulated rules for the separate villages and families. Once written, regulations took on a life of their own. Some areas of behavior, however, never were the subject of extensive formal commentary.[84]

The foodways of the Shakers, for example, varied from village to village. The Millennial Laws of 1821 offered relatively little guidance on these matters. Believers were to be content with the "common" diet, not indulging their appetites or asking for special provisions unless illness required. The kitchen was declared the province of the cooks and normally off-limits to other family members (fig. 13). These regulations were designed to maintain order and to curb natural impulses. Specific orders prohibited eating raw or unripe fruit and nuts, cucumbers without salt or pepper, and freshly baked bread. The society's dietary ordinances in the early decades of the nineteenth century did not extend beyond these few constraints. As a result, the food that was served reflected local supplies and regional preferences. Seafood, for example, was a special treat in the eastern villages, but not among the Kentucky Shakers, where southern cuisine was more evident. Menus fluctuated with the seasons and with the capacity of the families to preserve and store foodstuffs. Fresh vegetables and fruits made the summer and autumn fare more nutritious and varied—for Believers and non-Shakers alike. In general, the members of the society ate well.[85]

During the 1830s the society was caught up in a spirited debate over the ascetic principles espoused by Sylvester Graham, a Presbyterian minister and health reformer who advocated "temperance, a vegetarian diet, and sexual continence" as the solution to problems plaguing Jacksonian America. Graham contended that the ills of American society stemmed, in part, from the growing practice of eating bread made from refined flour. In time he espoused a comprehensive theory of diet and physiology. His meteoric public career as a lecturer and writer brought him fame and gave his ideas widespread popularity. The Shakers, not surprisingly, found elements of his program very attractive. By the mid-1830s Believers at several villages were adopting elements of his recommended regimen, which included, in addition to the use of unbolted flour, giving up coffee, tea, and chocolate as well as other stimulants, forgoing rich and highly seasoned

13. Dinner at Mount Lebanon
Arthur Boyd Houghton illustrated the "quaint, quiet costumes" of the Shakers and
their "staid expression of countenance." (*The Graphic,* 7 May 1870.)

foods, abandoning meat, and drinking cold water. Graham also recommended abstinence from alcohol and tobacco.[86]

Priscilla J. Brewer has shown how the principles of Grahamism divided Shakers at several villages, but for most Believers the practice of
these dietary reforms had at best a short life. Members of the Harvard society, for example, who had been among the first to experiment with a
vegetarian diet, began to back off that regimen in mid-1836. There is little
evidence that the western Believers ever found these ideas particularly attractive. A few Shakers became deeply committed to these reforms and
regarded them as useful tools for furthering the basic objectives of the society. Ephraim Prentiss argued that the boys under his care at Watervliet,
New York, were more manageable when on the Graham diet, and he became zealous on the subject. Others, including the central ministry, did
not share his enthusiasm, and as a result the United Society did not adopt

an official policy on Grahamism. Brewer has suggested that this indecision was symptomatic of weakness on the part of the leaders at New Lebanon and a contributing factor to the precipitant decline of the society. On the contrary, the ministry's ambivalence was consistent with well-established patterns, leaving many areas of communal life, including food and drink, open to local custom and choice.[87]

The care of the sick was another area for which the 1821 regulations provided only limited guidance. The Millennial Laws affirmed the principle of the right to ask for assistance, but ill Believers were to "apply to the Physician in their own family," not to those in other families or in the world. Special consideration was given to the sick in both food and drink, including the use of wine and cider. Throughout the period the Believers experimented with all kinds of health regimens, including medical and manipulative therapies that were popular in the world, such as certain heroic procedures, the use of botanicals, Thomsonianism, and hydropathy. When Asenath Clark was ill in 1839, for example, she tried several remedies, including bloodletting, "a puke and the vapor bath," water from Saratoga springs, and "mustard poultices." In 1844 the Whitewater village began using the water cure with considerable success, having previously employed the Thomsonian system. When their own physicians were unsuccessful, the Believers consulted with doctors from the world. Local practice varied greatly from village to village. The Shakers occasionally attributed recovery to the gift of faith healing. Calvin Green, for example, was instrumental in curing sores on an infant, a success that he credited to an "implanted faith that brot forth fruit."[88]

The official rules of the society mandated high standards of communal cleanliness and neatness. The Millennial Laws required the proper disposal of garbage and other refuse as well as "filthy" substances of any kind. The interiors and exteriors of buildings were to be kept orderly and in good repair. Even the streets surrounding the dwellings and the dooryards were to be cleared regularly of "hay, straw and dung &c." These statutes had positive implications for the general health of the Shakers. By contrast, the written regulations contain little that is explicit about matters of personal hygiene. The Believers apparently reserved such concerns for private instruction. A collective discomfort with public conversation about bodily functions characterized the Shakers. Their records are silent about provisions for toilet facilities or recommendations concerning bathing. One must assume also that information concerning bodily processes was handed on by word of mouth from older to younger members. The onset of menstruation, the proper sanitary procedures to be followed, and the changes attendant on menopause—none of these topics appear in family journals or personal diaries. Likewise, the physical changes within young men at puberty, the occurrence of nocturnal emissions, and other signs of physical maturation—these, too, are notably absent in the written records. Yet as Louis J. Kern points out, the Shakers spoke frankly and at length about sexual processes when they condemned marriage, adultery, prostitution, and masturbation or when they threatened the judgments of God on those driven by passion. Sexual taboos, therefore, touched both the public and the private side of a Believer's experience.[89]

The tension between communal order and individual taste manifested itself in Shaker dress, an area of considerable change during the first century of the society's existence. The earliest Believers had no distinctive costume that set them apart from their contemporaries in the world. Only with the passage of time and their failure to keep pace with changes in style did the Shakers become peculiar or different in their apparel. Uniformity of clothing gradually developed among the Believers during the early decades of the nineteenth century, but even when ministerial recommendations were issued, personal choice and regional variations persisted. Similar clothing had the obvious advantage of signaling union, order, and equality within the society. Yet the Millennial Laws of 1821, surprisingly, offered no specific injunctions concerning the style or pattern of dress. These statutes did speak, however, to issues of economy and neatness. Believers were not to dispose of footwear or garments simply because they were old or out of favor. Nor were they to wear "ragged" apparel at any time, even when working. The central ministry periodically emphasized a concern for the quality of materials and workmanship in the production of clothing. They also issued condemnations of conformity to worldly styles. Nevertheless, the standardization of dress among the members of the society, in the words of Beverly Gordon, "was by no means ever achieved."[90]

Shaker clothing styles thus evolved in rather unconscious fashion. During much of the mid-nineteenth century, the women typically wore a long one-piece dress with a full skirt, a white collar, and a kerchief pinned in a distinctive triangular pattern. A white cap and a bonnet as well as an apron were also standard. Few elements of this costume were distinctive to the Believers, for these were traditional patterns of rural dress from earlier generations. Numerous visitors commenting on this apparel remarked how it masked the female figure. Shaker brothers standardly were fitted out in a white shirt, trousers, a vest, a jacket or coat, and a hat. When working, they were likely to wear tow trousers, a frock open at the throat, and a leather apron if needed. The clothing for children often followed adult styles, though age and status in the society were reflected by head coverings. Girls, for example, adopted the white cap at the age of fourteen, when they left the children's order and assumed adult responsibilities. Most of this clothing was made by the Believers, women sewing for themselves and male tailors for the men. After midcentury there was an increase in the purchase of ready-made clothing from the world.[91]

A diversity of practice also seems to have characterized the care, management, and education of children within the society. Shaker caretakers had the difficult task of supervising young charges who had been indentured to the society by parents or guardians for economic, personal, or disciplinary reasons as well as caring for orphans, homeless youths, and other children who entered the villages with adult family members. The Believers placed a heavy accent on inculcating proper, respectful, and virtuous behavior. It was the Shakers' hope that years of exposure to their values would convince the young people to remain in the society when they reached maturity. To that end they were trained in crafts and practical skills and integrated as much as possible into the life of the community. They were instructed in Shaker beliefs and practices and included in most religious meetings. As a matter of principle, the society formally avoided the use of corporal punishment. Yet the precise nature of disciplinary practices in different families varied with the individuals in charge. There were numerous discipline problems as well as claims of child abuse from outsiders. As the nineteenth century wore on, fewer youths chose to stay in the villages when they reached the age of decision.[92]

The formal schooling given Shaker children—boys in the winter and girls in the summer months—had an overwhelmingly practical bent as they were prepared for citizenship within the society. Only such fundamentals as were consistent with that end were initially supported. The classical pattern of learning was condemned as worldly, unnecessary, and undesirable. Seth Y. Wells, appointed superintendent of all Shaker schools in 1832, was the principal spokesperson for the society on these matters and a significant influence on the education of the children. He was responsible for encouraging the building of schoolhouses at the villages and for cultivating an increasingly positive attitude toward formal instruction. Although Wells warned against knowledge for its own sake, the practical effect of his work was to move the Believers closer to the educational standards of the larger culture. As the nineteenth century progressed, Shaker educators gained considerable reputation, even though many within the society still feared the outcome of such schooling. An account published by Hervey Elkins, who grew up in the Children's Order at Enfield, New Hampshire, reveals the two sides to the youthful existence among the Shakers—hard work, discipline, and supervised activities as well as close friendships and wholesome recreation. Later Elkins served for several years as the schoolteacher at that village. His unquenchable thirst for humanistic knowledge ultimately led him to leave the society after fifteen years in the community. His departure was prophetic, for in subsequent decades education would become one of the most corrosive forces within the society.[93]

Each of these aspects of Shaker family life—food, clothing, treatment of the sick, hygienic practices, care and education of the children—had the potential for becoming a point of contrast between the Believers and the people of the world. And yet it is a mistake to assume that difference or to posit a rigid uniformity on these matters within the United Society. The scattered villages and the separate families within them often reflected diverse practices. The reality of Shaker pluralism has too often been overlooked. The Believers wished to be distinguished from the world, but they often chose different ways of establishing that distinction. The fundamental step for every member was separation from the natural family and integration into a Shaker family. In this way a threshold was crossed and an old way of life left behind. All members passed through this liminal state as they discarded established relationships and sought to create new bonds with their fellow Believers. Working and worshiping together forged links that strengthened the family. Written regulations and oral traditions shaped a collective mentality. Physical boundaries between the world and the Believers   stone walls and fences—reminded the members that they were to be separate and distinctive.[94]

The Shakers were not always successful in satisfying their converts. There has never been a systematic study of the wayward in the society—those who came and quickly left, those who joined but did not participate wholeheartedly, and those who remained as members for many years before departing for the world. That there were many of these not-so-faithful Shakers is clear from the society's records, though only the vocal and the most infamous apostates have attracted extensive commentary. Hundreds were attracted to Shakerism at one stage in their lives and later rejected it. These short-term Believers form a significant but neglected segment of the society.[95]

Among the forms of resistance to Shakerism perhaps the most common was running away. Children and youths, often indentured or bound over by their parents or guardians, fled from the Believers with striking frequency. Family journals throughout the society record in astonishing detail the steady stream of youthful rebels who tried to escape the Shaker confines. Usually pursuit by the Believers followed their departure. Parents sometimes returned the runaways; others successfully eluded capture. Shaker journals customarily offered uncharitable comments about the fugitives. Elisha Pote at Alfred declared that a "scattering" of young members in that village had "returned like dogs to their *vomets,* as sows who might have been washed, to their *wallowing* in their filth." When Ann Sabins was carried off to the world in 1844 from New Lebanon, the ministry expressed delight "because she had long been a corrupter in the family." Later that year at the same village Norman Traver was reclaimed by his father; he was denounced by the Believers as "a youth having despised his birthright" in the church and as "a very ungrateful & unthankful creature." Braman Wicks and Christana Yon were branded as "flesh hunters" when they left for the world in 1847. Often the desire to leave became contagious after the departure of an influential person. In the spring of 1863, for example, the Second Family at Mount Lebanon lost six young men in less than four weeks, following the departure of their elder. The first to depart was denounced as a "dishonest pretender." The harsh and spiteful language reflects the deep disappointment and sense of betrayal felt by the Believers.[96]

The youthful runaways come as no surprise because many of them lived among the Shakers against their will; they did not choose to be residents in the villages. But the records are equally full of individuals who came to the society to explore the possibility of joining and subsequently left. The Shakers often dismissed these inquirers as "winter Shakers" or "bread and butter" Believers, implying that they were interested only in such short-term physical benefits, as food, shelter, and clothing. That dismissal, however, is too facile and overlooks the failure of Shakerism to satisfy many who encountered it. The disappointed persons, often condemned in the society's records, illustrate the exclusive dimensions of sectarian life. Their trial among the Shakers—a few days, a few weeks, or several months—was crucial for the decision to remain or depart. At Watervliet, Ohio, on seventy-one separate calendar days in 1857, the ministry took note of persons seeking admission or leaving for the world. Some were young children or youths, others single adults or heads of families. Those who came to the village as well as those departing all had reasons. The inquirers formed a human stream from which the Believers ultimately attracted most of their long-term converts. And yet the roads leading to the Shaker villages also led away from them.[97]

Another category of not-so-faithful Believers was composed of those who from time to time disobeyed or resisted the principles of union and order and yet stayed within the community. This group is less visible in the standard accounts of Shaker history because they put the lie to the notion of harmony within the society. Every village and every family included such persons who influenced the collective course of activity. Discontent with the decisions of the leadership, complaints about working conditions, and disgruntlement with the food that was served were some of the manifestations of internal dissent. Yet rather than leave the society, some discontented members decided to remain and to voice their views within the community. Some agitated openly for change; others were too reticent to murmur in public. The Believers who did not leave found something in the society that outweighed the source of their complaints. Acknowledging the presence of these dissenters among the ranks of the Believers is important for a balanced view of social realities.[98]

Other Believers, sometimes after many years in the ranks, no longer found Shakerism satisfying. Usually we learn of these individuals through the church records, where they were commonly maligned for their decision to leave the society. Few apostates wrote about their feelings at the time of departure; most of them went silently into the world. But it is unwarranted to conclude that these individuals contributed little to the society or that they had no continuing affection for it. Numerous persons who held high positions in the society left after many years of involvement, such as Robert Baxter.

> No word of Robt. nor has he been heard of since except that he was a most filthy creature brim full of a reprobate sense & fully ripe for a dissolution from any relation to the Chh. So it may be recorded that on Wednesday April 16th Robert Baxter left the society, after spending 20 years in family leadership, and holding claim to all the honors & distinctions of a shaker Elder, & serving as a beacon to exhibit the contrast between the profession & practice of the pure self denying princeples of the gospel.[99]

Some Believers left the society for new and more demanding callings. Leonard Jones, a Believer at Pleasant Hill, for example, found Shakerism acceptable for a time. In 1823 the ministry in Kentucky reported with pleasure his arrival, but he immediately created a stir by bodily tossing a heckler out of a public meeting. Jones, they concluded, "did what he did, as he supposed, upon the same principal, that Christ made a scourge of small cords, and drove certain ones out of the temple." The next day he confessed his sins and subsequently was "very zealous" in his commitment, often speaking and praying in public. The ministry concluded that he would "make a useful Man in the Gospel, if he abides faithful." Jones served the Kentucky village in a variety of ways for some years, assisting the trustees and befriending his fellow Believers. Yet his religious zeal proved uncontrollable. He frequently received visions, but he repeatedly violated both the spirit and the letter of Shaker regulations. On one occasion, he "molested" some young sisters in the community to ascertain "what progress" they were making in the gospel. For that he was disciplined publicly and reassigned to the Gathering Order. Several times he wandered off from the village for a considerable period, and yet managed to retain the good graces of the leaders. When Jones finally departed from Pleasant Hill for the last time, he became a member of the Endless Life Society. As a member of that group, he signed a petition in December 1832 addressed to Henry Clay in hopes of securing a plot of land on which to build a "near paradise" and to plant "the tree of life." For Jones, who was always something of a maverick, the Shakers were only one step toward his ultimate goal.[100]

In her study of communal movements in America, Rosabeth Moss Kanter identifies three problems facing every community that seeks to maintain itself: the retention of members, the cultivation of group cohesiveness, and the development of conformity. In the opening decades of the nineteenth century these were not particularly pressing issues for the United Society. The membership was expanding, the Believers were experiencing a growing sense of community, and many seemed eager to "bear the cross." Centripetal forces appeared to be prevailing as the society moved into the middle of the nineteenth century, and the social situation of the Shakers seemed secure.[101]

But appearances are often deceptive. By 1835 considerable membership loss was occurring, especially within the ranks of the younger members. The federal structure, the separate villages, and the family system of the society had created far more diversity within the ranks than has traditionally been recognized. And there was also considerable dissent among the Believers who stayed within the society. In other words, there were grounds for growing concern about the degree of uniform commitment that the United Society enjoyed from its members. As a result of this centrifugal tendency within the society, the maintenance of boundaries—real and symbolic—became increasingly difficult for the Believers.[102]

And yet the Shakers thrived in antebellum America. According to Kanter, they were able to incorporate the "commitment mechanisms" necessary for successful communal organizations: sacrifice and investment, renunciation and communion, mortification and transcendence. Converts who joined a Shaker family renounced their natural relations, sacrificed the pleasures and prerogatives of their former situations, and emptied themselves, submitting to the will of the leaders. By these actions they attempted to make a clean break with their past. At the same time, the new Believers integrated themselves emotionally into the Shaker family, invested whatever resources they possessed in the community, and accepted the value system of the society. By these processes they attached themselves to the United Society. In Kanter's judgment, when intentional communities fail to establish such mechanisms, commitment is lacking and the result is rapid decline. But when these dynamic processes are fully operative, the community thrives. Kanter regards the Shakers as highly successful in cultivating commitment among a majority of the Believers.[103]

The Spiritualistic Revivals

No period of the United Society's history has attracted more attention and speculation than the years of spiritualistic activity beginning in the late 1830s and extending into the 1850s. Shaker historians, pointing with pride to this outpouring of gifts, have compared it favorably with the first century of Christianity. Sympathetic non-Shakers have depicted the period in much the same way. Critics and opponents of the Believers, by contrast, quickly seized on the frenzy of the revivals and attacked the beliefs and practices of the society. They ridiculed the ecstatic activity and pointed to the widespread religious commotion as a sign of the weakness of the society. More recent attempts to explain these phenomena often resort to reductionist solutions, making the religious dimensions of the revivals a manifestation of social, economic, or psychological tensions. There is an element of truth in each of these judgments. The Era of Manifestations was a time of unusual gifts as well as of strange behavior, and the circumstances of the society did have a direct bearing on these activities. But none of these explanations reckons sufficiently with the force of established religious traditions within the society. The spiritualistic revivals were precisely that—the resurgence of religious beliefs and practices already present among the Believers.[104]

The standard account of the period begins with the report of some extraordinary behavior among "a class of young girls, ten to fourteen years old," in the Gathering Order at Watervliet, New York. In August 1837 several of these "children" became "absorbed" in unusual trancelike activities in which their "senses . . . appeared withdrawn from the scenes of time." They spoke of communicating with "angels" and of journeys "to heavenly places." These events marked the beginning of the "remarkable period" known subsequently as Mother Ann's Work. Commentators often describe the society in the years leading up to this period as plagued by worldly values, including materialism, religious indifference, and formalism, as well as by the loss of concern for union and order. This approach, however, isolates the events at Watervliet from the strong tradition of ecstatic behavior and spiritual gifts within Shakerism. The practical effect is to heighten the distinctiveness of the revival period and to contrast it with the preceding decades.[105]

A more balanced approach situates the Era of Manifestations within the full sweep of the society's history. The fundamental concept of gift had never disappeared from the Shaker religious consciousness. At every village there were recurrent expressions of experiential spirituality in visions, dreams, voices, leadings, prophecies, healings, miracles, and the like. Contrary to many depictions, religious life among the Believers did not drift uniformly downward after the passing of the first and second generations of charismatic leaders. That impression is an unfortunate by-product of the term *revival*—one borrowed from the evangelical tradition that implies a period of religious activity more prosperous than those preceding it.[106]

The evidence of recurrent spiritual gifts before 1837 is abundant. The missionary journal of Benjamin S. Youngs, for example, records numerous extraordinary happenings in 1801. During one storm he had a vision of a "very large multitude of Sheep feeding in beutiful green pasture." On another occasion "God himself in Shape like a man" appeared at his bedside in a dream and told him that he was "to be mortified & brought down." Four years later, while preaching in the Ohio Valley, Youngs noted a range of unusual gifts, including the healing of a child, prophetic visions, inspired dreams, powerful "operations" during worship meetings, speaking in tongues, and divine judgments on those attacking the Shaker gospel. At one meeting a woman had a "gift of Songs within her breast which could be distinctly heard across the room." She beat notes on "her breasts" as if on an organ and danced to the music.[107]

In 1810 new converts at Pleasant Hill were experiencing "very mortifying scenes." After confessing their sins, they fell into "exercises," several of which caused special comment. Some wallowed in mud until covered from head to foot. Others pounded on furniture until "their hands were so sore & swollen that they could not use them." Lucy Smith, a village leader at the time, was the recipient of frequent visions, including one in 1821, in which two sisters appeared at her bedside accompanied by a bright and beautiful light "like a great double rose." Others not in positions of leadership at the same village likewise experienced visions and revelations. The gift of miraculous healing was reported among the Believers in various locations. At New Lebanon in 1825, for example, Esther Williams dislocated her back, having fallen from a barn loft, but she was instantly healed and joined in the dance as proof. Conversations with notable spirit figures were part of the Shaker tradition. Emily Pearcifield, a twelve-year-old at South Union, in 1835 traveled in vision to the spirit world, where she saw Jesus, Ann Lee, and other founders of the society.[108]

Similar spiritual phenomena took place throughout the 1830s. On 9 January 1831, for example, Rufus Bishop noted "an unusual outpouring of the gifts of God—tongues, visions &c." at a meeting of the First Order in New Lebanon. At the beginning of February 1832 he reported that Joshua Stone, while in an Albany prison for refusing military obligations, saw a vision of "the heavenly host," including Ann Lee. The cell, Stone stated, "was illuminated as bright as noon day!" In late winter 1834 Bishop recorded a "Remarkable increase of the fruits of the gospel" at both New Lebanon (fig. 14) and Hancock. At a meeting on 1 March 1835 the sense of "union and blessing" was such that Believers felt and saw many of their "departed friends" present. In January 1836 Bishop noted "Extraordinary meetings in the Chh. both for length & goodness." A month and a half later the gift of humility and repentance prevailed throughout the Second Order with "great manifestations of the power of God," especially among the children and youths. In October Bishop recorded power manifest in "tongues & divers operations"; in December he witnessed "uncommonly good" meetings at the First Order.[109]

On 4 January 1837 the central ministry noted a "Remarkable Vision" received by James Smith, a resident at Watervliet. Toward summer Rufus Bishop wrote, "The believers in this society have been waking up to life, zeal & power for some weeks past. Even the public meetings are full of demonstrations of power, in diverse operations & gifts of the Spirit." The ministry journal for 12 August contains a long description of the vision of Gidion Kibbee, who saw a large "company of heavenly host" with Ann Lee at the head, marching through the village three to four feet off the ground. Kibbee believed that "some new Era or great event" was about to happen to the Believers. Bishop thought that Kibbee had been given a "privilege to look into the invisible world." This was less than a week before the beginning of the stir among the children at Watervliet.[110]

14. The Religious Dance
Arthur Boyd Houghton recorded the worship activities of female Believers at Mount Lebanon—bowing, kissing, and touching. (*The Graphic,* 14 May 1870.)

The 1837 "revival" therefore was not the beginning of something totally new, for this kind of religious activity had taken place many times through the years. The children at the South Family "seem to be very much wrought upon," it was reported, "they have diverous [sic] gifts, shaking turning and singing and the like." These activities continued until almost midnight each night, and word spread to other families at Watervliet and to nearby Shaker villages. The religious excitement mounted even higher in the weeks that followed as the girls began to see visions. On 31 August fourteen-year-old Ann Mariah Goff, during the time "for retiring before meeting," saw a "female spirit" dressed in white who, in the service that followed, kissed all the sisters, labored with them in the circular dance and the shuffle, and sang songs of mourning for sinners and encouragement for the obedient. Goff herself, observers said, took part in the meeting "as usual," nothing appearing unusual to those present.[111]

Throughout September, similar manifestations were repeated at Watervliet, but in greater abundance. Spectators, astonished at these doings, thronged the public meetings. As the activities continued week after week, more and more Believers reported visions of the invisible world. Some described "the happified state of the Saints in light," others the "dark & dismal dungeons" where the wicked groaned in "awful distress." Although revelations and visions had been part of the society's past, never had they occurred in this number or with such agreement. These events even made "believers" out of some skeptics among the Shakers. Rufus Bishop wrote, "Some believers acknowledge that they have heretofore had doubts concerning the truth & reality of such gifts, but they will now say they must believe their own eyes."[112]

Accounts of the manifestations became more elaborate, offering greater detail concerning the circumstances, personnel, actions, and messages. Many visions mirrored the real life situations of the Believers, taking place in spirit dwellings filled with chairs, staircases, double doors, and rooms where sisters and brothers marched and sang. The instruments encountered leaders from the past, dead members of their natural or Shaker families, angels, and unknown figures. They commonly declared parts of their visions "beyond description." Increasingly, when taken in a trance, the religious subjects appeared "insensible" to their surroundings. On numerous occasions the "visionists," as they came to be called, had to be carried to their retiring room "like a lifeless person."[113]

The excitement at Watervliet and the growing public spectacle demanded the attention of the New Lebanon ministry. In early October 1837 Rufus Bishop offered "counsel" to the Second Family concerning the "supernatural gifts." He judged that these evidences of "the condescending goodness of God" were intended to strengthen faith in "the work of God" and to highlight the "state of rewards & punishment beyond the grave." He warned the instruments against "letting their sense rise or taking the honor of those gifts to themselves," and he urged that they "keep their joining to their Elders & to the living body or they would suffer great loss." The central ministry's position was clear: the gifts were of God, but they must be used to support union and order within the society.[114]

Even Rufus Bishop may have had some doubts. Following one "lively public meeting," he observed privately: "on the whole I considered it a good powerful meeting; but to be honest about the matter I think there was rather too much of the wind, fire & earthquake to satisfy Believers who have had a long & fruitful travel." He was not alone in his questioning; a number of others were also unpersuaded. The next day Bishop visited the elders at the Second Family and instructed them about "their duties in governing the meetings." The following Sabbath he noted a good meeting, one without "much supernatural operations, & no trances." Bishop believed his attempt to curb excesses had succeeded, but subsequent events proved him wrong.[115]

The visions of Ann Mariah Goff were one measure of the accelerating changes. On 7 November 1837, despite her protest that the family might not want her to go so often, Goff traveled with a spirit companion to a large "square building" where she was taken to Ann Lee's room. There, after proper introduction, Goff was seated on Lee's "right hand." The room contained thirty chairs different in "shape" from any she had ever seen and a table on which was a book "as large as a twelve light window." Lucy Wright then entered the room and sat on Lee's left. "Both Mothers were dressed in shining white robes, with crowns on their heads. . . . Their faces shone very bright, and their countenances were very smiling." Lee instructed Goff to tell the brothers and sisters to "repent & humble" themselves and to put away pride. She said that the Believers were "too noisey to be the people of God"; they must stop quarreling, talking "saucy," and telling lies. "She said we must be industrious & improve all our time," Goff reported, "& that we must not waste anything, for if we did we would have to suffer for it." Lee also exhorted the Believers to "keep order" and be "neat." Some, she said, thought "too much" of themselves and "talked too much about the gifts of God" and "made light" of them. Goff was told not to "labor any more with the girls unless they would be solemn."[116]

When Goff asked for a sign because some of the brothers and sisters "had no faith" in her visions, Ann Lee agreed to accompany her on the return to Watervliet. Before departing, Goff was given a tour of the square house with its beautiful flowers and trees. There she also "stroked" an angel, a creature with the head and face of a man, a long neck, and feet and legs like a man—"very beautiful, but difficult to describe." Covered by "white feathers" and with a ring of golden feathers about its neck, the angel both walked and flew. On the return trip Ann Lee pointed out the "clear" and "transparent" houses, where the brothers and sisters, the "boys and girls," with crowns on their heads lived, as well as the "dark colored & very muddy" location of the world's houses.[117]

The next evening Goff received another vision, which lasted five hours. The spirit of Ann Lee returned and announced her intention to "preach the gospel." Goff, taken in trance, was told to repeat all that Lee had said; she became literally the voice of "Mother Ann" speaking to the society. The message was of an impending "great day of judgement": the wicked would destroy the Believers "like bears," and all would be "separated." Mother would protect the faithful, Goff declared, but the unfaithful would be tormented in "that awful place" until they repented. Lee urged the Believers to "think of God, and the Lord Jesus & Mother Ann, and all the good Spirits" and pray to them for protection. While in trance, Goff named "individuals in the family that Mother said were out of the way in certain things." Those attending Goff during the vision reported that they had "never heard such powerful & convicting preaching proceed out of the mouth of any one." [118]

News of the religious stir at Watervliet spread rapidly across the society through the network of correspondents and visitors from other villages. In their letters the central ministry commented at length on the "wonderful manifestations from the spiritual world." Likewise, individual Believers felt compelled to describe the events occupying the center of attention in the village. Benjamin S. Youngs, recently recalled from the West against his will and resident at Watervliet, wrote of "multitudes" at both Watervliet and New Lebanon crowding the meetings and of "*Unknown tongues*" spoken by the youths, especially the "young girls." The "extraordinary exercises" taking place, according to him, included "Powerful *shakings* & *quakings*, testimonies, promises, threatenings, warnings, predictions, prophecies, *Trances*, revelations, visions, songs, and dances." The trances, he added, often lasted as long as seven hours. Among the gifts, repentance was foremost   "the most earnestly taught and the most earnestly sought for." Isaac N. Youngs, sent to Watervliet to transcribe the visions, reported that the "celestial visits" made it seem "as tho the veil between this & the other world was made almost transparent." Seth Y. Wells enumerated for the ministry at Canterbury the variety of gifts he had witnessed, including visits from an "antedeluvian of a very tall stature" and from the native American princess Pocahontas. Reports such as these fanned the excitement. [119]

Accounts of similar gifts and exercises at outlying villages soon were circulating throughout the society. In the East, for example, the Harvard ministry described "an uncommon outpouring of the spirit" in January 1838. The meetings of the Believers were filled with "zeal and power" as well as with "many supernatural gifts." By the end of February similar "precious and glorious" gifts were increasing at Enfield, Connecticut. There some "saw lights and unbodied spirits"; others heard the sound of angels flying. Much weeping and crying accompanied the gifts of humiliation and mortification. In March "deep conviction and repentance" were wrought among many at Enfield, New Hampshire, especially the younger members of the society, who "found a great increase in their spiritual travel." One young sister, Julian Willard, was "entranced six days."

Throughout the eastern villages there were frequent communications with the spirit world. Some visions provided encouragement for individual Believers; others identified persons in the society who required special efforts by the elders. In the case of "Poor little Edwin Myrick (the Simpleton)" at Harvard, the ministry reported "truly astonishing" communications through him, including "most pointed testimonies against sin."[120]

In the West extensive "involuntary exercises" occurred among the Believers at South Union during the spring of 1838. In June two sisters in the Gathering Order "were carried away in a trance to the world of Spirits." These phenomena did not begin in a sustained way at Union Village until summer under the encouragement of Freegift Wells. In August he read a description of religious exercises at Pleasant Hill, after which "the power of God" moved through the assembly "almost like electricity." Individuals heard "heavenly sounds" and experienced "supernatural operations." Among the first instruments at Union Village was five-year-old Amittie Ann Miller. One young boy at the village reportedly lay in a trance for thirty-seven and a half hours. Letters telling of the visions in the East were read in the meeting at North Union in late July. Seven days later Richard Pelham recorded in his diary that "Polly C. was exercised" and speaking in "unknown tongues," and that three girls had visions after the public meeting. One week later he observed abundant religious exercises and operations throughout the village. At a meeting less than a year later, he noted eighteen "male visionists" on the floor at once (fig. 15). By April 1839 correspondents were reporting that the "good work" had spread generally throughout the western villages, producing the same "good fruits."[121]

As the months passed, the spiritual gifts increased in abundance. Some manifestations were of a conventional nature, including messages of all kinds, anthems and laboring songs by the hundreds, and new marches and dances. The celestial sources for these resources seemed never to run dry. Often the messages and songs were in unknown tongues and required interpretation. Some, however, stood without explanation, spirit languages in no need of translation. Comfort and encouragement, counsel and admonition—this was the substance of the communications to individuals and groups, whether written, spoken, or sung. A few messages attacked members who were "obstinate" or "out of union." At a New Lebanon meeting, Martha Brainard "drove" out Thirza Horton, who later confessed that she was a "hypocrite." These communications of reproof became especially controversial. New laboring exercises seen in vision were introduced among the Believers. The Heavenly March and the Square Check,

15. The Whirling Gift
Among the religious exercises during Mother Ann's Work was the gift of turning
swiftly. Some Believers whirled so rapidly while in ecstasy that they eventually fell
prostrate on the floor. (David R. Lamson, *Two Years' Experience Among the Shakers*,
1848.)

for example, first revealed to instruments and then approved by the ministry, expressed the principles of mortification and union through action and
accompanying song. These new exercises, according to Daniel W. Patterson, brought into the meetings "elements of secular folk dance previously
shunned in Shaker worship," including performance with partners. Bowing to each other as an expression of humility became a major part of the
new manner of laboring.[122]

Other manifestations from the spirit world bordered on the bizarre,
raising the eyebrows of even the most believing Shakers. At Watervliet,
New York, Sarah Simons was "used" by "some invisible hand" like a mop
being scrubbed across a dirty floor. Oliver Prentis "shook mightily" and
rolled about the meetinghouse. At Union Village the Believers were required "to stoop down and eat simplicity off of the floor"—an action which
many acknowledged defied common sense. Elsewhere brothers and sisters acted "drunk with new wine" or obsessed with the gift of laughter.

Some instruments conducted powerful wars with evil spirits. The language spoken by the visionists in these encounters often breached acceptable standards.[123]

Yet the collective religious imagination of the society knew no limits. The mediums brought to the Believers gifts of another kind—imaginary spiritual "things" patterned after earthly objects: colorful balls and other playthings, golden chains and jeweled necklaces, fine clothing, treasure boxes, fruit baskets, musical instruments, lovely handkerchiefs, birds, flowers, and other wonderful presents the likes of which the Shakers did not possess in everyday life. In fact, some were items the Believers explicitly condemned as worldly. The instruments bestowed these gifts on the recipients with considerable ceremony and, in turn, received due expressions of gratitude and affection. These exchanges, interpreted as signs and seals of love and faithfulness, often involved elaborate mime. Eating, drinking, washing, planting, harvesting, fighting, and countless other ritual actions—all in mime—filled the meetings as the Shakers obeyed the commands of the visiting spirits. The Believers, at least most of them, seemingly never tired of this playful spiritual activity. The central ministry, too, expressed its approval: "it does my soul good to see this shaking," wrote Rufus Bishop.[124]

With each passing year there were new developments. In 1838 Philemon Stewart, a thirty-four-year-old Believer, entered the ranks of the instruments at New Lebanon marking the expansion of the group of visionists. In April he became "useful & conspicuous . . . in the heart-searching work," the ministry observed, and he began to deliver a series of messages. By year's end Stewart had moved into the First Order and was listed as one of the principal instruments at the village. He and others so identified made the reception of spirit messages into a special vocation. Stewart soon was playing a pivotal role in the society's affairs as a chosen vessel, communicating God's will to the Believers. Ultimately he became the "most prominent" as well as the most controversial instrument in the society. At other villages, too, older members began to occupy central roles as instruments in the revival. At Pleasant Hill forty-year-old Sarah Poole, a Believer since 1808, was the first to receive messages; she also received the most messages and became the most influential of the visionists.[125]

The most celebrated spiritualistic development of 1841 was the visitation of Holy Mother Wisdom, the female aspect of the deity. The Believers prepared for her announced advent by putting their villages in order and purifying their hearts. The ministry at New Lebanon even ritually washed their feet to make ready for "this great & blessed privilege." On the appointed day in April, Holy Mother Wisdom spoke through Miranda Barber, a chosen instrument, telling of the intention to "set a Mark on every person over 18 years of age, that when the destroying Angels should be sent forth they know who were vessels of mercy, & who were by their own works excluded from the protection of God." After bestowing "Gold Breastplate[s] set with pearls & precious stones of 35 colors" on the men and "Robes of needlework, covered with flowers of 18 Colors" on the women in the central ministry, as well as many "comforting words" on both, Wisdom worked her way through the ranks of the church. Each Believer repeated these words: "I am bound for the Kingdom of Heaven, O bless me with thy blessing! give me wisdom, strength & power O Holy Holy Mother!" The "divine parent" then spoke words of encouragement or admonition, set a mark on each member, and placed around each person's head a "Gold band" on which was written, "Touch not mine Anointed."[126]

In the months that followed Holy Mother Wisdom appeared at additional meetings with an expanding stream of messages. The Believers, in turn, sought more rigorous ways to prepare themselves properly for her presence. They adopted regimens that included early rising, eating bread and water, total fasting on given days, kneeling in prayer facedown, walking the Narrow Path (a solemn march introduced in 1840), abstaining from all labor, and performing the "searching work" as a step toward repentance. On one occasion Miranda Barber fasted for seven days on bread and water. In December 1841 the visit of Wisdom to New Lebanon consumed more than a week. She examined the members of every family at the village, speaking "love and blessing" to each Believer through the instruments. The response to these visitations was highly enthusiastic. August II. Grosvenor testified, "I felt morer [sic] thankful then for any thing I ever received befor in my life." Rufus Bishop called these visitations, which subsequently spread throughout the society, "the greatest condescension that ever was to mortals since the creation of the world."[127]

The solemnity occasioned by the deity's presence as well as a growing reluctance to display their gifts and exercises before the world led to the ministry's decision in 1842 to suspend the public meetings, where spectators from the world observed Shaker worship. This move was also motivated by fear that the activities of the instruments would provoke a new wave of public derision and harassment. Accordingly, announcements were posted at the villages restricting all but the "chosen people" of Zion. Those coming "with unclean hands and defiled hearts, to make sport of the work of God" were threatened with "sore affliction and distress." The wooden sign erected in front of the meetinghouse at New Lebanon on

1 May 1842 read: "Enter not within these gates, for this is my Holy Sanctuary saith the Lord[.] But pass ye by, and disturb not the peace of the quiet, upon my Holy Sabbath."[128]

The decision to suspend the public meetings came at an opportune moment, for later in 1842 the Believers took in "native spirits" in great numbers. Throughout the Shaker villages the spirits of American Indians possessed the instruments, causing them to speak and act in boistrous and savage ways, unusual even for the visionists. The wild actions were rationalized as a special test of the instruments. Native songs and messages were often "translated" into primitive English. One song attributed to the chief Contoocook opens: "Me love me hills and mountains   Me love me pleasant groves   Me love to ramble round as me feel as me choose." Another native song included the lines: "In me canoe me will go to Mudder   Dare me will sing lobe lobe lobe." Soon spirits from other foreign lands were crowding into the meetings. Although the decision to close the meetings was in tension with the society's hopes to attract new members, the Shakers promised that those genuinely seeking "information" concerning "the religious faith and principles" of the Believers would be "duly attended."[129]

The ritual innovations of the Shakers reached their most elaborate expression in the "feast of the passover," first held on the top of East Mountain at New Lebanon in the spring of 1842. There a site was selected and a "spiritual fountain" erected under the direction of the central ministry and a chosen group of instruments. On 1 May the members of the Church Order celebrated the feast at the "appointed spot on the summit," and on subsequent Sabbaths other families from the village participated in a similar ritual that sometimes consumed nearly eight hours. Later in the year leaders from other villages came to take part in the celebration, thus becoming acquainted with the rite, which they afterward carried back to their own locations. The central ministry issued an order that all villages were to prepare a sacred site for an outdoor feast to be held twice a year, normally in the spring and the fall.[130]

The physical arrangements at the sites, although they varied from village to village, were quite elaborate, as the situation at Harvard demonstrates. The Harvard ministry first participated in the passover feast at New Lebanon on 29 July 1842. Exactly one month later some ninety Believers at Harvard met at a select spot called the Holy Hill of Zion, where there was "speaking, singing, and dancing and marching." In mid-November a large group turned out to work further on the site. During the autumn a total of six hundred hours was invested in clearing, excavating, leveling, and enclosing the sacred location. The next spring seed was sown and an engraven marble slab was placed in the center of the clearing, which was surrounded by a low fence set in a hexagonal pattern. On one side of the Fountain Stone was the authorizing command and the date of erection, 23 November 1843 (fig. 16). On the other side was an inscription inviting those who sought healing, but warning others "polluted with sin" not to violate the enclosure lest judgment fall on them. It was May 1844 before all of these arrangements were complete.[131]

Although the "mountain feasts" varied from place to place, certain activities characterized the celebrations at all the sacred sites (fig. 17). The Believers at Tyringham, for example, on the occasion of one feast in 1844, assembled at ten o'clock in the morning and, while singing, marched "in regular order" up the hill to Mount Horeb. Halfway to the fountain they paused and were urged to be obedient to the will of their "heavenly Parents." At the gate of the enclosure they met Elder Nathaniel Deming and entered together, forming a "double circle around the fountain." There the company listened to addresses from the leaders, received gifts through the instruments, sang, testified, and marched. The Believers were encouraged to "improve" the "privilege" of meeting at this site and to labor with zeal. Then at the invitation of the elders they "washed" in the fountain and "drank" from it. They also drank wine and ate manna, clapped their hands "in token of union," and shouted thanks in the direction of New Lebanon. At noon they spread a "very rich feast" on tables and ate the white grapes, oranges, and other fruits sent in love from the spirit world and drank "the pure waters of life." All ate in order and were satisfied. Another discourse followed the spiritual meal, this one featuring the advantages of a mediating Mother, who not long afterward "arrived in her beautiful Chariot" to visit and bless her children. The "blessed Savior" and many others also bestowed gifts on the gathered Believers. These proceedings—all in mime—closed with a special call for obedience to Deming, who gave to all his love and blessing. Heavenly spirits accompanied the Believers halfway down the hill on their return to the village.[132]

At the time of the inauguration of the passover feasts, new spiritual names were adopted by the various villages. The sacred sites at each location likewise were given special designations. These place-names continued to be used in public and private long after the Era of Manifestations (see table 2).[133]

In the spring of 1842 Philemon Stewart received a series of special revelations, published by the society in 1843 as *A Holy, Sacred and Divine*

THE WORD OF THE LORD.

Hearken, O ye children of men, to this, the word of the Lord your God, yea, read, understand and give heed to the same. For with the finger of my own hand have I written it, and at my word was it engraved on this stone, which I have caused to be erected here, and called by my name,

THE LORD'S STONE.

Thus saith Jehovah, Behold! here have I opened a living fountain of holy and eternal waters, for the healing of the nations.

Here have I chosen a sacred spot, and commanded my people to consecrate and sanctify it unto me, their Holy God.

Here shall my name be owned, feared and praised, and I alone will be adored by the nations of the earth, and unborn millions that shall pass this way, shall bow in reverence to this, the work of my hands, saith the Holy One of Israel, *The Great I AM, the Almighty Power.*

Therefore, let the stranger from afar and the traveller behold this work with sacred reverence and pass by in the solemn fear of his God. And let none presume to trifle with this mystery, lest in my fierce anger I stretch forth my hand against them.

For whosoever shall step upon this holy ground, or lay their hands on this stone, with intent to do evil, or to injure it in any way, shall in no wise escape the justice of my righteous power. And in my own time will I, even I, bring an awful curse upon them, saith the *Eternal Judge of all, and Overruling Power of Heaven and Earth. Whose word is truth. Amen.*

16. Groveland Fountain Stone
This stone, engraved by Isaac N. Youngs, was erected at Groveland on 18 May 1843
The text reads:

THE WORD OF THE LORD

Hearken, O ye children of men, to this,
the word of the Lord your God; yea, read, under
stand and give heed to the same. For with the finger
of my hand have I written it, and at my word
was it engraved on this stone, which I have caused
to be erected here, and called by my name.

THE LORD'S STONE.

Thus saith Jehovah, Behold! here have I opened
a living fountain of holy and eternal waters, for
the healing of the nations.
Here have I chosen a sacred spot, and
commanded my people to consecrate and
sanctify it unto me their Holy God.
Here shall my name be owned, feared and
praised; and I alone will be adored by the nations
of the earth; and unborn millions that shall pass
this way, shall bow in reverence to this, the work
of my hands, saith the Holy One of Israel,
The Great I AM, the Almighty Power.
Therefore, let the stranger from afar, and the
traveller, behold this work with sacred reverence,
and pass by in the solemn fear of his God. And let
none presume to trifle with this my work. Lest in my
fierce anger I stretch forth my hand against them.
For whosoever shall step upon this my holy
ground, or lay their hands on this stone with
an intent to do evil, or to injure it in any way,
shall in no wise escape the justice of my
righteous power. And in my own time will
I, even I, bring an awful curse upon them,
saith the *Eternal Judge of all* and the
Overruling Power of Heaven and Earth,
Whose word is truth. Amen.

(Courtesy New York State Museum, Albany.)

17. Mountain Meeting
Engraving depicting religious activities by the Believers at the fountain stone site.
(David R. Lamson, *Two Years' Experience Among the Shakers*, 1848.)

Roll and Book. Originally in two parts and numbering more than four hundred pages, this volume typifies the spirit messages of the revival period. According to his own account, on 4 May Stewart was summoned by an angel to the Holy Fountain at New Lebanon, where he wrote down "the sentences of [the] Eternal God and Creator" as read to him from a sacred roll. The dictation process required fourteen days to complete. The angel, identified as Al'sign te're Jah', later returned and inspired testimonies to the authority and authenticity of the revelations that were printed in the second part of the volume. The publication explicitly identifies Stewart as a chosen instrument, tested through "deep tribulation," and claims for itself a status and function equal to the Bible.[134]

   The *Sacred and Divine Roll* contains moral counsel, biblical quotations, historical observations, and theological reflections, all represented as the product of spirit revelation. In the volume Stewart exhorts Believers to humility and threatens the consuming wrath of God if they disobey the divine commands. Those who obtain the gospel inheritance on earth, however, are assured "a peaceful mansion of rest . . . when they had done with things of time." The central figure in the spirit communications is Ann Lee, and the primary function of the publication is to buttress the society's

Table 2
Spiritual Names for Shaker Villages and Feast Sites in the 1840s

Village	Spiritual Name	Sacred Site
Alfred, Maine	Holy Land	Holy Hill of Zion
Canterbury, N.H.	Holy Ground	Pleasant Grove
Enfield, Conn.	City of Union	Mount of Olives
Enfield, N.H.	Chosen Vale	Mount Assurance
Groveland, N.Y.	Union Branch	Holy Ground
Hancock, Mass.	City of Peace	Mount Sinai
Harvard, Mass.	Lovely Vineyard	Holy Hill of Zion
New Lebanon, N.Y.	Holy Mount	Mount of Olives
North Union, Ohio	Holy Grove	Jehovah's Beautiful Square
Pleasant Hill, Ky.	—	Holy Sinai's Plain
Sabbathday Lake, Maine	Chosen Land	Mount Hermon
Shirley, Mass.	Pleasant Garden	Holy Hill of Peace
South Union, Ky.	Jasper Valley	Holy Ground
Tyringham, Mass.	City of Love	Mount Horeb
Union Village, Ohio	Wisdom's Paradise	Jehovah's Chosen Square
Watervliet, N.Y.	Wisdom's Valley	Center Square
Watervliet, Ohio	Vale of Peace	Holy Circle
Whitewater, Ohio	Lonely Plain of Tribulation	Chosen Square

claims concerning her. Stewart cites at length scriptural passages in support of the twofold coming of Christ. By the "second manifestation of the
same spirit," he writes, Ann Lee was constituted a "spiritual Mother, the
second Anointed One, who now stands in her proper lot and place, with
her blessed Lord and Savior." The "foundation of the kingdom" was completed by that spirit first appearing "in the *female witness*." William Lee
and James Whittaker were also assigned special roles as the second and
third witnesses. Stewart thus situated the founders, especially Ann Lee,
within the framework of biblical prophecy.[135]

The second part of the *Sacred and Divine Roll* contains the testimonies of ancient prophets, holy angels, and living witnesses who certify
the divine origins of Stewart's revelation. The prophets Jeremiah, Ezekiel,
Elisha, and Isaiah, as well as other biblical figures including Noah, Simon
Peter, and John the Revelator, and Holy Mother Wisdom, too, testify to the
truthfulness of the publication. In addition, more than seventy living Believers in various villages, many of them prominent instruments and lead-

ers in the society, stated publicly their belief in the special character of these spirit communications. The testimonies by the Shakers, also received by inspiration, were regarded as evidence of the miraculous nature of the publication. Stewart wrote, "And the spirit and substance of all herein contained, I pronounce and declare to all the inhabitants of earth, to be solemn and unalterable truths of God; and that which will stand for the same, in the endless ages of eternity."[136]

The text of the *Sacred and Divine Roll* contains directions for its own printing, circulation, preservation, and use. The volume was to be distributed to the rulers of the world, who were exhorted not to dismiss it, lest they fall on difficult times. Religious leaders were directed to place the publication side by side with the Bible in their pulpits and to use it for the edification of their congregations. Copies were to be kept in every Shaker meetinghouse, where God would position "four angels" to guard the "sacred work." It was to be read regularly in the assemblies of Believers, and the anniversary of the date when it was brought to earth by the angel (2 February) was to be observed as a day of solemn worship. The self-declaration of scriptural status, the claims made by Stewart throughout the process of dictation and publication, and the emphasis on supporting witnesses force comparison between the *Sacred and Divine Roll* and another new scripture, one published little more than a decade earlier in western New York, namely, the *Book of Mormon*. Both texts appeared overanxious to establish their legitimacy as new bibles, both displayed language similar to the King James Version of the Bible, and both effected a targumizing process through the amplification and extension of scriptural themes and stories. Both were also accorded mixed receptions.[137]

The initial reception accorded the *Sacred and Divine Roll* throughout the society was highly positive. Before its publication, the volume was read in its entirety at several eastern villages by Philemon Stewart and Giles Avery, and thus it had been critiqued by a number of leaders. The editors acknowledged that the publication was not totally clear in every respect, and therefore a few notes of explanation were appended, including one stating explicitly that Stewart stood in full union with the "visible leading authority of the Society" in the process leading to the printing. The Believers distributed copies to society members as well as to prominent persons in the world, religious and political leaders alike, in America and elsewhere. Bishop John Hughes of New York sent copies to Pope Gregory XVI in Rome. Leaders of European governments also received the publication. The king of Sweden and Norway expressed his pleasure at receipt of the *Sacred and Divine Roll* through his chargé d'affaires in the United

States. Not all outsiders, however, thought favorably of the volume and its author. One critic called it "an Awful Compound of Antichristianity, Arianism, and popery." Another called Stewart "a deluded Enthusiast, Exceedingly ignorant, and very dangerous." Still another denounced him as "a Monomaniac" who was deluded by Satan. These judgments certainly contributed to the rapidly declining fortunes of the volume and to the society's decision to withdraw it from public circulation before the end of the decade. Philemon Stewart's fall from favor in the society also influenced that decision.[138]

The outpouring of spirit manifestations during these years was accompanied by the promulgation of many new communal regulations. The instruments frequently delivered messages to the entire society, often as gifts to the ministry or village leaders. Sometimes these communications were specific injunctions to be incorporated by the ministry into the society's rules. The visionists received messages that condemned common practices within the villages. The spirit of Ann Lee spoke out against "unnecessary freedom" with dogs and cats; another called on members to give up reading unprofitable books. Still others censured the keeping of journals by individuals, the use of rocking chairs by young persons, and the wearing of "green veils" by sisters. There were repeated calls for purging all "idols" from Zion. Several large collections of rules were given by inspiration to the Believers between 1839 and 1845, when the central ministry authorized a revision and expansion of the Millennial Laws. In the spring of 1840 Rufus Bishop took note of a "book containing 'Divine Rules and Laws of the Church' given by Father Joseph and Mother Lucy." As early as July of the same year these laws were being read publicly to the church in a context filled "with great solemnity & the fear of God." These communications and others ultimately were combined with earlier regulations by a committee appointed by the central ministry. The result was a new and extended version of the Millennial Laws, the joint product of tradition, revelation, and administrative decision. These communal regulations circulated throughout the society in manuscript form in 1845; they were read annually to the Believers on the anniversary of Ann Lee's traditional birthday.[139]

No single event marked the close of the revival period, unlike its opening in 1837. The commitment to spiritualism, in fact, never disappeared completely from the society. Like a storm, the revival gradually dissipated, losing its force and direction. Because the religious situation was different in each village, the spiritual manifestations often reflected local circumstances more than the will of the central ministry at New Lebanon.

For some Shakers the loss of interest in the revival came quite early. Many of the Believers in Maine, for example, including James Pote, who had served as the Elder Brother at Alfred, had "very little if any faith" in the manifestations by early 1845, especially in the *Sacred and Divine Roll* and the activities at the fountain sites. After the middle of the 1840s the spiritual energies invested in the revival began to lessen throughout the society. The Shakers were no longer preoccupied with the spirit visitations. Furthermore, a number of departures by prominent instruments shook the Believers' faith in these gifts. One of the earliest to defect, in 1839, was Elleyett Gibbs at Watervliet, who had been the recipient of many "heavenly Songs, Visions & messages." According to the ministry, she was "unwilling to live so strict a life as the gospel requires." Even more disturbing was the apostasy in 1846 of eight young members, including the instruments John Allen and Mary Wickes of the Church Family at New Lebanon. Rufus Bishop expressed the society's dismay: "this feels awful beyond description, & has caused many tears, & is such an occurrence as this family never experienced before since we began to gather together in the year 1787."[140]

The Legacy of the Manifestations

The religious commotion of the revival period threatened the stability of the United Society. Early in the Era of Manifestations, Seth Y. Wells gave voice to a fear that gripped the leadership when he wrote, "A ship or even a little boat, with a sufficient weight of ballast, will go safely through the water with spreading sails; while another without ballast is in great danger whenever her sails are spread; because she is greatly exposed to be upset with the first blast of wind that blows." Wells and others spoke of the need to balance the spiritual gifts with sufficient humility, meekness, and repentance because pride lurked nearby, tempting the instruments and threatening to destroy union and order.[141]

The central ministry acknowledged the "good" that the "wonderful work" was accomplishing, including "overthrowing infidelity," but they warned that those who could see into the spiritual world would be "lost after all their great gifts" if they did not attend to the "orders and instructions" given for the protection of the Believers. The leaders likewise observed that sometimes the "want of true wisdom in the instruments" and their failure to "try the Spirits" led them astray. When false spirits were at work and the inspired visionists did not agree, a "shock of confidence" swept through the membership and also challenged the authority of the elders. The instruments gave fresh voice to the claims of the charismatic tradition within Shakerism, a heritage extending back to the Age of the Founders and expressed anew in the spirit visitations and ecstatic behavior. The leaders of the society, by contrast, reminded the Believers of the principles of union and order on which the society had been gathered and built by the second and third generations of Shakers. They warned that "the true watchmen of Zion's walls" must "look out . . . for the enemy." "Yea," the New Lebanon ministry wrote, "and Mother has given to the Ministry and Elders here, spiritual spectacles that they may see clearly and not be deceived by false spirits." The fundamental issue at stake was the proper relation between gift and order.[142]

During the height of the revival, confusion abounded. Everywhere religious excitement rose to fever pitch. The "visionary scenes" proved so captivating that much time was "spent day & night about them." Young children reversed traditional roles as they addressed the ministry in the name of their divine and heavenly parents as well as on behalf of revered leaders from the past. At times it seemed that "scarcely a youth or child [was] destitute of the power of God," a marked departure from earlier complaints. Unusual spirit visitors filled the meetinghouses week after week— angels with strange names, natives speaking foreign tongues, biblical figures from ancient times, political figures from America's past. New songs had to be learned, dances practiced, and preparations made for spiritual feasts and celebrations. Trances repeatedly interrupted the flow of daily activities, sometimes meetings lasted into the early morning hours, and a few special rituals even took place in the middle of the night. The regular routines of the Shakers fell victim to the manifestations.[143]

Tensions developed within the society between the supporters of charismatic gifts and the advocates of structured order, as well as among various factions hoping to exploit such discord for their own purposes. Conflict between the instruments and the ministry became almost inevitable, each claimed to speak the will of God, one by direct inspiration and the other by virtue of ministerial authority. This was not, however, a simple struggle between gift and order, for both parties viewed their own activities as divinely inspired. The instruments looked to visions and revelations accompanied by ecstatic experiences; the ministry appealed to the sanctity and responsibilities of their office. At stake in this struggle were control of the category of gift and the future direction of the United Society.[144]

Early in the revival the central ministry perceived the special dangers in the manifestations and took steps to curb the centrifugal forces unleashed by the charismatic activity. They began to require instruments to open their visions to the leaders separately, in this way discouraging collusion, checking extremism, and thus testing the integrity and consistency of the messages. The ministry authorized scribes to write down the communications in order to preserve them and also thereby to control the spirit texts circulating throughout the villages. They urged local leaders to be active in counseling the instruments and in maintaining control over the meetings. The elders continually preached humility and obedience as the responsibility of all, including those who were inspired. The ministry encouraged older and more experienced instruments in an effort to neutralize the youthful inclinations of many visionists. Similarly, mature Believers who were active seers were placed in positions of leadership at the local villages. The prominence accorded Philemon Stewart may be explained, in part, by this strategy. In time, the ministry even involved themselves in the selection of new visionists. Three brothers at Watervliet, for example, were chosen for that role in 1840. But the ultimate step in the effort to control the gifts came when members of the central ministry and other society leaders began to receive spirit communications themselves.[145]

The ministry had few alternatives as they sought to retain leadership in the society. If the leaders at New Lebanon had condemned the spirit visitations and messages, they would have been rejecting the oldest tradition in the society, one closely associated with the founders. But by welcoming the manifestations and the religious energies released by the wave of spiritualism, the ministry was creating a potentially explosive situation. The only reasonable middle ground was to support and attempt to control the course of the revival itself, using it as a tool for reforming and disciplining the members of the society. "I felt an uncommon gift, for me," wrote Rufus Bishop, "to urge the necessity of keeping every order & counsel which had been given for our protection and increase; Showing that in all ages of the world, God always noticed and protected his people when they obeyed the laws and statutes which were given them." That strategy, difficult as it was to implement, explains the seemingly contradictory positions occasionally taken by the ministry. Ultimately, they prevailed in the contest, but at the expense of accepting a number of the assumptions informing the visionists.[146]

The situation during the revival was even more complex, however, for the tension between gift and order fueled existing conflicts among the Shakers. The manifestations strained relations between generations when the younger, inexperienced members seized the religious initiative. The generational gap was especially evident in the contrast between the cool reception accorded the native spirits by the ministry and the youthful Believers' exuberance for those uncontrolled and uncontrollable visitors. The predominance of women, especially young girls, within the ranks of the instruments provoked the latent hostility of some Shaker males toward female leadership. The central ministry took the initiative to select more males as visionists in an effort to balance the expanding female role within the society. Likewise, an extended spirit visitation by the Almighty Father in 1842 followed the stay of Holy Mother Wisdom; he, too, moved systematically through the ranks of the Believers, blessing some and judging others.[147]

The long-standing tension within the society between East and West and the struggles between local and centralized authority were caught in the contest between gift and order. The revival raised questions concerning freedom and regulation among the Believers. Individuals led by the spirits often defied conventional rules and boundaries because, by definition, the visionists operated outside the realm of the ordinary. Community leaders, by contrast, sought to strengthen the centripetal elements within the society by featuring the authority of the central ministry, the primary symbol for the regulated communal life. Spirit possession, as I. M. Lewis has shown, traditionally has been used as an oblique strategy of aggression by those outside power structures. Individuals or parties seeking to be free from the Shaker establishment possessed potentially powerful allies in the instruments. Local traditions gained reinforcement from the seers. At times, ironically, the ministry found itself defending the letter of the law against the spirits.[148]

During the revival those Believers less enthusiastic about visions and revelations sometimes found themselves on the defensive. Calvin Green, one of the most respected and influential Shaker leaders, expressed reservations concerning some of the manifestations. Green, for example, became involved in a dispute over the "correctness & genuineness" of Philemon Stewart's role as an instrument. Because of his misgivings, Green was singled out for criticism by the visionists in the spring of 1838 and forced repeatedly to confess "his wrongs in feeling & acting against Order & government." Richard McNemar, a pillar of western Shakerism since 1805, found himself in conflict with Freegift Wells, the newly appointed leading elder at Union Village. Wells, the symbol of centralized eastern authority in the West, was an enthusiastic supporter of the revival. He regarded McNemar and several other westerners as potential competitors for the loyalty of the people. McNemar's resistance to the revival, combined with some resentment at having been passed over for leadership in the village, led to open conflict. The instruments at Union Village became pawns in the struggle, condemning Malcolm Worley as well as McNemar and calling for their dismissal. McNemar sought redress by traveling to New Lebanon in 1839, where his physical health deteriorated rapidly, despite counsel and support from the ministry and soothing messages from the spirit of David Darrow. Later that year he returned to the West and was formally reconciled with Freegift Wells. A few months later, still something of an outsider, he died. Seth Y. Wells, another Shaker theologian noted for his lifelong commitment to education, was himself in some tension with the anti-intellectualism of the instruments. Following Wells's death in 1847, Rufus Bishop stored away the "French, Greek & Latten books" belonging to Wells with the comment that they "will be useless among us, unless some learned person comes in among us."[149]

The mixed character of the revival's legacy is no less evident in the multitude of recorded spirit messages. No systematic count has ever been made of the communications received by the Believers during the revival. The number certainly is in the thousands, perhaps even tens of thousands. The central ministry directed local authorities to transcribe the spirit communications. The messages, in turn, were copied and circulated throughout the society. These texts, in both oral and written form, assumed the character of sacred scripture among the Shakers. Held in high regard as products of direct inspiration, they were read and reread in both public and private. Their value was not perceived to be limited to the original intended recipients. (This parallels canon formation in other religious traditions.) Only when claims for authority were made in the name of the visionists instead of those of the spirits was the status of the documents questioned. Controversy erupted, for example, over the *Sacred and Holy Roll,* no doubt fueled by personal animosities toward Philemon Stewart. The spirit messages were used liturgically in the Believers' meetings and became the source of inspiration for preaching, exhortation, and moral counsel. The ministry attempted to control which messages became part of the expanding informal canon by invoking the principle of consistency with other inspired writings and public testimonies, including the Bible.[150]

Great care was taken in the writing, preservation, and storage of the documents, a further reflection of the reverence accorded these texts. According to the Believers, the spirits spoke to the instruments who conveyed the messages to the Shakers. Recorders committed the spoken words to paper, and scribes then copied and recopied these texts for circulation among the members. The small booklets, composed of neatly cut pages carefully stitched to paper covers, often of denim blue, and written in matching ink, testify to the special attention given the manuscripts. These features set them apart from family journals, routine correspondence, and conventional discourse. Most of the booklets, numbering in the hundreds, are in excellent condition. Scribes also recopied the individual texts into larger collections that circulated among the villages.[151]

In the spirit messages the instruments gave voice to such traditional Shaker values as obedience, humility, repentance, union, and order. They also expressed some not-so-conventional notions, among them a mental delight with the forbidden "things" of the world and the loss of restraint in word and deed. During the revival traditional communal restrictions remained in force, but the spirits were not bound by them. Sometimes the instruments expressed antinomian impulses in the name of the visitors; in doing so, they crossed forbidden boundaries. More frequently the visionists voiced comfort and encouragement as well as counsel and warning. They continually gave free reign to their religious imagination. Repressed feelings were expressed in discourse and action, creating a moment of collective spiritual play without parallel in American religious history. The following text from Ohio is typical.

> My Beloved brother   you have spent a good long lifetime here on this earth. you have binn faithfull With the care entrusted to you. and I have some encouragement for you   as you have binn faithfull in bearing your cross and as you have come to the years of old age you have need of encouragement   your days will soon be closed on this earth. and I want you to take fresh hold of mothers work and persevere till I come after you. though you think the time long to come home to the glorious City do not be discouraged   there is room prepared for you   I want you to gether your sense on spiritual things and feel more giveness to come home when you are sent for   I send you a bigg boll of encouragmet to strenghen you and encourage you till I shall come after you   I want you to labour for more life and zeal in Mothers work and feel yourself prepared to come home. here is a box of humilaty and a box full of sugarplums and a box of love and simplicaty   I want you to take these and give a box out every meeting to the brethren and sisters till all is given out. I have nothing more but my love and blessing I want you to have   you may divide with the brethren and sisters by holding up your right hand and saying I will be mothers little baby.[152]

The Era of Manifestations divided contemporary observers and still separates those who look back on it today. Spiritual gifts ultimately exist in the eye of the beholder. The revivals proved dismaying to the leaders of the society because it was impossible to establish objective standards for separating legitimate from inauthentic gifts. There was no satisfactory way to settle the argument between those who regarded the revival as silly and those who saw it as an outpouring of divine blessings. Nor was it possible to halt the activities by administrative fiat. Once the spirit visitations caught the collective imagination of the Believers, the gifts could not be stopped. The revival had to run its course before the ministry could hope for a return to more normal spiritual patterns. Even then the prospect of new outbursts of spiritualism was never far away. Shakerism, with its notion of continuing revelation and an open canon, allowed for continual expressions of the extraordinary.[153]

One of the most enduring aspects of the Era of Manifestations was its musical legacy. A truly astonishing number of song texts and tunes was received by inspiration through the visionists. No exact count exists, but Daniel W. Patterson suggests that in the decade preceding 1848 some 3,850 new songs were sung at New Lebanon alone, most of which were received at that village. One instrument at Harvard, Joanna Randall, received 62 within a three-month period in 1844–1845. Most gift songs were "irregular and strange," reflecting the marks of the inspiration process and the lack of musical training among the Believers. A few were to accompany new laboring exercises introduced to the society through the visionists. The Shakers' compulsion to record the gifts has resulted in a large collection of manuscript hymnals containing both texts and musical notations. Some of the songs, not surprisingly, reflect tunes and techniques from the secular music of the day. "Cords of Love," for example, echoes the musical theme of the ballad "The Death of Queen Jane." This part of the Shaker religious heritage bears the stamp of its nineteenth-century context, too.[154]

No one gift song is typical of the period, although it has become fashionable in recent years to single out "Simple Gifts." According to one tradition, this song was to be sung as a quick dance and may have been composed by Joseph Brackett at Alfred in 1848. Although it has become well known in the second half of the twentieth century, thanks in part to Aaron Copland's use of its theme in his *Appalachian Spring* suite, there is evidence that it was already popular among the Shakers during the revival period. Its words and tune present a positive image of childlike innocence, humility, and spiritual play—all principal themes of the Era of Manifestations.

'Tis the gift to be simple, 'tis the gift to be free;
'Tis the gift to come down where we ought to be;
And when we find ourselves in the place just right,
'Twill be in the valley of love and delight.
When true simplicity is gaind,
To bow and to bend we shan't be asham'd
To turn, turn will be our delight,
'Till by turning, turning we come round right.

A different mood is evident in a song attributed to the spirit of Issachar Bates, received in 1851 by Louisa Youngs at New Lebanon. Here the strenuous, zealous side of the revival sounds forth.

Depart all thats evil   go away from me
I'll be a valient warrior   I will be free
I will not be bound   by any foe
For heaven I'm bound   to heaven I'll go.

The musical heritage of the period played a role in the community after the manifestations had subsided. Many of the songs continued to be used in worship, some preserved in written form and others handed down by oral tradition.[155]

Among the most unusual "texts" from the revival period are the drawings produced by the Believers, visual depictions of the gifts that were received. These artifacts, much more limited in number (192 extant by one count) than the messages and songs, first came to light outside the community in the 1930s. The records of the society are frustratingly silent about these works of Shaker religious art, which on the surface conflict with communal prohibitions against pictorial representations. During the Era of Manifestations the religious imagination of the Believers also found expression in graphic form. A few instruments drew and painted what they saw or received by inspiration. A small number of members, most of whom were at Hancock or New Lebanon, produced the surviving drawings. The visual gifts are filled with balls, boxes, and baskets, trees and flowers, horns and harps, crowns, cups, and clocks, birds, geometrical forms, strange machines, and extensive inscriptions. Many contain notations explaining their origins, such as: "Beloved Sister Anna, Receive this, with my never ending love and blessing, Polly Laurence. Given by Mother Lucy's permission, *with a bright Jewel of her love. June 1853.*"[156]

The charm of these spirit drawings, described by some critics as folk art, is the product of more than simply the visual effect. "The Tree of Life," by Hannah Cohoon, perhaps the best known of all the drawings, expresses by color, shape, and movement her view of the reality of the spirit world. Cohoon, who had been at Hancock since 1817, was sixty-six years old when in 1854 she "received a draft of a beautiful Tree pencil'd on a large sheet of white paper bearing ripe fruit." The spirit subsequently showed her details concerning the leaves and the fruit as well as the colors to be used. Finally, according to the inscription, on 1 October "Mother Ann" told Cohoon the name of the tree through "the hand of a medium." The bright red and green spheres—the fruit—vibrate as the viewer glances from one to another while the movement of the branches and the fluttering of the checked leaves refuse to allow the eye to rest. Cohoon has successfully created "the illusion that her tree rustles with a living spirit." For the Believers "The Tree of Life" evoked images of the church: as the tree was to bring forth good fruit, so those joined to the church, even the remotest branches, were to do the same.[157]

Yet not all the spirit drawings would so easily grace the face of greeting cards. The "prophetic signs" received by Miranda Barber, illustrations for a book "Written by the Prophet Isaiah," depict future "cataclysms of nature" that will strike the earth, such as fire, wind, hail, and earthquakes (fig. 18). The artist, a member of the Church Family at New Lebanon and a prominent instrument during Holy Mother Wisdom's visits, used simple but bold shapes to picture these future violent occurrences. The contrast is striking between her heavy apocalyptic images and the finely textured filigree in Polly Reed's gifts—whether line drawings in blue ink cut out in the shape of hearts, palms, and stars, or watercolors on conventional squares and rectangles. Reed, twenty-five at the time of her earliest pieces, had been among the Shakers for eighteen years. An airy quality and a sense of transparency dominate her paintings; the delicate material objects seem to float free of gravity. The leaves in the 1848 painting for Joanna Kitchell, for example, appear featherlike; the "Dish of Fruit" from the native spirits struggles to contain the items placed in it; and the yellow "Wings of holy power, from Fr. Issachar" confirm the ethereal intentions of the artist (fig. 19). The gift drawings reinforce the primary spiritual objectives of the Believers during the revival.[158]

The spirit texts—spoken, written, sung, and drawn—conveyed a new sense of intimacy with the founding generations. Believers coming to maturity in the 1830s lacked personal knowledge of the early leaders; even the traditions concerning the past seemed remote. The spirit visitations brought back to life the figures of Ann Lee and the early leaders as well as

18. And There Will Be Terrible Winds
Miranda Barber's gift drawing in June 1843 predicted upheavals in nature. The text
reads: "And there will be terrible winds in the earth and fire and hail, and dreadful
earthquakes." (Courtesy the Western Reserve Historical Society, Cleveland, Ohio.)

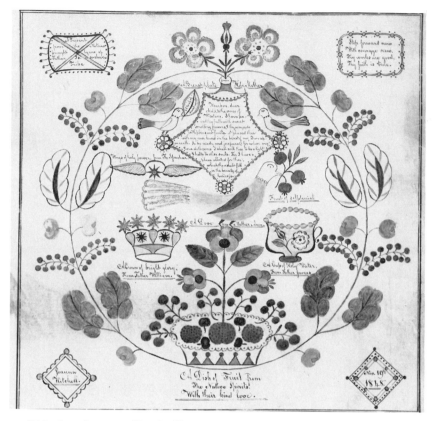

19. Gift for Joanna Kitchell

Polly Reed's gift drawing, dated 19 November 1848, was brought by natives of "Father Issachar's Tribe." The tokens of affection from the spirit world include a breastplate, wings of heavenly power, a cup of holy water, fruit of self-denial, a crown of bright glory, and a dove. The text in the breastplate reads: "Hearken, dear child, to the voice of Wisdom, I have paved thy path with sweet smelling flowers, & thy wayside with pleasant fruits. I placed thee with my own hand in the heart of my Zion upon earth. So be ready and prepared; for when my time doth come I shall call thee to be a light and help to other souls. For I have a place allotted for thee, which thou shalt fill in the beauty of holiness." (Courtesy the Western Reserve Historical Society, Cleveland, Ohio.)

scores of other former Shakers. Kitty June Regan documented the significance of this renewal. "While in meeting," she wrote, "Mother Ann came to revisit her children also Father William & Father James with many of the holy angels to have meeting with us and at the close of our meeting Mother Ann Father William and Father James took their leave of us which was verry affecting." The instruments provided detailed accounts of these spiritual parents and supplied unavailable "historical" and "biographical" data. The younger generation of Believers thus became acquainted with their predecessors in the faith, and the visionists answered a host of questions concerning the biblical, historical, and political past.[159]

The most striking aspect of the theological legacy of the revival period is the stimulus the spirit messages provided for reflection on the nature of the deity. In earlier periods, when Shaker theologians systematized the society's evolving beliefs they articulated the concept of a duality in God, a notion derived logically from the observed order in the natural world. That male-female dichotomy was, in turn, reflected in Jesus and Ann Lee, the Beloved Son and the Beloved Daughter. The dual nature of the godhead thus served to support the messianic mission of Lee. About the deity itself there had been relatively little reflection. The revival changed all that, with the detailed reports of the visitations by Holy Mother Wisdom and the Eternal Father. Now, in spite of the earlier disclaimers by Shaker theologians, the feminine and masculine aspects of God "took on flesh" and acquired personalities. They were no longer abstractions. The Believers conversed and became intimate with them: they ate and drank, washed and bathed, danced and sang together. Holy Mother Wisdom possessed all the traits of an ideal mother, the Eternal Father those of a male counterpart. Each filled conventional roles—the loving, tender mother and the stern, potentially wrathful father. Yet both had the capacity for love and justice, mercy and power.[160]

The revival period also provided new impetus for highlighting the roles of Ann Lee and Lucy Wright in the society's traditions. The same communications that accented the female aspects of God underscored the centrality of these women in the history of redemption. Many of the spirit gifts involved these two figures as well as actions traditionally associated with women. The concern for the motherly qualities of the deity and the celebration of acts of female solicitude—providing food and clothing, expressing tenderness and mercy, displaying love and affection—stamp many of the messages as overtly female in perspective. The domestic character of these discourses is further evidence of the general feminization of

American religion during the nineteenth century. In this way, too, the Shakers were participating in the cultural mainstream.[161]

Paulina Bates at Watervliet, New York, represents the culmination of the tradition of spiritualistic reflection. Her visionary messages were published by the society in 1849 as a companion volume to Stewart's *Sacred and Divine Roll*. The editors of *The Divine Book of Holy and Eternal Wisdom*, Calvin Green and Seth Y. Wells, defended the book's title by stating that "Holy and Eternal Wisdom is the Mother, or Bearing Spirit of all the works of God" and that this publication was "revealed through the line of the female, being Wisdom's *Likeness*." They also testified that "nothing short of the spiritual anointing of heavenly *power* and *wisdom*" could be responsible for "these sacred writings" that were conveyed through an "unlearned" instrument. When Rufus Bishop first heard some of the words received by Bates from Holy Mother Wisdom, he exclaimed, "truly it was some of the sublimest sentences that ever entered my ears, & I was at once convicted that the mortal Instrument never composed it."[162]

The messages received by Bates, who was called "a prophetess unto the Most High," addressed both the inhabitants of the world and the Shakers themselves. Her tone was urgent as she warned of an impending judgment on sinners who were not "prepared by being armed with a Christ-like spirit." She chided, for example, those "who pretend to be sanctified ministers of the gospel" but do not demonstrate the high calling in their lives. Bates attacked the sins of passion that were an abomination before God, including all kinds of fornication. She urged acceptance of the "straight path" of the Shaker gospel. "Man in a state of nature is like wild uncultivated land, which must be subdued before it is fit to receive good seed: so must the heart of man be subdued by confession and repentance, before the seed of the gospel can be planted and profitably cultivated in it." Confession, obedience, and submission to order, according to her, were essential steps toward salvation.[163]

In a section entitled "Word of Mother Ann to the lost inhabitants of the earth," Bates reflected on the life and message of the founder. She extolled Lee as a model: "Mother Ann was a woman of a remarkable strong constitution, of extraordinary powers and invincible fortitude of mind." Even her childhood, described in glowing detail, was paradigmatic for those who wished to be her living spiritual children. Lee's natural infants, by contrast, died tragically. But this, too, Bates turned to providential ends, echoing the judgments of Wisdom. The editors added the following footnote: "It may seem strange to some that Mother should ascribe the death of her infants to the mercy of God; but it must appear evident that the

great work to which she was called, would not admit her to be incumbered
with a family of children; therefore God in mercy took them from her in
the innocence of infancy." During the revival the image of Ann Lee
evolved further. Although the historical facts about the founder lay
shrouded in relative obscurity, during the Era of Manifestations the instruments filled in details concerning Lee's personality and message.[164]

Bates had special counsel for women who thought that they existed
to "be the glory of man, the crown of his enjoyments, and the bright morning star of his existence." That assumption is mistaken, she proclaimed.
"Ye are not called to become defiled and polluted, and to wallow in fleshly
gratifications as a sow walloweth in the mire." There is a better way to "act
the part of a mother, and a bosom friend to your companion." That superior way involves care and cheerfulness in household duties. "Lay your
hand to the distaff," wrote Bates, "and know that it is the diligent hand
that maketh rich, and idleness is the sure threshold to destruction." Likewise, she advised, avoid a "clamorous tongue," do not seek amusement
abroad, and "keep a clean habitation." These traditional Shaker admonitions were intended both for women of the world and for female Believers.[165]

Among the least enduring aspects of the revivals were the religious
ceremonies that came into existence during Mother Ann's Work. Although
some dances and marches remained in use for a time, many quickly passed
from the scene. Special rituals such as the "cleansing gift," or sweeping,
had been abandoned before the end of the 1840s. The hand motions that
later accompanied some songs may have been residuals of such activities,
but the evidence is not conclusive. The mountain feasts were discon-
tinued within a few years. Even at New Lebanon, where the passover
gatherings had come into being, these rituals disappeared and were not
even featured in the collective memory. Not only were the feasts no longer
celebrated, but the sacred sites at the villages soon fell into disrepair, and
some were violated by outsiders. In 1846 the enclosure at New Lebanon
was vandalized: stone altars were desecrated and the fountain stone "de-
faced & broken down." Rufus Bishop wrote, "O Lord God! what can we
ask at thy Almighty hand only that the words of thine own mouth may be
fulfilled speedily upon the author of this sacrilege, that he may, for thine
honor, be brought to repentance." A few years later, the feast ground returned to its natural wild state without extensive commentary from the
ministry. In 1861 the central ministry buried the fountain stone that had
been erected on Holy Mount with the hope that "some hundreds or thousands of years" later someone might exhume it and wonder at its inscription. The Shakers did not establish permanent shrines at these locations.

The rapid desacralization of the holy spaces, aided by a sense of collective embarrassment about the feasts, reflects the underlying Protestant disposition of the Shakers.[166]

The impact of the revivals on the Believers' way of life was considerable for a time. The visiting spirits first called for renewed commitment to traditional patterns of communal living; they reminded the Believers of their obligation to maintain neatness, cleanliness, quiet, civil conversation, and other virtues consistent with the Shaker principles of union and order. But before long the spirits were making greater demands through the instruments, including fasting and other acts of physical mortification, such as prolonged bowing and kneeling. These regimens were designed to promote spiritual purification. The deprivation of food and sleep also contributed to heightened religious sensitivities. The Shakers regarded these disciplines as gestures of believing and belonging. Within a few years the society had received countless prescriptions and prohibitions affecting almost every aspect of personal and communal life. Regulations concerning dress, diet, and daily routines poured forth from the instruments. In some cases, they were rescinded by the ministry shortly after their reception. In other cases, the Believers ignored the new statutes and persisted in their established habits. The 1841 ban on coffee, tea, and pork was a case in point; repeated injunctions by the central ministry failed to secure compliance by all Believers.[167]

The 1845 Millennial Laws are the fullest expression of the corporate asceticism that swept through the ranks of the society. In these expanded regulations the spirit of the revival found expression. Claiming the status of "divine revelation," these "holy laws" sharpened the boundaries between the society and the world, raised the standards of purity among the Believers, and enlarged the areas of supervision by the leaders. Several rules focused on appropriate behavior in the worship setting. "All should go into the meeting in the fear of God walking on their toes," read one of the orders. Another called for abstaining from "meat or fish . . . on the Sabbath . . . except in cases of ill health." The 1845 version expanded the laws dealing with "Intercourse between the Sexes" by specifying forbidden practices. For instance, "cologne water, or any kind of perfumery" was to be avoided before attending meetings, the seats of the brothers and sisters in the meetinghouse were to be no closer than five feet, and all "whispering or blinking" (winking) was prohibited. On the practical side, "Sisters must not mend, nor set buttons on brethren's clothes, while they have them on." The regulations tightened restrictions on relationships with animals and pets, on the use of items "superfluously finished, trimmed or ornamented," and on interaction with the world's people. In other words, it was a systematic attempt to reform and regulate the total environment of the Believers. This ascetic zeal persisted as long as the visitations were under way, but it slacked quickly once the outbursts subsided. By May of 1860 a revised version of "Rules and Orders" eliminated some of the "more exotic features" of the 1845 regulations.[168]

The revivals had indirect economic consequences that have received little attention from historians. The disruptions caused by the spirit visitations inevitably took their toll on the productive activities of the Believers. The instruments sometimes were in trances for hours; those attending were also deflected from normal routines in shop or field, kitchen or Office. During these years religious meetings often occupied more hours than was customary and were more frequent. Although it is impossible to measure exactly the decline in productivity and the attendant losses, the revival clearly did not aid the Believers' efforts to deal with the impact of the panic of 1837.[169]

One enduring result of Mother Ann's Work was the continuing interest in spiritualism among the Shakers after the Era of Manifestations had waned. The belief in spirit communication gained widespread popular support in America after midcentury. The Believers followed this expanding cultural interest with both curiosity and delight. The excitement generated by the "rappings" associated with the Fox sisters in Rochester, New York, affected the society, too. Soon members were hearing "Mysterious Knockings" in answer to questions posed and seeing tables "moved without any possible visible agent." These and other "wonderful manifestations" convinced the Believers of the existence of "an invisible power & agency" that worked to the "confusion of infidels." Mediums from the world visited the villages. The subsequent disclosures of fraud and chicanery did nothing to dampen the Shakers' enthusiasm, for spiritualism became for them and many other Americans a "scientific" defense of religious faith and a guarantee of claims concerning the afterlife. Belief in the reality of the spirits provided solace and comfort to those bereaved by the deaths of family members or friends. This was not lost on the members of the United Society, who confronted death with increasing frequency after 1850 because of the aging of the membership.[170]

Finally, the manifestations confirmed for the Believers a deep sense of their distinctiveness. They spoke of this era as greater than any dispensation since the day of Pentecost. In a subtle but important way the Shakers were claiming for themselves a spiritual superiority over earlier generations, including even the founders. That hubris worried some in the society and no doubt contributed to the growing disenchantment with the revival.[171]

The Changing Situation

Rhetoric cannot mask the failure of the revivals to redirect the evolution of the sect. The Believers were rapidly assimilating into the culture of the United States. Members of the United Society were increasingly conforming to the ways of the world, having abandoned their radical sectarian past. Although they maintained a continuing commitment to certain elements of their tradition—the principle of celibacy, the practice of confession, and communal arrangements—by 1860 the society was changing rapidly. These developments did not please all the Believers.[172]

On the eve of the Civil War, Isaac N. Youngs, then sixty-seven, took stock of the state of affairs and came to a pessimistic conclusion. "In a spiritual view the Chh," he wrote, "is wading thro' much tribulation, and are greatly exposed to feel discouragement, from various causes." He contended that the extensive business enterprises of the Shakers requiring hired help were creating an "undesirable" situation damaging to the Believers' "spiritual travel." Likewise, the members had become "more & more tasty, about clothing, and articles of fancy, the use of high colors, of paint, varnish, &c, . . . than is virtuous or proper." These changes, Youngs maintained, were a product of the expanding intercourse with American society. "It is a day of great improvements, in the world," he noted, "a day of much free thinking and freedom of investigation, every man may judge for himself, &c and this spirit, where there is so much freedom as now unavoidable exists between Believers and the world, insinuates itself powerfully among Believers, which is very injurious to their advancent [sic] in the gospel."[173]

Youngs was not alone in his assessment; reports from various locations throughout the society echoed similar judgments. At Union Village in 1860 "temporal things" were "prospering," and "Spiritual food" was abundant, but "very few Seem to have a realis [sic] for it." The same year Groveland began to hire outside help, and Eldress Lydia Dole wrote of troubles with the "social and spiritual condition" there. When the Enfield, New Hampshire, leadership filed its annual report in 1861, the central ministry declared it a "mournful" account. Even the church at New Lebanon was not immune to these problems; "disorderly union between Brethren & Sisters" had become a major concern there. In the spring of

1861, after visiting with the families at nearby Watervliet, the New Lebanon ministry issued the following summary judgment: "Truly we must say, by conditions we realize in our own bishopric, and those we are advised of by letter from other societies that Zion is wading through deep waters of sufferings and tribulation, much apostasy, much weakness, darkness & loss." The same elements "rending assunder the kingdoms of the world" were also "surging" in the ranks of the Believers, especially "a worldly carnal sense and feeling."[174]

The war raging between the North and the South was another, if not the most obvious, sign of deep-seated ills in America. From the standpoint of traditional Shaker values, participation in the conflict was unthinkable, even if the moral offense of slavery was acknowledged. Before the outbreak of hostilities, the leaders at the North Family in New Lebanon had warned against "partaking of any party spirit that is now existing without in relation to John Brown's invasion at Harpers Ferry." In the midst of the conflict, the central ministry left no doubt about the society's official position. Writing to Canterbury, they stated: "*Believers*, who are *obeyers*, cannot, under any circumstances engage in military servitude of *any name or nature*." This counsel was directed toward Shaker brethren between the ages of eighteen and forty-five who were conscripted. Many, if not most, of those drafted refused service and were fined, though not all resisted. At Union Village, for example, a number of the younger members enlisted on the side of the Union. In the fall of 1862, Benjamin Gates and Frederick W. Evans, acting on behalf of the society, traveled to Washington, D.C., where they met with Abraham Lincoln and other government officials and successfully secured a reprieve for a young Believer named George Ingals. In addition, they received instructions for how other Shakers, if drafted, might attempt to certify their "nonresistant principles, and conscientious scruples" and thus avoid service.[175]

Yet the society, East and West, was inevitably drawn into the conflict. At New Lebanon, the Shakers observed "a day of fasting and prayer" appointed by Lincoln on 4 January 1861. They held a meeting lasting more than four hours filled with exercises, including singing, marching, speaking, and praying. Wartime levies increased the burden of taxation on the Believers. As Giles Avery noted in 1863, the taxes were "enormous." The draft also continued to cause grief. At Shirley, for example, three members of the North Family were called up in 1863. Two were exempted for physical reasons; one failed to report or find a substitute, and he was arrested as a deserter. After extensive negotiations, he was released and excused for poor health. As early as mid-1861 the villages in Kentucky were experiencing hardship at the hands of the secessionists. The Shakers south of the Ohio River hoped to maintain a neutrality consistent with their pacifism, but that plan nearly drove them into poverty as their resources were taxed to the limit by passing armies, both Confederate and Union. The demands for food and lodging exceeded their capacity to meet them. Hay and fodder were requisitioned by the soldiers. Horses and wagons owned by the Believers were "pressed" into service by military officers or paid for with worthless southern scrip. Thievery by guerrilla bands was common; fires, too, destroyed property. At South Union, twenty thousand oak fence rails were burned in federal camp fires.[176]

The anguish and desperation of southern Believers cry out from the pages of their wartime journals. The Kentuckians called the conflict "the most singular and sad spectacle that has ever been witnessed since the creation of the world." Those taking part in it, they wrote, ignore the "unparalleled prosperity, peace & happiness" that the United States government had provided and "rise up without any cause, except disappointed ambition, rivalry & jealousy, and go to fighting like dogs, and butchering & murdering each other, and glorying in their deeds of blood like demons." The Shakers in Kentucky repeatedly were forced to feed large companies of soldiers that moved through their villages or encamped on their lands. One account from the autumn of 1862 tells of "ragged, greasy and dirty troops" in the streets of Pleasant Hill. "Large crowds marched into our yards & surrounded our wells like the locusts of Egypt," wrote the observer, "and struggled with each other for the water as if perishing with thirst; and they thronged our kitchen doors and windows, begging for bread like hungry wolves. We nearly emptied our kitchens of their contents, and they tore the loaves and pies into fragments, and devoured them as eagerly as if they were starving. Some even threatened to shoot others if they did not divide with them." By contrast, the elders at New Gloucester wrote in early 1863 that things were "prospering in general and nothing serious disturbs the calm repose of the Sabbath." For the Kentuckians, however, there was no sanctuary from the war.[177]

During the war years the Shakers came to regard Abraham Lincoln as a special friend and benefactor. In 1864 he thanked them for the gift of a "very comfortable chair" they had sent him, perhaps in gratitude for his favorable decision on the conscription issue. The Believers also followed his activities with concern. In early 1865, when the strain of the war was showing on Lincoln, Evans and Gates wrote to the president:

Esteemed frid,

We are impressed to invite you to our quiet home in Mount Lebanon, as a place of rest for body and mind.

If you prefer, come incog. leaving the President in Washington, to be worshippd and worried by the "Sovereign People." We will meet and receive you as sympathizing friends, brothers and sisters in Christ, who regard you as a servant of God to humanity, on the outer wheel.

We will ask for no favors, and you shall hear no complaints; nor any petitions, except to God for the restoration of your health and that you may be strengthened to accomplish your allotted task in the order of Divine Providence.

Committe in behalf of the Shaker Order

> F. W. Evans,
> B Gates.

Less than a month later, the president was dead, the victim of assassination. Eleven days earlier, according to a later account, Cecelia De Vere at Mount Lebanon had dreamed of a "great crime" perpetrated "at a theatre."[178]

The Shakers were being drawn out of their isolation in other ways, too. They themselves seemed increasingly intent on reaching some accommodation with the larger culture. Perhaps the Believers were driven to this strategy by fears about declining numbers. The membership, 3,627 in 1840, had slipped to 3,489 by 1860, and the losses continued to accelerate. Since the effort to revitalize the society in a traditional religious manner had not succeeded, alternative paths were being explored.[179]

In May 1860 the Millennial Laws were modified, reorganized, and issued anew. These "Rules and Orders" no longer embodied the intense ascetic spirit of the Era of Manifestations. The regulations were reduced to three categories: orders relating to essential religious practices, such as separation from the world, confession of sin, and matters of purity; conditional orders dealing with business, health, and daily routines that were subject to amendment as required; and counsels, or supplementary orders, addressing a variety of topics in detail, items that might be altered as local leaders saw fit. Built into the structure of the 1860 regulations was a spirit of accommodation. This new flexibility soon began to have an impact.[180]

The society's regulations had long declared that the leaders were to monitor and approve all reading matter. Even the Millennial Laws of 1860 stated that "No Books, Pamphlets, or Almanachs of any kind, are allowed to be brought into the family, without the knowledge and approbation of the Elders." Traditionally, the Believers had feared the contaminating influence of books. But a new spirit was becoming evident at Mount Lebanon. Eliza Taylor, a member of the central ministry, wrote in 1864: "Books written upon moral culture, also those pertaining to the arts & sciences of industry, are useful & necessary for Believers to study and practice to a certain extent." (Novel reading, by contrast, would continue to draw negative comment a decade later.) Although Taylor expressed a general caution about religious publications from outside the society, a new openness informed her remarks. The Believers no longer feared the printed word; now they began to seek it out. This small change was symptomatic of a larger switch in perspective.[181]

The fashions of the world were mentioned with increasing frequency in family journals and Shaker records. Looking glasses—formerly forbidden by the Millennial Laws, but now found in growing numbers throughout the villages—mirrored more than the visual image of the Believers; they also reflected a rising concern within the society for style and physical appearance. For men, wigs became popular. Gifts and presents exchanged among members, proscribed by earlier rules, no longer were confined to the spiritual exotica of the Era of Manifestations or to modest tokens of affection; now they included such typical Victorian niceties as cologne and jewelry. Dietary strictures enforced during the revival period were abandoned as the Believers resumed many of their former foodways. Coffee and tea, for example, were available again at several villages before the end of the 1850s. At Pleasant Hill these beverages were initially allowed only at breakfast. Meat eating, even pork, was again debated. Among the Shaker brothers, controversy erupted in the 1850s over beards, signaling a departure from earlier standards calling for clean-shaven faces. Clothing styles changed during the latter years of this Middle Period, allowing more individualism. The Believers began to ignore older rules concerning the decoration and furnishing of their dwellings. As a result, discussions of decorating schemes, wallpaper, carpets, and similar amenities appeared in the public records.[182]

The early severe regulations on the movement of Shakers in the world had been designed to restrict contact with outsiders. After the Era of Manifestations, travel beyond the boundaries of the villages became commonplace, and not just for those Believers responsible for errands and commerce. Outings involving a few members as well as large groups were frequent. Travel to public resorts for recreation or health became common, too. Anna White told of a visit in 1873 to Old Orchard Beach on the Maine coast, where she and other Believers from the North Family at Mount

Lebanon enjoyed the beach and "bathing" in the ocean. An elder and nine young sisters from Sabbathday Lake also spent a day there in late summer 1875. There were regular visits to nearby towns and cities for amusement. The Shakers at South Union enjoyed a day at the fair in nearby Bowling Green, Kentucky. The diaries from these years echo the delight of the Believers in these activities. Such pleasures increasingly replaced the spiritual play of earlier times.[183]

For some conservative Believers, these changes were conclusive evidence of a turn toward worldliness and away from authentic Shaker principles. That was the viewpoint informing Philemon Stewart's manuscript "The Word of the Lord Against the Physical Sins of his Zion," which he received from "the spirit of God." The elders to whom he submitted it, however, rejected the message, telling him to "cease writing anything more to them in the line of Inspiration." Hervey L. Eads at South Union was a far more influential voice for traditionalism within Shakerism. He spent his entire life within the society, having been born in 1807 shortly before his parents joined the community. Educated and trained within the community, at the age of twenty-nine he became the associate of Benjamin S. Youngs in the ministry at South Union. In 1844 he was transferred to Union Village, where he remained, serving in a variety of capacities, until the outbreak of the Civil War, when he returned to Kentucky. For the next three decades until his death, Eads served in the ministry in Kentucky. From that position he became the most articulate and forceful spokesperson for conservative Shaker values.[184]

Many Shakers, however, viewed reconciliation with the world as inevitable and welcomed the reorientation of the society. Powerful voices celebrated new ideas and called for abandoning the radical sectarianism of the past. The most prominent of these Shaker progressives was Frederick W. Evans, an elder at the North Family at New Lebanon. Born in 1808 at Leominster, England, at the age of twelve he emigrated to America with his father and brother George. Binghamton, New York, became their home, and there Evans began to pursue "books and learning." He also acquired a trade and later entered school in Ithaca, where he read philosophy and literature. He and his brother eventually issued a series of working-class publications espousing philosophical materialism and radical politics. They advocated land rights, an end to debtor prisons, equality for women, the abolition of slavery, and delivery of the mails on the Sabbath.[185]

Evans also became a convert to socialism, and in 1830 he set out to find or to found a satisfactory community. In June he visited the Shakers at New Lebanon, who at the time he "supposed were the most ignorant and fanatical people in existence." He was, however, "surprised and impressed by the air of candor and openness" as well as by "the quiet self-repose" he encountered. At the end of a week, he declared the Believers "a society of infidels"—the "highest compliment" he could pay them. He wrote,

> My reason for so concluding was, that all that I, as a philosopher, had repudiated and denounced, in the past religious history of mankind, as false and abominable, and as having turned this earth into a real hell, while they were cutting each other's throats about imaginary heavens and hells, the Shakers also repudiated and denounced, only in stronger terms than I was master of; the power of a man or people for truth and good being measured by their capacity for indignation, and for the "wrath of God revealed from heaven against" falsehood and evil, in all their multifarious forms.

Evans's conversion to Shakerism was not the result of these convictions, however, but rather the product of a series of angelic manifestations, or nightly visitations. These experiences, intermittent over three weeks, restored his "faith in the supernatural" and convinced him of "the existence of a spiritual world, of the immortality of the human soul, and of the possibility and reality of intercommunication between souls in and spirits out of the mortal body." [186]

According to his own retrospective account, Evans came to regard the Shakers as "religionists who were also rationalists," people willing to test their faith by their works. The society's belief in a dual God was confirmed by their commitment to women's rights and "equal suffrage for men and women." The Believers' communal life was an expression of the "Materialistic Socialism" he valued so highly. The spirit visitations at New Lebanon persuaded him "that a God did exist" and that such revelations were dependable. For Evans, choosing Shakerism was therefore a turn toward fideism from agnosticism (fig. 20). Within a few years he rose to a position of leadership in the North Family and soon emerged as the most articulate advocate for progressive Shakerism. [187]

The female counterpart to Evans at the North Family was Antoinette Doolittle, a New Englander, who joined the Shakers at the age of fourteen against the wishes of her family. Many years later she recalled that something "like a voice" directed her, "Go to the Shakers, visit, and learn for yourself who and what they are!" Doolittle began attending prayer meetings, which seemed to open "the way of life and death"; soon she chose the "path" that she would follow for the rest of her life, a way that led to

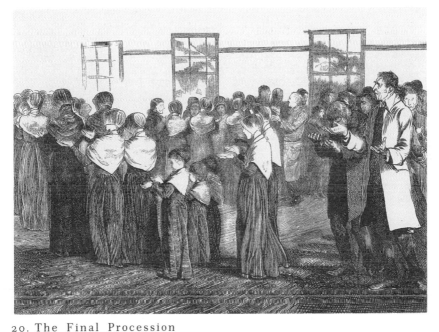

20. The Final Procession
Arthur Boyd Houghton portrayed the Believers at Mount Lebanon in solemn exercises,
palms outward and upward, men and women in separate ranks, the older members
leading the younger. In the center singers clap, keeping time. Frederick Evans is the
tall figure on the right. (*The Graphic*, 14 May 1870.)

leadership at the North Family and considerable public reputation. She
left behind evangelical Christianity and became a powerful spokesperson
for women within Shakerism and for the society's progressive faction.
Doolittle's impact on the Believers and on the outside world was multiplied
severalfold by her influence on a number of talented young women at the
North Family.[188]

Not all seekers during the Middle Period found the society so satisfactory. Some, in fact, revealed the growing inability of Shakerism to sustain the loyalty and commitment of converts and inquirers. Michael H.
Barton, a much-traveled young man of thirty-three, and formerly a Quaker
preacher by his own account, visited the Harvard village on his way west
to "join with the Mormonites." Author of a serial publication entitled
Something New, a proposal for reform of the alphabet, Barton was seized
with conviction and "gave himself up to become a humble Shaker." His
conversion in the autumn of 1831 attracted a great deal of attention. The

Harvard ministry wrote that he appeared "to be a man of sound mind and good abilities." Although married, Barton testified that he and his wife "had no confidence in the flesh and had kept themselves." Over the next ten months Barton's activities were regularly noted in village records— meeting with one or another elder, traveling on business, or addressing public meetings. He quickly gained the confidence of the leadership. Even Seth Y. Wells at New Lebanon was impressed with his linguistic pro- posals, although he was doubtful about how quickly the public would ac- cept them.[189]

But all signs were not favorable. Early in Barton's stay among the Shakers, to the embarrassment of the Massachusetts leaders, he violated society conventions by writing "out of order" to Calvin Green and other leaders at New Lebanon. By late summer 1832 Barton had become en- tangled with another convert of Quaker background, Warder Cresson, a contemporary and probably a former acquaintance, who hailed from a wealthy Philadelphia family. Cresson, also intensely religious, had partici- pated in the conflicts that resulted in the Hicksite separation within Quakerism. He had attacked the wealth and privilege of many in the So- ciety of Friends and called for the cultivation of greater spiritual virtues. By early 1829 he had left the Quaker meeting, and the next year he pub- lished a rousing denunciation of the Friends in Pennsylvania. In his pub- lication he also addressed social issues, including bank charters, lotteries, taverns, and political corruption. He echoed Robert Owen's call for "so- cial communities" based on equality for all, especially the working class. Cresson expressed his approval of Shakerism by inserting in his text an excerpt from the *Testimony*.[190]

Cresson was living with his family in the New Lebanon area by 1831, but his involvement with the Shakers began to cause the Believers consternation when he fell under the influence of a "zealous enthusiast from England" who came to America to warn of "terrible judgments" about to befall the land. The two traveled around Philadelphia, preaching and prophesying on the streets. By April 1832 they were shouting their message outside the meetinghouse at New Lebanon. On at least one occa- sion, Cresson even carried on inside the Shaker meeting. In mid-Septem- ber Barton and Cresson joined cause and departed from the society, intent on "a religious tour." The ministry at Harvard said that "confinement to the cross" was too much for Barton to endure; the leaders at New Lebanon regarded Cresson as mentally unbalanced. Barton became a controversial lecturer, displaying his charismatic gifts—healing, prophecy, and speak- ing in tongues—in the Millerite movement; Cresson pursued his interests in religion, reform, communal societies, and Near Eastern politics. In 1844 he received a commission as the first American consul to Jerusalem. Four years later he converted to Judaism and settled permanently in Palestine.[191]

Another unusual convert to Shakerism during the Middle Period was Rebecca Cox Jackson, a free black woman who left her husband and extended family in the Philadelphia area to become an itinerant preacher. Born in 1795, her earliest religious nurture had been in the context of the African Methodist Episcopal Church. According to Jean McMahon Humez, Jackson spent her adult years questing for "a spiritual 'family' that would integrate her religious life and her personal and social relationships into a seamless, shining fabric." She was a visionary who followed the lead of dreams and inner voices. On the basis of such instructions, Jackson renounced sexual intercourse with her husband and began a routine of rigorous self-discipline in her search for sanctification. She was gifted in a variety of ways.[192]

Jackson's first contact with the Shakers came in the fall of 1836 at Watervliet, New York. Seven years later, in 1843, she visited the village again and was attracted by the Believers' collective way of life and by their commitment to the principle of holiness. They, in turn, seemed to have been impressed with her spiritual powers. From 1847 to 1851 Jackson and her intimate friend Rebecca Perot lived at the South Family, which was the Gathering Order at Watervliet. She worked as a seamstress in the village, but also preached frequently in public meetings. She left the Albany area for Philadelphia, where despite resistance from the leadership at Watervliet, she attempted to recruit other blacks to her new faith. At the same time she became heavily involved in the practice of seance spiritualism. In 1857 Jackson returned for another year to the New York village. Before her second departure, she secured the official blessing of Eldress Paulina Bates for her undertaking in the City of Brotherly Love, where she and Perot began to hold Shaker meetings in 1859. They gathered a small group of Believers in that city, mostly black women, who lived at several sites. This urban cell of Shakers continued under Perot's direction after Jackson died in 1871.[193]

During the Middle Period the United Society drew new members from Millerism, another popular religious movement that gained widespread attention throughout the United States in the 1840s. The Millerites were the followers of the "adventist" preacher William Miller, a deist turned Baptist, who had calculated a timetable for the return of Christ to the earth. His apocalyptic message struck a responsive chord among

Americans in the late 1830s and early 1840s. Large numbers joined the cause, and even more were drawn into the excitement. The Shakers were no exception. In the summer of 1842 a Millerite lecturer named Beach (probably Augustus Beach) visited the North Family at New Lebanon and tried to convince the Believers, using biblical prophecy, that "Christ would make his second Appearance and this world would be consumed by fire" in the next year. The ministry noted his sincerity, but opined that they would be glad "to have the world burned up" and they did not care how soon, because they believed the world was "the lust of the flesh." [194]

When the Millerite prophecies concerning Christ's return were not fulfilled, disappointment and disillusionment gripped many of the adventists. Some, though chastened, recovered sufficiently to remain committed. Others pursued new religious options, including Shakerism. The Believers welcomed the disappointed, hoping to attract them into the society. In the East, for example, the central ministry permitted the adventists to hold a camp meeting on land at Enfield, Connecticut. Immediately following that gathering, the Believers conducted their own public meeting, with six to seven thousand "spectators." On that occasion the sisters served one thousand meals of baked beans and "meat with puddings." In the West, Believers from Whitewater attended adventist gatherings in Cincinnati. Estimates of the number of former Millerites who converted to the society range as high as two hundred in the West, many of whom joined the Whitewater community outside Dayton. Substantial numbers also converted in the East, especially at Harvard, Canterbury, and Enfield, New Hampshire. [195]

Among the Millerite converts none was more prominent than Enoch Jacobs, who had served as editor of the *Western Midnight Cry,* an adventist newspaper in Cincinnati. Following the Great Disappointment, he used the publication—renamed the *Day-Star*—to discuss the merits of Shakerism. Jacobs, who had been present at the Enfield camp meeting, proved extremely effective in attracting former Millerites to the society in both the East and the West. The Believers, in turn, assisted with the printing and distribution of his newspaper. Late in 1846 he, his wife, and his family took up residence at Union Village. Lawrence Foster has suggested that Jacobs and other Millerites found the society attractive because the Believers took seriously the second coming. Yet many adventists, including Jacobs, had great difficulty with the principle of celibacy. In mid-1847 he left the society, announcing that he preferred to "go to hell with Electra his wife than live among the Shakers without her." Unfortunately for the

Believers, a large number of the other adventists also departed within a few years.[196]

In 1848 Pleasant Hill was visited by Anders Bloomberg and Olof Stenberg, missionaries sent by Erik Jansson, the leader of Bishop Hill, a utopian community founded in 1846 near Galesburg, Illinois. These dissidents from the Church of Sweden recognized a measure of common cause with the Shakers. The Janssonists believed in the perfectibility of human nature and the possibility of living without sin. More than twelve hundred followers had journeyed to America, eight hundred of whom settled in Illinois. The residents of Bishop Hill, however, did not live a celibate life, and the Shaker principle of "the cross" soon divided the two missionaries. Only Bloomberg was persuaded by the Believers, and he and his family joined the community at Pleasant Hill. In 1850 Jansson was murdered by a disgruntled follower involved in a matrimonial conflict. His death and recurrent economic problems brought Bishop Hill to the brink of collapse. In the mid-1850s a number of Janssonists left that colony and entered Pleasant Hill. Among these converts was Anna Jansson, the widow of the former leader. Her stay, however, was short, as were those of many others who came from the Illinois community. "Swedish blood," wrote one Shaker, "is as much opposed to the Cross as any other."[197]

Bloomberg, an exception to this general pattern, became an elder at the West Lot in Pleasant Hill. In 1866–1867 he journeyed to his homeland to assist a number of families who had accepted Shaker ideals. After ten months, he returned to America with several Swedish converts, and others followed later. Eventually nearly sixty immigrants came to Pleasant Hill from Sweden. Once again, however, most of these newcomers stayed only a short time. The keeper of the ministry journal at Pleasant Hill was soon noting the steady departure of these persons by references to the "Swede Stampede" and "Swede trotting." This outreach effort was at best a limited success, although the 1880 census listed 13.7 percent of all Shakers in the United States as foreign born.[198]

The diversity of newcomers in the Middle Period can also be charted by the admissions to one family during a restricted period. The North Family, or Gathering Order, at South Union recorded twenty newcomers between 21 July and 21 October 1872. John Rees Cooper, the First Elder at that family, identified ten of the twenty as between twenty and forty years of age; nine of the individuals were not identified by age, although three were children and one an elderly woman (see table 3). Three persons were foreign born, one each from England, Scotland, and Germany. Five were described as suffering some bodily disability. Nearly all were

Table 3
North Family Converts at South Union in 1872

Name	Age	Vocation	Comments
John Dudley Smith*		Tailor	Walks with cane
Edward Louis Pottinger*	23	Schoolteacher, merchant, farmer	
William Richardson Meason*	28	Farmer	Something wrong with left eye
Sally his wife*			
Three children*			One child died
William Denis Roy*	20	Tailor	Something wrong with right eye
J. William Williams*	40	Shoemaker, Baptist exhorter	Diseased eyes
Reubin Gaines	Returned from world		Pitiable looking object
Sarah Horn*	Returned from world		Looking none the better
Charles Herman Ludwig*	23	Painter	One deformed foot
John Hopper	40	Farmer	Englishman
John Becker†		Gardener	German
Margaret Marks†			
James Graves	21	Farmer	
George Mason	41	Carpenter, chairmaker	
John Alexander Dickson	34	Carpenter	Scotchman
Charley Brown	34	Broom maker	
Louisa McCuen	71		

* Left between 21 July and 21 October
† Left between 21 October and 21 December

listed as skilled in trades or agriculture. By the end of the three months, ten of the twenty had left South Union, one had died, and eight of the remaining nine had spent fewer than forty-five days at the village. Three months later two more had left. The data suggest an astonishing movement of newcomers in and out of the society. The motives of these individuals are unclear.[199]

None of the converts discussed above merits the label "typical." All were part of the increasingly diverse population drawn to the society.

Some stayed with the Shakers only a short time, others for the balance of their lives. The United Society offered each something that was attractive at least temporarily, but these individuals also imported their own ideas and experiences into the community. These were years of growing demographic complexity within the United Society. The principal lines of division were no longer only between generations, the East and the West, and central versus local authority. Now a new schism emerged within the society, between a progressive party centered on the North Family in New Lebanon and a traditionalist faction identified with the central ministry and scattered leaders throughout the society.[200]

By 1860 the leadership at New Lebanon had passed into the hands of Daniel Boler and Giles B. Avery on the male side and Betsey Bates and Eliza Ann Taylor in the female order. The ministry who had directed the fortunes of the society for nearly three decades of the Middle Period had passed from the scene. Ebenezer Bishop, chronically ailing for many years, died in October 1849 "as calmly as if he was falling asleep, just as the Sun was falling below the horizon." He was followed less than a year later by Ruth Landon, and Rufus Bishop died in August 1852 while on yet another trip to the West. Asenath Clark, the last of the four who had succeeded Lucy Wright, died near the end of 1857, thus closing a remarkable period of continuity in the leadership at New Lebanon. Their average age at the time of death was seventy eight. Their successors, by contrast, averaged only fifty in 1857. This transfer of authority therefore also represented a shift to a new generation. For the first time, too, one of the members of the central ministry was not a native easterner. Daniel Boler had joined the society in South Union, Kentucky, but he had served as an elder in the Church Order in the East for nearly twenty years before joining the central ministry. Giles Avery had logged many years as an elder in the Center Family at New Lebanon before being advanced to the leadership of the society. Likewise, Betsey Bates had been an eldress in the Church Order at New Lebanon for nearly two decades before being elevated in 1852. Five years later Eliza Ann Taylor joined her as second in the female lead.[201]

These same decades witnessed the passing of a generation of intellectual leaders. Seth Y. Wells, one of the society's principal theologians in the East, died in 1847 at the age of eighty "He testified his unshaken confidence in the gospel of our holy Savior, and blessed Mother to the last," reported his long-time associate and friend Calvin Green. At his funeral two instruments confirmed his testimony "in a very impressive manner." Benjamin S. Youngs, Wells's counterpart in the West for many years, died in 1855 at eighty-one, and his brother, Isaac N. Youngs, died in 1865 at the age of seventy-two. Two other leading figures from this period, Calvin Green and Freegift Wells, died in 1869 and 1871 at the ages of eighty-nine and eighty-six, respectively. Boler and Avery attempted to carry forward the more traditional outlook. They were joined in this task by several individuals, including Hervey L. Eads at South Union, Alonzo G. Hollister at Mount Lebanon, and Henry C. Blinn at Canterbury, to name but a few. None of these Believers, however, would leave as deep a mark on the society's beliefs as the intellectuals of the preceding generation.[202]

As the years passed, the society seemed less sure of itself and of its ability to attract and retain new members. Defections continued without abatement at nearly every village. Cornelia Vaughn and Josephine Shephersan, for example, ran away from Watervliet, New York, in the summer of 1867. Some of the brethren went to search for them and found them "in bed in a tavern" about a mile from the village. They brought the two girls back, kept them for the night, and the next day returned Josephine and a younger sister to their mother in Albany. Harsh words were common for those who abandoned the ranks of the Believers. When fourteen-year-old Lizzie Chapman left the First Order at Mount Lebanon, the ministry described her as "coarse, worldly, [and] vile." After his departure from the Second Family, Otis Barker was called a "dishonest pretender." When nearly a dozen members of the Clement family jointly defected from the South and Second families, the official record declared that they had returned "to the world, from which they had never been spiritually cut off." The language reflects the Believers' deep fears and anxieties about these losses.[203]

Along with apostasy went continuous legal problems throughout the Middle Period. The Believers at Pleasant Hill reported in 1828 that they had paid out nearly $5,000 over the previous two years to apostates and lawyers, and owed $2,700 more. Furthermore, their legal struggles with a group of defectors were not yet finished. They were forced to lobby with the Kentucky legislature for laws to protect their property from seizure. All of the villages faced nuisance suits from apostates and short-term members. In 1844 the ministry at New Gloucester reported with relief that John Pierce had relinquished the idea of suing for wages not paid him by the Shakers during the time they had taken in him and his family, "bringing up his children and paying his debts." Had he persisted, they wrote, it "would be like being hung and paying forty shillings." Litigation involving the custody of children entrusted to the society plagued the Shakers. The

Believers at New Lebanon struggled with William Pillow for nearly four years over indentures. At Hancock during the same period, John Irving tried to remove his children from Shaker custody by force before turning to the courts. These legal struggles, repeated at nearly every village, cost the Believers money, time, and goodwill. When they lost court cases, the settlements were often expensive. In 1871, for example, the central ministry reported a new debt of $6,000 at Enfield, New Hampshire, as the result of a lawsuit. The net effect of the increasing interaction with American society was therefore mixed.[204]

The View from the Outside

During the middle decades of the century, a growing number of outsiders visited Shaker villages and recorded their conflicting impressions. Among the visitors were many persons of prominence, including writers and celebrities. James Fenimore Cooper, after inspecting Hancock, New Lebanon, and Watervliet, praised the outward appearance of the settlements. In spite of the order and cleanliness, however, he depicted the Believers as "deluded fanatics" because of their strange worship activities. Ralph Waldo Emerson was equally condescending about the life situation of the Shakers, which he described as a "protestant monastery," a place inhabited by "a set of clean, well disposed, dull & incapable animals." He made it clear that he had no desire to put on their "drab cowl." Charlotte Cushman, a popular entertainer on the American stage, was moved to verse by her contacts with the Believers.

> Mysterious Worshippers!
> Are you indeed the things you seem to be,
> Of earth—yet of its iron influence free
> From all that stirs
> Our being's pulse, and gives to fleeting life
> What well the Hun has termed, "the rapture of the strife"?

She, too, evoked the image of the "monking band," contrasting the plight of the sisters with the "mirth and revelry" of a bridal scene in the world. To Cushman, Shaker women seemed "cold and passionless."[205]

Other individuals associated with Transcendentalism in New England also wrote about the society. Elizabeth Peabody, an educational reformer interested in communal experiments, complimented the Shakers for their material success, but criticized them for the prosperity in their communities, which had cultivated "the desire of wealth" among them.

Another casualty of their "fanaticism," she added, was "personal individuality." Charles Lane, an editor and social reformer in England who came to America and financed the short-lived experiment at Fruitlands, Massachusetts, called on the Shakers at nearby Harvard more than once. In 1843, following a visit in the company of Bronson Alcott, Lane wrote favorably about the communal arrangements, although he thought the Believers had become too dependent on a cash economy for the purchase of meat, milk, coffee, and tea. He recommended a diet free from such foods, which would provide greater economic and spiritual freedom. Lane read several Shaker publications, including the *Summary View*. When Fruitlands disbanded in 1844, he and his son joined the Believers at Harvard for seventeen months before returning to England. In a published letter he later suggested that the Shakers were often unfairly slandered. Yet he, too, criticized them for "spiritual despotism" and mistaken judgments about education.[206]

Foreigner travelers often stopped at Shaker villages, drawn by curiosity and local reputation. Touring America between 1827 and 1831, the English gentlewoman Frances Trollope found herself too fatigued to visit the village at South Union, but she had no reluctance in echoing the "shaking Quaker stories" brought back by some gentlemen companions. The Shakers, she wrote, became "rich and powerful" when they established colonies. Their products were of the highest quality, but their religious activities were "most grotesque." Another English woman and writer, Harriet Martineau, visited the Believers at New Lebanon and Hancock a few years later. She, too, found their material accomplishments exceptional, but was harshly critical of their religious and social patterns. "If happiness lay in bread and butter, and such things," she wrote, "these people have attained the *summum bonum*." Their "way of life," by contrast, she found visibly absurd: "all dull work and no play." Martineau had little patience with the principle of celibacy or with the Believers' religious exercises, which she found repulsive. She accused them of pride and vanity and castigated them for mental and intellectual grossness. The Swedish novelist and reformer Frederika Bremer, after visiting New Lebanon and Canterbury, called the Shaker villages "the most rational, and probably the happiest of all conventual institutions." She viewed the society as a "misunderstood sect and a refuge for people in need."[207]

Perhaps the most celebrated traveler from abroad was Charles Dickens, whose contact with the Shakers at New Lebanon came on a single day in June 1842, at the height of the Era of Manifestations. To his consternation, he was barred from observing the worship services, for the meetings had been closed to the public. In his observations on America, Dickens published an extremely negative account of the Believers, depicting their life as grim and foreboding. He poked fun at the physical appearance of the persons who inhabited this "gloomy silent commonwealth." Although he acknowledged their reputation for honesty and fairness in business transactions, he accused them of destroying the "healthful graces" of life and its "innocent pleasures." He described their worship as "unspeakably absurd" and "infinitely grotesque," though he had never witnessed it himself. Content to parrot hostile judgments about the Shakers, he charged that they took in as "proselytes, persons so young that they cannot know their own minds" on religious matters. Dickens, no friend of "closed religious societies," lumped the Shakers "among the enemies of Heaven and Earth, who turn the water at the marriage feasts of this poor world, not into wine but gall." [208]

Other commentators also had differing reactions. Horace Greeley, after "some personal acquaintance," praised the Believers for conquering the appetites of "Lust, Avarice, Ambition, Revenge" and banishing "Pauperism and Servitude." He also complimented them on their "spirit of devotion to the common good." The German socialist Friedrich Engels, after reading travel accounts, declared the Shakers the "first people to set up a society on the basis of community of goods in America, indeed in the whole world." He described their situation as ideal because they were "free, wealthy and happy." Thomas Low Nichols, one of the founders of the Memnonia colony in Yellow Springs, Ohio, pointed to the "striking peculiarities" of the Believers, but praised their accomplishments, even though their life was spartan. He found "the perfection of order and neatness" everywhere at Union Village. Another traveler, by contrast, spoke disparagingly about the "pale and sickly hue" of the sisters and the "bad complexions" of the men at that Ohio location. [209]

After visiting the Believers at Canterbury in 1831, Nathaniel Hawthorne wrote, "On the whole, they lead a good and comfortable life, and if it were not for their ridiculous ceremonies, a man could not do a wiser thing than to join them." At that time he may have been toying with the idea of joining the society. He later changed his mind and became openly hostile, influenced perhaps by his reading of Thomas Brown's *Account of the People Called Shakers*. After an 1851 visit to Hancock, even the physical accommodations of the Believers became the object of his attack. Commenting on arrangements in the dwellings, he wrote, "The fact shows that all their miserable pretence of cleanliness and neatness is the thinnest superficiality; and that the Shakers are and must needs be a filthy set. And then their utter and systematic lack of privacy; the close function of man with man, and supervision of one man over another—it is hateful and disgusting to think of; and the sooner the sect is extinct the better—a consummation which, I am happy to hear, is thought to be not a great many years distant."[210]

Hawthorne drew on his knowledge of the Shakers in the composition of two short stories published during the 1830s. "The Canterbury Pilgrims" tells of the encounter between a group of pilgrims going to Canterbury and two young lovers fleeing the village by night for a new life in the world. Each of the pilgrims relates a tale of sorrow and woe. Even true love, they warn, ultimately will betray and lead to misery. Their narratives, Hawthorne observed, were "shadowy omens of disappointed hope and unavailing toil, domestic grief and estranged affection, that would cloud the onward path of these poor fugitives." Despite all this, the "melancholy band" of pilgrims continues on to Canterbury, a place of security like "that other refuge of the world's weary outcasts, the grave." The two lovers, Josiah and Miriam, also go on their way "with chastened hopes" to "an untried life."[211]

Hawthorne incorporated many of the same themes into a second piece of fiction. "The Shaker Bridal," a tale set in an imaginary village, focuses on the transfer of authority from the aging Father Ephraim to Adam Colburn and Martha Pierson, two faithful Believers who in their former life had been childhood friends and youthful lovers. Misfortune had struck both, and they deferred their marriage. After many years Adam proposes that they join the Believers. "Martha, faithful still, had placed her hand in that of her lover, and accompanied him to the Shaker village." There they find "security against evil fortune," but for Hawthorne it was the same "peace and quiet" found in the "gloom and coldness" of the tomb. Now years later the two have been chosen to lead the village as the Father and the Mother. Standing before the assembled elders, they are to pledge their faithfulness to the society. Adam declares with confidence his readiness to accept the trust. Martha, who possesses "a woman's heart," pales and trembles, looking more and more "like a corpse in its burial clothes." She speaks the proper words, but her heart breaks and she sinks "down at the feet of her early lover." Hawthorne used the parody of a wedding to equate joining "this strange people" with accepting a living death.[212]

Herman Melville resorted to a different form of ridicule in his fiction. His acquaintance with the Shakers came both from visiting and from reading the *Summary View*. In *Moby Dick* he places a series of jeremiadic warnings for Captain Ahab in the mouth of an eccentric prophet named Gabriel, who had been "nurtured among the crazy society of Neskyeuna

Shakers." According to Ishmael, in the "secret meetings" of the Believers Gabriel had descended through a trapdoor to announce the "speedy opening of the seventh vial, which he carried in his vest-pocket." Melville's ridicule played on a caricature of prophecy and apocalyptic. Critics have suggested that Melville also may have used Warder Cresson, whom he met on a journey to the Middle East, as a prototype for Nathan, his central character in the long poem *Clarel: A Poem and Pilgrimage to the Holy Land*. The spiritual odysseys of Cresson and Nathan both led ultimately to Judaism. In Melville's judgment, Shakerism was linked inescapably with religious extremism.[213]

Artemus Ward, the nineteenth-century humorist created by Charles F. Browne, viciously satirized the Believers in *Vanity Fair*. On an imaginary visit to a Shaker village, Ward coaxed two young sisters, "as putty and slick lookin gals as I ever met," to play "Puss in the corner," after which he attempted to kiss them (fig. 21). On another occasion, he found the grumpy Elder Uriah and an older Shaker hugging and kissing "like young lovers in their gushingist state." They explained their actions, he quipped, as the product of a fit over which Uriah had no control. Ward complimented the Believers for their cleanliness, neatness, and industry, but he declared their religion "small pertaters." "You mope away your lives here in single retchidness, and as you air all by yourselves nothing ever conflicks with your pecooler idees." On balance, he observed, "It's a unnatral, onreasonable and dismal life you're leadin here." The laughs he drew were at the expense of the Shakers, whom he portrayed as oversexed, naive simpletons.[214]

These depictions by outsiders reinforced a growing popular image of the Shakers as exemplars of cleanliness and industry as well as advocates of strange sexual ideas and bizarre religious practices. The apparent tension between these viewpoints made the Shakers all the more interesting to a curious public. The Believers' preoccupation with physical cleanliness was seen by some as a cover for their unnatural sexual habits. Their reputation for hard work seemed inconsistent with their devotion to strange spiritual labors, especially during the Era of Manifestations.[215]

Some outsiders capitalized on the Believers' paradoxical image. Beginning in 1846, a group of former Shakers from Canterbury traveled throughout the country, offering paying audiences public performances patterned after the Believers' worship. They reenacted ecstatic gifts, such as whirling and trances; they marched, danced, and sang. These concerts by apostates were a source of special aggravation to members of the society who took out advertisements in newspapers disclaiming any associa-

21. Artemus Ward among the Shakers
"When we broke up, sez I, 'my pretty dears, ear I go you hav no objections, hav you, to a innersent kiss at partin?'" (From [Charles Brown Farrar], *Artemus Ward, His Book,* 1865.)

tion with these shameless mockeries. During the same period, Shakerism became a subject for melodrama. In 1848 Daniel Pierce Thompson, a Vermont novelist, wrote a brief tale entitled "The Shaker Lovers," which told of two young Believers in love who wished to escape from the society. The villain in the story was a Shaker elder who was both a zealot and a "voluptuary." Thompson's work was the basis for a one-act drama of the same name performed as early as 1849 in Boston and several other cities. The play also included singing and dancing. Public curiosity increasingly focused on the problems created by celibacy and on the unique worship patterns of the Believers. No longer were the founders or the doctrines of the society at the center of contention. Absorption into the world of popular culture was itself a further measure of accommodation with the world. Outsiders no longer feared the Believers. Ridicule was a sufficient weapon against any remaining threat from the society.[216]

By contrast, one of the most sympathetic portraits of the Shakers in the popular media during this period came from Benson John Lossing, a well-known American historian and "the first of the great American photojournalists." Lossing, who lived in Poughkeepsie, visited New Lebanon for two days in 1856 and was hosted much of the time by Frederick Evans. Lossing inspected shops, spoke with Believers, and attended a public meeting as well as a union meeting. Throughout his stay he took notes and made pencil sketches, using a camera lucida. The following year Lossing published an unsigned essay illustrated with eighteen woodcuts in *Harper's New Monthly Magazine,* a major national periodical. This article played a significant role in shaping a more positive public image of the Shakers.[217]

"Order and Neatness there held high court with a majesty I had never before seen," wrote Lossing. He was equally complimentary of the Shakers' business ventures, which he observed were "carried on with exact economy." In spite of the "contempt and ridicule" heaped on their meetings, he found the worship curious but "deeply impressive," the exercises "graceful" and the music "beautiful." Lossing's description of the society's beliefs, drawn in part from their own publications, was restrained and largely nonjudgmental. His account of its history was matter-of-fact, except when he declared that Ann Lee had become "a *Pontifex Maximus*—a very Pope in authority," a characterization bound to arouse animosity among many readers. He closed his essay by complimenting the Believers for their hospitality and benevolence, their integrity and faith. Lossing was confident that it was "impossible for any candid man, after becoming acquainted with their character, to regard them otherwise than with the deepest respect." His text and the accompanying woodcuts presented the Shakers in a very favorable light.[218]

Little more than a decade later, the English traveler William Hepworth Dixon published an even more complimentary portrait of the Believers in his *New America,* a publication that went through multiple editions in both England and America as well as several translations before 1870. Through his work thousands learned about the Shakers. Dixon, who set out to examine the forces at work in American society, celebrated the "large love of Liberty" and the "deep sense of Religion" that were influential throughout the United States. He was especially interested in the operation of those "master passions" in three religious experiments that attracted his curiosity—Mormonism, the Oneida community led by John Humphrey Noyes, and the Shakers. Of the three, he was most positively impressed with the Believers.[219]

Dixon devoted six chapters to the physical circumstances, social principles, history, and religious beliefs of the Shakers. He found Mount Lebanon "prim and yet picturesque," a place of "peace and innocence" he likened to Eden. Each of the buildings, no matter how used, "has something of the air of a chapel." But he was especially impressed with the agricultural accomplishments and skills of the Believers, who "get more out of the earth by love" than others get by craft. "The Granary is to a Shaker what the Temple was to a Jew," wrote Dixon, who spent his time at the North Family with Evans and Doolittle, whom he described as possessing a "wedlock of the soul." He also compared the residents at Mount Lebanon to monks and nuns who "live for God alone." The village, he observed, "strikes you as a place where it is always Sunday." The Believers are "never angry, never peevish, never unjust."[220]

Dixon believed that Mount Lebanon had a "magnetic power," and the Believers a spiritual and moral force beyond their numbers. He commented extensively on their spiritualism, which he linked with the notion that Ann Lee "did not die, as mortal men and women die," but rather was "transfigured and transformed." Accordingly, she lives forever among her resurrection children, where "there is no marriage; only love and peace." The Shakers, Dixon reported, did not condemn marriage for others, but they did regard their own regenerate, celibate existence as superior to the life of generation. He also noted that the society had benefited from the revivals in America. In sum, he wrote, "Mount Lebanon is the centre of a system which has a distinct genius, a strong organization, a perfect life of its own, through which it would appear to be helping to shape and guide, in no slight and unseen measure, the spiritual career of the United States." Dixon was one of the first observers to romanticize the Shakers. He created the image of an idealized society in the face of a rapidly changing, deteriorating situation.[221]

The Closing of the Middle Period

By 1870 all factions in the United Society agreed that drastic steps were needed to offset the "universal declension in the religious element." In the judgment of many Believers, religion had "lost its vitality" throughout the United States. In June the central ministry wrote a circular letter to the villages in which they lamented the "unfaithfulness in Zion" evidenced by declining numbers. A few "weak souls," they noted, were even intimating that the gospel was "running out." But, the ministry declared, "God forbid that his Zion should perish; for, She is His vicegerent on the earth." As a partial corrective, the leaders at Mount Lebanon proposed that the Believers "in every society and family" unite each Sabbath evening at half past seven in a "universal gift of prayer," beginning on 7 August and "continuing until God shall return unto Zion in mercy." On the designated date, the Believers at Pleasant Hill and elsewhere did exactly that, substituting a prayer meeting for a regular union meeting. In addition to this concert of prayer, the central ministry recommended that every opportunity be taken to spread "the Gospel Testimony among the world" to bring stability to the United Society and to reverse its membership losses.[222]

During these last years of the Middle Period, the Believers launched an active missionary program, the likes of which had not been seen in the society since the days of the western expansion. Select members traveled alone, in pairs, or in large groups, and lectured about the Shaker gospel to those who would listen. Emmory Brooks, while visiting the eastern villages, preached at Hartford, Connecticut, where he reported considerable success in gaining a sympathetic audience. In the West, by contrast, Thomas McRae's "preaching trip" into Nicholas County, Kentucky, was not a success. After two weeks he returned to Pleasant Hill, "having cast his bread upon the waters, but made no proselytes." Frederick Evans (fig. 22) and George A. Lomas, a talented young Believer from New York City, headed a delegation of Believers lecturing at a joint meeting of Shakers and spiritualists in Troy, New York, in March 1872. Their presentations and that of Antoinette Doolittle were later published. The Shakers sponsored "missionary meetings" patterned after the manner of other protracted religious gatherings. In June 1872, for example, Evans, Doolittle, and leaders from Alfred, Sabbathday Lake, Shirley, and Harvard, as well as singers from Canterbury and Enfield, New Hampshire, participated in a series of public meetings at Portland, Maine. On one occasion, the local media reported, the attendance was estimated at three thousand persons. Similar gatherings, also in concert with the spiritualists, were held at Cleveland, Ohio, and Farmington, Maine, as well as at Albany, Brooklyn, and elsewhere.[223]

One series of missionary meetings in Boston involved more than fifty Believers from several villages. While in that city they lodged at the Marlboro House, where they organized themselves into the "regular order of a Shaker family." The meetings were held at several locations, including the Music Hall, which they filled to capacity. The Believers marched "in

22. Frederick W. Evans
An elder at the North Family at Mount Lebanon, New York, Evans was the leading
spokesperson for progressive Shakerism. (Courtesy Shaker Museum and Library, Old
Chatham, New York.)

Shaker fashion" between their hotel and the meeting place, attracting
considerable curiosity from the public. The Canterbury singers greeted
those entering the hall with traditional Shaker songs. Union meetings
held before the services were filled with "spiritual manifestations." Frederick Evans presided on the platform, lecturing and answering questions
from the audience. These gatherings took on the character of public performances, "sacred theatre" of a kind different from that in the Age of the
Founders. Here the curious and the inquiring might find entertainment or
information. The Believers, performing for the onlookers, hoped to impress with song and dance and speech.[224]

The United Society also sent missionaries abroad to spread the word.

In July 1871 Evans took the first of two trips to England, where he held a variety of meetings. He was accompanied on the trip by his friend James M. Peebles, "one of the better-known spiritualist lecturers" in America. Writing from London, Evans told of widespread interest in "the subject of Shakerism." When he spoke at St. George's Hall, W. H. Dixon chaired the meeting. According to Peebles's recollections, "members of Parliament, distinguished journalists, noted clergymen, secularists and spiritualists" were present. Evans "shocked" the audience with his radical social ideas, but he "delighted" them with his simple, sincere religious appeal. Shakerism and spiritualism were linked closely wherever Evans and Peebles traveled. The trip abroad, a homecoming of sorts for Evans, was considered a great success. He wrote, "If a Shaker Society could be founded here, I see nothing to hinder its succeeding." When he sailed for America on 24 August, "a party of proselytes" accompanied him. In the years that followed, a few more persons of English extraction joined the society, but they were never great in number.[225]

The most significant missionary initiative undertaken by the society was the inauguration of a monthly publication, initially entitled *The Shaker*, which sold for fifty cents per annum. This journal, "devoted to the exposition of religion, according to Shaker theology," carried on its masthead a favorite Bible passage of the Believers from Haggai 2:7, "I will shake all nations, and the desire of all nations shall come; and I will fill this house with glory, saith the Lord." First edited by George Lomas at Watervliet, New York, it also had a board of editors composed of eighteen leading male Shakers from various villages. The opening "Salutatory" announced the intention "to treat of a more excellent way of life, than is the ordinary practice of the multitudes." The publication aimed to disclose "'the pearl of great price,'—Christ, or the kingdom of heaven on earth," by "explaining the peculiar testimony and life of the people, called *Shakers*."[226]

The initial issue further clarified the agenda of *The Shaker* by stating that its purpose was "to keep before the public mind" the differences between the "angelic life" and an earthly existence. Among the distinctive concerns of an angelic life, it stated, were the practice of celibacy, the advocacy of peace, the denunciation of private property, freedom from political parties, and temperance reform—causes that were to receive their due in the periodical's pages. In addition, the editor promised to answer correspondence and to publish items of interest concerning the history and present situation of the society. Lomas closed with a dramatic call for support: "Friends of reform—lovers of wisdom—servants of God—aid us; bless our efforts to do good. Extend the cause of Christ to the notice of your neighbors; and let us all seek to walk 'the way,' learn 'the truth' and live 'the life'—being imitators of the beautiful Jesus—Christ."[227]

The Shaker sought to explain Shakerism by providing basic information about the society. The writers attempted to persuade by appealing to both reason and revelation; they were not shrill or ill-tempered in their statements. The pages of the periodical mirror the new spirit of accommodation and reconciliation among the Believers. The contributors located the United Society for their readers within the larger Christian tradition, using language familiar to many outside the community. They spoke of the Shakers as "the legitimate fruit of the Reformation" who must be counted as witnesses to the truth "during the gloomy reign of Antichrist." They represented the members as "law-abiding" persons who consecrated their property to "the support of the Gospel." The Believers accepted Jesus as a "guide" and an example for living, "the *Saviour* of men par excellence." Reactions to the journal from outside the society were quite favorable, especially from the ranks of kindred spirits. The *Banner of Light,* an important spiritualist weekly published in Boston from 1857 to 1907, complimented *The Shaker* in its columns and remarked on the great "sympathy" felt for the society. In the years that followed, the Believers came to regard the periodical as a primary means for representing their views to the world and for reaching potential converts.[228]

The society also mounted a spirited defense against outside criticism. Lomas, for example, answered an assault published by Josiah Gilbert Holland, one of the founders and the editor of *Scribner's Monthly.* Holland, who had dismissed the "doctrines" of the Believers as "an insult to the Christian world," scorned the Shaker practice of celibacy as "unnatural" and "selfish." He suggested that they lived a tortured, passion-driven life of self-denying hypocrisy. "The best thing the Shakers can do is to pair off," he wrote, "and go to separate housekeeping." Lomas accused Holland of ignorance and misrepresentation. In an extended justification of Shaker attitudes, he was careful not to condemn marriage, but rather contrasted it with a "superior good." Lomas quoted a sage who had said, "Marriage peoples the earth, but Celibacy increases the forces of heaven." He was also quick to point out that Jesus, the "much adored exemplar" of the Shakers, had been celibate.[229]

The most prominent Shaker apologist during this period was Frederick Evans, who emerged in the public eye as the leading spokesperson for the society. His skills as a writer and lecturer catapulted him into the limelight. Growing prominence in the missionary meetings, especially the one at Boston in November 1868, brought him an invitation to write "an autobiographical account of [his] experience as a seeker after truth." That request led to the publication of the "Autobiography of a Shaker" in the *Atlantic Monthly* in 1869. Later the same year he reissued the text in book form, with the addition of an essay called "Revelation of the Apocalypse" and some excerpts from Peebles's volume *Seers of the Ages*. Evans invited "both Rationalists and Religionists" to examine his story. He was confident that the volume would dissuade those who thought that Shakerism was "the extreme of ignorance and fanaticism." To that end he presented an image of Ann Lee as a gifted visionary and seer worthy of being considered with such recipients of "true science" as Confucius, Plato, Jesus, and Swedenborg, and he offered an interpretation of the Apocalypse that featured "the history of seven churches, from the Pentecostal to the Shaker Church." Evans also included information for those who wished to consider joining the society.[230]

And people were interested in the Shakers. When someone, either to stem the tide running against the society or out of spite, placed the following classified advertisement in the *New York Herald* and the *New York Sun* in January 1874, the response was overwhelming. It read: "WANTED. Men, women and children can find a comfortable home for life, where want never comes, with the *Shakers,* by embracing the true faith, and living pure lives. Particulars can be learned by writing to the *Shakers, Mt. Lebanon, N.Y.*" As a result, the Believers received 135 letters of application or inquiry within the space of five days. Of these, they reported, two-thirds were from young men, most of whom displayed "intelligence, culture, and earnestness of spirit." The Shakers, in turn, wrote to many of the inquirers, sending them copies of the monthly periodical. Giles Avery helped members of the North Family respond to this flood of correspondence.[231]

For the serious seeker, Evans offered in the journal a detailed description of the society and its requirements from the progressive perspective. The "first requisite" of membership, wrote Evans, is faith—"a belief induced by evidence consequent upon rational inquiry and scientific investigation—that the same Christ Spirit that created the primitive Pentecostal Church, composed of Jewish Israelites, has made its 'Second Advent' upon this earth, and has created Pentecostal Communities, composed of Gentile Israelites." This conviction leads to the confession and forsaking of all sins, including riches and poverty, as well as a host of attendant problems stemming from "false organic laws," such as "riotous living," unhealthy food, "poisonous medicines," and "body-deforming dresses." The Pentecostal principle, "All things common," also applies to this religious community, making possible charity for the poor. Likewise, the United Society is ordered and subject to regulations, for total liberty makes "human association" impossible. Evans then spelled out Shaker attitudes toward the dedication of personal property, the situation of married couples, and the process of probationary membership. Those who join this church, he stated, "become partakers of the sufferings of Jesus." Their worship involves them in "divers operations" led by the spirit, including sometimes "solemn or joyful dances."[232]

About the same time, the Believers were being visited by Charles Nordhoff, an American journalist who was examining the "successful Communistic Societies" in the United States. He hoped that his research might offer "useful hints toward the solution of the labor question" plaguing America. He was also concerned about problems resulting from the "idleness, selfishness, and unthrift in individuals." To that end Nordhoff traveled throughout the country, visiting such groups as the Amana Society, the Harmonists, the Zoar Separatists, the Oneida Perfectionists, and other communal societies, including fourteen Shaker sites. He drew on written sources, too, in his research. Believers throughout the society noted his visits favorably in their family journals. When Nordhoff published a book in 1875, he devoted more than 140 pages to the Shakers' history, beliefs, and practices as well as to detailed descriptions of individual villages. He cited available statistics on membership, acreage, and financial conditions. He concluded his volume with some comparative observations on the communistic societies he had studied. Although he was positive about the history of communal associations in general, he was not uncritical in his reflections. Nordhoff's *Communistic Societies* is the most instructive account of the Believers published by an outsider during the first century of the Shaker experience in America.[233]

Nordhoff declared that the Shakers were the "oldest" and "most successful" communistic society on the continent. He found them "to be in a more or less prosperous condition." In 1874 the United Society comprised fifty-eight families at eighteen sites with a total of 2,415 members. Adult women outnumbered men 1,189 to 695; females under twenty-one outnumbered male youths 339 to 192. According to his figures, the Believers owned nearly 50,000 acres of land at their principal sites and an equal amount elsewhere. He counted more than 350 hired laborers working among them. When summarizing their fundamental principles, Nordhoff cited Frederick Evans, who was his principal host at Mount Lebanon: "revelation, spiritualism, celibacy, oral confession, community, non-resistance, peace, the gift of healing, miracles, physical health, and separation from the world" (fig. 23). Nordhoff also featured the Shakers' notion that "the sec-

23. A Group of Shakers
This engraving from Charles Nordhoff's *Communistic Societies of the United States* (1875) depicted the Believers as scowling and stern. The Shaker seated on the right is holding a copy of *The Shaker*.

ond appearance of Christ upon earth" has taken place "and that they are the only true Church." He found the Believers "industrious, peaceful, honest, highly ingenious, patient of toil, and extraordinarily cleanly."[234]

The most valuable section of Nordhoff's account of the Shakers is his village by village description. He typically locates a site geographically and then describes the numerical and ethnic makeup of its families, the date of their gatherings, the vocational pattern of the residents, their landholdings, and the basis for the village economy. In addition, he often comments on the state of the buildings, the general prosperity of the location, the presence of medical facilities and libraries, the dietary habits of the residents, their entertainment and musical activities, and other distinctive practices. Although his Shaker hosts stressed the unity among Believers at the separate villages, more than any previous observer Nordhoff appreciated the diversity within the society. He wrote, "To the outer eye one Shaker is much like another; but the New Hampshire and Kentucky Shakers are as different from each other as the general population of one state is from that of the other, both in intellectual character and habits of life; and the New York Shaker differs again from both."[235]

Nordhoff documented the striking variations found among the villages in 1874. At most sites he was impressed by the outward signs of prosperity, but he observed that the buildings at New Gloucester showed "signs of neglect" and that those at Harvard were "not all in first-rate order." At Mount Lebanon, he noted, few of the Shakers ate meat; by contrast, at Enfield, New Hampshire, nearly all were "meat eaters, and they use both tea and coffee." Nordhoff recorded that at several villages a few older men were "allowed to chew tobacco." At Enfield, Connecticut, a few "take snuff." At Shirley, he wrote, one Believer "both smokes and snuffs." The reading materials available at the scattered locations varied widely in quantity and accessibility, but newspapers apparently were abundant at all locations. Nordhoff observed that Watervliet, New York, had "a branch" in Philadelphia composed of "twelve colored women"—Rebecca Jackson's colony. South Union, too, he reported, once had included a "colored family, with a colored elder," but when numbers declined the remaining blacks there were placed with the whites. He witnessed African Americans working for white Shakers only at Pleasant Hill, where "two colored women" and a young boy were hired as kitchen help for the sisters. At several villages, Nordhoff observed an abiding commitment to spiritualism, an aspect of Shakerism that attracted a disproportionate amount of attention in his volume. He also discovered copies of the *Sacred and Divine Roll* and of the *Divine Book of Wisdom* on public display in the western societies, though one elder suggested "that their best use was to burn them."[236]

Nordhoff did not romanticize the Shakers. He recognized that despite their history and prosperity, they were "decreasing." He rejected identifying them as "fanatics," however, because there was "room in the world for various and varying religious beliefs." Although he praised them for their commerce and industry, he criticized their aesthetic principles— especially those expressed in architecture and women's clothing—as bereft of beauty, homely at best. The Believers' preoccupation with "personal comfort, neatness, and order," a trait they shared with other communitarian groups, Nordhoff attributed to their being "a parcel of old bachelors and old maids," who fixate on such matters. Nonetheless, the "systematic arrangement of life" in communes, he acknowledged, might well account for some of their charm. Nordhoff confessed his surprise at finding communitarians "cheerful" and "healthful." He discovered that these communistic societies gave their members a "serenity of spirit" and a certain relief from the "follies" of everyday life. Yet they also demanded hard work and "perseverance," for "one can not play at communism." Nordhoff was not naive about the future; he did not think such societies would increase rapidly in the coming years.[237]

Not only did the membership not increase, but the Believers continued to suffer disasters. Fire devastated several villages in the early 1870s. Seven buildings were destroyed at Groveland in 1871. In November 1872 Watervliet, New York, sustained the loss of barns, feed, and supplies in two devastating conflagrations. Perhaps the most severe blow of all came at Mount Lebanon in 1875. Twice in February raging fires struck the village. On the sixth, eight buildings in the Church Family were "entirely consumed," including the dwelling house and the sisters' shop, in a blaze set by Charles Harris, a hired man. The loss sustained by this "most destructive fire ever experienced by Believers" was estimated at $100,000, for which there was no insurance. Thanks to the efforts of neighbors and the Pittsfield fire brigade, adjacent buildings, including the meetinghouse, were spared. Among those injured was Elder Daniel Boler. Eldress Harriet Goodwin was rescued "by ladder, from an upper window." Three weeks later, the herb house burned, a loss calculated at no less than $50,000. Only the heroic efforts of those fighting the fire, some of whom protected themselves from the intense heat with wet carpets, saved both the big barn and the meetinghouse. Giles Avery summarized the reaction to these events in four words: "Awful times beyond expression." Later that year Thomas Hammond at Harvard wrote, "It seems to be the lot of God's people, to bear afflictions & tribulation."[238]

In spite of the manifold difficulties of these times, the world of the Believers included a number of fixed points that allowed members of the society to find physical and religious satisfaction as Shakers. The primary institutions that defined the United Society stayed in place: the family structure with leadership divided between elders and eldresses; the division between spiritual and temporal concerns, the latter being the special province of the trustees, deacons, and deaconesses; and the central ministry at Mount Lebanon, which enjoyed remarkable stability during the Middle Period. The physical landscape of the Shakers was also familiar. Landmarks identified favorite terrain and sacred space. A few spots took on the character of shrines. Some of the Shaker buildings had well-known histories. Maps and village views helped to disseminate these details through the society. Even geographic and symbolic boundaries remained essentially the same in 1875.[239]

The patterns of daily life, too, were fairly constant for most Believers: prescribed times for eating and sleeping, for work and worship. The religious dimensions of Shakerism, though inescapably altered by the Era of Manifestations, still centered on the practice of confession, the virgin way of life, the pursuit of purity, the joint interest, and distinctive spiritual exercises. One such ritual was the "yearly sacrifice or judgment work" performed at each village near the end of the year. Preparation for that activity now commonly included certain ascetic regimens and dietary restrictions. The collective memory as well as traditions and testimonies from earlier generations bound the Believers together. The sense of family persisted on several levels and embraced all those who had ever been part of the Believers. Deep friendships and close relationships continued to characterize the society, as the rich documentary record of journals, diaries, and letters attests.[240]

No figure was more central to the ongoing stability and vitality of Shakerism than Ann Lee. Through story, song, gift, and vision, she lived on in each family, an ever-present maternal spirit. The Believers directed an astonishing amount of attention to her. The annual commemoration of her birthday near 29 February included singing songs dedicated to her and retelling stories about her. In the observance of 6 August as the day of the landing in America, she figured prominently, too. Even her physical appearance was a growing preoccupation among the Believers. In 1835 it was determined to move the remains of Ann Lee, her brother William, and Lucy Wright into the "common Burying Ground" at Watervliet, and the reburial became the occasion for the "examination of the relics of Mother Ann," which consisted of her skull and other bones. Before being reinterred in a new coffin, her remains were placed on display, "and all, or nearly all, both old & young, male & female through the Society came to be eye witnesses of the scene." As the years passed, the Believers lost none of this interest. Often they visited the sites that had figured in her life, for instance, "the old grant house" where she and the elders had been "so abused by the wicked." In 1869 Evans described his image of Lee: "Her complexion was fair; she had blue eyes, and light chestnut hair. Her countenance was expressive, but grave, inspiring confidence and respect. Many called her beautiful." Two years later a "psychometric portrait" purporting to be of Lee appeared in *The Illustrated Annuals of Phrenology and Physiognomy* (fig. 24). George Lomas explained that "a test medium, or psychological expert," not the artist, had identified the picture as Lee. Lomas suggested that although many Shakers believed the portrait to be "genuine," he himself doubted its authenticity. He thought the "features of the lower face" unattractive by comparison with the extraordinary beauty of the "brain-house." The cult of Ann Lee continued to grow.[241]

One final indication of the growing difficulties confronting the United Society was the debate concerning the closing or relocating of several vil-

24. Psychometric Portrait of Ann Lee
This wood engraving, purportedly copied from a canyon picture by a person named
Milleson in New York, accompanied a phrenological analysis of Ann Lee. The portrait
appeared again in *The Phrenological Miscellany* of 1882.

lages. For some time the Shakers in Maine had been exploring the possibility of selling at least a portion of their holdings and starting over again in
"a more genial clime and better soil." They had given an English agency a
year's option to attempt a sale of the Alfred site, but the firm was unsuccessful. By the end of 1870 they had placed the property in "other hands in
America for the same purpose." In August the ministry at Mount Lebanon
had opened formal conversations with the Believers at Tyringham about
the possibility of "selling out the place" and moving to a "more favorable
locality," most likely Enfield, Connecticut (fig. 25). They reached an agreement in principle to do so, if they could find a buyer willing to pay enough so
that the society would not take a major loss. Within a few months the talk
of "that place breaking up" had spread throughout the society.[242]

25. Shaker Village, Enfield, Connecticut
Engraving of the Church Family buildings at Enfield. (From Charles Edson Robinson,
A Concise History of the United Society of Believers, 1893.)

During the closing years of the Middle Period, many villages were
experiencing precipitant numerical decline. At Groveland, for example, 81
Believers were on the rolls at the close of 1864, 56 in the First Family and
25 in the Gathering Order. By the close of 1872, the membership had
shrunk to 52 Shakers, 38 and 14, respectively, in the two families, representing a drop of more than 35 percent in less than ten years. At Pleasant
Hill on 1 January 1869 members numbered 385; by the end of 1875 that
figure had declined to 234, a loss of more than 39 percent in six years. Of
all the villages, Tyringham was the most vulnerable. In 1874 Nordhoff had
dismissed Tyringham as "small" and having "no noticeable features." He
listed only seventeen Believers at the site. It is not surprising, therefore,
that the Shakers decided to close that village and sell the property. In June
1875, almost hidden in *Shaker and Shakeress*, the following brief notice
appeared: "The Tyringham Society of Shakers has removed to the Enfield
Society, Connecticut." Thus the Believers brought to an end a village that
had existed for more than eighty years, the first to be closed in the East. In
doing so, they opened a new chapter in Shaker history.[243]

American historians normally do not lump together the middle decades of the nineteenth century, what I have called the Middle Period of
Shaker history, because of the searing, knifelike effect of the Civil War.

The common descriptive category "antebellum," for example, signals the typical dividing line at 1860. And yet the Shakers require a different historical timetable to reflect the distinctive rhythms of their communal experience. The Believers went through their own Sturm und Drang before the internecine struggle in America. The stress and strain of the Era of Manifestations marked the high point of the Middle Period of the society's history. During the revival Shaker leaders were tested sorely when the members triggered a remarkable burst of religious activity, and the ensuing contest issued a variety of results.[244]

The hierarchical system of government in the United Society emerged from this period shaken but intact, thanks in part to the stability and practical wisdom of the leadership at New Lebanon and to the lack of an organized alternative. The federal structure of the society, the persistent localism of the villages, and the independence of the separate Shaker families worked against formation of an effective coalition that might have challenged the central ministry. The leaders coopted the revival and ultimately turned it to their advantage. The members of the society—especially the more youthful Believers—for a time occupied center stage, wielding immense influence over the course of daily events. During these years of commotion and confusion, routines were altered and rules broken. There was no lack of excitement or anticipation. For many, the revivals were one prolonged, protracted meeting packed with charismatic and ecstatic activity.[245]

In the short run, the religious traditions of the United Society—worship patterns, theology, hymnody, scriptures, and practical spirituality—were expanded and revitalized by the spirit visitations. Mother Ann's Work renewed and enriched the lives of the members, although with the passing of the manifestations those effects faded quickly. For a time the new asceticism commanded by the spirits and codified in several collections of statutes, including the 1845 Millennial Laws, prevailed. Yet the spiritual disciplines, the dietary prohibitions, and the strict controls on daily activities were of limited duration. By 1860 a new and less stringent version of the communal regulations was being circulated by the central ministry. This revised code marked a public retreat from the severe asceticism of the revival period. Perhaps the most enduring religious aspect of the period was the notion that the Shaker concept of gift was not a closed category and that such revitalization might occur again at any time. In other words, Shakerism not only was concerned about the past, but also was open to the future.[246]

The impact of the manifestations on the economic order of the Shakers was considerable. The revivals distracted the Believers at an especially critical moment, when the full force of the panic of 1837 was hitting the United States. The spiritualistic commotion upset the structures of daily life and displaced work priorities. The attention of the leaders was diverted by these outbursts. One result was that the trustees operated with increasing independence from the elders. This growing separation between the temporal and spiritual orders in turn contributed to expanding economic problems at many villages.[247]

In the social order the immediate effect of the revival was to strengthen the sense of community in the face of special difficulties with the rising generation. But that unity fell apart when factions began to differ over the interpretation of the gifts and to compete for power in the society. The revival did little to stop the exodus of the young, which, ironically, included a number of prominent instruments at several villages. What began with the promise of attracting new converts to the society became within a few years the cause for closing the public meetings and restricting the observation of the manifestations to members only. In the long run, therefore, the Shakers neither strengthened their internal sense of community nor attracted many new members through the revival. These failures set the stage for a number of initiatives by the society designed to reach out to the non-Shaker world, including the launching of a missionary program and the inauguration of a monthly periodical.[248]

The Middle Period established the outer limits of Shaker sectarianism. From the 1850s onward the Believers in general increasingly accommodated the patterns and standards of the world and moderated their drive to be distinctive. In the aftermath of the revival the progressive wing of the society, under the leadership of Frederick Evans, Antoinette Doolittle, and others at the North Family in New Lebanon, emerged as the leading public representative of the United Society. Eventually these North Family leaders rivaled the central ministry and, in the eyes of many outsiders, overshadowed the more conservative leaders. The sectarian perspective was further compromised by the greater individual freedom exercised by the Believers and the growing hospitality rendered by them to outsiders. These changes were accompanied by a general decline in the level of tension with American society. Even during the Civil War the rapprochement with the larger culture continued.[249]

By the close of the period, the Shakers had been resident for more than one hundred years in their adopted homeland. During that first century in America Shakerism had changed in a number of significant ways.

Some of these developments intensified what might be called primitive impulses within the society. Among the points of continuity with earlier times was the Believers' identification with Ann Lee and the other founders, a relationship newly intensified by the spirit visitations. The same communications expanded the Shakers' creative reflections about the deity, whose image became more familiar and personalized as a result of the revival experiences. Likewise, the commitment to celibacy, alternative family patterns, and communal living remained fixed. By contrast, although the joint interest continued to be the basic economic principle, the society participated increasingly in the national economy. Union and order still headed the society's social agenda, but achieving them became more difficult.[250]

By 1875 Shakerism had become openly pluralistic—one of the most striking developments of this period. The sense of community suffered as factions divided over the interpretation of the manifestations and struggled for power within the society. The outpouring of gifts, reminiscent of the Age of the Founders, seemed to promise new success in attracting converts. That prospect did not materialize, however. On the contrary, the 1840s were the beginning of numerical decline: the losses sustained during the revivals were an omen of the impending downward curve in membership. The United Society had not been permanently revitalized.[251]

PART

FOUR

In the Van

of an Advancing

Host:

The Transformation

of the Society

1876–1947

The celebration of America's centennial in 1876 was marked by patriotic observances across the nation. Although all parts of the country were not prospering equally, many Americans struck a cheerful note in their assessment of the state of affairs in that anniversary year. The United States had weathered the Civil War and now was regrouping for further advancement. Even the South, facing complex problems with the failure of Reconstruction, was struggling to rebuild. A note of optimism echoed through the chambers of government and business, education and religion, as well as in the halls of the Centennial Exhibition at Philadelphia.[1]

Progress was the watchword of the day and the apparent goal of all enterprises. In politics the spirit of reform motivated many, manifesting itself in efforts to improve the circumstances of workers, immigrants, women, and the poor. In the world of business, new manufacturing techniques and the organization of finance capitalism transformed the workplace and the industrial order, creating both economic prosperity and glaring inequity between owners and workers. In education the expanding influence of science was immense on how knowledge was obtained and on the imagined prospects for the future. Darwinism, one aspect of the new science, challenged prevailing assumptions concerning the origin and destiny of the human race. In religion, efforts to push beyond traditional creeds and practices toward universal truths and values created controversy. A host of new movements, including emergent forms of modernism and fundamentalism, added to the complexity of America's expanding religious pluralism. Materialism gained its share of adherents at the same time that alternative spiritual practices attracted many who had rejected the established orthodoxies.[2]

The Shakers marked the national centennial with reflections on the past and the future. Ann Busby at Mount Lebanon composed a three-stanza hymn entitled "Centennial Blessings," celebrating the victory brought by the "cross of Christ." Now the "unfettered" spirit, she wrote, may pursue the "heavenly way" by "confession and repentance." Busby hoped that 1876 would bring "blessings" on the "rulers" of the nation and especially on the "gospel testimony" of Zion, that all may be prepared "for the coming of the Lord." Elizabeth H. Webster at Harvard was even more specific in her aspirations for the "centennial year." In a poem by that name she expressed her desire that the anniversary would result in "freedom for all" and peace for every nation. In particular, Webster hoped that 1876 would "give To all of her daughters so brave, The freedom her sons have, to be and to live." Frederick Evans expressed his longing for a republic of citizens free from "debt, war, poverty or riches" and uninfluenced by sectarian theology. He criticized the Centennial Exhibition for closing on the Sabbath, arguing that sabbatarianism was a violation of "the rights and consciences" of Americans by "a committee of bigoted, persecuting theological tyrants" and a subversion of the constitutional principle of the separation of church and state.[3]

Two years before the nation's celebration, the Shakers had marked a different centennial, the anniversary of their founders' arrival in America. There had been no special speeches or displays of fireworks in the villages to observe the occasion. From family journals it appears that on 6 August 1874 the Believers went about their daily routines much as usual, although they had earlier discussed what might be an appropriate way to commemorate the event. In a meditation on Ann Lee's journey to America and her subsequent struggles published that October, Elizabeth H. Webster applied the lessons of Lee's experiences to nineteenth-century Believers, urging them to imitate her courage, love, and self-denial. In that way, she suggested, the members of the society might "keep a joyful centennial" in their hearts, even "though it find no outward demonstration." Webster closed her contemplations with a prayer for a further harvest of "souls" from the world:

> Hail, thou victorious gospel!
> And that auspicious day
> When Mother safely landed
> In Hudson's lovely bay![4]

By 1876 the parallels between the growth of the United States and the development of the United Society were becoming less instructive. The nation had survived the Civil War and was about to enter the modern era with a burst of renewed energy. Industrialization, urbanization, immigration, geographical expansion—these and other forces were reshaping and reinvigorating the nation. The national centennial marked a milestone in the forward journey of American society. By contrast, the Shaker anniversary occurred within a context of impending geographical retreat, numerical decline, and institutional retrenchment.[5]

For the Believers the period between 1876 and 1947 was a time of creative adjustment to rapidly changing circumstances. Women played increasingly prominent roles in the society's leadership, making more of the decisions involving governance, theology, and the life of the society. Endless accommodations to pressing social and economic realities forced members of the community to alter established patterns. The liberalization of Shakerism took its toll, both internally and externally. The Shakers beat a steady geographical retreat as site after site was abandoned. Between 1876, when the property at Tyringham was finally sold, and 1947, when the last Believers at Mount Lebanon left for Hancock, fifteen Shaker villages were forced to close their doors.[6]

By the midtwentieth century the United Society was but a shadow of its former self. And yet it is a mistake to dismiss this period of Shaker history as insignificant because of the society's declining numbers or changing viewpoints. Many within the community manifested a remarkable spirit of dedication and commitment during this Time of Transformation. The Believers displayed an intellectual and social courage that won for them new respect and admiration from their fellow Americans. This was a period of major reorientation in the relation between the Shakers and American culture in general.[7]

Declining Membership and Geographical Retreat

The closing decades of the nineteenth century contrast sharply with the society's years of expansion in the early 1800s. The dominant institutional reality shaping the experience of the Shakers after 1876 was the precipitant numerical decline in the ranks of nearly every village. After the closing of Tyringham, the society struggled to maintain itself and to shore up its collective sense of community in the face of seemingly insurmountable odds. In spite of the loss of membership, the Believers did not lose heart. Their confidence and commitment, though sorely tested, found repeated expression. One stouthearted resident of the Second Family at Watervliet, New York, struck a characteristic Shaker note in 1886: "Our number is small but the feeling is strong."[8]

Such sentiments did not alter the demographic realities. Federal census figures reflect the changing fortunes of the Shakers. William Sims Bainbridge has calculated that in 1880 the United Society numbered 1,849 Believers. That figure does not include temporary residents or inquirers who may have stayed for short periods at one of the villages. Using the figures from twenty years later, Bainbridge determined that by 1900 the total had dropped to 855 persons. In other words, the society experienced a 54 percent drop in membership during the last twenty years of the nineteenth century. These figures are broken down by village in table 4.[9]

Tyringham was not to be an isolated closing. In 1889 the Shakers completely abandoned North Union. Once composed of three units—the Center, or Church, Family; the East, or Gathering, Family; and the Mill

Table 4
Shaker Population in 1880 and 1900

Location	1880	1900	Decline (%)
Alfred, Maine	55	39	29
Canaan, N.Y.	57	—	100
Canterbury, N.H.	158	106	33
Enfield, Conn.	103	92	11
Enfield, N.H.	144	68	53
Groveland, N.Y.	41	—	100
Hancock, Mass.	35	16	54
Harvard, Mass.	54	36	33
Narcoossee, Fla.	—	6	—
New Lebanon, N.Y.	283	125	56
North Union, Ohio	47	—	100
Pittsfield, Mass.	48	27	44
Pleasant Hill, Ky.	203	34	83
Poland, Maine	27	—	100
Sabbathday Lake, Maine	43	41	5
Shirley, Mass.	40	12	70
South Union, Ky.	99	55	44
Union Village, Ohio	165	44	73
Watervliet, N.Y.	136	90	34
Watervliet, Ohio	46	15	67
Whitewater, Ohio	65	49	25
Total	1,849	855	

Family—numbering more than two hundred members, this village experienced a declining membership long before 1880. Despite earlier prosperity based on profits from mills, diversified agricultural activities, and some light manufacturing, most notably broom making, the decreasing numbers steadily moved North Union toward bare subsistence. And yet the Believers in northern Ohio remained enterprising. When they no longer had sufficient numbers to harvest broomcorn, they rented out their lands. They also hired outside labor to continue broom production and capitalized on a quarry on their property by selling stone to the world. Nevertheless, the claims of North Union's leaders aside, the village operated for years on a thin margin.[10]

The disintegration intensified in the late 1870s and throughout the following decade. In 1876 William Reynolds noted "the lack of government" at the Center and Mill families as well as financial trouble at the Mill Family. James S. Prescott, who had served for years as an elder, schoolteacher, and trustee at North Union and whose interests in theology and spiritualism brought him considerable reputation, resigned in the fall of 1877 because of ill health and old age. He was then seventy-four. Subsequent leaders appointed by the ministries at Union Village and Mount Lebanon proved disappointing. The annual economic reports from the three families in 1881 reveal the precarious situation of the Believers in Cuyahoga County. In that year the Center Family reported excess expenses of $729 on a total income of $3,167, and the Mill Family reported a deficit of $12 on an income of $2,626. Only the East Family realized a profit, $9 on an income of $2,184. Collectively, the Believers at North Union spent $732 more than they earned in 1881. The principal sources of their income remained brooms, milling fees, rents, and the sale of timber and stone. By this time they had become heavily dependent on outside suppliers for basic foodstuffs and such items as dry goods, coal, medicine, wine, and tobacco. The largest single outlay during the year in all three families was for hired labor because there were not enough members to do the work.[11]

The situation at North Union continued to worsen. Although the Believers owned more than 1,373 acres of land, the village was no longer profitable. By July 1885 the East Family had broken up and been absorbed into the other two units. The East House Farm, including the dwelling and other buildings, was rented to "some German and Bohemian families." Some Believers leveled charges of "maladministration" against the leaders. James Higgins of the Center Family, for example, accused Eldress Clymena Miner of endangering his health through her unwillingness to secure proper medical treatment for him. In his old age, James Prescott seemed oblivious to reality, declaring repeatedly that North Union was experiencing "*financial* prosperity." Other Believers at the village who disagreed began to see themselves surrounded by "*ominous*" signs. When a gas balloon failed to ascend during a Fourth of July celebration in 1886, one Shaker judged the incident portentous, signifying "that the rising hopes and expectations of believers cannot be realized at the present." The same observer interpreted the firing of cannons on that occasion as symbolizing contemporary conflicts, the tightrope of an acrobat as "the straight line of obedience" needed by the Believers, and the explosion of an old "Shaker Mill" as a sign of "the downfall of original Shakerism in

Ohio." These premonitions were apt, unlike the more sanguine speculations of a self-styled "German Prophet" in Cleveland. Phillip Hering had predicted in 1882 that the society soon would have "more Shakers" than it knew "what to do with"—a prophecy never fulfilled.[12]

The death of Prescott in 1888 provided the occasion for the leadership of the United Society to close North Union, by that time reduced to thirty-four Believers. On 1 August 1889 the members of the Mill Family moved to Union Village and Watervliet, Ohio; on 15 October the Center Family followed. The trustees of the society at Union Village leased the gristmill to local operators for a specified period. They had considered a plan to drill for gas before selling the principal acreage at North Union, hoping thereby to increase the selling price. That idea was rejected, however, and a few years later, after consulting with the trustees at Mount Lebanon, the land was sold to T. A. and Lawrence Lamb for $316,000. They, in turn, sold it for $1,365,000 to the Van Sweringen family, who developed the property commercially.[13]

Three years after North Union closed, the central ministry made another difficult decision. This time Groveland was the targeted village. Initially located at Great Sodus Bay on Lake Ontario, this settlement had been troubled through much of its history. The original capital investment in the tract of land involved both private subscriptions and loans from eastern villages that were not paid back for many years, and then only in part. In 1837, little more than a decade after establishing the village, the Believers in western New York had been forced to sell their site. The Sodus Canal Company, exercising the right of eminent domain, planned to build a waterway connecting the Erie Canal with Lake Ontario through the Great Sodus Bay. The relocation of the Believers to Groveland some fifty miles southwest necessitated a new start, and the community in western New York never fully recovered from that setback. Part of the New Lebanon bishopric, the village was not easily integrated into the administrative structure of the United Society. Geographically it was neither part of the eastern bloc nor a true western settlement. In its location lay both its principal advantages and its drawbacks. As long as the Erie Canal was the route of travel between East and West, the village was a primary way station for travelers within the society. The distance from New Lebanon and Watervliet in the eastern part of the state, however, isolated Groveland and added to the difficulty of supervising its development.[14]

Groveland, also called Sonyea, an Indian name for the area, began a sharp decline in numbers after 1860, when it dropped below 100 members for the first time, having averaged 125 Believers during the previous

twenty-five years (fig. 26). In 1860 there were only twenty-nine men between the ages of fourteen and eighty; women and young children formed
an increasingly large percentage of the village population. The Believers
were unable to sustain their agricultural, milling, and manufacturing activities. Few of the children raised by the Shakers, upon coming of age,
chose to stay with the society. In addition, a series of departures by trusted
and experienced leaders—Daniel Dryer, Jesse Leonard, and Lucius
Southwick—shocked and further crippled the struggling community.
Southwick, for example, who had served for more than thirty years as the
first trustee at the village, apostatized in 1864 and shortly thereafter married Sarah Ann Sizer, a Believer at Groveland for more than twenty-five
years. He was accused of having embezzled community funds, but the society reached a financial settlement with him instead of going to court.
The losers on this occasion were the Believers, not the apostates.[15]

Despite its location on the "psychic highway" in western New York,
Groveland never managed to attract large numbers. The reluctance of the
Believers in the midnineteenth century to seek converts aggressively left
them at a disadvantage compared with their evangelical neighbors in the
"burned-over district." When railroads displaced canals as the primary
means of east-west transportation, the site lost much of its significance for
the United Society. Declining membership and economic pressures persuaded the central ministry in 1892 to close the village, which was sold
two years later to New York State and converted into the Craig Colony for
Epileptics. The Believers at the site moved to Watervliet, New York. It
could be argued that the Shakers should have cut their losses at Groveland
long before.[16]

The closing of North Union and Groveland was a severe blow to the
Believers remaining at those locations, some of whom were long-time residents and often elderly. Eldress Polly Lee, for example, was seventy-two
when she left Groveland for Watervliet in 1892. She handled the adjustment remarkably well and with good spirit. Years later, by contrast, when
the central ministry determined to close the Second Family at Watervliet,
New York, Eldress Rachel E. MacDonald, sixty-five years old, adamantly
refused to move or be moved. "Eld. Rachel still holds the fort," it was reported. She won the day with her stubbornness, and the family dwelling
was not shut down until her death in May 1913.[17]

The impact of declining numbers in the society was not limited to
those settlements that were shut down completely. After the 1870s, almost
every Shaker village was forced to consolidate its position by reducing the
number of families and absorbing members into other units. Poland Hill,

26. Shaker Village, Groveland, New York
Photograph from the 1890s showing the meetinghouse completed in 1842 (on the right), the four-story brick East Family dwelling built in the late 1850s, and a variety of shops. (Courtesy New York State Museum, Albany.)

for example, the North Family, or Gathering Order, at Sabbathday Lake, had sometimes served as a refuge for those out of favor with the leadership in Maine. It had developed a less than favorable reputation within the society and was a frequent topic of discussion among the leaders. As early as 1872 the central ministry debated what to do with Poland Hill. In November 1877 the leaders at Mount Lebanon were involved with the "rectification of some prominent evils" at the site. By 1882 only nineteen persons remained in that family, six males and thirteen females. The sale of Poland Hill, which at one time had comprised more than 500 acres and eighteen major buildings, was finalized in 1899 for $7,500 on a ten-year note, and the last members were transferred to Sabbathday Lake. The new proprietors, the Ricker brothers, who owned the nearby Poland Spring House resort, planned to convert the site into "a very beautiful place" for their guests.[18]

The Shaker settlements at Canaan, New York, further illustrate the effect of declining numbers on individual families. Divided between the Upper and Lower families, Canaan was part of the New Lebanon settlement, even though it was removed four or so miles from the center of the village. The Canaan families, functioning as part of the Gathering Order, exercised a measure of independence sometimes not fully perceived. Beginning in the 1870s, both families found themselves in an increasingly precarious situation. In 1878, for example, Lower Canaan listed only six brothers and sixteen sisters, nine of whom were children. In 1884 that family was dissolved and its property sold. Less than fifteen years later the Upper Family was also broken up.[19]

The situation of Upper Canaan during its last decade is instructive because it typified the dilemma facing many Shaker families. In 1875 the Upper Family consisted of eleven males and twenty-two females, the average age of the males being forty-six and that of the females, thirty-nine. Five years later there were fourteen males in the family averaging thirty-two years of age and twenty-two females averaging thirty years. In 1885 eight males averaged fifty years of age, and nineteen females averaged thirty-one years (see table 5). The most striking aspect of these figures is the increase in the percentage of youthful members in the family. But the relative stability of the younger members varies greatly when males and females are compared. Of the eleven males in the family in 1875, only two remained in 1885, Granville Sproat and Clawson Middleton, aged seventy-five and eighty-two, respectively. Furthermore, of the eight males on the 1880 roster who were not part of the family in 1875, only one remained at Upper Canaan in 1885. The turnover in male membership was very high. By contrast, nine of the eleven females in the family in 1875 remained in 1885, three of whom were sixty or older—Eliza Brown, sixty; Maryann Manning, seventy-three, and Emily Sears, eighty-one. Correspondingly, of the six females on the 1880 roster not part of the family in 1875, four remained on the rolls in 1885. In other words, the female population of the Upper Family displayed much greater stability during this decade than that of the males.[20]

When the statistics from Upper Canaan are compared with data for the Mount Lebanon Church Family from the same years, three observations are in order. First, the size of the two groups is not comparable: in 1875 the Church Family, comprising of twenty-eight males and sixty-six females, was nearly three times the size of Upper Canaan. A decade later the Church Family was approximately two and a half times as large. Second, in both families women were predominant in numbers as well as in stability of commitment to the society. Finally, the Upper Canaan figures suggest that the pool of potential leadership talent on the female side was adequate, relative to the whole, in both number and experience. These statistics provide a context for understanding the observation of Alice Braisted, one of the nine women who resided at Upper Canaan between

Table 5

Age Distribution by Percentage: Upper Canaan and Mount Lebanon Church Families, 1875–1885

Age Group in Years		<16	16–59	>60
	1875			
Upper Canaan				
	Male	18.2	45.5	36.4
	Female	13.6	63.6	22.7
	Combined	15.1	57.6	27.3
Mount Lebanon Church Family				
	Male	30.0	40.0	30.0
	Female	10.8	50.0	39.2
	Combined	17.5	46.5	36.0
	1880			
Upper Canaan				
	Male	50.0	28.6	21.4
	Female	27.3	63.6	9.1
	Combined	36.1	50.0	13.9
Mount Lebanon Church Family				
	Male	31.0	45.2	23.8
	Female	25.7	32.4	41.9
	Combined	27.6	37.1	35.3
	1885			
Upper Canaan				
	Male	25.0	25.0	50.0
	Female	36.8	42.1	21.1
	Combined	33.3	37.0	29.6
Mount Lebanon Church Family				
	Male	29.6	22.2	48.2
	Female	16.9	37.3	45.8
	Combined	20.9	32.6	46.5

1875 and 1885. In 1881 she wrote, "One by one they pass from our ranks, leaving the younger ones to carry on the work, to sustain & build up the cause of truth for truth will ever exist, though Zion's numbers may be reduced to one third of what they are yet there will always be a few, who will take the work of God as it is, & feel that His yoke is easy, & His burden is light."[21]

The most obvious fact about Upper Canaan is that there were too few productive members to maintain an independent family. And yet the leadership at Mount Lebanon seemed intent on prolonging the community's existence. In 1895 the central ministry spent a day at Canaan, reporting "a lovely little band of true workers there," whom they encouraged by giving the leaders "the title of Elder & Eldress" as in other families. The ministry was reluctant to close the site completely. Less than two years later, however, they reversed their position, shutting down the Upper Family and moving its remaining members to other New Lebanon locations. The society, for the moment, retained the ownership of the properties. The experience at Upper Canaan seems to confirm the observation Lawrence Foster has made about the fluidity of membership at Mount Lebanon's Second Family, where "large numbers of children were taken in for relatively short periods of time," most of whom subsequently left.[22]

No Shaker location was immune from problems related to the declining membership, not even the village where the central ministry resided. In 1872, more than a decade before the closing of Lower Canaan, the East Family at Mount Lebanon had been relocated and its buildings turned over to seven or eight "world families" of hired help, including a cobbler, broom makers, farmers, gardeners, and a carpenter. The Shakers did not sell the site, however, for they nourished the hope that someday things might be different. "Who knows but it may yet be occupied by families of young Believers." The same difficulties were cropping up at other eastern villages, too. At Harvard, for instance, it was reported in 1877 that there was a "want of competent persons for burdenbearers."[23]

In the West, the circumstances of some Shaker families had become desperate by the 1870s. In spite of substantial numbers at Pleasant Hill, the situation was appalling in the eyes of eastern leaders. They described the East Family there as "lacking" a gift "in every sense." The West Family at Pleasant Hill, composed of seven males and twenty females, was in an equally sad state: "insubordination & want of enterprise both temporal and Spiritual reigns supreme." At South Union the easterners discovered that "One young man by name of John Crach, & five Sisters" were located in the West Family "just to keep out the Negroes," a reference to the large number of freed slaves drifting around the countryside during Reconstruction.[24]

The problem of insufficient numbers was not unrelated to other difficulties faced by the society. Giles Avery, second in the central ministry, recognized the widespread implications of declining membership (fig. 27). More than a decade before the closing of North Union, he wrote, "There is universal distress, in these days, among believers on account of the paucity of numbers, and a lack of ability to manage business, or to keep a suitable spiritual gift for protection; the future prospect of keeping the various Shaker organizations in tact, looks very dubious, unless the work of the Lord calls into Zion very soon, a class of souls largely developed in spiritual understanding, and considerably progressed in a travel out of themselves, and into a Gospel consecration." Avery was not raising groundless fears, but rather was echoing sentiments expressed in other locations, too. Even at Pleasant Hill the people wept "as they talk[ed] of their fading condition spiritual & temporal."[25]

The declining numbers undermined the Believers' capacity to sustain a level of economic production consistent with the standards of the past and necessary for a stable future. Similarly, the ability of the society to maintain its properties, including grounds and buildings, was in constant jeopardy. By 1889 the building occupied by the boys at South Union was described as "awfully dilapidated, worse than multitudes of stables in the eastern states, very far worse." Trying to keep such structures in repair was an unending drain on Shaker resources. These run-down conditions also made the society less appealing to outsiders, and therefore attracting new converts became all the more difficult. Priscilla J. Brewer has discussed at length the implications of the declining numbers for the pool of potential leaders. It became increasingly problematic to persuade members to accept positions of responsibility. Families went for long periods of time without appointed leaders. Daniel Boler and Giles Avery, for example, were unable to prevail on George Price to serve as a trustee at Mount Lebanon; he objected and "utterly refuse[d]" their request. The crisis in membership and the economic instability fed on one another, leading to additional problems.[26]

After the turn of the twentieth century, the decline in numbers accelerated. Between 1900 and 1947 twelve more Shaker settlements were forced to close because of shrinking numbers and limited economic resources: 1908, Shirley; 1910, Watervliet and Whitewater, Ohio, and Pleasant Hill; 1912, Union Village; 1917, Enfield, Connecticut; 1918, Harvard; 1922, South Union; 1923, Enfield, New Hampshire; 1931, Alfred; 1938,

27. Giles B. Avery
Avery served as a member of the central ministry at Mount Lebanon, New York,
for more than thirty years. (Courtesy Shaker Museum and Library, Old Chatham,
New York.)

Watervliet, New York; and 1947, Mount Lebanon. Census figures for the
opening decades chart a similar decline. Membership in the society fell to
516 in 1906, 367 a decade later, 192 in 1926, and 92 in 1936.[27]
 As a result of these closings, the central ministry and the trustees of
the society—sometimes in concert with the leaders of the besieged villages—were involved almost continuously in legal and financial transactions. The trustees in particular played a central role in the sale of land,
buildings, furnishings, livestock, equipment, and other assets at the locations being abandoned. They served as agents in negotiations with potential buyers and with lawyers. Nearly all the initial transactions at these
sites involved the sale of outlying farms, woodlots, or other isolated proper-

ties. Many properties had already lost their income-producing capacity and the buildings fallen into disrepair. When members of the Mount Lebanon ministry made a western tour in 1889, for example, they found facilities at South Union in a deplorable state. Eldress Harriet Bullard wrote, "Disorders of various kinds exist to blight this once flourishing society."[28]

The situation at Shirley was typical. The loss of members and economic pressures forced leaders to sell parcels of land in an effort to stave off complete dissolution. Shirley had never completely recovered from the Phoenix factory disaster. In the mid-1880s the community found itself without sufficient fluid assets to pay current expenses, much less to meet outstanding mortgage and tax payments. By early 1886 the circumstances were so desperate that Elder John Whiteley used three English sovereigns given him as a personal gift to buy eight barrels of flour for the community. He wrote, "It does at times seem too much to bear patiently or otherwise. I have struggled hard to keep up—and shall try to do so. Yet there is a limit to human endurance!" In February Whiteley reported debts of $1,461 for hired help, overdrawn checks, medical bills, equipment, and livestock. Shirley could not meet these obligations. An earlier trade of New Hampshire pasture lands owned by the Shakers for a nearby farm had proved disastrous: the debtor on the lands fled to Canada and the bank holding the mortgage foreclosed. Whiteley rushed to liquidate other properties, including the Fitchburg farm and the Brick Tavern lot, to pay the outstanding debts. (Ironically, in the midst of these dire financial circumstances, Elder Whiteley "donated" land to the town of Shirley for a park "with the proviso, that it shall be called Whiteley Park"—a move that provoked a written rebuke from Eldress Maria Foster.) The subsequent sale of other parcels of land only delayed the inevitable. In 1904, the year before Whiteley died, Joseph Holden, a member of the central ministry, was chosen as his successor. Only a handful of sisters and one brother remained at the village. In October 1908 Shirley was sold to the Commonwealth of Massachusetts, a transaction involving 889 acres of land, twenty-six buildings, livestock, and other items. The central ministry received $43,000, and the site became the location of the Shirley Industrial School for boys. The remaining Believers were dispersed among Harvard, Hancock, and Mount Lebanon.[29]

The ministry and trustees attended to the needs of the Believers at the villages being closed. When the first sites were abandoned, the residents commonly moved to nearby villages. As more locations were given up, however, fewer resettlement options remained. The society frequently had to make alternative financial arrangements for the remaining Shakers, often at considerable expense. In 1918, for example, when Harvard was sold for $60,000 to Fiske Warren, a "social experimenter," the handful of Shakers there chose different paths. Eldress Josephine Jilson and four other sisters relocated at Mount Lebanon, all but one joining the North Family. Several years later, Laura Beal, one of "the Harvard Club" who became "disenchanted" at her new home, was given $1,000 to settle old claims before returning to live in Ayer, Massachusetts. Nathaniel Nilant, the sole surviving male at the village, was placed in a local residence where his board was paid by the society. Hattie Whitney signed a discharge, severing her relationship "as a covenant member" and accepting a sum of $1,850 plus an assortment of furniture, bedding, clothing, "household conveniences," and a sewing machine. Myra McLain received a small monthly stipend as well as a supply of clothes, household furnishings, and domestic items. Mary Jane Maxwell was admitted to a "home for Aged people in Brockton, Massachusetts" under the terms of a contract releasing the society from all further claims.[30]

At Union Village the economic pressures of the closing decades of the nineteenth century left a mixed legacy. Under the management of James Fennessey, who took over as trustee, the village slowly lifted itself out of debt and back to a stability. They were thus able to enjoy the home improvements made during the 1890s. Their land, 4,005 acres, was rented out to farmers who worked it for shares, raising corn, wheat, oats, cattle, and hogs. But the community's numerical situation was not so favorable. In 1907 only thirty-three Believers remained at the village, twenty-seven of them over seventy years of age, and five over eighty. One visitor that year described the site as "an ideal old folk's home, with its beautiful grounds, fine orchards and splendid farms; its spacious, cheery, richly furnished and equipped buildings well fit it to supply physical needs and comforts and its soothing, restful, pervading quietude." What struck him most was the solitude. Even the worship pattern, no longer distinctive, was subdued. Since the old meetinghouse had been abandoned, the residents "sing, pray and speak, much in the fashion of a Methodist prayer-meeting." When the Shakers are gone, this observer wrote, it would be fitting if the site became "an old folks' home and a religious institution."[31]

On 15 October 1912 the trustees at Union Village, who now included Arthur Bruce at Canterbury, signed a sale agreement with officials of the Church of the United Brethren in Christ, who intended to use the properties for an orphanage. The transaction included the 4,005 acres and all buildings. The sale price was $50,000 in cash and a ten-year note for

$275,000. The agreement also provided that the seventeen Shakers on the premises might use Marble Hall and some of the adjacent service facilities for ten years, free of charge. By 1920 eleven of these last residents had died, three men had left, and the last three sisters were transferred to Canterbury. Yet the years of joint occupancy had not been peaceful. Numerous complaints were registered by Shakers and non-Shakers alike about the "meanness" of James Fennessey, who made life miserable for his fellow Believers. L. O. Miller, an official of the United Brethren church and a friend of Arthur Bruce and Irving Greenwood, lobbied the leadership at Canterbury for a $50,000 debt reduction in the 1920s. He also asked for one of "those fine old tall, hall clocks" at Canterbury, which they subsequently sent him. Many years later the Otterbein Home at the Union Village site gave up the care of children and became exclusively a retirement center. It is now owned by the United Methodist Church.[32]

The closing of South Union was even more complicated. As early as 1915 the central ministry and the society's trustees had contemplated selling the Kentucky property, but the transaction was not completed until 1922, at which time the eastern leaders assumed all responsibility for the undertaking. There were nine Shakers at South Union, several of whom were aged or incapacitated, and all of whom were "very anxious for a cash settlement and all the goods they can lug away." They were given the option of moving to one of the remaining eastern villages, but distance and a lack of contact had separated these few western Believers from their counterparts on the East Coast. As a result, none of the Kentuckians made that choice. Seven of the nine agreed to monetary settlements of $10,000 apiece. That arrangement drew sharp criticism from local lawyers, who declared that $10,000 was "a meagre provision" and totally inadequate for the "board, lodging, doctors' bills, washing, clothes and incidentals" of those advanced in years and unable to support themselves. The proposed settlements, they wrote, "are not looked upon as especially generous in view of the fact that the bulk of the estate is to be transferred elsewhere." Seven of the South Union Shakers initially relocated in Kentucky. Two of the seven, William Bates and Elizabeth Simmons, were married. Walter Shepherd, who supervised the closing and arranged the financial settlements, took Josie Bridges, who had mental problems, to Mount Lebanon. The most difficult decision involved Elder Logan Johns, eighty years old and too ill to be on his own, although that was his wish. Eventually Johns was taken by train to the East, accompanied by the farm manager, Joseph Wallace, whose lease on Shaker lands was bought out for $15,000. Approximately half of the amount realized from the sale of South Union and its contents was spent on the remaining Kentucky Shakers, the balance reverting to the control of the eastern Believers.[33]

With the sale of South Union in 1922 to an investment company, western Shakerism came to an end after more than a century of continuous existence, a victim of the society's inability to maintain sufficient economic strength and religious identity at sites in the Ohio River valley. By this action the United Society ended its formal presence west of the Appalachians. The Believers could no longer represent themselves as a national organization following this retreat, which required a reorientation in the society's distinctive sense of geography. Watervliet, New York, was once again the westernmost Shaker location. After 1922 the society embraced only seven eastern villages. In spite of the negative significance of these developments, the remaining Believers at times still echoed the spirit of an earlier judgment expressed by the central ministry: "But, though the number be few who stand the purifying furnace in Zion, the few are the flower of Heaven that yet Shall be fruitful, and, with their songs of Thanksgiving for Salvation make glad the City of God."[34]

The Feminization of the Society

The feminization of the United Society accelerated dramatically in the decades surrounding the turn of the twentieth century. Although women had always played an especially significant role in the Shaker experience compared with their counterparts in most other religious groups, during this period they achieved more than the parity theoretically possible under the covenants and Millennial Laws of the community. Shaker women began to dominate nearly every aspect of the society's life. Feminization within Shakerism, therefore, by contrast with developments in America that historians have described at length as the "cult of domesticity" and the doctrine of "two spheres," involved the increasing empowerment of Shaker women.[35]

One aspect of the feminization process was purely demographic. From the beginning, according to the best statistics available, women outnumbered men in the United Society. In the post-Tyringham years, however, the ratio of women to men increased so much that by the end of the century 72 percent, or nearly three out of four Shakers, were women—a slightly higher percentage if young children are excluded. This proportion continued to climb in the following decades. Women made up 83 percent of the society in 1916, 86 percent in 1926, and 88 percent in 1936.[36]

On this basis William Sims Bainbridge suggests that Shakerism was becoming "a women's sect." He concludes that because of their experiences with children, especially males, who left the society upon reaching maturity, the Believers accepted fewer boys late in the nineteenth century. Furthermore, widows with children and siblings without parents abounded, making the case that as the century wore on the society had become "a refuge rather than a revolution." Family journals from the second half of the nineteenth century support Bainbridge's contention. Within the space of four months in 1873, for example, the North Family at South Union took in eight women unaccompanied by husbands, each of whom brought between one and four children or dependents. Equally striking is the departure of the majority of these twenty-six individuals in a short time, with only a few ultimately remaining in the village. Nevertheless, it is unfair to dismiss these inquirers as "winter Shakers," thereby depreciating the legitimacy of all such individuals. People in distress did turn to the Shakers for assistance, and many of them subsequently left the community. But a substantial number of those who became lifelong Shakers, especially women, also entered the society under precisely these circumstances.[37]

But the feminization of Shakerism involves more than statistics. During these decades of retrenchment a cadre of talented female leaders emerged among the Believers. These women, in larger numbers than ever before within the United Society, began to fill roles traditionally reserved for males. In part this was because so few men remained in the society, and many of them were elderly and unable to carry a full burden of responsibilities. Yet these Shaker women were also very capable, resourceful, and energetic. They rose through the ranks, establishing their credentials within the society. Not since the time of Lucy Wright had women exercised so much power.[38]

The expanding role of women is especially evident in the pages of the Believers' monthly publication, first issued in 1871. The Shaker, renamed several times, is an invaluable resource for the society's history during the last three decades of the nineteenth century. Despite a bias in favor of the progressive party centered at the North Family in New Lebanon, this journal remains the single best reflection of the manifold changes sweeping the society during these years, including the rising significance of female leaders. The Shaker was never intended to be the voice for only one faction in the society. Rather, as George Lomas announced in the first issue, it was to communicate to the world the "ideas of life and happiness as viewed from the Shaker platform" without a show of "erudition" or "speculative theories of a theological nature." In other words, it was to serve as a public testimony to the Shaker way of life and thought.[39]

Although its first editorial board was all male, *The Shaker* offered an unusual opportunity for women to gain a public voice. Because copy was needed to fill the columns, contributions from everyone were welcome on the editor's desk. Furthermore, several of the leading supporters of the publication, including Giles Avery and Frederick Evans, were among those most inclined to accent the female side of Shakerism. The first issue featured Ann Lee's role as a "divinely inspired leader, and a *spiritual mother,* and the Eldress" of the early society. The Believers were identified as "sons and *daughters* of God" at a time when sex-exclusive language was the cultural norm. In explaining the basic beliefs of the sect, Evans spoke of the special significance Shakers attached to the "female of the earth" as revealed in the second coming. The first issue also contained the initial installment of a biography of Ann Lee, a long dialogue among Shaker sisters in the "Juvenile Department," an article on the duality of the deity that argued for gender balance within nature and the godhead, two signed essays submitted by Shaker sisters, and a poetic answer to Charlotte Cushman's query that resoundingly defended the life choice of "a SHAKER GIRL." In other words, the publication opened on a note that was overtly responsive to women.[40]

The contents of the Shaker periodical varied through the years, but the basic editorial policy remained constant, namely, to represent the society's ideas and activities to readers inside and outside the society. The editor, members of the central ministry, other leaders, and Believers from all the villages submitted materials. The journal included theological, philosophical, and scientific reflection and speculation; moral and spiritual meditation, counsel, and exhortation; and advice on health, agriculture, and domestic concerns. Its pages also featured correspondence from readers with responses, special articles for children or younger persons, historical documents, excerpts from other publications, Bible study materials, hymns and poems of all kinds, death notices, "Home Notes" from the scattered Shaker sites, and beginning in 1878, advertisements for Shaker products and other items. The journal therefore had something for everyone—Believers as well as readers from the world.[41]

Few, if any, of these categories were reserved exclusively for male contributors. Shaker women soon were writing articles for every section of the journal. They did not hesitate to adopt both a hortatory and an admonitory voice. Nor did they confine themselves to the sentimental tones that were expected of women as guardians of virtue and piety in the outside world. The Shaker sisters moved boldly into the area of speculative thought, even though the Believers in general continued to deny that they were engaged in writing theology, which they preferred to distinguish from religion. The theological arena was traditionally reserved for the ministry, the elders, and other male religious functionaries, but now the women of the society became active participants. Jane Knight, a member of the North Family at New Lebanon, for example, submitted a short essay on the biblical concept of the New Jerusalem, which she equated with the "Shaker Order." She contended that the organization of this earthly city mirrored a heavenly pattern. Unity, purity, simplicity—these were the marks of the new order, where the "true, legitimate sons and daughters" of God live like angels, forsaking "false systems" and natural relationships. "The spirits call for more of the angelic," wrote Knight, "less of the Adamic. We need to learn to 'dwell in everlasting burnings,' until self-pride and all that is not godly and true is consumed in the soul."[42]

This openness to contributions from women became even more explicit in 1873 when a destructive fire at Watervliet, New York, made it impossible for George Lomas to continue as editor of *The Shaker.* He was forced to assist with the rebuilding efforts at the village. Frederick Evans and Antoinette Doolittle were chosen to serve as editors in his place. In accepting the "chief editorship," Evans announced that consistent with "our fundamental idea of a *duality* in the Divine government of the universe, and also in our Society organizations, the *Shaker* will henceforth contain a department edited by Eldress Antoinette Doolittle, open to contributions from the Sisterhood of our Order; and to her such contributions, and other communications from females, both within and without the Shaker fraternity, may be addressed." He further justified this move by the widespread interest of "the outer world" in topics relating to "woman's rights, duties, and privileges." Evans also changed the name of the journal to *Shaker and Shakeress,* and he divided the eight pages with Doolittle, who was identified as Editress for the second half of each issue. In her inaugural issue she called on her "dear sisters" to unite in the effort to "advance the good cause" of the society through this publication.[43]

Doolittle's "Appeal" struck a highly responsive chord among Shaker women, who began immediately to submit essays and poetry on a host of topics. Many submissions reflected traditional themes in both language and subject matter. Some wrote of Shaker family life in sentimental tones. Nancy C. Danforth at Canterbury began an essay entitled "Our Christian Home" this way: "Home! how many sweet associations cluster around the name; a place where father and mother, brothers and sisters dwell in love and peace, and sound of discord should never enter." Yet, she wrote, the "blessings of a gospel home" surpass those of any earthly abode because of the "love and good will" found within it. The "Christian communistic home" is free of immorality, selfishness, and sensuality. All possessions have been "dedicated and consecrated to the service of God and his people." The "Christ Spirit" pervades this dwelling, and its inhabitants seek to live holy and blameless. "We would invite all who are truly sick of sin," wrote Danforth, "and earnestly desire to 'lay their heavy burdens down,' to seek this home, 'beyond the wind and tide' of earthly strife, and find that peace and rest their spirit's [sic] crave." In the communal home, according to her, "the order and harmony of heaven itself" had been realized.[44]

Other contributions by Shaker women were less traditional in perspective. Many spoke with determined voice for a particular cause. Ruth Webster at Union Village, for example, attacked time-honored theological arguments that countenanced the subordination of women. Ever since the expulsion of Adam and Eve from the Garden of Eden, she observed, women have been reproached for "leading mankind *into* sin." On that basis they have been forced to accept domination by men, especially in religious matters. Webster, however, declared that women were no longer responsible for the sinful condition of humanity. "About one hundred years ago God raised up a woman," she wrote, "and endowed her with wisdom to bring forth a testimony by which mankind might be led *out* of sin." As a result of the witness of Ann Lee, things had changed. Thousands had been affected by the "efficacy" of her testimony. "Henceforth," Webster warned, "let every one who continues in sin after hearing the gospel testimony, bear the reproach himself, and not cast it on woman. If mankind had been as ready to have been led *out* as *into* sin, long, ere this, lewdness would have ceased in the land, and long since, war would have been no more." In other words, according to Webster, acceptance of Ann Lee's testimony would also lead to social reform.[45]

Ann Lee was a favorite topic of these "scribling" Shaker women, to borrow a term from Nathaniel Hawthorne. The founder became all things to the female Believers. Some composed poetic tributes and hymns of praise to "Mother Ann"; others offered less sentimental portraits. Aurelia Mace at West Gloucester wrote:

O my Mother, my blessed Mother,
Her name to me is dear,
I'll praise her name
I'll spread her fame,
And kings and priests shall hear.

Cora C. Vinnes at Mount Lebanon penned the following verse:

> She came, our Mother, with a heart of steel,
> Bringing a courage worthy of the strife,
> And with a soul baptized with love and zeal
> She gave her life.

The figure of Ann Lee was a source of spiritual encouragement. On the one-hundred-and-twentieth anniversary of Lee's arrival in America, Emma B. King at Canterbury celebrated "the integrity of purpose which fitted her as a pure agent to disseminate light and truth to the world, and to reveal a way of salvation to all souls." King rejoiced in the religious accomplishments of "Mother Ann." A few years earlier Martha J. Anderson at Mount Lebanon, who gained considerable reputation as a writer, speaker, and singer, had drawn on the founder's image for political purposes. Anderson wrote, "The real mission of Ann Lee was to uplift and release woman from the thralldom of sin and set her in her proper place as the helpmeet and equal co-worker with man in all the duties and services of life. She struck the key-note to woman's emancipation, and it has sounded through the world ever since her message of truth was given." For these Shaker women religion, politics, history, and home were not sharply separated spheres.[46]

The Shaker publication provided women an expanding role within the society. Letters published in *Shaker and Shakeress* testify to its liberating impact. Several Believers expressed the "great satisfaction" and the sense of sisterhood they experienced through the journal. Hester A. Adams, the ranking eldress at Sabbathday Lake, combined traditional female virtues with a reminder of the special role of Shaker women when she wrote, "I am prompted by love to cast my mite into the Lord's treasury." She reassured her sisters throughout the society who felt the burden of their life choice, "We have a Father's strength to uphold, and a Mother's love to cheer and encourage." Betsey Ann Hollingsworth at Hancock expressed her delight with the periodical because it offered a "full manifestation of the Christ Spirit in both male and female." Hannah E. Potter's letter is perhaps the most revealing. "I have not been accustomed, nor do I feel qualified," she penned, "to write for the press; yet I possess so lively an interest in what I consider a *living cause,* of vital importance." She expressed special thanks that the journal was now "a medium through which Sisters, as well as Brethren, can present their views, and express their desires, and be heard." Potter testified that she had escaped the "bondage of the flesh" and the suffering associated with carnality because of the second appearance of the Christ Spirit in the female and the example provided by Ann Lee. Potter conveyed the exuberance of one who wants to shout a joyful secret for all to hear.[47]

Not all Believers were equally thrilled with the change of title in 1873 or with the division of responsibilities between Evans and Doolittle. After three years of the joint editorship, George Lomas resumed his former position in 1876 and, after thanking Evans and the others, promptly changed the title back to *The Shaker,* adding an explanatory line to the masthead, "A Dual Advocate of Christ Principles." Lomas defended his action by suggesting that a proper understanding of the original title amplified rather than detracted from the dual principle. Yet he promised that *The Shaker* would illustrate belief in "a brotherhood and sisterhood in Christ, where impartiality of rights is fully prevailing." He also urged that all friends of the journal support it in every way. Lomas expressed the hope that both brothers and sisters would contribute their "best thoughts on religion and science generally, on philosophy, physiology, on cooking and all domestic duties; on farming, gardening, building, mechanical improvements and moral truisms."[48]

In 1879, on the occasion of the one-hundredth issue of the journal, now entitled *The Shaker Manifesto,* Lomas restated its goal, namely, to illustrate "the plain, undraped purity and unselfishness of genuine Christian life." Despite this high ideal, however, the society struggled to maintain the financial solvency of the enterprise. The editor repeatedly pleaded with and cajoled his fellow Believers for subscriptions and subventions. At its height, the journal had several thousand subscribers, but the hope of expanding the circulation was never realized. The situation reached a crisis several times, and at one point the central ministry contrived a system of head taxes on the villages to support the publication. Nevertheless, testimonies of satisfaction by Believers and outsiders continued to be printed on its pages. At least one sister perceived the special role of this journal in the lives of Shaker women. Rebecca A. Shepard at Canterbury identified the publication as a "bond of union" among the Believers, a blessing worthy of continued sacrifice. She also suggested that the sisterhood, in particular, ought to continue their support of the periodical because it is a "Herald of Freedom," proclaiming the glad tidings of "'Woman's rights,' in the best, truest sense of the term." Therefore, she asked, how could we give it up?[49]

During the closing decades of the nineteenth century Shaker women began to assert greater authority within the society. By contrast with the achievements of Ruth Landon and Asenath Clark, Betsey Bates and Polly Reed—all respected members of the central ministry during the Middle Period—the accomplishments of later female leaders such as Antoinette Doolittle, Leila S. Taylor, Aurelia Mace, Anna White, Catherine Allen, and Emma J. Neale were of a different order (fig. 28). The women of the Middle Period focused their attention and energies principally on the needs and concerns of their own sex within the society. That was the time-honored pattern of internal administration among the Believers. The new generation of Shaker women was more assertive and active in society affairs involving both males and females. These younger leaders took seriously the social and political implications of the Believers' religious views, and as a result they sought to establish greater parity within the society. They were supported in this effort by the growing women's rights movement in the United States.[50]

Antoinette Doolittle was the first Shaker woman of this new breed to achieve prominence. She exercised immense influence on the sisterhood through her position as an eldress at the North Family and her reputation as a spokesperson for Shakerism. But Doolittle did not confine her public presentations to women. She became an accomplished platform lecturer, accustomed to addressing large mixed audiences. She also wrote extensively in a sophisticated manner. In one typical essay, she examined the meaning of the common phrase "the *mystery* of the Gospel." Doolittle was convinced that the endless "theological discussions" on this subject had produced little insight. In her explanation, she began with the assumption that every "human mind" possesses an "intuitive sense" capable of discerning truth. That sense, however, has been corrupted. As a result, she concluded, the "mystery of God" is the product of the mixing of good and evil. The "*unperverted* Natural Order" knows no such disharmony; mystery and misery came to the human race because of the abuse of generative powers. Truth, therefore, contains no mystery, according to her. However, she wrote, where "so much reliance [is] placed upon the atoning blood of Jesus and the pulpit eloquence of a hireling priesthood, . . . the *mystery* of iniquity will continue to work." Nonetheless, Doolittle was optimistic, for she believed that "spiritually progressed, honest, earnest souls" do exist, watching and waiting for the sounds of truth, "who live a pure, celibate life for conscience sake." The "star of *Purity*" rising on the "spiritual horizon," she contended, was the sign of an approaching "brighter and more perfect day." Doolittle, who wrote more copy for the journal than any other woman, set a literary example for Shaker sisters of all persuasions.[51]

28. Antoinette Doolittle and Anna White
Doolittle and White both served as eldresses in the North Family at Mount Lebanon, New York. Doolittle died in 1886, White in 1910. (Courtesy Shaker Museum and Library, Old Chatham, New York.)

One of the most prolific Believers to follow in her footsteps was Aurelia G. Mace at Sabbathday Lake. Her father was Fayette Mace, an eccentric Universalist minster, and her mother, Sarah, an early women's rights activist. Aurelia, who signed the covenant in 1858 at the age of twenty-three, served as Second Eldress at the village from 1860 to 1880 and as trustee during the last fifteen years of her life. Mace was a regular contributor to the Shaker periodical, and she also wrote a series of letters to a Bangor newspaper in the mid-1880s. She subsequently collected these and other writings and issued them as *The Aletheia: Spirit of Truth*. On the title page, Mace printed Theodore Parker's words, "God is our Infinite Mother; She will hold us in her arms of blessedness and beauty forever and ever." Mace dedicated the book "To 'My Ten,' Gems of Priceless Worth," the young girls she supervised and taught as a schoolteacher. The goal of a Shaker, she wrote, "is to live the pure life which Jesus lived and taught" by subduing the animal and cultivating the spiritual nature.[52]

By disposition Mace was an essayist, her writings ranging widely over diverse topics (fig. 29). She wrote historical vignettes, meditations on religious topics, eulogies to former acquaintances, and public lectures. All reflected her preoccupation with the Christ Spirit in its various manifestations. In one letter Mace defined Christ as "the Anointing Power" available to everyone. "Inasmuch as Jesus became the Christ and as Ann Lee became the Christ," she wrote, "so may all be in possession of the same spirit to that degree which they make themselves worthy by good works." This same force, she informed the Russian novelist Leo Tolstoy, is the "foundation" of the Shaker community. Likewise, it was this Christ Spirit that was responsible for persuading the first convert to Shakerism in Maine, Nathan Merrill. And this same spirit would spread the Shaker testimony in years to come. Even the physical layout of *The Aletheia* lent an air of spirituality to the publication. Twenty-two formal portraits of Believers from the second half of the nineteenth century grace its pages. In every case the subject of the photograph is gazing away from the camera into a distant realm. These saintly figures lend an aura of otherworldliness to Mace's testimony. Each photograph also includes a tribute—a citation in prose or a short verse. The uniform caps and berthas of the women strike a note of monastic uniformity and dedication; the males, by contrast, appear almost indistinguishable in dress from their worldly counterparts. Mace tried to create the impression in her volume that all the Believers were one in pursuit of the spirit of truth, but even in appearance, only the women were united.[53]

29. Sisters from Canterbury and Sabbathday Lake
Formal portrait made late in the nineteenth century that includes Aurelia Mace of
Sabbathday Lake (holding the book) and Dorothy Durgin of Canterbury (second from
the right, seated in the chair). (Courtesy Shaker Museum and Library, Old Chatham,
New York.)

The crowning intellectual achievement by Shaker women during
these decades of change was the publication in 1904 of *Shakerism Its
Meaning and Message* by Anna White and Leila S. Taylor. These two eldresses at the North Family, standing in a line descending from Doolittle,
personified the progressive spirit. They were supremely confident that
Shakerism as "a system of faith and a mode of life" was relevant to the
twentieth-century world. In the text White and Taylor celebrated in detail
the accomplishments of the Believers. The volume is therefore both history and theology. They devoted half of the four hundred pages to retelling
the story of the society, beginning with the Camisards in France, the
Wardleys in England, and the "soul struggles" of "a bright, active little
girl" growing up in a "lowly cottage" in Manchester. This girl-turned-
woman became the conduit for "some of the most remarkable spiritual
phenomena the world has seen—electric streams from Deity." From Ann
Lee emerged "a great religious movement" that has defeated "monopoly,

immorality, intemperance and crime" within its midst and created a context where purity, freedom, equality, and industry prevail. White and Taylor then carried the account of the society's history up to the turn of the twentieth century, charting the social, economic, political, and religious changes within Shakerism. Their volume was the most comprehensive historical statement ever written by members of the society.[54]

The second half of *Shakerism Its Meaning and Message* was a description of the religious beliefs and experiences of the Shakers. The approach in this portion was more theological than historical, though often the two were inseparable. White and Taylor wrote about the spiritualistic heritage of the Believers, suggesting that the origins of the society were tied to "[v]oices and visions" and that the Shakers were the "First Modern Spiritualists." The authors identified the leading religious principles of the Believers: the duality of God and the corresponding equality of the human sexes; the indwelling of the Christ Spirit and the process of working out salvation by becoming "one with God"; the joint practices of celibacy and confession of sins; and the community of goods. All were to be understood as the fulfillment of biblical prophecy. These principles, they contended, were responsible for the Believers' accomplishments in such areas as industrial production, publications, and music.[55]

This 1904 volume, called by one scholar "the last major Shaker public statement," was essentially an exercise in apologetics, a defense and explanation of the faith. It was one with the missionary effort launched by the society in the 1860s and 1870s because it attempted to extend the influence of Shakerism outside the boundaries of the community. Nowhere was that purpose clearer than in the closing chapter, "A Look into the Future," where Anna White depicted Shakerism as "but another name for advanced Christianity," which calls for men and women who are "honest, true-hearted, desiring purity, strength, brotherhood and sisterhood, the attainment of self-control, contentment, spiritual happiness, willing to work for soul development, for the good of others, for the uplifting of humanity—those who will confess their sins, and depart therefrom." According to the authors, the United Society offered an answer to those seeking the meaning of life as well as to those troubled by the prospect of death. Only now, they wrote, was the world "beginning to ring with the reverberations of the Divine messages" that the Shakers represented in such causes as the rights of labor, medical freedom, animal protection, temperance, and sexual equality. White and Taylor declared that in this context the Shaker sister was "the freest woman in the world." They were confident that Shakerism embodied "the underlying truths of God-life in all ages" and that a new age was dawning in which more and more individuals would find "their true home" in that faith and practice.[56]

After reading about a meeting of the Equal Rights Club of Hartford, Connecticut, at which the idea of a Divine Mother in the world's religions was examined, Anna White wrote to that organization in 1903 describing the Shaker belief in the "Motherhood of God." White attacked religious leaders of the past who had created that "'horrible man-made monster of cruelty' that 'Bluebeard God' of Cotton Mather and Jonathan Edwards," a god untouched by the feminine. Furthermore, she pointed out, the "gift of the Mother Spirit" that was revealed in ancient India and Persia had been received by Ann Lee and imparted to the "quiet centres of practical Christian Communism" in America for the past century and a quarter. To the Shakers, too, White wrote, "the universe is one harmonious whole, and the eternal Cosmic energy is the Mother of the universe." This statement was perhaps the most expansive expression of the feminine principle in Shaker theology during this period.[57]

These intellectual accomplishments notwithstanding, the majority of Shaker women during the Time of Transformation still were preoccupied on a daily basis with domestic tasks—not with theological reflection, political action, or writing poetry. Family journals confirm the heavy burden of pressing household responsibilities for the average female Believer. An unending string of domestic chores confronted the women of the society, a situation worsened by declining numbers and the aging process, especially the shrinking percentage of men in the community. Not even the rotation of work assignments softened the impact of these steady demands. The situation of an unnamed seamstress at Watervliet, New York, in 1891 was typical, as her journal makes clear. She was regularly involved in a continuous cycle of washing and ironing as well as dressmaking. Sickness among family members added to her burdens. She wrote, "Met is a little better. I have all I can do to do her work and tend the chickens. Magie helps me so I can get some dressmaking along. Eva is in the garden. Sts. Annie and Co is mending." There was no liberation from these tasks for Shaker women.[58]

The domestic orientation of the sisters' daily activities did not change as the society moved into the twentieth century. These enterprises, in fact, became more essential to the economic survival of the remaining families. Anna Goepper of the South Family in Watervliet, New York, provides a glimpse into the world of Shaker women in the early twentieth century. Goepper, in her early forties in 1912, was a native of Germany who entered Union Village in 1878 at the age of seven. After moving to Watervliet in 1910, she was assigned much of her time to baking and kitchen responsibilities. Her journal provides a revealing picture of her obligations. On 25 July 1912, for example, Goepper made twelve pies for a dinner at which fifteen paying guests were expected, only to discover later that they were not coming. On that occasion, she expressed her frustration—"Quite a mean piece of business, I think"—because the sisters had "worked hard all forenoon, & went to a great deal of extra trouble." Dinner guests were a regular source of income for the family. Six "young lady clerks" from Albany once ate both dinner and supper, paying fifty and twenty-five cents, respectively, for the meals. On 21 February 1913, Goepper noted that she had been serving in the "bake-room" sixteen consecutive weeks. Later she recorded twelve weeks of kitchen duty and that she had made three hundred pies during her job rotation. At harvest time the demands for food increased dramatically. "Threshers come tomorrow," she wrote. "They are expecting about ten men for dinner counting our hired hands."[59]

The other women at the South Family were equally busy with their chores: picking huckleberries in nearby swamps, canning raspberries, churning butter, caring for the sick, and cleaning the hired men's house, which included exterminating bedbugs, were but a few of the tasks. They were also "working every minute getting ready for the Christmas sale." The girls were "almost killing themselves," wrote Goepper, preparing items for sale; even Eldress Annie Case labored for that cause. At the preholiday sale the Shaker sisters displayed a variety of "fancy goods" produced throughout the year. In the decades following the Civil War, declining membership made heavy agriculture and manufacturing activities less feasible, so the items produced by the Shaker women became increasingly critical to the society's economy. These goods were sold in the Office at the villages, at nearby hotels and resorts, and by traveling salespersons. The same tasks occupied the sisters at every village. "Should you call in to see us in the present week you would find us about as when you were here," wrote one sister at Canterbury, "busily making sweaters or fancy work &c. caring for company, gathering peas, beans or currants beside the usual household duties so necessary to a well regulated home." Although these activities were taxing, they were also satisfying to the Believers and an important source of income for the families.[60]

The catalog of goods for sale by Shaker women was impressive, both for its variety as well as for the skill and creativity displayed in the items. Among the fancy goods were ornamental boxes made of wood or cardboard as well as woven poplar containers for storing sewing items, jewelry, and other incidentals; lined carriers and oval boxes; pincushions in various shapes and sizes; balsam-filled pillows; sieves; baskets and brushes; woven palm-leaf fans; crocheted pieces of various kinds; and dolls dressed in traditional Shaker clothing. Some villages increasingly relied on the sale of comestibles including applesauce, horseradish, pickles, baked beans, jams, and jellies. Candies, too, became a source of income—chocolates, nuts, preserved orange peel, and maple sugar. The sisters knitted sweaters, stockings, shawls, mittens, and other coverings. They also made the famous Dorothy cloaks, named after their designer, Eldress Dorothy Durgin of Canterbury. As the number of Shaker brothers declined, these items carried an increasingly heavy share of the income-producing burden.[61]

The pressures of daily work and economic survival created a strong bond of sisterhood among Shaker women. Goepper filled her journal with expressions of love and affection, friendship and camaraderie. She and her Shaker sisters worked hard, but they were also able to relax and enjoy themselves. For entertainment they played the card game Flinch and listened to the Victrola. On her birthday, Goepper had a party with cake, crepe-paper streamers, caps, and noisemakers. At the celebration they listened to "Uncle Josh pieces" and "Artful Annie's two Step" on the phonograph. Afterward she wrote, "It was grand, and the nicest birthday I ever had in my life. It was a very jolly evening for all of us, and one long to be remembered." She received a number of gifts, including stationery, hose, a "tidy," and a bottle of perfume. Goepper clearly had a zest for life. When she lost a bet on the presidential election of 1912, she paid her friend by treating her to a turkey dinner in Albany and attending Proctor's Theatre. "We had a grand time," she wrote, "& don't you forget it." This bonding among the sisters no doubt strengthened their commitment to the community (fig. 30).[62]

Another shift in the economic sphere occurred during the Time of Transformation. For a variety of reasons, after 1880 the society began to place women in the position of village trustee. Before that Shaker sisters had been relatively uninvolved in the "financial management" of the society. The work of the sisterhood was not even calculated regularly in annual reports until sometime after the Civil War. After 1880, however, as Karen K. and Pamela J. Nickless have shown, the role of trustee was distinguished from that of deacon, the trustee being the only party responsible for legal and financial transactions with the outside world. In the 1870s some tension developed between the sexes over these financial arrangements. One former Shaker, recalling his years as a member of the society, noted that men "kept all the books of account, and in their names

30. Group of Shaker Sisters
Stereoptican view of Believers at Canterbury produced by W. G. C. Kimball, a Concord, New Hampshire, photographer. (Courtesy Jerry Grant, Old Chatham, New York.)

were made all deeds and titles to real estate." That pattern changed
quickly, however, as the number of males decreased and as female Believers occupied increasingly important roles. No women served as trustees
before 1880, according to the Nicklesses, but after that date several did.[63]

The emergence of these "new Shaker women" corresponded with
the changing situation of women in America near the end of the nineteenth century. Mary P. Ryan has described this as a time when American
women moved in significant numbers into the social and economic
spheres, even though they were still heavily encumbered by their "domestic associations." In other words, they were torn between their desires and
the controlling realities. Carroll Smith-Rosenberg, writing about the appearance in the late nineteenth century of "the single, highly educated,
economically autonomous New Woman," has said, "The New Woman
constituted a revolutionary demographic and political phenomenon. Es-
chewing marriage, she fought for professional visibility, espoused innovative, often radical, economic and social reforms, and wielded real
political power." The new breed of Shaker women, like their non-Shaker
counterparts, formed the vanguard of twentieth-century Believers.[64]

The World of Finance Capitalism

The last stronghold of male domination in the United Society was
the financial and legal arena. What earlier had been the prerogative of the
"order and office of deacons" under the Millennial Laws of 1821, by midcentury became the designated responsibility of the society's trustees. It
was they, for example, who held consecrated property in their own names
on behalf of the society. They, and only they, legally could incur debt, hold
bonds, transfer property by sale or mortgage, and enter into contracts with
persons outside the society. The trustees were the chief financial officers
of the society. As the nineteenth century progressed, they became involved in a range of increasingly complex undertakings.[65]

In theory, the trustees were subject to the advice and counsel of the
elders and the ministry: the temporal realm was subordinate to the spiritual in Shakerism. And in many instances, the record provides evidence of
close interaction between elders and trustees. In fact, however, as the
nineteenth century wore on, the office of trustee became increasingly autonomous. Practical circumstances often dictated the necessity of independent judgments. Trustees were forced to make decisions at locations
far removed from the village meetinghouse. They did not always have the
time or opportunity to consult with the elders or the ministry. Conse-

quently, they often acted without consultation or prior approval from society leaders.[66]

The trustees exercised immense financial power because the collective resources of the villages and the society were substantial. Although there is no reliable estimate of the overall worth of the society during this period, intermittent financial reports exist for individual families and villages. Yearly reports, however, did not reckon the value of real estate or capital improvements. In general, they confined their attention to sales information and the inventory of goods, livestock, and services. The annual data provide little basis for estimating the combined monetary worth of the United Society. Outsiders assumed that the society was very wealthy. In court, for example, a lawyer once asked Robert Valentine, a Mount Lebanon trustee, if the society's real estate holdings in New York State alone were worth 10 million dollars. Valentine refused to answer directly or to offer an estimate. Opponents of the society repeatedly charged the Shakers with not paying their fair share of taxes—a charge the Believers refuted vigorously. Outsiders petitioned the New York legislature for a law requiring annual disclosure of the society's assets. In 1883, when the central ministry sought to distribute the cost of publishing *The Shaker Manifesto* across the society, they wrote a circular letter requesting each village to submit "a statement of its entire amount of wealth, rendering . . . an honest report of the same, as near as the Leaders of society can approximate it." Not surprisingly, they did not receive uniform responses from the trustees who were responsible for supervising those assets.[67]

By the closing decades of the nineteenth century, the financial base of the society had narrowed considerably. The failure to attract new converts meant that the stream of newly consecrated lands and goods dried to a trickle. After midcentury the shrinking and aging of the membership reduced substantially the supply of cheap labor. The Believers were forced to hire more outsiders to run their farms and shops. The product line gradually shifted as fancy goods and other domestic items became the primary articles for sale. The one constant in the economic equation was the land, which in many locations had appreciated substantially over time, even though the higher values could not be tapped without mortgaging or selling the property. Handling real estate was the exclusive responsibility of the trustees.[68]

Many Shaker trustees were skillful in their management of the society's resources. They took advantage of the community's ability to produce labor-intensive agricultural products and manufactured goods at lower prices than their competitors. These financial managers became

knowledgeable about production costs, the marketplace, distribution systems, and profit margins. They interacted regularly with suppliers, merchants, lawyers, and bankers. The trustees moved with ease among people
of the world, and for the most part the Shakers were successful in these
capitalistic arenas. They were known for both honesty and shrewdness.
Outsiders continued to hold many of their products in high esteem. The
seed industry at South Union during the 1870s and 1880s is a good example. The Kentucky Believers filled orders from that state and Tennessee
as well as from Mississippi and Arkansas. Their customers were pleased
with the merchandise and frequently solicited the Shakers' judgment on
business matters.[69]

The skilled management of Shaker enterprises was also evident
in the chair industry at the South Family in Mount Lebanon. Under
the direction of Robert M. Wagan, this business expanded in the 1860s
and 1870s. When demand rose, a new chair factory was built in 1872,
equipped with machinery that made possible increased productivity—as
many as two dozen chairs a day. Wagan's mass production methods and
new marketing techniques, including the circulation of catalogs, brought
increased success to the endeavor (fig. 31). A special exhibit of Shaker
chairs was mounted at the Philadelphia Centennial. The growing reliance
on machine work resulted in more standardized products. By the 1880s
the Shakers were purchasing some parts for their chairs from outside
suppliers. Wagan's management of the chair industry was extremely successful. After his death in 1883, one obituary notice credited him with
establishing "a nation-wide market for Shaker chairs," a market that continued for several more decades.[70]

By the second half of the nineteenth century many earlier prohibitions restricting intercourse with the world appeared archaic. Now the
trustees traveled extensively on business. Benjamin Gates even journeyed
to Europe. Trustees standardly entered into rental contracts, signed the
indenture papers of children entrusted to the Shakers, bought and sold
assets, and worked closely with attorneys to defend the society in court.
David Parker, the trustee at Canterbury, signed a contract with Aaron
Woodman, who agreed to work the Mount Morris farm for the Shakers at
annual wages of $500. At Enfield, Connecticut, the trustee was required
by state law to provide a list of persons who had lived at least five years
with the Shakers in order to establish the society's liability for maintenance of these departees if they became impoverished. The trustees signed
deeds granting the right of way for railroad construction across Shaker
lands. They also invested surplus funds, a practice that began before the

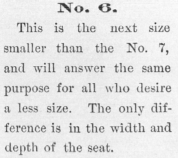

No. 6.

This is the next size smaller than the No. 7, and will answer the same purpose for all who desire a less size. The only difference is in the width and depth of the seat.

We have this chair with or without rockers or arms. See price list.

31. Chair Advertisement
Chairs made at Mount Lebanon advertised in an 1876 catalog. (Courtesy Shaker Museum and Library, Old Chatham, New York.)

Civil War. Early in the century land was purchased with excess funds, some tracts ostensibly for woodlots but others for lumber, some nearby, others remote from Shaker villages. These purchases document the beginnings of finance capitalism among the Believers, who invested with the hope of substantial returns.[71]

Before long the trustees were making investments not only in real estate, but also in commercial paper. When Richard Bushnell, the trustee of the North Family at New Lebanon, listed the family's financial assets in 1858, nearly 50 percent of the total $54,275 was in corporate bonds, including the New York and Erie, the New York Central, and the Illinois railroads. He also itemized "Bonds & Mortgages on real Estate in different Places," ranging from houses and lots in Albany, Hudson, and Pittsfield to shares in the United States Hotel in Pittsfield. Likewise, he recorded debts due on brooms and garden seeds as well as promissory notes from individuals. The North Family and others possessed a diversified portfolio of investments. During the 1850s the Church Family at Mount Lebanon invested in farmland and timber lots in Michigan. In 1873 they sold a farm in that state, and payment included the transfer of deeds for two lots and houses in Niles, Michigan, and four in Chicago. Members of the ministry took part in these transactions as well. In 1872, for example, Giles Avery purchased a mortgage bond from Louisville. In the same year he lent Benjamin Gates $500 for investment in Georgia at a rate of 10 percent per annum. His records reveal investments in the American Book Exchange and the Atlantic Pacific Rail Road Tunnel Company. In other words, the Shakers entered the world of corporate finance almost as soon as it emerged in America.[72]

In the decades after the Civil War, the incorporation of America occurred with dizzying speed. As Alan Trachtenberg has demonstrated, such transforming influences as the impact of the railroad and factory system, the westward expansion, the effect of technology on communications, the growth of cities, and the rise of the modern corporation created modern America. Old assumptions about work and wealth were discarded as new opportunities beckoned. Speculative fever swept the country during the closing decades of the century. Some investors acquired immense wealth and resources; others were dragged into debt and poverty. It was a glorious time for successful risk takers, who left their names on industrial and commercial empires. For many others, these were years of dashed hopes and dreams. Incongruous as it may seem, the Believers took part enthusiastically in the Gilded Age.[73]

The Shaker trustees controlled sufficient assets to emerge as serious players in the financial markets. They gained additional economic leverage with the closing of the villages. One unintended result of retrenchment, beginning with the closing of Tyringham, was an increase in the capacity of the trustees and other leaders—East and West—to participate in the game of finance capitalism. The last Shakers left the site at Tyringham long before the society sold all of the property. Negotiations with potential buyers were still under way in 1876, months after the few remaining Believers had been relocated at other New England villages. The deal finally struck with Dr. Joseph Jones in Honesdale, Pennsylvania, involved cash, promissory notes, and a large tract of timber land in Pike County, Pennsylvania. The agreement included the North Family at Mount Lebanon. Frederick Evans, though an elder at the North Family and not a trustee, was heavily involved in the negotiations. (Perhaps that explains why he was later named, along with two trustees, in a suit filed by Mary Charlotte Byrdsall to recover funds after she left the society and why, shortly before his death in 1893, Evans signed a sworn statement turning over all assets and debts to trustees Benjamin Gates and Robert Valentine.) Although it is impossible to follow the paper trail in the Tyringham sale, speculative fever clearly had become a factor in the society. That transaction ultimately resulted in a substantial financial loss because the Shakers were unable to realize a profit from the production of timber on the land in Pennsylvania.[74]

For the next half century or more, land became the primary source of cash for the trustees. They raised money for expenses and investment purposes by selling outlots, woodlots, timber tracts, farms, houses, and other real estate that the Believers had accumulated through the years. Sometimes the sales involved very small amounts. The Hancock Church Family, for example, sold two houses and small lots during the first years of the twentieth century for $350 and $200, respectively. The Believers at Shirley, by contrast, were able to realize more than $2,500 from the sale of the Mark Holden farm. As the years passed and the village closings accelerated, the Shakers came into larger sums of money. The sale of Shirley to the Commonweath of Massachusetts in 1908 netted the society $43,000. In 1910 Peter F. Sering purchased the Whitewater site, including approximately 780 acres, for $40,000. Frances Hall sold the last parcel of the South Family at Watervliet, New York, approximately 444 acres and standing buildings, to Leonard and Catharina Bol for $15,500. The sale of Harvard to Fiske Warren in 1918 brought the society $60,000—one-third in cash and the remainder over five years on a 6 percent mortgage.[75]

From this time forward society trustees and members of the ministry engaged in an astonishing amount of wheeling and dealing, frequently without consultation or authorization and sometimes for personal financial advantage. Many Believers, of course, carried out their responsibilities with integrity, to the best of their abilities, and in a traditional manner. Some had little room to maneuver, however, especially when the circumstances were desperate. Matthew B. Carter, for example, first in the Union Village ministry during the 1880s, presided over that site during a difficult decade. Several persons there in positions of responsibility violated the society's trust. Uncontrollable events also took their toll. A tornado struck the village in 1886, inflicting considerable damage. An arsonist set a costly fire at the South Family. But Carter contributed to the problems by authorizing loans totaling $16,000 to the Dayton Furnace Company, a firm developing a hot-air furnace. In spite of public assurances from Joseph Slingerland that there was "nothing loose going on about that Business," by the end of the decade the Believers in Ohio were forced to acknowledge a bad investment. They could not recover their own funds and also had to cover the losses of Mary and Louisa Gass, who had invested privately in the venture. Late in 1889 Carter lamented, "The wrighter is trying to use what little ability he has to sustain and maintain the cause of Believers." In fact, however, he was incapable of handling these financial matters. Giles Avery admitted that some Shakers were making bad investments with devastating results. "It is a time of great tribulation and spiritual dearth among Believers quite generally—Some families & societies much more active than others. Believers in some societies have, by bad management, become indebted to the world! This has produced great loss of members, loss of spiritual gift, & withall occasioned the breaking up of families. Oh, Would to Heaven all *could,* & *would,* learn wisdom & practice it."[76]

Benjamin Gates served the Believers with distinction for many years as a trustee. Admitted to the society at the age of four in 1821, Gates had known no other life. A tailor by training, his childhood and education within the community exposed him to a wide range of occupations, from agriculture and timbering to carpentry and blacksmithing. These experiences combined with native diligence to make him a natural candidate for major responsibilities. In 1856 he became a trustee at New Lebanon. During the following decades, he represented the interests of the United Society in a variety of financial, economic, and legal circumstances. Gates played a pivotal role, for example, in establishing a business relationship with Andrew Judson White, who owned a small pharmaceutical firm in New York City and London. A. J. White became the primary distributor of medicinal products manufactured at Mount Lebanon, including extracts, pills, and plasters. The most successful product was the Shaker extract of roots, later marketed under the name Mother Siegel's Syrup. White's firm published promotional literature, including a series of "so-called Shaker almanacs," which contained testimonials for his medicines. Gates traveled to Europe in 1878 to assist in stabilizing the English markets for White's enterprises. In 1887 Gates represented the North Family in Chicago, where "a dishonest lawyer," according to society records, was "trying to steal" some city lots owned by the Shakers. He went to Union Village as a troubleshooter to assess the economic problems there. In the same year he advised the leadership at New Lebanon to close down the seed industry (fig. 32) and to transfer needed resources and personnel to the medical extract business, pointing out that it was costing the Believers $5,000 per year for "imbecile help" to maintain the production of extracts. He also represented the central ministry at the sale of North Union in 1889. In 1903 at age eighty-four, Gates was finally released from all public responsibilities.[77]

Although he was a sophisticated manager, as his extant correspondence reveals, Gates's speculative hunches were not always sound. He played an instrumental role, for example, in launching the short-lived settlement at Narcoossee, Florida. In late 1894 when the North Family at Mount Lebanon was greatly agitated by the "Florida fever," he pushed for action. "Benjamin Gates our trustee is very anxious to purchase some land

32. Seed Label

Garden seed label from Mount Lebanon, probably from the 1880s. (Courtesy Shaker Museum and Library, Old Chatham, New York.)

down there, and start a family there," wrote the keeper of the family journal. Gates was part of the advance group that scouted the area before the purchase in 1896 of more than 7,000 acres in Osceola County for $94,500. He became the informal head of the Florida colony called Olive Branch. Some of the Believers had doubts about the wisdom of this venture. One of those involved, Andrew Barrett, feared that financial considerations might become dominant. Early in the venture, he wrote: "When I see the greed of money step in and engross our whole attention I begin to think we have forgotten the primary object of our exit into Florida. . . . To me this was not intended as merely a *speculative scheme* for a quiet and comfortable home with a chance to make a few dollars to still keep the thing a running. If God is in it I don't believe he wants any such Business." By contrast, Calvin Reed at Mount Lebanon had received a spirit message from Giles Avery, assuring the Believers that "the glory and hand of God" rested on the "investment in Florida." Gates prevailed in spite of the debate about the colony among the Believers. He did, in fact, hope for a successful business enterprise at Narcoossee. It was his decision to raise pineapples as the primary commercial crop in the first years.[78]

Levi Shaw, a contemporary of Gates, was one of the principal trustees at the North Family. His career illustrates another aspect of trustee activity during the closing decades of the nineteenth century. Shaw was the agent and wholesale dealer for carpet and rug beaters manufactured at Mount Lebanon. In the public eye, he operated as the owner of that business. Trustees at other villages advertised themselves in similar ways. On letterhead, for example, they appeared as the proprietors of Shaker enterprises. "A. L. Johns, Trustee" was printed on promotional literature for South Union's cattle business, "John Whiteley" on labels for cayenne put up at Shirley, and "William Dumont Trustee" on a display card for Tamar Laxative produced at Sabbathday Lake. These trustees were responsible for giving an account of the funds they handled, but in practice they operated with relative autonomy. Late in the century it became common at many villages for the same person to serve as both trustee and elder. Trustees became accustomed to being involved in litigation on behalf of the society. Shaw, for example, was party to a suit against Olive Hand, a neighbor in Columbia County, in which boundary lines and timber rights were at stake. Court records demonstrate his business acumen, although the Believers lost that suit. Shaw's wisdom in the following matter is harder to discern. In 1898 he and Timothy Rayson signed a contract with Charles M. Comstock of Windsor, New York, agreeing to equip and fund an expedition to prospect for gold in the Klondike. The lure of great wealth beckoned the partners. "Alaska and the N.W. Territorii are rich in minerals," wrote Comstock's brother, "and there will be fortunes taken out for the next 100 years and not exhaust it." Comstock's honesty, however, was questionable: he wrote more than one check to Shaw without sufficient bank funds to cover them. Nevertheless, three years later the partnership was still in place.[79]

The full extent of Shaker involvement in speculative activities becomes clearest with Joseph Slingerland, another Believer of long standing (fig. 33). He had been admitted to the Church Family at New Lebanon in 1854 at the age of ten. In 1889 Slingerland was sent to Union Village and appointed second in the ministry in order to deal with the deteriorating financial situation in the West. Once on the scene, he acted with relative disregard for local feelings. He became directly involved in the decision to close North Union by refusing to pay the taxes on that property, which Union Village had been assisting with for a number of years. Slingerland unsuccessfully tried to force the closing of Watervliet, Ohio, in the same way. Instead he sold their livestock and other movable properties to pay the tax bill. To the Believers at these villages, his decisions appeared arbitrary and dispiriting. Slingerland was also the driving force behind an expensive renovation program at Union Village. Under his direction, the

33. Joseph Slingerland
Slingerland spearheaded the financial reorganization of western Shakerism and the modernization of Union Village, Ohio, in the 1890s. (Courtesy Shaker Museum and Library, Old Chatham, New York.)

Believers repaired buildings, fenced fields, and set out new orchards. Most of the farmland, except for gardens and orchards, was then rented to outsiders. The most striking "improvement" was the transformation of the Office, built in 1810, from a traditional plain Shaker building to a turreted Victorian edifice, complete with columned porch, ornamented cupola, marble floors, walnut paneling, ornate staircase, and modern sanitation facilities. Not all the residents at Union Village welcomed Marble Hall (fig. 34) and the other changes. In fact, newspapers depicted the Ohio village as being victimized by eastern appointees intent on taking control of western resources.[80]

In the midst of these activities, Slingerland also traveled extensively. In 1894 he joined three eastern brethren, including Benjamin Gates, on their first trip to Florida, to look for "land suitable for Believers to live on."

34. Marble Hall, Union Village, Ohio
Facade of Marble Hall, as the Office at Union Village came to be known, after modernization. (Courtesy Shaker Museum and Library, Old Chatham, New York.)

That expedition and the subsequent founding of the settlement at Narcoossee whetted Slingerland's appetite for a similar undertaking. In 1897
and 1898, under his leadership, Union Village purchased two pre–Civil
War plantations on the Altamaha River—Altama and Hopeton—thirteen
miles from Brunswick, Georgia, and more than 7,000 adjacent acres.
Using assets derived in part from the sale of North Union properties, the
Ohio Believers paid $13,000 in cash for Altama and its 2,000 acres. The
former owners had raised sugar, cotton, and rice on these lands with slave
labor; at the time of purchase the fields were overgrown and the mansion
in disrepair. Later the same year the Ohio Believers purchased more than
7,000 additional acres and a number of city blocks in the town of White
Oak, Georgia. They paid $16,500 for that acreage and bought the lots on
contract.[81]

The Georgia enterprise went badly from the start. Slingerland and
Eldress Elizabeth Downey led a small delegation of settlers to the site in
early 1898. The Believers at Union Village, however, were not united in
support of the undertaking. The financial strain of starting this outpost

was severe. Livestock and goods were sent in abundance during the first months of 1898, causing Oliver Hampton to write, "I hope this is the last loaded car that is to go to Georgia." Things did not go smoothly in Georgia. Two of the Believers left the colony less than three months after it was founded and were married shortly afterward. By 15 April Slingerland and Downey had returned to Ohio. "So the Georgia Colony is broken up at present," wrote one of the Believers. "What may be the future is not known at this time." In June Slingerland was off to New Mexico with a friend. The Georgia colony survived, however, and the White Oak location became the center of activities. In April 1899 one visitor found a handful of Believers there, "struggling to establish a community home." Later observers reported that the Shakers had built a "modern" three-story house for $20,000 with all kinds of conveniences, including indoor plumbing serviced by an artesian well. Yet by the end of 1902 the entire Georgia enterprise had folded. The failure of the undertaking left the Ohio Believers with mortgaged properties to sell. (They had used the land as collateral in 1899 to borrow $30,000.) Eventually they sold the plantations to John W. Crow of Chicago and the White Oak holdings to a group of local sportsmen.[82]

In 1903 James H. Fennessey, the last trustee at Union Village, described the financial legacy of Joseph Slingerland's speculative activities. During his tenure Slingerland had traded Georgia land for a building in Chicago on which a $100,000 mortgage existed. When the property lost $8,000 in its first year, Fennessey, at the advice of an attorney, paid the $8,000 and transferred the deed to the party holding the note, thus cutting the society's losses and releasing it from a $100,000 debt. He estimated the loss in this exchange at $48,000. Slingerland had $50,000 in notes against him in Cleveland and New York City, which by mortgaging the Watervliet, Ohio, property he was able to pay off for $40,000. He had also mortgaged Altama for $20,000. "What he did with the money we do not know," wrote Fennessey. "We are compelled to pay Eighteen hundred dollars back interest on this Twenty thousand debt." Both Altama and White Oak were ultimately sold at substantial losses. But even that was not the end of Slingerland's financial misdealings. He had purchased a hotel in Saint Paul, Minnesota, by acquiring a mortgage of $67,500 at 5 percent interest. When mortgage, taxes, and insurance were combined, the society "never received a dollar income from the property." Even more speculative was his purchase for $75,000 of a cemetery in Memphis, Tennessee, which by 1903 had cost the society more than $100,000. "It is a property that nobody wishes to invest in," wrote Fennessey. "In fact, there

are few people who want to get in it, & few who ever get out." Fennessey
reported that he had given "a Mr. L. Lamb" an option to buy it for $48,000,
and he was determined to accept "that sum or anything near it." Slingerland's investments—whether the product of poor judgment, inexperience,
or unscrupulousness—were devastating for the society.[83]

It is even more difficult to be charitable about the activities of Robert
Valentine, another long-term trustee at Mount Lebanon. He, too, had entered the society as a child, at the age of nine in 1831. He served for many
years in the position of trustee. Like Gates, Shaw, and Slingerland, he was
involved in a myriad of typical financial transactions, from purchasing
25,123 acres of land in Rowan County, Kentucky, in 1891, to buying
shares in the Electric Scene Company in 1896. But Valentine crossed the
line of propriety and legality in 1896, when in association with the Otis
Realty Company, he took out leases in his own name on properties in New
York City, including three hotels, one of which was located on Broadway,
as well as a group of lots on West Eighty-second Street. Valentine accepted
large bonuses for signing the papers and received early rents with little or
no intention of paying the mortgages on the income properties. On 20 May
1901, August Ludemann brought suit against Valentine in a New York
court, charging fraud and deception. The transcript of the proceedings is
an astonishing record of Valentine's duplicity. He had deceived both the
society and the parties involved in these transactions. In his testimony
under oath he employed every possible dodge to extricate himself from the
charges. Valentine lost the suit and was ordered to pay $2,000 and 5 per-
cent interest to Ludemann. The society, however, lost more than money,
although relatively few of the Believers apparently were aware of these financial operations. Valentine, a high official, had betrayed the community's trust by falling prey to the mores of the day. He had proved unable
to resist an opportunity to enlarge his own fortune. It is not clear how
much he took from the society. It is clear, however, that long before the
Ludemann trial he was involved in questionable activities with unreliable
associates. One business partner, Thomas S. Smith of New York City, constantly sought Valentine's cooperation on speculative investments, including milk processors, "rubber belts," mica, a cure for chills and fever, and
real estate of all kinds. More than once Smith promised that the investments would "make money steadily."[84]

Shortly after the turn of the century, Shaker women played increasingly prominent roles as society trustees. They were not immune, of
course, from the same problems that confronted the brethren. Yet it appears that they were less given to speculative ventures and, in general,

more conservative in economic outlook. Emma J. Neale and Sarah Burger, for example, sold real estate, arranged timber sales, negotiated the right of way for railroads, and tried to recover some portion of the bad investments made by their predecessors. And they did all of this in the most difficult of times for the society. In general, these women brought a new measure of stability to the office of trustee.[85]

By the opening decades of the twentieth century the United Society was fully integrated into the American economy. Individual families still accepted the principle of joint interest, but the society no longer consistently enforced the earlier regulations. Some members had bank accounts of their own. The society was thoroughly enmeshed in the market economy, both as producer and as consumer.[86]

Financial records from the period reveal that the Shakers made substantial investments in a variety of industries. Hancock's trustees spent $2,000 on 10 shares of La Zacualpa Rubber Plantation Company in 1908; a few years later they bought stock in the Fisk Rubber Company. In 1915 they reported to the tax assessors a diversified portfolio of 2,709 shares of stock, including such issues as Bigelow Hartford Carpet, Southern Pacific, Otis Elevator, American Telephone and Telegraph, American Locomotive, Third National Bank, and United States Smelting and Refining. In 1919 South Union reported a smaller and less diversified set of holdings, including bank stocks, bonds in the Terry Coal and Coke Company, and Liberty Bonds and Savings Stamps. The last of these was valued at $15,000. Both villages also reported their livestock, and in that category South Union was far superior to Hancock. In 1919 South Union owned 81 head of cattle, 43 of which were registered. In addition, they listed 16 mules, 6 horses, and 120 hogs, 15 of which were brood sows. In 1915 Hancock possessed only 11 calves, 4 pigs, and 6 horses.[87]

In 1935 the Agricultural National Bank of Pittsfield acknowledged receipt of a variety of securities for Emma J. Neale at Mount Lebanon. Included were 543 shares of stock, a mix of common and preferred issues, in such firms as American Bank Note Company, AT&T, General Electric, New England Power, Radio Corporation of America, and Springfield Gas Light. In addition, the Mount Lebanon portfolio included $27,450 worth of interest-bearing bonds issued by transportation and energy companies including Detroit City Gas, Manitoba Power, Newport & Fall City Street Railway, New York State Electric & Gas, and Sierra and San Francisco Power. On another occasion the same bank acknowledged receiving $70,000 from Neale. They then purchased for the Shakers more than $62,000 worth of bonds in railroads and utilities, placing the balance in two savings accounts. Mount Lebanon therefore had substantial holdings at this time, especially considering the small number of Shakers at that site. Not all the remaining villages possessed similar portfolios, but they did have other successful enterprises, such as the extract business at Canterbury and the production of Tamar Laxative at Sabbathday Lake.[88]

But the profit motive and even speculative fever did not destroy all bonds of community among the scattered villages. The Believers' sense of union continued to manifest itself in acts of charity and mutual support. In 1900, for example, when Mount Lebanon faced an impending deadline on a note of nearly $35,000 to A. J. White, the leadership—because they had "little money"—asked for assistance from the other settlements. The central ministry visited all the eastern societies, except Enfield, New Hampshire, to request donations. "At Each place The Ministry found the People ready and willing to assist so far as they were able." As a result, the society was able to raise sufficient funds to satisfy the creditors immediately. Then the ministry refinanced the balance of the debt. Hancock alone gave $4,000 to assist Mount Lebanon. The very next year Hancock sent $1,000 to Alfred when fire destroyed a dwelling there. The Shakers also continued their tradition of offering assistance, both money and gifts in kind, when tragedy struck their neighbors or distant persons. Pleasant Hill, for example, donated $50 to yellow fever sufferers in 1878; in 1918 Mount Lebanon contributed $50 to the American Committee for Armenian and Syrian Relief; and in 1927 Canterbury gave $2,500 to the Margaret Pillsbury General Hospital Campaign Fund. These expressions of union and charity never disappeared completely from the Shaker scene.[89]

During the Time of Transformation, the society moved beyond brooms and seeds into the world of finance capitalism. The traditional adage, "Hands to work, and hearts to God," seemed far removed from the activities of modern trustees. Now the economic well-being of the Believers was inseparably linked to market forces driven by industrialization and urbanization. The rural villages remained the physical location of the Shakers, but the forces shaping their lives were increasingly those of the city. The male trustees who had played so central a role during this time of retreat were unable to resist the lure of speculation. Their decisions brought the society to the brink of economic disaster.[90]

The Impact of Modern Thought and Life

The pace of modernization within the United Society accelerated dramatically during the last decades of the nineteenth century. One Believer in western New York captured the new outlook with a brief sentence: "Happily we at Groveland are among the class known as disciples of the new and better way, advocating best systems of being and doing, thinking and acting." *Modernization*, as employed by historians of culture, implies more than just the use of laborsaving devices, themselves symbols of a larger process. It describes the change in outlook that accompanies the development of modern institutions—technological, industrial, commercial, educational, governmental. It also delineates movement away from the patterns found in traditional societies. With the change in world view, old ways of life erode, community standards lose their force, and time-honored boundaries fall. Modern men and women seek self-mastery and personal fulfillment, relishing engagement with the larger culture. They accept outside standards as the measure of their activities.[91]

Modernization was evident throughout Shaker society during this period, even among the most conservative members. The Believers eagerly embraced the symbols of modern life and, in doing so, revealed a changing world perspective. New means of transportation, sources of power, complex machinery, and communication devices transformed community life and came to symbolize the views of modern Believers. These developments elicited considerable public comment from the Shakers, who, like other Americans, were captivated by the implications of such changes.[92]

Before midcentury the railroad had already begun to transform the way Shakers traveled and transported their goods. By 1876 the Believers commonly moved by rail between their scattered villages. Travel by "car" reduced substantially the time spent on the road for the leaders and their representatives. In 1889, for example, when three members of the central ministry visited the western settlements, the actual time in transit between Mount Lebanon and Union Village via New York City, Philadelphia, Baltimore, and Cincinnati was less than thirty-six hours. In other words, the journey was reduced to a matter of days instead of the weeks required early in the century. Trustees and sales representatives used the railroads, covering long distances more quickly and transporting large quantities of goods more efficiently. Seed routes were redrawn to correspond with the locations served by the tracks. The distribution of everything from brooms to fancywork was made easier. Rail facilities close at hand reduced transportation costs and made new markets accessible. The Believers transported livestock and various perishable goods over the rails: cattle from Hancock to New York City, pigs from Union Village to Cincinnati, milk from Alfred to Boston.[93]

For these and other reasons, the Shakers sought ready access to railroad depots and sometimes even made economic concessions to ensure that. As early as 1852 trustees at New Lebanon signed a contract with the Lebanon Springs Rail Road Company. Subsequent agreements reveal the high value placed on such access. In 1881, for example, the same village received $5 for a right-of-way involving more than 6 acres. Thirty years later the trustees at Mount Lebanon—Emma J. Neale and Sarah Burger—accepted $1 for more than 21 acres from the Troy, Renssalaer & Pittsfield Railroad Company. Early in this period the Shakers at Enfield, Connecticut, pointed with pride to a new track within 125 rods of their buildings. The completion of the railroad bridge over the Kentucky River near Pleasant Hill was an occasion for celebration among the Believers.[94]

The increasing reliance on railroads drew the Shakers physically into closer proximity with all segments of American society and tied them even more tightly into the nation's economy. Rather than fearing these developments, however, the Believers welcomed the arrival of the tracks and eagerly embraced the new opportunities. Growing dependence on this means of transportation also worked subtle changes on Shaker villages. The trains ran on fixed schedules, and the Believers were forced to adjust communal patterns to correspond with the clock of the outside world. Family members began to record the hour and the minute of Believers' arrivals and departures at the stations. The society also joined the rest of America by investing heavily in the expanding railroads. Pleasant Hill, for example, purchased Texas Pacific bonds worth $5,000 in the 1880s. As late as the mid-1930s the trustees at Mount Lebanon were placing large amounts of money in railroad securities.[95]

Steam power, the energy source driving the railroads, was harnessed by the Believers for other uses. As early as 1873 the Shakers at Sabbathday Lake used a steam engine, adapted by Hewitt Chandler, to produce barrel staves. By 1876 at least one building at Mount Lebanon was "warmed by steam," to the delight of its inhabitants. Four years later the Believers at Harvard declared their "experiment" of heating buildings a grand success. The Center Family introduced steam heating at Whitewater in 1897. Steam replaced waterpower at several mill sites throughout the society, eliminating the need to construct and maintain elaborate systems of ponds, sluices, floodgates, bridges, and waterwheels such as those supporting the Canterbury mill complex. The ministry at Pleasant Hill noted with pride their purchase of a steam engine for the gristmill in 1884. The Believers at Watervliet, New York, in 1890 threshed their oats using a steam-driven machine, and in the same year steam boilers were installed in the laundry at Mount Lebanon. In 1899 Levi Shaw bought a steam sawmill for Mount Lebanon. Steam power had the virtue of being more predictable and efficient, requiring fewer attendants. As an alternate source of heat, it had other advantages, too; it was, for example, cleaner. Steam heat reduced the number of woodburning stoves in the villages, thereby lessening the risk of fire.[96]

The telephone made an impact on the United Society during this same period. The Shakers who visited the Centennial Exposition probably saw Alexander Graham Bell's first crude instrument displayed in Philadelphia. The formation of commercial telephone companies during the next decade made possible the refinement of his invention and the spread of its use over long distances. The Believers, however, were forced to wait for the telephone lines, which came to rural areas later than to cities. In the meantime some Shakers improvised their own local systems. In 1878 George Caldwell rigged limited service between two buildings at South Union, which did not become part of a telephone system until 1910. The ministry at New Lebanon acquired its first telephone, which allowed them to communicate with Albany, in 1883. They correctly anticipated that the new instrument would save them "many journeys." The New England Telephone Company installed telephones at Canterbury in 1901, the same year that both Whitewater and Pleasant Hill acquired telephone service.[97]

Everywhere the arrival of Bell's invention was greeted with delight. The telephone made possible instant communication between villages without the hardships of travel or the time delays of the postal service. Believers at scattered locations could now consult on matters of importance and also exchange news and information. How often the Shakers used the telephone in its earliest years is difficult to determine, since there are only occasional references in the written sources. The increased availability of this means of communication probably contributed to the general decline of letter writing among the Believers. Never doubting for a moment the significance of the invention, the Shakers demonstrated their faith in it by investing heavily in American Telephone and Telegraph securities.[98]

Electricity had an even more dramatic impact on the society. In 1881 Benjamin Gates bought five "Light Machines" for $750 from Dynamo Electric Machines of New York. By the end of the decade there was extensive discussion at Mount Lebanon concerning the possible applications of electricity. "The next improvement must be Electric Lights—for house and Streets," declared Frederick Sizer. In some Shaker villages electricity was generated initially on site. At Canterbury, for example, in 1910 the Believers constructed a large powerhouse, which contained a gasoline-powered generator and a large number of storage batteries, for $8,000. The direct current produced by this system lighted sixteen buildings at the New Hampshire location until the arrival of alternating current in 1925. Batteries first powered "an electric call bell" connecting the ministry shop and the office at South Union. Electric lights came to Shirley in 1904, to Harvard nearly a decade later in 1912, and to Hancock in 1919. Rural electrification did not reach the South Family at Watervliet, New York, until after November 1934. On Thanksgiving of that year the sisters there were forced to listen to their battery radio set because the power lines were three poles short of their dwelling.[99]

Electricity eventually replaced the indoor use of candles and lanterns at all the villages, thereby further reducing the danger of fire. In the North Family at Mount Lebanon, a single light bulb was installed in the cooling room in late 1921. This new power source aided the Shakers with other tasks, too. Two months after electricians installed a "light plant" at South Union, for example, the Center Family purchased an "electric churn." Electric refrigeration units permitted longer, safer storage of produce and perishable commodities. In 1895 Maria Witham at Enfield, Connecticut, forecast the future: "we believe electricity will make us independent of ice in a few years; it is in the air, that creamers and cooling-rooms, will be refrigerated by machinery." Collectively, the Believers expressed their confidence in this new technology by investing in electric utilities and other related securities, even though on at least one occasion their investments turned sour. In 1903 it was reported to Benjamin Gates that the society's fifty shares of Portelectric Company had "no Market value." In this case, the Shakers had "made a very poor investment."[100]

Perhaps no modern invention captured the imagination of the Shakers more than the automobile powered by the internal-combustion engine. The opening years of the twentieth century revolutionized that young industry in America with the development of mass production, assembly lines, and interchangeable parts. The attraction of owning a motorized vehicle spread quickly among the ranks of the Believers. In 1905 a Clinton, Massachusetts, newspaper reported fifteen Shaker sisters taking turns riding with "Two young men from Boston" in their automobiles. Sabbathday Lake decided to buy a Selden for $2,100 in late 1909. At South Union in 1914, one Believer observed: "Everything quiet but the autoes and they go past at full speed." Within a few years, family journals regularly reported the purchase of automobiles. The North Family at Mount Lebanon, for example, bought a "small Overland auto" in the autumn of 1918; less than two years later Walter Shepherd, first in the central ministry, brought home a new Studebaker "for the family." In April 1915 South Union purchased its first automobile; by July 1921 the Center Family at South Union had acquired its fifth auto, a Dodge roadster, for $3,815. They had previously owned a Reo, an Empire, a Studebaker, and a Case.[101]

The automobile immediately influenced Shaker life patterns. Although it did not replace the use of trains for long distances, the auto permitted access to locations not served by railroads. Soon it became common to "motor" to nearby towns and cities as well as to visit fellow Believers at other villages. Speed and convenience were additional benefits of this means of transportation which so enchanted the Shakers and other Americans. Yet the rising popularity of automobiles brought new problems. When winter arrived, the North Family was forced to buy a "closed top" for their Studebaker so that they could use it in cold weather. William Bates at South Union may hold the distinction of being the first Shaker involved in an automobile accident. In 1920 he injured his arm when the community's car "turned over in a ditch—on a bad road." Three years later an explosion and fire destroyed four buildings at Mount Lebanon when a lantern ignited gasoline fumes while an auto was being refueled at the North Family.[102]

The Believers used their vehicles for both work and pleasure, as numerous photographs attest. In 1918 as the sisters at Canterbury prepared to pick fruit they posed with apple baskets on the back of their one-and-a-half-ton Federal truck. The photographer, interestingly, framed the truck rather than the Shakers. Other pictures show Believers from Canterbury visiting at Sabbathday Lake (fig. 35). The Shakers recorded with the camera their pride in ownership. Numerous photographs taken on recreational outings feature an automobile as the centerpiece and Believers crowding around it. The first car at Alfred, a Pierce-Arrow, was photographed with a group of Shakers standing in the background. The first auto at Sabbathday Lake, a Selden, was pictured with Delmer Wilson at the wheel. At Hancock the first car was a Cadillac; Ricardo Belden was usually the driver. The Believers became known for their automobiles. One newspaper in 1919 reported, "Among the finest cars seen at the Shaker funeral were those owned by the Shakers themselves. All the communities have them now. They go on the theory that the best is invariably the cheapest in the long run." The Believers first used a "motor driven funeral coach," appropriately, at the interment of Walter Shepherd. The automobile broke down the last barriers of space and time separating the Believers from the outside world.[103]

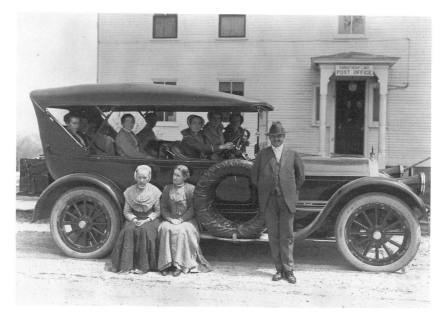

35. An Automobile Outing
Believers from Canterbury, including Irving Greenwood, pose with their automobile
in front of the Post Office at Sabbathday Lake. (Collection of the United Society of
Shakers, Sabbathday Lake, Maine.)

But even the automobile did not satisfy fully the insatiable thirst of
the Believers for new technology. The *Cleveland Plain Dealer* announced
that the Shakers living at Union Village "proposed to buy an aeroplane
from the Wright brothers and operate it for their own pleasure." Although
they already possessed an auto, the Ohio Believers wanted "to try other
means of travel," and it was reported that they had sufficient financial resources, "about $1,000,000 in property and cash," to do so. The accuracy
of this report is impossible to determine, but it does reflect the excitement
of the age. One of the first Believers to fly was Irving Greenwood, a member of the society at Canterbury who advanced to the central ministry in
1933. That year he flew to Chicago, a trip that attracted considerable attention from the membership.[104]

In the 1920s the radio became a new source of information and entertainment for the Shakers as well as for other Americans, and another
link between the two worlds. In 1923, three years after the establishment
of broadcasting stations in the United States, the North Family at Mount
Lebanon acquired its first receiver. A year later at Canterbury, Irving

Greenwood, who was gifted mechanically, built a crystal set for the community that included external speakers, making it possible for the sisters to listen as they worked in the kitchen. In the following decades the radio was an increasingly important form of amusement for the Believers, especially those who were aging and infirm. Bertha Lindsay recalls that the Shakers at Canterbury sat up long hours in the chapel, past the regular retiring time of nine o'clock, listening to radio dramas that sometimes lasted "until after one o'clock in the morning." Another sister wrote, "We sure go for the radio when we can not be outside, [and] always find something of interest." Even more than the print media, it brought the sounds and events of American life into Shaker dwellings—the Cadman hour, the Rose Bowl, music from the Roxy Theatre in New York City, a speech by Clarence Darrow. Even members unable to travel could "walk the streets" of the land through this "miracle."[105]

By the turn of the century the Shakers were becoming thoroughly "modern Believers," not simply because they welcomed new technologies and inventions but also because they no longer feared close relations with the world. In 1905 Arthur Bruce wrote, "Improvements seem to be the order of the day and we must move to keep pace with the demands of the day." Life in the remaining Shaker villages came to resemble that in the rest of American society. Long-standing traditional practices among the Believers passed from the scene. Community life was transformed in externals as well as in its inner workings. Only a few fixed points remained—a sense of family, a cooperative ethic, celibacy, and the legacy of land. Even these occasionally came under pressure.[106]

The physical world of the Believers was changing rapidly, too. The landscape of the villages was no longer "sociopetal," to use the language of Dolores Hayden; it no longer encouraged the easy formation of relationships or a sense of community among the members. The visual boundaries of some families were broken by decaying fences, intersecting highways and railroads, and intruding utility lines. The scars of fires lingered in blackened beams and overgrown cellar holes. Unsightly structures surrounded by debris stood within eyesight. Outsiders occupied buildings within the village complex, carrying on their worldly business in leased or rented property. Even the new buildings at several sites conflicted aesthetically with the spare lines of the past. Victorian facades, weighty porches, single doors—these and other features created debate and controversy at Union Village, Hancock (figs. 36 and 37), and Sabbathday Lake. Gates painted bright red and blue clashed with earlier regulations. In a few locations dirt lanes gave way to "expensive macadamized pavements" and

36. The Office, Hancock, Massachusetts

The Hancock Office, or trustees' house, was constructed around 1813 and enlarged in 1852. It remained a classic example of Shaker architecture until 1895. (Courtesy Shaker Museum and Library, Old Chatham, New York.)

37. The Remodeled Office, Hancock, Massachusetts

The Office at Hancock was modernized in 1895 and transformed into a Victorian structure, complete with tower and porches on the outside, as shown here, and flowered wallpaper on the inside. (Courtesy Shaker Museum and Library, Old Chatham, New York.)

overgrown dooryards to "well-kept lawns" celebrated as signs of "prog
ress" by those who thought of the Shaker homes as "missionaries." At the
North Family in Mount Lebanon a "water reservoir" holding half a million
gallons stood tall as a protection against the threat of fire. The architectural unity of the antebellum villages lived on more in memory than in
reality.[107]

The interiors of the buildings were also undergoing transformation.
Kitchens were modernized, bathroom "closets" installed, sewage and water
systems upgraded, woodburning stoves replaced. The Center Family at
Mount Lebanon, for example, installed a tile floor in the kitchen in the
hope of keeping out "those pestiferous rodents that inhabit our cellars and
gain access to the kitchen to the annoyance of the cooks." In addition, the
Believers redecorated their dwellings consistent with the fashions of the
day. Oliver Hampton reported approvingly from Union Village that the sisters had whitewashed the kitchen and painted the ceilings and moldings
"in lively colors." Wallpaper became something of a rage among the Shakers. In 1914 the North Family at Mount Lebanon made its choices for the
halls from "sample books" supplied by a local painter. Individual taste became the grounds for such decisions rather than traditional community
standards. In 1929 even the rooms in the building occupied by the central
ministry were wallpapered, including Emma Neale's retiring room. Past
prohibitions against worldly fashions carried little weight among twentieth-century Believers.[108]

Uniform appearance, another mark of the members of the United
Society throughout much of the nineteenth century, gradually gave way to
greater individual choice. In women's clothing, concern for fashion be
came a factor in style changes. Beverly Gordon points out that the wearing
of berthas instead of triangular neckerchiefs was itself a fashion statement. Variations were allowed in cut and materials. The use of lace,
rickrack, fringe, velvet, and ruffles reveals the Victorian influence. By the
1890s some Shaker women were also wearing "fashionable blouses that
were probably made in the world" as well as jewelry, including "breastpins
and rings." Others retained more traditional clothing patterns. The Dorothy cloak is an interesting example of Shaker apparel becoming fashionable in the world. By the late nineteenth century some sisters wore their
hair in contemporary styles; others continued to wear white caps at all
times, although the caps went through numerous modifications during
the Victorian period. At Union Village the sisters gave up wearing caps in
1895. After 1876, Shaker men in general "gradually stopped dressing in a
specifically Shaker style." They tended to purchase "ready made" gar-

ments in the world, and thus their clothing was almost indistinguishable from that of outsiders (fig. 38). Male Believers also increasingly resembled their counterparts in the world in terms of how they wore their hair and whether they chose to be clean-shaven or bearded. The spirited debate concerning beards no longer divided the community. John Patterson MacLean reported that the Shaker men at Union Village in 1895 were allowed "to wear the hair in such style as suited the individual." Photographs taken during these decades provide confirming evidence of such changes.[109]

Work routines among the Believers were changing. The brothers spent much of their time supervising hired men who handled many of the heavy tasks. The male Shakers looked after the aging buildings, maintained machinery and equipment, and carried on specialized production, such as the herbal and medicinal extract business. Frederick Evans and Hamilton DeGraw, both preoccupied with scientific farming, represented one aspect of this specialization. Evans worked especially with the orchards at Mount Lebanon. DeGraw, a dedicated horticulturist who moved to Watervliet, New York, when Groveland closed, was involved with developing hybrid strains of vegetables and flowers. He and others constructed an elaborate irrigation system for twenty-five hundred strawberry plants. At Enfield, Connecticut, an "experiment with Japanese buckwheat" proved a great success. Daniel Offord, by contrast, was more mechanically inclined; "ever busy where pipes are concerned," he was frequently repairing or replacing the plumbing at Mount Lebanon's North Family.[110]

The Shaker sisters bore an especially heavy burden as the remaining families struggled to stay solvent. Dairies and gardens, orchards and berry patches, required regular attention. Products and produce had to be prepared, preserved, and canned. The sisters at Enfield, Connecticut, for instance, processed 6,500 pounds of butter in 1889. And the daily responsibilities of cooking and baking, cleaning and polishing, washing and ironing, sewing and mending, never ended. These were the domestic chores Jessie Evans at Canterbury had in mind in 1899 when she wrote that "muscular Christianity holds full sway six days in the week." On one occasion Timothy Rayson at Mount Lebanon observed: "The Sisters have just about finished spring's cleaning, there are so many buildings to be cared for it comes quite hard on them." By 1906 the sisterhood at Union Village was "so reduced" that they did not have the capacity to bake their own bread, and as a result for the first time purchased bread from outsiders. The women also participated in income-producing activities, including light manufacturing. At several locations, for example, they made custom

38. Shakers at Upper Farm, Pleasant Hill, Kentucky
Photograph documenting the diversity in clothing styles among the Kentucky Believers. (Courtesy Historic Photographic Archives, Shakertown at Pleasant Hill, Ky., Inc.)

shirts. The sisters at Enfield, New Hampshire, produced about six dozen
shirts per month for Hewin & Hollis of Boston. Their work involved both
hand sewing and Wheeler and Wilson sewing machines. Typewriters
were purchased at Canterbury in 1907 and at Sabbathday Lake in 1911, to
the delight of Shaker writers.[111]

The presence of outsiders, especially laborers, within the Shaker
community frequently led to conflict and controversy. The hired men were
expected to abide by certain rules while dwelling in the villages, but frequently they did not. Persistent and recurrent problems stemmed from the
use of alcohol and resulting drunken behavior. Obnoxious and bothersome
conduct, often targeted at the younger sisters, was common. Thievery was
another problem. Fires, set by angry or careless laborers, were even more
costly. Paying guests, too, at times seriously disrupted village life. During
this period visitors became more frequent as the Shakers used their vacant
facilities to produce income. In 1897 the Believers at Pleasant Hill opened
the Shaker Hotel, formerly the East Family dwelling, under the direction
of Jane Sutton. The Ann Lee cottage at Mount Lebanon became a source
of revenue after it opened for boarders in 1906 under the supervision of

Emma Neale. Interaction with these outsiders on the premises was another way the world influenced the society.[112]

One persisting conflict at the South Family at Mount Lebanon illustrates some of these problems. During the second decade of the twentieth century the sisters' repeated clashes with hired men produced a steady stream of complaints directed to the aging William Anderson, who served as both elder and trustee for that family (fig. 39). The laborers hired by Anderson, it was reported, were a "disgrace" and a "menace." Often carousing in "saloons," they were "indecent" and destructive of both their dwelling and their equipment. The situation deteriorated to the point where the sisters refused to abide the laborers' presence any longer, and they announced that decision to Anderson in writing. He, in turn, became defensive and stubborn. He wrote, "But when the female part of this place, rise up, and *say*, on a certain date *so & so will be done* and *such & such must be done,* and put the threat in black & white with their *Signatures,* then the only Alternative I had was to utter my ultimatum." From then on Anderson refused to pay any of the sisters' bills, and he notified their creditors not to accept further charges on their accounts. When Eldress Sarah Collins pleaded with him, reasoning that if he did not carry out his responsibilities they could not continue under those conditions, Anderson reportedly said, "there's the street, you can take it." After months of wrangling, the elder finally turned over control of the farm to the sisters, but he did not give up all the family's assets. In fact, over the next few years the situation went "from bad to worse," according to the Believers. Appeals to the leadership of the society had little effect. In 1918 four members of the family called the situation "a perfect disgrace not only to a Shaker community but to this justice loving country America." They pleaded with the ministry to take some action, or to assist them in civil courts, to clear away "the accumulations of evil doings of the past years." Anderson was never disciplined, and after his death in 1930 stocks and bonds worth $8,000 were found in his safe deposit box in Pittsfield.[113]

The alternating rhythm of work and worship, so definitive of the Shaker experience in earlier decades, passed from the scene at several villages during these years. At some sites public worship disappeared almost completely, and at others services were held only with great irregularity. Julia Neal concludes that during the last twenty-five years of South Union, "few services of any kind were held" except when eastern leaders visited. Recreation occupied a larger place in the activities of the society's members. The sisters still picked berries, but they looked beyond those tasks for their leisure activities. They continued to organize husking bees,

39. William Anderson
An elder in the South Family at Mount Lebanon, New York, Anderson was a controversial figure in the opening decades of the twentieth century. (Courtesy Shaker Museum and Library, Old Chatham, New York.)

but they also played croquet on the lawn. The Shakers joined other Americans in pursuit of amusement and relaxation. They planned outings to Orchard Beach and Lake Winnepesaukee. Individuals went to the White Mountains and to Mackinaw Island; small groups took "vacations," some to established resorts, others to metropolitan areas. A trip to Barnum's show, the zoo in Cincinnati, or a county fair—these kinds of diversions filled the family journals. Many Believers traveled to other villages to see friends; some journeyed to visit their natural families; others took trips for health reasons. Few if any of these modern Believers would have been content to live by the restrictions that formerly governed all travel outside the settlements.[114]

Social occasions gradually replaced religious rituals as the high points of the year for many members. National holidays were often observed with elaborate festivities. On 4 July 1899 the South and Second families at Mount Lebanon celebrated the nation's birthday at Lake Queechy in the town of Canaan, "a beautiful, pacific lake" bounded by groves and cottages. At noon the group was seated in a pavilion, where they feasted on "a rich repast of the fruits of the orchard and garden"— language that calls to mind the mountain feasts of the 1840s. Rather than ecstasy and sacred dance, however, "reading, singing with speech-making and mirth generally ruled the dining hall of the rustic flag-draped shelter." Boating and racing also were "a merry feature of the day." Elder Ernest Pick took snapshots of the occasion with his Kodak. A Fourth of July celebration at Pleasant Hill included "innocent recreations, amusements, singing, reading" and patriotic speeches as well as a great feast shared with "tenants, & work hands, black & white, & some of the neighbors." Two or three fiddles also "crept in rather unawares," and the crowd enjoyed the "fine music." Other national holidays—Lincoln's and Washington's birthdays and Thanksgiving—were observed as well with some regularity.[115]

The Believers often entertained themselves and others with music, now no longer limited to gift songs and anthems. Singing classes spread through the society beginning in the 1860s and 1870s, and with that instruction came musical influences from outside. Pianos, organs, and other instruments soon were the pride of the Shakers (fig. 40). An orchestra was formed at Canterbury. The Believers continued to use music as a principal way to communicate with one another. A group of "seven happy songsters," junior members at Hancock, presented a "musical reception" for visitors from Mount Lebanon. A Canterbury quartet under the direction of Dorothy Durgin toured Shaker sites and also sang for the world's people. In 1897 that group gave concerts at Sabbathday Lake and at the nearby Poland Spring House in Maine. The repertoire of these singers included religious hymns, both Shaker and non-Shaker, as well as secular songs. Henry Blinn underscored the financial possibilities of the Canterbury group when he wrote, "This is a venture, but possibly they may bring back about as much gold as though they went to Klondike."[116]

The changing attitude toward Christmas among the Believers was another measure of the influence of American culture. The earliest Shakers had shared with many Protestants a distaste for festivals. During the Formative Period, however, Joseph Meacham had established Christmas as the time for an annual ritual of confession. The 1845 Millennial Laws

40. Two Sisters with Saxophones
Two unidentified sisters at Canterbury display their interest in secular music.
(Courtesy Canterbury Shaker Village, Canterbury, New Hampshire.)

mandated that on that day all members "should make perfect reconciliation, one with an other; and leave all grudges, hard feelings, and disaffection one toward an other, externally behind on this day; and to forgive, as
we would be forgiven." It was to be a moment of sober reflection and personal accounting, a time for recommitment to the society's fundamental
principles of union and order. This "Christmas gift" was also called the
"Yearly Sacrifice." One early account included foot washing in this process of reconciliation. Still in this vein, on Christmas day in 1874 the Be-

lievers at Sabbathday Lake took part in extended religious meetings, which were "attended by Ministering spirits, producing a heavenly spiritual influence." Two years later the scene had changed dramatically; holiday festivities at the same village now included a number of practices that had gained popularity in America, namely, a decorated tree, the exchange of gifts, caroling, and abundant food. "A Christmas tree! Who ever heard of such a thing before in Shaker village, New Gloucester?" exclaimed one Believer. This switch from confession to celebration gradually spread throughout the society. By the turn of the century Christmas among the Shakers appeared almost indistinguishable from that of the rest of the American population. In 1908 Delmer Wilson at Sabbathday Lake dressed up like Santa Claus.[117]

Yet the annual fast seems to have lingered longer than other ritual practices. Whenever and wherever it was observed, this ritual functioned as a powerful reminder of previous outpourings of spiritual gifts. One typical account of fast activities merits full citation.

> This day is devoted to Fasting and Prayer, each individual for themselves studying their own hearts to see what is there not owned by the spirit of God in the light of truth, and an honest confession is made of what conscience condemns, by every true Believer. In thus making sacrifices of self and a selfish nature a renewal of the Believers of Christ is gained and the soul is enabled to enter more deeply into the work of God and more efficient in the work of salvation. The labors of the day having been faithfully performed, the Church assembled at 7 o'clock in the evening for worship and there recieved refreshings from the spirit of the Lord.

The annual sacrifice, or day of confession, was perhaps the most distinctive continuing expression of Shaker religion.[118]

The "Florida fever," which spread through the society after 1894, was another manifestation of a changing outlook among the Believers. Glowing reports from Narcoossee told of the warm climate, luxuriant vegetation, and prospects for success in the southland. Enchanted by these accounts, some in the Northeast talked of a move to the Southeast, reviving an idea discussed earlier in the century. Public controversy broke out over this suggestion. Supporters of the proposal, including members of the Center Family at Mount Lebanon, received numerous spirit messages urging them to "press the prosecution" of the enterprise with "untiring zeal." Even mediums outside the society confirmed "the hand of God" in the southern plantation. By contrast, another Believer expressed delight that this "fever" had not reached the North Family at Mount Lebanon, for they would not know how "to cure it." She wrote, "There is a majesty in Mt. Lebanon not to be found in the sand beds of the south; and our lovely village is truly a city set on a hill that will not be hidden."[119]

The proposal to move to the South never gained sufficient support within the ranks of the society to make it a reality, although enchantment with the southern colonies continued for some time. For those experiencing the severe winters of the Northeast, the "balmy breezes" of the South were enticing. In February 1899 Andrew Barrett wrote from Olive Branch, "To pass through an orchard of one or two thousand trees, and inhale the sweet fragrance, is a thing to gladden the heart of every lover of nature." Visits to the Florida colony by the society's leaders, ostensibly for official business, became commonplace. These journeys frequently took place during the winter months. In 1898 Joseph Holden, Harriet Bullard, and Emma Neale traveled to Narcoossee. In 1901 the ministry at Union Village—Joseph Slingerland and Elizabeth Downing—left for Florida on 1 October and returned to Ohio exactly six months later. Family journals regularly reported winter "vacations" taken by the older members and leaders of the society. Others justified extended stays in the South for medical reasons. One physician suggested that Alonzo Hollister would live "much longer" if he resided in Florida instead of New York. Only "modern Believers" could have enjoyed the luxury of such prolonged holidays.[120]

Even before 1900 the Shakers no longer maintained the fiction of the simple life. They had become eager participants in nearly every aspect of modern life and thought. Earlier generations of Believers, by contrast, had aspired to self-sufficiency and separation from the world, adopting an aggressive work ethic to accomplish that end. Their fabled inventiveness—the flat broom, the clothespin, the circular saw, to name the most commonly cited items—was an unintentional by-product of their religious ethic. During the Time of Transformation, however, the invention of labor-saving devices was often consciously driven by economic considerations. The washing machine patented by the Shakers at Canterbury won a gold medal at the Centennial Exposition in 1876, but it also produced income for that village. The Believers welcomed such "conveniences—the foundation of modern living." In 1890, a few days before his death, Elijah Myrick of Harvard sounded the same theme. He wrote, "The results of experience and experiments in every department of life interest all—are aids to help keep abreast of the improvements of the times. Success and failures are our educators. . . . So we may all profit by information, investigation and observation, often saving time and trouble." Myrick described a

number of specific changes at Harvard consistent with this outlook—a
new windmill for pumping water, a sewage system for the dwelling house,
a boiler and steam system for heating, power, and laundry, and the in-
stallation of bathroom "closets." For him and others, these improvements
were the ultimate measure of success.[121]

Reconciliation with the World

After 1876 the United Society no longer embodied the radical sectarian attitude that once had defined its relation to the world. That harsh
critique gave way in the closing decades of the century to a reformist impulse, especially among members of the society's progressive wing. Rather
than simply condemning the world and trying to flee from it, many
Shakers now wished to change things for the better. They came to see
themselves as agents for the transformation of American society. Although
but "a little body," the Believers possessed "a great soul" and aimed at the
"construction of a true Christian order, . . . a new millennial earth." Now
they felt a compelling sense of responsibility for the world.[122]

These reform sentiments were given fullest expression in the writing and labor of the North Family at Mount Lebanon (fig. 41). Frederick
Evans, perhaps more than any Believer, personified this spirit within the
society. His motto was "Cease to do evil." While serving as the editor of
Shaker and Shakeress, he itemized the principal evils—individual and social—that needed to be suppressed. Evans's list anticipated the interests
of progressive Shakers over the next several decades. Among the individual evils he identified were processed flour, meat, liquor, narcotics, condiments, tea and coffee, and impure air and water. He also believed that
pressing social ills derived from perpetual land tenure, poverty, war, slavery, masculine domination, usury, and the perversion of spiritualism. To
correct these abuses, Evans and other like-minded members devoted their
time, energy, and resources to a variety of causes, and in doing so they
joined with other reformers of the Gilded Age.[123]

Dietary reform remained a favorite concern for some Believers, even
after the specific prohibitions in the 1845 Millennial Laws were no longer
enforced. Grahamism never completely lost its hold on the society. Evans,
one of the most committed, pointed to the "general derangement of physical functions" caused by the use of "Superfine Flour" stripped of its bran.
In 1886 he summarized the positive experience of the North Family,
which for many years had ground their own wheat "coarsely," used it "unbolted," and baked it without leaven. So committed was he to "pure" flour

41. North Family, Mount Lebanon, New York
Engraving showing the buildings of the North Family against the background of surrounding mountains. On the left is the North Family residence; at center, moving
toward the horizon, are a workshop, the laundry, and brothers' quarters. In the distance is the curved roof of the village meetinghouse. (From Charles Edson Robinson,
A Concise History of the United Society of Believers, 1893.)

that he doubted "whether really good men and women—Christians—can
be raised upon poor bread, made of adulterated materials and chemically
corrupted by leaven." Daniel Fraser had earlier argued that the feeding of
ancient Israel in the wilderness by manna underscored the importance of
a proper diet. "The non-procreative man and woman, the virgin sons and
daughters of God," particularly needed foodstuffs appropriate to their way
of life instead of those derived from the standards of the world. "The
nearer we come to the grains and fruits," he concluded, "the nearer we
come to the order, and benefits of a manna diet." Evans previously had
written, "I quite agree with the God of Israel, that the first step in the work
of human redemption is to make and eat good bread."[124]

Only a few Shaker families or individual members practiced vegetarianism or Grahamism, but those few were vigorous advocates for the
cause. Evans argued that people who justified by Darwinian principles
"the killing of dumb animals" unable to "plead their own rights" were
committing gross "deception." Ernest Pick, a member of the Second Fam-

ily at Mount Lebanon who came from Austria, contended that vegetarianism was "one of the means" whereby the millennium would be realized.
He noted that the "primitive home of man" was the Garden of Eden, not a
slaughterhouse or stockpen. Therefore, he reasoned, the fallen race cannot "reach perfection" until they are content "to subsist on fruits and
grains (simple and primitive fare which nature offered unsullied by
blood)" in a new garden home, a "veritable heaven on earth" (fig. 42). Pick
thought that "an almost unconscious loss of the desire for flesh foods" was
growing over all the land and that "many are almost vegetarians without
knowing it." But the cause was not as popular as he believed, not even
among the Shakers.[125]

   In 1894 Anna White eulogized Evans for his pioneering role in opening "a new and startling revelation to the pork-eating—beef-lovers" among
the Believers, who "dip their hands in blood and deck their tables with
dead carcasses." She chided those Shakers who had forgotten Evans's prophetic counsel in order to appease their "depraved appetite." Daniel Offord
called on the "followers of Christ in the second appearing" to be "guiding
lights to a progressing world" in these matters. He proposed, for example,
that "flesh meats" be entirely prohibited among those who "go down to
Florida to start a new organization" and that all others follow the practice
for five years. By that means, he hoped, the Shakers might reach "a spiritual baptism that will instill new life into the waste places." For Evans,
Offord, and the others, dietary reform was a step toward the ultimate goal
of Shakerism.[126]

   Evans also condemned the use of condiments—salt, pepper, mustard, vinegar—because they contributed to the "physical deterioration" of
the human body by "destroying the natural taste" of foods and by "creating unnatural tastes and appetites." Similarly, tea and coffee were evils to
be avoided, for they were drinks that cultivated vanity. Food was to be
natural and untainted, water clear and free of impurities. Spring water at
Harvard, boasted Elijah Myrick, was the "Cheapest & Best" life insurance
in the world, therapeutic and healthful to all who drink it. He claimed that
Shaker water "[i]nsures against disease and premature death; and extends
the lease of life, giving health and opportunity to leave a richer legacy to
posterity than any stock company extant." The general principle was as
follows: "The people of God should be as clean in the air they breathe, as
in the food they eat, the clothes they wear, or the houses in which they
live."[127]

   The Shaker reformers reserved special comment for liquor, which,
they contended, disabled those who imbibed, maddening the brain. Al-

42. A Shaker Family Gathering Apples
John H. Tarbell photographed children gathering apples under the supervision of the
Believers, at Enfield, New Hampshire. (From *New England Magazine*, 1910.)

cohol "dethroned" reason and "seared" the conscience. For this reason, like other Americans committed to the expanding prohibition movement, Alonzo Hollister argued for total abstinence from all beverages containing alcohol. He cited both chemical analyses and ethical judgments to support his view. Albumin in the brain is hardened by contact with alcohol just as "strong heat hardens the white of an egg," he wrote, making that organ "impermeable" to "nobler sentiments," including intellectual and religious reasoning. As a result, the faculties that govern the soul and the body are cut off, and "the coarse, strong, selfish, brutal propensities" take charge, with disastrous results, as demonstrated by the behavior of "inveterate topers." Even "moderate drinking" would lead down the same road. Therefore, wrote Hollister, abstain from that "first draught" and "break off immediately" if the habit has been formed. "Be thou henceforth a total abstainer, for the good of your friends, for the good of your country, for the good of humanity, and for your own best good now and ever after." To bolster his position, Hollister compiled a scrapbook of newspaper clippings that featured the virtues of temperance.[128]

But practice among the Believers was not uniform on these matters. The evidence indicates that the Shakers were not of one mind about drinking hard cider, beer, wine, and other liquor. Formal regulations were issued repeatedly by the ministry, suggesting that temperance was not the standard practice. Financial logs tallied substantial expenditures on alcohol. Family journals identified individuals who drank heavily and created problems for the society. These accounts often referred to the drinking habits of hired men. In the South Family at Watervliet, New York, the hired help once broke into a locked storage room and became intoxicated on hard cider. Other workers returned from Albany inebriated. But it was not simply outsiders who caused problems. At Groveland an inquirer named Joseph Lisk (alias J. Watkins)—an intelligent, educated young man—was forced to leave because he was "familiar with *bad* spirits." In an apparent act of revenge, he then broke into the cellar, stole some wine, and vandalized jars of fruit and preserves. Abigail Crossman, writing of these events, concluded that he had been "ruined by the destructive *cup!*" Even Shaker leaders were not immune to these difficulties. At the South Family at Watervliet, New York, Elder Isaac Anstaat had a serious problem with alcoholism. Anna Goepper made numerous references to his "queer spells," signaling the severity of the situation. In one entry she noted, "Eld. Isaac generally has a *queer spell once a week.*" During these drinking bouts Anstaat failed to eat meals for extended periods, and he was also unable to keep appointments. Sometimes he returned from business trips "with a 'queer spell' on" that lasted until the next evening. No wonder Goepper wrote, "If there is anything I despise on the earth it is a mess of drunken men around." These circumstances motivated some Believers to participate in the national temperance movement by attending rallies and supporting local lectures.[129]

Among Shakers in the North Family at Mount Lebanon at the end of the century, no one was more committed to social reform than Catherine Allen (fig. 43). She worked tirelessly on behalf of a host of causes, always seeking to link her support of particular undertakings to the religious principles of Shakerism. In a paper Allen delivered to the Social Improvement Society at Mount Lebanon, she set out to answer the following question: "How far is it the duty of Believers, and to what extent will it be profitable for them to co-operate with and sustain the various reform movements of the outside world, and through what means should they co-operate?" Her essay reveals both the depth of her convictions and the sense of mission that motivated her and other progressives.[130]

43. Catherine Allen
A spokesperson for the reform-minded North Family at Mount Lebanon, New York,
Allen served in the central ministry until her death in 1922. (Courtesy Shaker Mu-
seum and Library, Old Chatham, New York.)

Allen contended that the spiritual truth revealed to the Shakers empowered them to destroy evil and all forms of bondage and to lead the cause of progressive reform in the world. True religion emancipates humanity. Therefore Believers ought to support "every movement which tends toward reform and the general progress of the race." Allen also responded to objections against this activist stance by some members of the society. She rejected the notion that small numbers or limited means should deter "active co-operation." On the contrary, she contended, the Shakers, "as a people long accustomed to seclusion," needed to be educated about their "relation and duty to the outside world." To that end, Allen wrote, "We must allow our customs and habits of thought and life to be remolded, not in conformity to the spirit of the world, but by the progressive spirit of the age." Self-denial, she argued, the product of the "Christ spirit," was the foundation of "every true reform." Therefore she urged her fellow Believers to support such causes by writing articles, signing petitions, speaking at conventions, and joining organizations in order to "increase our power for good." [131]

Catherine Allen called for radical social and political changes. She attacked laws and institutions that favored "class privileges in any shape," charging that "enormous monopolies" and the "system of wage slavery" were crippling the nation. She feared that the crisis at hand might lead to revolution unless "true democracy" was restored in America. Among the "necessary" reforms Allen proposed were universal suffrage, the secret ballot, the total separation of church and state, the taxation of church properties, land reform, the abolition of usury, inheritance taxes, a bimetallic currency, compulsory education for minors, equal access to "higher branches of learning," municipal ownership of utilities and "systems of transportation and communication," an end to exclusive rights to inventions, and free legal assistance. She recognized that these changes would require the complete reconstruction of society. Monopolies and injustice would end only after citizens "learn that the Great Ruler of all, is Father and Mother" and that social institutions must reflect the principle of "Universal Brotherhood." [132]

Women's rights were a special concern of all progressive Shakers, and not just of the women. Yet it was the sisters who most consistently spoke on this issue. Antoinette Doolittle, for example, openly challenged the assumptions that allowed males to dominate the primary institutions of government and religion. She denounced the "bondage and servitude" that kept women out of "legislative halls" and gave them no voice in the tribunals of government. The only exception, she noted, was when they were taken into those chambers as wives of government officials, dressed "like gayly plumed show birds, to attract attention" rather than to take part in the governing process. The stated rationale for this pattern of oppression, Doolittle acknowledged, was the transgression in Eden, after which "a voice was heard saying: 'He shall rule over thee.'" In the churches of the land, the "opinion" of Saint Paul that women should not be heard in the church explained why no ministers "dare to allow a woman to occupy their pulpits," even though female lecturers traveled widely and were treated with respect when they expressed their ideas about human problems. Perhaps women ought to "withhold their contributions" from such churches and with those funds "build a few small churches wherein they could feel at home and give expression to their own religious views and convictions" apart from male domination.[133]

Catherine Allen, who advanced to the central ministry in 1908, was also a leading advocate for women's rights. In spite of the Believers' traditional prohibitions against involvement with political parties, she supported a petition drive in favor of suffrage. In 1895 the Shakers at Mount Lebanon, female and male, took time out from a "busy season of house cleaning and seed sowing" to sign petitions in hopes of securing "an equal voice" for women in governance. Allen urged all "true and intelligent" women to give their strength to the cause. "Together they [women] have been degraded," she wrote, "together they must rise." Allen linked the political bondage of women to the "thraldom to sensual passions," which she regarded as the root of all social problems. She also believed that placing the ballot in the hands of women would lead to an upgrading of moral standards for men, and thus ultimately to the "[p]urification of the social life of the sexes." By denying "false appetites and unjust systems," vital life forces would be conserved for the "redemption of the race." For Allen the issues of suffrage, religion, and reform were inextricably bound together.[134]

In 1907 Allen addressed the annual executive meeting of the National Council of Women held in conjunction with the Jamestown Exposition commemorating the tricentennial of the settlement of Virginia. In her speech she wove together the history of women's suffrage and that of Shakerism. In her opinion, the "brave women" who worked for emancipation in earlier decades were sustained by the force of truth and a "Divine Energy." That group, she stated, included Ann Lee, who "proclaimed the inherent equality of man and woman" as well as the notion of "God as the All Father-Mother." Allen recognized the critical relation between these two ideas. "Ever do man's concepts of Deity find reflex in human affairs," she wrote, and as a result religious ideas about God provide the basis for "cooperation between man and woman in all the relations of life." For that reason, she pointed out, the Shakers had always preferred the term "Equal Rights" to "Woman's rights." It was the cooperation of brothers and sisters that had produced the high standards of the society. For one hundred thirty years the Shakers had endorsed the principles of universal peace, one standard of morality, and equal suffrage—the goals of the National Council of Women.[135]

As the years passed, Catherine Allen's enthusiasm for social reform did not flag. She followed her own advice and enrolled as a supporting member in a diverse group of organizations. Animal rights was an issue of special concern to her. Between 1915 and 1920, for example, she held memberships in the Vivisection Investigation League, the American Humane Association, the National Association of Audubon Societies, the R.S.P.C.A. Fund for Sick and Wounded Horses, the American Red Star Animal Relief Society, the Animal Rescue League, and the New York Anti-Vivisection Society. She favored cooperation among different religious communities and supported the newly formed Federal Council of Churches of Christ in America as well as the American Branch of the World Alliance for Promoting International Friendship through the Churches. The fate of children was another favorite cause. Allen gave money to the National Child Labor Committee, the New York Kindergarten Association, and the French Tubercular Children's Fund. She contributed to the National Temperance Society and Commission on Temperance and to the United Committee on War Temperance Activities in the Army and Navy. In the aftermath of the First World War, she supported several relief agencies, including the National Allied Relief Committee, the General Relief Committee, and the French Heroes Lafayette Memorial Fund. To all of these causes, Allen gave both verbal and financial support.[136]

What made the Shaker progressive program distinctive from that of other reformers during the Progressive Era was its unique combination of social reform and Shaker ideology. Daniel Offord, another North Family leader during this period, combined the fervor of an evangelical preacher and the social conscience of a muckraker with the religious principles of a Believer. He regarded Jesus and Ann Lee "as the greatest reformers that have ever blessed the earth" because their practice was consistent with their preaching. Offord linked Jesus with land reform because he "had no place to lay his head." Jesus was also the "greatest hygienist" because he healed the sick and helped those in distress. "It is my faith that the spiritual power manifested by Jesus upon the bodies of the people, will be manifested in far greater perfection in the Church of Christ in the latter day," wrote Offord. For that reason he challenged Believers to continue the "warfare against the powers of darkness." In particular, Offord called for renewal of the commitment to celibacy. "Let the testimony roll, as thunder from Mount Zion, and let the lightnings play, and the battles of shaking be renewed; that every heart may be inspired with Mother's gift to hate the flesh vehemently." [137]

There is some irony in Offord's fervor, for less than six years later he left the society in the company of Mabel Franklin. The Center Family journal includes the following entry: "The North Family are in sore tribulation over the defection of Elder Daniel Offord for whom there has been great love and affection for his faithfulness and zeal as a Believer." In the Church Family journal Joseph Holden wrote, "Daniel Offord left Society last night sometime. What a pitty." Offord went on a western adventure accompanied at least for a time by Franklin. His precise whereabouts and activities during the next three years are unclear. During his travels he invested money in several western land schemes. In November 1898, however, Offord, "recently from Colorado," visited Mount Lebanon. In March of the next year he was again fixing pipes, and by 1902 he was reinstated to the eldership, accepted back apparently without recrimination (fig. 44). [138]

The complete separation of church and state was an issue of concern to many progressives in the United Society. Frederick Evans repeatedly warned of dire consequences from the union of civil and ecclesiastical forces. In that situation, he cautioned, religionists "will think they are doing God, and Christ, and the Holy Spirit good, and acceptable service in restraining heretics and infidels, Quakers and Shakers, Free-thinkers and Spiritualists." He vowed not to rest until "fighting, monopolizing, persecuting theologies" were purged forever from courts and legislatures. Evans also linked the Shakers' refusal to vote with the principle of absolute separation. He argued that the United Society did not believe in any "union" between church and state. He characterized the founders of the American republic as religious "skeptics" who had left Christianity and were determined to be free of "theology and all forms of ecclesiasticism." Furthermore, he noted, whenever church and state have been mixed, "holy inquisitions and unholy religious wars" have resulted. Not voting therefore was consistent with the rigorous application of the separation of church and state. He also applauded a court ruling against reading the Bible in public schools, urging that prayer and all such activities be "confined to the church." Daniel Offord warned that if government came

44. Daniel Offord
Offord was a leading member of the North Family at Mount Lebanon, New York, until
his death in 1911. (Courtesy Shaker Museum and Library, Old Chatham, New York.)

under the control of the "so-called Christians," liberties would vanish and "everybody will be compelled into the narrow limits of their creed, and circumscribed by their very unchristian practices." On these grounds he opposed Sabbath laws and ordinances restricting health practices. "And when the Christian God gets into the constitution of the United States," he wrote, "we can bid farewell to Liberty."[139]

Poverty and a series of related issues troubled many Believers. Daniel Fraser, another English convert and resident at Mount Lebanon, underscored the anomalies of American capitalism. He pointed to the fundamental inconsistency between the existence of "many millionaires" in the United States and the "logic of a republic." Through their financial power the wealthy exercised more control than did "the monarchs of the old world." The accumulation of riches by capitalists was producing, in turn, "want, discontent, degradation, and crime" among the laboring class. He thought that the disparity between these two groups was greater in the nineteenth century than it had been in the fifteenth century. Fraser feared for the well-being of the American republic, and he urged those in positions of power to discover ways "to secure a healthful distribution of all the products of labor, and thus avert impending evil." He proposed a number of economic steps, including land reform and an end to usury. Fraser wanted every citizen to be a landowner. He hoped that these reforms might begin to restore the notion of a just "social compact." To that end, he urged, "Form Committees. The ballot is in your hand. Put this matter through. Work cordially with all classes."[140]

Oliver C. Hampton at Union Village thought that the adoption of Edward Bellamy's ideas might bring an end to the "selfishness" plaguing American society and a beginning to true equality and "the genuine Christ life." Bellamy, author of the best-selling novel *Looking Backward,* had offered an optimistic vision of a utopian nation in the year 2000. There was some sentiment among the North Family at Mount Lebanon in favor of the "single tax" theory of Henry George, who had proposed to tax the unearned increment related to landholdings in order to redistribute wealth. George H. Baxter at Enfield, New Hampshire, by contrast, sounded a more traditional note, suggesting that the way to stay free from the "monopolizing greed of the world" was to fulfill "the spiritual and industrial" responsibilities demanded by the society.[141]

The peace movement also occupied the attention of progressive Shakers. For many years Evans served as a vice president of the Universal Peace Union, a small radical peace society organized by the Quaker Alfred Love in 1866. Drawing on the principles of love and nonviolence, the union expanded its designs for a "force-free America" into a number of related fields of reform, including civil rights for blacks, improved native American relations, and women's rights. The membership of this organization, which never became large, was composed principally of religious sectarians, with women forming at least a third of the group. Beginning in 1882, Evans, Doolittle, and other Believers from the North Family regularly attended conventions sponsored by a branch of the union at Salt Point, New York. They also took part in similar meetings elsewhere. Anna White, who became an eldress at the North Family, was especially active in this cause. She was also involved with the Alliance of Women for Peace, an international organization with headquarters in Paris. White gathered hundreds of women's names on a petition calling for disarmament and was appointed an officer of the alliance in New York State. In 1890 Evans published *The Conditions of Peace,* a letter he had sent to his friend Alfred Love.[142]

Involvement in the peace movement peaked in 1905 when the Believers at Mount Lebanon sponsored a "Peace Convention." The announcement for the gathering declared that the intention was to bring pressure to bear on the government of the United States. The publicized speakers represented a variety of perspectives. Lawyers and clergy, educators and activists, women and men, were on the program. Women's organizations, peace associations, and religious groups were also represented. Three sessions were scheduled for 31 August. Among those on the program were the spiritualist James Peebles, Rabbi Charles Fleischer of Cambridge, Massachusetts, and Elizabeth B. Grannis, who was the president of the National Christian League. Refreshments and entertainment were to be supplied by the Shakers, and the Rutland Railroad provided special rates to New Lebanon.[143]

On the appointed day the meetinghouse at Mount Lebanon was arranged with chairs, a speaker's platform under a canopy decked with bunting, and vases of flowers in each window. Tricolored bunting was also stretched on pegs behind the platform. Photographs show an attentive audience made up of Shakers and many outsiders. Anna White was one of the Believers who addressed the assembly in the afternoon. She both bade them welcome and challenged them to respond to the noble cause. White made clear the commitment of the Shakers to the undertaking. She said, "You may think that, cloistered as we are from the outside world, pursuing the even tenor of our ways, the larger affairs of life, those pertaining to country and nation and not directly affecting us, would not enlist our sympathy nor engage our attention. It is far otherwise. No citizen is more thoroughly alive to the interests of state or nation than are the Shakers. In the Peace of the nation is our Peace." The assembly adopted a series of specific resolutions proposed by Leila Taylor, Catherine Allen, and Henry S. Clubb of the National Vegetarian Society. All were based on the assumption that "wars are equally barbarous and equally unnecessary, . . . and to be regarded only as a return to primitive savagery." Included among the resolves were pleas for the international arbitration of disputes, the reduction of all armaments, the establishment of commercial waterways as neutral zones, the interdiction of war loans, the strengthening of the judicial power of the Hague court, and commendation of President Theodore Roosevelt's efforts to effect peace between Russia and Japan. This gathering represented the climax of the reformist spirit in the society.[144]

The Shakers also adopted progressive views on a number of other issues, some of national concern, some largely intramural to the society. In 1899 Oliver Hampton at Union Village gladly signed a petition "for the abolition of capital punishment." He was persuaded that "that awful relic of barbarism . . . should have been wiped from our Judicial system long ago." William Reynolds at the same village earlier had mounted a multifaceted attack on the use of tobacco, even though he acknowledged that in the past the Shakers generally had been "tobacco users." He recalled "social meetings" where the air was "blue with the fumes of the weed!" Now he was repulsed by the thought of the Believers' dwellings ever again being "polluted" by fumes or saliva. "We accept with joy the light that science has shed upon the subject—that it has, as usual, taken the hand of our religion, declaring tobacco no less respectable than rum, and that it is a moral and spiritual degenerator, and a physical disorganizer." In 1873 Frederick Evans republished "Twelve Reasons Why No Rational Being Should Use Tobacco." Among the reasons given were moral, medical, financial, aesthetic, and social arguments for abstaining. Alonzo Hollister's clippings against smoking included an emotional appeal: "Ah, boys! if you could only understand how much harm you do yourselves by smoking those nasty cigarettes!"[145]

The Shaker reformers also attacked funeral and burial practices popular in the late nineteenth century. The progressives criticized embalming, ornamental coffins, unsightly graveyards, and "extravagantly expensive cemeteries," such as Auburn and Greenwood. Evans and others argued that burial grounds ought to be made into public parks planted with trees, creating "splendid groves of valuable timbers all through the nation." George Lomas proposed that graveyards, called "God's Acre," ought to be more than burying places. They should be living acres in which "corn or wheat, or potatoes, or flowers, or other merchandize" are grown. All these ill-placed cultural practices, the Shakers charged, were a product of the "doctrine of the resurrection of the body." The contrary belief—spiritualism—repudiates the notion of a physical resurrection and leads to rational funerals. Otis Sawyer at Sabbathday Lake extended the argument against lavish monuments, flowers, and shrubbery in cemeteries by calling these practices "idolatry" and a wicked use of money, which should be spent instead on "living objects of charity" who are suffering. "Virtues are more enduring than granite," he wrote, and the appropriations expended on burials "should be used for the elevation of the downcast, homes for the destitute, and for charitable and religious purposes generally." The Shakers pointed to the economy and simplicity of their own funerals and cemeteries. They buried their dead in a plain pine coffin and a simple white pall. They also used simple grave markers. Yet even those within the society did not agree on all these issues. Aurelia Mace's "last request" was to have her body embalmed. At her funeral "she lay in the casket wreathed in the beautiful floral tribute of dear friends."[146]

The progressives carried the reforming impulse to a comical conclusion in their attack on carpets. Their arguments drew together several concerns, both spiritual and temporal. The following unsigned piece stated the position clearly.

> Carpets are injurious to health, so far as the lungs are concerned. They accumulate dirt, and hold it as a reservoir. Every motion of persons, things in the room, or even of the air, causes it to rise in an impalpable powder, to be seen only in the rays of sunshine that may chance to get into the room to fade the colors of the carpets. Therefore, to preserve the carpets and the accompanying furniture in their beauty, carefully exclude the light; and, to exclude the dust, keep the windows closed; and, to preserve the health of the family, let them live in other rooms, with no carpets, plenty of air, and floods of sunshine.

The author's logic turned on the Shakers' preoccupation with health, cleanliness, and purity. The humor stemmed from the extreme to which the progressives carried their position.[147]

These reforms were all linked to an expanding commitment to education. No more striking evidence can be found than the Self-Improvement Society organized in 1891 under the leadership of Catherine Allen. This organization aimed to improve the "habits and manners" of the younger sisters at the North Family and to cultivate the appreciation of "substantial, interesting and beautiful things." The sisters in this association promised to avoid slang, sarcasm, and white lies and at the same time to observe correct grammar and pronunciation. At each weekly meeting they were to bring a selection from their reading and a sample of their writing to be shared. This activity was "for the cultivation of consecutive thought, the expansion of mental capacity, the promotion of freedom, correctness and confidence, and the edification and educational benefit" of those in the organization. No longer was learning confined to the practical or the spiritual; now it was measured by a different set of canons. The advertisements for magazines and journals in *The Shaker Manifesto* also revealed this broadening of intellectual horizons, as did the efforts of the Lebanon Literary Union formed among the Church Family at Mount Lebanon. On the program for 11 March 1884, for example, were such topics as the early history of religion, etiquette, the biography of Matthew Arnold, and popular superstitions.[148]

The Shaker program of progressive activities blended well with that espoused by religious and secular reformers of the day. Walter Rauschenbusch and Stephen S. Wise, Richard T. Ely and John Commons, Francis Willard and Jane Addams—these and others driven by a vision of the future hoped to create a better world. Muckrakers and liberal clergy, union organizers and cultural critics, millennialists and utopians alike, all believed that life could be better. In that conviction they were joined by many Believers.[149]

In a paper entitled "The Golden Age," Catherine Allen gave final form to her vision of a better earth. Drawing on traditional Shaker conceptions of an ideal world, she presented her ideas concerning a "pure democracy." At the root of the problem, according to her, were the "love of greed," oppression by corporations, the competitive system, and the "iniquitous system of finances," which have created war, poverty, and crime. The "New Heavens and New Earth" will come into existence when natural wealth is shared with everyone, educational opportunities are equalized, cooperation replaces competition, women gain full citizenship, laborsaving machinery is used for relief instead of oppression, the "desire for tobacco, liquor, and other forms of indulgence" disappears, a vegetarian diet is adopted by all, prisons and "pauper houses" are converted into schools, and there is no need for doctors, lawyers, or clergy. Then all nations will be "one great family" speaking one language with "one Bible and one religion." "Progress is eternal," wrote Allen, and someday the "glory of the Millennium" would be established.[150]

Varieties of Religious Experience

By the end of the nineteenth century the "varieties of religious experience" within Shakerism, to borrow a phrase from William James, defied easy categorization. The situation among the Believers paralleled the expanding pluralism within America. No one event signaled the growing religious diversity in the United States more than the World's Parliament of Religions, held in conjunction with the Columbian Exposition in Chicago. At that gathering in 1893 "Christians and Jews, Mohammedans, Buddhists, Brahmans and followers of about every religious creed in the civilized world met in one grand assembly . . . for the first time in the history of the world." A spirit of toleration unparalleled in American history prevailed. Leaders representing highly divergent perspectives appeared on the same lecture platform—among them James Cardinal Gibbons of the American Catholic hierarchy, the Congregational minister and advocate of the Social Gospel Washington Gladden, the Theosophist Annie Besant, the Buddhist H. Dharmapala, Bishop William Arnett of the African Methodist Episcopal Church, and Daniel Offord from the North Family. In his address Offord affirmed, "Our object is to enfold all who would rise above the propensities and develop the superior life."[151]

Within the United Society, too, a kind of pluralism was emerging, not marked by separate denominations or rigidly defined factions, but rather by contrasting strains of spirituality. Several distinguishable religious patterns surfaced among the Shakers during the Time of Transformation. All were allowed to stand side by side with no attempt to create the fiction of unity. Many Believers, in fact, celebrated the tolerance that permitted variety. "We condemn none who differs," wrote Offord. These religious positions were not mutually exclusive, however, for individual Believers frequently reflected more than one of these strains in their beliefs and practices.[152]

Spiritualism was the religious choice of many Shakers. The spiritualistic tradition among the Believers embraced more than the spirit communications manifested in the years before the Civil War or the popular preoccupation with psychic phenomena in the following decades. Spiritualism rather was a sophisticated metaphysical outlook, which, to use the language of Charlotte Byrdsall, consisted "of the development of the indwelling, God-implanted germ in the hearts of . . . [individuals] which will be a key to the chambers of human souls, and reveal true character." This rudimentary force imparted knowledge, restored health, showed the utility of life, and pointed to a future state of existence. Antoinette Doolittle described this element as a "vitalizing principle in human hearts" and the "main spring of action." She was unwilling to restrict access to this "Creative Power" to Christians; pagans, the followers of Hinduism, and the devotees of Greek and Roman deities were moved by similar beliefs. "Faith in spirit intercourse was never more prevalent among earth's inhabitants," she wrote, "than at the present time."[153]

Perhaps spiritism is a more accurate name for this perspective, because for the Believers direct communication with the spirits through visions and seances was only one aspect of their faith. And yet the occult was an important demonstration of the reality of spirit power. The concern with psychic phenomena showed no sign of flagging in the society. Shakers, both East and West, eagerly participated in spiritualistic conferences and in private demonstrations of spirit power, including materializations through mediums, clairvoyants, and seances. Making visible the surrounding spiritual beings was one of "the beautiful and important wonders of our day," wrote Cecelia Devyr. How to explain such phenomena was not equally clear to her. Nevertheless, she stated, the "laws that govern materialization" cannot be ignored without peril. Some "perceive sights and sounds" and others do not, a situation that would prevail until "the science of the soul" was fully operative.[154]

Spirit communications were commonplace among the Believers during this period. Early in 1878 George Lomas reported in *The Shaker Manifesto* that Mount Lebanon might "become a Mecca for those who are now, materialistic unbelievers in truths of spirit returns and physical embodiments." "Scores of Shaker spirits" were said to have materialized there. These visitations, Lomas noted, had taken place under "Shaker supervision," making it impossible to ascribe them to fraud. In 1908, some fifteen years after the death of Frederick Evans, Daniel Offord reported that the members of the North Family had the impression that Elder Frederick wanted to communicate with them, but they were unable to receive his message properly. Rebecca A. Hathaway at Canterbury told of hearing voices many times from "spirit connections" that spoke directly to her and comforted her. In the 1920s Delmer Wilson at Sabbathday Lake recorded a series of dreams he received. One occurred after he had been reading extensively about spiritualism. According to Wilson, the "holy power" of such moments was "too great for mortal mind, even in slumber." A firm believer in spirit communication, he testified: "I doubt not but our departed ones do often return to us to help & instruct us and in turn help themselves."[155]

The Believers eagerly joined forces with the larger spiritualist movement in America, affirming the reality of spirit and the significance of this belief. The society's long-standing relationship with James M. Peebles, called "our dear friend," testifies to this association. He lectured frequently at various villages, and the Shakers eagerly read and often reprinted his writings. They corresponded with him regularly. According to Peebles, the spiritualists believed in a living God, Jesus as "a man approved of God," and a continuous "afflatus" of the Spirit "from the Christ Heavens." Inspiration was evident in prophets and poets, in gifts, dreams, and trances, and in other spirit demonstrations. In death, mental and spiritual existence continued, and progress was possible. "I believe in salvation through Divine obedience—through Christ," he wrote, "just as I believe in buds and flowers and harvests through the quickening sunshine." Peebles was confident that both religion and science were compatible with these doctrines and that these beliefs would "tend to better the world." He also stated that Christianity, Shakerism, and spiritualism were "the trinity of the resurrection state."[156]

Peebles included a description of Shakerism in his history of spiritualism, a work that charted the changing fortunes of spirit belief throughout the ages. He placed the society among the "genuine silver-glimmerings" of spirit that flashed through the "spiritual midnight" created by Roman Catholicism, Protestantism, and a *"paganized Judaism."* He situated the Believers alongside Jakob Böhme, George Fox, William Blake, and Emanuel Swedenborg in a chapter entitled "Churchianic Spiritualism." Peebles wrote of Ann Lee's "remarkable" visions and revelations, which provoked hostility from both priests and magistrates. He also compared the Shakers to the Essenes, ancient Jewish sectarians who once lived near the Dead Sea in Palestine. He complimented Evans and James Prescott for their involvement with the spiritualist movement and quoted William Hepworth Dixon's opinion that the Believers held strictly to the "dogma of the existence of a world of spirits." Peebles declared that the Shakers were "the neatest, healthiest, the most pure-minded and kind-hearted souls of earth" and praised them for their "system of rational living."[157]

The Believers subscribed to spiritualist publications and read them with regularity. Anna White, for example, after perusing in the *Banner of Light* an account of a youthful clairvoyant and clairaudient, delivered the essay "True Spiritualism" at the Unity Church in Pittsfield. She restated a common view within the society, namely, that the modern spiritualist movement in America "originated in the Shaker Order" several years before the Fox sisters in Rochester attracted national attention. Spiritualism's success was prophesied by the "ruling spirit" among the Believers. White equated true spiritualism with biblical accounts of angels visiting the earth and voices sounding from heaven. The only persons, she wrote, who have truly obeyed the call are the Shakers, who are "in the world," but "not of the world." Their "new order" would lead to "the long looked-for Millennium." White declared spiritualism "a means of salvation from the gigantic sins of the world," and therefore a "step toward the consummation of the Kingdom of Heaven in earth." Shaker spiritualists were optimistic about human nature and the future; they welcomed signs of progress, in the world of science and other arenas. Most progressive Believers stood in this camp. They regarded their commitments to social reform and to spiritualism as highly compatible and mutually reinforcing.[158]

Shaker spiritualists declared that the "truths of the Divine life" were not confined to any particular "sects or parties." They welcomed insight wherever it was found, whether in Eastern religious traditions, Christian Science, or harmonial philosophies. When the Believers spoke of the Christ spirit, it was not restricted to Shakerism or even to Christianity. Members of the society looked for kindred spirits outside their villages. Hamilton DeGraw at Watervliet, New York, read with interest an article in the *Phrenological Journal* about Swami Vivekananda, a representative of the Vedanta movement who was the talk of the crowds at the World's Parliament of Religions. In his Chicago lecture Vivekananda had declared that Krishna "taught that a man ought to live in this world like a lotus leaf, which grows in water but is never moistened by water—so a man ought to live in this world—his heart to God and his hands to work." The swami quickly gained celebrity status as he traveled throughout the country. DeGraw was delighted that this "young Hindoo monk" was calling for renunciation of the "lower life" and the practice of celibacy. Thus he exclaimed, "To all such the hand of fellowship is extended of whatever race, color or creed." Anna White received correspondence from Frances Ellen Burr suggesting that Shakerism was "at one with the teachings of the Vedanta." William Anderson, elder at the South Family at Mount Lebanon, purchased astrological charts during the second decade of the twentieth century from such diverse locations as The Hague in Holland and Crown Point, Indiana. He also had his handwriting analyzed by an expert in England. The Believers at the North Family developed a friendship with members of the American Society for Psychical Research, which was organized in 1885. The membership of this research organization, devoted to systematic inquiry about the reception of information by humans outside normal sensory channels, included the distinguished American educators William James, Josiah Royce, Charles Eliot Norton, and G. Stanley Hall.[159]

The same impulse to reach out to others motivated Frederick Evans
to propose that the United Society consider joining forces with the Koreshan Unity founded by Cyrus Read Teed. Teed, a practitioner of eclectic
medicine and a visionary, established a church and cooperative home in
Chicago in 1888 after two decades of lecturing throughout central New
York. Known to his followers as Koresh the prophet, he taught a theory of
"cellular cosmogony" that rejected the Copernican view of the earth. He
proposed that the universe had emanated from a single source, God, and
that the earth was concave. Teed also had a vision of the "Divine Motherhood" and believed in a dual godhead. The society he formed accepted
his views on "mental science and metaphysics" as well as "alchemy, rein-
carnation, celibacy, [and] communism." Some three hundred joined his
church in Chicago. In 1894 the community relocated in Estero, Florida,
where they acquired large agricultural holdings and also interacted with
the Shaker colony. Nothing came of Evans's proposal, although the Believers continued to feel a bond with the Koreshans. When Teed died in 1908,
his followers split into several factions.[160]

The Shakers recognized common cause with other outsiders, too.
The pastor of a Universalist church in Marshalltown, Iowa, corresponded
with Charles Clapp at Union Village about their common interest in spiritualism. He was gathering "accounts of Spirit phenomena wherever they
have occurred" and hoped to acquire Shaker books dealing with "medi-
umship." The members of the North Family at Mount Lebanon shared
their enthusiasm for spiritism with their long-time friend and correspondent Laura Holloway Langford. Langford, an affluent, cultured woman
who purchased the Shaker farm at Upper Canaan in 1906, exchanged
letters with the Believers for thirty-five years, beginning in 1874. A talented author and editor, she was especially interested in women's issues,
social reform, and religion. (She also published a Buddhist cookbook.)
Helena Blavatsky, the founder of the Theosophical Society, was her close
friend. Langford became a patron and benefactor of the Shakers. She
wrote on their behalf, marketed their produce, and made proposals for the
use of their vacant properties. The Believers, in turn, regarded her with
special affection as a kindred spirit.[161]

Following the death of Langford's second husband in 1902, Anna
White wrote to console her friend. White's epistle was occasioned by
strong thoughts of Laura, proving in her opinion "that telepathy is as real
as is spirit communication." White thought that Colonel Langford had
understood the "inner workings" of Shakerism even though he had not
experienced extended contact with the Believers. "If he still lingers on this

side," she wrote, "please convey to him our help our strength in passing over—our kind remembrance and love. He may soon meet some of our people and then he will know more." Laura need have no fear about his ultimate destiny, for he had risen above his passions and "fulfilled the higher law of his being."

> Your faith in immortality will help dispel the clouds of grief, and the thought that he will be with you still will be a comfort to you in many a weary hour. You will miss his bodily presence; that can never be replaced, but the spirit may be so quickened as to know him better even than when in the body.

She closed the letter with lines from a poem entitled "Beautiful Death."[162]

Spiritualism's rejection of death as final made it attractive to persons affected by the changing attitudes toward death and mourning in the late nineteenth century. Spirit communication provided consolation for the living and hope for the dead. Shaker families, too, it was assumed, remained intact across the barriers of time. Elaborate circumlocutions developed whereby it became unnecessary to use realistic language about death. In the Shaker magazine, the list of those who had died at the villages appeared under the heading "To Evergreen Shores." Family journal entries throughout the society employed similar references. Andrew Fortier "departed . . . across the dark river unto the Ever green shore," Rhoda Hollister "took her flight to the better land," Ann Buzley "departed to the Spirit land of souls," Otis Sawyer "passed to the spirit home," Ruth Barry "passed to spirit life," Dorothy Wright took "her exit from the mortal part," Henry Blinn "passed from sight," Matilda Reed passed "from our earthly vision," and Annie Dodson passed "from the mortal to the immortal state." Rarely was the explicit language of death or dying used, although it was reported that Galen Richmond "dropped dead" and that Ann Eliza "died . . . mid terrible agonies." At Shaker funerals it was common to receive communications from the deceased, and such contacts often continued for years afterward.[163]

Dreams were frequently the means through which Believers received spirit messages. Catherine Allen published her "visionary dream" of the judgment of souls, where all the living and former leaders of the society were seated in "a spacious hall dedicated to religious purposes." From this assembled body emanated a white aura; the atmosphere surrounding them was "dense with spiritual force." At the center was an altar on which glowed a "quenchless flame" of God's pure love. A song pleaded, "Come to the Judgment! Enter the flame and be purified." This scene produced in Allen the "power of conviction" and a desire to be "cleansed from sin." In spite of her reluctance to reveal all in front of the assembled witnesses, she decided to "lay bare" her condition and to confess. "O beloved Ones! Anointed of Christ,—in mercy to my poor soul do witness for me." Allen realized how flimsy were her excuses and how potent God's love. In her dream, many others, too, were "deeply exercised" as they claimed their privilege. Another Believer, at Union Village, while praying before going to sleep, saw "two bright suns in the North eastern horizon (toward Mt. Lebanon)," which were interpreted as signs that "a revival might spring up among believers, conducted by both Christ & Mother as representatives of the Dual principle in Deity."[164]

The spiritism of the Shakers also manifested itself through their interest in Christian Science, the religious movement begun in 1875 by Mary Baker Eddy. Metaphysical in outlook, yet practical in its concern for healing, Christian Science attracted considerable attention from the Believers. Christian Science lecturers visited the villages from time to time, delivering their distinctive message. Eddy taught that the material world was an illusion, as were sin, sickness, and death. Those who understood the spiritual nature of all reality would be freed from the grasp of false ideas and empowered to demonstrate their oneness with the Divine Mind. Eddy also stressed that the concept of God, although impersonal, incorporated both masculine and feminine aspects. Individual Shakers consulted Christian Science practitioners and healers. William Ryan at Watervliet, Ohio, requested the assistance of a "Christian Science doctor" in 1894; four sisters at the same village also visited his office in Dayton. The *Christian Science Journal* in 1907 reported that Anna White had been cured of a serious illness. Other Believers, too, identified closely with the basic ideas of Christian Science. Oliver Hampton, for example, described himself as "a Christian Scientist (albeit not of the Eddy stripe) and," he wrote, "we C. S. don't allow ourselves to talk about sickness and pain but only health and consolation." He suggested that dwelling on symptoms "is one of the most fruitful ways to create sickness on earth." Not all the Believers, however, were equally persuaded. When Eldress Rachel McDonald of the South Family at Watervliet "asked for a christian science treatment in the middle of the night," family members "telephoned for some old fraud of hers, and she gave her an absent treatment." Anna Goepper judged that the treatment "done about as much good as to spit against the wind." Two days later the eldress died.[165]

The difficulty of defining Shaker spiritism is evident in the case of Aurelia Mace at Sabbathday Lake, one of the most creative women in the society. Like others, she was preoccupied with the concept of the Christ spirit, but for her Jesus and Christ were not to be confused. The former, she stated, "gained the Spirit of Christ by his good works." Mace was equally comfortable using the expression "Buddha the Christ." Jesus and Buddha were both recipients of a higher transforming spirit. Describing a successful meeting in 1896, she wrote: "There was something there that came from far above us. Something that is past words to describe. Every little one, even the smallest child felt the influence of the Spirit." This "something" made progress possible. Following the logic of her position, Mace agreed with Alonzo Hollister and others who proposed changing the name of the society to the Alethians, meaning the "spirit of truth." In her opinion, "Calling Shakerism 'Christ's Second Appearance' has been a mistake from the beginning, and that mistake entered into our fundamental name. Christ has appeared in thousands, and is the atmosphere or Spiritual life of all good." Mace understood the Christ spirit to be the "Love which clasps like air."[166]

Shaker spiritualism, or spiritism, was a comprehensive world view that allowed the Believers to make sense of their daily experience as well as to understand the larger universe of which they were a part. It drew on traditional ideas from the society, but it was responsive also to the world of late-nineteenth-century America. At its core were a rejection of materialism and an affirmation of the primacy of spirit. The unity of reality, the capacity of human beings, and a higher destiny—these were the themes sounded by Shaker spiritualists. Death posed no ultimate threat, grief was a passing stage, and immortality a proven fact. In the words of one Believer, "We mourn not, as those who have no hope." Shaker spiritism promoted equality of the sexes, toleration of divergent religious traditions, and freedom of thought. It was perhaps the most creative strain of late-nineteenth-century Shaker religion.[167]

One attack launched against Shaker spiritualism came from the American novelist William Dean Howells. His own religious skepticism and his abiding commitment to artistic realism colored his depictions of the Shakers in a series of writings, including four novels. His own first-hand experience with the Believers came at Shirley in 1875. He published his impressions in the *Atlantic Monthly* the next year. Though complimentary about many aspects of their existence, Howells had no patience with celibacy, which he regarded as an affront to "elemental humanity." In each of his novels involving Believers, a young couple confronts the tension between the Shaker principle of celibacy and the attraction of marriage. Choosing the angelic life instead of marriage was cause for attack by

Howells. Shakerism and spiritualism, according to him, were too concerned with the beyond and not enough engaged with "the ethical application of spiritual truth." He condemned the Believers' romanticism and idealism. They, in turn, dismissed his assessment of Shaker spiritism as not well informed in a short review of *The Undiscovered Country*.[168]

An evangelical strain of spirituality constituted a second religious perspective within the society during this Time of Transformation. This tradition was not new to the Believers, for during the first century of Shaker history many, if not most, converts had been drawn from Protestant evangelical churches. At that time, the attitude of the Believers toward those churches had been basically antagonistic. In the post–Civil War years, a resurgent conservative Protestantism carried forward its crusade for a Christian America, drawing on revivalist techniques, holiness principles, biblical dispensationalism, and antimodernism, forging a new coalition. Some Shakers responded positively to aspects of the evangelical agenda.[169]

The Shakers were frequent participants at camp meetings, prayer meetings, and revivals. Sometimes they attended with the intention of testifying to their own distinctive beliefs. Other times they took part heartily in the activities. Family journals routinely record these visits. Giles Avery noted in 1876 that about fifty Believers from Mount Lebanon had attended an evening revival in Lebanon Valley. He judged it "quite a good meeting." Others went to Albany to listen to Henry Ward Beecher. The Shakers at Pleasant Hill spent all day at a camp meeting where Thomas DeWitt Talmage, a prominent minister, was preaching. The Believers followed with great interest the revival meetings conducted by Dwight L. Moody and Ira Sankey. Henry Blinn and Elijah Myrick attended a series of meetings at the Tabernacle in Boston, after which Blinn featured his observations—a mixed report—on the front page of *The Shaker*. He was not impressed with Moody's "spiritual" qualities. Nevertheless, Blinn wrote, "That he is earnest, and in sympathy with his work, no one can doubt; and he is evidently as much a servant of God in that revival as a Shaker may be in his quiet home." Blinn was impressed with Moody's rhetorical skill in addressing a congregation of seven thousand.[170]

The Shakers sometimes invited the revivalists and other Protestant ministers into their villages or allowed them to use their facilities. In 1879 a preacher from Indiana spoke in the meetinghouse at Pleasant Hill on "Holiness & Peace." The following year in the same village three Methodist ministers took part in a "Call Meeting"; one preached a sermon at the Center Family. In 1885 two Baptist ministers baptized their new converts in the West Family pond at Pleasant Hill; a crowd of one thousand was in attendance, including most of the society members. The next year the Believers canceled their own meetings to attend a camp meeting on their land. In 1902 they invited a large company of the Salvation Army from the pine grove at Lebanon Springs into the meetinghouse at Mount Lebanon, where they sang and marched together with much spirit. Photographs taken on that occasion reveal more outward uniformity among the members of the visiting group than among their hosts. The occasion was declared "a mutual blessing" in the ministry's journal. The next year the Salvation Army was back at the village again. At Sabbathday Lake in 1907, clergy from Rumford Falls and Portland, Maine, visited the Shakers and joined with them in song and prayer.[171]

The Believers established Sunday schools at their villages. During the nineteenth century the Sunday school, perhaps more than any other institution, became the primary transmitter of the "culture of evangelical Protestantism." In 1876 the Shakers at Canaan joined with the Methodists in attending a "sabbath-school concert." At Pleasant Hill in 1887 classes were held at nine o'clock on Sunday morning. The central ministry visited the Kentucky location in 1889 and found to their dismay that the Sabbath school being conducted there included both Believers and the world's people, that the lessons taught "a false theology," and that their songs spoke of being saved through the blood of Jesus. In 1894 the sisters at Sabbathday Lake conducted a Sunday school composed of nineteen students in three classes, with Elder William Dumont serving as superintendent. For instruction, they used a publication by Alonzo G. Hollister and materials produced and distributed by the American Sunday School Union. At Mount Lebanon it was customary to conduct a quarterly review of the Sabbath school classes.[172]

The Believers also began to pay more attention to the Bible. *The Shaker Manifesto*, for example, contained a regular column entitled "From the Bible Class," in which traditional expository methods were used to derive moral and spiritual advantage from biblical texts. These explanations often did not refer to distinctive Shaker beliefs. Flora Rothwell at Canterbury, for instance, wrote about "the new love" that "characterizes the disciples of Christ, who are ever ready to bear and forbear, give and forgive, and . . . willingly suffer pain to alleviate another's sorrow." After contrasting the "selfish love of the natural heart" with the love of God, Rothwell concluded her reflections with a meditation on the excellence of Jesus' love. The article contained nothing uniquely Shaker. In 1899, the last year of *The Manifesto,* Henry Blinn wrote two front-page editorials on the value of scriptural study. The opening paragraphs of the first read:

> The searching of the Scriptures is always new and interesting. It is like the storehouse of precious treasures—the eye never tires of seeing, nor the ear with hearing. Those who have not grown to appreciate the study of the wonderful Book, will be more or less like those, who have eyes, see not the many beautiful things which God places before them.
>
> We should study the Scriptures that we may be the better able to understand what the best inspiration of all ages has instructed men to do in the work of practical righteousness.

According to Blinn, the Bible confirmed Shaker beliefs.[173]

Alonzo G. Hollister used biblical materials to support and buttress his belief in spiritualism. He described how evil spirits as well as good exerted control over mortals. He suggested that "the paradise of devils & damd spirits" exists just outside the earth's atmosphere, where dwells the "Prince of the power of the air," described by the Apostle Paul in Ephesians 2:2. Virtue and vice both involve a struggle of wills, and the strongest will prevails. Jesus triumphed over the prince of evil and thereby created a heaven filled with "emancipated Spirits in Light" who enlighten those who obey "Mother Ann's gospel." Hollister was also fascinated by biblical study aids. David Skeene, "inventor of the famous Bible Chart," reportedly once displayed a twelve-foot-square chart at Mount Lebanon, to the apparent delight of the Believers.[174]

There was a corresponding rise of interest in the figure of Jesus, as numerous articles in *The Manifesto* attest. Elijah Myrick at Harvard concluded that Jesus was "a man like us," and therefore the Believers could be persons such as he. "What one has done another can do." His example might be an inspiration, whereas "*[d]ependence* [emphasis mine] on pattern saints and saviors, has ever been an incubus on human advancement." Abraham Perkins at Enfield, New Hampshire, itemized the virtues that Jesus embodied. Jesus was celibate, peaceful, meek, truthful, just, sober, and honest. These principles define a true Christian and a Shaker, too, wrote Perkins.[175]

The religious language of the Believers was at times indistinguishable from that of the evangelical tradition. Benjamin Dunlavy, an elder at Pleasant Hill, used classic Protestant logic to explain a disastrous fire in 1876. Despite the mental and physical suffering caused by the calamity, the Shakers had reasons to be thankful, among them that their "chastisement was not heavier." He also warned of the fleeting character of material goods. "While earthly riches make to themselves wings, and fly away," he wrote, "the treasures of heaven abide in the soul forever." Dunlavy used the "fiery ordeal" to school the Believers in proper attitudes. The Shakers sounded apocalyptic themes familiar to many Protestant millennialists. Arthur W. Dowe, a "Believer" who attempted to found a Shaker community in San Francisco, wrote of the "great and terrible day of the Lord" that had already begun. That work, he wrote, will continue until "a full and final separation shall be made between good and evil." The Pleasant Hill Believers allowed a "colporteur for a Bible & tract society" from Allegheny, Pennsylvania, to lecture for three consecutive nights in the village. The speaker was a follower of Charles Taze Russell, founder of the Watch Tower Bible and Tract Society, the organization that later was known by the name Jehovah's Witnesses.[176]

Shaker worship, when it existed at all, increasingly resembled Protestant worship services. When the eastern ministry visited Pleasant Hill in 1889, they discovered that the younger members in Kentucky were completely unfamiliar with traditional Shaker songs and exercises. Long before the closing of Enfield, Connecticut, the Believers there had stopped holding public services; they worshiped in their rooms without any exercises. At South Union few religious meetings were held at all in the twentieth century. Apparently the same was true at Mount Lebanon before it was finally abandoned. When meetings were held, they reflected fundamental changes, such as an end to the exercises and marching, the incorporation of instrumental music, the highlighting of the sermon, and the use of Protestant hymns (fig. 45). Pleasant Hill stopped "stepping, shuffling, & marching" at the end of 1885. The use of organs in worship was being debated fiercely within the society late in the century. Ministers from neighboring churches began to officiate at Shaker funerals. In 1894, for example, the Reverend Goodloe of Harrodsburg conducted a funeral in the Pleasant Hill meetinghouse. The pastor and choir of the Christian church in Harrodsburg presided at James W. Shelton's burial in 1910. In that same year the Reverend Eleanor B. Forbes of Gray, Maine, "spoke words of sympathy and comfort to the stricken family" at the memorial service for Aurelia Mace. Evangelicalism influenced Shakerism in many ways.[177]

A third identifiable strain of spirituality within the society was espoused by Believers who called for a return to a more sectarian perspective and to earlier religious patterns. These Shaker restorationists adopted a pessimistic view of the contemporary situation, declaring that "an infidelic

45. Shaker Meeting
This rare photograph, taken in the meetinghouse at Sabbathday Lake, Maine, on
20 September 1885, shows seating arrangements, patterns of dress, and a crowd
of outsiders behind the first two rows. (Collection of the United Society of Shakers,
Sabbathday Lake, Maine.)

element" was "almost universally manifest." They looked back wistfully to
the Age of the Founders, hoping to recover the ardor and commitment of
that earlier era. Often they singled out particular beliefs or practices and
made them a test of the faith. They voiced the hope that free-flowing charismatic gifts might return. During their last years of tenure in the central
ministry, Daniel Boler and Giles Avery frequently spoke on behalf of the
primitivist cause. In 1877 the ministry received a gift urging the families
to read the "biographies and teachings" of the founders in the *Summary
View* and to "call to mind Gospel precepts." A few years later, in his
Sketches of "Shakers and Shakerism," Avery reduced the theology of the
Believers to twenty-three propositions. One criticized classic Protestant
doctrine: "Jesus's death on the cross of wood constitutes no part of the
plan of salvation instituted by our Heavenly Father; it simply operated to
delay its progress." Another affirmed classic Shaker views: "Every soul
must work out its own salvation by practicing the self-denials of Jesus."[178]

  Henry Blinn was another Believer intent on recovering the past. In
The Life and Gospel Experience of Mother Ann Lee, first published in

1882, he described the "Primitive Church, showing plainly a manifestation of the spirit of Christ and the purifying gospel work as taught by Ann Lee." He believed that the original principles on which Shakerism had been founded remained sufficient. "Separation from the world, confession of sin, purity of spirit, and a united inheritance are the essentials," he wrote. In his volume Blinn retold the story of the founders, using the testimonies of the early Believers about Ann Lee. He featured a fundamental tension between the Shaker gospel and the values of the world. He hoped to revive a similar spirituality in the late nineteenth century, which no doubt was also an underlying motive when Giles Avery reissued the *Testimonies* in 1888. A number of changes were made in the text consistent with the contemporary cultural and religious situation. During these years *The Shaker Manifesto* also published a large number of tributes to Lee's memory.[179]

The most articulate of the Shaker traditionalists was Hervey L. Eads of South Union (fig. 46). Eads, the ranking elder in Kentucky, became an accomplished preacher and lecturer as well as a sophisticated writer. These achievements were the more remarkable because he was largely self-taught. Eads was a steady contributor to the Shaker periodical, often opposing the progressive views of the North Family at Mount Lebanon. His most significant publication, however, was a collection of addresses and writings entitled *Shaker Sermons: Scripto-Rational,* first published in 1879 and reissued within a decade in four enlarged and revised editions. This work harks back to the rational theological tradition of the early nineteenth century associated with Benjamin S. Youngs and John Dunlavy. (Eads served with Youngs in the ministry at South Union.) It also represents the culmination of the apologetic tradition within Shakerism.[180]

Blinn, in the preface to Eads's volume, declared that *Shaker Sermons* defended the fundamentals of Shakerism: "Virgin Purity, Non-resistance, Peace, Equality of Inheritance and Unspottedness from the world." Eads used both philosophical and theological arguments. Although he employed a self-effacing style, he was as comfortable citing Plato and Locke as he was making a semantic point on the basis of Alexander Cruden's concordance to the Bible. Religious and secular history figured in his arguments, but his most frequent appeals were to the interpretation of the Bible and to common sense and reason. Eads was knowledgeable about traditional theological issues as well as contemporary critical questions. He sought to reaffirm and restore Shaker traditions. It is a mistake, however, to see him simply as echoing the past. In fact, he actively responded to the world of nineteenth-century American thought, specifically to the views of the freethinker Robert Ingersoll, the Pres-

46. Hervey L. Eads
This engraving by J. C. Buttre was used as a frontispiece in Eads's *Shaker Sermons: Scripto-Rational* (1879). Eads was forced to defend his inclusion of the portrait in the publication.

byterian preacher Thomas DeWitt Talmage, James McCosh, the Scottish philosopher who became the president of Princeton College, and Henry Ward Beecher.[181]

Eads addressed theological issues in order to defend Shaker beliefs. In an address entitled "God Immutable," he examined the nature of the deity by attacking the logic of the "divines" who made Christians believe "that the terms *unity* and *trinity* are synonymous." He ridiculed those who, "whilst they declare that the *Son is the Father,* still hold that *there is a Father aside from the Son.*" This kind of specious reasoning, he contended, was the basis for "the triple-God doctrine" that was presented as a mystery beyond human comprehension that had been revealed in the Bible. But, Eads declared, God is not mysterious "to those to whom He is revealed."

Miracles are next urged upon you, especially the great, grand miracle of miracles, "revealed in God's word," that the Infinite Jehovah, the Creator of worlds, beyond thought, focalized himself in a woman, became a baby, a boy, a man, then permitted His fellow man to kill Him that He might reconcile it with His sense of justice to admit the sinner into Heaven, especially all who were simple enough to believe the story!

This proposition "is entirely beyond the power of belief to any educated and unbiased mind." Having destroyed the grounds for traditional trinitarianism to his own satisfaction, Eads went on to propose the proper understanding of "the son the 'Man, Christ Jesus.'" In his explanation he drew on the text of 1 Timothy 2:5, the meaning of the Greek and Hebrew terms for *anointed,* several noted authorities, and finally the parallel between the names "John the Baptist" and "Jones, the Sheriff." In sum, he wrote, the "good man, godly man, or God-man, if you please," left an ex ample that others could follow—a salvation that is attainable "in this life."[182]

Alonzo Hollister, a self-proclaimed "Shaker historian and a defender of orthodoxy," used his talents as a scribe, editor, and writer to maintain traditional beliefs and practices. Although he labored in the medical extract business at Mount Lebanon for more than four decades, he spent an enormous amount of time collecting, copying, and preserving documents from the past. He used the lives and testimonies of the early Believers to uphold traditional Shaker views. He was especially interested in the concept of progressive revelation. Hollister thought that all revelations, including the Bible, must be consistent. He did not subscribe to modern historical canons; on the contrary, he used history to defend the "truth." He also felt no compunction about altering documents to reflect orthodox beliefs.[183]

Hollister was the author of numerous religious tracts, several of which related to eschatological themes. *Divine Judgment, Justice and Mercy,* published in 1895, addressed a range of traditional issues relating to the final judgment and the millennium. He interpreted the classic apocalyptic texts of Daniel and Revelation as forecasting a "work of universal reconstruction." Hollister was also the author and editor of a set of Bible study lessons entitled *Pearly Gate of the True Life and Doctrine for Believers in Christ.* This catechetical work, published in 1895, with supplements issued erratically over the next decade, was for the instruction of "the young in faith." Its intention was to present to inquirers and learners, the leading principles of our Gospel, with reasons for the same, and to prove by Scripture and reason, and from revelation and experience that the gospel of Jesus Christ and of Ann the Word, is the Power of God unto salvation, to every one that obeyeth. Also that it is the Gospel of the great world Harvest, the general Resurrection, and the Final Judgment foretold in the New Testament revelation.

For example, Hollister asked, "Can God be seen by mortal sight?" The response was, "Nay, for God is Spirit, which cannot be seen with mortal eyes. Jon i: 18. Ch. v: 37." Hollister included a chapter called "The Scriptures of Truth," which explored the significance of the Bible. He was a staunch and consistent defender of biblical revelation, which he called "the sun of the religious and mental world." He also contended that an attack on the Bible was "a blow at spiritual mindedness." Hollister used the scriptural lessons to support traditional Shaker views.[184]

The Shakers looked with interest at other religious groups, often with curiosity, but sometimes with admiration at elements in those traditions. Mormonism, founded by Joseph Smith in 1830, stirred renewed debate throughout America after the Civil War; its practice of polygamy provoked outrage and persecution. One of the earliest efforts of the Mormons to convert the Shakers had ended in an unfriendly exchange. In 1831 Smith had written, "And again, verily I say unto you, that the Son of Man cometh not in the form of a woman." No longer competitors by 1885, the Shakers could afford to be a bit more charitable about the Latter-day Saints, who had outstripped them in every way. Louis Basting at Mount Lebanon wrote a spirited attack on polygamy, but in the same essay described in detail the charismatic gifts manifested among the Mormons, their remarkable missionary successes, and their achievement of turning a "barren wilderness" into a fertile land through their commitment to "order and sobriety and general thrift." Two years later a Mormon elder addressed an assembly of Believers at Groveland, seeking to "rectify false reports of their Church" and to outline the nature of their faith. He had no success, however, in gaining converts.[185]

The Believers had a remarkably charitable view of another contemporary sect, the followers of John Humphrey Noyes. Although the Shakers and the Perfectionists possessed very different beliefs and practices, they managed to express a measure of mutual respect. William Hinds, a disciple of Noyes and editor of the Oneida *Circular*, visited Shaker villages before writing his *American Communities,* which included a sympathetic account of the Believers even though the two groups held completely opposite views on sexual relations. Noyes had instituted a system of "complex marriage" in his community at Oneida, New York, based on the assumption that sexual intercourse was the highest possible form of spiritual communion. He attacked monogamy as "selfish love" and substituted a social arrangement in which men and women had sexual relations with varied partners. By 1879 the residents of New York State had become enraged by Noyes and the Perfectionists. Yet in an account of a gathering of ministers who wanted to eject Noyes and his followers from the region, the Believers castigated the ministers and their churches for sanctifying conventional marriages, a form of legal "libertinism or prostitution." "We are not championing complex marriage," the Shaker writer editorialized, "but we have made the most searching investigations into the mysteries of Oneida complexity of life, and while it is far from Shakerism, it is, we truthfully believe, vastly purer than some of the most respectable marriages of to-day." The Believers were able to muster this charity for the Perfectionists in part because both communities practiced the principle of common property.[186]

Spiritualism, evangelicalism, restorationism—these were the basic elements that constituted the religious pluralism among the Believers by the end of the nineteenth century. *Pluralism* is the correct term because none of these traditions of spirituality was elevated to the level of a new orthodoxy. All stood on equal ground, and sometimes even side by side within the same person. In other words, there were multiple ways for a Shaker to be religious.[187]

The Issue of Decline

As the realities of post–Civil War Shakerism became apparent, one question was asked most frequently by Believers and outsiders alike: "Are the Shakers dying out?" The faithful raised the question in order to answer it in the negative. Non-Shakers inquired for a variety of reasons, including perhaps the hope that "an institution so antagonistic to the elements of a worldly life . . . might die out"; so Giles Avery thought in 1879 when he set out to answer the question. Avery looked back into history and noted that only four villages had been closed during the previous century: West Union in Indiana, Sodus Bay in New York, Gorham in Maine, and Tyringham in Massachusetts. He acknowledged, however, that there had been "ebbs and flows" in the society relating both to the life of the spirit and to conditions in the outside world. He also granted the need for more Believers at the present. But he affirmed that never before had the "Shaker testimony" exercised so much power. Avery described the times as "revolutionary," and yet he was confident that Shakerism was part of God's providential plan for history. "Shakerism is not *'dying out,'* nor preparing to die; and, were every vestige of its present trophies of earthly gains, or the entire numbers who profess its faith, to be swept from the earth at once, the mental and spiritual light and truth in vigorous operation, would, phoenix-like, suddenly raise it again into immortal glory, prosperity and renown. *Shakerism never can 'die out!'*" This resounding declaration was the standard response of the faithful.[188]

The previous year George Lomas had addressed the same question several times in *The Shaker Manifesto*. To the Believers themselves, his remarks were primarily hortatory. "The times are dull," he conceded, "spiritually; the heavens now seem unusually closed to the impartation of heavenly gifts; . . . but these *trials* of our faith, will *prove* the faithful worthy of the grandest promotions." Therefore he urged, "Let us take heart, and fling doubt and despondency to the winds. Let us, and all the world realize, that our maintenance as a spiritual organization entirely depends upon its genuine religious revivals." The tone of these admonitions suggests that many Believers may have needed convincing. To outsiders, Lomas declared that the success or failure of Shakerism did not "depend on numerical calculations." Although the Believers were few in number, he wrote, the "Shaker influence" was felt throughout the world in various reform movements, as well as through "thousands who claim they 'are more than half Shakers.'" "We are not on the decline," he proclaimed.[189]

Similar affirmations echoed through scores of other essays and comments on "the Shaker problem." One editorial concluded, "Shakerism being the harvest of the world's good, its career is quite in its infancy," even if the present times were lean. Another Believer looked forward "to the better time coming." Yet another declared that the "work of Shakerism is the climatic [sic] process of man's strife for the Kingdom of Heaven." The present phase was but a "halt in the march of religious progress," and the march would soon begin anew. "When names, and sects, and parties shall have passed away, true Shakers will be found to possess a kingdom eternal, while the world, and its elements, will be burned up by the fire of truth." A fourth commentator affirmed that "the dispensation of Christ's Second Appearing" was still in "its spring time." Four years after the turn of the twentieth century, Anna White and Leila Taylor wrote confidently, "Are Shakers Dying Out? Yea! dying out and up. Men and women die— advance, go to higher planes, to spheres of greater radius than earth, where we hear of them actively engaged along the same lines as on earth—the spread of truth among humanity. Is Shakerism Dying? Nay! not unless God and Christ and eternal verities are failing."[190]

Such public affirmations did not end the questioning, nor did they stem the growing tide of uneasiness and fear expressed privately by many within the society. It was impossible for the Believers to ignore the evidence of severe institutional decline by the end of the century. The United Society had been unsuccessful in recruiting significant numbers of new converts. William Sims Bainbridge has found "pathetically high rates of loss" in membership between 1880 and 1900. In addition, increasing numbers of the members were elderly and infirm. Their care became a major task for many within the society. The mentality of old age began to dominate the Shakers, and for good reason. In 1900, 32 percent of the 855 Shakers were sixty or older, with 51 members eighty or above. Physical disabilities, the fear of sickness, the threat of long-term care, loneliness, the loss of independence, anxieties about insufficient resources—these were the preoccupation of many Believers. Even Martha J. Anderson's poetic effort to put a friendly face on aging failed to avoid the language of weariness and sorrow, loneliness and despair.[191]

Old age became a regular topic of conversation among the Believers, who struggled to put that stage of life in a positive light (fig. 47). Julius Assman at Canaan acknowledged that it was rare to "see truly happy and venerable old age." Yet, he argued, because human progress advances the soul from the "lower animal nature" to the higher "angelic condition," it stands to reason that an older person is better able to practice duty and self-denial. Advancement in years, therefore, should correspond with progress in "true spiritual life and power." In 1878 the Shakers at Albany boasted about the large percentage of members at Watervliet who were more than seventy years of age and acting "as if in their prime." Sadie A. Neale spoke of aging as part of the inevitable cycle of nature. "*Growth* and *decay* are stamped upon the face of all existence. To-day we live in a material form; to-morrow our existence may be elsewhere." In autumn, she wrote, Mother Nature mourns, attired in brown and sere dress. Yet even in this "feeble form" lies the "germ of rejuvenated life." Therefore, Neale concluded, "seeming decline leadeth not unto death, but in reality unto a resurrection of life through all futurity."[192]

These attempts to find a bright side to aging appear alongside the regular necrology in the pages of the Shaker periodical. In May 1881, for example, *The Shaker Manifesto* listed eight deaths in the society: Chloe Chaffin (eighty-five) and Sallie Ann Tucker (sixty-four) at Enfield, New Hampshire; Mercy Dring (seventy-six) at Harvard; Mary Peterson (sixty)

47. A Typical Occupation
John H. Tarbell captured the repose of an elderly Shaker at Enfield, New Hampshire,
patiently carrying on with domestic tasks. (From *New England Magazine*, 1910.)

at Sabbathday Lake; Thomas Giles (eighty-three) at North Union; Elizabeth Whiteley (eighty) at Shirley; and Eliza Sharp (eighty-four) and Sarah Bates (eighty-eight) at Mount Lebanon. On the same page was a tribute to Dolly Saxton, who was approaching her one-hundred-and-sixth birthday, and a notice from the editor, George Lomas, announcing that he had decided against publishing "mortuary notices" of recent deaths because they would consume an entire issue if printed in full. As a result, "respectful mementoes" commonly were issued as separate publications and, in some cases, accompanied by a formal portrait.[193]

The Shakers greeted death in various ways; they responded with both anguish and guarded confidence. One sister at Pleasant Hill in 1886 reported five deaths in two weeks from the "flux," with two more expected shortly. "It seems as quick as one dies," she wrote, "the other get sick." In 1912 Anna Goepper at Watervliet, New York, lamented, "So much sickness and death and everything seemed to come in a heap together, and none of us seem to have much heart for Christmas." Genevieve DeGraw at Mount Lebanon managed more bravado in the face of widespread mortality. Her simple verse stated her faith.

> One by one they're passing on,
> Friends we long have known;
> But we'll meet them all again
> In our spirit home.

The Believers eulogized Zelinda Smith at Enfield, New Hampshire, for her "Christly culture and faithful work." She was "an example of nobility safe to imitate." Thomas Steadman, a member for sixty years at the same village, had been the overseer of the large barn and the stock. "In that realm where man is judged, not by scholarship, position or profession, but by his life acts," it was written, "Brother Thomas will reap a rich reward." Smith and Steadman died a day apart in 1899, causing their friends to write: "We perceive the on-coming messenger for others who must soon pass beyond Eternity's curtain."[194]

The most infamous death involving a Shaker was at the Olive Branch community in 1911. Sadie Marchant, a proselyte who suffered from an advanced stage of tuberculosis, requested and received chloroform from Egbert Gillette with the full knowledge of Elizabeth A. Sears, who had been her nurse. This mercy killing was a feature story in newspapers across the country. Both Gillette and Sears were arrested. It is noteworthy that the local newspaper, the *Kissimmee Valley Gazette,* spoke kindly of the Shakers and declared their belief in Gillette's "innocence of evil intent." The grand jury refused to indict the two, and they were released. Charges were subsequently dismissed. The notoriety of Marchant's death did not, however, help the cause of the Florida settlement.[195]

In 1899 the Believers responded to another kind of "passing" with similarly mixed feelings. In that year it was decided to end publication of *The Manifesto* after twenty-nine years. The editor, Henry Blinn, announced that possibly it had "accomplished all the good it can for the present" and would go into "retirement" until called forth by "another wave of enthusiasm." Among the reasons he cited for that decision were changing times and economic distress at several villages. The announcement was greeted by some as though a close acquaintance had died. "How sad it is to part with a friend and such a helpful friend, too, as THE MANIFESTO has been!" wrote Ada Cummings at Sabbathday Lake. "Is there no doctor that can be called in to administer the right kind of medicine that would restore it?" Fidelia Estabrook at Hancock was certain the publication "will not be forgotten or that its people will be forsaken." She added, "We will miss the little monthly chat with our Brothers and Sisters in other homes, but must learn to converse by thought waves." Jesse Evans at Canterbury responded to the news by reminding the Believers that they were "children of one rich inheritance . . . upon which the sun can never set." The loss of the periodical was a major blow to communications within the United Society. "Notes About Home," in particular, had created a "family circle" where unity and common purpose were reinforced. After 1899 there was no regular exchange among the scattered villages and little systematic public representation to the world.[196]

Old age, death, and institutional decay contributed to the steady closing of villages in the opening decades of the twentieth century. The relatively few family records that survive from these sites for this period of the society's history tell a not-so-glorious story. A few entries from a Whitewater journal, for example, document the final dissolution of the Center Family. Charles Sturr, a trustee since 1878 and later an elder, died on 18 March 1910. At the time it was noted: "we find at his death some bad *mistakes*." Approximately two weeks later Eldress Amanda Rubush and Pearl McLean left "their Shaker home" to live among relatives in the world. Rubush, seventy-nine, had been in the leadership since 1878, having lived among the Believers for sixty years. McLean, a much younger woman of twenty-seven, had resided with the Shakers since childhood. A few days later Frederick Young, forty-five, also left for the outside. Young and McLean later returned to claim a generous share of "household things." At that point only three "old members" of the family remained, and the

Mount Lebanon ministry ordered the western ministry to take possession of the property. The keeper of the journal noted, "The home is badly run down and no money in the treasury to meet the coming necessities! But God is good, and I dont believe he will see his servants deprived of the necessary parts of life—So we will toil on to the end." In the following months, under the supervision of Joseph Holden and Arthur Bruce from the East, the properties were sold to a judge from Cincinnati. The final departures from Whitewater were recorded only in private journals.[197]

By contrast, a year later an account of the declension of Enfield, Connecticut, appeared in the pages of the *New York Times* under the headline "The Last of the Shakers—A Community Awaiting Death." The reporter who visited Enfield described it as a "quaint, ghostlike colony of religious fanatics" with twenty-two members still committed to chastity and sainthood. Emily Copley, the eldress who was interviewed, was too sick to conduct a tour of the village, but she answered a variety of questions. She spoke of the former days of power and wealth when hundreds of Believers filled the buildings. But, she added, "I've seen them die off one by one until there are only a few of us left." When asked if she intended to attempt to keep the belief alive, she responded: "It is almost too late now. We have hoped and tried, but without success." The young people of today, she said, are too restless and interested in things of the world. The reporter asked, "And then when you are gone, your religion will cease to exist?" Copley replied, "It appears so, and I am afraid the time is coming quickly. We have lost a great many of our dear brothers and sisters in the last year, and many of us are ready to follow them." Copley appeared reconciled to her own demise and to that of the society. In fact, Enfield did not close for another eight years. More than two decades later another unidentified eldress was quoted as saying, "Oh! I know we're disappearing, but what of it? We've done our work. . . . We've served our time. Yea! and if we go, something else that's maybe better will take our place."[198]

Not all the Believers accepted defeat or viewed their situation so pessimistically. An eighty-year-old Groveland sister considered her old age to be filled with blessings, including "the priviledge of the present Season of Life, released from the burdens, cares, & toils of the past; a quiet residence, surrounded by *long proved* & kind young friends, feeling the *rich* blessings of *Home sweet Home*, not only a shelter from the storm, but in loyal *hearts*, unmoved by surging winds, & cruel tongues of slander." Another Believer thought perhaps too much attention was being given to "departed saints" and not enough to the "pure and brave souls who are at present in the battle of life." He reminded others, "Those who have past to the evergreen shores faithfully performed their duty. We are here to perform ours."[199]

And many of the remaining Believers did perform their duties faithfully. Those efforts, however, largely went unnoticed and unrecorded. The interest of outsiders in the Shakers waned rapidly during the 1920s and 1930s. The society's members no longer posed any threat to the religious communities of America, and therefore the churches ignored them. Occasional brief notices in local newspapers measured the numerical decline but offered little insight into the life situation of the remaining Believers. One four-inch column dated 29 November 1937 announced that the Albany colony of Shakers had now dwindled to seven "survivors" led by eighty-one-year-old Eldress Anna Case and Hamilton [DeGraw], who was eighty-three. The other members were Mary Frances and Grace Dahm, Frieda Sipple, Ella E. Myer, and Anna Goepper. Judging from Goepper's personality in earlier years, it is likely that this group was cohesive, affectionate, and supportive. Similar long-standing friendships existed in all the remaining families.[200]

Even in the most adverse circumstances, individual Believers managed to carry on with dignity and commitment. This was true at Mount Lebanon, too, where by the mid-1920s the financial situation had become desperate, fueled by the developments already discussed and aggravated by the national economic collapse. The ministry had been trying for years to sell portions of the holdings. By the mid-1920s, a number of agents were contacting Emma Neale concerning the sale of the Church Family and other properties. One of the more unusual contacts was through Fred M. Seiverd of Cleveland, Ohio, who attempted to arrange an on-site visit to Mount Lebanon for Robert H. Tannahill, curator of the Detroit Museum, whom he described as "a connoiseur of all kinds of antiques" and "a buyer for a large number of America's richest men." According to Seiverd, Tannahill represented Henry Ford, who was especially "interested in preserving just such [historical] places." Ford did not purchase the Mount Lebanon property, but in 1930 the Lebanon School bought 300 acres, forty buildings, and their contents from the Church Family for $75,000. The Shakers paid a sales commission of 5 percent to George H. Cooper, Jr., for the transaction. The school was eventually renamed the Darrow School in honor of the Darrow family, on whose acres the Church Family was built.[201]

One year before the sale, the Mount Lebanon ministry made an important decision concerning the management of the society's funds. A meeting was held in July 1929 to discuss how the Shakers' assets should be handled. The leaders decided to place them in a trust administered by a bank. To that end, in August the church covenant was amended as follows:

> Realizing the need at this period of our Society's history, of meeting the changed and changing conditions brought about by our depletion in membership, and our lack of qualified ability, in some cases, to care adequately for our surplus and invested funds, it is hereby recommended that where Society trustees feel unequal for the best care of such funds, they shall have liberty under the guidance and authority of the Parent Ministry, to place such funds under the care and management of the Trust department of a suitable Bank having such facilities.

This financial decision, apparently unopposed at the time, had major implications for the society in later decades.[202]

The Depression added to the problems at Mount Lebanon, now consisting only of the North Family. Taxes, insurance, and other expenses forced the Believers to sell furniture and other objects. Early in 1939 Lillian Barlow wrote to a friend in Brooklyn, New York, who had purchased many of these items, "The Holidays have come and gone and we are all in good health and spirits, facing the New Year with as much courage a[s] possible." But the situation continued to deteriorate. When an attempt to sell the farm in 1940 fell through, Ella E. Winship, the trustee, despaired: "everything has been so uncertain that we have hardly known which way to turn." The Shakers were no longer able to pay their farm manager, and so they allowed him to use the land, house, equipment, and stock for occupancy. They appeared to be facing financial disaster.[203]

The situation for individual Shakers at Mount Lebanon was bittersweet. Some managed to be philosophical about the dilemma. Sadie Neale, who had come to the village in 1855, was an uncomplaining, resilient, contented Believer. She had served the society faithfully as a weaver, schoolteacher, assistant to George Lomas at Watervliet on *The Shaker*, postmistress, and orchard deaconess. She handled difficult circumstances and aging rather stoically. In 1932 Neale observed, "Every material thing has its birth, growth and decay." A decade later she wrote, "I am as lame as ever and cannot get around very well." Yet in the spring of 1945, while all the world was in an uproar over the Second World War, at age ninety-six Neale wrote, "We had a very pleasant Easter, but a very quiet one. No one came to see and we went to see no one—but we were happy among ourselves. . . . I am nearing the end of my journey." Two years later she died, having been forced by circumstances to leave her home at Mount Lebanon and relocate at Hancock.[204]

Sarah Collins, another elderly Believer at Mount Lebanon, seemed to find strength in her daily tasks. Collins, who had come to the society as a child during the Civil War, was the last survivor of the South Family. Tireless in pursuit of her responsibilities, she spoke with pleasure about the process of aging. "I am glad I outlived all the members up there that I lived with so many years," she wrote. Collins had worked in the chair industry during times of great prosperity, and after those days were past, especially after the chair factory was destroyed by fire, she and Lillian Barlow continued to build and repair chairs as well as braid rugs. A local reporter observed, "With the hands of an artist she weaves the tape in making the seats and uses shellac in touching up the woodwork of some of them." Collins personified the traditional Shaker ethic: she found great satisfaction in her work. "I love this old Place," she wrote of Mount Lebanon in 1934. She tried to make the best of her situation, but even she had moments of doubt. "Wonder if death ends it *all*," she wrote. Yet her faith prevailed: "What ever comes in this world or the next I am *sure* of *my* Passport."[205]

Martha Wetherell seemed a bit more disturbed about the realities confronting Mount Lebanon. In 1935 she conceded to a friend in very unsteady hand, "My best days of workmanship are over, having just passed my eightieth milestone." Steps posed a special problem for her. Yet she had no intention of giving up. Seven years later she explained the new leadership situation in the society. Frances Hall had been appointed to deal with business affairs, she noted, but no other appointments had been made. "My radio has filled the place of ministry for years; so that is not new." Later she underscored again the special role of the radio in her life: "for the ministry, we listen to all the *good* programs of the several broadcasting companies over the air so we miss nothing in that line. We are all elderly enough to do as we ought, so no other appointment seems necessary." When Lillian Barlow became seriously ill in 1942, Wetherell feared that it was the "beginning of the end." Barlow was especially loved and esteemed by all, inside and outside the family circle. "We certainly are a dependant people," Wetherell observed. Less than a month later she wrote, "Sister Lillian left us yesterday very suddenly for the Evergreen Shores. It will be a difficult matter to fill the many places she has left. It is a terrible shock to us all. Sisters Sarah and Carrie are bearing up under it as well as could be expected. . . . We are wondering *What next*." At the time Barlow was eighty-six. Her fellow Believers in the family included one eighty-eight-year-old brother and six sisters, aged, respectively, ninety, eighty-one, seventy, sixty-six, sixty-four, and fifty-five.[206]

The leadership situation in the society, as Wetherell implied, had become somewhat ambiguous by the 1940s. Arguably the most powerful position in the society during the first half of the twentieth century was that of the trustee, who controlled the purse strings. Yet the evolution of the temporal and spiritual offices had been such that often the two were held by the same person and therefore not distinguished sharply. The last men to serve in the central ministry were Arthur Bruce at Canterbury, appointed a trustee in 1892 and an elder in 1919, and Irving Greenwood, also of Canterbury, who became first in the central ministry in 1933. Bruce, known as a "talented musician and a lover of horses," died in 1938, and Greenwood, the last brother at Canterbury, a year later. At the beginning of 1940 the society leaders included Ella E. Winship and A. Rosetta Stephens at Mount Lebanon, Frances Hall at Hancock, and Josephine E. Wilson at Canterbury. It is easy to conclude that Hall exercised the greatest influence of the four because of her position as trustee and because of her dominant personality. Wilson, appointed to the central ministry in 1939, died in 1946. That year Emma B. King, who had served as an eldress at Canterbury since 1913, was elevated to the parent ministry. Shortly after her selection, a change became apparent. King aggressively asserted leadership and over the course of the following years became a dominant force in society affairs.[207]

King wrote a long "pastoral" letter, for example, to three of the last sisters at Mount Lebanon, who were "disturbed" by the call to "take up a cross in moving" to Hancock   Grace and Mary Dahm and Jennie Wells. Although sympathetic, King minced no words. She stated that the Believers had become "very selfish" in wanting to keep open large homes with only a few residents. This pattern had been "a constant drain upon our Shaker funds," she wrote. Therefore it was a "moral and economic necessity" to consolidate. King also claimed that rumors concerning conflicts with the residents at Hancock village and with Frances Hall were unfounded. She verbally chastised the three for their independent spirit: "Self appointed leadership always engenders inharmony and bitterness and conflict and insubordination has no place in a Shaker home. . . . We are supposed to renounce our own opinions and humbly submit our judgments & will to the wisdom of the appointed leaders, not try to dictate what they shall say and do, but come and go as we are asked." Frances Hall, King added, had been unjustly charged with "disloyalty to her trust." She was "among the most efficient Trustees" and had carefully conserved the society's funds. "It is not the right of any Shaker Sister to take the leaders to task in this way and the blessing of God will never come to one who does it. We had better pray for light to see ourselves and reform." King closed her stern rebuke with these words: "Accept, please my love and interest for you and be the brave, wise, good sisters you know how to be, we need you every one."[208]

King demonstrated her determination to take charge of the society in another protracted confrontation. Jennie Wells, the principal subject of a winsome portrait of the Mount Lebanon family published in 1947 in the *New Yorker,* had been invited by the Reverend John Schott to visit Cleveland Heights in Ohio. She was eager to accept the invitation. King, however, made it clear that the ministry thought the trip inappropriate and would not consent. The needs of the society were too great at the moment, especially in view of the impending move to Hancock. "Sacrifices of desire and pleasure are required of us all," she reminded Wells. Furthermore, King doubted whether any Believer could adequately represent contemporary Shakerism, for "today we are just humble sisters struggling to do the best we can under many adverse conditions, and publicity is not to be desired." A month later, writing again to Wells, this time in confidence, King addressed herself to the matter of "giving away home business and talking unwisely with outside friends." She chided Wells for representing herself as a Shaker "authority" and for speaking indiscreetly. King cited several disturbing comments from the *New Yorker* article, including Wells's opinion that Eldress Rosetta was "out of her mind" and that Frances Hall had mismanaged Shaker funds. In saying such things, Wells had overstepped her authority. The article caused "much hurt" among the Canterbury sisters, according to King. "I beg of you to refrain from gossip and careless speech and don't give away knowledge of news which belongs among ourselves." King, exasperated with Wells's insubordination, closed with a stern admonition: "Are you working with us or against us? and is this your ideal of Shakerism? Would recommend that you think on these things." King also informed Schott that the Shakers had "no intention of selling excess furniture," which they valued highly, either at auction or to antique dealers.[209]

The Shaker principles of self-denial and sacrifice did little to soften the blow for the elderly Believers who were forced to leave their established homes and resettle in a different family at a new location. Routines were often strange and rules sometimes more restrictive. Frieda Sipple, formerly at Watervliet, complained that at Hancock "Eldress Fanny runs the home [and] not one thing done without asking." Sipple was apparently accustomed to more latitude under Anna Case. Mary Dahm, also relocated from Watervliet, wrote a heart-wrenching letter to a friend, telling of her sadness and loneliness.

> Any little reminder of my home and friends is a great comfort at the present. The sisters are very kind but this dark house is very depressing to an already broken heart. [T]he hills smother me and this room crushes me. Home is where the heart is and mine is not here. I hope and trust that God in His own way may bring a little comfort and peace to my heart. At present all I can do is make the best of a bad bargain.

The year after the closing of Mount Lebanon, Dahm wrote of Sipple's death: "We feel dreadfully bad; as we had planned to have a few happy years together. Fate seems to have decreed it otherwise."[210]

Each remaining village had its own leaders who, with varying degrees of success, guided the local fortunes. During the 1930s and 1940s all those in charge were elderly sisters. The presiding eldress at Mount Lebanon, for example, was Emma J. Neale, who was eighty-six in 1934. She occupied that position for another nine years. At Hancock, Fannie Estabrook, named eldress in 1929, was in charge; in 1947 she was seventy-seven years old. Anna Case, the lead at Watervliet before the closing of that village, was born in 1855. Prudence Stickney, born in 1860, presided at Sabbathday Lake, and Marguerite Frost, who assisted Emma B. King at Canterbury, was seventy-nine at her death in 1971. These women were all resolutely committed to Shakerism. They did not necessarily agree, however, about the proper strategies for the society's survival, the standards of behavior, or the religious patterns that should prevail.[211]

Yet strong bonds—personal and historical—tied together the remaining sites. In the midst of the Depression, for example, at the urging of Arthur Bruce, Emma J. Neale sent a series of checks to Sabbathday Lake to assist that village in staying out of debt. Prudence Stickney thanked Neale profusely each time, calling her an "angel of mercy" during a time of "so much sickness and death." The financial troubles in Maine were compounded, according to Stickney, by the influx of people from Alfred, which was closed in 1931 and sold to the Brothers of Christian Instruction. The arrival of the Alfred Believers meant more expenditures for "sickness, operations and hospital bills." And yet Stickney was unwilling to call the Alfred Believers "a burden." She did not want to "say anything to hurt their feelings" because they were "a very happy family." Stickney had great personal affection for Emma Neale and worried about the future of the society. "I think of all the few remaining brave souls," she wrote, "and talk to our dear departed saints about it, but the answers never come back." She proposed that the "Lead ones" from the various villages meet to discuss the problems.[212]

Other outsiders also had suggestions for the Believers. In the spring of 1947 a New Hampshire attorney, who had been associated with the Shakers for more than twenty years and handled some of their tax affairs, offered an unsolicited professional opinion to Emma B. King. "It would seem that should the four remaining Societies become amalgamated into one, both as to membership and location," wrote A. W. Levensaler, "it would relieve the burden of difficulties that might arise in the future, tend toward more efficiency in administration and a saving of money by a reduction of expenditures." Telephone and travel costs might be reduced and urgent business transacted more easily. Furthermore, he warned, given trends in real estate, rising rates of taxation, heavy government spending, and the high cost of living, those who owned real estate and had fixed incomes were likely to lose their "properties and homes" because they would be unable to pay rising tax bills. The legal result would be seizure by local governments for "non-payment of taxes." Levensaler closed his letter by reminding the Believers that "in union there is strength."[213]

The fifteenth of October 1947 was a significant day in Shaker history, for on that date the last of the Mount Lebanon Shakers relocated at Hancock. This move, engineered by Emma King, brought to an end one hundred sixty years during which the Lebanon site had been the principal seat of authority for the United Society of Believers, the symbolic center of the organization. The closing of Mount Lebanon was a public admission of defeat and a signal to the world that the society recognized its desperate circumstances. At Hancock village Frances Hall was in charge. The contents of the remaining Mount Lebanon buildings were removed and probably shipped to Hancock. Most of the documents from the New York village went to Canterbury, where King was located. After this date Shakers remained at only three locations—Hancock, Canterbury, and Sabbathday Lake. In abandoning Mount Lebanon, the society was acknowledging that a new stage had been reached in the evolution of Shakerism. Old age, death, and departures—in a word, decline—had become the story of the Shakers.[214]

Many of those who have written about the Shakers have employed the terms *decline* and *failure* to explain what happened to the society. Six years before the close of Mount Lebanon, for example, Marguerite Fellows Melcher declared, "The Shaker story is the story of an adventure which,

by worldly standards, failed." Six years after the close of the primary loca
tion of the central ministry, Edward Deming Andrews concluded his historical account with the chapter "Decline of the Order." Both authors were
content to measure success and failure by statistical standards. On any
such quantitative measure, by 1947 the Shaker movement was a failure,
for it had declined to a point of numerical insignificance. There is no dis-
guising that, despite the offense this language gives to the Shakers of today or to their devout friends. And yet quantitative measures of success or
failure are insufficient to reckon with the complex realities represented by
Shakerism in the twentieth century. *Decline* is a poor word to describe
these qualitative concerns. The comparative study of other religious communities suggests that sects frequently "decline" rapidly. In that respect,
the Shakers are an exception. There is more to the story during this period
than the obvious institutional failure.[215]

These years of transformation, which opened on an optimistic note
at the centennial celebrations, closed in another key. Now the principal
rituals conducted by the Shakers were those of death and mourning. The
Believers were preoccupied with farewells to their friends, their homes,
their possessions, and their traditions. As village after village closed and
the radius of the society narrowed, some of the "world's people" gathered
round to comfort and grieve with the Shakers. These "friends" from the
outside also began to look with interest on everything the society possessed—its books and manuscripts, its furniture and tools, its buildings
and land, even its hymns and melodies—to the growing annoyance of the
Believers. Librarians and archivists asked and begged for documents and
artifacts; collectors and dealers pursued, bought, and stole objects; Aaron
Copland borrowed "Simple Gifts" for the score of the ballet *Appalachian
Spring*. From these remains of the society would later arise a host of new
enterprises.[216]

The changes were more dramatic from 1876 to 1947 than during
any other period of Shaker history. The United Society shrank from a
strong national organization with immense resources—human, financial,
intellectual, and religious—to three small families of aging Believers in
New England. At all three locations the Shakers were keenly aware of the
limitations imposed by these circumstances. They were dependent on out
side laborers for assistance with farming and other major tasks. Illness potentially threatened their personal and financial well-being. The struggle
to survive forced everyone, including the elderly, to contribute—in the
garden, the shop, and the kitchen. Producing fancy goods was not a hobby

for the Believers, but a major source of income. With some notable exceptions, the Shakers no longer possessed a unified world view. Their identity
as Believers was now tied more to the particular site, the web of family
relationships, and the patterns of home life.[217]

There was some continuity with the earlier tradition. Celibacy and a
sense of community were still fixed points within the society. The physical
stage on which the principal events were played out was the same, though
reduced greatly in size and altered somewhat with the passage of time.
Hills and mountains, rivers and ponds, orchards and trees, buildings and
cemeteries, fences and roads—many familiar landmarks remained and
their mere presence was a reminder of the past. That is why the final departure from Watervliet in 1938 and from Mount Lebanon in 1947 was
so significant. The Believers were saying farewell to sacred space, holy
ground whereon formative events for their traditions had taken place. At
those sites, too, the founders and leaders from earlier generations were
buried.[218]

Most of the defining marks of the Believers from the past had gradually disappeared or changed. The clothing and physical appearance of the
Shakers, the daily routines they followed, the ways they amused themselves, their interactions with the world—these dimensions of their lives
were increasingly oriented to the outside culture. Some observers have
equated these changes with decline. Others have pointed to demographic,
economic, and social forces outside the society that contributed to the evolution of Shakerism. Sociologists have attempted to explain the development of sectarian and utopian communities on a more theoretical level.
One recent study attempted to identify the factors likely to affect the
"chances for survival of communes." Among the most significant were
physical setting, economic autonomy, authority structure, ideological
foundation, homogeneity of members, and population control. The authors, Karen H. Stephan and G. Edward Stephan, found that "communities having a single religious faith practiced by all members tended to
survive for longer periods of time than did communities favoring a plu-
rality of religions or no religion at all."[219]

The Stephan study is useful for understanding the evolution of the
United Society. During the nineteenth century the Shakers scored well on
every survival test. Yet the seeds for disintegration were present. Using
the measures employed by the Stephans, it is possible to identify a number
of factors contributing to the institutional decline of Shakerism after 1876.
Although the physical setting of the Shakers was fixed at the village sites,
the sale of parcels of land and outlying farms reduced the productive

acreage. The Believers, who had never been totally self-sufficient, became fully integrated into the national economy during this period. They engaged in financial speculation and on numerous occasions fell into crippling debt to outside parties. Even for food and clothing, they began to turn to sources outside the society. The Believers retained the covenant and still demanded that converts accept its provisions. At many villages, however, the authority structure broke down and the disciplinary power of the leadership was severely compromised. Another striking change was the total absence of male leadership by the end of the period.[220]

The population of the United Society was never totally homogeneous, although the vast majority of members were white, English speaking, evangelically oriented persons with either agricultural or domestic experience or skills as mechanics or artisans. As the century progressed, converts came from a greater diversity of religious backgrounds. The interaction between Believers and nonmembers expanded rapidly through hired help, frequent travel, growing business involvement, and friendships with the world's people.[221]

The Shaker experience during this period confirms the principal observation of the Stephan study, namely, that the most critical factor affecting the chances of survival was the practice of a single religious faith. The Shakers lost that integrating center as the society became more secularized and modernized. Major portions of the common life were separated from their earlier religious moorings. For many, the link between the temporal and the spiritual sphere had weakened, if not broken. The sectarian principle of separation from the world had been abandoned for the alternative strategy of becoming a vanguard of reform, leading the world toward a better tomorrow. The work ethic, once sanctioned as the highest form of worship, became simply a necessity for survival. Traditional worship forms disappeared, some by ministerial directive, others for lack of knowledge or because of a certain embarrassment.[222]

Yet Shakerism was not dead, and the modern people called Shakers were Believers. Contrary to the impression created by many, the progressives of the late nineteenth century and the less traditional members of the twentieth century had as much right to claim the name "Shaker" as Believers who counted themselves among the conservatives. There never had been only one kind of Believer in the society. It is the nature of religious communities to change even though the members of those groups are often unaware of it. The most striking evidence of the society's residual vitality during the first half of the twentieth century was the renaissance of Shakerism after 1950.[223]

PART

FIVE

I Almost

Expect to Be

Remembered

as a Chair:

The Rebirth

of Shakerism,

1948 to the

Present

The United States emerged from the Second World War, a conflict fought to end a demonic scourge, only to face a battery of newly bewildering and frightening circumstances. The atomic age brought the specter of nuclear attack and the necessity for shelters, real or imaginary. The Cold War replaced former enemies with the forces of communism. A new age of international tension opened, and limited warfare flared up with frightening regularity during the decades that followed. Political tests for patriotism became commonplace as Americans learned to live in the "global village."[1]

Changes were no less dramatic on the domestic front after mid-century. The postwar economy took off despite the fears of many who remembered the Depression. Urbanization accelerated as metropolitan areas dominated even far-off rural locales. By 1950 two of every three citizens lived in cities, an increasing number of them in the suburbs, where look-alike houses with attached garages were built by the tens of thousands and filled with mass-produced furnishings, including that miracle of the age, the television set. The culture of consumerism created new anxieties for this emerging affluent society.[2]

Religious organizations in America began to enjoy an institutional prosperity that surprised even the experts. The postwar revival seemed to many, in the language of Robert Wuthnow, "a time of new beginnings." Among the aspects of this spiritual boom were a statistical increase in organized religious activity across the spectrum of denominations, a resurgence of Protestant revivalism epitomized by the success of Billy Graham, and a wave of "popular interest in generalized forms of religion." Americans employed a host of useful pieties against the anxieties of the times. A "deeply felt religious faith—and I don't care what it is"—was all that really mattered, said Dwight D. Eisenhower.[3]

For the Shakers, however, there was no prosperity, only anxiety. In a world of rapid change the dwindling band of Believers struggled to survive, an apparent anomaly in modern America. The members of the United Society presented a study in contrasts with the rest of American society. They did not participate in the economic surge of the postwar years. Their rural villages provided, at best, a limited sanctuary from the hustle and confusion of the times and from the pervasive urban culture. The buildings at Hancock, Canterbury, and Sabbathday Lake, filled with handcrafted Shaker furniture and other objects, were falling into disrepair. The aging members had their hands full just caring for the immediate needs of their fellow Believers. In 1948 the parent ministry at Hancock sounded a melancholy theme. "We are now just a group of older people," wrote Frances Hall and Emma B. King, "trying to care for each other, maintain our homes, doing what good we can and salvage what good we can from Shaker history of the past."[4]

The Believers of the twentieth century seemed to take refuge in the past rather than looking to the future. Many appeared resigned to the inevitable end of the society. Where once a proud spirit of independence and a sense of self-sufficiency had characterized the members of the United Society, now a different way of thinking prevailed. Fear and desperation alternated as the elderly Believers felt themselves losing control of their environment, becoming increasingly vulnerable to outside forces. Sickness and death were a constant preoccupation as the Shakers struggled with the process of aging. Many were content to "follow the quiet routine of home life" with its simple pleasures rather than attempting to stem the tide of change. Some dared to hope that the Believers might be "memorialized" in an appropriate last will and testament—perhaps "the American way of life as exemplified by the Shakers."[5]

By midcentury the preoccupation with survival had effectively displaced attention from traditional religious matters. There were no revivals in the meetinghouses, few meetings at all. Apart from celibacy, few distinctive elements of the Shakers' sectarian witness remained. Problems with domestic help, worries about the sale of fancy goods, fears that unexpected bills might not be paid—these were the topics of daily conversation and private correspondence. There was almost no public side to Shakerism. Even at Sabbathday Lake, where perhaps more of the religious traditions had endured, no public meetings had been held in the meetinghouse since 1888. It seemed that the world had passed the Shakers by, and the rest of America had forgotten them. Several observers— not unfairly—presumed to write the obituary of the Shakers. In 1951 Caroline B. Piercy declared that "we can not say that Shakerism was a total failure, for many things which they believed and practiced have been incorporated in our social and civil life and have not passed with the closing of their doors." Two years later, in his concluding tribute to the Believers, Edward Deming Andrews wrote: "And as the world slowly absorbs another dissident faith, much remains to record the seeking, and in some measure the finding, of truth, and beauty, and light." For both Piercy and Andrews, Shakerism had banked its fires once and for all, and soon only the legacy of the society would remain.[6]

But not everyone in the community was willing to see the United Society die out. To paraphrase Mark Twain, the report of the Shakers' death had been greatly exaggerated. In the mid-1960s a handful of Believers at Sabbathday Lake began to fight extinction. Their struggle coincided with an unexpected explosion of interest in Shakerism, or more accurately, in the image of the Shakers and in their material culture. By the 1970s the Believers were no longer alone in the fight for survival; they were surrounded by a rapidly expanding group of devotees and by a host of satellite enterprises that fed in parasitic fashion on their experience. These were years of accelerating turmoil in America—urban conflict, the civil rights movement, an unpopular Asian war, a sexual revolution, cultural ferment, and political disillusionment. In these circumstances the image of the Shakers became an increasingly powerful and appealing cultural force.[7]

These developments left their mark on the society, which in the 1970s experienced a rupture of relations between the two remaining villages, Canterbury and Sabbathday Lake. To the consternation of nearly all parties involved, the conflict became public, and friends of the Shakers began to choose sides. Within the society the schism involved ecclesiastical, financial, and legal questions. On the outside, the expansion of satellite industries—historical, commercial, and educational—continued without abatement. These enterprises constitute what might broadly be called the "world of Shaker," a remarkable example of contemporary popular culture.[8]

Today Shakerism comprises two different parts: the remnants of the United Society of Believers and the host of people and organizations involved in the world of Shaker. It is difficult to escape the conclusion that it is the second element that has become the driving force in the relationship. Projections of future prospects, therefore, must take both into account.[9]

Waiting for the End

"It is hard for those on the outside to comprehend the burdens, anxieties and inner workings of our organization," wrote Emma B. King late in 1947, "and how much careful planning it requires with our present few members to meet the needs of the aged and feeble and keep these large homes running successfully." On King's shoulders rested the principal burden of leading the dwindling number of Believers. Gifted and resolute, this diminutive woman—remembered by some as Emma Be King—guided the society through the difficult postwar years. King, who had served for more than thirty years in the leadership at Canterbury before being advanced to the central ministry in 1946, eventually became first in the lead and also served as trustee for the society.[10]

King's style of leadership was direct and to the point. She dealt with bothersome outsiders, for example, in a polite but candid manner. After responding in detail to a series of requests for information about the Shakers from a correspondent in North Canton, Ohio, King brought the exchange of letters to an abrupt end: "because of pressure of home responsibilities, I would appreciate having the correspondence close with this issue." King could also be warm and sensitive with friends and family members. In a letter to a "Pal of many years," Agnes E. Tuttle, she consoled the ninety-two-year-old, who was confined to a nursing home, by discussing the impact of "old age" and noting that the years were taking their toll on all the Believers at Canterbury, too. [11]

King and her colleague in the ministry Frances Hall presided over the society at a time when the complete disappearance of Shakerism seemed almost inevitable. That was the basic assumption informing a pictorial essay that appeared in *Life* magazine in the spring of 1949. The commentary accompanying the photographs of Canterbury village and its sixteen sisters described a way of life that had "almost vanished." By contrast with the vitality of an earlier century, now all that remained was a group of "[s]hy and old" women who were trying to carry on some of the society's traditions. The caption at the bottom of the opening page read, "To see what the women of Canterbury are doing before they and their religion die together, turn the page." Subsequent photographs showed a medicine cabinet filled with "old Shaker remedies," white-capped elderly sisters gathered for worship in the chapel of the main dwelling, another group standing for prayer before meals, and others sewing and weaving. The final page carried the banner "Death of a Sect" and a photograph of the stone monument at the Canterbury graveyard bearing the single word "Shakers." The essay stated that the Believers had become "very philosophical" about the disintegration of their sect and "resigned to the death of their movement. They feel that they have been a nucleus for good works in the world and that their missionary work can now be perpetuated by public social agencies. As one old Canterbury sister summed it up: 'The good just won't be concentrated in one spot any more.'" [12]

Charles C. Adams, director of the New York State Museum, thought it was "too bad" that these magazines had to "pester the Shakers." The *Life* essay produced a flood of inquiries about the society. Some of the writers were looking for a refuge from their problems. One woman in California declared, "I have been terribly hurt in the past. I can't get used to the petty meanness and cruelty of men. I hate them. Can I come and live in your colony?" A polio victim wrote, hoping for help in regaining health and mobility. Another reader proposed turning Canterbury into a Christian home for children and the aged. Some simply were attracted by the physical image of the Shakers. "I liken you to my Great Aunt," one correspondent told Emma King. Several were motivated by spiritual or religious interests. A self-identified representative of the "Faithists," who believed only in the Creator, suggested founding a colony where orphans and unwanted infants might be raised in order to avert the imminent end of Shakerism. One visionary, who reported that his soul had left his body and that he had visited Satan, was drawn by the herbal lore of the Believers. A physician in Florida was also interested in the Shakers' use of herbs, as a possible supplement to his practice of "drugless therapy." Those who wrote spanned the full spectrum of ages. A seventy-six-year-old vegetarian offered his suggestions for survival to the Shakers. One week later a letter arrived from a nineteen-year-old who wrote, "I said to myself that surely people like this would welcome a convert who comes with true spirit and real hope. Therefore, I decided to write you to see if it would be possible for me to join you." The Shakers at Canterbury responded to many of these letters, but they showed no intention of admitting new members.[13]

By June 1951 the membership of the entire society had dropped to forty: seven sisters and one brother at Hancock, fifteen sisters at Canterbury, and sixteen sisters and one brother at Sabbathday Lake, as well as a "group of girls under school age." The three remaining families faced continual financial problems. By the end of the Second World War the buildings at Hancock, for example, were "shabby and forlorn," the fields "sadly neglected" and full of "golden-rod," and the fencing badly rusted. Canterbury confronted a series of "excessive bills" because "extensive repairs" had to be made on the electrical system installed in 1910. The threat of fire left the Believers no choice. "These old homes require considerable money for their upkeep," wrote Emma King. For that reason the Believers tried to hold down costs by leaving buildings unheated when possible. In 1950 the sisters living in the Office at Canterbury issued a formal invitation to five others in the village to join them in their "steam-heated dwelling" for the winter months. "Great expense would be saved in Electricity, Stove-oil and wood," they wrote, "and a much reduced rate of insurance on the risks of an old building." Yet the Office was not large enough to accommodate all the Believers at the site. To meet expenses and to "obtain funds for maintenance," the Shakers continued to sell items that they loved, including furniture and other objects. The situation went from bad to worse at Canterbury. A hurricane moved through New Hampshire, wreaking havoc on buildings and property alike. King admitted, "we unfortunately had neither time nor funds to do much that should be done for the safety and prescrvation of our buildings." And always there was more to do. "I am kept so busy with the needful problems that arise," wrote King, "that much remains unfinished."[14]

The Shakers constantly engaged in "business" activities to meet daily expenses. The two remaining brothers, Ricardo Belden at Hancock and Delmer Wilson at Sabbathday Lake, were occupied with a variety of tasks; for Belden these included repairing clocks and sewing machines, and Wilson made oval boxes (fig. 48) and supervised the orchard. In 1950 Belden was eighty years old and Wilson seventy-seven. The sisters at all three locations were consumed with the production of "fancy goods." In November 1952, for example, Emma King reported that the sisters at Canterbury were making sale items for the next summer. The following December Ethel Peacock described the sisters at Sabbathday Lake as so busy with Christmas sale goods that they had "no chance to breathe hardly." This routine seemed never to vary. Year after year they prepared "fancy articles" for the gift shop, bazaars, holiday sales, and summer visitors. Sometimes the sisters "had little time for visiting" even when friends came, for which Mildred Barker apologized in 1955. The Believers traveled regularly to nearby resorts to sell their goods. Eva Libby carried out that responsibility for the Maine Believers for many years. In 1956 Mildred Barker and Ethel Peacock helped with the task "to increase home funds." King summarized the prevailing Shaker attitude when she wrote, "Good business is a need all around."[15]

But there was more to Shaker home life than work. Scattered correspondence and published recollections suggest that recreation often accompanied certain domestic tasks. Community endeavors allowed for conversation and singing. Visitors from outside the family were welcomed because they offered friendship and diversion from routines. Picnics and other outings were regular features of Shaker life, especially on national holidays. Like many Americans, the Believers continued the practice of taking vacations. In 1955, for example, the sisters at Sabbathday Lake went to the Maine coast in midsummer. The next year the Believers at Canterbury took a "pleasure excursion" after the close of the tourist season and before winter arrived in New Hampshire. In the 1950s television replaced radio as a source of both information and entertainment. The Shakers at Canterbury were given a television set by friends in 1953. Bertha Lindsay recalled vividly the arrival of that newest form of communication in the village, and she suggested that the sisters were especially interested in educational programming. She did not say what they thought of the more frivolous programs.[16]

48. Delmer Wilson
Wilson in his shop at Sabbathday Lake, Maine. (Collection of the United Society of
Shakers, Sabbathday Lake, Maine.)

Aging and dying continued to be primary topics of conversation
within the ranks of the Believers. Emma King stated the situation with
stark clarity: we continue to be fully occupied, she wrote, with "illness,
deaths, and pressure of home responsibilities." As a result, even support
for worthy causes often had to be delayed. In 1954, for example, persistent
problems with illness at Canterbury required the sisters who were well to
serve as nurses and cooks, "caring for home necessities"; they thus had
little opportunity to make goods for sale. Occasionally, death surprised one
of the younger members. "Ours was a rather quiet Christmas," King wrote
early in 1956, "saddened by the sudden and unexpected passing of one of
our sisters on December 5th 64 years old. It was a great shock to us all."
More frequently, the objects of attention were the very elderly. When an
eighty-five-year-old had a heart attack, fear and faith alternated in the
hearts of the sisters. "These are the cold, bare facts, the home anxiety and
worry lies too deep for words, all we can do is trust and hope, and believe

that whatever is right for her and for us, in Gods loving wisdom will be."
The affection of the members at different villages for one another was
revealed in Mildred Barker's expression of love and concern for Emma
King. She wrote, "I realize what a great anxiety you have in watching the
health of the older ones, and far too often you fail to think of your own
strength. . . . Please speak my love and blessing for all in your family but
keep a large share for our dear Eldress Emma."[17]

In spite of these realities and the gloomy prognostications of outsiders concerning the society, Emma King refused to accept the notion
that Shakerism had been a failure just because it was dying out as a communal institution. On the contrary, she wrote, "I think it is quite time that
the decline of the Shaker Movement took on a New Look and was presented to the public in a New Light." As a result, in the fall of 1956 she
wrote a small tract entitled *A Shaker's Viewpoint*. This was the first major
statement published by a Shaker leader in more than three decades. King,
who had taught school at Canterbury for many years before assuming the
position of eldress, was an able writer. It was her intention to refute the
commonplace judgment that Shakerism was a failure. That opinion, she
felt, did not reckon sufficiently with the earlier prosperity and accomplishments of the Believers. She also addressed the causes for the decline
of "Shaker homes." Wars and economic depressions had reduced the
Shakers' funds, competition had destroyed their industries, the modern
world had seduced their young people, and the resulting membership loss,
especially among brothers, had crippled the society. And yet, she declared,
"many noble men and women lived and died in the faith, worthy examples
of Christian loyalty to Shaker principles."[18]

The "passing of the Shaker homes," according to King, did not prove
that the United Society had failed. "We are not depressed," she affirmed.
"It is all in the process of evolution. . . . The material homes may fail but
the Shaker experiment is no failure." Its principles continued to exist. The
"light and truth" of Shakerism had been adopted by contemporary religious groups, industrial organizations, and charitable institutions. Many
young persons educated at Shaker villages had retained the influence of
the Believers' values. She continued,

> No, Shakerism never has been nor ever will be a failure. "The hands
> drop off but the work goes on." God has permitted us in our humble
> way to do much good. The principles, the light and truth will live on
> forever. There may be a new awakening, souls lighted by its truth
> and revelation, but I very much doubt its manifestation will again

take the original form of organization. Times have changed and the world moves forward.

King compared the Shakers to "torch bearers" who run for awhile, and then pass the torch to others. The Believers intended to be true to their trust, facing the future with courage. "We mean to go down gloriously." After completing her essay King wrote, "I claim no particular merit to the article but have written as I feel, deploring the gloomy aspect which is so often pictured regarding the Shakers."[19]

King's interpretation of the decline of the United Society did nothing to change the course of events. The next three years, in fact, proved to be the final days of the Hancock village. In March 1957, the same month in which King's essay was published, Frances Hall, first in the central ministry and the last trustee at Hancock, died at the age of eighty-one. Hall had played an active role in the society, especially after the closing of Mount Lebanon. She had also presided over the gradual dismemberment of Hancock. Numerous holdings had been sold, and many buildings, including the meetinghouse, had been torn down or moved to lighten the tax burden and the problems of maintenance. Hall's death probably triggered the final arrangements for disposal of the village. In 1959 the central ministry sold 550 acres of woodland north of the highway to the Commonwealth of Massachusetts, thereby adding that tract to the Pittsfield State Forest. As part of the transaction, the state took over perpetual care of the Shaker cemetery at the site. Emma King wrote, "The transfer of this land is another step in disposing of outlying lands connected with the Hancock Shaker colony." Later that same year Ricardo Belden died at the age of eighty-nine. His death left only three Believers at the village: Eldress Fannie Estabrook, who was "ailing," and two sisters, Mary Frances Dahm and Adeline Patterson.[20]

It was in these circumstances that Emma B. King, newly advanced to first in the ministry, made perhaps her most significant decision (fig. 49). Following Hall's death, King apparently discovered the full extent and size of the society's financial resources, including its stock portfolio, cash, and real estate. That knowledge moved her to action. In 1959, with the help of lawyers from the firm of Sheehan, Phinney, Bass, Green & Bergevin in Manchester, New Hampshire, King established the Shaker Central Trust Fund. It was initially administered by a six-person board of trustees composed of one representative from each of the remaining villages and a lawyer chosen by each. This fund derived from moneys obtained through the sale of properties and assets at the villages that had been closed. (Neither

49. Emma B. King
The most significant member of the central ministry in this century, Emma B. King of Canterbury, New Hampshire, made a number of critical decisions that shaped the subsequent fortunes of the society. Here she is photographed in the trustees' Office at Hancock in 1957. (Photograph by William Tague; courtesy Shaker Museum and Library, Old Chatham, New York.)

the society nor the attorneys have ever revealed the amount of these resources.) The stated purpose of the trust was to provide for the care and
needs of the covenanted members of the society, to assist in the preservation of the Shaker heritage, and to promote the understanding of Shakerism. King's fiscal conservatism laid a secure foundation for the future of
all the covenanted Believers. She was, in effect, following the path laid
down by the ministry in its 1929 decision to seek the assistance of knowledgeable financial managers. King was planning ahead. "Our leaders today face some serious problems regarding our homes," she wrote, "and we
feel the responsibility to be cautious, wise and far seeing for the good of
those who will still live after our work is done." The trust fund was her
primary provision for the future. That decision had immediate consequences for the aging and infirm, whose well-being had become the concern of all. The funds in the Shaker trust, of course, continued to grow as
additional assets were sold. For example, it took the Believers several years
to dispose of the North Family property at Mount Lebanon, for which they
were asking $75,000.[21]

In the autumn of 1959, word began to circulate that Hancock village
was for sale at an asking price of $200,000. Included in the proposed sale
were 974 acres, more than half of which was woodland, with much of the
rest in pasture or under tillage. There were eleven major buildings and ten
lesser structures. Several groups were potentially interested in the site, including a firm hoping to establish a racetrack with pari-mutuel betting.
The prospect of the village becoming a site for a racetrack caused the
Shakers to include a number of restrictions in the sale offer, including prohibitions against gambling, penal facilities, and the sale of alcohol on the
premises. Another group, the Hancock Shaker Village Steering Committee, under the leadership of Lawrence K. and Amy Bess Miller, already
had been contemplating a strategy to preserve the Shaker heritage in
Berkshire County. After a number of meetings between representatives of
the steering committee and lawyers for the Shaker Central Trust Fund,
the central ministry, now composed of King, Ida F. Crook from Canterbury, and Gertrude M. Soule from Sabbathday Lake, on 29 June 1960
accepted an offer of $125,000 from the Miller party on the understand-
ing that the site would become a museum. At the same time the Shaker
leaders voted formally to close the Pittsfield-Hancock community, which
had been in existence since 1790, and to transfer its remaining assets to
the Shaker Central Trust Fund. (Local lore among members of the Pittsfield financial community suggests that "several million dollars in cash and
securities" left the area because of this decision.) In a formal announce-

ment, Emma King expressed delight that the land and buildings at Hancock would be devoted to the "preservation of the Shaker traditions and
the education of others in the Shaker crafts and industries." The three remaining elderly Believers at the site were to be cared for in the Pittsfield
area. The closing date for the final transaction was set for 14 October
1960. Less than a month before that date Fannie Estabrook died at the age
of ninety and was buried in the Hancock cemetery, the last Believer to be
interred in that graveyard.[22]

Now only two "homes" remained, and the Shakers at Canterbury
and Sabbathday Lake closed ranks at their respective sites. The language
of "family" and "home" took on greater significance. The Believers at
these two locations came to resemble extended farm families more than
purposeful religious communities. By the end of 1961, however, these
families had no covenanted male members. The last brother at Sabbathday Lake, Delmer Wilson, died that year. The Shaker women were forced
to rely even more on farm managers and hired help, neighbors and
friends. Fields were rented, crops shared, firewood cut, and orchards
tended by others.[23]

The Believers, understandably, were increasingly guarded with outsiders. They commonly expressed dissatisfaction with their treatment by
the news media. The Shakers preferred to maintain a collective privacy
and to avoid public attention. Emma King had stated the society's position
in 1949. "As a people we do not care for much publicity," she wrote; "if it
brought us financial aid we might accept it graciously but there has been
so many write-ups, lectures, books and news-paper articles published
[in] recent years and people have taken such erroneous ideas about the
Shakers that we are quite weary and averse to it all. We get more annoyance and burden out of the publicity than help." The passage of time only
increased the Shakers' defensive posture. In 1961, following the publication of a misleading article in *Time*, Mildred Barker determined "to never
again give even a tiny interview for magazine publication."[24]

The historian attempting to write about this period of Shaker history,
unfortunately, will find few primary resources. By contrast with the nineteenth century, for which the abundance of records is overwhelming,
source materials for the twentieth century are much less accessible.
Thirty years of central ministry journals in the custody of the attorneys for
the Shaker Central Trust Fund are not available for inspection. The records at Sabbathday Lake after 1919, both correspondence and journals,
have also been placed off limits by the Maine Believers. The primary
sources that are available, including some correspondence and interviews,

have been collected by individuals, museums, and libraries. Until additional records are opened, misinformation and speculation will likely continue.[25]

By the middle of the 1960s there were signs of differences in spirit between the two remaining villages. The sisters at Canterbury seemed almost fatalistic about the future. The end was near, and nothing they could do would change that. Even though Emma King had rejected the concept of failure, the New Hampshire family found its primary identity with the Believers of the past. Their understanding of the society's ultimate purpose trumpeted the glories of earlier times. A short essay by Marguerite Frost entitled *About the Shakers* is a striking example. The three parts of the essay deal successively with the English experience of the founders, especially Ann Lee, the early growth and organization of the society, and the industrial accomplishments of the Believers. Within this framework Frost sketched the Shakers' beliefs about God, their basic social principles, and some of the reasons for what she called the "diminution" of the society. Only in a brief closing paragraph did she address the issue that was primary in her day, the future of Shakerism. "That is in God's hands and there is no safer place. It is an ever-living call that God sends out to His children; there will always be a few, at least, who hear and answer. Forms will differ, but 'unto them that look for Him shall He appear the second time'. As for us, we shall live one day at a time, striving to do our best and leaving the outcome to Him who called us to walk the Shaker path."[26]

The sisters at Sabbathday Lake seemed less willing to accept this pessimistic scenario. In spite of the sorrows and difficulties of the moment, several of them looked toward the future. Mildred Barker, who had been appointed trustee of the society in 1950, embodied this optimistic spirit in a quiet way. In a talk at the Shaker Historical Society in Cleveland, Ohio, she said of Shakerism, "It is good and therefore of God and no good is ever a failure." In that judgment she stood shoulder to shoulder with Emma King. A comment about her trip to Cleveland suggests the different perspective at Sabbathday Lake. Writing at the age of sixty-three, Barker told of her airplane ride to Ohio, the first she had ever taken. "It was one of the most thrilling experiences I have ever had," she wrote, "if not the very most. My first plane flight left me ready to go again any time." Barker's thoughts were oriented to the future. The same year she was "trying desperately" to fill the library at Sabbathday Lake with whatever Shaker sources she could find. "There is much that we do not have," she wrote. In this action, too, she was looking ahead. The seeds of this optimism had been planted by earlier Believers in Maine. In the midst of the Depression, while Sabbathday Lake was struggling to survive, Eldress Prudence Stickney had become upset and angered by a radio program that "had a slam about the few old women that were left at Lebanon." She wrote a letter of complaint to the station, but she also offered a resounding affirmation to her fellow Believer Emma Neale. "If this is God's work," wrote Stickney, "and I know it is, it will be carried on, and it will not grow by crying it down. We need [the] faith of our fathers, and their hours of hard labor for souls."[27]

By 1964, however, circumstances had become more desperate at Canterbury. A letter from King to a dear friend, quoted here at length, speaks volumes about the spirit prevailing at that village.

Dorothy writes me you are quite feeble and are getting anxious to hear from me. I am sorry not to see you or write oftener but I too have troubles. During the Fall, Eldress Ida, Sister Lillian, Alice and Marguerite were very sick and it was all we could do to keep things going. Our Christmas was a quiet one but it was a worrisome time for me. I went to the Hospital every day to be sure the sisters had every kind of care. They are all now in duty but they are not young and strength returns slowly, and it is evident their best days are over.

Very few of our friends can realize what it means at our ages to carry on our home with so few members but it is our home, we love it and it has done so much to make us what we are that we mean to be loyal and support it as long as life lasts.

Soon after Christmas I came down with a heavy cough and cold. I was somewhat better when I came down with pneumonia and was seriously ill, confined about 5 weeks followed by a period of convalescence as strength only returned slowly.

I am on duty now and quite well for 90 years but am trying to catch up with business. . . .

I am sorry your strength is failing and that you cannot enjoy better health but we have to make the best of life while it lasts. I do not forget you though my responsibilities do not permit the seeming intimacies of the past. I love, think and pray for your health, happiness and comfort and wish for you the best in life but I must meet my responsibilities as well as I can and be faithful. The rest I must leave to God and trust he will understand my inability to do more.

I love you Nellie and ask God to bless and comfort you. You and Rebecca and I have been good friends through life. We will act well our part and patiently wait our reunion. God bless and make you as happy and comfortable as possible

It was the very next year, in this atmosphere of distress, that King, in association with Gertrude M. Soule at Sabbathday Lake, decided to close the
membership of the society.[28]

The Beginnings of a Shaker Revival

Around midcentury, when it appeared that the United Society was
passing completely from the scene, the first stirrings of a new chapter in
Shakerism's story were felt. The signal event was the publication in 1953
of Edward Deming Andrews's monograph *The People Called Shakers*. This
modest-sized volume, which told in charming and sympathetic fashion
the tale of the society before 1870, became the centerpiece in a renaissance of historical interest in the Shakers. Reissued a decade later in an
enlarged edition that included footnotes, Andrews's account became the
standard introduction to the Believers for thousands, if not tens of thousands, of readers. The 1963 edition remains in print today. Andrews, of
course, was not the first outsider to write the history of the Shakers, but
his work has had an influence that far exceeded expectations at the time
of publication. To understand the full dimensions of that impact, it is necessary to examine the efforts of others before him.[29]

Two early-twentieth-century pioneers stand out in the record of
those who contributed to the historical understanding of the Believers.
One was a prolific author as well as a collector and seller of Shaker documents. The other published nothing himself, but was responsible for assembling the premier collection of Shaker writings. These two men, John
Patterson MacLean and Wallace H. Cathcart, occupy a distinctive place
in the history of Shaker studies. Both cultivated close relationships
with prominent Believers who, in turn, served as the suppliers for their
acquisitions.[30]

MacLean has been described as a "peripatetic Ohioan" who changed
jobs with some regularity. He studied medicine and surgery at the Eclectic
Medical Institute in Cincinnati; he also held degrees from Saint Lawrence
University and National Normal University. Employed for a time at the
Western Reserve Historical Society in Cleveland, early in the century he
began writing a series of essays on the Shakers of Ohio. With the help of
Alonzo Hollister at Mount Lebanon, MacLean compiled and published in
1905 his *Bibliography of Shaker Literature*. In the same year he issued a
short biography of Richard McNemar. He also published sale catalogs of
Shaker publications, items that he was securing through his contacts with
Hollister and his visits to the communities, both East and West. In effect,

he became the society's agent for distributing books and manuscripts to private individuals and various libraries. Among the institutions buying materials from him were the Library of Congress, the Ohio Archaeological and Historical Society (later the Ohio Historical Society), the New York State Library, and the Western Reserve Historical Society. The Shakers also contributed and sold materials to other major libraries, including the Boston and New York public libraries. Hollister, the self-appointed guardian of the society's documents, thought this distribution of literature might attract new converts. In 1907 nine of MacLean's essays were reprinted in book form as the *Shakers of Ohio*. Essentially a chronicle of events, the volume remains valuable today because it contains extensive citations from Shaker manuscripts, some of which are no longer extant. MacLean was delighted that the Believers thought his articles thorough and fair.[31]

MacLean's interest in the Shakers was more than historical, however, because he received a commission on the sale of Shaker items. He was also a practicing Universalist preacher. In general, he avoided passing judgment on Shaker theology and religious practice, but in the introduction to his collected essays he stated unequivocally: "The Shakers do not and never did worship Ann Lee." He offered other correctives, too, to what he regarded as mistaken opinions. He noted, for example, that relatively little discipline was exercised among modern Believers. Twentieth-century Shakers enjoyed the "comforts of life" and were given the "widest latitude" in matters of belief. "They are of the same flesh and blood as other people," he wrote, contrary to views of outsiders. Because of negative reports, they had suffered considerable persecution. Even today, he wrote in 1907, lawyers and financiers take advantage of the society, "fleecing" the members of their limited resources. MacLean saw much to admire in their religious dedication. "Whatever the world may think," he wrote, "yet the simple fact remains that Shakerism has been an active example of the quiet life and simplicity of habits as well as an intelligent view of the Creator." After Hollister's death in 1911, MacLean's special relationship with the Shakers began to weaken, in part because of the aggressive collecting tactics of Wallace H. Cathcart.[32]

Cathcart entered the world of Shaker through his association with the Western Reserve Historical Society. A lover and collector of books long before joining the society, in 1907 he became its first full-time president and later its director. Cathcart's interest in Shakerism was fed by his own religious commitments to the Baptist church and by his proximity to the former North Union site. He had also read MacLean's bibliography. In part at the suggestion of Joseph Slingerland at Union Village, Cathcart wrote to

Hollister asking for assistance in building a collection of Shaker materials. Unfortunately for Cathcart, Hollister regarded Slingerland as a disgrace to the society because of his dishonest financial dealings and was not terribly interested in cooperating. Cathcart visited the remaining Ohio communities, seeking to acquire items, but without much success. He again sought out MacLean, who agreed to help because he had fallen out with the Ohio Archaeological and Historical Society. Cathcart wrote to Hollister once more, requesting his help. Hollister, however, had died, and Catherine Allen, who had been assisting in channeling materials to MacLean, read the letter. This was the beginning of a long association between Cathcart and Allen.[33]

Cathcart had to convince Allen that the Western Reserve Historical Society was a more deserving location for valuable documents and publications than the Library of Congress, which had become the repository of the largest Shaker collection, thanks to MacLean's control of the trade. Cathcart pointed out that the Library of Congress had not organized the materials they had received and that the Western Reserve had an excellent fireproof facility. He cultivated his friendship with Allen carefully, and by the end of 1911 she had decided to give him first choice on items for sale and to introduce him to others within the society who might assist in building the Shaker collection in Cleveland. Soon boxes were coming to him from widely scattered villages. Allen herself, as she traveled from family to family on official business, often searched through vacant buildings for items. At Watervliet, New York, she reported, "Yesterday, a cup board from which [the] key had long been lost was opened from the back & I have found a few real treasures." Among the items was the manuscript of Benjamin S. Youngs's *Testimony*. Although the pace of collection would slacken with the years, the cooperation between Cathcart, Allen, and other prominent Believers ultimately resulted in the formation of the largest collection of Shaker materials in the world. Allen was convinced that this effort would aid future historians and give the Believers themselves insight into their place in history. "Our history belongs to the nation and to the world," she wrote, "and is it our bounden duty to use every reasonable means in having it preserved and perpetuated thro' historical libraries."[34]

During these years other individuals began competing for Shaker materials. Several libraries hoped to establish their reputations on the strength of Shaker collections. The librarian at the Berkshire Athenaeum in Pittsfield, H. H. Ballard, petitioned Anna White for assistance in making his institution "the fifth largest collection of books on Shakers in the world." His own engagement with the society was "from a librarian's standpoint," he acknowledged, whereas some found the Believers' "line of thought" attractive, and still others wanted the records for genealogical purposes. "I want to get *every scrap* of paper ever printed on, or *written on*," he wrote. Ballard hoped to mount "a sort of Shaker St. Louis Exposition for all time." In 1903 Richard T. Ely, professor of economics at the University of Wisconsin, wrote to the North Family at Mount Lebanon asking for pamphlets, periodicals, and books. He had visited there some twenty years earlier and had spoken at length with Frederick Evans and Daniel Fraser. An outspoken advocate of the Social Gospel, in his writings Ely encouraged cooperation over competition and social solidarity instead of individualism. He began gathering a set of publications dealing with American communities because of their "value for the student of history and social science." Daniel Offord responded to the request by sending a few books, although he also told Ely that the society was "burdened with debt" and therefore could not donate the publications. That same year Edward Brockway Wight, an undergraduate at Williams College in nearby Williamstown, Massachusetts, visited Mount Lebanon seeking publications. Anna White said of Wight, "like MacLean [he] wants all of Shaker literature he can lay his hands on   So it goes." Wight, who was especially interested in the sociological side of communal life, with the help of his father acquired a substantial private collection of both imprints and manuscripts. In 1931 the Wight Shaker Collection was presented to Williams College, where it became the centerpiece for an expanding body of research materials.[35]

One year after that presentation, the first major publication by Edward Deming Andrews appeared under the auspices of the New York State Museum, a handbook to accompany an exhibit of Shaker artifacts. In it Andrews focused on the agricultural and manufacturing processes and products of the Believers. He portrayed the Shakers as progressive entrepreneurs, economic pioneers whose material success was a product of their sense of "spiritual destiny" as well as of their mastery of practical technique. He admired their material culture and respected their world view. His evidence, drawn largely from New Lebanon sources, included such items as medicinal herbs, oval boxes, baskets, clothing, and chairs. Andrews concluded that for the Believers "the artistic coincided with the religious conscience" and that in their communities "utilitarianism [was] raised into the realm of undeniable charm and a quiet and pure beauty." This first volume contained the seeds of Andrews's lifelong interpretive viewpoint. "The Shaker brethren and sisters were ever aware that theirs was a high calling," he wrote, "and that they labored for the greatest Employer of all."[36]

Andrews's publication was the result of a decade of rising interest in the Shakers and sustained interaction with them at several villages. Andrews and his wife, Faith, first became interested in Shaker material culture in 1923. Andrews, who had received his undergraduate degree from Amherst, was working on his doctorate in the history of education at Yale University. He and his wife became "collectors-dealers in colonial and post-colonial artifacts," both as a hobby and as a source of income. Years later, after he was unable to secure a university appointment, he served for fifteen years as the dean of students and head of the history department at Scarborough School in New York State. Edward Andrews also collected manuscripts. The bibliography for the museum handbook itemized seventy-two separate manuscripts owned by Andrews, part of the author's own "extensive collection" of items he had acquired from the Believers.[37]

Edward and Faith Andrews visited the Shaker villages frequently during the years of greatest distress for the society. These "Antique Pilgrims," as they were once called by the Believers, seemed to be interested in everything that could be obtained—furniture, clothing, tools, books, and manuscripts. The Shakers treated them cordially, but privately they recorded mixed judgments. In her personal diary, Sadie Neale recorded eight different occasions in 1929 on which at least one of the Andrewses was at Mount Lebanon, mostly to examine old furniture or other artifacts. Neale's patience wore thin from time to time. On 27 August, for example, she noted: "Andrews couple come in afternoon. Select two or three old pieces and use considerable of my time." In February Emma Neale was forced to tell the Andrewses that they could not visit the closed buildings because of the cold weather. In 1930 Josephine Wilson at Canterbury wrote to assure the professor and his wife that the things they had left behind would be kept in "safe storage" and that a few more things had "come to light during Housecleaning time."[38]

Andrews's scholarly interests also received a mixed response from his Shaker acquaintances. Walter Shepherd, at the time a member of the central ministry, responded negatively in 1931 to a request for data on the current membership of the society. "We do not wish to advertise the poverty of our present membership," he wrote. "All the families feel this way—especially Elder Arthur [Bruce]. He would not I am sure give out any figures." Shepherd expressed his appreciation for Andrews's interest in Shaker history and stated his confidence that whatever he wrote about the society would be "judicious and friendly." Edward and Faith Andrews also established a strong friendship with the Believers at Sabbathday Lake. Eldress Prudence A. Stickney wrote to them with some regularity. In 1932 she articulated her delight that the Believers had "such loyal friends," who defended their cause and understood their way of life. Stickney complimented Andrews in a letter to Charles C. Adams. She was especially taken with the "spiritual Reverence for higher and divine things" that made Andrews's work so successful. "I am very fond of he and Mrs. Andrews. Lovely people. . . . They have been here a number of times."[30]

In 1937 Edward Andrews published an illustrated study of Shaker furniture in which he examined the Believers' craftsmanship in more detail. He identified a number of distinctive features, such as the absence of brass and the use of exposed dovetailing, which he interpreted as religion penetrating into the workshop. He concluded that everything in Shaker culture was "subordinate to religion" and reflective of the "primitive scriptural dogmas" revived by Ann Lee and other early Believers. Objects became "texts" for Andrews to read. An oval box, he wrote, was "more than an enclosure or a receptacle, to be crudely nailed together to answer an immediate need; construction must be painstaking, even in so common an object, if its true usefulness were to be insured. The geometric grace and simplicity of such pieces are symbolical of a people's urge for perfection, even in that work of the hands which was to go forth into the world." This admiration and reverence for Shaker objects became another trademark of Andrews.[40]

The illustrator for *Shaker Furniture* was William F. Winter, Jr., a gifted photographer from Schenectady. He began studying the Shakers sometime in the early 1920s. Winter struck up a friendship with Sarah Collins, at the time eldress in the South Family at Mount Lebanon. She gave him, he recalled, "virtually unrestricted license to come and go as I wished, and where, over the entire property." He roamed and photographed as he pleased. Later he "enjoyed the same broad privilege" at other sites. In June 1933, for example, he described his situation at Hancock, where he was living and working. He had an apartment and a darkroom in one of the smaller buildings. "In fact I have a whole building," he wrote, "the main room is large and beautifully furnished, almost entirely with Shaker furniture. This is my laboratory, or Studio, for the purpose of developing, studying, and working up material pertaining to the theory and technique of pictorial photography. Expenses are low, environment beautiful, the Shakers wonderful. Having a great time. In addition, I am making some photographs for Andrews, photographs of some of his things." From these visits came a portfolio of black-and-white photographs of Shaker objects and settings as well as portraits of some of the remaining Believers, including Collins, Rosetta Stephens, Sadie Neale, and Anna Case. Winter's work came to public notice through a series of exhibitions in the early 1930s. Winter, Andrews, and Charles Adams collaborated on several projects, including the New York State Museum exhibit and another at the Berkshire Museum, before Winter's untimely death in 1939.[41]

Winter's photography created an apposite Shaker image to accompany Andrews's interpretation. Contrary to the impression he created, however, Winter did not always find the scenes he photographed; he frequently arranged them. By his own account he occasionally removed "an object which obviously did not belong in the picture; or something which did belong was moved in the picture space." Although he suggested that "for the most part things were photographed as they were," a close examination of the illustrations in Andrews's volume reveals otherwise. Winter repeatedly used the same corner setting for totally different scenes. In one photograph a trestle table and eight low-back chairs are arranged in front of a window with a blind; in another, three sewing stands are situated with two rockers and a rug in front of the same window with the blind (fig. 50); in yet a third photograph, the same corner of the room with the window and blind becomes the background for a bed, a chair, and an electrostatic machine, ostensibly an infirmary location. In other words, the three scenes were not "photographed as they were"; all were contrived for the camera. All convey the visual impression of the spare life, free of clutter. The straight lines of floors and peg boards, the bright reflective surfaces of plain walls and wooden floors, the careful balance of the objects—these visual cues created an impression of Shaker purity and simplicity, union and order, orthodoxy and traditionalism. Winter's photographs reinforced Andrews's frozen view of the Believers.[42]

The Andrews-Winter interpretation of the Shakers almost immediately had an expanding influence. Constance Rourke, widely regarded as one of the most perceptive observers of American culture in the period, wrote a review of *Shaker Furniture* for the *New York Herald Tribune* in which she singled out Winter's photographs for special comment. She suggested that the pieces grouped together conveyed "the simplicity of the communal dwellings or shops in earlier years. The beauty of Shaker crafts is ascetic, and it is also functional. No ornament appears." That same astringency became a major theme in her essay "The Shakers," published posthumously in 1942 with an introduction by Van Wyck Brooks. She saw the rejection of sacramentalism, the commitment to the principle of equal-

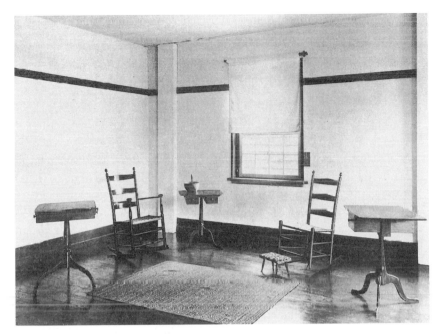

50. Shaker Interior: Sewing Stands and Chairs
These sewing stands were designed to permit two Shaker sisters to work together on
sewing tasks. (Photograph by William F. Winter; pl. 15 in Edward Deming Andrews,
Shaker Furniture, Yale University Press, 1937.)

ity, the freedom of the dance, the unadorned lines of the furniture, the
willingness to suffer persecution, and the notion of travel (implying both
labor and progress) as all of a piece; they involved a rejection of the world
and the creation of an alternative world view. Rourke wrote about the
Shakers as part of her larger defense of American culture, in its diversity of
form and aesthetic, against those who saw Europe as the only measure of
cultural worth. The purity and simplicity of American folk art became additional grounds for withstanding attacks from abroad.[43]

Andrews extended the scope of his studies with his publication in
1940 of *The Gift to Be Simple,* a catalog of Shaker songs, dances, and rituals. The book consists mostly of the texts and tunes that he had collected
and descriptions of worship activities. The artifacts and exercises, Andrews explained, gave voice and form to the "mystic afflatus" present
within the society. These expressions of Shaker "folk culture" possessed
"a curious primitivism and child-like innocence." The "gospel simplicity"
of the songs and dances paralleled the functional simplicity of furniture

and shop products. Both expressed "self-discipline and self-denial." Andrews used these Shaker texts as a preacher and proselytizer—to suggest that the Believers' "experiment in primitive Christianity has been replete with lessons of value to all mankind."[44]

Three women wrote historical books about the Shakers in the years immediately preceding the publication of *The People Called Shakers.* Each was stimulated in her interest by personal circumstances. Marguerite Fellows Melcher, raised in Enfield, New Hampshire, had a Shaker great-aunt and great-uncle. She wrote of Shakerism as a spiritual adventure that brought the Believers economic security and contentment for more than a century. They, in turn, left a material legacy that was the product of their handwork. Julia Neal grew up and attended college in Kentucky, where she had memories of visiting the Shakers before they left South Union. Her account of the history of that village drew heavily on manuscript journals she read while pursuing a master's degree in English at Bowling Green. She described the Believers as a virtuous people who made a substantial contribution to American life. As a child, Caroline B. Piercy listened to her mother tell stories about family contacts with the Shakers at North Union. She subsequently discovered the immense resources of the Western Reserve Historical Society and used that collection to write the history of the Believers in northern Ohio. Piercy depicted the Shakers as a people with a "passion for perfection" who worked for harmony and influenced the course of American history. All three authors reflected the collective search for viable forms of community life in a day when American democratic values were under siege.[45]

These efforts by outsiders to tell the story of the society were not always appreciated by the Shakers, even though they sometimes kept their judgments to themselves. When Marguerite Melcher's play "Rose in the Wilderness," described by one critic as a "serious study of a spiritual ordeal in a Shaker community," was produced in 1949 by the Abbe Practical Workshop at the Master Institute in New York City, it brought unwanted publicity to the Believers. The play included vivid dance scenes. It was reported that the production was going to "strain even further, the already strained tolerance of Mrs. Melcher" at Canterbury village. "She is not aware, I think," wrote one friend of the Believers, "(because their sweet courtesy would make them gentle with a guest always) that they feel such resentment over her BOOK (Shaker Adventure). . . . And [the play] will hurt them, offend and affront their self-respect too." The Shakers thought such productions distorted public understanding of the society.[46]

One outsider, by contrast, who gained the confidence and trust of Emma B. King and other Believers was John S. Williams, a New York broker and gentleman farmer in Old Chatham, New York. Around 1935 he began collecting furniture, tools, and other items from Mount Lebanon, and subsequently from the other remaining sites. In addition to buying from the Believers, Williams assisted them in finding outlets for their fancy goods and other home products. Sometime in the late 1940s he decided to transform his personal collection into a private museum, and for that purpose he adapted barns and other buildings on his farm. He also continued searching for Shaker artifacts. In 1949, for example, he paid the Believers at Canterbury $275 for a washing machine and $150 for a fire engine. He was confident that both objects would make fine additions to the museum because they demonstrated "Shaker workmanship" and "inventive genius." Emma King voiced her strong support for his undertaking. "Nothing would please us more than to have your Shaker Museum rank first in the country and represent and perpetuate the spirit and work of the Shakers for coming generations," she wrote. The Shaker Museum at Old Chatham was granted a charter by the state of New York in 1950, and it opened in midyear. The first director of the museum, H. P. Clawson, reported to King in September that 150 people were visiting per week.[47]

The launching of the museum seemed to whet Williams's appetite for collecting. Throughout the 1950s both he and Clawson maintained friendly relations with the Believers at Canterbury and Sabbathday Lake. The Williams family visited the Shaker sites often. They also became steady customers for pickles, jam, and vinegar. The Shakers, in turn, toured the museum. When John Williams lost a son in 1953, Emma King sent the family a letter of comfort and encouragement. "Feel His Presence as a sustaining power confident that all will be well," she wrote, "and you will meet again in that better country." By this time she had decided to place her confidence in Williams's capacity to preserve the historical legacy of the Shakers, the material culture as well as the documents. She promised not to sell to "any other party" what he needed for the museum. She also made a gift of the Canterbury fountain stone to the museum, trusting that Williams appreciated "the sacred and devotional use" to which it had formerly been dedicated and would not commercialize it. King regarded Williams's role as custodian of the Shaker legacy to be providential. "While we love to know our treasures of historical worth are being preserved to the world for years to come," she wrote, "the financial aid has been a great blessing to us and we thank God and you for making possible this assistance."[48]

It was in the context of this expanding interest in the society that *The People Called Shakers* appeared in 1953. In it Andrews told the story of the Believers from their English origins through the years of the American Civil War. He dealt only in passing with the nineteenth century after 1865 and not at all with the first half of the twentieth century. Andrews's interpretive framework dictated these chronological limits because the portrait he painted of the Shakers allowed little or no change of the kind that took place in the society after 1876. According to him, the "consolidated goodness" of the Shakers gave rise to a

> tangible heritage. The songs and dances and rituals; the inspirational drawings and paintings; the craftsmanship which so truly exemplifies principle; the buildings bespeaking integrity and purpose; the surviving products, stamped with the seal of a uniform excellence, of a progressive industry; the labor of hands in every sphere— products (in Thoreau's words), of "some unconscious truthfulness, and nobleness, without even a thought for the 'indweller'." . . . The forces which operated within and upon the church evolved forms by which it is not unjust to judge the cause.

Andrews found the Believers' record to be one of "truth, and beauty, and light."[49]

Andrews laid the foundation for the contemporary sentimentalized image of the society. One result of his approach to the Shakers was the loss of critical perspective. Homer Eaton Keyes, a close friend of the Andrewses and editor of *Antiques,* suggested that if Andrews had confined himself "to a purely objective investigation," the results would have been "barren." He had to win the confidence and cooperation of the remaining Shakers. "Adequate interpretation of the accumulated findings demanded more than knowledge, more than sympathetic insight," Keyes wrote. "It involved the exercise of that extremely subtle gift of duality whereby it is possible to become spiritually merged in the extrinsic while yet preserving an unclouded intellectual point of view." Unlike Keyes, I do not think Andrews possessed that "subtle gift," or that any scholar can or should attempt to obtain it. To merge spirituality with the Shakers is to become a Believer. The Believer's perspective is necessarily different from that of the scholar. Andrews lost sight of that difference.[50]

For both the general public and those with cultivated interests in the United Society, *The People Called Shakers* quickly became the canonical source on the subject. Rarely does a single scholar dominate a field as Andrews has the study of Shakerism. The reasons for that dominance are complex. Until the present volume there was no equivalent introduction available. Andrews rescued the Believers from the fringes of American life, removing them from the realm of the bizarre. He made the Shakers appealing, not threatening. He identified them with qualities that many Americans admire—a solid work ethic, inventiveness, sincerity, honesty, commitment to religion, practicality. He showed their heroic side in their willingness to suffer persecution for what they believed. He situated the Believers in serene agricultural villages, worlds apart from the urban landscape of the twentieth century and from the conformity of the suburbs. Andrews created a good feeling about the Shakers. In a word, he made them highly marketable.[51]

Andrews reduced the religious dimensions of Shakerism to the principle of "primitive Christianity revived." He identified authentic Shaker religion with spirit-directed impulses and charismatic gifts. He associated the early Believers with a biblical world view and an ethical integrity reminiscent of New England Puritanism. When the members veered away from the model of primitive Christianity as he understood it, they were deemed inauthentic and even offensive to Shaker ideals. He assumed that only one form of religious leadership could be effective, namely, "[s]trong spiritual guidance." He concluded that the rigorous asceticism of the 1845 Millennial Laws was the "standard" for behavior within the society at all times—an erroneous conclusion that has created widespread misunderstanding. Andrews mistakenly declared that the "mechanics of modern spiritualism . . . offended the Shaker mind." These errors and others reflect a static model of sectarian development that does not do justice to the variety of religious activity within Shakerism during its more than two centuries of American experience. Andrews wished for union and order within the society. At times he seemed blind to the Believers' great difficulty in living up to those high ideals. He shut his eyes to conflict and dissent among faithful Shakers. In sum, Andrews saw what he wanted to see and thus romanticized the Believers. He celebrated their faith because he himself had been nurtured by their "spiritual as well as material 'gifts'." As he wrote, "Precious were these fruits of the Shaker tree of life."[52]

An early reviewer of the 1953 history suggested with classic understatement that Andrews had been "not unsympathetic" to the Shakers. In fact, he and his wife took great pride and pleasure in their close relationships with the members of the remaining Shaker communities. Yet the Believers themselves exercised a certain restraint in their reactions to the volume. In August 1954 Marguerite Frost at Canterbury told the Andrewses that she had not yet "had time or opportunity with a copy" of the

book. "Therefore I did not and do not want to give you half formed opinions," she wrote. Four months earlier, however, Frost had sharply critiqued the volume in a letter to Charles Adams. In her judgment, it was
"well written" and gave evidence of "a great deal of work." But, she continued, "I and we are disappointed in it. . . . I realize it is a difficult thing to
place one's self in the position of people who lived two hundred years ago
but it can be done if you have sympathy. Unless one has spiritual rapprochement with the subject would it not be better not to attempt [to]
write a book about them. I never did admire the 'debunking' way of writing a book. . . . Dr. Stone, a friend of ours, said what I felt, 'Dr Andrews
lost a golden opportunity.'" In other words, Frost was unwilling to tell Andrews truthfully what she thought of his book.[53]

In the years following the publication of *The People Called Shakers*,
an increasing number of outsiders came to share the opinion that the
"fruits" of the Shakers were, indeed, worthy of attention. The Andrewses
themselves took a major step toward making their extensive collection of
artifacts available to a wider public. In 1957 they announced an agreement to transfer their Shaker holdings to the School of Fine Arts and the
American Studies Program at Yale University. There the artifacts and
documents would make possible the intensive study of the Shaker order as
a "microcosmic civilization," thereby fostering an awareness of "the
richness and range of the American experience," in the words of Professor
David M. Potter. Yale University appointed Andrews a "Consultant on
Shaker History and Culture." The Andrewses mounted an exhibition in
the Sterling Library at the university with considerable fanfare. When a
disagreement later developed over plans for the collection, it was withdrawn from Yale.[54]

One significant study offering a different view from Andrews's
appeared in France in 1955, the work of the sociologist and former Do-
minican Henri Desroche. Desroche examined Shakerism as a form of
"socioreligious dissent," related both to traditional religious sectarianism
and to emergent forms of socialism. The Shakers were for him at the same
time conservative and innovative. Although Desroche acknowledged the
importance of Andrews's work, which, he wrote, "cannot be consulted too
often," his approach was very different. Drawing on European traditions of
scholarship, including the intellectual dialogue between Marxism and social Catholicism, he compared the Believers with other sects, Christian and
non-Christian. He regarded the centrality of "family" and the rejection of
conventional marriage as the most significant aspects of Shakerism. He
compared this "ascetic feminism" to the behavior of other religious groups,

such as the Buddhists, the Montanists within early Christianity, and other post-Reformation sectarian communities. Most significant, Desroche did not sentimentalize the Believers. Perhaps because he had no personal contact with the society and conducted his studies on the basis of published texts alone, he was insulated from the charm and attraction of the Shakers. Desroche's intellectual agenda in the book was primarily political, not religious.[55]

Far more in tune with the expanding revival of interest in the Shakers was *The Believers*, a sentimental novel by Janice Holt Giles. Giles, who published "more than 20 books which sold in excess of three million copies," set her melodrama at South Union. The novel was written from the standpoint of Rebecca Fowler, a faithful wife who, against her deepest wishes, accompanies her fanatical husband, Richard, into the Shaker community. There she struggles against the society's regulations and, in particular, against enforced separation from him and her children. Giles featured the ways in which celibacy destroyed the bonds of marriage and the family. At last Rebecca leaves the village and divorces her husband, only to marry another with whom she lives happily ever after. At the end of the tale, Richard is indicted and condemned by Giles for going "against nature"; for that reason, too, she thought, the Shakers in general were "doomed." Giles, through Rebecca, offered her summary judgment of the Believers. "The most devoted of them were good people, as they saw goodness. My quarrel with them was that their conception of goodness made no allowance for any other man's, and that, I felt, was . . . the tyranny of innocence." Although she ultimately condemned the society by defending Rebecca's decision to leave, the net effect of Giles's novel was to arouse considerable curiosity about the Shakers, and thereby to contribute to the rising interest in the society.[56]

Charles Sheeler, the American painter and photographer, used his media to express an interpretation of the Believers. He became acquainted with them in the 1920s, and thereafter Shaker objects and buildings began to appear in his paintings. He was drawn to the artistic study of Shakerism as part of his larger concern with native traditions of American workmanship. During the 1930s and 1940s he painted a variety of Shaker buildings and objects and produced several photographic studies. His paintings feature geometric shapes, straight lines, and plain surfaces. Simplicity borders on severity in his compositions, which employ shadow and angle to great effect. Sheeler, who was also a collector of Shaker artifacts, attracted the attention of the historians of Shakerism, including Constance Rourke and Edward Andrews. His paintings on Shaker themes are the most distinguished of any American artist to date. They are also highly compatible with Andrews's spiritualizing approach to the Shakers.[57]

Controversy among the Believers

Within Shakerism no single principle has received more attention through the years than union. From unity came societal strength, and from its lack came weakness. "o UNION thou great source of strength ever abide with us, for thou art our life, our all!" wrote one Believer at Pleasant Hill in 1890. Mary Johnston continued, "Have we not realized how harmoniously we progress when all are united in heart and spirit for the interest of each other and the glorious cause in which we have engaged? Herein lies our success or defeat." The "journey in time," according to her, was "too short" for "needless strife and discord." Pointing to the motto of the United States, *E pluribus unum,* meaning "one from the many," Johnston suggested that the parallel with the United Society of Believers led naturally to the question "Are we being truly a united people?"[58]

The most obvious fact about the United Society of Believers in the years after 1960 was the palpable erosion of the sense of unity between the two remaining families. The reasons for this growing schism among the Shakers were complex. The Maine community, for example, had enjoyed a long tradition of independence throughout its existence. Sometimes that spirit had manifested itself in open conflict with the central ministry; other times it was reflected in geographical isolation and distance from the centers of power in the society. The financial problems at Sabbathday Lake had kept the community on the edge of poverty for years. Yet through much of the twentieth century the Maine society had managed to maintain itself, due partly to a conservative social and religious position. In the words of Prudence Stickney, Sabbathday Lake was striving "to keep the old fashioned gospel." In addition, the Believers in the Pine Tree State had retained a more optimistic faith in the future of the society.[59]

Canterbury, by contrast, had always been more closely associated with the leadership at Mount Lebanon. The New Hampshire site had served as the seat of a bishopric ever since its founding. In the nineteenth century, when the Maine villagers fell from favor, they were placed under the disciplinary supervision of the New Hampshire ministry. Canterbury had been a prominent and wealthy village throughout its history. It also became a center of intellectual influence, especially during the years when Henry Blinn was the editor of *The Manifesto.* There was an especially strong bond between Canterbury residents and the Shaker progressives at the North Family in Mount Lebanon. It is not insignificant that when leadership of the society left the New York location, much of the power went to Canterbury through the persons of Arthur Bruce, Irving Greenwood, and Emma King. Finally, it was the ministry at Canterbury that was most influential in deciding to close the ranks of the society in 1965.[60]

Perhaps it was natural that the last two villages should become competitors. Each seemed intent on survival, but what they meant by that goal differed considerably. Canterbury was content to separate the ultimate fortunes of the society from its institutional forms. For them the society's legacy involved the principles and ideals of the Believers as well as their past accomplishments. The Shakers at Sabbathday Lake, by contrast, rejected that view, insisting that communal structures would continue to carry the tradition into the future. Maine Believers remained committed to family order and the joint interest as essential testimonies. Conflict between the two villages was almost inevitable as the drama of decline unfolded.[61]

The stage was set for the contest in 1965 by the decision of Emma King and Gertrude Soule to close the membership of the society. According to unconfirmed reports, one of the motivating factors was King's worry that the assets in the Shaker Central Trust Fund would attract new members interested in the money rather than in the religious life of the community. This fear was not totally abstract, for each time the Shakers were publicized in the media, the villages received a spate of inquiries from persons interested in joining them or suggesting how the society might spend its resources. According to one source, it was at the advice of the attorneys in the Manchester firm handling the Shaker trust that the ministry decided to close the membership. It is impossible, at present, to confirm the precise motives for that decision or the immediate reaction of the members at the two remaining villages. Neither the Believers nor the attorneys in Manchester handling the trust will discuss these matters.[62]

Personality conflicts may have been another factor involved in this unusual decision by the ministry—unusual in the sense that from its inception at the time of Ann Lee until 1965, the Believers had always been watching and waiting for new ingatherings. No historical precedent existed within the society for barring from entrance those who accepted the Shaker gospel. In fact, Sabbathday Lake had a continuous history of welcoming inquirers and kindred spirits. Although the last person to sign the Shaker covenant in Maine was Frances Carr in 1948, throughout the 1950s and 1960s numerous individuals spent varying lengths of time in

the community, often exploring the possibility of a permanent relationship. One of these friends of the Shakers, Theodore E. Johnson, turned
out to have more than a passing interest in Shakerism. He would, in time,
become a prominent Believer and the center of a firestorm of controversy.
Johnson's story is inextricably linked to the quarter-century of controversy
within the society.[63]

Johnson, a New Englander by birth, held an undergraduate degree
from Colby College. In 1953–1954 he studied medieval Latin literature in
Strasbourg, France, as a Fulbright scholar. In 1955 he received a master's
degree from Harvard University School of Education in the teaching of
classics. Between 1955 and 1957 he was enrolled as a special student at
Harvard Divinity School. Johnson was a member of the Episcopal Church
and attended a parish administered by the Cowley Fathers of the Society of
Saint John the Evangelist. He first discovered the Shakers through his
work as a librarian. According to his own testimony, he had always been
attracted to the monastic life. In October 1957 he went to Hancock village,
where he met Ricardo Belden and Mary Frances Dahm. They urged him
to visit Sabbathday Lake because of his spiritual interests, and he did. He
found the Shaker community in Maine far more attractive than traditional
Christian monasticism. Johnson subsequently took a job at the Waterville
Public Library in Maine, and he was able to spend an increasing amount
of time with the Shakers at Sabbathday Lake. Beginning in the late 1950s,
he also assisted the Believers in organizing their library.[64]

Soon Johnson was spending weekends and evenings at Sabbathday
Lake. By 1960, although he still worked in Waterville, he had a room in
the trustees' Office at the village. Mildred Barker records his entry into the
community as 28 May 1960—a date that probably should not be confused
with his becoming a member. He subsequently became director of the
Shaker Library and editor of the *Shaker Quarterly,* a new publication
launched in 1961. He also was appointed director of the village museum.
These first years of Johnson's association with the Believers were also Delmer Wilson's last. According to Johnson's own account, he spent long
hours with Wilson during his final illness in the second half of 1961. (Interestingly, Johnson expressed disappointment that Wilson, who was preoccupied with the farm, "did not have strong spiritual interests.") During
these initial years of Johnson's friendship with the Shakers, Gertrude
Soule, a member of the society's ministry, was the ranking Believer at Sabbathday Lake.[65]

It is impossible to determine precisely how Johnson's presence at
Sabbathday Lake affected the ministry's 1965 decision to close the mem-

hership. Johnson had begun almost immediately to play a significant role in the religious life of the Maine community. Following Wilson's death, he "took over the lead in the public meeting." Soon he emerged in the eyes of the Believers as well as those of the observing public as the most prominent public spokesperson for the family. He lectured about the Shakers frequently, both at the village and elsewhere. His knowledge and professional training served him well in these tasks. Richard Morse, the Manchester attorney who has been most closely associated with the administration of the Shaker Central Trust Fund from its inception, was quoted in 1980 as saying that "the decision to close membership was made 'after extensive consultation with all the remaining members of the then two societies'" and by the members of the ministry, including Gertrude Soule. This is both significant and difficult to understand, for the obvious effect of the ministry's decision was to bar Johnson and others like him from the society, a move that appears to be in tension with his expanding role in the Maine family. Whether that was the primary intention of the decision remains unclear. It is revealing, however, that the "Home Notes" from Sabbathday Lake throughout the 1960s document Johnson's central role in the family. One of the earliest references to "Brother" Theodore Johnson was in 1962. In the 1960s he was often referred to as simply Theodore Johnson or Mr. Johnson.[66]

The conflict erupted in late 1971 when Eldress Gertrude Soule, whose appearances in "Home Notes" during the 1960s are surprisingly limited, left Sabbathday Lake for Canterbury, ostensibly to help care for the sick. Following a second journey to New Hampshire, she chose never to return to the village in Maine. Two years later Soule spoke with a Portland, Maine, newspaper reporter about the controversy. She explained that the ministry's decision was provoked by the death of the last covenanted Shaker brother. "When Elder Delmer Wilson died in 1961," she stated, "we lost our last Head Brother. This meant that we could not admit a new male member because we would not have a male counsellor to instruct him." She continued, "We ruled against accepting young women as members because young people do not want to accept the discipline, the rules and regulations which govern our way of life. . . . Young people are interested in and attracted by the Shaker religion and faith, but the discipline of our living is not acceptable to them. We have had bad experiences in some Shaker communities." Soule contended that this decision would not mean the end of Shakerism. On the contrary, she said, "It is only the Shaker way of life in a Shaker family that will come to an end. I wish that every room in every Shaker residence were filled. However, our religion was started by God; God will see it continues in some way. He will take care of it." Soule was restating the Canterbury position, which separated the essence of Shakerism from the practice of community life.[67]

Despite Richard Morse's statement that all the members at both villages were consulted, not all the Believers were pleased with the ministry's decision. By 1973 Mildred Barker, who held the position of trustee in the society, publicly stated her opposition to the ban on new members. "No one has the right to shut the door of the church on anybody who sincerely seeks to enter it," she declared. Following Soule's departure from Sabbathday Lake in 1971, Barker emerged as the spiritual leader and formal head of the community in Maine. Technically, she remained a trustee, but she often played the part of the family's eldress. She was supported in her opposition by a number of the other sisters at the village. A year earlier the Sabbathday Lake Shakers had defied a directive of the ministry at Canterbury to eject Theodore Johnson from the community. As a result, the Shaker Central Trust Fund stopped sending $3,000 per month to Maine to support the family. The officers of the trust, however, did continue paying the taxes and insurance at the Maine site, as well as a modest $10 per week for each covenanted sister. The issue was clear. The ministry at Canterbury did not regard Johnson as an authentic Shaker; the sisters at Sabbathday Lake, by contrast, accepted him fully as their spiritual brother.[68]

Johnson did not say a great deal in public about the controversy. He did, however, suggest (correctly, one might add) that this was not the first time the Shakers had divided on issues of practice or belief. In an interview more than a decade after the controversy had been aired in public, Johnson revealed the intensity of his feelings about the situation. He noted, for example, that initially he had experienced pleasant associations with Emma King and the other Canterbury members, even though he felt that some of the Believers there were "very jealous of Sabbathday as more active, more strongly traditional religiously." He also discerned a "feeling of superiority" on their part. "I've often said that Canterbury in those days had the aura of one of those Portuguese convents for ladies of noble birth," he stated. Moreover, Johnson continued, "The Canterbury people were always very much concerned with the so-called 'niceties' of life that have nothing to do with Christianity nor the gospel in the Shaker tradition. They were very much concerned about how they seemed to the world. At Sabbathday I was impressed by people just being themselves, where at Canterbury there was mask-wearing."[69]

Johnson also charged that the religious interests of the Canterbury residents were far removed from the Shaker tradition. (On this judgment, he was historically inaccurate, given the diverse strains of spirituality in the society after 1876.) During the 1950s and 1960s they were, he suggested, more interested in Eastern religions, the occult, psychic research, and Edgar Cayce than in traditional Shakerism. "So the spiritual life, if there was any, then, rather turned me off or frightened me," he said. "It had nothing to do with Christianity and represented a number of popular fringe movements." Johnson thought that Canterbury gave the impression of a "commercial enterprise"; the gift shop seemed to be the most important location at the site. By contrast, he said, at Sabbathday Lake the "things that were essential had been maintained with fidelity." He personally was attracted to Shakerism because of its sense of vocation—its call for commitment, community of goods, and family relationships.[70]

During the 1970s and 1980s Theodore Johnson became a highly controversial figure. He seemed an easy target for his critics, who depicted him as a self-styled "scholar and sage," one who thought he could "save the Shaker religion" even though, in their judgment, that went beyond his capacity and ability. One critic, writing to Gertrude Soule at Canterbury, ridiculed Johnson's wearing of a clerical collar, dubbing him "His Grace, the Archbishop of Teddy-Poo." He wrote, "I hope he doesn't think Shaker elders dressed like priests!" Johnson himself admitted that some Believers were suspicious of him and disliked him. Rumors and innuendos also circulated, calling into question his motives and intentions. On one occasion Richard Morse reportedly opposed Johnson's inclusion on the program of a Shaker seminar at the Museum of American Folk Art in New York City. To his fellow Believers at Sabbathday Lake and many others, however, Johnson was much beloved and highly respected. They saw him as gifted, in the traditional Shaker sense of that term—a natural leader who was able to inspire, educate, and counsel others. It is impossible to avoid comparing his activities with those traditionally assigned to a Shaker elder. Johnson served the Maine family as the functional equivalent of an elder during the 1970s and 1980s, which no doubt added to the ministry's hostility toward him.[71]

The decision to close the membership and the subsequent controversy over Johnson's status occurred at a time when the youth of America were rebelling against middle-class values and institutions and seeking alternative world views and social structures. The surge in communal activity during the 1960s and early 1970s often involved sexual promiscuity and experimentation with the drug culture. Perhaps that is why Gertrude Soule spoke of the ministry's fear and distrust of the young people "attracted by the Shaker religion and faith," whom she said were unwilling to accept the "discipline" of the Shaker life. Her response to the youth culture of that era was shared by many other Americans, especially those who were older. The Believers in Maine, however, did not fear youthful inquirers. Johnson was convinced, had the ministerial ban not existed, that "as many as 50 men and women would have sincerely sought and gained admission as covenanted members. And today [in 1973] we would have 20 or 30 men and women here, ranging in age between 25 and 45. Shakerism would have become again a vital, ongoing force." No one will ever know if he was correct, but the public record from the 1960s through the 1980s shows a steady stream of inquirers and friends—kindred spirits—moving in and out of Sabbathday Lake.[72]

In 1979 Frances Carr at Sabbathday Lake wrote to the editor of the *Portland Press Herald,* expressing publicly her dismay over the New Hampshire position of not admitting new members "for fear that they would be exploited by 'charlatans' eyeing the nearly 2000 acres of real estate." The Maine Shakers, Carr contended, had no such worry because their covenant "contains stringent safeguards" protecting their properties. "The Covenant," she added, "also requires that 'the door must be kept open for the admission of new members of the Church.'" Carr went on to describe the realities of Shaker life.

> To be a Shaker in the last quarter of the twentieth century is to take on a great personal burden; it is not an easy life. We have been impressed by the personal integrity and courage of those young men and women who would make their spiritual home with us. We prefer to be encouraged by the admonition of our leader, Mother Ann, who said, "Open the windows and doors and receive whomsoever is sent."

The conflict became increasingly public during these years.[73]

In May 1980, Tim Clark, a reporter for *Yankee* magazine, published an important article on the controversy under the title "Shattering the Shaker Image." In the piece he took aim at the stereotypical view of the Believers, and he also probed into the background of the controversy, quoting almost all the parties involved, some firsthand, others through previously published sources. Clark reportedly received a measure of cooperation from Richard Morse in advance of publication, but a misunderstanding over editorial review of the article by the attorney led to the threat of a lawsuit after publication. The Sabbathday Lake Believers were, on the whole, pleased with Clark's essay. Mildred Barker wrote, "There is much in it that has needed saying for sometime." She did object, however, to placing the responsibility for the conflict on Theodore Johnson. She continued, "To be sure, what he represents and has represented for over twenty years is certainly a source of contention. The real root of the difficulty lies, however, in the refusal of us all here to accept the efforts of non-Shakers to end Shakerism. . . . Our desire to continue Shakerism and our absolute objection to being told what to do by lawyers, not Brother Ted, is the crux of the matter." Johnson himself worried that the article might affect the daily life of the community, its younger members, and himself if the question of his "genuineness" as a Shaker became its focus. "Strangely," he wrote, "the questions as to the nature of my life here all seem to come from collectors, museum personnel, and would-be-historians of the movement who live at some geographical remove from us." Local people had no such problem, they "take me very readily for what I am," he observed.[74]

In this controversy over the admission of new members, Sabbathday Lake mounted a religious argument. The Maine Believers contended that those who accept the Shaker gospel and its attendant discipline should be embraced within the family. For them, a spiritual judgment was the primary consideration. By contrast, the New Hampshire ministry defended its ecclesiastical position on administrative grounds. They attempted to protect the purity of the society by eliminating the possibility of new members. I have never read any attempt to justify Canterbury's action on theological grounds. On the contrary, the rationale for the ministry's action appeared to be protection of the interests of the existing covenanted Believers. There are certain ironies attached to these respective positions. The conservative Maine Believers were more open to contemporary culture, and the progressive Canterbury Shakers returned to a more rigid variety of sectarianism. From the outside, it is difficult to understand the rigidity of the Canterbury position. One wonders if in their hearts the New Hampshire Believers would not have preferred to see an expanding society rather than a dying institution. At the same time, it must be acknowledged that the actions of the Sabbathday Lake community produced the first structural schism within American Shakerism. By 1980 two Shaker societies, small as they were, existed in America. From the standpoint of religious considerations, that situation made little sense. From the standpoint of the attorneys, whose responsibility it is to protect the interests of their clients, the dilemma was an unfortunate but necessary standoff. The conclusion is unavoidable that the attorneys have exercised considerable influence over the course of the controversy.[75]

The passage of time has done relatively little to temper the feelings of the two parties to this controversy, although now much of the public exchange is between friends of the two villages. Sometimes these salvos are direct and undisguised, other times more subtle. In 1985 a documentary film, "The Shakers: Hands to Work, Hearts to God," was produced by Ken Burns and Amy Stechler Burns. This production, which aired on public television stations throughout the nation, led to the publication two years later of a trade book drawing on the same materials. Both items were well received. The cinematography was stunning, as were the photographs in the volume. Both productions spoke directly in support of the Canterbury view on the contemporary controversy. The film was the more subtle of the two. It showed the two villages, but managed to do so without any clue to the viewer that there were three male Shakers in Maine. The book was even more explicit. It contained a foreword by Bertha Lindsay in which she stated, "While we may have closed our doors to new members, we have never closed our hearts, and we still welcome any young people to talk with us. We feel that we are still witnessing for our church and for God, so nothing is going to be lost." In the epilogue the authors wrote, "Today, Shakerism endures, not through the active practice of thriving communities, but through the power of the spirit that has been left behind." Shakerism speaks, they wrote, through the women "immersed in the struggle for godliness."[76]

Sabbathday Lake has had its defenders, too. No defense or account of the Maine Believers has been more explicit or compelling than the volume by Gerard C. Wertkin, a long-time friend of the Shakers. His book, *The Four Seasons of Shaker Life,* used text and photographs to describe the life rhythms of contemporary Believers at Sabbathday Lake. Wertkin has visited the village often since 1966. He and his family appear frequently in "Home Notes." One Sunday morning, for example, Mildred Barker noted that Wertkin, although Jewish by tradition, united "in testimony, first in Hebrew from the Torah," and that he then expressed "the reverence he holds for the Mother's Gospel." Wertkin wrote his book "to record the life of a living Shaker community" as well as its "hopes for the future." The first photograph in the book is a family portrait, showing five sisters and three brothers (fig. 51). The last photograph looks in on Theodore Johnson and Arnold Hadd at prayers. The pages in between document the vitality and energy—physical and spiritual—that Wertkin finds among the Maine Believers. He also addresses explicitly the question of the future. "Beginning with one or two individuals in the late 1950s," he wrote, "and accelerating in the 1970s, seekers, at first tentatively and later with greater boldness, have found their way to the Church. The possibility of a new generation of Shakers is no longer an academic question." A 1990 BBC documentary on the Maine community, an attractive cinematic pro-

51. The Sabbathday Lake Shakers
Sitting, left to right: Minnie Greene, R. Mildred Barker, Marie Burgess, Frances A.
Carr. Standing: Elsie A. McCool, Theodore E. Johnson, Wayne Smith, Arnold Hadd.
(Photograph by Ann Chwatsky; courtesy Ann Chwatsky, Rockville Centre, New York.)

duction that makes much the same point, seems a calculated response to
the earlier Burns film. In a celebration of the family life at Sabbathday
Lake, the English producer, Jane Treays, did not even mention the existence of Canterbury, thereby leaving the viewer with the impression that
the Maine Believers were the only living Shakers.[77]

Individuals who first encountered the Shakers in their youth have
often become the most loyal defenders of the two villages. June Sprigg, for
example, developed a close relationship with the ministry at Canterbury.

In 1975 she wrote to Gertrude Soule, "This is just a small gift from one who's received infinitely more in love and kindness from you than she can ever repay. I love you, Eldress Gertrude, and I'm going to miss you so much. . . . I know sometimes your heart is hurting." Sprigg's publications through the years have avoided addressing directly the controversy surrounding the new members at Sabbathday Lake, thus in effect taking the side of Canterbury. Michael Taylor, who first met the Shakers at Sabbathday Lake while he was working on his dissertation at Harvard University, has become an outspoken defender of the Maine Believers. His review of Robley Edward Whitson's anthology of Shaker spirituality, for example, is a not-so-veiled attack on what he calls "the presuppositions of ecumenical mysticism," which, he charges, were approved and supported by Eldress Gertrude Soule of Canterbury. Taylor regards much of Whitson's work as "outrageous" and not representative of authentic Shakerism. Taylor, by contrast, traces the continuities in Shaker spirituality from Ann Lee to the contemporary Believers at Sabbathday Lake.[78]

The controversy concerning membership hinges on the definition of a Shaker. Canterbury maintained that the essential criterion for being a Shaker was having signed the church covenant before the year 1965. Sabbathday Lake said that a Shaker is defined by acceptance into the community of fellow Believers. Both assumed that knowledge and understanding of the society's traditions and beliefs and a willingness to submit to the communal discipline were prerequisite. Canterbury reflected the perspective of the ecclesiastical establishment; Sabbathday Lake held out for local autonomy. The New Hampshire Believers rested their case on the authority of the ministry; the Shakers in Maine grounded their practice on spiritual credentials. Canterbury celebrated the legacy of the past and was determined to safeguard it at all costs. Sabbathday Lake believed that the traditions of the past could prosper in the future. The division between the villages was not imaginary, for the two were headed in opposite directions.[79]

The Selling of the Shakers

The historical revival, which began modestly in the early decades of the twentieth century before the controversy between Canterbury and Sabbathday Lake, became the foundation for a vast array of commercial undertakings, many of which were linked only indirectly to the United Society. During the first century of the Shaker experience in America, in theory at least, temporal issues in the society had been subordinate to spiritual concerns. The trustees answered to the ministry, handwork was a form of worship, and activities in the meetinghouse sometimes displaced shop routines. That all changed during the second century of the Believers' history. By the 1960s the United Society was in jeopardy of being swamped by a rising tide of commercial enterprises.[80]

Responsibility for this surge of Shaker commercialism cannot be placed exclusively on greedy outsiders interested in making money at the expense of the society. The economic circumstances of the Believers, in fact, were the principal driving force in the inauguration of this commercialization of Shakerism. As the Believers became more desperate for funds to deal with their expenses during the decades of plummeting membership, to raise cash they turned with increasing regularity to the sale of furniture and other objects from their homes. In February 1949, for example, Emma King wrote, "The old-time relics are dear to us and only the immediate need of money would induce us to part with them." The next month she struck much the same note when corresponding with H. Phelps Clawson about the museum at Old Chatham. "I deeply regret that we are forced to sell that which we love in order to obtain funds for maintenance but it is a great satisfaction to know that they fall into good hands who will reverently care for them, and preserve them for historical value and enlightenment for future generations."[81]

Until the death of Frances Hall in 1957, the members of the society were apparently unaware of the full extent of the assets controlled by the society's trustees. The Shakers sold furniture and other antiques because they were in need, not because they wanted to be rid of these items. They regarded the collectors with mixed feelings. Friends and dealers lingering nearby seemed a bit like vultures, watching and waiting for anything and everything they could seize. Sometimes even "friends" of the Shakers, to whom the Believers rendered every public courtesy, were privately castigated for their insatiable appetite for "things Shaker." When these customers did not pay for their purchases promptly, the Believers were forced into the awkward situation of reminding them of their obligations. The Shakers sometimes were subjected to tedious explanations of why the collectors were unable to pay higher prices for particular pieces. It appears that the buyers frequently took advantage of the elderly Believers.[82]

Although the first participants in the Shaker furniture and antique arena were the Shakers themselves, a major secondary market soon developed. Among those trading in it were many of the same persons directly involved in the revival of historical interest in the Shakers. The prime examples were Edward and Faith Andrews, who were antique dealers long before they discovered the Shakers. According to their own account, their interest in Shaker artifacts began as something of an accident. One September afternoon in 1923 as they were scouring the countryside for collectibles, the Andrewses stopped at Hancock village because they had heard about the delicious bread that could be purchased there. They were welcomed by a Shaker sister and bought the bread. "In the long clean 'cook-room,'" they wrote, "we saw much besides: a trestle table, benches, rocking chairs, built-in cupboards, cooking arches, all beautiful in their simplicity." They added, "Later, eating the bread, we knew that our appetite would not be satisfied with bread alone," and it was not. Before several decades had passed, the Andrewses had assembled perhaps the largest private collection of Shaker artifacts and antiques. They sold inferior pieces to a "few discriminating customers who sensed their unique quality." In 1927, when they brought their investments to the attention of Homer Eaton Keyes, the editor of *Antiques,* he asked them to write an article on the interpretation of Shaker antiques. "On that autumn evening," they wrote, "our interest became a calling." Their calling also paid interest and more in the years that followed.[83]

Edward and Faith Andrews became preoccupied with the pursuit of Shaker items. Friends and family initially scoffed at their new interest, but when the Andrewses sold two Shaker trestle tables "at a considerable profit, they were impressed." Soon the couple was scouring every standing building that had ever been inhabited by the Believers for objects. In the Ann Lee cottage at Mount Lebanon, they spotted an unusual cat dish and asked for it. "Sadie [Neale] wondered why we should want a cat dish," they wrote, "but said we could have it." It turned out to be a rare piece of early signed pewter. On another occasion they "coveted" a distinctive stand next to an aging brother's bed on which he laid his watch at night. Their request was refused, but seven or eight years later when Brother Ferdinand "was no longer in time, the sisters kept their promise to let us have what time had withheld so long." Less than a month after the death of her sister Emma, Sadie Neale recorded the arrival of the Andrewses, who made "some special inquiries." At the Second Family at Mount Lebanon they later had problems obtaining the permission of Lillian Barlow, the last Shaker woman in that family, to buy furniture. "She had a strong sentimental attachment to any piece of Shaker workmanship—to sell it was to part with a part of her past; to admit, perhaps, that there was no future for one of the oldest New Lebanon families." Yet the Andrewses were persistent and managed to "obtain, or more properly speaking, successfully beg several pieces from this loyal Shakeress." In their recollections about collecting, Edward and Faith Andrews inadvertently reveal the

subtle ways in which they and others pressured the aging Shakers to surrender their possessions. These "friends" of the Believers, in turn, made
substantial profits and built impressive private collections.[84]

The next step in the evolution of the Shaker antique market was the
mounting of major shows such as the exhibition at the New York State
Museum at Albany in 1930, an exhibit in 1932 at the Berkshire Museum
in Pittsfield, Massachusetts, another in 1934 at the library in Lenox, Massachusetts, and the display "Shaker Handicrafts" at the Whitney Museum
in 1935. By the 1960s exhibitions of this kind were commonplace. These
and other widely publicized events fed the rising interest and sweetened
the market prospects for collectors and dealers. Such exhibitions also created customers for books about Shaker furniture. In this area, too, as in
almost every category of endeavor related to the Believers, the Andrewses
led the way. In the 1940s and 1950s, only a few others were prepared to
write about Shaker furniture. After the publication of *Religion in Wood* in
1966, however, the reading public could choose from a growing number of
volumes on the subject. Some described authentic Shaker pieces; others
were designed to assist those who wished to build their own "Shaker
furniture."[85]

Specialized books on furniture became the model for publications in
other areas of Shaker material and domestic culture. Baskets and clothing
attracted attention, both from historians and from practicing artisans.
Shaker architecture, too, became the subject of study. The cultivation of
herbs by the Believers was of interest for both culinary and medicinal
uses. In 1950, for example, Edward and Faith Andrews published a bro-
chure entitled *Shaker Herbs and Herbalists* to accompany an exhibition at
the Berkshire Garden Center in Stockbridge, Massachusetts. More than
twenty-five years later Amy Bess Miller published a major study on Shaker
herbs. The interest in this topic has grown, in part from the "reopening" of
the herb business in 1969 at Sabbathday Lake under the leadership of
Theodore Johnson. By the late 1970s the Maine Believers were devoting
ten acres to the cultivation of herbs, and they were conducting a mail-
order business that has become a major source of income. This undertaking profited from the changing eating habits of Americans.[86]

Shaker cooking has always been of popular interest, starting with
the observations made by nineteenth-century visitors concerning the food
served by the Believers. Cookbooks have become a unique genre in the
field of Shaker studies and with a certain legitimacy, for Shaker manuscripts contain many recipes. The Believers frequently exchanged these
items. As early as 1882 a collection of recipes attributed to the Shakers

was published under the title *Mary Whitcher's Shaker House-Keeper*. This volume advertised Canterbury's medicinal products, including its sarsaparilla syrup. A Shaker cookbook was one of the few books that the Andrewses did not write, although they discussed foodways in their other studies. One of the earliest works concerned with the Believers' cuisine was by Caroline B. Piercy, the author of the history of North Union. She came to this interest through her mother, who had carefully collected recipes from the Shakers. Piercy, who mixed historical anecdotes with recipes, thought that the Believers' kitchens were "as sacred to them as were their meeting houses." Therefore their "luscious pies, dumplings and dainty flummeries" must be seen as concrete expressions of their religious perspective. Correspondingly, she imagined that the sisters, "endlessly preparing delicious food for their enormous households," did not look on this task "as a labor, but as a glorious opportunity to serve God joyously by feeding his children." Piercy's uncritical perspective, which seems to ignore the hard work involved in kitchen duty, has been echoed in subsequent publications.[87]

Two recent Shaker cookbooks require special attention because they are literally more than that and were written by contemporary Believers. They appeared within a year of each other, one by Frances Carr of Sabbathday Lake and the other by Bertha Lindsay of Canterbury. Both offer abundant recipes—some traditional and others contemporary—and an astonishing amount of detail about twentieth-century life in the two villages. Carr's volume allows a glimpse into family life in the Maine community during her years as a Shaker. Through her prose the reader meets a number of Believers, including Ethel Peacock, Prudence Stickney, and Delmer Wilson. The recipe section confirms her observation that the arrival of the new brothers over the past twenty-five years "introduced a more sophisticated trend" into the community's cooking. Carr includes, for example, recipes for Brother Ted's Swedish Meat Balls and Brother Arnold's Lasagna with Meat Sauce. These inclusions are the only hint of the contemporary ecclesiastical controversy. Bertha Lindsay's cookbook, edited by Mary Rose Boswell, focuses on the past eighty years of culinary traditions at Canterbury. Although Lindsay was the last surviving member of the parent ministry, she spent a great deal of her more than eighty years at the village cooking for the community. Interspersed with her recipes are Lindsay's recollections, generously illustrated with photographs, from the first four decades of the twentieth century. There is no explicit reference to the contemporary conflict in this volume, although Lindsay's afterword echoes the perspective of Canterbury on Shakerism's future. "The Shakers are being honored throughout the country at this time. There are many exhibits and many shows in different places honoring the ones who made the furniture. But the furniture will not last as long as the philosophy of the Shakers, and I am proud that I have been a part of this culture and perhaps in my small way can add a little bit to people's happiness by what I can say or do for them." Both cookbooks provide valuable insider information on twentieth-century Shakerism.[88]

The establishment of museums and the restoration of the historic Shaker sites have contributed substantially to the growth of the Shaker market. The museum and tourist trade at both Sabbathday Lake and Canterbury set the pace. Both locations offered tours of their facilities long before the wave of interest in historic preservation. (In fairness, however, it must be noted that Clara Endicott Sears, a pioneer in the museum field, moved the trustees' Office from Harvard to Prospect Hill in 1920, where it became part of the Fruitlands Museums.) During the middle decades of the century tourists at the Shaker villages generated substantial revenues for the fragile economies of the Believers. The visitors during the summer season were customers for the fancy goods in the Office shops. The Believers at both sites took great pride in this activity. "Home Notes" made repeated reference to the growing numbers and to each family's preparations for their arrival. In 1966, for example, Mildred Barker reported that the winter days were filled with "making aprons, holders and toys, or whatever we feel will interest the callers at the Gift Shop in the summer." Two years later, at the close of the tourist season, Bertha Lindsay announced a record number of tourists—5,189. Yet the most elaborate museums were not at Canterbury or Sabbathday Lake, but at the sites of former villages.[89]

The restoration effort launched in 1960 at Hancock progressed rapidly, thanks to the energy and financial support of local patrons and people from across the country. Less than a year after the site was obtained, the village was opened officially to the public. At that time only a few rooms in the Brick Dwelling and the first floor of the Sisters' Shop were available to visitors. In the course of the following years additional buildings were restored, gardens planted, and surrounding grounds refurbished. The process of repairing, restoring, and refurnishing the structures required more than a decade and large amounts of money. The village was also able to import a Moses Johnson meetinghouse from Shirley in 1961, thanks to the Sabbathday Lake Believers, who learned of its availability. At one point the most celebrated edifice at Hancock, the round stone barn built in 1810, was in danger of total collapse. Its restoration was underwritten in 1968 by Frederick and Carrie Beinecke. The artifacts needed to fill the restored buildings were purchased or donated by benefactors and friends. Included among these contributions were items from the Andrews collection of Shaker furniture and other objects, which had previously been given to Yale University and then withdrawn. Edward Andrews served as the curator at Hancock for the first three years of its operation. A library of books and manuscripts was assembled through a similar process.[90]

Hancock Shaker Village has become the leading Shaker restoration on the East Coast. During its first year of operation, 4,500 people visited the site. A decade later, annual attendance had jumped to more than 40,000. By 1984, 800,000 people had visited the restored village. Hancock is now a complex of enterprises—the historic site and museum open to tourists April through October, educational programs and workshops, a research library and publications program, replica reproduction through the Community Industries Program housed at the site, craft demonstrations, and special events. The revenues supporting this diversified operation are generated by museum and class fees, the sale of food, souvenirs, herbs, books, furniture, and other items, fund-raising events, private contributions, and occasional government grants for specific projects. Under the leadership of Amy Bess Miller and the professional staff and with the assistance of local boosters and volunteers, Hancock has become a major force in promoting the interest in Shakerism.[91]

Shakertown at Pleasant Hill, Kentucky, the leading Shaker restoration in the West, was developed at the same time as Hancock. The challenge at the Kentucky site, however, was much greater, because all of the former Shaker properties at Pleasant Hill were in private hands. There had been some talk in the 1940s of establishing a Shaker museum at the Pleasant Hill site, but nothing came of it. In 1960 a group of Kentuckians reopened that conversation and the next year formed a nonprofit educational corporation to begin raising funds. At the time the village included "a country store, a Shell filling station, and a row of large stone and brick buildings along either side of an asphalt highway and a half dozen frame buildings, some with sagging roofs and some leaning on their foundations." At the center of this cluster was the old meetinghouse, where the Shakertown Baptist Church held regular worship services. Thanks to the personal signatures of several trustees of the new corporation, all of the central properties at the site, with the exception of the meetinghouse land, were purchased for around $400,000. Several years later the Baptist congregation agreed to surrender the meetinghouse in exchange for a new church and parsonage about a mile from that location. At the head of this financial undertaking was Earl D. Wallace, who served as chairman of the board of trustees from its founding until his death in 1990. Wallace, a former executive in the petroleum industry, used his financial experience and extensive business and personal contacts to great advantage.[92]

Wallace chose James L. Cogar, a former curator at Colonial Williamsburg, as executive director of the village. Cogar, in turn, was largely responsible for the development of a master plan that enabled the corporation to apply successfully for a $2 million loan from the U.S. Department of Commerce. Restoration at the site began in 1964, guided by detailed architectural drawings. The engineering challenge was daunting because the village was to be restored to its antebellum status, but was also to include fully modern housing facilities with all utilities hidden from view. Wires were placed underground, plumbing and heating snaked through solid walls, and the original decor of the buildings restored. Thousands of visitors came to observe the restoration activity before it was complete, but the first stage was finished and the museum officially opened in April 1968. More than half of the buildings at the site, however, had not yet been touched.[93]

Additional funding was secured through loans and outright gifts from major benefactors, facilitating the restoration of other structures and the purchase of surrounding farmland and outlying sites. After the state of Kentucky built a bypass for U.S. Route 68, the asphalt road was removed from the center of the village. By 1974 the second stage of restoration had been completed, at which point eight buildings were used for Shaker exhibitions, two for the sale of craft products, books, and other items, one as a restaurant seating 116 persons, nine for guest houses, and several others for staff facilities. Under the management of James C. Thomas, Shakertown at Pleasant Hill has become a major tourist attraction and a center for educational activities. By June 1987, more than 3 million tourists had visited the site. In 1987 alone there were 250,000 visitors. By contrast with Hancock, the restoration effort in Kentucky was not aided in any substantial fashion by the living Shakers, although they were not uninterested. Local and regional boosterism played a major role in this enterprise. Earl Wallace himself scoffed at the religious beliefs and practices of the Shakers. He found the site attractive because of its place in Kentucky history and culture.[94]

Hancock and Pleasant Hill are the premier Shaker restorations, but the surge of interest in Shakerism has fueled the efforts of preservationists and friends of the society at other sites, too. Since 1962, a ten-day Shaker Festival has been held annually at South Union, featuring an outdoor drama entitled "Shakertown Revisited," which tells the story of the village in both song and dance. In 1971 a group of South Union friends succeeded, with state assistance, in securing sufficient funds to purchase two buildings at the site from the Benedictine order, including the Center Family dwelling; this complex is now the Shaker Museum, featuring displays of furniture, farm implements, and inventions. In 1977 individuals in the Albany, New York, area formed the Shaker Heritage Society, devoted to "preserving the memory of the Believers" through lectures, conferences, exhibitions, workshops, and children's programs. This group has spearheaded efforts to develop a cultural and educational center at the Watervliet location, where eight Church Family buildings remain, all part of Albany County's Ann Lee Health-Related Facility. In 1983 the Shaker Heritage Society joined with the Believers in New Hampshire and Maine in an effort to save the cemetery in which Ann Lee is buried from being overrun by a baseball stadium and parking lots. The stadium was built, but the graveyard was also protected. More modest museum and preservation efforts are under way at Mount Lebanon Shaker Village, a corporation organized to assist the Darrow School in caring for the twenty-five original Shaker buildings on the school's property; at Lower Shaker Village in Enfield, New Hampshire; at the site of Union Village, now the Otterbein Homes owned by the United Methodist Church; and at Groveland. In each of these locations local historical and business interests have combined to support preservation and restoration efforts.[95]

Several significant Shaker museums or permanent exhibitions of Believers' objects are not located at former village sites. The largest of these is the study collection of objects and documents at the Shaker Museum and Library in Old Chatham, New York. Other noteworthy exhibits scattered throughout the country and overseas include those at the Henry Francis du Pont Winterthur Museum in Delaware, which was the recipient in 1967 of the Edward Andrews Shaker library, the Boston Museum of Fine Arts, the Metropolitan Museum of Art in New York City, the Warren County Historical Society Museum in Lebanon, Ohio, and the American Museum at Bath in Great Britain. At these locations, as at the historical restorations, visitors pay fees to tour the facilities. These institutions regularly sponsor seminars and lecture series on Shakerism. In 1987, for example, the Shaker Museum in Old Chatham hosted a seminar on Shaker furniture and design, which participants paid $275 to attend; the following year the topic was "Shaker Religion in Context." In 1989 a conference on Union Village held at the Warren County Museum drew several hundred participants. There seems to be no limit to such activities. In addition, craft demonstrations, herb and cooking workshops, and antique festivals are commonplace at these museums and well attended.[96]

The efforts of the preservationists have not always been successful. Several times in recent years fire has destroyed historic landmarks. In 1972 the North Family barn at Mount Lebanon was consumed by fire; less than a year later the Church Family barn at Canterbury burned. Both were huge structures reflecting the agricultural activities in those villages. Some buildings deteriorated to the point where they had to be razed. After standing empty for fifteen years, the North Family dwelling at Mount Lebanon was demolished in 1973. Efforts by local Shaker enthusiasts to save buildings at Whitewater, Groveland, and Enfield, Connecticut, have been thwarted by real estate developers and private owners. The most striking instance of failure to date is the unsuccessful attempt to save the facilities at Mount Lebanon, despite the determination of several organizations intent on that goal, a sophisticated historical archaeological project that is under way, and a $1 million grant from the New York State Office of Parks, Recreation and Historic Preservation. The problem stems in great part from the financial difficulties of the Darrow School, which owns the former Church Family and North Family properties. Massive funds are needed simply to stabilize the facilities. In 1990 the school sold its Shaker artifacts and furniture to Ken and Maria Luisa Hakuta for $650,000 to raise operating funds. The Hakutas, who agreed to keep the collection at the site for at least ten years, later moved it to Washington, D.C.[97]

Specialized publications designed specifically for those interested in the United Society have played a major role in the development of the Shaker market. In the fall of 1971 the first issue of the *World of Shaker* appeared, a quarterly published by the Guild of Shaker Crafts at Spring Lake, Michigan. This guild, established in 1965 by Betty and Ken Kammeraad, dealt in "authentic Shaker Furniture, replicas, and accessories." The eight-page oversized publication was "devoted exclusively to the many aspects of Shaker lore both past and present." It was to serve as a "clearinghouse" for "everything that is Shaker inspired." The editor continued,

> Our purpose is to present a readable potpourri of Shaker history, design, historical sites, special events, kitchen hints, antiques, decorating tips and a wealth of other Shaker information. . . . So much has taken place and likewise continues to be done to preserve Shaker tradition, we feel it should be shared as widely as possible. The Shaker story is a fascinating one and in many ways speaks today

with as much vitality and beauty as it did when Shaker communities flourished from Maine to Kentucky.

This undertaking, the editor stated, was based on "great respect for the principles and contributions of these gentle people." The annual subscription price for the publication was one dollar.[98]

The first issue of the *World of Shaker* documented a wide range of interests. The feature article was a reminiscence about Marguerite Frost written by Irene Norman Zieget, who had acquired a large collection of artifacts from the Believers that she later donated to the Philadelphia Museum of Art. The publication included ideas for how Shaker design might be used by "decorator-conscious homeowners," "Shaker" recipes reflecting "the goodness that could be expressed through good food," and reviews of new books. The first issue also contained excerpts from the 1845 Millennial Laws and photographs of Shaker objects and scenes from historic restorations. Much of the content was either implicit or explicit advertising. One article reported on a Chicago exhibit of photographs and artifacts; another described South Union's summer festival; a third featured the two-hundred-thousandth visitor to Shakertown at Pleasant Hill. Paid advertisements described the Shaker Museum at Old Chatham, reproductions available through the Shaker Workshops in Concord, Massachusetts, and items for sale from the Guild of Shaker Crafts. A special section called "Antique Market" consisted of small notices for persons wishing to buy, sell, or trade Shaker items.[99]

During the next six and a half years the *World of Shaker* published news and information about the Believers, past and present, as well as about the rapidly expanding world of Shaker. Eulogies regularly appeared, reporting the deaths of the remaining Believers. Historical restorations and museums were the primary subjects of coverage. In 1974, the year of the Shaker bicentennial in America, considerable attention focused on events commemorating the arrival of the Shakers from England. In all these years there was no indication of the schism between the leadership of the society at Canterbury and the Sabbathday Lake Believers. On the contrary, each issue delicately balanced its coverage of the two active Shaker sites. In November 1977 the magazine stopped publication.[100]

But the *World of Shaker* was soon resurrected. In 1978 Paul and Diana Van Kolken, whose interests in Shakerism stretched back over a decade, purchased the *World of Shaker,* changed the name of the magazine to the *Shaker Messenger,* and began publication in 1979 from Holland, Michigan. The stated purpose of their publication was to keep "readers up to date on current events in the world of Shaker with reports from Shaker communities, restorations and museums; book reviews, study papers, antique shows, songs and seminars." The editor, who lectures widely on the Shakers, serves as a sales agent for craftspeople at shows and runs a mail-order book business. The *Shaker Messenger,* with more than a thousand subscribers, has become a leading gauge of the state of affairs within the larger world of Shaker. Disdained by some because of its commercialism and the lack of rigor in its essays, it is nonetheless a major link among the scattered friends of Shakerism.[101]

The *Shaker Messenger,* like its predecessor, contains a variety of news and information items. It also has even more paid advertisements, which reflect the expanding range of commercial activities within the world of Shaker. The sophistication of the advertising varies considerably. One full-page ad assures the reader, "In the past 20 years we have helped build major private and public collections. If you are considering selling part or all of your collection and would like to do so in a discreet, professional manner, we will buy or represent your furniture or accessories in the marketplace without the risks of a public auction." Another notice trumpets the fact that a cabinetmaker is "accepting orders for a limited edition (100) of dovetailed Shaker carriers" of cherry wood, with maple handles and pine bottoms, approximately 11 × 7 × 8 inches in size. The price of these reproductions is $125 plus shipping and handling. Significantly, the ad states, the perceived value of these objects is much greater: "This is the identical carrier that Willis Henry mistakenly auctioned as 'an original Shaker carrier' in September 1985 for $3800."[102]

Following the prices of Shaker antiques through the late twentieth century is likely to produce a feeling of vertigo. The market has come a long way from when Edward and Faith Andrews paid Sabbathday Lake $6 for a table, $25 for a bureau, $10 for a yellow sink, $15 for a workbench, and $5 for a spool bed. In 1973 the *World of Shaker* reported on the first auction of Shaker artifacts in Manhattan. At that sale a good large oval fingered box sold for $180, a "Very Nice Pine Two-door Cupboard" 94 inches high for $725, and a "Red-Stained Twenty-One Drawer Storage Chest," 82 × 104 × 18 inches, for $3,750. Each year the *Shaker Messenger* celebrates the new sales heights. The annual Willis Henry auction has become more than a sale; it is a cultural event, the ultimate measure of Shaker worth. Astonishing levels were reached in 1989 when two pieces were sold privately from the Darrow School collection, a 96-inch tall cupboard with drawers for $200,000 to entertainer Bill Cosby and a Benjamin Youngs tall clock for $165,000 to businessman Ken Hakuta. In 1990, when the British Broadcasting Corporation filmed its documentary on the Shakers, the producer felt compelled to attend the Willis Henry auction to represent the full span of the Shaker enterprise in America. On that occasion television talk-show hostess Oprah Winfrey paid $220,000 for a pine work counter, setting a new record price for a single Shaker item (fig. 52).[103]

In 1989 a new magazine entitled *Shaker Spirit* was announced by James E. Betts, the founder of *Early American Life*. The prospectus for this publication stated: "SHAKER means many different things to people. Purity and functionalism in furniture and utensil design . . . Simplicity of life . . . Devotion to hard work . . . Quality workmanship and honest value . . . And a philosophy of life and religion that is without compromise. . . . Our research (and our own feelings) tell us that the time is right for SHAKER SPIRIT. We are not Shakers, but the 'spirit' is somehow in all of us." The publisher promised that the magazine would include suggestions on how to "modify parts of the Shaker philosophy" so that they could be applied to today, directions for making an oval box "the fast and easy way," information on Shaker songs and dances (the "aerobics of yesteryear"), and drawings for "what a Shaker one-family house would have looked like if there had been such a thing." Subscriptions were twenty-four dollars per year.[104]

Shaker Spirit was more crassly commercial in its approach than any previous Shaker publication. The opening essay in the first issue was an interview with Willis Henry, president of Willis Henry Auctions Inc. Entitled "Antiques Report: A Hot Market That's Not Cooling," the article was designed to impress the reader with the investment possibilities of Shaker collecting, even though Willis himself cautioned against playing it as a "growth market." The writer, by contrast, repeatedly implied the positive prospects for investors. One photograph pictured a tall chest that sold at auction in 1988 for $99,000. Reference was also made to the sale of the Karl Mendel Shaker Collection of 196 pieces, which sold for $652,000. Mendel was identified as a "retired New York school teacher who had the foresight to collect Shaker items 20 years ago." Another essay in this inaugural issue depicted the Shakers as "World Champions" in developing new products, including the circular saw, the flat broom, and the clothespin—by now a cliché. Betts calculated that the Believers were responsible for "one invention per 161 Shakers," by contrast with the rest of the world's population who produced only one new product for every 54,474 people. The magazine included full-color photographs of idyllic scenes at Pleasant Hill. The second issue contained the plans of a Shaker house for today, that is, a modern home "inspired" by Shaker architecture. Russell

MOVERS AND SHAKERS

52. Movers and Shakers
Cartoon by Don Bousquet that first appeared in *Yankee* magazine. (Courtesy Don Bousquet, Narragansett, Rhode Island.)

Swinton Oatman, a trained architect, drew up the plans, which resembled "contemporary period vernacular" except for such differences as "larger and more numerous windows, simplified trim and detailing, and separated equal entrances." A closer examination reveals little that is distinctively Shaker in the working drawings, which are available from the architect for $150. "Shaker Showcase," another section of the second issue, featured a variety of items for sale: a Tree of Life sterling silver pin shipped in a velvet box for $52.50, an eight-drawer wooden chest of "a unique Shaker style in both appearance and function" for $2,030.00 plus shipping, a $29.95 videotape on how to make oval boxes, and a two-step "step stool" made of cherry wood modeled after one "attributed to the New Lebanon community" for $190.00 plus $12.00 shipping.[105]

Other publications also reflect the strength of the Shaker market. Shaker gift books proliferate, filled with exquisite photographs of the society's artifacts and scenes from the living villages and the restorations. The photographers and artists who create these volumes have carried the presentation of Shaker material culture to the level of an art form. Linda Butler's black-and-white photos draw the observer into the still lifes. By contrast, the bright tones of the photographs in L. Edward Purcell's volume press objects into the viewer's consciousness. Photographic essays of Shaker objects abound. Women's magazines, books on crafts and antiques, publications describing country living—all are crammed with pictures. The pieces of furniture at the museum in Old Chatham displayed in *Antiques* magazine, for example, seem to stand as art objects in their own right.[106]

There is even a world of Shaker for children. In 1978 the Viking Press published a Shaker alphabet book filled with more than "one hundred real and imagined animals," each one more charming than the next. *Cobblestone,* a children's magazine, devoted an entire issue in 1983 to the Shakers, which included an interview with Bertha Lindsay, historical essays, a map study, a time line, and directions for making a Shaker doorstop. *A Cut and Assemble Shaker Village* in H-O scale, which includes the round barn at Hancock, an instructional book, and cutouts, recipes, and awards, is available for schoolchildren ages eight to twelve. Mary Lyn Ray has written an award-winning children's book about Cornelia French, who came to New Lebanon at the age of two and spent her life as a basketmaker. Shaker coloring books and paper dolls are on the market. Now children can learn about the Believers even before they can read.[107]

This does not exhaust the full range of the Shaker marketplace, which has become international with the opening of a Shaker store in London. Videocassettes are available on various crafts associated with the Believers. It seems as though almost anything that has a link to the Shakers can be sold. Sweater manufacturers enjoy a special advantage because of the "Shaker-knit-stitch." The advertising employed by manufacturers plays on the popular association of quality with the Shakers. The *Land's End* catalog features "A Shaker *Polo*" that uses the "easy-moving half-cardigan stitch the Shakers found so necessary to their hardworking lifestyle. (Spend five minutes on a Shaker chair, and you'll know why they kept moving from sun-up to sun-down. They had no comfortable place to sit down.)" Block's, a national clothing firm, works an inversion of sorts on the image by featuring "Shaker knit sweaters to shake 'em up at school." A "Shaker style" ski rack using "hardwood pegs" is available through Yield

"(A) the Shakers didn't work from kits, and
(B) they were religiously motivated."

53. The Shakers Didn't Work from Kits . . .
Drawing by Donald Reilly; © 1982 The New Yorker Magazine, Inc.

House in New Hampshire. *USAir Magazine* featured a long article on Shaker furnishings. Full-color calendars present the same objects. The name Shaker carries a clear connotation for many Americans. The *New Yorker* exploits the image in cartoon (fig. 53); Garrison Keillor advertises Shaker chairs alongside Powdermilk Biscuits in Lake Wobegon.[108]

The Ecumenical Shakers

By the 1960s Shakerism had become much more than the Believers; in fact, the world of Shaker was threatening to overshadow the Shakers themselves. There is some irony in that name the world of Shaker for the founders of the society and their early followers had withdrawn from the world because they regarded it as evil and carnal. In the late twentieth century the Believers were embraced by the world, which fed on them in parasitic fashion. The Believers welcomed this embrace, however, and a symbiotic relationship developed in which both parties were nurtured. As a result, in the case of the United Society, what began as a radical sect became a culture-affirming movement. But what about the religious beliefs and practices of the Shakers in the second half of the twentieth century?

The Believers at Canterbury and Sabbathday Lake followed somewhat different paths. Both families claimed to represent authentic Shakerism and defended their contentions by looking to the past. In fairness to both, it must be said that their respective arguments were equally valid. They simply drew on different traditions and precedents. The religious outlook of the Shakers at both villages was influenced by their diverse judgments concerning a strategy for the future. The Believers at Sabbathday Lake thought of themselves as religious conservatives, patterning themselves self-consciously after their predecessors; those at Canterbury, adopting a more eclectic approach, pursued a less structured spiritual life. The Maine family's perspective was akin to that of the restorationists of the late nineteenth century; Canterbury reflected the progressive and evangelical strains of spirituality. Both were ecumenical, extending the hand of fellowship to other denominations. Yet their openness to other religious perspectives did not enable them to reach out to each other.

Bertha Lindsay, recalling the routines at Canterbury in her youth, described a pattern of recreational and religious activities that alternated throughout the week. Monday evenings were spent playing games and Tuesdays singing. On Wednesdays the discipline of the society was discussed at a "young people's conference." Sometimes, however, they substituted a "prayer service." Thursdays were for family singing and Fridays were free. Lindsay continued,

> On Saturday evenings we had another prayer service. And then, of course, our Sunday worship and Sunday School came on the following day. In the afternoon, we sometimes had a young people's prayer service, and, in the summertime, we held it in the Old Church, which was such a lovely place to have a service. On Sunday evenings, Sister Lillian Phelps would start playing the piano, and, before long, many of the younger people came in to join her in singing. We often sang gospel songs because we learned the songs of other churches as well as our own.

Lindsay's recollections underscore the evangelical flavor of the religious life at Canterbury and the openness of the Believers to influences from other churches. The language she used seemed more Protestant than Shaker. She spoke of services instead of meetings and of the Old Church instead of the meetinghouse. Yet even in New Hampshire some traditional religious activities persisted. Ethel Frost described her feelings in 1919 as she formally entered the society's covenant. She wrote, "The sacred privilege of signing our names to the covenant of our beautiful Church we are sure secured this relationship with God's own people."[109]

But in the years that followed, traditional Shaker religious activities nearly disappeared at Canterbury. There are few references in correspondence or "Home Notes" after 1960 to regular religious meetings. Such gatherings may have taken place without notice, but the absence of public commentary is significant. Individual Believers in New Hampshire maintained private devotional patterns with a deep faith both in God and in their cause, but an organized religious life was no longer the center of attention. The Shakers relied increasingly on community churches in the area, which they visited when they pleased, or on services held in the chapel to celebrate anniversaries and special occasions. One Thanksgiving, for example, a number of Believers attended the Congregational church in nearby Tilton. The Canterbury sisters developed close friendships with neighboring ministers to whom they turned in times of distress. Groups from nearby churches sometimes conducted worship in the chapel at the village.[110]

The Believers at Canterbury were confident in God's direction of their individual and collective existence. Their faith seemed secure in the face of anxieties. The "Home Notes" from late 1961 express readiness for the new year, which would bring "new responsibilities . . . and new opportunities for Christian service." Whatever the year ahead might bring, Bertha Lindsay wrote, "we rest in the assurance that, 'We cannot drift beyond His love and care.'" The same theme echoed through other public reports. In 1968 Lindsay noted, "We cannot foresee what the future holds in store, but this we do know, God has been good to us. With grateful hearts we face the future with courage." Lindsay's own religious identification at this time was first and foremost Christian. In many of her published comments of a spiritual nature, there is little that can be identified as distinctly Shaker. One exception was the "Home Notes" for 1966, where, recalling Ann Lee's birthday in February, she suggested: "let us renew our faith in the teaching of our great leaders and consecrate our lives anew to more dedicated service, presenting to the world our firm belief in the brotherhood of man in peaceful existence." Here Lindsay equated peace and brotherhood with the essence of Shaker teachings.[111]

The Canterbury Believers continued their earlier interest in spiritualism. In 1962 Bertha Lindsay reported that, in accord with a "desire for greater spiritual attainment," many of the members had joined the New Hampshire Society for the Study of Psychical Research organized by Charles "Bud" Thompson, who lived and worked at the village. In subsequent years "Home Notes" told of the continuing activities of this group. In 1963 the society sponsored a presentation on "the Essenes and the Dead Sea Scrolls," in 1964 a lecture by Swami Paranpanthi from India, and on another occasion a talk by an astronomer. Lindsay linked these educational activities with "traditions" begun by Dorothy Durgin and Henry Blinn, "both of whom were always anxious to bring worthwhile knowledge into our home." During these years Marguerite Frost penned a poem about death.

> She has not died. She has not gone
> Nor traveled very far.
> 'Tis only mist that lies between
> There really is no bar.
>
> But God who gave will never take
> He keeps our loved ones near,
> They bless us in our daily round;
> If we but speak, they hear.

Spiritualism in its broadest terms retained considerable appeal for the Canterbury Shakers.[112]

Marguerite Frost wrote more extensively about her religious views in a 1963 publication entitled *The Shaker Story*. This short tract, cast in a historical mode, told of the origins of the society, its gathering and geographical expansion, the achievements of the Believers, and the changing circumstances of the twentieth century. Throughout the narrative Frost made numerous observations about the religious dimensions of Shakerism. None is more revealing than her description of the spiritual insights of the founders. Ann Lee, according to Frost, had found the secret of life; that is, that "meditation and contemplation" are the proper means for "perceiving Divine Reality." A "latent Living Christ" resides in the human spirit; prayer and contemplation are the way to achieve union with that "Indwelling." She declared that "the Second Coming of Christ is a spiritual experience brought about in the individual soul." Lee, Frost contended, "did not think of herself as a 'female Christ' nor 'Ann the Word'." Lee always regarded Christ as "her Head and Lord." The first Shakers who followed her and the other founders were "humble, earnest Christians."[113]

Frost challenged the popular image emerging in the world of Shaker by criticizing those who thought the Believers "made a religion out of work." They were neither simply "hand-minded" nor simply intellectual. The Shaker way, wrote Frost, was to realize the "surrounding spiritual world in daily living." That was the reason for their interest in spiritualism and psychic experiences. The Believers lived with an understanding of the "nearness of the Other World." Frost was confident that the millennial church would "go on forever" because "the Spirit of the Inner Christ is still in the hearts of men and women awaiting its discovery." She contended that Shakerism had never been "a proselyting faith"; instead the Believers were working to bring about "a climate in which souls could become fully developed spiritually." The few "living members" in the two communities, she wrote,

> still walk our daily path believing that the greatest force in the universe is the love of God which fills all immensity and the second greatest power is interior prayer whereby man finds his union with God. Our aim is in the words of one of our early ministers, "Let every breath be a continual prayer to God." Our Shaker homes have been like caskets of priceless jewels where precious human souls were dedicated to a life of unselfish and unstinting service—each giving of his heart and his hand—loving not with a selfish love but with a universal love, consecrating and reconsecrating his life and his soul, dedicated to making the Kingdom of Heaven a living, personal reality.

Frost's views represent a liberal appropriation of the Shaker tradition.[114]

In the 1980s the Canterbury Shakers became interested in television preachers. "We watch Dr. [Robert] Schuller on Sunday. We're very fond of him," Bertha Lindsay said in 1986. Schuller's "Hour of Power," originating each week from the Crystal Cathedral in southern California, offered the New Hampshire Believers a steady diet of "possibility thinking." Lindsay also enjoyed listening to tape recordings of the New Testament read by Gregory Peck. Speaking about her understanding of Shakerism, Lindsay stated, "We are simple people who believe in Christ. Like good Christians everywhere, if we live by his teachings we are good people and good Shakers. We feel that the Christ spirit comes to each person individually, differently, not at the same time." She also suggested that "anyone can live a Shaker life anywhere, because it is very simple: just live by the teachings of Christ and meet everyone in a brotherly spirit with a lot of love, because that is what the world needs today." On another occasion Lindsay said, "I don't think Shakers are different in the least from other Christian sects, because we do believe in Christ's teachings, and we believe in the Bible."[115]

The religious situation at Sabbathday Lake was more consciously imitative of conservative Shaker beliefs and practices. Eldress Prudence Stickney had sounded that note when she spoke of the effort of the Maine Believers to retain "the old-fashioned gospel." Yet that determination on the part of the leadership did not necessarily produce a thriving religious situation. Again, personal faith and commitment seem to have outshined public religious observance before 1960. Without access to family records, it is impossible to determine precisely the frequency of religious meetings at Sabbathday Lake. What seems clear from the records after 1960 is that the members of the community themselves perceived a significant revival of spiritual activity at the village. In 1963, for example, Mildred Barker wrote, "History was once again made this year as we held Sunday services in our old Meeting House for the first time since 1888. The services were beautiful and inspiring, blest we feel by a 'host unseen' as well as by the friends here with us who in heart and spirit love and bless Mother's gospel as we do." One of the friends was Theodore Johnson. There is no doubt that his presence was a major catalyst for a revival of Shaker spirituality at Sabbathday Lake.[116]

Abundant evidence documents the rising tide of religious activity among the Maine Believers. The inaugural issue of the *Shaker Quarterly,* edited by Johnson, pointed to the "unchanged and unchangeable" truths on which Shakerism rested. That conviction became the foundation for a new appreciation of traditional Shaker religious practice. And yet there was a significant difference between the traditions of the past and the "new Shakerism" at Sabbathday Lake. This new Shakerism had a liturgical, biblical, and ecumenical cast. The festivals of the Christian church year were now superimposed on the Shaker calendar. The Bible moved to center stage in the worship activities of the Maine Believers, assuming greater importance than Shaker writings from the past. The new Shakers consciously reached out to other Christian groups in the spirit of unity.[117]

Theodore Johnson was the leader of the revival at Sabbathday Lake. His Episcopalian background and scholarly interests in the Middle Ages nurtured these new directions. The "Home Notes" in the *Shaker Quarterly* began to reflect the conjunction between liturgical sensitivities and the society's traditions. The "special blessings" of the "Advent season" were the topic of Mildred Barker's comments in 1970. She added, "We joined in praying that Mother's special spiritual gifts of the season would find an abiding place in the heart of each one of us and that peace might start just where we stand." In 1973, Barker described the celebration of the feast of Pentecost in the "old meetinghouse," where the "seven-fold gifts of the Spirit" were evident in both song and testimony among those present. The meeting was "deeply moving," she reported, in part because the ranks of both brothers and sisters "were equally filled for the first time within the memory of anyone now living." In other words, the meeting-house was filled with friends and kindred spirits. Barker wrote, "We hope that this may be a spirit indication of things to come."[118]

Early in Johnson's years at Sabbathday Lake, religious routines at the village were reestablished and new elements added. Weekly worship now occupied increasing importance in the life of the family. "One hun-dred per cent attendance has been the rule of the day at both our Sunday services and midweek prayer meetings," wrote Mildred Barker early in 1964. "Sweet refreshment and spiritual uplift always seemed to be found where two or three were gathered together in Christ's name." In the fall Johnson organized a weekly Bible class for the sisters, which produced a positive response. In 1967 the Maine Believers organized "The Fellowship of the Holy Spirit," an organization committed to regular intercession for "the ever growing work of the divine Father Mother . . . on earth." Those across the nation who joined this fellowship were remembered in both public and private prayers. As the years passed, the celebration of Shaker anniversaries was given more prominence in the public records. The fam-ily also continued the tradition of an annual reading of the "Church Cove-nant and Orders." In these meetings Johnson served as the leader and preacher. He also commonly offered homilies on the scriptural lessons for the day or on the anniversary events. His sermons, some of which have been transcribed, wove together biblical, liturgical, and traditional ele-ments. On Transfiguration Sunday in 1986, for example, Johnson ex-plored the meaning of the "new creation." He declared that it was "nothing other than the entry of a soul into that metamorphosized, that changed state, [which] is at the heart of the work of the Gospel." He asso-ciated this realization with the work of the "ever-blessed Mother" [Ann Lee], who called for leaving behind "those things that are of the world."[119]

During the past three decades, in part under the influence of Johnson, Shaker worship has taken on new significance at Sabbathday Lake. The services, held in the 1794 meetinghouse during the warm months and in the family meeting room in the dwelling the rest of the year, have become occasions for mutual support among the Believers and outreach to friends. The simplicity of the setting—the bare space filled simply with benches (and now a lectern, too)—underscores the sense of tradition. Worshipers enter the meetinghouse through two doors—men on the left and women on the right. The Shakers and those gathering with them sit in silence before the service, facing each other across the room, with only a nod of recognition to friends. At the announced hour, the silence is broken by song, scripture readings, a homily by one of the Believers based on the biblical texts that have been read by the family in advance, testimonies, prayers, and more song. Hymns from the Shaker past live on among the Believers. There are no hymnals. One voice strikes the beginning line and all who know the words and the tune join in. (Sometimes not even all family members are able to sing along.) Visitors often sit silently, joining in perhaps only on the well-known lines of "Simple Gifts."[120]

The testimonies of the modern-day Believers constitute a second sort of sermon. One by one, in an almost perceptible internal order, the Maine Shakers rise to express their gratitude to God and affection for one another, their hopes and concerns. Some testimonies are reflective and discursive, even theological, occasioned perhaps by events of the past week and of the days to come or suggested by the biblical readings. Others are short and almost formulaic, but seemingly no less sincere. Together they provide a measure of the collective spirit of the family. Friends of the Shakers testify, too. The prayers of the community invoke the names of distant friends, other Christian communities, and kindred spirits who have asked to be remembered. In these services the old and the new stand side by side. The songs and the testimonies partake of the past; the lectern, an occasional vase of flowers, set biblical lessons, the homily, recognition of the liturgical calendar, the presence of outsiders within the worshiping ranks—these and other features mark change. Gone are the dances and marches, the ecstatic behavior, the diatribes against the world. In their place remain some "motions" (clapping, bowing, stomping) to accompany a few songs, the heartfelt testimonies, and an overwhelming sense of unity.

But Johnson exercised even greater influence on the spiritual life of the Maine community and the surrounding group of friends through his historical and theological writings in the *Shaker Quarterly*. He edited a variety of significant documents from the society's past, including such important texts as the Millennial Laws of 1821 and Calvin Green's biographical account of Joseph Meacham. His introductions to these editions became the vehicle for religious reflections on the Shaker tradition. He also wrote essays on theological topics. His contributions to the *Quarterly* confirmed the intention of the Maine Believers to return to the classic sources of the tradition for new inspiration.[121]

The clearest statement of Johnson's theological perspective appeared under the signature "Confrater" in the spring of 1963. This "homily" embodies the essence of the new Shakerism. Johnson began with the premise that everyone and everything has a purpose. To yield to that purpose is to know God's will. "The Shaker is one who has heard this call and . . . strives to live in accordance with that Will." The Shaker church, he wrote, is "but a part of *the* Church." It represents a revival of apostolic Christianity shaped by the spiritual experiences of Ann Lee. The Believers are called to witness to holiness through lives of humility and love as taught in the New Testament. The spirit of Christ in their midst produces unity, community of goods, and the acceptance of authority. These traditions, Johnson contended, are not anachronistic. "Shakerism has a message for the twentieth century—a message as valid today as when it was first expressed. . . . Shakerism teaches God's immanence through the common life shared in Christ's mystical body." In this one article Johnson summarized the theological agenda for the new Shakerism.[122]

The most systematic statement of Johnson's understanding of Shakerism was in an address at a conference at Hancock in 1968. He began with the concept of the "indwelling presence of Christ," and from that basic principle spoke of unity and simplicity as the major theological emphases of the tradition as expressed in the life of community. Then he turned to a number of classic theological concerns. God, he said, is one, but possesses "the male characteristics of strength and power" and "female characteristics of compassion and mercy." Many, he charged, have misunderstood Shaker Christology. "Mother Ann was not Christ," he wrote, "nor did she claim to be." The second coming of Christ was in the church. Johnson called Shakerism "suprasacramental" because the baptism of the Holy Spirit is more important than water baptism, and every meal that is shared is a eucharist. Heaven and hell are spiritual, not physical, and there is "an intermediary state" where the soul "still benefits from the prayers and spiritual labors of the living church." Shaker worship is open to the movement of the spirit. The Bible, although important, is not the final expression of God in history. These ideas, according to Johnson, all derive from the availability of Christ's spirit.[123]

In his lecturing, preaching, and writing Johnson underscored how the society had evolved through its two centuries of experience. What began in protest against a secular culture, he declared, had become "a highly workable modus vivendi" with the world premised on the notion that "God's kingdom lies everywhere." The "physical isolation" of the first Believers had given way to the quest for building "a deeply recessed place of inner quiet." Johnson stated that Shakerism was fundamentally "a way of life" manifest in a community characterized by absolute surrender to the will of Christ. He was confident that Shakerism possessed a powerful "germ of truth" that held great promise for the larger Christian community. Johnson's views echoed the ecumenical spirit of the 1960s. The Second Vatican Council of the Roman Catholic Church, for example, encouraged many of the same concerns. The new Shakers, therefore, were reflecting the religious mood of the times.[124]

Theodore Johnson's work as a historian and theologian had a ripple effect on the study of Shakerism. The library at Sabbathday Lake attracted students and scholars who consulted with Johnson on their research projects. Some of these individuals were personally interested in Shakerism and spent time, at the invitation of the Believers, in the community. Several inquirers became advocates for the new Shakerism, sometimes publishing their work in the *Shaker Quarterly*. John Morgan, one of the theological defenders of the Maine Believers, described Shakerism as a form of "radical Christianity," the "social incarnation" of the Christ spirit first manifest in Jesus and Ann Lee. Morgan judged Shakerism to be essentially experiential and communal. He applied the category of "realized eschatology" to the tradition, stating that the second coming of Christ was in the community and that "at-one-ment" with God through Christ was the Shaker doctrine of salvation. Morgan praised the Shaker community for its unique contributions to Christianity.[125]

The ecumenical interests of the Sabbathday Lake Shakers became apparent in other ways, too. In the years following Johnson's arrival at the village, the Maine Believers developed close relationships with the members of other religious communities in the Northeast. These friendships were nurtured through correspondence and on-site visits. The "Home Notes" tell of frequent contact with other groups living the monastic life.

> We still enjoy a long-lasting friendship with the sisters of the Abbey of Regina Laudis at Bethlehem, Conn. We hear from Mother Piea almost monthly as well as corresponding with Mother Prisca who is now the Superior at the Monastery of Our Lady of the Rock in Washington state. We continue to be in touch with the monks of Weston, Vermont as well as the Monastery of Christ in the Desert, the Star Cross Monastery, the Benedictine Grange, our brother at New Skete

in Cambridge, New York and our brothers at Gethsemane Monastery in Kentucky.

These friendships strengthened the commitment of the Maine Believers to the Christian heritage as well as to the communal life.[126]

The Sabbathday Lake Believers also extended the hand of fellowship to churches in their immediate neighborhood. The Shakers were asked to offer the invocation at the New Gloucester Congregational Church's bicentennial in 1965, an invitation they readily accepted. Mildred Barker commented favorably after the fact about the "spirit of Christian unity" that was present in that gathering. On another occasion the members of the local Congregational church asked permission to join the Believers in an evening prayer service. The resulting meeting, which included song, testimonies, and prayers, was declared "a most spiritually uplifting experience." It was followed by friendly conversation and snacks. The whole evening was "blessed by the Spirit of ecumenicalism," wrote Barker.[127]

It would be a mistake to imply that the religious renewal of Shakerism at Sabbathday Lake was solely the result of Theodore Johnson's entry into the community. That he was the primary mover and a catalyst for this spiritual revival seems clear, but within the community there were other important contributors. Della Haskell, an older sister at Sabbathday Lake, wrote several essays for the early issues of the *Shaker Quarterly*. In one she addressed the question "What is Shakerism?" Her answer was simple: it is "actualized Christianity—a life of sympathetic understanding and service." Following the model provided by Jesus and Ann Lee is the way of the Believer. The Christ life comprises a number of essential features, including virgin purity, brotherly love, equality, simplicity, humility, and obedience. The pursuit of these virtues is a lifelong work. Haskell displayed a strong pastoral instinct in her writings. A second essay dealt with the concept of faith in the face of "burdens, duties, responsibilities and perplexities." Her counsel was direct: "We must build a little fence of trust around each day," she wrote, "and close out everything that does not belong in it." In a commentary on the parable of the rich man in Luke 12, Haskell advised: "Fill a worthy place, however humble; fill it well, so as to honor God and bless the world."[128]

A far more prominent figure in the religious revival at Sabbathday Lake was Mildred Barker, a society trustee and powerful personality within the community. During the exact same years that Theodore Johnson was emerging within the community, Barker was gaining public recognition as a spokesperson for Shakerism. Barker, more than Johnson, came to symbolize in the mind of the public the resurgence of interest in

Shakerism and the new religious vitality. Her charm and forthright manner endeared her to thousands, whether through the print media, film and
television, or personal contact. Barker wrote extensively on behalf of the
cause of contemporary Shakerism. She composed historical essays, theological reflections, and "Home Notes" throughout the 1960s, 1970s, and
1980s. She managed more effectively than any other person, Johnson included, to convey the spirit of the Shaker tradition and the determination
of the Maine Believers to move into the future. Johnson was the most articulate public representative of the new Shakerism, but "Sister Mildred"
was its spiritual center.[129]

A sampling of Mildred Barker's writings reveals a wide range of interests. She wrote the only history of the Alfred community, where she
first entered the society as a child. She also chronicled the development of
the Sabbathday Lake village. Her writings display a mix of pride in traditional Shaker elements and an openness to the future. In discussing the
authority of the Bible, for example, she distinguished between the "Word
of God" and the "Scriptures," contending that the Word is greater than any
book. The Bible, she wrote, was not the "only revelation of the Word of
God." Divine revelation would never cease, according to prophecies contained in the Bible itself. "Each new dispensation must meet with new
issues and conditions peculiar to its time." The Shakers, Barker stated,
had found a new revelation "through the advent of Mother's ministry."[130]

Music occupied a unique place in Mildred Barker's religious world.
Her "love of song" and her faithful memory for texts and tunes were the
vehicles for preserving important elements in the Believers' heritage.
Daniel W. Patterson spoke of her special musical role when he dedicated
his magnum opus to her. Barker wrote about Shaker songs and sang
them, too. One that she learned as a young child from Pauline Springer, a
gift song from "a little bird" during the Era of Manifestations, speaks its
simple message in a playful tune.

> Mother has come with a beautiful song,
> Ho ho talla me ho.
> She's come to bless her children dear,
> Ho ho talla me ho.
> And Christ your Savior will be near,
> Ho ho talla me ho.

The preservation of such songs reflects the traditionalism of the new
Shakerism at Sabbathday Lake.[131]

The "Home Notes" that Barker wrote through the years are even

more revealing of her formative influence on the spiritual direction of the
Maine family. They carry the reader into the family circle, which despite
all the publicity surrounding the contemporary Believers remains closed.
The pleasures of the family at Christmas, for example, radiate through the
reports. Christmas Eve included carol singing and a buffet supper around
the Christmas tree. "Christmas Day opened with a beautiful Christmas
Service," wrote Barker in 1966, "which brought home to us the fact that
Christmas is not fir trees, tinsel and gifts, but 'Christ within us.'" She continued, "He finds entrance only when, as at Mother Ann's injunction, we
follow and make 'reconciliation one with another.'" Barker did not sentimentalize her faith, for in the same issue she denounced the reenactment
of Shaker dances in the meetinghouse at Hancock Shaker Village. She
found such efforts to re-create that which was sacred to the Believers "dis-
tasteful" and urged "all lovers of the Shaker heritage" to write the individuals responsible for those "hurtful travesties."[132]

In the early 1970s, after the open rupture with Canterbury, Mildred
Barker began to write longer "Home Notes." In 1974, for example, she
published a day-by-day account of family activities from October through
December. Her record functions much like the family journals of the nineteenth century, and for at least a moment she opened a window into family
life. Barker wrote about the impact of the weather in Maine, the unending
daily chores, the struggle to maintain the buildings, the coming and going
of friends, the pleasures that visitors brought to the family, the centrality
of worship within the community, the affection expressed among the
Believers, their joy in sharing their faith with others, the delight they derived from good food and hospitality, and the apprehensions that arose
when outsiders represented the Shakers to the world. For those who wish
to read about the community life of the new Shakers, no more useful ave-
nue exists than Mildred Barker's "Home Notes" from the past several
decades.[133]

A number of outsiders have attempted to join cause with the ecumenical Shakers. One of the earliest spiritual colleagues of the Believers
at Maine was Robley Edward Whitson, at the time a Roman Catholic
priest and professor of theology at Fordham University. In the 1960s he
emerged as a friend and student of Shaker history, often visiting Sabbathday Lake to use the library. He had a hand in giving an award to Mildred
Barker in 1965 for her artistic contributions to the Shaker tradition. In
1967 Whitson established the United Institute for the purpose of "the renewal of Shakerism." He was driven by a vision of Christian unity and sincerely believed that "the Shaker Way of Life in Christ" might assist in

transforming "the Universal Church." A few years later, however, he became caught up in the conflict between the two villages. Whitson ultimately chose the side of Canterbury, and as a result he lost all favor in Maine. When he published a volume on Shaker spirituality in 1983, Gertrude Soule wrote the preface, in which she spoke of "a new world committed to the unity of the Truth." It was this volume that Michael Taylor, in defense of Sabbathday Lake, attacked as an "outrageous" reading of the Shaker tradition.[134]

The high point of Shaker ecumenism was in the spring of 1979 when Yale Divinity School in New Haven sponsored the symposium "Visible Theology: Emblems of Shaker Life, Art, Work, and Worship." The stated purpose of the gathering was "to see Shaker life and faith as an example of Christian life made visible." The conference was intended as an explicit critique of the tendency to allow the interest in furniture to obscure the life embodiments of the Shaker faith. Among the speakers were Believers (Theodore Johnson and Mildred Barker), Shaker scholars (June Sprigg, Daniel Patterson, and Robley Whitson), and historians from the Yale faculty (Roland Bainton and Sydney E. Ahlstrom). No Believers from Canterbury took part in the symposium. The program included a worship service led by the Shakers. This assembly provided the ecumenical Shakers a public forum and a new measure of intellectual respectability. The ideal of Christian unity, however, was not sufficiently powerful to bridge the gulf separating the two villages.[135]

The Shaker Myth: A National Treasure

There is a connection between the recent ecumenism of the society and the unprecedented popularity the Shakers are enjoying today. The members of the United Society have become both a curiosity and an object of admiration. Their reputation is higher than ever before. Television documentaries and news clips, cookbooks and coloring books, gift books and doctoral dissertations, how-to-do-it kits for those who are handy or "not so handy" and samplers for those who sew, antique shows and auctions, record-breaking crowds at historical restorations and museums, high-priced seminars for collectors and informal study groups for Shaker enthusiasts, newsletters in abundance and a national computer network devoted exclusively to Shakerism—these phenomena all confirm that Shakerism is a growth industry. Americans have taken this small society into their hearts and their homes. They have adopted the Shakers as "family" and are literally buying stock in the enterprise.[136]

In no area is this clearer than in the realm of material culture and collectibles. The Shaker antique and replica industries are thriving. Authentic Shaker pieces command astonishing prices at public auctions and through private transactions arranged by dealers, prices so high that few can contemplate owning them. The manufacturers of replicas (both those who sell finished products and those who provide kits) have put the look alikes, or the almost look alikes, within the reach of thousands. Old pieces as well as modern counterfeits enjoy the advantage of association with Shakerism. Their prices rise with the surge in Shakerana. Often it is impossible, even for the trained eye, to tell the two apart. The contemporary "gold standard" for pricing Shaker objects is the report of auctions that are watched more closely by dealers than the Dow Jones average. Faithful reproductions, too, slide higher with this index, and even the prices of the items advertised in the back pages of women's magazines and craft publications edge upward as the Shaker name works its magic. No wonder the lawyers for the Shaker Central Trust Fund have moved against individuals or firms who seek to use the Shaker label.[137]

Once feared, hated, and persecuted, now the Shakers are darlings of American popular culture. In 1986–1987 a major grant from United Technologies Corporation made possible a spectacular exhibit of Shaker objects at the Whitney Museum of American Art in New York City and the Corcoran Gallery of Art in the nation's capital. In his foreword to the catalog for the exhibition, Tom Armstrong, the director of the Whitney Museum, spoke of the "privilege" that organization had in presenting these examples of "indigenous American art." The chief executive officer of United Technologies declared his corporation's pride in being associated with this "extraordinary exhibition." June Sprigg, the curator of collections at Hancock Shaker Village and the author of the catalog, described how the "harmony of proportion" in Shaker pieces transformed "common objects into works of uncommon grace." Others have described the Believers' furniture as "religious furniture." One lover of Shaker things wrote, "One can feel the sincerity, the drive for perfection, the dedication to religious principles when studying a fingered box, a kitten-head basket, a whisk broom with its delicately tapered handle, a wall cabinet built to hold tools." She continued, "It's an experience not felt by everyone. But if one has felt it, that person understands the tremendous attraction things Shaker have for some of us." This collector was describing a religious experience—her religious experience, not that of the Shakers.[138]

Marjorie Procter-Smith, a theologian and student of Shaker history, has suggested that Shaker artifacts have become icons for many who are part of the world of Shaker. An icon is a material representation of a spiritual reality, a sign of something greater than itself. Icons possess a sacramental quality because they become the bearers of grace or power. They reveal, instruct, and inspire. Artifacts are useful in their own right; icons are treasured because they point to something beyond themselves. Shaker chairs were for sitting; oval boxes contained loose objects; clocks kept time; mitten forms shaped hand warmers; and wood planes cut molding. Yet today photographers etherealize these objects, and critics write about their spiritual qualities. Many contemporary commentators fail even to take note of how the Believers used these objects.[139]

Shaker artifacts have played a critical role in the midtwentieth-century popular response to the Believers. The Andrews synthesis, which still reigns in most circles, depends heavily on the interpretation of objects as primary texts. The beauty and simplicity of an oval box, for example, led Edward Andrews to conclude that the maker of the box had been committed to values consistent with beauty and simplicity. That form of argumentation is most persuasive when historical evidence is available to establish the actual motives and feelings of the artisan. If objects of comparable beauty and simplicity can be mass-produced for a commercial market or created by hired help who do not share the religious and communal world view of the Shakers, the spiritual interpretation must be called into question. In other words, spiritualizing material objects in the absence of explicit evidence is both poor history and suspect criticism.[140]

The love affair with the Shakers can be explained in part by the American preference for "things" rather than ideas. For those who are part of the world of Shaker it is far easier to praise the qualities of Shaker design than it is to explain coherently the distinctive religious ideas of the early Believers. In particular, since many of the Shakers' traditional beliefs are in fundamental opposition to twentieth-century values, there is little to praise in the estimation of most Americans. Celibacy has few advocates in modern America apart from those who are cloistered. The joint interest, or sharing of goods, is an offense to the cardinal principle on which the nation's economy rests, namely, the right of private property. Unquestioning obedience to higher authorities has lost much of its appeal in an age when officials entrusted with public responsibilities have violated those trusts. Humility, simplicity, and self-denial—what could be more out of step with the individualism and consumerism of the late twentieth century? Shaker objects, by contrast, are not offensive and do not talk back or tell of conflict and dissent. Chairs and candle stands, buckets and baskets, can be read like Rorschach blots—any way you wish. In these projections we reveal as much or more about ourselves as we do about the makers of the objects.

Another factor that explains the current love affair between the Shakers and Americans is the size of the society. It is easy to be hospitable to a sect that is so small. The handful of contemporary Shakers threatens no one socially, economically, or religiously. Not all sectarian groups reach this point in their evolution. In fact, many other nineteenth-century religious communities that have endured do not enjoy this public favor. Anti-Mormonism, for example, is a favorite pastime for many Americans. Christian Scientists are experiencing a wave of cultural criticism because of their distinctive pattern of spiritual healing. The Jehovah's Witnesses have never endeared themselves to the general population. The Shakers therefore are something of an exception. By midcentury most people looked on the Believers as harmless, if not pitiable.[141]

This cultural embrace of the Shakers has occurred during a time of tumultuous changes in American society. In the years following the Second World War, new fears arose, generated by the atom bomb and international communism. Other anxieties were triggered by the expansion of suburbia, the growth of inner-city ghettos, and the general drive for affluence. During the 1960s Americans quarreled over the conflict in Vietnam, the civil rights movement, the youth culture, and the War on Poverty. In the following years new social issues surfaced that held implications for everyone—the contest for equal rights for women, the debate concerning sexual mores, the concern for protecting the environment, and the crusade to preserve traditional family values. According to many observers, these and other problems have led to a crisis of self-confidence in America. Some commentators suggest that Americans have lost faith in their own world. Many are looking for new stability and security, for common values and principles they can respect. These factors also have been used to explain the resurgence of evangelical Christianity in the 1970s and 1980s.[142]

In these circumstances the popular image of the Shakers has much to offer those who wish for a better world. Fantasies about a society where peace and order prevail may help some modern Americans cope with social realities. A people who sought perfection in everything they did may be a useful model for those who wish to teach morality to the next generation. Visiting a postcard-perfect sanitized historical restoration may motivate some to work harder at protecting the environment from modern wastes. Imagining someone sweating profusely in the field or in the kitchen as they labor, humming to themselves the tune of "Simple Gifts," may inspire a few hourly workers to get through another shift. These and other projections all derive from a mood of collective nostalgia. Most Americans prefer this popular image of the Shakers of the past to the present reality of a ruptured society.[143]

Contemporary artists have reinforced this image of Shakerism. In Kathy Jacobsen's oil painting of the round barn at Hancock, even the cows look orderly and tidy. Nothing is out of place. Her depiction of the mob attack on the Believers at Shirley, Massachusetts, in 1783 sets the dark of the night and the violence of the attackers against the brightness and order of Elijah Wild's house. Constantine Kermes's Shakers stand tall and straight, the embodiment of righteousness and spiritual rigor. He leaves little to the imagination. The woman in *Shaker Harmony,* unemotional in her features, stands near a wood stove and a rocking chair holding oval boxes in her hands; a broom hangs from a peg board (fig. 54). Sister Karlyn Cauley annotates her Shaker-like drawings with poetic homilies. She titled one of a tree bearing leaves, needles, and fruit or blossoms all at the same time "The song that lives during the Heart of winter becomes the soul of spring." Only in Jack Gaughan's rendition of the hippie "New Shaker" do we find any questioning of the popular image.[144]

In the fall of 1989 *National Geographic* magazine published a stunning photographic essay on the Shakers. The author, to her credit, did not ignore the contemporary controversy among the Believers. And yet Cathy Newman could not escape repeating stereotypical judgments of the society. Brilliant glossy photographs of Shaker icons draw the reader from page to page—a stack of oval boxes on a candle stand, the round stone barn at Hancock, Joshua Bussell's map of the Alfred village, ladder-back chairs hung on pegs framing double doors in a dwelling house. Contemporary Believers posed for the camera, too—Mildred Barker and Frances Carr in a generational portrait, Bertha Lindsay with her dog, Arnold Hadd and Wayne Smith chatting on a meetinghouse bench. The quotable quotes included Ann Lee's "Hands to work and hearts to God," the text of "Simple Gifts," and Amy Bess Miller saying, "Even their *soil* was perfect. . . . Not a rock or a pebble in it." All of these predictable elements appeared under a subtitle that implied that the "boundary between heaven and earth" blurred in the Shaker society. According to her own account, Newman simply wanted to write a story that was both "informative" as well as "warm and human." She succeeded admirably, but she also restated the central myth of the world of Shaker; that is, that the Believers and what they produced are somehow greater than life—truly a national treasure.[145]

It may seem strange or even irreverent to include this discussion of the Shaker myth in a history of the United Society of Believers. Yet the fact is that the most powerful element within Shakerism today is the idealized image of the Shakers found in both popular culture and the academic

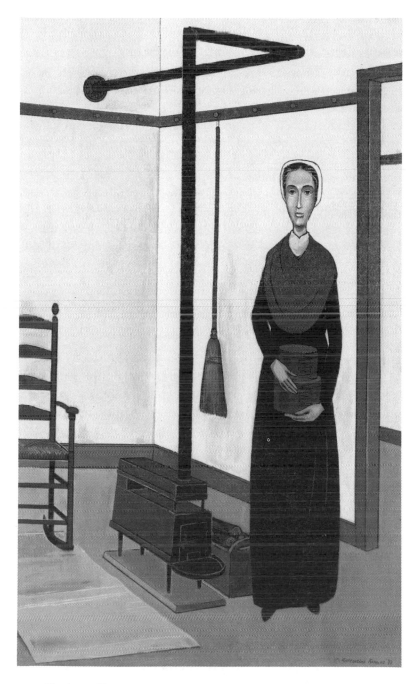

54. *Shaker Harmony*
Painting (1978) by Constantine Kermes. (Courtesy Constantine Kermes, Lancaster, Pennsylvania.)

world. One of the most direct statements of this perspective comes from the pen of the editor of the *Shaker Messenger,* Diana Van Kolken.

> For over two hundred years [the Shakers] have lived quietly in se-cluded communities, sharing a simple life and seeking perfection in everything they do, from cooking to carpentry.
>
> Dedicated to the glory of God, Shaker perfectionism can be seen in the serene beauty of their villages, in the gracefulness of their furniture and crafts, and in their qualities of character—devo-tion, thrift, humanity, ingenuity.
>
> America is a land of pioneers, dreamers and idealists, who dared to explore new frontiers and to create a new society. The Shakers were spiritual pioneers, and when we look at them, we see something of ourselves.

Van Kolken's comments are instructive. She would have us see the Shakers as simple and serene, idealistic and ingenious. Indeed, she writes, in the Shakers we see ourselves—pioneers and doers, "shakers and mov-ers" (so to speak)—and, she implies, we like what we see, both in them and in ourselves.[146]

One of the most respected voices in the world of Shaker today, bridg-ing the popular and professional spheres, is June Sprigg, who represents the second generation of scholars committed to the Andrews synthesis. Her introduction to the Whitney and Corcoran exhibition restated that perspective forcefully.

> The men and women who became Shakers were ordinary people, but the circumstances in which they chose to live produced an ex-traordinary opportunity for creativity. To a degree that we can scarcely imagine, the Shakers were free of distractions. They stayed at home, worked quietly, and gave a part of each day to meditation. They eliminated the tyranny of petty decisions. Communal life pro-vided uniform clothing, meals, a daily routine, and job assignments. It also freed them from financial worries. No one relied solely on his or her work for survival, and none made cheap second-rate goods to get by. With ample work space, the best of materials, and business-minded colleagues to market what they made, Shaker artisans could concentrate wholly on their work. Celibacy released Shakers from the demands of conventional marriage and parenthood.

The same sentiments echo through Sprigg's other publications.[147]

These observations are shared by many professional historians. In an award winning volume, one of the most respected historians of America's religious life called the Believers' communities "one of the American marvels. . . . In a simple Yankee way these Shaker villages were, in fact, idyllic: the wants of life were fully, even abundantly supplied; the clean-lined functional buildings, spotless interiors, gracefully practical furniture, wonderful cattle herds, fine herb gardens, and perfectly tended fields all witnessed to organizational, social, and economic success." The late Sydney E. Ahlstrom liked what he saw in the Shakers.[148]

This image, this ideal, remains powerful, especially to those of a serious religious bent. One inquirer in 1985 wrote, "In this terribly corrupt and disloyal order of life that exists in the 'outside world' I find that I turn to communities such as yours; and the Amish; and find a certain calm & peace to know that there are alternatives to the ever-quickening pace at which us 'city-dwellers' must live to escape from harms way." Another wrote, "My soul is 'hungry' and I very earnestly desire hearing from you." A few years earlier a correspondent, after complimenting the Shakers at Canterbury on their "pure selfless love," confessed, "To live quietly in my own house and to be a Shaker in my heart . . . to live with such pure intent seems to be the only intention worth devoting a life to."[149]

Unfortunately, Van Kolken, Sprigg, Ahlstrom, and many others drawn to the Shakers have chosen to look selectively at the story of the United Society. They have glossed over the enigmatic personalities and strange behavior of the founders. They have ignored the repressive qualities of the communal order and its coercive features. They have created an illusion of homogeneity within the society that never existed. They have failed to perceive the fault lines that have flexed repeatedly under the stress and strain of controversy within the society. Tensions existed between leaders and followers, men and women, young and old, easterners and westerners, progressives and traditionalists, intellectuals and charismatics, Canterbury and Sabbathday Lake. It is a truism (but one that stands up well under close historical examination) that the United Society of Believers has never been united in the simple sense that we have been led to believe. The contemporary conflict of the past two decades therefore is not without precedent in the Shaker experience. In fact, such problems have been recurrent throughout more than two hundred years of Shaker history in America. Even at its height as an organized society, factions and parties vied for power and influence. It is impossible to retain the romantic view of Shakerism after immersing oneself in the written records, especially the journals and the letters. The realities described in the primary sources destroy sentimental projections.

Some fear that if the Shakers are seen as human, they will somehow become less interesting, remarkable, or marketable. For that reason it is rare to discover an account of the Believers that includes "warts and all." The guides at restorations, museums, and even the remaining two villages sometimes contribute to this problem. Often they possess only minimal knowledge about the society. While visiting a restoration with a group of graduate students, I heard an interpreter fail to distinguish between the Amish and the Shakers. On a different occasion, another guide declared confidently, "All the Shakers are gone." It is equally troubling to discover that interpreters at each of the remaining villages do little to inform their visitors about the existence of the other family or the issues that separate the two communities. Although basic facts about Shaker beliefs may go unexplained, some guides are able to describe in detail the properties of the layers of paint on a doorsill, the construction and operation of the laundry facilities, or how silkworms led to the production of raw silk. The religious ideas of the early Shakers, by contrast, appear offensive to many. (Maybe that is why the meetinghouse at Canterbury has been filled with furniture and farm implements.) Avoiding such topics seems prudent.

The textbook accounts of Shaker history remain antiseptic, repeated over and over in documentaries, gift books, cookbooks, and every other medium. Yet it is a mistake to make the Shakers bigger than life. The story of the Believers is all the more engaging when they are viewed in their full humanity and when the society is evaluated according to categories derived from comparable social and religious organizations. The United Society has an unusual, even remarkable, record of achievements. It does not need to be sentimentalized or romanticized.

The time has also come to acknowledge the religious diversity within the Shaker experience. Unfortunately, in part as a result of the prodigious scholarly output of Edward Deming Andrews, we have been left with the impression that Shaker beliefs and religious practices were formulated by Ann Lee and perpetuated by her followers with a consistency that belies the historical process and the human condition. In this volume I have attempted to place the United Society within a developmental framework. Sects and churches, religious societies and communities, pass through stages. The context in which such development occurs is also in constant flux. Perhaps we need to remind ourselves that Ann Lee was a product of the eighteenth century and that Bertha Lindsay and Mildred Barker were shaped by their twentieth-century experiences.[150]

I am inclined to believe that the remaining Believers have a much better sense of the realities surrounding the Shaker experience than do most of the friends and patrons who have gathered around them. Life is difficult for members of the society today. They live under constant public scrutiny, and the attention they receive is out of proportion to the reality they represent. The contemporary Shakers are in danger of becoming symbols, living icons.

Occasionally, a protesting voice has been raised against the romantic image, suggesting an imbalance. But these have been rare in the world of Shaker. John Cornforth, an Englishman who visited several historic sites, spoke of the "tendency to turn Shakerism into a cult of early American virtue." He thought that the revival of interest in the Shakers was a direct result of the "sense of order and security" lacking in America, especially in the aftermath of the Watergate scandal. The filmmaker Tom Davenport, who produced a documentary entitled "The Shakers," suggested that Americans were "romanticizing" the Believers as they disappeared, because of a "swing back to Shaker-like values," including an interest in peace, personal religion, and communal living.[151]

Another kind of critique has come from creative writers who have been attracted to the figure of Ann Lee. Robert Peters presents episodes in poetic form from Lee's early life as he imagines it. He attempts to explain her sexual prohibitions through reflections on her psychological development and early experiences. His explicit tales are not in tune with the literary canons of the world of Shaker. Even more offensive to Shaker enthusiasts is a fictional account by the award-winning English novelist John Fowles. *A Maggot*, Fowles contends, is not a biography or a historical novel, though he chose to give the child born out of wedlock at the end of the account the name Ann Lee. A "convinced atheist," Fowles acknowledges that he was obsessed with the Shakers, to whom he considered dedicating the novel. He confesses "a very considerable affection and sympathy" for the society, which for most people, he suggests, means little more than "a furniture style and an ultra-puritanism." He admires their fortitude in the face of opposition. Fowles adds, "Something in Shaker thought and theology (not least in its holding that a Holy Trinity that has no female component cannot be holy), in its strange rituals and marvellously inventive practical life, in its richly metaphorical language and imaginative use of dancing and music, has always seemed to me to adumbrate the relation of fiction to reality." He points to a parallel with novelists, who "also demand a farfetched faith, quite often seemingly absurd in relation to normal reality." In a strange sort of way, Fowles seems to have caught the uniqueness of Shakerism more accurately than have many of the friends and patrons of the society.[152]

A most unusual critique of the world of Shaker appeared in 1986 in the single issue of the *Shaker Smalls Newsletter* put out by David Serette of Sebasco, Maine. In 1969 Serette was the manager of a radio and television station in Portland. He surfaced in the "Home Notes" at Sabbathday Lake in 1974 as Brother David, who was preoccupied with a photographic project. Two years later he was included in an official portrait of the Maine family. His newsletter of 1986 represents a strange amalgam of satire and sarcasm, bitterness and cynicism. *Shaker Smalls* is a spoof of the *Shaker Messenger*'s preoccupation with artifacts. But Serette also wrote a fictional account of a "Spiritual Pilgrim" arriving at the Maine village and settling in. (Such pilgrims typically, he wrote, have "religious commitment," but they have not found the right situation for it. They possess "only a foggy idea what Believers believe and are even more ignorant about day to day life in the Community.") Serette depicts the sisters as gullible and naive, taken in by this traveler, who soon is exercising undue influence on the family's life and activities. Several references to *MAD* magazine and the *National Lampoon* provide an obvious context for understanding this publication. He mocks the white caps of Canterbury and the yeas and nays at Sabbathday Lake. But perhaps *Shaker Smalls* is more significant than it first appears. It may be the most recent example of apostate literature. Serette appears disillusioned with the new Shakerism just as others before him did not always find full satisfaction in the society. That, too, is part of the Shaker reality.[153]

Looking to the Future

A century ago Charles Edson Robinson wrote a series of essays on communism and Shakerism, which were printed in altered form by the Shakers at Canterbury in 1893. In the preface to that volume the author made evident his sympathy with the society by such observations as "No Shaker was ever known to make a false statement in relation to any business transaction whatever." Robinson obviously had not encountered Nathan Sharp, Edward Chase, Isaiah Wentworth, Robert Valentine, or Joseph Slingerland in his researches. He also raised a question about the future of Shakerism, asking specifically whether the Believers would manage "as a body to pass the two hundredth mile-stone of their years," given the uncertainties of the late nineteenth century. His own answer was: "That Shakerism will endure the ravages of time as long as other Christian denominations exist, we see no reason to doubt." Robinson's prediction was nearly accurate. He could not be expected to anticipate the contemporary schism, for he had listed among the cardinal virtues of Shakerism the fact that it constituted "one household, one faith."[154]

The Shakers did, indeed, reach the two-hundredth anniversary of their founders' arrival in America, and they celebrated that bicentennial in 1974 with considerable fanfare. A major conference was held on 3–6 August in the meetinghouse at Sabbathday Lake, which included worship services, singing meetings, scholarly presentations, a photographic exhibition, and a tour of the other Maine villages. Theodore Johnson gave the last paper at the meeting, "a discourse on the gospel of Mother Ann, her thought, her philosophy and her hopes for the Shakers." The following week, on 11 August, the Believers at Canterbury sponsored a service of commemoration in the maple grove outside the meetinghouse. Gertrude Soule, Bertha Lindsay, and Miriam Wall all spoke to the assembly. The principal speaker, however, was Robley Whitson. The Concord, New Hampshire, choir provided music for the service. In October another bicentennial gathering took place in Cleveland, Ohio, cosponsored by the Shaker Historical Society and the Western Reserve Historical Society. It featured three days of lectures, tours, exhibits, and performances. Soule, Lindsay, and Wall also attended that meeting. On no occasion during the anniversary year were Believers from Canterbury and Sabbathday Lake present at the same event. And yet, surprisingly, there were no comments concerning this anomaly in any of the public reports of these activities. Those who were part of the world of Shaker preferred to imagine that the United Society of Believers was still united. They did not breach in public the code of silence concerning the Shaker schism.[155]

Historians make notoriously bad prophets, and I am no exception. When I began teaching more than twenty years ago, I recall predicting that before many more years were past my students would be reading the final chapter in the Shaker story. I based that judgment on widely available assessments of the likely fortunes of the few remaining members of the United Society. There seemed to be an irrefutable logic leading toward that outcome. Many other sectarian communities had followed the same passage from glory to extinction. At that point I had not met any of the Shakers personally, nor had I confronted their history in its complexity. I accepted without question the simple story of the rise and fall of the Believers. What I needed to hear was the retort of Mildred Barker to a tourist who "whisked through the small museum at the Shaker village, admiring the spare, elegant furniture. 'Too bad no Shakers are left,' he clucked. '*I'm* left,' she snapped."[156]

Much has changed since 1970, and a different assessment of future prospects for the Shakers is now in order. The religious revival at Sabbath-day Lake, the acceptance of younger members into that community, the emergence of a nationwide network of Shaker friends and benefactors, the continued growth of the commercial side of Shakerism—these and other factors have altered dramatically the society's prospects. But it would be equally uninformed and naive to predict a rosy future for the Shakers or a period of rapid growth. At present, the society is walking a fine line be-tween the possibility of extinction as a religious organization and an un-certain, but not necessarily gloomy future.[157]

The cast of main characters in this drama has been reduced dras-tically over the past few years. Four leading Shakers have died, one unex-pectedly, three in the natural course of events. All were principals in the controversy between the two villages. On 20 April 1986, Theodore Johnson, a "portly man," died suddenly and without warning at the age of fifty-five, victim of a cerebral hemorrhage. His death "came as a total shock" to the Sabbathday Lake family and friends. The community had steeled itself for the eventual loss of Mildred Barker because of her ad-vanced age, but Johnson's demise was an unanticipated blow. He had come to personify the revival of Shakerism in Maine. Johnson was Sab-bathday Lake's principal public spokesperson, its historian, theologian, charismatic leader, and pastor. His loss to the family and community was immense. In her published eulogy Mildred Barker wrote, "The [Shaker] community had not had such a theologian since the passing of Elder Al-onzo Hollister of Mt. Lebanon, N.Y. in 1914. . . . What a gatherer of souls Brother Ted was! His vitality and zeal for the gospel and his home so con-sumed him that he soon became the brightest star of this home. He was kind, lowly, humble and loving to all. No book could contain all his good works." Friends of the Shakers wrote letters of tribute and comfort to the family. "He was a great man amongst a great people," Michael Taylor stated. "We know that he is gone to be with God, with Jesus and Mother in the kingdom," wrote Stephen Marini. Johnson was buried in the commu-nity cemetery. None of the elderly Shakers from Canterbury attended the funeral.[158]

Two years later, at Canterbury on 11 June 1988, Gertrude Soule died in her sleep at the age of ninety-three. She had been a member of the so-ciety for more than eight decades, having been placed at Sabbathday Lake as a child following the death of her mother. Soule had been part of the ministry since her appointment in 1957. She served with Emma B. King during the years when the Shaker Central Trust Fund was established and when the membership of the society was officially closed. Yet those were not the memories cited at the service held in the dwelling house chapel or in later eulogies. Soule was remembered for her love of children, birds, and the seacoast and for her "sparkling sense of humor and a bent toward whimsy." After coming to Canterbury from Sabbathday Lake in 1971, she had spent long hours with Bertha Lindsay, greeting the stream of tourists who visited the village. Her religious faith was simple and not articulated often in print. She once said, "Our mission is to live as near as we can to Christ's teachings." Frances Carr and Arnold Hadd from the Maine community attended Soule's funeral. She was buried in the cemetery at Canterbury.[159]

On 25 January 1990, Mildred Barker died at Sabbathday Lake at the age of ninety-two, having been ill with cancer for several months. Barker had been a member of the society for more than eighty-five years, first as a resident at the Alfred village. She had served as trustee since 1950. Personable yet strong willed, she was regarded as the spiritual leader of the Believers in Maine. During the last thirty years of her life she became something of a celebrity because of media attention. She made substantial contributions to the study of Shaker history and culture through her writings, her recollections of the musical heritage of the society, and her support of the library at Sabbathday Lake. It was she who led the Maine Believers through the difficult years following the rupture with the parent ministry. Frances Carr declared Barker "the greatest Shaker who ever lived." Others remembered "Sister Mildred" lifting her voice in simple songs. She was buried in the cemetery at Sabbathday Lake.[160]

The last of the four leaders to die was Bertha Lindsay, the sole surviving member of the Shaker ministry. She died on 3 October 1990 at Canterbury at the age of ninety-three. Orphaned as a young child, Lindsay had been placed with the New Hampshire Believers in 1905 when she was seven years old. She was educated in the community's school. After turning twenty-one, she signed the church covenant. Lindsay spent many years cooking and baking for the Believers. From 1944 to 1958 she supervised the community's fancy work trade. In 1967 she became the second eldress at Canterbury, and three years later she succeeded Marguerite Frost as the Canterbury eldress and also became a member of the parent ministry. She served in that capacity with Gertrude Soule, who was her close companion for nearly two decades. Lindsay's personal charm and remarkable personality, despite blindness after 1970 and failing health, were her most distinguishing marks. She always found time to talk with schoolchildren or to greet visitors at the village. She played a central role in the formation of the museum at Canterbury, which became Shaker Village,

Inc. Declared "the heart and soul of the Village" in one tribute, Lindsay never swerved from her confidence in the society's principles. By her own request, there was no funeral or public ceremony following her death. Staff members, trustees, and volunteers honored her with "a private memorial service" and by ringing the village bell. That service was attended by Frances Carr, Arnold Hadd, and Leonard Brooks from Sabbathday Lake.[161]

The deaths of Johnson, Soule, Barker, and Lindsay within five years marked a major turning point in the story of contemporary Shakerism. By early 1991 only one Shaker sister, Ethel Hudson, remained at Canterbury; she was ninety-four (fig. 55). In addition, one uncovenanted woman had stayed at the village for many years. In 1991 there were eight Shakers residing at Sabbathday Lake. Four were sisters who joined the society before the membership rolls were closed: Elsie McCool, Minnie Green, Marie Burgess, and Frances Carr. Two of them are in their eighties, two in their sixties. There are also two recent additions to the sisterhood, Margaret Haskell and June Carpenter. The two brothers at the village are Arnold Hadd and Wayne Smith, aged thirty-four and twenty-eight, respectively, in 1991 (fig. 56). Both have been part of the family for more than a decade. The ministerial succession that began with Joseph Meacham ended with Lindsay's death. Frances Carr and Arnold Hadd have assumed leadership responsibilities at Sabbathday Lake.[162]

It is always difficult to make adjustments following the death of family members. The Shakers are no exception to that human rule. At Canterbury there is no longer a functioning family of Believers. Ethel Hudson, who has lived as a recluse for years, is directly dependent on services provided by the staff hired by the nonprofit corporation Shaker Village, Inc., which was formed in 1969. The Canterbury family is one step away from extinction, an end to which Soule, Lindsay, Hudson, and the lawyers for the Shaker Central Trust Fund reconciled themselves.[163]

Sabbathday Lake faces perhaps the greater challenge. Mildred Barker's death was sad, but not tragic. Family and friends felt deeply the pain of loss. But the Shakers have never regarded death as unnatural or unacceptable. The death of Johnson, however, was different because it was assumed that he would be centrally involved in the life of the community for several decades. He played a role in the society unsurpassed by any other contemporary Believer. Johnson, for example, was president of the nonprofit corporation the United Society of Shakers, which was formed in 1971 in response to the conflict with Canterbury. His death created a vacuum at the head of the family's organization and activities. The Maine

55. Ethel Hudson
Hudson was brought to the village at Canterbury, New Hampshire, at the age of seven.
Now in her nineties, she is the last Shaker at Canterbury. (Photograph by Sam Abell ©
1989 National Geographic Society.)

56. Arnold Hadd and Wayne Smith
These Shaker brothers are seated in the meetinghouse at Sabbathday Lake, Maine.
(Photograph by Sam Abell © 1989 National Geographic Society.)

Shakers faced major difficulties if other family members were unable to step immediately into the breach created by Johnson's death.[164]

Frances Carr brings to her task of leadership strength of character, religious commitment, seemingly boundless energy, and a determination to carry Shakerism into the future (fig. 57). She was one of the most ardent backers of Theodore Johnson and of the policy of admitting new members to the community. For years she worked in the shadow of both Barker and Johnson. Yet she has never minced words. In 1974 at the age of forty-seven she said, "I think some people wish we would just pass away, so they could say what they wished about Shakerism without fear of contradiction from us. . . . Ten years ago, people came to Sabbathday with an interest in our antique chairs and gadgets. Now, people come with an interest in the Shaker way." Carr's many skills are complemented by a strong will, a deep loyalty to family and place, and maternal instincts that manifest themselves on both the interpersonal and the organizational level. She is a capable woman on whose shoulders now rests an immense responsibility. Her credentials as a bona fide Shaker have never been questioned. She has demonstrated her abilities in the kitchen and the meetinghouse, the Office and the lecture hall. Few ambassadors of Shakerism have been more effective in reaching those outside the society with the essence of the community's experience. Carr has now been set apart by circumstances beyond her control. It appears that she will lead the society into the twenty-first century, stewarding its assets, protecting its traditions, and nurturing its members.[165]

In her role as an eldress—whether she is called that or not—Frances Carr will be assisted by other members of the family. The contributions of Marie Burgess will be quiet ones and may go almost unnoticed. That is often the Shaker way. Arnold Hadd will likely assume an increasingly important role as a spokesperson for the community. He has already begun to write in defense of the society's history and traditions, his essays appearing in the *Shaker Quarterly*. He will take over the role of society historian and theologian. Wayne Smith is the prime mover in the family's agricultural activities. Although neither Hadd nor Smith has the professional training or the breadth of life experience that Johnson possessed, in their contrasting ways, one more reflective, the other more gregarious, both bring to the society needed skills, religious dedication, and love for the family.[166]

And a family it is! Six months before Mildred Barker's death, the following typical report was published in the *Shaker Quarterly*.

57. Mildred Barker and Frances A. Carr
Mildred Barker, seated, and Frances Carr, standing, photographed in the dwelling at
Sabbathday Lake, Maine, in front of the portrait of two earlier sisters at the village.
(Photograph by Sam Abell © 1989 National Geographic Society.)

Sister Mildred, who just celebrated her 85th anniversary in the Shaker faith, may be working in her office or overseeing a crew of floor sanders who are laboriously—and noisily—refinishing the main floor hallway. Brother Arnold is probably in the cellar print shop, printing material for the big conference to be held here this month.

Sister Marie is likely to be baking her terrific bread and Sister Minnie making potholders, while Meg is no doubt in the garden. Brother Wayne may be caring for the sheep or the herb and tea business, where his brother Stephen works. And Sister Frances? Well, she's everywhere!

Here is yet another version of the myth. In spite of all these willing hands and hearts, the years ahead will be a severe test for the Maine Believers.[167]

Other parties on the scene will continue to influence the future course of events for Shakerism. Staff members at both villages have made major investments in these respective causes, rendering frontline assistance to the Believers in both temporal and spiritual affairs. At Canterbury the most prominent supporter, until his retirement in the autumn of 1990, was Charles "Bud" Thompson, who was appointed the first director of Shaker Village in 1971. For years he had been a confidant of the ministry and a primary interpreter of the site. Some observers have suggested that Thompson played a role at Canterbury somewhat similar to that of Johnson in Maine. At Sabbathday Lake, Leonard Brooks, a long-time associate of the Believers and a kindred spirit, was appointed director of the museum in 1987. He now functions centrally in the administration of the Maine village. Trained professionals work in the museums and libraries at both Canterbury and Sabbathday Lake.[168]

At both sites a circle of friends, supporters, and religious inquirers form a much-extended family stretching beyond the confines of the Believers themselves. These associates, grouped at both villages into dues-paying organizations, assist in a variety of ways. They raise funds for particular causes and donate hundreds of hours of volunteer labor in the kitchen, shops, and gardens as well as at special events, whether it be conducting a conference or painting fences. They spread the word about the Shakers in their own locations and sometimes function directly as apologists for the Believers. Some of these friends associate exclusively with one or another village, thereby taking sides in the conflict between the Shakers. This national network of supporters is without parallel among other religious groups in America. The friends of the Shakers are often

committed religious individuals who are active in their own denominations, and yet also drawn to Shakerism. This is in part because the contemporary Believers are extremely effective apostles for their faith. For
many outsiders, a visit to a Shaker village constitutes a spiritual retreat, a
moment of internal refreshment.[169]

The world of Shaker also has a stake in the future of the society. It is
convenient, though not essential, for antique dealers and collectors to
point to a few remaining Shakers. The Believers provide an interesting
topic for conversation with potential customers. As long as wealthy individuals in America, looking for ways to invest their funds, are attracted to
the beauty of early American artifacts, the market for Shaker items likely
will remain strong. Quality antiques gain value with time. It is less clear
that the reproduction, replica, and craft markets will sustain themselves in
the same manner in the future. These enterprises are more directly dependent on economic and cultural cycles and a continuing interest in early
American decor. The rhythms of popular culture are subject to passing
fancy in a way that the value of collectible antiques is not. The future prospects of a considerable part of the world of Shaker are therefore perhaps
less secure than many involved in it might wish.[170]

The academic study of Shakerism is also subject to shifting tides of
interest. The cultural preoccupation with communitarian living in the
1960s brought increased attention to Shakerism and other historic communal experiments. The feminist movement of the 1980s brought the Believers new scrutiny from those concerned with the role of women in the
society. It is impossible to predict what new scholarly inquiries will surface
next and how they will affect academic research on the Shakers. However,
a variety of professional organizations and informal study groups are committed to the examination of communal societies, specifically the Shakers.
These groups are likely to sustain a high level of interest into the foresee-
able future. The immense body of resources available for the study of
Shakerism, much of which has not been exhausted by researchers, will
also encourage continuing scholarly investments. In addition, the growing
professionalization of museums and library staffs augurs well for future
efforts in the field.[171]

The most puzzling and unpredictable element in the future of
Shakerism is the role of the Shaker Central Trust Fund and the attorneys
who protect those assets. Because the documents under which the trust
was constituted are not public, outsiders can only speculate about these
matters. The primary intention of the trust, reportedly, is to provide for
the needs of the covenanted sisters. When that responsibility is fulfilled,

the balance of the assets is to be used to support historic preservation of the Shaker sites and understanding of the Believers' traditions. Many questions remain, however. Will the attorneys for the trust attempt to take possession of Sabbathday Lake after the last covenanted sister is dead? Will the new Shakers at that location be given any support from the funds? Will the conflict that began in the 1960s finally be laid to rest, or will a protracted legal struggle ensue?

There is a tradition among the Shakers that Ann Lee, looking to the future, spoke about a time when the number of Believers would decline to the point that those remaining would not be sufficient to bury their dead. At that moment in history, it is said, there will be a new outpouring of interest in the Shaker gospel and the society will be reborn. Both Canterbury and Sabbathday Lake have seized on this tradition to support their respective projections into the future. Canterbury has employed the account to buttress its belief that the society's fortunes lie in God's hands, and that therefore the Believers must trust the decision of the ministry. As Bertha Lindsay said, "We're not surprised how few Shakers are left. . . . Prophecy said our numbers would diminish. Still, we keep order. The hands drop off, but the work goes on." Sabbathday Lake regards this prophecy as one being fulfilled in their own community, and therefore they move confidently into the future. The Maine Believers have written, "Our Blessed Mother taught that salvation unto souls comes by generations and that so long as one person in a generation had the saving inner knowledge of the Gospel the work would go on." These conflicting interpretations demonstrate that such sayings can be used in more than one way.[172]

It is tempting to draw parallels between the situation today and that in 1774. The inauspicious beginnings of the society in America involved a handful of Believers gathered around a powerful woman. Over the course of several years they rose above adverse circumstances, not without defections, and managed to plant the seed of their faith in the new land. Frances Carr is not Ann Lee, nor does she aspire to be thought of as a founder. But she and the youthful family members at Sabbathday Lake hold in their hands the future of the United Society of Believers. The world of Shaker, by contrast, lies beyond their control, as do the assets, for the moment, of the trust fund. The image of the Shakers seemingly belongs to anyone who wishes to use it. There is no longer any doubt that there will be Shakers in America for many years to come.

ABBREVIATIONS

The abbreviations below refer to Shaker manuscript collections

DeWint
Henry Francis du Pont Winterthur Museum, Winterthur, Delaware

DLC
Library of Congress, Washington, D.C.

InU
Indiana University, Bloomington

KyHM
Mercer County Historical Society, Harrodsburg, Kentucky

KyLoF
Filson Club, Louisville, Kentucky

KySP
Shakertown at Pleasant Hill, Harrodsburg, Kentucky

KyU
University of Kentucky, Lexington

MeSl
United Society of Shakers, Sabbathday Lake, Maine

MPH
Hancock Shaker Village, Inc., Pittsfield, Massachusetts

MWiW
Williams College Library, Williamstown, Massachusetts

N
New York State Library, Albany

NhCa
Shaker Village, Canterbury, New Hampshire

NN
New York Public Library, New York City

NOC
Emma B. King Library, Shaker Museum, Old Chatham, New York

NSyU
Syracuse University, Syracuse, New York

OClWHi
Western Reserve Historical Society, Cleveland, Ohio

OHi
Ohio State Historical Society, Columbus

NOTES

Preface

1. Edward Deming Andrews and Faith Andrews, *Religion in Wood: A Book of Shaker Furniture* (Bloomington: Indiana University Press, 1966), xiii; transcript, "The Shakers: Hands to Work, Hearts to God" (New York: Non Fiction Television, 1984), 2.

2. Edward Deming Andrews, *The People Called Shakers: A Search for the Perfect Society* (New York: Oxford University Press, 1953), reissued in an enlarged edition (New York: Dover, 1963); Priscilla J. Brewer, *Shaker Communities, Shaker Lives* (Hanover, N.H.: University Press of New England, 1986); Daniel W. Patterson, *The Shaker Spiritual* (Princeton: Princeton University Press, 1979); Clarke Garrett, *Spirit Possession and Popular Religion: From the Camisards to the Shakers* (Baltimore: Johns Hopkins University Press, 1987). Marguerite Fellows Melcher, *The Shaker Adventure* (Princeton: Princeton University Press, 1941), is a sympathetic portrait, not a general history.

3. Chronology plays an important role in this account. Subjective criteria—success and failure, prosperity and decline—too often have governed the periodization of the society's history. I have attempted to eliminate the need for religious or cultural consensus by selecting significant public events, such as the deaths of leaders and the opening or closing of major villages, as dividing points. The division of the story into five parts allows each to be read independently as well as in continuity across time. In the citation of primary sources, the original spelling has been retained. *Sic* is used sparingly.

Part One

1. *New-York Gazette and the Weekly Mercury,* 8 Aug. 1774, pp. 1, 4; *New-York Journal; or the General Advertiser,* 18 Aug. 1774, p. 4; Charles Royster, *A Revolutionary People at War: The Continental Army and American Character, 1775–1783* (Chapel Hill: University of North Carolina Press, 1979), 25–53.

2. One later reference to Lee's revelation appears in Benjamin S. Youngs, *The Testimony of Christ's Second Appearing Containing a General Statement of All Things Pertaining to the Faith and Practice of the Church of God in this Latter-day* (Lebanon, Ohio: Press of John M'Clean, 1808), 24 (hereafter cited as Youngs, *Testimony*).

3. See Suggestions for Further Reading.

4. David S. Lovejoy, *Religious Enthusiasm in the New World: Heresy to Revolution* (Cambridge: Harvard University Press, 1985). 1. The classic description of enthusiasm within Western Christianity is Ronald A. Knox, *Enthusiasm: A Chapter in the History of Religion with Special Reference to the Seventeenth and Eighteenth Centuries* (New York: Oxford University Press, 1950). The literature on the definition of sectarianism is vast. The pioneering work of Ernst Troeltsch, published originally in Germany and translated by Olive Wyon as *The Social Teaching of the Christian Churches* (London: George Allen and Unwin, 1931), sets the terms for discussion. On the English background, see Christopher Hill, *The World Turned Upside Down: Radical Ideas during the English Revolution* (New York: Viking, 1972). The tension between a sect and its surroundings is developed by Benton Johnson, "On Church and Sect," *American Sociological Review* 28 (1963): 539–549, and William Sims Bainbridge and Rodney Stark, "Sectarian Tension," *Review of Religious Research* 22 (1980): 105–124.

5. Extracts from the Register of Baptisms at the cathedral, cited in William E. A. Axon, *Lancashire Gleanings* (Manchester: Tubbs, Brook, and Chrystal, 1883), 80; photocopy of the parish record of Manchester reproduced in Flo Morse, *The Shakers and the World's People* (New York: Dodd, Mead, 1980), 12; Cathedral Burial Registry cited in

Axon, *Lancashire Gleanings*, 82. The surnames Standerin, Stanley, and Standley are all linked with Lee's husband.

6. *Virginia Gazette*, 9 Nov. 1769; p. 1; Edward Chamberlayne, *Angliae Notitia; or, The Present State of England; with Divers Remarks upon the Ancient State thereof* (1694), cited in the *Oxford English Dictionary*, ed. James Augustus Henry Murray, 13 vols. (Oxford: Clarendon, 1933), 9:605.

7. *Virginia Gazette*, 9 Nov. 1769, p. 1.

8. Records of the constables of Manchester, cited in William E. A. Axon, "The Early Shakers in Manchester," *Manifesto* 22 (1892):193–194.

9. Ibid.; photocopy of the records of the Quarter Sessions from *Prescott's Manchester Journal*, 31 July 1773, reproduced in Morse, *Shakers*, 14.

10. For the relation between enthusiasm and antinomianism, see Lovejoy, *Religious Enthusiasm*, 35–38, and Philip F. Gura, *A Glimpse of Sion's Glory: Puritan Radicalism in New England, 1620–1660* (Middletown, Conn.: Wesleyan University Press, 1984), 49–92.

11. The most instructive account of early Quakerism is George Fox, *The Journal of George Fox*, ed. John L. Nickalls, rev. ed. (Cambridge: Cambridge University Press, 1952). For changes within Quakerism, see Hugh Barbour, *The Quakers in Puritan England* (New Haven: Yale University Press, 1964), 234–256, and Richard T. Vann, *The Social Development of English Quakerism, 1655–1755* (Cambridge: Harvard University Press, 1969), 197–208. Contemporary scholars differ over the question of Quaker influence on the Shakers. See Lawrence Foster, *Religion and Sexuality: Three American Communal Experiments of the Nineteenth Century* (New York: Oxford University Press, 1981), 24, who regards it as a major factor, and Clarke Garrett, *Spirit Possession and Popular Religion: From the Camisards to the Shakers* (Baltimore: Johns Hopkins University Press, 1987), 141–142, who makes a more persuasive case for "broad currents of prophetism" and similar forms of piety.

12. Hillel Schwartz, *The French Prophets: The History of a Millenarian Group in Eighteenth-Century England* (Berkeley: University of California Press, 1980), 71.

13. Ibid., 211, 122–123, 229; Garrett, *Spirit Possession*, 35–58.

14. Schwartz, *French Prophets*, 212 n. 41; Garrett, *Spirit Possession*, 141–147. The Whitefieldian connection is a basic premise of Stephen A. Marini, *Radical Sects of Revolutionary New England* (Cambridge: Harvard University Press, 1982).

15. Many Shaker traditions concerning the English phase of the society's history are of limited usefulness, though they are repeated often in print. See Edward Deming Andrews, *The People Called Shakers: A Search for the Perfect Society*, 2d ed. (New York: Dover, 1963), 3–13. Andrews expresses caution about these legends, but Garrett is even clearer, calling many of the stories "completely untrue or considerably elaborated." *Spirit Possession*, 149–150.

16. *Rivington's New-York Gazetteer; or, The Connecticut, Hudson's River, New Jersey, and Quebec Weekly Advertiser*, 11 Aug. 1774, p. 3.

17. Van Rensselaer land tax list of 1779, original in the New York State Library, Albany, photocopy reproduced in Dorothy M. Filley, *Recapturing Wisdom's Valley: The Watervliet Shaker Heritage, 1775–1975*, ed. Mary L. Richmond (Albany, N.Y.: Albany Institute of History and Art, 1975), 11–12, 20–21.

18. See Youngs, *Testimony,* and Rufus Bishop and Seth Y. Wells, eds., *Testimonies of the Life, Character, Revelations and Doctrines of Our Ever Blessed Mother Ann Lee, and the Elders with Her; Through Whom the Word of Eternal Life was Opened in this Day of Christ's Second Appearing: Collected from Living Witnesses* (Hancock, Mass.: J. Tallcott and J. Deming, 1816) (hereafter cited as Bishop and Wells, eds., *Testimonies*).

19. Bishop and Wells, eds., *Testimonies,* 5–6, 10–11, 50–52.

20. Ibid., iii–iv.

21. See Youngs, *Testimony,* 6–8, for reasons why the earliest Shakers did not publish in their defense. The most sophisticated and satisfactory reconstruction of this period is Garrett, *Spirit Possession,* 140–159.

22. The variety of available documentary materials is evident in Mary L. Richmond, *Shaker Literature: A Bibliography,* 2 vols. (Hanover, N.H.: University Press of New England, 1977), and Kermit J. Pike, *A Guide to Shaker Manuscripts in the Library of the Western Reserve Historical Society* (Cleveland: Western Reserve Historical Society, 1974). The Shaker Museum and Library at Old Chatham, New York, possesses a piece of dress cloth associated with Ann Lee. The Fruitlands Museum at Harvard, Massachusetts, has a rocking chair linked with her. See Morse, *Shakers,* 50, for a picture of the chair.

23. Youngs, *Testimony,* 26; James Thacher, *Military Journal of the American Revolution* (Hartford, Conn.: Hurlbut, Williams, 1862), 141–142, cited in Garrett, *Spirit Possession,* 162; *Boston Gazette,* 2 Nov. 1778, p. 1.

24. Filley, *Recapturing Wisdom's Valley,* 11–12.

25. David J. Goodall, "New Light on the Border: New England Squatter Settlements in New York during the American Revolution" (Ph.D. diss., State University of New York at Albany, 1984), 3, Marini, *Radical Sects,* 52–53; James West Davidson, *The Logic of Millennial Thought: Eighteenth-Century New England* (New Haven: Yale University Press, 1977); Ruth H. Bloch, *Visionary Republic: Millennial Themes in American Thought, 1756–1800* (Cambridge: Cambridge University Press, 1985).

26. Valentine Rathbun, *An Account of the Matter, Form, and Manner of a New and Strange Religion, Taught and Propagated by a Number of Europeans, living in a Place called Nisqueunia, in the State of New-York* (Providence, R.I.: Bennett Wheeler, 1781), 4. For a fuller description of the social context, see Patricia U. Bonomi, *A Factious People: Politics and Society in Colonial New York* (New York: Columbia University Press, 1971), and Goodall, "New Light."

27. Theodore E. Johnson, ed., "Biographical Account of the Life, Character, & Ministry of Father Joseph Meacham the Primary Leader in Establishing the United Order of the Millennial Church by Calvin Green 1827," *Shaker Quarterly* 10 (1970): 25–26.

28. Johnson, ed., "Biographical Account," 26–27; Marini, *Radical Sects,* 47–48; Garrett, *Spirit Possession,* 169–171.

29. See Bishop and Wells, eds., *Testimonies,* 17, 39, 134, 166, 174, 228, 296, 365–366.

30. Ibid., 73–74; Garrett, *Spirit Possession,* 167–169.

31. Goodall, "New Light," 225–235; Royster, *Revolutionary People,* 105–106; Victor Hugo Paltsits, ed., *Minutes of the Commissioners for Detecting and Defeating Conspiracies in the State of New York,* 3 vols. (Albany: State of New York, 1909–1910).

32. Paltsits, ed., *Minutes* 2:452–453, 461.

33. Ibid., 469–471.

34. Ibid., 504, 569–571, 573–575, 589; George Clinton, *Public Papers of George Clinton, First Governor of New York, 1777–1795—1801–1804,* 10 vols. (Albany: State of New York, 1899–1914), 6:420–421.

35. Paltsits, ed., *Minutes* 2:592.

36. Rathbun, *Account,* 3. On Rathbun, see Isaac Backus, *The Diary of Isaac Backus,* ed. William G. McLoughlin, 3 vols. (Providence: Brown University Press, 1979), 2:1094.

37. Rathbun, *Account,* 17–19. For a general statement on the value of apostate testimonies, see Garrett, *Spirit Possession,* 197.

38. Rathbun, *Account,* 3, 8, 12, 20–23. On the Separate Baptists, see C. C. Goen, *Revivalism and Separatism in New England, 1740–1800* (New Haven: Yale University Press, 1962), 208–257, and William G. McLoughlin, *New England Dissent, 1630–1833: The Baptists and the Separation of Church and State,* 2 vols. (Cambridge: Harvard University Press, 1971), 1:419–488.

39. Rathbun, *Account,* 4, 9.

40. Ibid., 3–5.

41. Ibid., 5–7, 12.

42. Ibid., 4.

43. Ibid., 7–8.

44. Ibid., 10–11, 13; Angell Matthewson, "Reminiscences in the Form of a Series of Thirty-nine Letters to his Brother Jeffrey," NN, Letter VII.

45. Rathbun, *Account,* 11. On the relation between rituals and the social order, see Mary Douglas, *Purity and Danger: An Analysis of Concepts of Pollution and Taboo* (London: Routledge and Kegan Paul, 1966), 69, 94, 128.

46. Bishop and Wells, eds., *Testimonies,* 82.

47. Ibid., 82–83.

48. See John R. Alden, *A History of the American Revolution* (New York: Alfred A. Knopf, 1969), 457–492.

49. See Margot Mayo, "The Incredible Journey of Mother Ann," *Shaker Quarterly* 2 (1962):42–52, and Garrett, *Spirit Possession,* 177–194. Mayo accepts the account in the *Testimonies* as historically reliable; Garrett is more critical of that source in his reconstruction of the journey. Useful information about the missionary journey is also contained in Matthewson, "Reminiscences," Letters V–VII.

50. Bishop and Wells, eds., *Testimonies,* 82–204.

51. Ibid., 309, 338, 343–344, 353; Marini, *Radical Sects,* 89–90.

52. Rathbun, *Account,* 6–7, 12; Bishop and Wells, eds., *Testimonies,* 30, 34, 137, 257, 344, 348–351. See also Jean McMahon Humez, "Images of Female Power in Early Shaker Oral Tradition and Literature" (paper presented at the National Historic Communal Societies Conference, Canterbury, N.H., October 1986).

53. Shaker traditions concerning persecution are illustrated in Bishop and Wells, eds., *Testimonies,* 94–96, 115–120, 151–152, 157–158.

54. Ibid., 128–129.

55. Ibid., 85ff., 134; Marini, *Radical Sects,* 50–51; Isaac Backus, *A History of New England. With Particular Reference to the Denomination of Christians called Baptists,* ed. David Weston, 2d ed., 2 vols. (Newton, Mass.: Backus Historical Society, 1871), 2:462–463.

56. Bishop and Wells, eds., *Testimonies*, 85; Edward R. Horgan, *The Shaker Holy Land: A Community Portrait* (Harvard, Mass.: Harvard Common Press, 1982), 20–24. See "Mother Ann Lee's Square House for Sale: Historic Site Not Suitable for Museums," *Shaker Spirit* 1 (May 1989):6.

57. Bishop and Wells, eds., *Testimonies*, 90 92, 100 101, 108; Sheila Culbert, "Sturdy Beggars and the Worthy Poor: Poverty in Massachusetts, 1750–1820" (Ph.D. diss., Indiana University, 1985); Douglas L. Jones, "The Strolling Poor: Transiency in Eighteenth-Century Massachusetts," *Journal of Social History* 8 (1975):28–54.

58. Bishop and Wells, eds., *Testimonies*, 94–96, 115–120, 151–152, 157–158, 162, 184–187, 200. For more on mobs in the revolutionary era, see Alfred F. Young, ed., *The American Revolution: Explorations in the History of American Radicalism* (DeKalb: Northern Illinois University Press, 1976).

59. Bishop and Wells, eds., *Testimonies*, 202.

60. The requirements for successful communitarian societies are described theoretically in Rosabeth Moss Kanter, *Commitment and Community: Communes and Utopias in Sociological Perspective* (Cambridge: Harvard University Press, 1972).

61. Historians have paid too little attention to this source problem. See, e.g., Andrews, *People Called Shakers*, 21–25. One noteworthy exception to this pattern of neglect is Garrett, *Spirit Possession*, esp. pp. 149–150.

62. The collection of testimonies edited by Bishop and Wells was supplemented more than a decade later by *Testimonies Concerning the Character and Ministry of Mother Ann Lee and the First Witnesses of the Gospel of Christ's Second Appearing: Given by Some of the Aged Brethren and Sisters of the United Society, Including a Few Sketches of Their Own Religious Experience*, ed. Seth Y. Wells and Calvin Green (Albany, N.Y.: Packard and Van Benthuysen, 1827).

63. My skepticism concerning the historical usefulness of the Shaker testimonies for the earliest period is shared by Daniel W. Patterson, *The Shaker Spiritual* (Princeton: Princeton University Press, 1979), xvi. This problem in Shaker studies is analogous to the task facing text critics who attempt to distinguish the message of Jesus from the kerygma of the earliest Christian church. See Rudolf Bultmann, *Theology of the New Testament*, trans. Kendrick Grobel, 2 vols. (New York: Charles Scribner's Sons, 1951–1955), 1:3–62, and Susan M. Setta, "The Appropriation of Biblical Hermeneutics to Biographical Criticism: An Application to the Life of the Shaker Founder, Ann Lee," *Historical Methods* 16 (Summer 1983):89–100.

64. Bishop and Wells, eds., *Testimonies*, iii–iv, vi–vii.

65. Ibid., 380, 396.

66. Ibid., 263–264, 346; Jan Vansina, *Oral Tradition: A Study in Historical Methodology*, trans. H. M. Wright (Chicago: Aldine, 1965), 143–147.

67. Bishop and Wells, eds., *Testimonies*, 273, 309.

68. Ibid., 247.

69. Sandra K. D. Stahl, "Personal Experience Stories," in *Handbook of American Folklore*, ed. Richard M. Dorson (Bloomington: Indiana University Press, 1983), 268–269.

70. Bishop and Wells, eds., *Testimonies*, 282. On the category "story worthy," see Stahl, "Personal Experience Stories," 268.

71. The value of apostate accounts is also affirmed by Foster, *Religion and Sexuality*, 51–54.

72. Amos Taylor, *A Narrative of the Strange Principles, Conduct and Character of the People known by the Name of Shakers: Whose Errors have Spread in Several Parts of North-America, but are Beginning to Diminish, and ought to be Guarded against* (Worcester, Mass.: For the Author, 1782), 7–9, 11, 15. See Marcus Allen McCorison, "Amos Taylor, a Sketch and Bibliography," *Proceedings of the American Antiquarian Society* 69 (1959):37–55.

73. William Plumer, "The Original Shaker Communities in New England," ed. F. B. Sanborn, *New England Magazine,* n.s., 22 (1900):304–306, 308–309. Plumer subsequently became governor of New Hampshire.

74. Benjamin West, *Scriptural Cautions Against Embracing a Religious Scheme, Taught by a Number of Europeans, who Came from England to America, in the Year 1776, and Stile Themselves the Church, &c. &c.* (Hartford, Conn.: Bavil Webster, 1783), 3–8, 10–11, 13.

75. The First Presbytery of the Eastward, *Bath-kol A Voice From the Wilderness. Being An Humble Attempt to Support the Sinking Truths of God, against Some of the Principal Errors, Raging at this Time. Or, a Joint Testimony to some of the Grand Articles of the Christian Religion Judicially delivered to the Churches under their Care* (Boston: N. Coverly, 1783), 83–84.

76. Garrett, *Spirit Possession,* 195–213. Angell Matthewson describes the circumstances in which naked dancing occurred and the justification for it in his recollections ("Reminiscences," Letter VII). The charge that Lee physically abused the sexual organs of her disciples is made by Daniel Rathbun in *A Letter from Daniel Rathbun, of Richmond, in the County of Berkshire, to James Whittacor, Chief Elder of the Church, called Shakers* (Springfield, Mass., 1785), 29–31.

77. For another judgment, see Marjorie Procter-Smith, *Women in Shaker Community and Worship: A Feminist Analysis of the Uses of Religious Symbolism* (Lewiston, N.Y.: Edwin Mellen, 1985), 10–25.

78. Bishop and Wells, eds., *Testimonies,* 202.

79. Ibid., 341–342.

80. Ibid., 351–352; *Albany Gazette,* 9 Sept. 1784 (quoted in Morse, *Shakers,* 43).

81. Filley, *Recapturing Wisdom's Valley,* 13.

82. Bishop and Wells, eds., *Testimonies,* 52–53, 87, 93, 271, 363.

83. James Whittaker to Josiah Talcott, 25 Feb. 1782, MPH.

84. Ibid.

85. Plumer, "Original Shaker Communities," 307; Garrett, *Spirit Possession,* 190; Andrews, *People Called Shakers,* 51–52; "A Collection of the Writings of Father Joseph Meacham, Respecting Church Order and Government; Evidently intended for Waymarks, for All Who Would or Should be called in Spiritual or Temporal Care in the Church," OClWHi VII B 59, pp. 93–95.

86. James Whittaker to Henry Van Schaack, 13 Nov. 1784, Van Schaack to Whittaker, n.d., NOC. Both of these are copies. See H. C. Van Schaack to Benjamin Gates, 16 Feb. 1866, NOC. See also Richard D. Birdsall, *Berkshire County: A Cultural History* (New Haven: Yale University Press, 1959), 79–84; Henry Cruger Van Schaack, *Memoirs of the Life of Henry Van Schaack, Embracing Selections from His Correspondence during the American Revolution, by His Nephew, Henry Cruger Van Schaack* (Chicago: A. C. McClurg, 1892); and McLoughlin, *New England Dissent* 1:664–670.

87 Bishop and Wells, eds., *Testimonies*, 361, 364; Whittaker to his relations, 9 Oct. 1785, in [Joseph Meacham], *A Concise Statement of the Principles of the Only True Church, according to the Gospel, of the Present Appearance of Christ. As Held to and Practiced upon by the True Followers of the Living Saviour, at New-Lebanon, &c. Together with a Letter from James Whittaker, Minister of the Gospel in this Day of Christ's Second Appearance, to his Natural Relations in England* (Bennington, Vt.: Haswell and Russell, 1790), 17–24. Henry Abelove speculates that the English Shakers may have derived "their doctrine of celibacy" from the negative attitude of John Wesley toward marriage. See *The Evangelist of Desire: John Wesley and the Methodists* (Stanford: Stanford University Press, 1990), 59, n. 36.

88. James Whittaker to Joseph Meacham, 23 May 1786, OClWHi IV A 77; Bishop and Wells, eds., *Testimonies*, 368, 378–380.

89. James Whittaker, "Last Will and Testament," 9 June 1787, OClWHi I A 20. A similar formula appears in the will of Ruth Trip, a Shaker at New Lebanon, dated 4 Feb. 1789. She commends her "Soul to God that gave it[,] hoping through the Merits of Christ Jesus my Lord to meet with Eternal Salvation." OClWHi I A 9.

90. "Some Account of the Tenets and Practice of the Religious Society called Shakers," *American Museum, or Repository* 1 (1787): 148–150.

91. For an insightful account of the beginnings of another American sect, see Jan Shipps, *Mormonism: The Story of a New Religious Tradition* (Urbana: University of Illinois Press, 1985). Shipps raises critical questions concerning the sources for the story of early Mormonism, in contrast to another account of the same period by Richard L. Bushman, *Joseph Smith and the Beginnings of Mormonism* (Urbana: University of Illinois Press, 1984). These two volumes illustrate the differences between outsider and insider history.

92. For different periodizations of Shaker history, see Warren Lewis, "What to Do after the Messiah Has Come Again and Gone: Shaker 'Premillennial' Eschatology and Its Spiritual Aftereffects," in *The Coming Kingdom: Essays in American Millennialism and Eschatology*, ed. M. Darrol Bryant and Donald W. Dayton (Barrytown, N.Y.: International Religious Foundation, 1983), 101–104.

93. On the growth of the Free Will Baptists and the Universalists during this period, see Marini, *Radical Sects*.

94. My accent on process and change in the development of Shakerism is in tension with much that has been written on the society.

95. For a contrasting approach to the traditions concerning Ann Lee, see Edward Deming Andrews, "Ann Lee," in *Notable American Women, 1607–1950: A Biographical Dictionary*, ed. Edward T. James et al., 3 vols. (Cambridge: Harvard University Press, 1971), 2:385–387. See also Stephen A. Marini, "A New View of Mother Ann Lee and the Rise of American Shakerism," *Shaker Quarterly* 18 (1990): 47–62, 95–114.

96. It is my contention, using terms proposed by sociologist Peter Berger, that "world construction" by the Shakers was not complete by 1787. Much of what we today identify as Shaker remains to be created. See Peter L. Berger, *The Sacred Canopy: Elements of a Sociological Theory of Religion* (Garden City, N.Y.: Doubleday, 1967), chap. 1.

Part Two

1. See Gordon S. Wood, *The Creation of the American Republic, 1776–1787* (Chapel Hill: University of North Carolina Press, 1969), 391–429; Richard Buel, Jr., *Securing the Revolution: Ideology in American Politics, 1789–1815* (Ithaca: Cornell University Press, 1972); and Robert E. Shalhope, "Republicanism and Early American Historiography," *William and Mary Quarterly*, 3d ser., 39 (1982): 334–356.

2. By designating these forty years as the Formative Period of the society's history I am implying that Shakerism designates an *organized* religious reality with identifiable forms and structures. During this stage of development charisma typically is replaced by structured offices as the basis of authority. Kerygma is systematized in doctrinal propositions. Rules and codes are formulated to govern interaction within the society and contact with the host culture. Fixed rituals take the place of more spontaneous worship patterns.

3. In 1826 the last major Shaker village was founded at Sodus Bay, New York.

4. See Rosabeth Moss Kanter, *Commitment and Community: Communes and Utopias in Sociological Perspective* (Cambridge: Harvard University Press, 1972), 75–125; Karen H. Stephan and G. Edward Stephan, "Religion and the Survival of Utopian Communities," *Journal for the Scientific Study of Religion* 12 (1973): 89–100; and Rodney Stark and William Sims Bainbridge, "American-Born Sects: Initial Findings," *Journal for the Scientific Study of Religion* 20 (1981): 130–149.

5. Eli Root to Edmond Crane and Thomas Fuller, 9 Aug. 1787, OClWHi IV A 19; Confession of Edmond Crain and Thomas Fuller, 12 Aug. 1787, OClWHi I A 6.

6. Bishop and Wells, eds., *Testimonies*, 22–24, 218–220; Theodore E. Johnson, ed., "Biographical Account of the Life, Character, & Ministry of Father Joseph Meacham the Primary Leader in Establishing the United Order of the Millennial Church by Calvin Green 1827," *Shaker Quarterly* 10 (1970): 28–29.

7. Johnson, ed., "Biographical Account," 22–25, 29. See also John H. Morgan, "The Baptist-Shaker Encounter in New England: A Study in Religious Confrontation in Eighteenth-Century America," *Shaker Quarterly* 12 (1972): 83–94, 152–163; 13 (1973): 27–32.

8. Johnson, ed., "Biographical Account," 29–32.

9. Meacham is generally credited with writing the *Concise Statement of the Principles of the Only True Church* . . . (Bennington, Vt.: Haswell and Russell, 1790). See also "A Short Information of my Order and famylis" (OClWHi I A 8), which bears the following later inscription by Alonzo Hollister: "If not written by Father Joseph, I think it must have been dictated by him, & written by him or one of his Assistants in gathering the Church. A.G.H. Mch. 1911." In 1850 Rufus Bishop attributed "A Collection of Writings" (OClWHi VII A 12) to Meacham.

10. Johnson, ed., "Biographical Account," 59.

11. Ibid., 25–27, 30.

12. Ibid., 31; Bishop and Wells, eds., *Testimonies,* 332–333; Calvin Green, "Biographic Memoir of the Life, Character, & Important Events, in the Ministration of Mother Lucy Wright," [1861], OClWHi VI B 27, p. 9; Clarke Garrett, *Spirit Possession and Popular Religion: From the Camisards to the Shakers* (Baltimore: Johns Hopkins University Press, 1987), 223.

13. Johnson, ed., "Biographical Account," 29–30.

14. Dorothy M. Filley, *Recapturing Wisdom's Valley: The Watervliet Shaker Heritage, 1775–1975*, ed. Mary L. Richmond (Albany, N.Y.: Albany Institute of History and Art, 1975), 14–15; Garrett, *Spirit Possession*, 227

15. For records of consecrated land at New Lebanon, see "Records Book No. 2," NN.

16. "A Memorandum Kept by Jethro [Turner]," OClWHi V B 75.

17. [Meacham], "Short Information."

18. "A Book of Records, kept By Order of the Deacons, or Trustees of the Church of New-Lebanon, in the Town of Canaan, County of Columbia, & State of N. York . . . Kept by Rufus Bishop," OClWHi I B 30.

19. "Covenant of the Church of Christ in New Lebanon, relating to the possession and use of a Joint Interest 1796," OClWHi I B 28.

20. Isaac N. Youngs, "Memorandum of the United Society for the Years 1780 to 1794 inclusive," OClWHi V A 3; single dated sheet, 11 Apr. 1791, OClWHi V A 3; David Meacham, "Directions to the Manafactory of wool Hatts in the Church To be Regalated and Don according to the followg order & Manner, 15 February 1791," OClWHi I A 10; Johnson, ed., "Biographical Account," 62–68.

21. [Meacham], *Concise Statement*, 1. At least one edition attributes the publication to James Whittaker. See Mary L. Richmond, *Shaker Literature: A Bibliography*, 2 vols. (Hanover, N.H.: University Press of New England, 1977), 1:145–146.

22. [Meacham], *Concise Statement*, 3–15.

23. Among those who have noted the absence of any reference to Ann Lee in the tract are Robley Edward Whitson, ed., *The Shakers: Two Centuries of Spiritual Reflection* (New York: Paulist Press, 1983), 44, and Priscilla J. Brewer, *Shaker Communities, Shaker Lives* (Hanover, N.H.: University Press of New England, 1986), 25.

24. Johnson, ed., "Biographical Account," 94–99. See also "A Collection of the Writings of Father Joseph Meacham, Respecting Church Order and government; Evidently intended for way-marks, for all who would or should be called in spiritual or temporal care, In the Church," OClWHi VII A 12.

25. Daniel W. Patterson, *The Shaker Spiritual* (Princeton: Princeton University Press, 1979), 73–74, 99, 107.

26. Joseph Meacham to Lucy Wright, [1796], OClWHi IV A 30.

27. Johnson, ed., "Biographical Account," 54–55.

28. Green, "Biographic Memoir," 24–25.

29. Youngs, "Memorandum," 3; Joseph Meacham to Lucy Wright, in "Collection of Writings," 91–92; Edward Deming Andrews, *The People Called Shakers: The Search for the Perfect Society*, 2d ed. (New York: Dover, 1963), 311 n. 91.

30. *Western Star*, cited in *Connecticut Gazette*, 11 Feb. 1796, pp. 1–2.

31. "Mother Lucy's Sayings, Spoken at different times and Under various circumstances," DLC sec. 88; "Petition to New York Legislature, 5 April 1800," OClWHi I A 10. The charges against the society parallel those leveled today against controversial cults. See also Frances A. Carr, ed., "Mother Lucy's Sayings Spoken at Different Times and under Various Circumstances," *Shaker Quarterly* 8 (1968): 99–106.

32. Seth Watkins to Joseph Meacham, 16 May 1788, OClWHi IV A 19; Meacham to Watkins, 7 June 1788, OClWHi IV A 30; William Johnson, *Reports of Cases Adjudged in the Supreme Court of Judicature of the State of New York: From January Term 1799, to January Term 1803 Both Inclusive; Together with Cases Determined in the Court for the*

Correction of Errors During that Period, 2d ed. (New York: Banks, Goulod, 1846), 251–253; Andrews, *People Called Shakers,* 205.

33. Reuben Rathbun, *Reasons Offered for Leaving the Shakers* (Pittsfield, Mass.: Chester Smith, 1800), 3, 6, 10, 13–23.

34. Ibid., 15, 24–28.

35. "Memorandum by Jethro [Turner]," 7 Nov. 1798.

36. Petition of Daniel Goodrich et al., November 1788, OClWHi I A 9; Moses Ashley to General Ashley, 6 Sept. 1790, Robert Rensalaer to Joseph Meacham, 16 Feb. 1793, OClWHi IV A 30; William Bentley, *The Diary of William Bentley, D.D. Pastor of the East Church Salem, Massachusetts,* 4 vols. (Salem, Mass: Essex Institute, 1905–1914), 3:426; receipts from New Lebanon relating to military fines, OClWHi II A 8.

37. Johnson, ed., "Biographical Account," 26; Green, "Biographic Memoir," 13–17; Angell Matthewson, "Reminiscences in the Form of a Series of Thirty-nine Letters to his Brother Jeffrey," NN, Letter XXIV. The phrase "petticoat government" occurs in New Lebanon Ministry to Alfred Ministry, 30 July 1816, OClWHi IV A 33.

38. For background on this period, see Robert H. Wiebe, *The Opening of American Society: From the Adoption of the Constitution to the Eve of Disunion* (New York: Alfred A. Knopf, 1984); Joyce Appleby, *Capitalism and a New Social Order: The Republican Vision of the 1790s* (New York: New York University Press, 1984); Sean Wilentz, *Chants Democratic: New York City and the Rise of the American Working Class, 1788–1850* (New York: Oxford University Press, 1984); and Nathan O. Hatch, *The Democratization of American Christianity* (New Haven: Yale University Press, 1989).

39. Green, "Biographic Memoir," 7, 9. See also Edward Deming Andrews, "Lucy Wright," in *Notable American Women, 1607–1950: A Biographical Dictionary,* ed. Edward T. James et al., 3 vols. (Cambridge: Harvard University Press, 1971), 3:681–682, and Frances A. Carr, "Lucy Wright: The First Mother in the Revelation and Order of the First Organized Church: A Faithful Fulfillment of Her Holy Calling," *Shaker Quarterly* 15 (1987):93–100, 128–132. The Carr essay reflects the attitude of contemporary Shakers toward Wright.

40. Green, "Biographic Memoir," 14–15; Calvin Green, "Biography of Elder Henry Clough," OClWHi VI B 24.

41. See Charles Roy Keller, *The Second Great Awakening in Connecticut* (New Haven: Yale University Press, 1942); Donald G. Mathews, "The Second Great Awakening as an Organizing Process, 1780–1830: An Hypothesis," *American Quarterly* 21 (1969): 23–43; Richard D. Shiels, "The Second Great Awakening in Connecticut: Critique of the Traditional Interpretation," *Church History* 49 (1980):401–415; and Robert E. Cray, Jr., "Forging a Majority: The Methodist Experience on Eastern Long Island, 1789–1845," *New York History* 67 (1986):285–303.

42. Green, "Biographic Memoir," 27–29. Eleven out of fourteen members of the Wells family were members of the society when they died. See "Record of a Remarkable Family," *Shaker* 6 (1876):59.

43. Thomas Brown, *An Account of the People Called Shakers: Their Faith, Doctrines, and Practice, Exemplified in the Life, Conversations, and Experience of the Author during the Time He Belonged to the Society. To Which is Affixed a History of their Rise and Progress to the Present Day* (Troy, N.Y.: Parker and Bliss, 1812), 14, 55.

44. Ibid., 18, 301.

45. Ibid., iii, 361–362.

46. Youngs's missionary journals are in manuscript collections at NOC, MWiW, and OClWHi. On Bates, see "Sketch of the Life and Experience of Issachar Bates," OClWHi VI B 18. Theodore E. Johnson edited the "Sketch" in *Shaker Quarterly* 1 (1961): 98–118, 145–163, and 2 (1962): 18–35.

47. Benjamin Seth Youngs, "Journey to the North," NOC no. 10,123, 28 July 1802, no. 10,124, 27 Oct.

48. Youngs, "Journey to the North," NOC no. 10,510, 30 June, 15 July 1802, no. 10,511, 24 Aug. 1802; Youngs, "Journey to the East," NOC no. 10,512, 14 Sept. 1802.

49. Green, "Biographic Memoir," 31–32; Youngs, "Journey to the East," NOC no. 10,512, 14 Sept. 1802.

50. Julia Neal, *By Their Fruits: The Story of Shakerism in South Union, Kentucky* (Chapel Hill: University of North Carolina Press, 1947), 10; John McGee to Thomas L. Douglas, 23 June 1820, *Methodist Magazine* 4 (1821): 191, cited in John B. Boles, *The Great Revival, 1787–1805: The Origins of the Southern Evangelical Mind* (Lexington: University Press of Kentucky, 1972), 57. The decision to send the missionaries is described in [Benjamin S. Youngs], "Early Watervliet Journal," NOC no. 10,514, pp. 82–83. See also Paul K. Conkin, *Cane Ridge: America's Pentecost* (Madison: University of Wisconsin Press, 1990).

51. See Malcolm J. Rohrbough, *The Trans-Appalachian Frontier: People, Societies, and Institutions, 1775–1850* (New York: Oxford University Press, 1978), and Boles, *Great Revival*, 9–11.

52. "Sketch of Issachar Bates," 56–57; John Meacham, Issachar Bates, and Benjamin Seth Youngs to New Lebanon Ministry, 31 Jan., 27 Apr. 1805, OClWHi IV A 66.

53. See F. Gerald Ham, "Shakerism in the Old West" (Ph.D. diss., University of Kentucky, 1962), chap. 1; Boles, *Great Revival*, 143–164; Barton W. Stone, *An Apology for Renouncing the Jurisdiction of the Synod of Kentucky. To which is Added a Compendious View of the Gospel, and a Few Remarks on the Confession of Faith. By the Presbytery of Springfield* (Lexington, Ky.: Joseph Charles, 1804); and [Richard McNemar], *Observations on Church Government, by the Presbytery of Springfield, To which is added, the Last Will and Testament of that Reverend Body: With a Preface and Notes* (Cincinnati, Ohio: John W. Browne, 1807).

54. "Sketch of Issachar Bates," 58; Richard McNemar to New Lebanon Ministry, 25 Sept. 1805, cited in Ham, "Shakerism in the Old West," 75–76; J. P. MacLean, *A Sketch of the Life and Labors of Richard McNemar* (Franklin, Ohio: Franklin Chronicle, 1905), 22; Meacham, Bates, and Youngs to New Lebanon Ministry, 27 Apr. 1805; J. P. MacLean, "The Shaker Community of Warren County: Its Origin, Rise, Progress and Decline," in *Shakers of Ohio: Fugitive Papers concerning the Shakers of Ohio, with Unpublished Manuscripts* (Columbus, Ohio: F. J. Herr, 1907), 63.

55. David Meacham, Amos Hammond, and Ebenezer Cooley to People in Kentucky and Adjacent States, 30 Dec. 1804, cited in MacLean, "Shaker Community of Warren County," 61–63.

56. Neal, *By Their Fruits*, 23–26; Boles, *Great Revival*, 157–159.

57. Stephen A. Marini, *Radical Sects of Revolutionary New England* (Cambridge: Harvard University Press, 1982), 39, 100. The eastern missionaries reported, "Many of the people here [in Ohio] have been in an expectation last fall, & through the winter that Something extraordinary would take place this Summer—Some have thought it would be only the extending & spreading of the Same light they had already received—But others believed there would be Some new Revelation which would cause an entire new

Revolution among those that had the light." See John Meacham, Issachar Bates, and Benjamin S. Youngs to New Lebanon Ministry, 1 June 1805, OClWHi IV A 66.

58. Meacham, Bates, and Youngs to New Lebanon Ministry, 27 Apr. 1805.

59. Turtle Creek Brethren to New Lebanon Ministry, 25 Sept. 1805, David Darrow and John Meacham to David Meacham, 19 Mar. 1806, David Darrow and John Meacham to New Lebanon Elders and Brethren, 5 June 1806, Turtle Creek Sisters to New Lebanon Sisters, 16 Aug. 1806, OClWHi IV A 66. See Robert P. Emlen, *Shaker Village Views: Illustrated Maps and Landscape Drawings by Shaker Artists of the Nineteenth Century* (Hanover, N.H.: University Press of New England, 1987), 32–37, for two early "maps" of the Ohio settlement, one sketched by McNemar.

60. Darrow and John Meacham to David Meacham, 19 Mar. 1806; Turtle Creek Sisters to New Lebanon Sisters, 16 Aug. 1806; David Darrow and Ruth Farrington to New Lebanon Ministry, 27 Jan. 1812, OClWHi IV A 68.

61. Meacham, Bates, and Youngs to New Lebanon Ministry, 1 June 1805; Believers at Turtle Creek to New Lebanon Ministry, 19 Dec. 1805, OClWHi IV A 66; Theodore E. Johnson, ed., "Violence at Turtle Creek: An 1805 Missionaries' Letter," *Shaker Quarterly* 12 (1972): 107–116; Union Village Ministry to Richard [Spier], 29 Nov. 1809, DLC sec. 248; Peter Pease to Richard Spier, 12 Sept. 1810, Richard McNemar to Proctor Sampson, 5 Jan. 1811, OClWHi IV A 68; Peter Pease to Richard [Spier], 10 Mar. 1811, DLC sec. 245; James Smith, *Remarkable Occurrences Lately Discovered among the People Called Shakers; Of a Treasonous and Barbarous Nature, or Shakerism Developed* (Paris, Ky.: J. R. Lyle, 1810); James Smith, *Shakerism Detected, Their Erroneous and Treasonous Proceedings, and False Publications, Contained in Different News-Papers, Exposed to Public View, by the Depositions of Ten Different Persons, Living in Various Parts of the States of Kentucky and Ohio* (Paris, Ky.: Joel R. Lyle, 1810); MacLean, "Mobbing the Shakers of Union Village," in *Shakers of Ohio*, 362–387. For another outsider's view, see James McBride, "The Shakers of Ohio: An Early Nineteenth-Century Account," *Cincinnati Historical Society Bulletin* 29 (1971): 126–137.

62. Meacham, Bates, and Youngs to New Lebanon Ministry, 1 June 1805; Benjamin S. Youngs to New Lebanon Ministry, 20 Mar. 1806, OClWHi IV A 61; Benjamin S. Youngs to Matthew Houston, 20 Oct. 1806, OClWHi IV A 52; Benjamin S. Youngs, "A Journey to the Indians, Miami near Lebanon, Ohio, 3d month 1807," DeWint. Emlen misinterprets the reference to "old believers" in his excellent study, *Shaker Village Views*, 34.

63. Darrow and Farrington to New Lebanon Ministry, 27 Jan. 1812; David [Darrow] and Ruth [Farrington] to Archibald [Meacham] and Ruth [Darrow], 9 Nov. 1811, OClWHi IV A 68; "The Way Union Village received its name From Elder David," OClWHi VII A 20; Ham, "Shakerism in the Old West," 88–89.

64. Ohio Ministry to Deacon Daniel, 15 Jan. 1807, OClWHi IV A 67; "Manuscript Journal Ohio," NOC no. 10,132, 9 May 1807; Mercer County Kentucky Ministry to [Lucy Wright], 13 Dec. 1809, OClWHi IV A 52; Lucy Smith to Dana Goodrich, 15 Aug. 1810, DLC sec. 248; Thomas D. Clark and F. Gerald Ham, *Pleasant Hill and Its Shakers* (Pleasant Hill, Ky.: Shakertown Press, 1968), 10–15. The text of the Pleasant Hill covenant appears in Daniel Mac-Hir Hutton, *Old Shakertown and the Shakers: A Brief History of the Rise of the United Society of Believers in Christ's Second Coming, the Establishment of the Pleasant Hill Colony, Their Beliefs, Customs and Pathetic End*, revised and enlarged by Jane Bird Hutton, 14th ed. (Harrodsburg, Ky.: Harrodsburg Herald Press, 1987), 15–25.

65. David Darrow to Daniel Mosely and Peter Pease, 11 May 1812, David Darrow to Richard Spier, 28 Nov. 1812, DLC sec. 245; MacLean, "Shakers of Eagle and Straight Creeks," in *Shakers of Ohio*, 270–346; Ham, "Shakerism in the Old West," 93.

66. Andrews, *People Called Shakers*, 70–93; Ham, "Shakerism in the Old West," chaps. 2–3; Caroline B. Piercy, *The Valley of God's Pleasure: A Saga of the North Union Shaker Community* (New York: Stratford House, 1951), 67–74; Julia Neal, *The Kentucky Shakers* (Lexington: University Press of Kentucky, 1977), 1–11.

67. David Darrow to Lucy Wright, 12 Jan. 1807, Ohio Ministry to New Lebanon Ministry, 31 July 1808, OClWHi IV A 67.

68. David Darrow and Brethren to David Meacham and Brethren, 18 Aug. 1806, DLC sec. 245; Ohio Ministry to New Lebanon Ministry, 31 July 1808; Peter Pease to Deacon, 1 Jan. 1809, DLC sec. 245; Ohio Ministry to New Lebanon and Watervliet Ministries, 4 July 1809, OClWHi IV A 67; "Sums of Money Sent to the Western States," OClWHi II A 17. Brewer's decision to limit the focus of *Shaker Communities* to the eastern societies produces a distorted picture, for eastern and western Shakerism had a major impact on each other.

69. As early as 1813 Darrow was referred to as Father and Ruth Farrington as Mother by western Believers. See South Union Ministry to New Lebanon Ministry, 1 May 1813, OClWHi IV A 60.

70. See, e.g., Malcolm Worley's letter of thanks to Lucy Wright, 9 Sept. 1809, OClWHi IV A 67, and Benjamin S. Youngs's testimonial in a letter to Ebenezer [Cooley], 2 Feb. 1806, OClWHi IV A 61. One western convert introduced herself by letter to the eastern sisterhood and testified: "to be Redeemed and purifyed from all Sin is my dayly labour—my determination is to bear the yoke of Christ" (Jenny McNemar to New Lebanon Sisters, 25 Sept. 1805, OClWHi IV A 66). More than two hundred extant letters were sent from Union Village between 1805 and 1826. See OClWHi IV A 66–70.

71. Green, "Biographic Memoir," 38.

72. H. H. Gerth and C. Wright Mills, eds., *From Max Weber: Essays in Sociology* (New York: Oxford University Press, 1946), 52, 153.

73. Ibid., 153.

74. "A Short Account of the People known by the Name of Shakers, or Shaking Quakers," *Theological Magazine* 1 (1795): 81–87.

75. Union Village Ministry to Lucy Wright, 16 Aug. 1806, OClWHi IV A 66; Darrow and John Meacham to David Meacham, 19 Mar. 1806; "A Candid Statement of Our Principles," OClWHi VII B 239. For the text of this manuscript, identified elsewhere as "Religious Exposition written at Turtle Creek," see Stephen J. Stein, "'A Candid Statement of Our Principles': Early Shaker Theology in the West," *Proceedings of the American Philosophical Society* 133 (1989): 503–519.

76. Stein, "'Candid Statement,'" 514–519. On the authorship of the document, see p. 514.

77. Union Village Ministry to Wright, 16 Aug. 1806. Brewer credits Wright with initiating the society's publishing effort. *Shaker Communities*, 35.

78. See the journals of Benjamin S. Youngs that describe his missionary journeys throughout New England in 1802–1803 (NOC nos. 10,123–10,125, 10,510–10,512).

79. Lucy Wright to Ohio Ministry, 9 Oct. 1806, OClWHi IV A 31.

80. Benjamin S. Youngs, "Manuscript Journal—Ohio 1806," NOC no. 10,130, pp. 5, 9; Benjamin S. Youngs, "Manuscript Journal—Ohio 1807," NOC no. 10,131, p. 3; David Darrow to David Meacham, 15 Jan. 1807, Ohio Ministry to New Lebanon Ministry, 12 Dec. 1807, John Meacham to Richard Spier, 16 Mar. 1808, Union Village Ministry to New Lebanon Ministry, 28 Dec. 1808, David Darrow to Richard Spier, 25 Dec. 1808, OClWHi IV A 67; Youngs, Testimony; David Darrow and Ruth Farrington to Lucy Wright, 10 July 1809, OClWHi IV A 67; David Darrow to Abiathar Babbitt, 13 Aug. 1814, OClWHi IV A 68.

81. Union Village Ministry to New Lebanon Ministry, 28 Dec. 1808.

82. Youngs, Testimony, 8, 10–11.

83. Ibid., 11, 593–599.

84. Ibid., 204, 277; Union Village Ministry to New Lebanon Ministry, 28 Dec. 1808. The publication Youngs cited frequently is Edwards's A History of the Work of Redemption, Containing, The Outlines of a Body of Divinity, in a Method Entirely New (Edinburgh: W. Gray, 1774), which also appeared in an annotated American edition (New York: T. and J. Swords, 1793).

85. Youngs, Testimony, 185–200, 223–227, 253, 369, 411–430.

86. See James West Davidson, The Logic of Millennial Thought: Eighteenth-Century New England (New Haven: Yale University Press, 1977); Ruth H. Bloch, Visionary Republic: Millennial Themes in American Thought, 1756–1800 (Cambridge: Cambridge University Press, 1985); Nathan O. Hatch and Mark A. Noll, eds., The Bible in America: Essays in Cultural History (New York: Oxford University Press, 1982), esp. pp. 3–100; and Henry F. May, The Enlightenment in America (New York: Oxford University Press, 1976).

87. Youngs, Testimony, 9–10, 416, 436–437.

88. Ibid., 431–442; Union Village Ministry to Wright, 16 Aug. 1806.

89. Youngs, Testimony, 436–439, 523–538.

90. New Lebanon and Watervliet Ministries to Ohio Ministry, 23 Feb. 1809, New Lebanon Ministry to Ohio Ministry, 23 Feb. 1809, Lucy Wright to David Darrow and Ruth Farrington, 12 Apr. 1809, OClWHi IV A 31.

91. New Lebanon and Watervliet Ministries to Ohio Ministry, 23 Feb. 1809; David Darrow and Benjamin S. Youngs to New Lebanon Ministry, 20 Apr. 1809, OClWHi IV A 67; New Lebanon Ministry to Ohio Ministry, 15 June 1809, OClWHi IV A 31; David Darrow and Ruth Farrington to Lucy Wright, 10 July 1809, OClWHi IV A 67; Benjamin S. Youngs to Seth Wells, 6 Sept. 1810, OClWHi IV A 68; Seth Wells and Calvin Green, eds., Testimony, 2d ed. (Albany, N.Y.: E. and E. Hosford, 1810).

92. Correspondence surrounding the publication of the third edition of the Testimony (Union Village, Ohio: B. Fisher and A. Burnett, 1823), illustrates this same pattern. See Union Village Ministry to New Lebanon Ministry, 8 Dec. 1821, 1 July 1823, OClWHi IV A 70, and Seth Wells to Eleazar Wright, 18 Feb. 1824, DLC sec. 246.

93. John Meacham to Lucy Wright, 17 Mar. 1815, John Meacham and Lucy Smith to New Lebanon Ministry, 20 Apr. 1817, OClWHi IV A 52; Lucy Wright to John Dunlavy, 13 Feb. 1818, New Lebanon Ministry to Pleasant Hill Ministry, 18 June 1818, OClWHi IV A 33.

94. John Dunlavy, The Manifesto, or a Declaration of the Doctrines and Practice of the Church of Christ (Pleasant Hill, Ky.: P. Bertrand, 1818), iii.

95. Ibid., v–vi. See Michael Brooks Taylor, "Developments in Early Shaker Ethical Thought" (Ph.D. diss., Harvard University, 1976), 223–245, for a useful discussion of the *Manifesto*.

96. New Lebanon Ministry to Pleasant Hill Ministry, 18 June 1818; John Dunlavy to Ebenezer Bishop, 22 Oct. 1818, OClWHi IV A 69. On Green, see Diane Sasson, *The Shaker Spiritual Narrative* (Knoxville: University of Tennessee Press, 1983), 189–209.

97. The *Testimony* gained the reputation of being the "Shaker Bible" (see Richmond, *Shaker Literature* 1:212). One correspondent wrote, "Some gain faith by reading 'Christ's Second Appearing,' doubtless more than are willing to bear the cross. Many will own that it is a good book, and but few that we hear of will venture to condemn it. Some will call it the Shaker's *Bible*, and will swear by it before a Justice of the Peace when there is no Bible at hand, for the Justice tells them that it is as good as any Bible." Undated fragment, OClWHi IV A 88.

98. See Jean McMahon Humez, ed., *Mother's First-Born Daughters* (forthcoming), concerning the limitations placed on Shaker women in the area of theology.

99. "Short Account," 81–83.

100. Richard McNemar, *The Kentucky Revival; or, a Short History of the Late Extraordinary Outpouring of the Spirit of God in the Western States of America, agreeably to Scripture Promises and Prophecies concerning the Latter Day: with a Brief Account of the Entrance and Progress of What the World Call Shakerism among the Subjects of the Late Revival in Ohio and Kentucky Presented to the True Zion Traveler as a Memorial of the Wilderness Journey* (Cincinnati, Ohio: John W. Browne, 1807; reprint, New York: Edward O. Jenkins, 1846), 3, 101–104, 121. Stone had leveled his charges in *Atonement: The Substance of Two Letters Written to a Friend* (Lexington, Ky.: Joseph Charless, 1805).

101. Youngs, *Testimony*, 5–11.

102. Union Village Ministry to David Meacham, 15 Jan. 1807, OClWHi IV A 67; Youngs, *Testimony*, 19–30.

103. Youngs, *Testimony*, 484. The healings appear as "Evidences accompanying the second Appearing of Christ" (pp. 467–486).

104. New Lebanon Ministry to Union Village Ministry, 15 June 1809, OClWHi IV A 31. The first edition of the *Testimony* reads: "and was married to a man named Abraham Standley, by whom she had four children who all died in infancy; which was a particular means of increasing her conviction of the deplorable loss of the human race" (p. 22). The second edition (1810) ends the sentence with "infancy" (p. xxvi).

105. New Lebanon Ministry to Union Village Ministry, 11 Nov. 1809, OClWHi IV A 31.

106. Rufus Bishop to David Darrow, 18 May 1816, New Lebanon Ministry to Union Village Ministry, 23 Jan. 1818, OClWHi IV A 33; Seth Y. Wells to Union Village Ministry, 25 Apr. 1822, OClWHi IV A 78.

107. Bishop and Wells, eds., *Testimonies*, iv.

108. Surprisingly little critical scholarly attention has been paid to the *Testimonies*. Two exceptions are Susan M. Setta, "The Appropriation of Biblical Hermeneutics to Biographical Criticism: An Application to the Life of the Shaker Founder, Ann Lee," *Historical Methods* 16 (Summer 1983): 89–100, and Jean McMahon Humez, "Images of Female Power in Early Shaker Oral Tradition and Literature" (paper presented at the National Historic Communal Societies Conference, Canterbury, N.H., October 1986).

109. Bishop and Wells, eds., *Testimonies*, iii–v.

110. Ibid., vi, 2.

111. Ibid., 2–5, 11.

112. Ibid., 26, 82, 90, 137, 262.

113. Ibid., 104–105, 145, 168–170.

114. Ibid., 205–213.

115. Ibid., 351.

116. Ibid., iv, 81, 98, 111, 127, 396.

117. Even Edward Deming Andrews expressed skepticism about the accuracy of the stories concerning the sufferings of the founders. He wrote, "It should be borne in mind that these accounts of persecution, as recalled by the participants, may understandably have been exaggerated and highly colored" (*People Called Shakers,* 305 n. 53). Less caution is evident in Marini, *Radical Sects,* 88–94.

118. Rufus Bishop to David Darrow, 18 May 1816; New Lebanon Ministry to Union Village Ministry, 23 Jan. 1818.

119. [Seth Y. Wells] to Benjamin S. Youngs, 1818, OClWHi IV A 77.

120. David Darrow to Lucy Wright, 14 Dec. 1818, OClWHi IV A 69.

121. Ibid.

122. Seth Y. Wells to Benjamin S. Youngs, 22 Feb. 1819, OClWHi IV A 77.

123. New Lebanon Ministry to Union Village Ministry, 27 Mar. 1819, OClWHi IV A 33. See also Bishop and Wells, eds., *Testimonies,* 204–213.

124. Eunice Chapman, *An Account of the Conduct of the People Called Shakers: In the Case of Eunice Chapman and Her Children, Since Her Husband Became Acquainted with that People, and Joined their Society, Written by Herself* (Albany, N.Y., 1817), 14, 58; Seth Y. Wells to Benjamin S. Youngs, 19 July 1817, OClWHi IV A 77. See also Nelson M. Blake, "Eunice against the Shakers," *New York History* 41 (1960):359–378.

125. Mary Marshall Dyer, *A Brief Statement of the Sufferings of Mary Dyer, Occasioned by the Society Called Shakers. Written by Herself. To Which is Added, Affidavits and Certificates. Also, a Declaration from Their Own Publication* (Concord, N.H.: Joseph C. Spear, 1818); Mary Marshall Dyer, *A Portraiture of Shakerism, Exhibiting a General View of their Character and Conduct, from the First Appearance of Ann Lee in New-England, down to the Present Time. And Certified by many Respectable Authorities* (N.p., 1822), title page, v.

126. Large sections of the *Portraiture* contain the texts of the affidavits. See, e.g., pp. 90–97, 141–201.

127. Dyer, *Portraiture,* 116; Richard McNemar, *The Other Side of the Question. In three parts. I. An explanation of the proceedings of Eunice Chapman and the Legislature, against the United Society . . . in the state of New-York. II. A refutation of the false statements of Mary Dyer against the said society, in the state of New-Hampshire. III. An account of the proceedings of Abram Van Vleet, esq. and his associates, against the said United Society at Union Village, Ohio. Comprising a general vindication of the character of Mother and the elders against the attacks of public slander—the edicts of a prejudiced party—and the misguided zeal of lawless mobs* (Cincinnati, Ohio: Reynolds, 1819); Calvin Green and Seth Y. Wells, *Summary View of the Millennial Church, or United Society of Believers, (Commonly Called Shakers.) comprising the Rise, Progress and Practical Order of the Society; together with the General Principles of their Faith and Testimony* (Albany, N.Y.: Packard and Van Benthuysen, 1823), iii–iv (hereafter cited as Green and Wells, *Summary View*).

128. Green and Wells, *Summary View*, v–xiv.

129. For example, the accounts of Job Bishop's last visitation with Ann Lee three days before her death are almost identical in Bishop and Wells, eds., *Testimonies*, 235–236, and Green and Wells, *Summary View*, 36–37.

130. Green and Wells, *Summary View*, title page.

131. Ibid., 76; Brewer, *Shaker Communities*, 215.

132. William Sims Bainbridge, "Shaker Demographics, 1840–1900: An Example of the Use of U.S. Census Enumeration Schedules," *Journal for the Scientific Study of Religion* 21 (1982):352; Brewer, *Shaker Communities*, 74–79, 147–150, 224; Robert F. W. Meader, "Another Lost Utopia," *Shaker Quarterly* 4 (1964):123–124; David R. Proper, "More Notes on 'Lost' Communities," *Shaker Quarterly* 6 (1966):45–47; Robert F. W. Meader, "Shepherds of the Hills," *Shaker Quarterly* 6 (1966):14–17; Robert F. W. Meader, "The Adirondack Shakers," *Shaker Quarterly* 7 (1967):99–106; Stephen J. Stein, "The Conversion of Charles Willing Byrd to Shakerism," *Filson Club History Quarterly* 56 (1982):395–414.

133. Green and Wells, *Summary View*, 76. See Robert S. Fogarty, *Dictionary of American Communal and Utopian History* (Westport, Conn.: Greenwood, 1980); E. G. Alderfer, *The Ephrata Commune: An Early American Counterculture* (Pittsburgh: University of Pittsburgh Press, 1985); Herbert A. Wisbey, Jr., *Pioneer Prophetess: Jemima Wilkinson, the Publick Universal Friend* (Ithaca: Cornell University Press, 1964); Beverly Prior Smaby, *The Transformation of Moravian Bethlehem: From Communal Mission to Family Economy* (Philadelphia: University of Pennsylvania Press, 1988); Karl J. R. Arndt, *George Rapp's Harmony Society, 1785–1847* (Philadelphia: University of Pennsylvania Press, 1965); Emilius Oviatt Randall, *History of the Zoar Society, from Its Commencement to Its Conclusion: A Sociological Study in Communism*, 3d ed. (Columbus, Ohio: F. J. Heer, 1904); and F. Gerald Ham, "The Prophet and the Mummyjums: Isaac Bullard and the Vermont Pilgrims of 1817," *Wisconsin Magazine of History* 56 (1973):290–299.

134. Travel accounts abound among the Believers during this period, including: "Journal of trips made by Elder Ebenezer and others from Mt. Lebanon to other communities," 1802–1804, OClWHi V A 6; "Journey from Alfred to Harvard" [by] Seth Y. Wells," 1822, OClWHi V B 1; "Journal of the trips made by the Harvard ministry to other Shaker communities," 1818–1830, OClWHi V B 37; "Journal of William Demming's Travel to Ohio & Ky," 1810, OClWHi V B 78; "Journal of a trip to Believers in Savoy Aug 1821," OClWHi V B 90; "Bro Seths Journey to Long Island 1819," OClWHi V B 299; and "Account of a journey to Busro," n.d., OClWHi V B354. Demming's account records the mileage covered each day.

135. Lucy Wright to David Darrow, 9 Oct. 1806, OClWHi IV A 31; Darrow to Wright, 12 Jan. 1807, OClWHi IV A 67; Wright to Darrow, 11 July 1807, OClWHi IV A 31.

136. Green and Wells, *Summary View*, 68–69, 75–76. The choice of South Union as the name for the village on the Gaspar River reflects the Shakers' sense of geography. That location was "the furthest south of all the other Believers." See Benjamin Seth Youngs to Lucy Wright, 2 May 1813, OClWHi IV A 60.

137. Marini, *Radical Sects*, 96. Brewer documents a "rising proportion of children and teenagers among the membership" in the East between 1800 and 1820 (*Shaker Communities*, 30). D'Ann Campbell in "Women's Life in Utopia: The Shaker Experiment in Sexual Equality Reappraised—1810 to 1860," *New England Quarterly* 51 (1978): 23–38, explains the success of the Shakers by deprivation theory.

138. Green and Wells, *Summary View,* 58–61.

139. "Record of Public Meetings," entries for 1 Nov. 1801, and 27 Oct. 1806, MeSl; Green and Wells, *Summary View,* 59, 63.

140. David Meacham, Joseph Meacham's younger brother, was the first deacon in the Church Family at New Lebanon. Archibald and John, sons of Joseph, served as elders at Busro and Pleasant Hill, respectively. Archibald, with Issachar Bates, was part of the leadership problem in Indiana, for which he was judged harshly (see Benjamin Seth Youngs to Lucy Wright, 17 Dec. 1818, OClWHi IV A 60). John was criticized repeatedly by both Wright and Darrow. See Lucy Wright to David Darrow and Ruth Farrington, 12 Apr. 1809, OClWHi IV A 31; David Darrow to Lucy Wright, 15 July 1809, OClWHi IV A 67; Lucy Wright to David Darrow, 13 Feb. 1818, OClWHi IV A 33; and Lucy Wright to John Meacham, 13 Feb. 1818, OClWHi IV A 33.

141. Alfred Ministry to Harvard Ministry, 4 May, 7 Sept. 1816, OClWHi IV A 1; New Lebanon Ministry to Alfred Ministry, 30 July 1816, OClWHi IV A 33.

142. See, e.g., "Covenant of the church of Christ in New Lebanon relating to the possession and use of a joint interest," 1795, DeWint; "A concise statement of the faith and principles upon which the joint union & covenant relation of Believers are formed: and the covenant of the Second family of the Society of Believers at New Lebanon," 1815, DeWint; "A concise statement of the faith and principles upon which the joint union and covenant relation of Believers are formed, the nature of that relation, and the order & manner of attaining and entering into it: and the covenant of the Second family of the New Lebanon United Society," 1827, DeWint; and the 1797 covenant at Shirley, NOC no. 9776. Other examples of early Shaker covenants are in OClWHi I A–B.

143. Rufus Bishop to David Darrow, 18 May 1816, OClWHi IV A 33; "A Book of Records kept by Order of the Deacons, or Trustees of the Church at New Lebanon, in the Town of Canaan, County of Columbia, & State of N. York," OClWHi I B 30.

144. Green, "Biographic Memoir," 51–52; "West Union Covenant, 1 March 1815," DLC sec. 249.

145. "Names of the Brethren and Sisters at Sabbathday Pond [and] at Alfred," MeSl.

146. Patience Emery, "The time of our rising in the Morning and lieing Down at night," 21 Feb. 1817, MeSl; "A few remarks upon learning and the use of books, for the consideration of the youth, among Believers," n.d., MeSl; "Manner of Address," n.d., DeWint; New Lebanon Ministry directive, 23 Nov. 1802, NOC no. 10,476; "A Copy given to all Believers in Relation to Spirits," 1800, OClWHi I A 24; Rufus Bishop to David Darrow, 2 July 1817, OClWHi IV A 33.

147. New Lebanon Ministry to unidentified ministry, 14 Feb. 1821, OClWHi IV A 34; Theodore E. Johnson, ed., "The 'Millennial Laws' of 1821," *Shaker Quarterly* 7 (1967):35–37.

148. Johnson, ed., "'Millennial Laws,'" 45–46, 49, 57.

149. Ibid., 50–53.

150. Ibid., 47–49, 54–55; Mary Douglas, *Purity and Danger: An Analysis of Concepts of Pollution and Taboo* (London: Routledge and Kegan Paul, 1966), 69.

151. Johnson, ed., "'Millennial Laws,'" 45–47; Molly Goodrich to Daniel Goodrich, 1816, DeWint. On the concept of liminality, see Victor Turner, *The Ritual Process: Structure and Anti-Structure* (Ithaca: Cornell University Press, 1977), 94–130.

152. Harvard Ministry to New Lebanon Ministry, 16 Jan. 1823, OClWHi IV A 22.

153. "Account of the Persecution at Harvard in the Year 1825," DeWint. Sexual improprieties, arbitrary authority, physical abuse of children, inhumane corporal punishment, drunkenness, despotism, sedition, and worshiping Ann Lee as God—the charges against the Shakers made by James Smith in 1810 were reprinted in Dyer, *Portraiture*, 308–327. These anti-Shaker arguments resemble closely the conspiratorial thinking discussed in David B. Davis, "Some Themes of Countersubversion: An Analysis of Anti-Masonic, Anti-Catholic, and Anti-Mormon Literature," *Mississippi Valley Historical Review* 47 (1960): 205–224.

154. Lucy Smith to Ruth Landon, 12 Aug. 1825, Pleasant Hill Ministry to New Lebanon Ministry, 1 Aug. 1826, OClWHi IV A 53.

155. The pattern of community development varied among the villages; on Harvard, see Edward R. Horgan, *The Shaker Holy Land: A Community Portrait* (Harvard, Mass.: Harvard Common Press, 1982), 47–70; on Pleasant Hill, see Clark and Ham, *Pleasant Hill and Its Shakers*, 16–37; and on Alfred, see R. Mildred Barker, *Holy Land: A History of the Alfred Shakers* (Sabbathday Lake, Maine: Shaker Press, 1986). See also Edward Deming Andrews, *The Community Industries of the Shakers* (Albany: University of the State of New York, 1932).

156. Timothy Dwight, *Travels in New England and New York,* ed. Barbara Miller Solomon, 4 vols. (Cambridge. Harvard University Press, 1969), 3:102–107; Sydney E. Ahlstrom, *A Religious History of the American People* (New Haven: Yale University Press, 1972), 494.

157. Herbert Schiffer, *Shaker Architecture* (West Chester, Pa.: Schiffer, 1979), contains photographs of all the buildings mentioned in this paragraph. See also Philip James Anderson, "The Simple Builders: The Shakers, Their Villages, and Architecture" (Ph.D. diss., Saint Louis University, 1969).

158. Samuel Johnson, Jr., "Diary, from Mt. Lebanon, 1790–1819," NOC; Rachel Johnson to Deborah and Susanna, 12 Sept. 1807, OClWHi IV A 67.

159. "Extract of a Letter from the Ministry at Lebanon," [1816], MeSl. See Joseph B. Hoyt, "The Cold Summer of 1816," *Annals of the Association of American Geographers* 48 (1958): 118–131.

160. Johnson, ed., "Biographical Account," 65; Green, "Biographic Memoir," 32; "Bro. S. Y. Wells, Tour to Eastern Bel. Schools," 1823, OClWHi V B 302; *A Juvenile Monitor: Containing Instructions for Youth and Children; Pointing Out Ill Manners, and Showing Them How to Behave in the Various Conditions of Childhood and Youth* (New Lebanon, N.Y.: The Shakers, 1823); Frank Gilbert Taylor, "An Analysis of Shaker Education: The Life and Death of an Alternative Educational System, 1774–1950" (Ph.D. diss., University of Connecticut, 1976), 137–179; Edward Deming Andrews and Faith Andrews, "The Shaker Children's Order," *Winterthur Portfolio* 8 (1973): 201–214.

161. Patterson, *Shaker Spiritual*, 99; Henry Bedinger to Mrs. R. Bedinger, 10 Dec. 1810, in Robert S. Franklin, ed., *Copies of Old Family Letters* (Charlestown, W.Va.: n.p., 1933), 25–27.

162. Patterson, *Shaker Spiritual*, 133, 149–150; *Millennial Praises, containing a Collection of Gospel Hymns, in four parts; adopted to the Day of Christ's Second Appearing Composed for the Use of His People* (Hancock, Mass.: Josiah Tallcott, Jr., 1813). See also Daniel W. Patterson, "Millennial Praises: Tune Location and Authorial Attributions of the First Shaker Hymnal," *Shaker Quarterly* 18 (1990): 77–94.

163. *Millennial Praises*, iii–iv, 16, 78, 96, 136; Patterson, *Shaker Spiritual*, 151.

164. Patterson, *Shaker Spiritual,* 201–202, 249–250. This discussion of song and dance draws primarily on Patterson's monumental study, which supplants the earlier works on the topic, including Edward Deming Andrews, *The Gift to Be Simple: Songs, Dances and Rituals of the American Shakers* (New York: J. J. Augustin, 1940), and Harold E. Cook, *Shaker Music: A Manifestation of American Folk Culture* (Lewisburg, Pa.: Bucknell University Press, 1973).

165. Patterson, *Shaker Spiritual,* 150, 230, 247–248; Isaac N. Youngs, "Narrative of Various Events Beginning April 1815," DLC sec. 42, 2 Apr. 1815; Matthew Houston to Seth Y. Wells, 23 Apr. 1821, DLC sec. 245; Shirley Ministry to New Lebanon Ministry, 12 Nov. 1825, OClWHi IV A 58; Union Village Ministry to New Lebanon Ministry, 24 May 1826, OClWHi IV A 70; "Nathaniel Taylor, Watervliet, [Ohio], Diary, 1823–1830," OHi no. 119, 30 May 1824.

166. Union Village Ministry to New Lebanon Ministry, 25 Mar. 1815, OClWHi IV A 69; Issachar Bates to Seth Wells, 12 Apr. 1815, DLC sec. 245.

167. Samuel Turner to Calvin Green, 1 Apr. 1820, DLC sec. 245; William J. Haskett, *Shakerism Unmasked, or the History of the Shakers; Including a Form Politic of Their Government as Councils, Orders, Gifts, with an Exposition of the Five Orders of Shakerism, Ann Lee's Grand Foundation Vision, in Sealed Pages. With Some Extracts from Their Private Hymns Which Have Never Appeared before the Public* (Pittsfield, Mass.: L. H. Walkley, 1828), 143–146.

168. Green and Wells, *Summary View,* xiv; *Millennial Praises,* 233.

169. The limitations of using the Civil War as a watershed in the history of Shakerism are apparent in Henri Desroche, *The American Shakers: From Neo-Christianity to Presocialism,* trans. John K. Savacool (Amherst: University of Massachusetts Press, 1971), 96–99.

170. For a different chronological scheme, see Warren Lewis, "What to Do after the Messiah Has Come Again and Gone: Shaker 'Premillennial' Eschatology and Its Spiritual Aftereffects," in *The Coming Kingdom: Essays in American Millennialism and Eschatology,* ed. M. Darrol Bryant and Donald W. Dayton (Barrytown, N.Y.: International Religious Foundation, 1983), 71–109.

171. Brewer marks Wright's death as a major turning point in the society's fortunes. *Shaker Communities,* 43–64.

172. South Union Ministry to New Lebanon Ministry, 1 May 1813, OClWHi IV A 60; New Lebanon Ministry to South Union Ministry, 30 Dec. 1815, OClWHi IV A 32; Hannah Goodrich to Lucy Wright, 17 Sept. 1819, OClWHi IV A 3; Rufus Bishop, "Day Book," OClWHi V B 85, 5–6 Feb. 1821; Freegift Wells to New Lebanon Ministry, 31 Jan. 1821, OClWHi IV A 77; New Lebanon Ministry to Harvard Ministry, 14 Feb. 1821, OClWHi IV A 34; "Account Book 1819 Kept by Calvin Green," OClWHi V B 80, 9–10 Feb. 1821.

173. New Lebanon Ministry to unidentified ministry, 14 Feb. 1821, New Lebanon Ministry to South Union Ministry, 14 Feb. 1821, OClWHi IV A 34; Hancock Ministry to New Lebanon Ministry, 20 Feb. 1821, OClWHi IV A 22; Ministry at Enfield, N.H., to New Lebanon Ministry, 5 Mar. 1821, OClWHi IV A 11; West Union Ministry to New Lebanon Ministry, 24 Mar. 1821, OClWHi IV A 85.

174. Pleasant Hill Ministry to New Lebanon Ministry, 1 Apr. 1821, DeWint.

175. David Darrow to New Lebanon Ministry, 22 Apr. 1821, DeWint.

176. Ibid.; David Darrow to New Lebanon Ministry, 8 Dec. 1821, OClWHi IV A 70.

177. "Records of the Church at Northunion Containing the Rise and Progress of the Church Commencing in the Year 1822 and brought down to the present year 1843," copied by J. P. MacLean, OClWHi V B 177; MacLean, "Rise, Progress and Extinction of the Society at Cleveland, Ohio," in *Shakers of Ohio*, 112–118; Mary Lou Conlin, *The North Union Story: A Shaker Society, 1822–1889* (Cleveland: Ohio: Ontario Printers, 1961), 1–3; Piercy, *Valley of God's Pleasure*, 75–82; Theodore E. Johnson, ed., "A Sketch of the Life and Religious Experience of Richard W. Pelham," *Shaker Quarterly* 9 (1969): 59.

178. MacLean, "Origin, Rise, Progress and Decline of the Whitewater Community of Shakers Located in Hamilton County, Ohio," in *Shakers of Ohio*, 227–238; "A Church Record Relating in Consecutive Order the Appointments to, and Removals from, Office of Ministry Elders Trustees & Deacons of the Church & Society of White Water From its Commencement, in 1823," OClWHi V B 357.

179. "Account of the Rise and Progress of the Church at North Union," OClWHi V B 177, preface, p. 4, entries for March–November 1822; "Church Record of White Water," entries for 1823–1831.

180. Union Village Ministry to New Lebanon Ministry, 7 June 1824, OClWHi IV A 70; MacLean, "Origin, Rise, Progress," 233–236; MacLean, "Shakers of Eagle," 317–325; Mary Lou Conlin, "The Lost Land of Busro," *Shaker Quarterly* 3 (1963): 57–59. On the continuing theological debate between the East and the West, see Union Village Ministry to New Lebanon Ministry, 3 Dec. 1821, Eleazar Wright to Seth Wells, 27 Oct. 1823, OClWHi IV A 70; Wells to Wright, 18 Feb. 1824, DLC sec. 173; and McNemar to Proctor Sampson, 4 July 1824, DLC sec. 245; Youngs, *Testimony*, 3d ed. (Union Village, Ohio: B. Fisher and A. Burnett, 1823).

181. Description of David Darrow's funeral, 28 June 1825, DLC sec. 245; Union Village Ministry to New Lebanon Ministry, 4 July 1825, OClWHi IV A 70.

182. Description of Darrow's funeral, 28 June 1825; Union Village Ministry to New Lebanon Ministry, 4 July 1825.

183. Union Village Ministry to New Lebanon Ministry, 4 July 1825. Richard W. Pelham eulogized Darrow as follows: "Father David was one of those great and good men, who bless and illuminate mankind once in a century. He was the center and soul of the gathering gift during his life and administration in the west" Johnson, ed., "Sketch," 75.

184. New Lebanon Ministry to West Union Ministry, 30 July 1825, OClWHi IV A 35; Union Village Ministry to New Lebanon Ministry, 3 July 1826, DeWint; New Lebanon Ministry to West Union Ministry, 12 July 1826, OClWHi IV A 35. The earlier conflict between South Union and Pleasant Hill over the use of *Mother* and *Father* is discussed in New Lebanon Ministry to Benjamin S. Youngs, 19 May 1821, OClWHi IV A 34. This letter contains reflections on the history of these terms, including Joseph Meacham's refusal to accept the designation Father until a year or two before his death. Hannah Kendal thought that using such parental language may have been a strategic mistake.

185. Union Village Believers to New Lebanon Ministry, 3 July 1826, DeWint.

186. "A Brief Narrative of the Religious Experience of Joseph Pelham," OClWHi VI B 3; Herbert A. Wisbey, Jr., *The Sodus Shaker Community* (Lyons, N.Y.: Wayne County Historical Society, 1982), 5–7. On the religious ferment in western New York, see Whitney R. Cross, *The Burned-Over District: The Social and Intellectual History of Enthusiastic Religion in Western New York* (Ithaca: Cornell University Press, 1950); Paul E. Johnson, *A Shopkeeper's Millennium: Society and Revivals in Rochester, New York, 1815–1837* (New York: Hill and Wang, 1978); Mary P. Ryan, *Cradle of the Middle Class: The Family in Oneida County, New York, 1790–1865* (Cambridge: Cambridge University Press, 1981), and Michael Barkun, *Crucible of the Millennium: The Burned Over District of New York in the 1840s* (Syracuse: Syracuse University Press, 1986).

187. Ronald E. Shaw, *Erie Water West: A History of the Erie Canal, 1792–1854* (Lexington: University Press of Kentucky, 1966); Wisbey, *Sodus Shaker Community,* 6–7.

188. Wisbey, *Sodus Shaker Community,* 6–11; Proctor Sampson and Calvin Green to New Lebanon Ministry, 10 Mar. 1826, Sampson and Green to Brethren and Sisters at Sodus, 15 Mar. 1826, OClWHi IV A 35; "A Record of the Commencement and Progress of Believers at Sodus and Portbay," OClWHi V B 21.

189. See, e.g., Olive Spence and Susannah Ellis to Eldress Esther, 6 Aug. 1831, NN, and "Tour thro the States of Ohio and Kentucky; By Rufus Bishop and Isaac N. Youngs. In the Summer of 1834," NOC.

190. See Bernard J. Siegel, "Defensive Structuring and Environmental Stress," *American Journal of Sociology* 76 (1970): 11–32.

191. Thomas F. O'Dea and Janet O'Dea Aviad, *The Sociology of Religion,* 2d ed. (Englewood Cliffs, N.J.: Prentice Hall, 1983), 24–26. See also Diane L. Barthel, *Amana: From Pietist Sect to American Community* (Lincoln: University of Nebraska Press, 1984), and Jonathan G. Andelson, "Routinization of Behavior in a Charismatic Leader," *American Ethnologist* 7 (1980): 716–733.

192. See Marini, *Radical Sects,* 172–176, for a celebration of the "revolution of the spirit" in the Shakers and other early anti-Calvinist sects. Charles E. Hambrick-Stowe has written: "Even seeming anti-ritualists cannot live without ritual, and iconoclasts cannot survive without images that give meaning to their lives. Ritual may be taken to mean activity that a society establishes to celebrate and renew commonly held perceptions, to be repeated at specified times by members of the society, either corporately or individually. Ritual activity thus expresses a society's understanding of self." *The Practice of Piety: Puritan Devotional Disciplines in Seventeenth-Century New England* (Chapel Hill: University of North Carolina Press, 1982), 51.

193. "Members live their religion by doing it, acting its rites, restating its memories, speaking its hopes, obeying its commands, thus gaining an identity and a world to live in." Ruel W. Tyson, Jr., James L. Peacock, and Daniel W. Patterson, eds., *Diversities of Gifts: Field Studies in Southern Religion* (Urbana: University of Illinois Press, 1988), 5.

194. The Shakers' polysemantic use of *gift* invites comparison with other religious groups for whom the same term is central. In American Pentecostalism, for example, gifts nurture both the experiential and the institutional aspects of the religion. See Elaine J. Lawless, *God's Peculiar People: Women's Voices and Folk Tradition in a Pentecostal Church* (Lexington: University Press of Kentucky, 1988), 51–52.

195. No modern biographies exist for Meacham, Wright, or Darrow.

196. Jean McMahon Humez has collected and edited the sayings and correspondence of Lucy Wright in *Mother's First-Born Daughters.*

197. Unfortunately, F. Gerald Ham did not publish his excellent dissertation, "Shakerism in the Old West."

198. Robert S. Fogarty has written of Wright, "She was a vital force in the society during a period when the Shakers experienced their greatest growth." *Dictionary of American Communal and Utopian History* (Westport, Conn.: Greenwood, 1980), 122.

199. Siegel, "Defensive Structuring."

200. Nathan O. Hatch mentions the Shakers only in passing in his perceptive study, *Democratization of American Christianity.* He contends that they, as well as the Mormons and the Oneida community, passionately sought a "new order" because they perceived "that there was no authoritative center" in the new republic (p. 65).

Part Three

1. See Richard D. Brown, *The Transformation of American Life, 1600–1865* (New York: Hill and Wang, 1976); David J. Rothman, *The Discovery of the Asylum: Social Order and Disorder in the New Republic* (Boston: Little, Brown, 1971); Anthony F. C. Wallace, *Rockdale: The Growth of an American Village in the Early Industrial Revolution* (New York: Alfred A. Knopf, 1978); and Mary P. Ryan, *Cradle of the Middle Class: The Family in Oneida County, New York, 1790–1865* (Cambridge: Cambridge University Press, 1981).

2. See Nathan O. Hatch, *The Democratization of American Christianity* (New Haven: Yale University Press, 1989), 3, and Jon Butler, *Awash in a Sea of Faith: Christianizing the American People* (Cambridge: Harvard University Press, 1990), esp. 225–226.

3. Seth Y. Wells to Sodus Elders, 11 Jan. 1835, OClWHi IV A 7; "Journal Kept by Giles Avery," 29 Feb. 1835, OClWHi V B 105; "Journal Kept by Joseph Hammond," 1 Mar. 1835, OClWHi V B 209; "Journal Kept by Freegift Wells," 1 Mar. 1835, OClWHi V B 293; "A Daily Journal of Passing Events; Begun January the 1st 1830. By Rufus Bishop, in the 56th Year of his Age," NN (hereafter cited as Central Ministry Journal 1830–1839), 1 Mar. 1835.

4. Edward Deming Andrews features this spiritualistic period in *The People Called Shakers: A Search for the Perfect Society*, 2d ed. (New York: Dover, 1963), 152–176.

5. See Clifford S. Griffin, *Their Brothers' Keepers: Moral Stewardship in the United States, 1800–1865* (New Brunswick: Rutgers University Press, 1960); Timothy L. Smith, *Revivalism and Social Reform: American Protestantism on the Eve of the Civil War* (Nashville, Tenn.: Abingdon, 1957); John L. Thomas, "Romantic Reform in America, 1815–1865," *American Quarterly* 17 (1965):656–681; Lois W. Banner, "Religious Benevolence as Social Control: A Critique of an Interpretation," *Journal of American History* 60 (1973):23–41; and Ronald G. Walters, *American Reformers, 1815–1860* (New York: Hill and Wang, 1978).

6. Anthony F. C. Wallace, "Revitalization Movements," *American Anthropologist* 58 (1956):264–281.

7. Louis J. Kern features the sexual function of ecstatic behavior during the spiritualistic period. See *An Ordered Love: Sex Roles and Sexuality in Victorian Utopias—the Shakers, the Mormons, and the Oneida Community* (Chapel Hill: University of North Carolina Press, 1981), 91–113.

8. Seth Y. Wells, "Mother Lucy's Last Visit to Watervliet," OClWHi V A 10, entry for 4 Feb. 1821; Calvin Green, "Biographic Memoir of the Life, Character, & Important Events, in the Ministration of Mother Lucy Wright," [1861], OClWHi VI B 27, p. 72. Babbit (1766–1847) was, in fact, only two years the senior of Ebenezer Bishop (1768–1849) and eight years older than Rufus Bishop (1774–1852). He was nine years older than Landon (1775–1850) and five years older than Clark (1780–1857).

9. Green, "Biographic Memoir," 72; Ruth Landon to Molly Goodrich, 22 Feb. 1822, OClWHi IV B 35; Calvin Green, "Biography of Elder Henry Clough," OClWHi VI B 24, p. 87.

10. On the male side, Rufus Bishop spent more time than Ebenezer Bishop on strictly administrative matters. Rufus was the more robust of the two; Ebenezer suffered long periods of illness from time to time. The division of labor between the two female leaders is less clear.

11. Administrative and political skills, expert knowledge, and a measure of professionalism are required of leaders who do not possess charismatic gifts. Rufus Bishop emerges from the record as the consummate religious bureaucrat.

12. Union Village Ministry to New Lebanon Ministry, 3 July 1826, DeWint; New Lebanon Ministry to Benjamin Seth Youngs, 19 May 1821, OClWHi IV A 34; Richard McNemar to Seth Wells, 14 June 1830, DLC sec. 245. Samuel Turner to Lucy Wright, 19 Aug. 1814, OClWHi IV A 52, includes a reference to Elder John Meacham "(or Father for So we call him here)." Seth Y. Wells to Eleazar Wright, 31 May 1824, DLC sec. 246, closes with the hope that the western Believers "will continue to be Father David's good children, for we acknowledge him [David Darrow] as a father in Zion." New Lebanon Ministry to West Union Ministry, 12 July 1826, OClWHi IV A 35, mentions the poor health of "Father Job" [Bishop] at Canterbury.

13. "Journies of the Ministry since the Decease of Mother Lucy," OClWHi V B 91. Local leaders traveled to New Lebanon with some frequency, too, especially when the central ministry was unable to visit all the villages.

14. "A Memorandum of Letters Sent to and Received from Our Friends in Different Parts," OClWHi IV B 5. For an account of the rapid expansion of the United States postal system during these years, see Wayne E. Fuller, *The American Mail: Enlarger of the Common Life* (Chicago: University of Chicago Press, 1972), esp. pp. 42–78.

15. "Memorandum of Letters." The Post Office, with its network of post roads, was a major "bond of union" among Americans in the years before the Civil War (Fuller, *American Mail*, 81–82). The Shakers took full advantage of this governmental service.

16. Harvard Ministry to New Lebanon Ministry, 16 Jan. 1823, OClWHi IV A 22. Seth Y. Wells, Calvin Green, and Isaac N. Youngs frequently served as scribes and letter writers for the central ministry.

17. J. P. MacLean, "Shakers of Eagle and Straight Creeks," in *Shakers of Ohio: Fugitive Papers concerning the Shakers of Ohio, with Unpublished Manuscripts* (Columbus, Ohio: F. J. Heer, 1907), 270–346; Mary Lou Conlin, "The Lost Land of Busro," *Shaker Quarterly* 3 (1963):44–60. McNemar's judgment appears in his poem "A Lamentation for West Union," in MacLean, *Shakers of Ohio,* 342–343.

18. Union Village Ministry to New Lebanon Ministry, 4 July 1826, OClWHi IV A 70; New Lebanon Ministry to West Union Ministry, 12 July 1826; MacLean, "Shakers of Eagle," 322–328.

19. MacLean, "Shakers of Eagle," 326. Earlier closings in the West had involved 30 Believers from Red Bank, Kentucky, who moved to Busro in 1809 and 150 Shakers from Eagle Creek and Straight Creek in Adams County, Ohio, who were resettled in Union Village and West Union in 1811. Ibid., 275–276.

20. Priscilla J. Brewer, *Shaker Communities, Shaker Lives* (Hanover, N.H.: University Press of New England, 1986), 223–224; Pleasant Hill Ministry to New Lebanon Ministry, 28 June 1828, OClWHi IV A 53.

21. "Membership Records of the South House," OClWHi III B 35, 11 Sept., 27 Oct. 1824; "Records of the Church at Watervliet, N.Y.," OClWHi V B 279, 11 Sept., 27 Oct. 1824. On religious controversy in western New York, see Glenn C. Altschuler and Jan M. Saltzgaber, *Revivalism, Social Conscience, and Community in the Burned-Over District: The Trial of Rhoda Bement* (Ithaca: Cornell University Press, 1983).

22. "Membership Records of the South House," 17 July 1826; "Register of Members, Watervliet, N.Y.," OClWHi III B 42; "Account of the Births and Deaths of Believers at Watervliet, N.Y.," OClWHi III B 43; "Records of the Church at Watervliet, N.Y.," 2 Nov. 1824; Daniel W. Patterson, *Gift Drawing and Gift Song: A Study of Two Forms of Shaker Inspiration* (Sabbathday Lake, Maine: United Society of Shakers, 1983), 85–86. Patterson identifies Mary Wickes as an instrument during the revival period. According

to him, she apostatized on 11 Sept. 1846. For the case of a man who sought solace with the Shakers because he was dominated by his wife, see Alfred Ministry to New Lebanon Ministry, 16 Feb. 1820, OClWHi IV A 1.

23. Samuel Turner to Calvin Green, 26 Apr. 1827, DLC sec. 245; William S. Byrd to Charles Willing Byrd, 9 Mar. 1828, Byrd Papers, InU; Stephen J. Stein, ed., *Letters from a Young Shaker: William S. Byrd at Pleasant Hill* (Lexington: University Press of Kentucky, 1985), 31, 84–87; F. Gerald Ham, "Shakerism in the Old West" (Ph.D. diss., University of Kentucky, 1962), 181–187. On Meacham's recall, see New Lebanon Ministry to Pleasant Hill Ministry, 18 June 1818, OClWHi IV A 33.

24. John Whitbey, *Beauties of Priestcraft; Or, a Short Account of Shakerism* (New Harmony, Ind.: New Harmony Gazette, 1826). Whitbey was influenced by Robert Owen's *A New View of Society; or, Essays on the Formation of the Human Character Preparatory to the Development of a Plan for Gradually Ameliorating the Condition of Mankind*, 4th ed. (London: Longman, Hurst, Rees, Orme, and Brown, 1818). For more on Owen and his ideas, see J. F. C. Harrison, *Robert Owen and the Owenites in Britain and America: The Quest for the New Moral World* (London: Routledge and Kegan Paul, 1969).

25. Samuel Turner, "Early Records of Pleasant Hill, Feb. 19, 1806–1836," KySP, 12–13; William S. Byrd to Charles Willing Byrd, 9 Mar. 1828.

26. Benjamin S. Youngs to New Lebanon Ministry, 8 Sept. 1828, OClWHi IV A 60. A copy of this letter appears in Stein, ed., *Letters*, 120–124.

27. "A Short Account of the Rise of Believers, and a Few of the Most Interesting Occurrences that have Taken Place since that Time," OClWHi V B 60, 8 June, 12 Oct. 1815; Alfred Ministry to New Lebanon Ministry, 21 June, 20 Nov. 1815, 12 Feb., 4 May, 7 Sept., 1816, OClWHi IV A 1. John Barnes had always been something of an eccentric. In the 1780s he and other Merry Dancers in Maine had engaged in bizarre behavior, including drunkenness and what was described as "indecent and immoral practices," before converting to Shakerism. See Clarke Garrett, *Spirit Possession and Popular Religion: From the Camisards to the Shakers* (Baltimore: Johns Hopkins University Press, 1987), 192.

28. Alfred Ministry to New Lebanon Ministry, 25 Jan., 9 Feb. 1831, OClWHi IV A 2.

29. New Lebanon Ministry to Alfred Ministry, 20 July 1831, OClWHi IV B 7.

30. Isaac N. Youngs, "Tour thro the States of Ohio and Kentucky; By Rufus Bishop and Isaac N. Youngs. In the Summer of 1834," NOC. For more on the trip, see Robert P. Emlen, *Shaker Village Views: Illustrated Maps and Landscape Drawings by Shaker Artists of the Nineteenth Century* (Hanover, N.H.: University Press of New England, 1987), 65–92, and Stephen J. Stein, "Community, Commitment, and Practice: Union and Order at Pleasant Hill in 1834," *Journal of the Early Republic* 8 (1988):45–68.

31. Youngs, "Tour" 1:78–104, 2:1–8; Union Village Ministry to Rufus Bryant, 26 Nov. 1834, OClWHi IV A 71; Rufus Bishop to Union Village Ministry, 7 Mar. 1835, OClWHi IV A 37; Samuel Turner to Rufus Bishop, 13 Oct. 1835, OClWHi IV A 54.

32. Turner to Bishop, 13 Oct. 1835, Samuel Turner to Jethro Turner, 17 June 1834, Samuel Turner to New Lebanon Ministry, 11 Apr. 1836, OClWHi IV A 54; "Church Record Book A," KyHM, 36; New Lebanon Ministry to Pleasant Hill Ministry, 22 June 1836, OClWHi IV A 54.

33. Brewer suggests that the four members of the central ministry were overly concerned with "maintenance of the status quo" and that they lacked a "progressive vision and imagination" (*Shaker Communities*, 96). Her judgments reflect a bias toward charismatic leadership.

34. The ministry journals document the daily routines that occupied the central ministry. Rufus Bishop, for example, worked as a tailor. The ministry also cut and split their own firewood. See Central Ministry Journal 1830–1839, 25 Feb. 1830, 30 Apr. 1836. The eldresses spent regular hours in their shop and frequently cared for the sick. See Ruth Landon to Molly Goodrich, 21 Feb. 1817, OClWHi IV B 35.

35. Opposition to female governance was persistent within the society. See, e.g., New Lebanon Ministry to Alfred Ministry, 20 July 1831.

36. Brewer, *Shaker Communities*, 143–145.

37. See Ferdinand Tonnies, *Gemeinschaft und Gesellschaft*, translated and edited by Charles P. Loomis as *Community and Society* (East Lansing: Michigan State University Press, 1957).

38. MacLean, "Origin, Rise, Progress, and Decline of the Whitewater Community of Shakers Located in Hamilton County, Ohio," in *Shakers of Ohio*, 245–246; "A Register of Stock &c of the United Society at New Lebanon, To be Taken Annually, Beginning January 1st. 1839," OClWHi II B 38. The category "bishoprick" first appears in Green and Wells, *Summary View*, 60. The grouping of villages within bishoprics changed from time to time.

39. David Darrow and John Meacham to David Meacham, 19 Mar. 1806, OClWHi IV A 66; David Darrow et al. to David Meacham et al., 18 Aug. 1806, Peter Pease to Deacon, 1 Jan. 1809, DLC sec. 245.

40. "Record of Public Meetings, Sabbathday Lake," MeSl, 1 Nov. 1801, 22 May 1802, 27 Oct. 1806; "Names at South Union," OClWHi III B 31, entry for September 1873; "The Covenant or Constitution of the Church of the United Society at Union Village Ohio," OClWHi I B 70. For examples of business records from this period, see OClWHi II A–B.

41. The pioneering study of the Believers' business enterprises was Edward Deming Andrews, *The Community Industries of the Shakers* (Albany: University of the State of New York, 1932). Priscilla J. Brewer has written, "The Shakers preferred to engage in legitimate occupations that earned them a spiritual reward first. If a monetary profit developed, that was merely a by-product" (*Shaker Communities*, 100). In my judgment, Brewer underestimates the daily realities confronting the Believers. See George Rogers Taylor, *The Transportation Revolution, 1815–1860* (New York: Rinehart, 1951).

42. Andrews, *Community Industries*, 60–65; Russell H. Anderson, "Agriculture among the Shakers, Chiefly at Mount Lebanon," *Agricultural History* 24 (1950): 113–120; "South Union Office Daybook," OClWHi II B 79, entries for 1835.

43. Ham, "Shakerism in the Old West," 237–238. The claims for Shaker inventiveness have been repeated often. See Anna White and Leila S. Taylor, *Shakerism Its Meaning and Message Embracing An Historical Account, Statement of Belief and Spiritual Experience of the Church from Its Rise to the Present Day* (Columbus, Ohio: Fred J. Heer, 1904), 310–318; Andrews, *Community Industries*, 39–45; and Flo Morse, *The Shakers and the World's People* (New York: Dodd, Mead, 1980), 133. Robert F. W. Meader offers a useful corrective: "Their mechanical ingenuity was and is legendary, though their innocent assumption of being the prime inventors of any number of mechanical devices will not stand up under scholarly scrutiny" (Edward R. Horgan, *The Shaker Holy Land: A Community Portrait* [Harvard, Mass.: Harvard Common Press, 1982], xix). On agriculture during the period, see Paul Wallace Gates, *The Farmer's Age: Agriculture, 1815–1860* (New York: Holt, Rinehart and Winston, 1960), and Christopher Clark, *The Roots of Rural Capitalism: Western Massachusetts, 1780–1860* (Ithaca: Cornell University Press, 1990), 195–313.

44. Andrews, *Community Industries*, 66–82; Margaret Van Alen Frisbee Sommer, *The Shaker Garden Seed Industry* (Old Chatham, N.Y.: Shaker Museum Foundation, 1972), 10–16; Nancy L. Hillenburg, "Shaker Trade Routes," *Shaker Quarterly* 18 (1990): 40–46; "Account Book of Salesmen," OClWHi II B 80; "Account of the Seed Business," OClWHi II B 34; "Account of Sales," OClWHi II B 78. For examples of broadsides, posters, labels, envelopes, and order forms related to the seed industry, see M. Stephen Miller, *A Century of Shaker Ephemera: Marketing Community Industries, 1830–1930* (New Britain, Conn.: Privately printed, 1988), 13–18.

45. Sommer, *Shaker Garden Seed*, 13, 49–51; "Account Book of Salesmen," 1 Nov. 1838 through 4 Feb. 1839; Calvin Morrell to Daniel Goodrich, 26 Dec. 1822, DeWint; Urban Johns to Eli M'Lean, 15 Dec. 1836, OClWHi IV A 61.

46. Andrews, *Community Industries*, 87–111; Amy Bess Miller, *Shaker Herbs: A History and a Compendium* (New York: Clarkson N. Potter, 1976); "Press Book," OClWHi II B 101; "Account of Sales"; Dorothy M. Filley, *Recapturing Wisdom's Valley: The Watervliet Shaker Heritage, 1775–1975*, ed. Mary L. Richmond (Albany, N.Y.: Albany Institute of History and Art, 1975), 55; Ham, "Shakerism in the Old West," 242. Elmer R. Pearson and Julia Neal, *The Shaker Image* (Boston: New York Graphic Society, 1974), 105, contains a picture of the New Lebanon vacuum pan.

47. "Cattle Sales S. Union Commencing 1827," OClWHi II B 68; Youngs, "Tour" 1:11, 2:3–4; Ham, "Shakerism in the Old West," 226–232; "Deacon's Journal of East Family [Pleasant Hill] Jan 1, 1843–Oct 5, 1882," KyLoF, p. 205; John M. Keith, Jr., "Ante-Bellum Agriculture of the South Union Shakers," *Filson Club History Quarterly* 51 (1977): 158–166.

48. "Blacksmith's Account Book," OClWHi II B 77.

49. Ham, "Shakerism in the Old West," 211–212; Anderson, "Agriculture," 119. The society's commitment to engineering and technology is illustrated in Youngs's "Tour."

50. David R. Starbuck, "The Shaker Mills in Canterbury, New Hampshire," *IA: Journal of the Society for Industrial Archeology* 12 (1986): 11–38. This valuable account and reconstruction of the water system provides an excellent model for work that might be done at other Shaker sites. See also Rebecca A. Bell, "The Canterbury Church Family Mills: 1797–1876," in *Historical Survey of Canterbury Shaker Village*, ed. David R. Starbuck and Margaret Supplee Smith (Boston: Boston University, 1979): 41–59, and Donald E. Janzen, *The Shaker Mills on Shawnee Run: Historical Archaeology at Shakertown at Pleasant Hill Mercer County, Kentucky* (Harrodsburg, Ky.: Pleasant Hill Press, 1981). Archaeological work has also begun at the West Union site in Indiana.

51. Ham, "Shakerism in the Old West," 247–248, 252; Alan M. Hall, "The Shaker Response to Industrialism: A Case Study of the Sabbathday Lake Shaker Community, 1848–1896" (master's thesis, University of Maine at Orono, 1979), 6, Caroline B. Piercy, *The Valley of God's Pleasure: A Saga of the North Union Shaker Community* (New York: Stratford House, 1951), 136–138.

52. "Account of Sales," entries for 1832; "An Account of the Sisters Work 1836. 1st Order Watervliet," OClWHi V B 315; Youngs, "Tour" 2:3–4.

53. Andrews, *Community Industries*, 229–248; Jerry V. Grant and Douglas R. Allen, *Shaker Furniture Makers* (Hanover, N.H.: University Press of New England, 1989), 17–21; Charles R. Muller and Timothy D. Rieman, *The Shaker Chair* (Winchester, Ohio: Canal Press, 1984).

54. Muller and Rieman, *Shaker Chair*, 3–4; June Sprigg, *Shaker Design* (New York: Whitney Museum of American Art, 1986), 19.

55. Martha Wetherbee and Nathan Taylor, *Shaker Baskets,* ed. Mary Lyn Ray (San-bornton, N.H.: Martha Wetherbee Basket Shop, 1988), 25–26, 79.

56. "South Union Office Daybook"; Eunice E. Bennet, "An Account of the Manner I have Spent the Money Given to me by my Good Brethren & Sisters at Watervliet and Elsewhere Beginning September-1-1826," OClWHi II B 99; "Deacon's Journal of East Family," 191–201.

57. "Urgent temporalities," for example, caused meetings to be cancelled on the Sab-bath in Kentucky. See "South Union Diary, July 21, 1872–Jan 29, 1878," MWiW, 25 Aug. 1872. Receipt signed by Sheffield Haywood, 8 Mar. 1831, OClWHi II A 11.

58. On economic developments between 1820 and 1860, see Richard D. Brown, *Mod-ernization: The Transformation of American Life, 1600–1865* (New York: Hill and Wang, 1976), 122–158.

59. MacLean, *Shakers of Ohio,* 90, 337–338; documents from Union Village and Water-vliet, Ohio, DLC sec. 262; "Church Records Union Village," OClWHi III B 34, pp. 156–158; "A Chh. Journal of Current Events from June 23d 1817 to June 1st 1846 By Daniel Miller," OClWHi V B 237, 10 Sept. 1835.

60. MacLean, *Shakers of Ohio,* 74–75, 92–94; documents from Union Village and Wa-tervliet, Ohio; Eleazar Wright to Solomon King, 24 Aug. 1829, DLC sec. 246; Richard McNemar to Seth Y. Wells, 17 Aug. 1831, DLC sec. 245; Central Ministry Journal 1830–1839, 11, 28 Oct. 1835, 29 Jan. 1836; Seth Y. Wells to Eleazar Wright, 10 Nov. 1835, Nathaniel Deming to Eleazar Wright, 13 Nov. 1835, DLC sec. 246; Eleazar Wright to Seth Y. Wells, 2 Dec. 1835, OClWHi IV A 71; J. R. Bryant to Eleazar Wright, 31 Dec. 1835, DLC sec. 249; New Lebanon and Watervliet Ministries to Union Village Ministry, 9 Apr. 1836, DLC sec. 263; Seth Y. Wells to Eleazar Wright, 12 Sept. 1836, DLC sec. 246; Luther Copley to Stephen Spinning and Andrew Houston, 30 Apr. 1837, OHi. Richard McNemar took the name Eleazar Wright after converting to Shakerism.

61. Wells to Wright, 10 Nov. 1835; Wright to Wells, 2 Dec. 1835; New Lebanon and Watervliet Ministries to Union Village Ministry, 9 Apr. 1836.

62. Horgan, *Shaker Holy Land,* 101–102; "Money received of the Phoenix Factory & money laid out on the Phoenix Factory & premises for repairs needed & demanded," OClWHi II A 11; "The Order & Succession of the Ministry," OClWHi III A 7; "A Regis-ter of Incidents and Events Being a Continuation from other Records kept by the Minis-try Kept by Giles B. Avery Commenced Oct 20th 1859," NN (hereafter cited as Central Ministry Journal 1859–1874), 9, 22 Nov. 1859, 8 Apr. 1861.

63. Hall, "Shaker Response," 56–87; Central Ministry Journal 1859–1874, 31 Oct. 1859; "Address on Deacons and Rules Pertaining to them," MeSl; Ministry at Watervliet, New York, to Daniel Dryer, 12 Dec. 1859, Ministry at Watervliet to Groveland Ministry, 19 Feb., 29 Aug. 1860, NN.

64. New Lebanon Ministry to United Society, 10 Oct. 1860, MeSl; Hall, "Shaker Re-sponse," 83; West Gloucester Ministry to United Society, December 1860, MeSl.

65. Hall, "Shaker Response," 87–167; Maine Ministry Correspondence, 26 Jan. 1870, 7 Apr. 1867, cited ibid., 90–91; John Kaime to Ministry at Watervliet, 15 Apr. 1862, MeSl; "Church Records, Vol. 1, 1872–1877, Sabbathday Lake," MeSl, 13 Apr., 3 May 1874.

66. "Diary 1818–1860 at Hancock," DeWint, 16 Feb. 1839; Central Ministry Journal 1830–1839, 30 Jan. 1836; Youngs, "Tour" 2 : 1; Receipt for William Jones, 8 Oct. 1855, OClWHi II A 13.

67. Hall, "Shaker Response," 103 118; "Universal Circular to Believers, Concerning Care about Indebtedness to the World To be Read Annually in Each Family 1864," NOC no. 12,171.

68. "From the Shaker Defalcation? The Other side of the Question," OClWHi I A 11, pp. 1-4.

69. See Hall, "Shaker Response," and Solomon Goddard to New Lebanon Ministry, 6 Feb. 1867, quoted in Ham, "Shakerism in the Old West."

70. See Thomas J. Schlereth, ed., *Material Culture Studies in America* (Nashville, Tenn.: American Association for State and Local History, 1982), 1–75, for an instructive discussion of the interpretive possibilities of artifacts.

71. William Sims Bainbridge, "Shaker Demographics, 1840–1900: An Example of the Use of U.S. Census Enumeration Schedules," *Journal for the Scientific Study of Religion* 21 (1982):352–365. Bainbridge revises previous estimates of the number of Shakers. He counts 3,608 white members in 1840 as the likely high point (p. 355). An earlier, almost standard figure of 6,000 members in the decade before 1860 is repeated in Andrews, *People Called Shakers*, 224. John McKelvie Whitworth lists more than 5,500 as the top figure in the 1850s in *God's Blueprints: A Sociological Study of Three Utopian Sects* (London: Routledge and Kegan Paul, 1975), 76.

72. Andrews incorrectly argues, "Each of the Shaker villages was like the others, not only in the organization of its religious and temporal affairs, but in its architecture, in its customs and folk ways, in its dress and the speech of its inhabitants, and in the general nature of its agricultural, horticultural and industrial art activities." *Communal Industries*, 13.

73. See Kermit J. Pike, *A Guide to Shaker Manuscripts in the Library of the Western Reserve Historical Society* (Cleveland: Western Reserve Historical Society, 1974), 31–46, for a list of family journals in the Western Reserve Historical Society. The expression of individualism within Shakerism has received almost no scholarly attention.

74. The study of village topography deserves more attention than it has received. At Hancock the valley floor was more than 600 feet below the peaks of adjacent mountains. See Dolores Hayden, *Seven American Utopias: The Architecture of Communitarian Socialism, 1790–1975* (Cambridge: MIT Press, 1976), 78, and Emlen, *Shaker Village Views*, 65–92. The Believers frequently commented on the scenic advantages of their locations. See Youngs, "Tour," vol. 1, entries for 2, 14 Aug. 1834.

75. Hayden emphasizes the linear quality of Shaker village life in her examination of the physical layout and construction patterns at Hancock in *Seven American Utopias*, 64 103. See also Emlen, *Shaker Village Views*, for pictorial representations of the villages.

76. Many twentieth-century coffee-table books create a false impression of Shaker space by using photographs of building interiors that are contrived and almost devoid of signs of life. John E. Murray explores the negative implications of the crowded living space in "Tuberculosis in a Shaker Commune: North Union, Ohio, 1822–1889" (unpublished essay).

77. Two outstanding examples of social history employing the methods of cultural anthropologists are Wallace, *Rockdale*, and Rhys Isaac, *The Transformation of Virginia, 1740–1790* (Chapel Hill: University of North Carolina Press, 1982).

78. "A Journal, Containing an Account of the Hand Labor Performed by the Sisters, And also their Shop Proceedings," OClWHi V B 239. See also Anita Danker, "Woman's Place in the Harvard Shaker Community," *New England Social Studies Bulletin* 43 (1985–1986):15–39.

79. "The Boys Journal of Work," OClWHi V B 137, entries for 1846.

80. Andrews, *People Called Shakers,* 109. For examples of the ministry's involvement in daily labor, see Central Ministry Journal 1830–1839, 25 Feb. 1830, 11 Mar. 1831, 30 Apr. 1836, and "A Daily Journal of Passing Events; Begun May the 19th 1839, at Watervliet; By Rufus Bishop, in the 65th Year of His Age," NN (hereafter cited as Central Ministry Journal 1839–1850), 4 May 1847.

81. "Account of the Sisters Work," entry for 31 Dec. 1836. Andrews speculates that job rotation was "more systematic" among women in the society. *People Called Shakers,* 110–112.

82. "Dye House Journal," DeWint, 5 Aug. 1854, cited in Brewer, *Shaker Communities,* 74; Benjamin Gates to Isaac N. Youngs, 20 Mar. 1826, 11 Dec. 1837, NOC. On bonding among women, see Carroll Smith-Rosenberg, "The Female World of Love and Ritual: Relations between Women in Nineteenth-Century America," in *Disorderly Conduct: Visions of Gender in Victorian America* (New York: Oxford University Press, 1986), 53–76, originally published in *Signs: Journal of Women in Culture and Society* 1 (1975). On same-sex intimacy, see John D'Emilio and Estelle B. Freedman, *Intimate Matters: A History of Sexuality in America* (New York: Harper and Row, 1988), 121–130. Louis J. Kern links Shaker use of the term *effeminate* with condemnations of homosexuality. See *Ordered Love,* 83–84.

83. "A Scetch of my Faith in Short in Relation to the Order of the Church and my Order in the Same," NOC no. 9570; Emmory Brooks to Elders, 14 Oct. 1868, N; Deborah A. Einhorn, "Family and Friends in Shaker Society" (B.A. thesis, Williams College, 1981), 120.

84. Theodore E. Johnson, ed., "The 'Millennial Laws' of 1821," *Shaker Quarterly* 7 (1967):36–40.

85. Ibid., 55, 58; Brewer, *Shaker Communities,* 106–107. See Carolina B. Piercy, *The Shaker Cook Book: Not by Bread Alone* (New York: Crown, 1953), for recipes identified with different villages. The literature about Shaker cooking may have misrepresented the uniformity of the Believers' diet, but it probably has not overstated the general abundance and richness of food during this period.

86. Stephen Nissenbaum, *Sex, Diet, and Debility in Jacksonian America: Sylvester Graham and Health Reform* (Westport, Conn.: Greenwood, 1980), x; "Brief Journal Kept by an Unidentified Resident at Shirley," OClWHi V B 199, 4 May 1835. See also James C. Whorton, "Patient, Heal Thyself: Popular Health Reform Movements as Unorthodox Medicine," in *Other Healers: Unorthodox Medicine in America,* ed. Norman Gevitz (Baltimore: Johns Hopkins University Press, 1988), 60–69, and Robert C. Fuller, *Alternative Medicine and American Religious Life* (New York: Oxford University Press, 1989), 30–34.

87. Brewer, *Shaker Communities,* 106–113; Ephraim Prentiss, "Report of Interesting Experiences with Boys in Regards to Health, Discipline, and Fleshless Diets," OClWHi VII B 258.

88. Johnson, ed., "'Millennial Laws,'" 50–51, 55; Central Ministry Journal 1839–1850, 25, 28 June, 3 Aug., 27 Sept. 1839; MacLean, "Origin, Rise, Progress," 250; "Biographic Memoir of Calvin Green," MeSl, cited in Daniel W. Patterson, *The Shaker Spiritual* (Princeton: Princeton University Press, 1979), 97. For additional background, see Gevitz, ed., *Other Healers,* 29–98; Fuller, *Alternative Medicine,* 12–37; William G. Rothstein, *American Physicians in the Nineteenth Century: From Sects to Science* (Baltimore: Johns Hopkins University Press, 1972); and Susan E. Cayleff, *Wash and Be Healed: The Water-Cure Movement and Women's Health* (Philadelphia: Temple University Press, 1987).

89. Johnson, ed., "'Millennial Laws,'" 54–55; Kern, *Ordered Love*, 89; Green and Wells, *Summary View*, 129–143.

90. Johnson, ed., "'Millennial Laws,'" 54; Rufus Bishop to David Darrow, 2 July 1817, OClWHi IV A 33; Beverly Gordon, *Shaker Textile Arts* (Hanover, N.H.: University Press of New England, 1980), 149.

91. These observations are based on Gordon's discussion "Clothing and Personal Accessories" in *Shaker Textile Arts*, 146–203. See Pearson and Neal, *Shaker Image*, for illustrations of these items.

92. *A Juvenile Monitor: Containing Instructions for Youth and Children; Pointing Out Ill Manners, and Showing Them How to Behave in the Various Conditions of Childhood and Youth* (New Lebanon, N.Y.: The Shakers, 1823); Edward Deming Andrews and Faith Andrews, "The Shaker Children's Order," *Winterthur Portfolio* 8 (1973): 201–214; Brewer, *Shaker Communities*, 74–77; Frank Gilbert Taylor, "An Analysis of Shaker Education: The Life and Death of an Alternative Educational System, 1774–1950" (Ph.D. diss., University of Connecticut, 1976), 90–136. Not all caretakers found their responsibilities with the children a pleasant assignment. See "Boys Journal of Work," entries for November 1844. For a detailed description of Shaker life from a boy's perspective, see the recollections of Nicholas A. Briggs in "Forty Years a Shaker," *Granite Monthly: A Magazine of Literature, History and State Progress* 52 (1920): 463–474, and 53 (1921): 19–32, 56–65, 113–121.

93. Seth Y. Wells, "A Circular Address to the Society at Watervliet Concerning the Education of Children," 26 Jan. 1832, DeWint; Taylor, "Analysis of Shaker Education," 137–179; Hervey Elkins, *Fifteen Years in the Senior Order of Shakers: A Narration of Facts, Concerning that Singular People* (Hanover, N.H.: Dartmouth Press, 1853), 80–84.

94. Full understanding of the internal diversity within the United Society awaits detailed examination of individual Shaker families.

95. Nineteenth-century Shaker records are sufficiently detailed to allow the systematic study of short-term Shakers. Journals regularly note arrivals and departures.

96. Elisha [Pote] to Joseph Brackett, 15 Dec. 1842, MeSl; Central Ministry Journal 1839–1850, 16 Jan., 16 Aug. 1844, 24 Aug. 1847; Central Ministry Journal 1859–1874, 22 Apr., 3–4 May 1863.

97. MacLean, "Watervliet, Ohio, Shaker Community," in *Shakers of Ohio*, 211–214.

98. The logic of sectarianism leaves little room for official recognition of less than fully committed members.

99. See Elkins, *Fifteen Years*, 101–102; Stein, ed., *Letters*, 32; and Richard McNemar, "Diary," DLC secs. 253–254, 17 Apr. 1835.

100. Pleasant Hill Ministry to New Lebanon Ministry, 7 May 1823, 12 Apr. 1825, OClWHi IV A 53; William S. Byrd to Charles Willing Byrd, 25 Jan. 1827, Leonard Jones to Charles Willing Byrd, 4 Feb. 1827, W. S. Byrd to C. W. Byrd, 25 Feb. 1827, Jones to C. W. Byrd, 12 Apr. 1827, W. S. Byrd to C. W. Byrd, 25 May, 31 July 1827, Byrd Papers, InU; Stein, ed., *Letters*, 26; *Richmond [Indiana] Palladium*, 2 Mar. 1833, p. 1.

101. Rosabeth Moss Kanter, *Commitment and Community: Communes and Utopias in Sociological Perspective* (Cambridge: Harvard University Press, 1972), 64–70.

102. Brewer, *Shaker Communities*, 113–114.

103. Kanter, *Commitment and Community*, 61–74.

104. Henry C. Blinn, *The Manifestation of Spiritualism among the Shakers, 1837–1847* (East Canterbury, N.H.: The Shakers, 1899); MacLean, "Spiritualism among the Shakers of Union Village, Ohio," in *Shakers of Ohio*, 388–415; Julia Neal, *By Their Fruits: The Story of Shakerism in South Union, Kentucky* (Chapel Hill: University of North Carolina Press, 1947), 153–154; Andrews, *People Called Shakers*, 152–176; Whitworth, *God's Blueprints*, 64–72; Kern, *Ordered Love*, 105–113; Lawrence Foster, *Religion and Sexuality: Three American Communal Experiments of the Nineteenth Century* (New York: Oxford University Press, 1981), 62–71; Marjorie Procter-Smith, *Women in Shaker Community and Worship: A Feminist Analysis of the Uses of Religious Symbolism* (Lewiston, N.Y.: Edwin Mellen, 1985), 174–219.

105. Andrews, *People Called Shakers*, 152.

106. See Jon Butler, "Enthusiasm Described and Decried: The Great Awakening as Interpretive Fiction," *Journal of American History* 69 (1982):305–325.

107. Benjamin S. Youngs, "Early Watervliet Journal, 1794–1803," NOC, 44–47; "Journal of One Year Tuesday Jany 1st 1805 to Tuesday Decr 31st," DeWint, 124–125, 128, 142–143, 206–207, 275–277, 283, 287–288.

108. Lucy Smith to Dana Goodrich, 15 Aug. 1810, DLC sec. 248; Pleasant Hill Ministry to New Lebanon Ministry, 1 Apr. 1821, DeWint; Stein, ed., *Letters*, 63, 66; New Lebanon Ministry to Archibald Meacham, 30 July 1825, OClWHi IV A 35; Neal, *By Their Fruits*, 137.

109. Central Ministry Journal 1830–1839, 9 Jan. 1831, 1 Feb. 1832, 13 Feb. 1834, 1 Mar. 1835, 10 Jan., 21 Feb., 2 Oct., 18 Dec. 1836.

110. Ibid., 4 Jan., 11 June, 12 Aug. 1837.

111. "Account of the Sisters Work," entry for 19 Aug. 1837; "A Vision Seen by Ann Mariah Goff—2d Family—Watervliet—August 31st 1837," OClWHi VIII B 233.

112. Central Ministry Journal 1830–1839, 3, 10, 24, Sept. 1837.

113. Ibid., 29 Sept., 1 Oct. 1837, 8 Feb. 1838. For detailed accounts of these early visions, see "Inspirational Messages Second Family Watervliet, N.Y. 1836–1839," OClWHi VIII B 233; "Inspirational Visions of Ann Mariah at Second Family Watervliet, N.Y. 1838," OClWHi VIII B 234; and "Watervliet, N.Y. Society of Believers Inspirational Messages, Nov 16 1837–Mar 19, 1841," OClWHi VIII B 235.

114. Central Ministry Journal 1830–1839, 1 Oct. 1837.

115. Ibid., 8, 9, 15 Oct. 1837.

116. "A Vision of Ann Mariah Goff, Second Family, Watervliet, New York, November 7, 1837," OClWHi VIII B 233.

117. Ibid.

118. "Ann Mariah Goff's Vision, Second Family, Watervliet, November 8th 1837," OClWHi VIII B 233. Lawrence Foster has pointed out parallels between the actions of the instruments and those of the youthful accusers of witches in colonial Salem in "Shaker Spiritualism and Salem Witchcraft: Social Perspectives on Trance and Possession Phenomena," *Communal Societies* 5 (1985):176–193.

119. New Lebanon Ministry to Jeremiah Tallcott and Elders at Sodus Bay, 14 Feb. 1838, OClWHi IV A 79; Daniel Boler to Abner Bedell, 8 Apr. 1838, OClWHi IV A 37; Benjamin S. Youngs to Eleazar Wright, 22 Nov. 1837, DLC sec. 246; Isaac N. Youngs to New Lebanon Ministry, 7 Dec. 1837, OClWHi IV A 79; Seth Y. Wells to Canterbury Ministry, 3 Apr. 1838, OClWHi IV A 37.

120. Harvard Ministry to New Lebanon Ministry, 24 Jan. 1838, OClWHi IV A 23; En field, Connecticut, Ministry to Hancock Ministry, 28 Feb. 1838, OClWHi IV A 9; En field, New Hampshire, Ministry to New Lebanon Ministry, 20 Mar. 1838, OClWHi IV A 12; Enfield, Connecticut, Ministry to Harvard Ministry, 24 Oct. 1838, OClWHi IV A 9.

121. Cited in Neal, *By Their Fruits*, 140; MacLean, *Shakers of Ohio*, 393–394, 396; "A Diary Commenced January, 1st 1837 by R. W. Pelham," OHi, 22, 29 July, 5 Aug. 1838, 9 June 1839; Austin [at Watervliet, Ohio] to Rufus Bishop, 5 Apr. 1839, DeWint.

122. Patterson, *Shaker Spiritual*, 316–385, esp. pp. 377–380; Central Ministry Journal 1830–1839, 1, 29 Dec. 1837, 7–8 Feb., 25 Mar. 1838.

123. Central Ministry Journal 1830–1839, 31 Dec. 1837, 20 Jan., 29 Apr., 11 Nov. 1838; MacLean, "Spiritualism among the Shakers," 398–399; Isaac N. Youngs to New Lebanon Ministry, 11 Dec. 1837, OClWHi IV A 79; Central Ministry Journal 1839–1850, 14 Mar. 1840.

124. Central Ministry Journal 1830–1839, 4–5 Nov. 1837. For accounts of activities in these meetings, see "Journal of Meetings Held on the 'Holy Hill of Zion' at which Messages were Given by the Holy Father. Collected by Daniel Myrick," OClWHi VIII B 103; "Journal of Meetings at which Inspired Messages and Communications were Received, Begun by Derobigne M. Bennett and Continued by Isaac N. Youngs," OClWHi VIII B 138; "Journal of Meetings Held in the Church Order at which Inspired Messages and Communications were Received, Kept by Joseph W. Babe," OClWHi VIII B 139; "Minutes of Sabbath Meetings Held on the Mount of Olives," OClWHi VIII B 178; and "Inspired Messages and Accounts of Meetings," OClWHi VIII B 282.

125. Central Ministry Journal 1830–1839, 19 Apr., 28 Sept., 1 Dec. 1838; Andrews, *People Called Shakers*, 153; Brewer, *Shaker Communities*, 125–126. See "Copies of Messages and Extracts of Messages from Mother Ann, through Philemon Stewart," OClWHi VIII B 112, and "A Brief Sabbath or Spiritual Journal; Together with Condensed Minutes of the Most Solemn, Prayerful, and Prophetic Feelings Breathed Forth to God at Different Times, from the Soul of the Writer, as Divinely Inspired," 7 vols., OClWHi VIII B 181–187. On Poole's prominence in Kentucky, see "A Record of Visions, Messages and Communications Given by Divine Inspiration in the Society at Pleasant Hill, Ky.," OClWHi VIII B 211, and "A Family Record of Messages and Communications by Divine Inspiration. First Order of the Church at Pleasant Hill, Ky.," 2 vols., OClWHi VIII B 212–213.

126. Central Ministry Journal 1839–1850, 10–13 Apr. 1841.

127. Ibid., 22–25 May, 16, 21, 23, 27–28 Nov., 17–19, 25 Dec. 1841; "A List of Presents from the Spiritual World Given to Augustus H. Grosvenor, Harvard," MWiW, entry for 28 July 1841. See also "Journal of Meetings by Bennett and Youngs."

128. Andrews, *People Called Shakers*, 162; Edward Deming Andrews and Faith Andrews, *Fruits of the Shaker Tree of Life: Memoirs of Fifty Years of Collecting and Research* (Stockbridge, Mass.: Berkshire Traveller Press, 1975), 45–50.

129. Central Ministry Journal 1839–1850, 3, 4, 18 Sept., 13 Oct. 1842, 8 Jan., 12 Feb. 1843; Shirley Ministry to Nathaniel Deming, 8 Mar. 1843, DeWint; Patterson, *Shaker Spiritual*, 351–356; MacLean, "Spiritualism among the Shakers," 399–401. An early abortive attempt to convert some Indians in 1807 may have predisposed the Believers favorably toward these native manifestations. See MacLean, "Shaker Mission to the Shawnee Indians," in *Shakers of Ohio*, 347–361.

130. Central Ministry Journal 1839–1850, 21, 29 Apr., 1, 8, 15 May, 29 July, 31 Aug., 14 Sept. 1842.

131. Horgan, *Shaker Holy Land*, 75–78. For a description of the feast grounds, see Robert F. W. Meader, "Zion Patefacta," *Shaker Quarterly* 2 (1962):5–17; David R. Lamson, *Two Years' Experience Among the Shakers: Being a Description of the Manners and Customs of that People, the Nature and Policy of their Government, Their Marvellous Intercourse with the Spiritual World, the Object and Uses of Confession, Their Inquisition, in Short, a Condensed View of Shakerism as It Is* (West Boylston, Mass., 1848), 56–58; and Piercy, *Valley of God's Pleasure*, 156–158.

132. "Record of Meeting on 5 May 1844," in "Spiritualistic Communications," N, 103–113. David Lamson's account of an 1843 fountain feast at Hancock appears in *Two Years' Experience*, 58–67. Lamson, who left the Shakers after two years, regarded these rituals as silly "nonsense" and "an outrage upon common sense" (pp. 65–66).

133. Henri Desroche incorrectly identifies Tyringham as the City of Union (*The American Shakers: From Neo-Christianity to Presocialism*, trans. John K. Savacool [Amherst: University of Massachusetts Press, 1971], 329). There is some uncertainty about several of the names. I wish to thank Leonard Brooks and Arnold Hadd for assistance with these identifications. Note that the Lonely Plain of Tribulation (Whitewater) is the only name with a negative connotation, making it a striking exception to the larger pattern.

134. *A Holy, Sacred and Divine Roll and Book; from the Lord God of Heaven, to the Inhabitants of Earth: Revealed in the United Society at New Lebanon, County of Columbia, State of New-York, United States of America. In 2 Parts* (Canterbury, N.H.: United Society, 1843), 1, 7, 11. This was the first book printed at Canterbury.

135. Ibid., 2–3, 30–31, 74, 79–80, 111–113.

136. Ibid., 401. Among those offering testimonies to the volume were Seth Y. Wells and Benjamin S. Youngs (pp. 371–381).

137. Ibid., 12, 148, 160–161, 177–179. For a discussion of targumizing, see Krister Stendahl, "The Sermon on the Mount and Third Nephi," in *Reflections on Mormonism: Judaeo-Christian Parallels*, ed. Truman G. Madsen (Salt Lake City, Utah: Publishers Press, 1978), 139–154. For an excellent example of Shaker targumizing, see "Wisdoms Vally: Words Spoken for Our Saviour While at the Center, by a Mortal Instrument; In Company with the Groveland Ministry, Sept 4th 1842," N.

138. "Otis Sawyer's Testimony," MeSl, 23 Aug. 1843; "David Snow's Testimony at New Gloucester," MeSl, 24 Aug. 1843; "Diary 1818–1860, Hancock," DeWint, 5–15 Dec. 1843; Central Ministry Journal 1839–1850, 15 Dec. 1843, 6 Feb., 27 Oct. 1844; Robert F. W. Meader, "The Vision of Brother Philemon," *Shaker Quarterly* 10 (Spring 1970):8–17; W. P. W. Owen to Allen Bong, 20 Jan. 1847, MeSl.

139. Central Ministry Journal 1839–1850, 12, 22 Mar., 6, 8 Apr., 13 May, 12 July 1840; Johnson, ed., "'Millennial Laws,'" 37–41. The text of the 1845 Millennial Laws appears in Andrews, *People Called Shakers*, 249–289.

140. Canterbury Ministry to New Lebanon Ministry, 2 Jan. 1845, OClWHi IV A 5; Central Ministry Journal 1839–1850, 3 Aug. 1839, 11 Sept. 1846.

141. Seth Y. Wells to Groveland Elders, 24 Apr. 1838, OClWHi IV A 37; Central Ministry Journal 1830–1839, 1 Oct. 1837.

142. New Lebanon Ministry to Jeremiah Tallcott and Sodus Elders, 14 Feb. 1838, OClWHi IV A 79; New Lebanon Ministry to South Union Ministry, 12 Aug. 1839, cited in Andrews, *People Called Shakers*, 173–174; Central Ministry Journal 1839–1850, 26 May 1839.

143. New Lebanon Ministry to Jeremiah Tallcott, 6 June 1838, OClWHi IV A 79; Central Ministry Journal 1830–1839, 1 Dec. 1837, 29 Apr., 11 Nov., 29 Dec. 1838, 14 Jan. 1839; Central Ministry Journal 1839–1850, 22 June, 7 July 1839, 16 Nov. 1841, 3 Feb., 4 Sept. 1842, 21 Sept. 1844.

144. The contest between gift and order, spirit and letter, freedom and control, is universal within religious communities.

145. Suzanne Youngerman, "'Shaking is No Foolish Play': An Anthropological Perspective on the American Shakers—Person, Time, Space, and Dance-Ritual" (Ph.D. diss., Columbia University, 1983), 437–438; Central Ministry Journal 1830–1839, 24 Sept., 1, 9 Oct. 1837, 28 Sept. 1838; Central Ministry Journal 1839–1850, 30 June, 10 Aug. 1839, 5 Apr., 5 Sept., 25 Oct. 1840, 30 Jan. 1842, 14 Sept., 25 Dec. 1845.

146. Central Ministry Journal 1839–1850, 2 Feb. 1840.

147. Ibid., 20 Apr., 25 Oct. 1840, 9 Jan., 16 Apr., 18 Sept., 20 Nov. 1842, 4 Apr. 1844.

148. I. M. Lewis, *Ecstatic Religion: An Anthropological Study of Spirit Possession and Shamanism* (Harmondsworth, Middlesex: Penguin, 1971), 18–36.

149. Central Ministry Journal, 1830–1839, 9–11 May 1838; Central Ministry Journal 1839–1850, 29–30 May, 5, 8 June 1839, 30 Oct., 14 Dec. 1847; J. P. MacLean, *A Sketch of the Life and Labors of Richard McNemar* (Franklin, Ohio: Franklin Chronicle, 1905), 52–63.

150. "Remarks upon Inspired Writings," OClWHi VIII B 173; "Rules for Recording Inspired Writings," OClWHi IV A 38; Peter Foster to Rufus Bishop, 17 Sept. 1849, OClWHi IV A 5. The manuscripts of the inspired writings in repositories throughout the country represent a largely untapped resource and invite scrutiny from individuals interested in the psychological, sociological, literary, linguistic, and religious dimensions of such texts. See Pike, *Guide to Shaker Manuscripts*, 69–89, for the vast holdings of the Western Reserve Historical Society.

151. See, e.g., "A Communication from our Ever Blessed Mother Ann. Written by Inspiration at Wisdom's Valley Aug. 10th 1842. Concerning Temporal Things," OClWHi VIII B 274; "Words of a Shining Roll, Sent from Holy Mother Wisdom to Brother Rufus Bishop. July 10th 1842," DeWint; "A Book Containing an Account of Some of the Particular Transactions of John Calvin; and His Entrance into the Spiritual World. Written by Himself, in Union with our Heavenly Parents, 1842," MWiW; "A Prophetic Message of Warning Delivered in the Night of June 11, 1842, by the Prophet Ezra, 1842," N; "A Card of Love and Notice from Blessed Mother Ann to Elizabeth Lovegrove. January 25th 1843," DeWint; "A Brief History of Mary Magdalen Written by Herself," MWiW; and "A Book of the Prophet Jeremiah; to Which is Added a Book in Two Parts from the Patriarchs Caleb and Joshua. Written by Inspiration, Lovely Vineyard, 1843," MWiW.

152. Spirit letter from E. Issachar to Alexander written by J. Dunlavy, n.d., OHi.

153. Separating authentic and inauthentic religious experience has been a recurrent concern of religious leaders in America. See, e.g., Jonathan Edwards, *Religious Affections*, ed. John E. Smith, vol. 2 of *The Works of Jonathan Edwards* (New Haven: Yale University Press, 1959), 8–52.

154. Patterson, *Shaker Spiritual*, 317, 337–338, 358, 377–379. More than four hundred manuscript hymnals are part of the collection of the Western Reserve Historical Society. See Pike, *Guide to Shaker Manuscripts*, 91–133. For a representative collection of songs from the revival period, see Patterson, *Shaker Spiritual*, 323–376. For a discussion of the laboring songs and exercises from the period, see ibid., 379–385.

155. Patterson, *Shaker Spiritual,* 349–350, 372–373.

156. Patterson, *Gift Drawing,* 11, 29, 43. The story of the disclosure of these drawings by Alice Smith is in Andrews and Andrews, *Fruits of the Shaker Tree,* 93–97. For photographs of spirit drawings, see Edward Deming Andrews and Faith Andrews, *Visions of the Heavenly Sphere: A Study in Shaker Religious Art* (Charlottesville: University Press of Virginia, 1969), and Patterson, *Gift Drawing.*

157. Patterson, *Gift Drawing,* 47–50; Jane F. Crosthwaite, "The Spirit Drawings of Hannah Cohoon: Window on the Shakers and Their Folk Art," *Communal Studies* 7 (1987):1–15. Andrews and Andrews, *Visions,* 71, contains a color plate of Cohoon's "Tree of Life."

158. Crosthwaite, "Spirit Drawings."

159. "A Journal in the Centre Family Commencing January 1st 1839 Pleasant Hill Mercer County Ky., Kept by Kitty June Regan," KySP, 24 July 1842. See Sally M. Promey, "Spiritual Spectacles: Shaker Gift Images in Religious Context" (Ph.D. diss., University of Chicago, 1988).

160. These visitations led to moments of theological reflection. After an extended visit by Holy Mother Wisdom, Rufus Bishop wrote: "I have attended to Her judgment in nearly every family both here & at New Lebanon, and in all places & cases I have no cause to doubt the presence of an all-seeing Eye—a Holy being that sees us through & through, & from whom it is impossible for us to conceal the least transaction, word or thought" (Central Ministry Journal 1839–1850, 27 Jan. 1842). Hester Ann Adams, an instrument at Canterbury, wrote, "How can I but love my Mother, who hath so often feed & nourished me in the hour of affliction. O blessed blessed Mother, can I ever deny thee and thine can I ever turn from thy pure way, and break the holy Covenant which I have made with thee, Nay, nay, I will ever stand firm and true unto the end, that I may meet my Heavenly Parents in peace, when I have done with the things of time." Adams to Ruth Landon and Asenath Clark, 30 Aug. 1845, OClWHi IV A 5.

161. Procter-Smith, *Women in Shaker Community,* 196–203. See Barbara Welter, "The Cult of True Womanhood: 1820–1860," *American Quarterly* 18 (1966):151–174.

162. Paulina Bates, *The Divine Book of Holy and Eternal Wisdom, Revealing the Word of God; Out of Whose Mouth Goeth a Sharp Sword* (Canterbury, N.H.: The Shakers, 1849), iv, vi, xxi; Central Ministry Journal 1839–1850, 17 Oct. 1843.

163. Bates, *Divine Book of Wisdom,* 2, 4, 14, 35, 41, 46, 61–62.

164. Ibid., 556–586.

165. Ibid., 517, 666–669.

166. Central Ministry Journal 1839–1850, 3 Sept. 1846; Meader, "Zion Patefacta," 5; "A Register of Incidents and Events Being a Continuation from other Records kept by the Ministry Kept by Giles B. Avery Commenced Oct 20th 1859," NN (hereafter cited as Central Ministry Journal 1859–1874), 19 June 1861.

167. Central Ministry Journal 1839–1850, 25 Feb., 9 Mar. 1844, 7 Oct. 1845, 27 Sept. 1847; Brewer, *Shaker Communities,* 131–135. "By understanding a religion according to its gestures, the researcher learns that believing is not one activity or state of mind and belonging another activity and state." Ruel W. Tyson, Jr., James L. Peacock, and Daniel W. Patterson, eds., *Diversities of Gifts: Field Studies in Southern Religion* (Urbana: University of Illinois Press, 1988), 5.

168. Andrews, *People Called Shakers,* 249–289. See also Johnson, ed., "'Millennial Laws'," 40–41.

169. For one account of the disruption of daily routines, see Elkins, *Fifteen Years,* 55–56.

170. New Lebanon Believer to Brother Oliver, 10 Nov. 1850, MeSl; Canterbury Ministry to Lovely Vineyard [Harvard] Ministry, 16 Apr. 1850, OClWHi IV A 6; "A Small Record Book Kept by Betsy Crosman Beginning Nov 1848," OClWHi V B 143, 28 Jan., 3 Oct. 1851, 31 July 1852; "Records, 1855–1873, Kept by Sister Anna White," NN, 22 Jan. 1855.

171. Central Ministry Journal 1839–1850, 25 May 1841.

172. See Brewer, *Shaker Communities,* 158–177.

173. Isaac N. Youngs, "A Concise View of the Church of God and of Christ, On Earth Having its Foundation In the Faith of Christ's First and Second Appearing," DeWint, 501–509.

174. E. Burnham to Edward Fowler, 20 Oct. 1860, MeSl; Central Ministry Journal 1859–1874, 11 Jan., 26 Feb. 1860, 29 May, 26 Dec. 1861; Herbert A. Wisbey, Jr., *The Sodus Shaker Community* (Lyons, N.Y.: Wayne County Historical Society, 1982), 27. For more on Groveland, see Part IV.

175. "Records Kept by Sister Anna White," 25 Dec. 1859; New Lebanon Ministry to Ministry at Canterbury, 19 July 1863, NOC; MacLean, *Shakers of Ohio,* 100–101; Central Ministry Journal 1859–1874, 28 Oct. 1862; C. Miller and D. A. Buckingham to Frederick Evans and Benjamin Gates, 12 June 1863, N. For a tally of able-bodied Shaker men at the time of the war, see Brewer, *Shaker Communities,* 174. The Shaker petition presented to Lincoln appears in White and Taylor, *Shakerism,* 182–183.

176. Central Ministry Journal 1859–1874, 4 Jan. 1861, 27 Jan. 1863; Horgan, *Shaker Holy Land,* 111–112. For the war's impact on the Kentucky villages, see Neal, *By Their Fruits,* 177–197, and Thomas D. Clark and F. Gerald Ham, *Pleasant Hill and Its Shakers* (Pleasant Hill, Ky.: Shakertown Press, 1968), 63–70. See also White and Taylor, *Shakerism,* 180–204.

177. "Journal and Yearly Census. (Jan. 1856–Feb. 1871) Civil War Journal," KySP, 1 Aug. 1861, 8 Oct. 1862, New Gloucester Elders to Alfred Ministry, 15 Feb. 1863, MeSl.

178. Abraham Lincoln to Friends, 8 Aug. 1864, NOC; Frederick Evans and Benjamin Gates to Abraham Lincoln, 19 [Mar.] 1865, NOC; White and Taylor, *Shakerism,* 366.

179. Bainbridge, "Shaker Demographics," 355.

180. Theodore E. Johnson, ed., "Rules and Orders for the Church of Christ's Second Appearing Established by the Ministry and Elders of the Church Revised and Reestablished by the Same, New Lebanon, New York May 1860," *Shaker Quarterly* 11 (1971): 139–165.

181. Johnson, ed., "Rules and Orders," 155–156; Andrews, *People Called Shakers,* 272–273; Eliza Taylor to Mary Whitcher, 1864, MeSl; "Ministrie's Journal, Kept by Giles B. Avery, of Mount Lebanon Columbia Co. N.Y.," NN (hereafter cited as Central Ministry Journal 1874–1890), 28 June 1874.

182. "Civil War Journal, Pleasant Hill," KySP, 1 Jan. 1856; "Sally Sharp's Journal at Union Village," DLC sec. 298, 19 Feb. 1856; "Family Journal Kept by Order of the Deaconesses of the East House, Pleasant Hill," KyLoF, 1 Jan. 1857; "Diary Kept by Wealthy Storer 1846–1854," DeWint, 2 Feb. 1848. See also Brewer, *Shaker Communities,* 158–177.

183. "Records Kept by Sister Anna White," 10 July 1873; "Church Records, vol. 1, 1872–1877," MeSl, 1 Sept. 1875; "South Union Diary July 21, 1872–Jan 29, 1878," MWiW, 1 Oct. 1874.

184. Charles Edson Robinson, *A Concise History of the United Society of Believers Called Shakers* (East Canterbury, N.H.: The Shakers, 1893), 69–74. The conservative faction within Shakerism was not a cohesive, organized entity, but simply a loose group of like-minded individuals.

185. Frederick W. Evans, *Autobiography of a Shaker, and Revelation of the Apocalypse with an Appendix* ([Albany, N.Y.]: Charles Van Benthuysen and Sons, 1869), 9–28. See also Frederick Evans to George Evans, 11 June 1830, OClWHi IV A 36.

186. Evans, *Autobiography,* 26–35.

187. Ibid., 35–41. Evans's account, which originally appeared serially in the *Atlantic Monthly* 23 (1869):415–426, 593–605, elicited a spirited letter of approval from a reader who also rejected trinitarianism and the ecclesiastical practices of "so called christian Churches." See F. W. Byrdsall to Frederick Evans, 29 Mar. 1869, NOC.

188. *Autobiography of Mary Antoinette Doolittle Containing a Brief History of Early Life Prior to Becoming a Member of the Shaker Community, also an Outline of Life & Experience Among the Shakers* (Mount Lebanon, N.Y.: [The Shakers], 1880), 20–21, 25.

189. Michael H. Barton, *Something New, Comprising a New and Perfect Alphabet Containing 40 Distinct Characters, Calculated to Illustrate All the Various Sounds of the Human Voice Designed also to Facilitate the Acquisition of any Foreign Language. To Which is Added, Stenography Made Easy; or, a New Theory of Short Hand Writing* (Boston, 1833); "A Journal of Thomas Hammond," OClWHi V B 40, 26 Oct., 1 Nov. 1831; "Joseph Hammond's Journal," OClWHi V B 205–206, 27, 30 Oct., 2 Nov. 1831, 12 Jan., 9 Mar., 22 Apr., 29 July, 12 Aug. 1832; "North Family Shirley Journal," OClWHi V B 190, 12 Jan. 1832; Harvard Ministry to New Lebanon Ministry, 9 Nov. 1831, 20 Feb. 1832, OClWHi IV A 23; Seth Y. Wells to Michael H. Barton, 4 June 1832, OClWHi IV A 36. Barton's publication was issued in twelve numbers between April 1830 and October 1832.

190. Warder Cresson, *Babylon the Great is Falling! The Morning Star, or Light from on High. Written in Defence of the Rights of the Poor and Oppressed* (Philadelphia: Garden and Thompson, 1830); Shirley Ministry to New Lebanon Ministry, 10 Dec. 1831, OClWHi V A 58; Frank Fox, "Quaker, Shaker, Rabbi: Warder Cresson, The Story of a Philadelphia Mystic," *Pennsylvania Magazine of History and Biography* 95 (1971):147–194. On the Hicksite separation, see H. Larry Ingle, *Quakers in Conflict: The Hicksite Reformation* (Knoxville: University of Tennessee Press, 1986).

191. Fox, "Quaker, Shaker, Rabbi," 155–194; "Joseph Hammond's Journal," 13 Sept. 1832; Harvard Ministry to Alfred Ministry, 16 Oct., 17 Dec. 1832, "Annie Williams' Journal," OClWHi V B 127, 23 Sept. 1832; Seth Y. Wells to Harvard Ministry, 25 Oct. 1831, OClWHi IV A 36; Seth Y. Wells to Ministry, 23 Sept. 1832, OClWHi IV A 6; David L. Rowe, *Thunder and Trumpets: Millerites and Dissenting Religion in Upstate New York, 1800–1850* (Chico, Calif.: Scholars Press, 1985), 63.

192. The most important study of Jackson is Jean McMahon Humez, ed., *Gifts of Power: The Writings of Rebecca Jackson, Black Visionary, Shaker Eldress* (Amherst: University of Massachusetts Press, 1981); see p. 9. See also Richard E. Williams, *Called and Chosen: The Story of Mother Rebecca Jackson and the Philadelphia Shakers* (Metuchen, N.J.: Scarecrow, 1981), and Diane Sasson, *The Shaker Spiritual Narrative*

(Knoxville: University of Tennessee Press, 1983), 158–188. The role of black women preachers in this period is the subject of William L. Andrews, ed., *Sisters of the Spirit: Three Black Women's Autobiographies of the Nineteenth Century* (Bloomington: Indiana University Press, 1986).

193. Humez, ed., *Gifts of Power*, 23–41.

194. Central Ministry Journal 1839–1850, 24 July 1842.

195. Ibid., 17 June 1846; "Diary by Wealthy Storer," 16–17 June, 10–16 Aug. 1846; MacLean, "Whitewater Shaker Community," 250–253; Brewer, *Shaker Communities*, 152–153.

196. Lawrence Foster, "Had Prophecy Failed? Contrasting Perspectives of the Millerites and Shakers," in *The Disappointed: Millerism and Millenarianism in the Nineteenth Century*, ed. Ronald L. Numbers and Jonathan M. Butler (Bloomington: Indiana University Press, 1987), 173–188, "Diary by Wealthy Storer," 16 Aug. 1846; N. Gordon Thomas, "The Millerite Movement in Ohio," *Ohio History* 81 (1972):95–107.

197. See Robert S. Fogarty, *Dictionary of American Communal and Utopian History* (Westport, Conn.: Greenwood, 1980), 58, 131; Paul Elmen, *Wheat Flour Messiah: Eric Jansson of Bishop Hill* (Carbondale: Southern Illinois University Press, 1976), 133–134; and Clark and Ham, *Pleasant Hill*, 61–62.

198. Andrews, *People Called Shakers*, 223; "Ministerial Journal Pleasant Hill 1868–1880," KyLoF, 8 Nov. 1868, 21 Jan., 10, 16 Feb. 1869; Neal, *By Their Fruits*, 234; Bainbridge, "Shaker Demographics," 357.

199. "South Union Diary 1872–1878," 21 July to 21 Dec. 1872.

200. The categories "liberal" and "conservative" do not do justice to the complexity of the opposing perspectives within the society after 1870.

201. Central Ministry Journal 1839–1850, 9 Oct. 1849; Thomas Whittaker, "From Jasper Valley to Holy Mount: The Odyssey of Daniel Boler," *Shaker Quarterly* 10 (1970): 35–45 Amos Stewart, the brother of Philemon, who had been brought to New Lebanon when he was nine years old, was appointed to the central ministry in 1849 at the age of forty-seven. He served as second in the lead under Rufus Bishop until Bishop died in 1852. Then Stewart advanced to first in the ministry where he remained until 1858, when he was released and selected as elder of the Second Family.

202. Calvin Green to John Lockwood, 8 Nov. 1847, NN. Some insight into the later troubled years of Isaac N. Youngs's life is available through his "Personal Journal," NOC. See also Grant and Allen, *Shaker Furniture Makers*, 35–51.

203. "A Journal Kept by the Deaconess of the Church Family at Watervliet Commencing Sept. 1, 1866," DeWint, 11–12 July 1867; Central Ministry Journal 1859–1874, 29 Sept. 1862, 22 Apr., 10 May 1863.

204. Francis Voris to Stephen Munson, 28 June 1828, DeWint; "Gass and Bonta against Wilhite and Others—a Society of Shakers," in *Reports of Select Cases Decided in the Court of Appeals of Kentucky During the Year 1834*, ed. James G. Dana, 3 vols. (Louisville, Ky.: Geo. G. Fetter, 1899), 2:170–203; Richard McNemar to Seth Wells, 15 Sept. 1830, 5 Apr. 1831, DLC sec. 245; Carol Weisbrod, *The Boundaries of Utopia* (New York: Pantheon, 1980) 122–134; *A Memorial Remonstrating Against a Certain Act of the Legislature of Kentucky, Entitled "An Act to Regulate Civil Proceedings against Certain Communities Having Property in Common"* (Harrodsburg, Ky.: Union Office, 1830); New Gloucester Ministry to Chosen Vale Ministry, 17 Nov. 1844, MeSl; Green to Lockwood, 8 Nov. 1847; Brewer, *Shaker Communities*, 148–150; Mount Lebanon Ministry to Watervliet Elders, 8 June 1871, OClWHi IV A 44.

205. James Fenimore Cooper, *Notions of the Americans: Picked up by a Traveling Bachelor,* 2 vols. (London: Henry Colburn, 1828), 2:328–331; Ralph Waldo Emerson to Charles Chauncy Emerson, 1 Jan. 1828, 7 Aug. 1829, *The Letters of Ralph Waldo Emerson,* ed. Ralph L. Rusk (New York: Columbia University Press, 1936), 1:224–226, 275–276; [Charlotte Cushman], "Lines: Suggested by a Visit to the Shaker Settlement, near Albany," *Knickerbocker* 9 (January 1837):46–47.

206. Elizabeth [Peabody], "A Glimpse of Christ's Idea of Society," *Dial* 2 (October 1841), 223; Charles [Lane], "A Day with the Shakers," *Dial* 4 (October 1843):165–173; "Letter from Charles Lane—The Shakers—Community &c.," *Regenerator,* n.s., 1 (October 19, 1846):239. See also Anne C. Rose, *Transcendentalism as a Social Movement, 1830–1850* (New Haven: Yale University Press, 1981), 52–56, 120–125, 197, and Priscilla J. Brewer, "Emerson, Lane, and the Shakers: A Case of Converging Ideologies," *New England Quarterly* 55 (1982):254–275. Lane subsequently exchanged letters with the Shaker David Richmond. See Mary L. Richmond, *Shaker Literature: A Bibliography,* 2 vols. (Hanover, N.H.: University Press of New England, 1977), 1:239–240.

207. Frances Trollope, *Domestic Manners of the Americans,* 2 vols. (London: Whittaker, Treacher, 1832), 1:194–196; Harriet Martineau, *Society in America,* 3d ed., 2 vols. (New York: Saunders and Otley, 1837), 1:310–315; Frederika Bremer, *The Home of the New World; Impressions of America,* trans. Mary Howitt, 2 vols. (New York: Harper and Brothers, 1853), 2:579–580.

208. Charles Dickens, *American Notes for General Circulation,* 2 vols. (London: Chapman and Hall, 1842), 2:217–220; Duncan A. Carter and Laurence W. Mazzeno, "Dickens's Account of the Shakers and West Point: Rhetoric or Reality?" *Dickensian* 72 (1976):139.

209. Horace Greeley, "The Social Architects—Fourier: A Lecture," in *Hints Toward Reforms, In Lectures, Addresses, and Other Writings* (New York: Harper and Brothers, 1850), 278–280; Friedrich Engels, "Description of Recently Founded Communist Colonies Still in Existence," in vol. 4 of *Karl Marx, Frederick Engels: Collected Works,* trans. Christopher Upward (New York: International Publishers, 1975), 215–216, first published in *Deutsches Bürgerbuch für 1845* (Darmstadt, 1845); Thomas Low Nichols, *Forty Years of American Life,* 2 vols. (London: John Maxwell, 1864), 1:31–32; Henry Howe, *Historical Collections of Ohio; Containing A Collection of the Most Interesting Facts, Traditions, Biographical Sketches, Anecdotes, etc. Relating to its General and Local History with Descriptions of its Counties, Principal Towns and Villages* (Cincinnati, Ohio: E. Morgan, 1854), 502. See also Carl J. Guarneri, *The Utopian Alternative: Fourierism in Nineteenth-Century America* (Ithaca: Cornell University Press, 1991).

210. Nathaniel Hawthorne to Louisa Hawthorne, 17 Aug. 1831, in *The Letters, 1813–1843,* ed. Thomas Woodson, L. Neal Smith, and Norman Holmes Pearson, vol. 15 of *The Centenary Edition of the Works of Nathaniel Hawthorne* (Columbus: Ohio State University Press, 1984), 213; Hawthorne, *The American Notebooks,* ed. Randall Stewart (New Haven: Yale University Press, 1932), 230; Seymour L. Gross, "Hawthorne and the Shakers," *American Literature* 29 (1958):457–463; James Franklin Farnham, "Hawthorne and the Shakers," *Shaker Quarterly* 6 (1966):5–13; Rita K. Collin, "Hawthorne Contemplates the Shakers: 1831–1851," *Nathaniel Hawthorne Journal* 8 (1978):56–65.

211. Nathaniel Hawthorne, "The Canterbury Pilgrims," in *The Snow-Image and Uncollected Tales,* ed. J. Donald Crowley, vol. 11 of *Works of Hawthorne* (Columbus: Ohio State University Press, 1974), 120–131.

212. Nathaniel Hawthorne, "The Shaker Bridal," in *Twice-Told Tales*, ed. J. Donald Crowley, vol. 9 of *Works of Hawthorne* (Columbus: Ohio State University Press, 1974), 419–425.

213. Herman Melville, *Moby Dick, or, The Whale* (New York: Harper and Brothers, 1851), 349–350; Melville, *Clarel: A Poem and Pilgrimage to the Holy Land,* 2 vols. (New York: G. P. Putnam's Sons, 1876); Melville, *Journal of a Visit to Europe and the Levant, October 11, 1856–May 6, 1857,* ed. Howard C. Horsford (Princeton: Princeton University Press, 1955), 143. See also Richmond, *Shaker Literature* 2:82, and Fox, "Quaker, Shaker, Rabbi," 192–193.

214. Artemus Ward, "On the Shakers," *Vanity Fair,* February 23, 1861, 94–95.

215. It is tempting to see these popular images of the Shakers as projections of the wishes or fantasies of those who wrote about the society.

216. Theodore E. Johnson, ed., "Prudence Morrell's Account of a Journey to the West in the Year 1847," *Shaker Quarterly* 8 (1968):54–55; "Record of Events of the Church Family, Union Village," OClWHi V B 230, 11 July 1847; D. P. Thompson, *The Shaker Lovers, and Other Tales* (Burlington, Vt.: C. Goodrich and S. B. Nichols, 1848), 5–43; Samuel D. Johnson, *The Shaker Lovers. A Drama, in One Act* (New York: Samuel French, [1857]).

217. Don Gifford, "Lossing and the Shakers," in *An Early View of the Shakers: Benson John Lossing and the Harper's Article of June 1857 with Reproductions of the Original Sketches and Watercolors,* ed. Don Gifford (Hanover, N.H.: University Press of New England, 1989), 59–69; "The Shakers," *Harper's New Monthly Magazine* 15 (July 1857):164–177. Charles I. Glicksberg erred in attributing this unsigned essay to Walt Whitman, in "A Whitman Discovery," *Colophon,* n.s., 1 (October 1935):227–233. The mistake was corrected by George J. Finney in an unpublished essay entitled "A Visit to the Shakers: Lossing not Whitman" (December 1940), cited in Gifford, "Lossing and the Shakers," 70.

218. Gifford, "Lossing and the Shakers," 32, 37–39, 51, 55, 57.

219. William Hepworth Dixon, *New America,* 4th ed., 2 vols. (London: Hurst and Blackett, 1867), 1:ix–x; Richmond, *Shaker Literature* 2:37–38.

220. Dixon, *New America* 2:80, 84, 86–87, 93–94, 97, 110.

221. Ibid., 2:89, 102, 106–107, 123–124, 134, 148.

222. New Lebanon Ministry, "Circular Epistle," 23 June 1870, NOC (another copy is at N); "Ministerial Journal, Pleasant Hill, 1868–1880," KyLoF, 7 Aug. 1870. For background on concerts of prayer among American evangelicals, see Stephen J. Stein, ed., *Apocalyptic Writings,* vol. 5 of *The Works of Jonathan Edwards* (New Haven: Yale University Press, 1977), 29–48.

223. Emmory Brooks to Polly Lee, 6 Jan. 1869, N; "Ministerial Journal, Pleasant Hill, 1868–1880," 23 Mar., 5 Apr. 1869; *Shaker* 2 (1872):35–38, 42–43; "Church Records, Volume 1, 1872–1877," MeSl, 9 June 1872; Theodore E. Johnson, "The Great 'Portland Meetings' of 1872," *Shaker Quarterly* 12 (1972):121–137; *Shaker* 2 (1872):56; *Shaker and Shakeress* 3 (1873):42–43.

224. White and Taylor, *Shakerism,* 206–208.

225. Frederick Evans to Albert Lomas, 4 Aug. 1871, OClWHi IV A 44; R. Laurence Moore, *In Search of White Crows: Spiritualism, Parapsychology, and American Culture*

(New York: Oxford University Press, 1977), 87; *Religious Communism. A Lecture by F. W. Evans (Shaker) of Mount Lebanon, Columbia Co., New York, U.S.A., Delivered in St. George's Hall, London, Sunday Evening, August 6th 1871; with Introductory Remarks by the Chairman of the Meeting, Mr. Hepworth Dixon. Also Some Account of the Extent of the Shaker Communities, and a Narrative of the Visit of Elder Evans to England. An Abstract of a Lecture by Rev. J. M. Peebles, and His Testimony in Regard to the Shakers* (London: J. Burns, [1871]); James M. Peebles to Editor, 3 Sept. 1871, in *Shaker* 1 (1871):73–74; Frederick Evans to Editor of the *Golden Age*, 11 Aug. 1871, in *Shaker* 1 (1871):79; White and Taylor, *Shakerism*, 208–209. On Peebles, see J. O. Barrett, *The Spiritual Pilgrim: A Biography of James M. Peebles* (Boston: William White, 1871).

226. "Salutatory," *Shaker* 1 (1871):1, 8.

227. Ibid., 1.

228. "Who Are the Shakers?" *Shaker* 1 (1871):1–2, 64; Moore, *In Search of White Crows*, 13.

229. [Josiah Gilbert Holland], "Shakerism," *Scribner's Monthly* 3 (January 1872): 369–370; Lomas, "Shakerism's Defense," *Shaker* 2 (1872):19–20.

230. Frederick W. Evans, "Autobiography of a Shaker," *Atlantic Monthly* 22 (1869): 415–425, 593–605; Evans, *Autobiography of a Shaker*, 3–4, 9, 59–60, 97, 149. See also James M. Peebles, *Seers of the Ages: Embracing Spiritualism, Past and Present; Doctrines Stated and Moral Tendencies Defined* (Boston: W. White, 1869).

231. *New York Herald*, 7 Jan. 1874, p. 12; *New York Sun*, 8 Jan. 1874, p. 4; *Shaker and Shakeress* 4 (1874):9; Central Ministry Journal 1874–1890, 10 Jan. 1874.

232. Frederick W. Evans, "Shaker Pentecost," *Shaker and Shakeress* 4 (1874):9–10.

233. "Church Records, Volume 1, 1872–1877," 29 Jan. 1874; "Journal No. 9. of the South Family. Commencing with the 10th of July 1868, Watervliet, New York," OClWHi V B 312, 6 Feb. 1874; "South Union Diary 1872–1878," 29 Mar. 1874; "Record of Events of the Church Family, Union Village," 3–4 Apr. 1874; "Private Diary Volume 4th Since the Year 1862 January 1 by William Reynolds," OClWHi V B 258, 3–4 Apr. 1874; Charles Nordhoff, *The Communistic Societies of the United States; from Personal Visit and Observation: Including Detailed Accounts of the Economists, Zoarites, Shakers, the Amana, Oneida, Bethel, Aurora, Icarian, and Other Existing Societies, Their Religious Creeds, Social Practices, Numbers, Industries, and Present Condition* (New York: Harper and Brothers, 1875), 17–19, 115–256; Richmond, *Shaker Literature* 2:89.

234. Nordhoff, *Communistic Societies*, 117–119, 256.

235. Ibid., 179–214, 396.

236. Ibid., 166, 183, 189, 191–194, 197–198, 206–207, 213, 245–251.

237. Ibid., 164, 168, 388–390, 398, 405–406, 417–418.

238. Mount Lebanon Ministry to Elders at Watervliet, 8 June 1871; *Shaker and Shakeress* 3 (1873):7, and 5 (1875):20, 25; Central Ministry Journal 1874–1890, 6, 28 Feb. 1875; Thomas Hammond to Alonzo Hollister, 29 Aug. 1875, OClWHi IV A 44. In August 1876 two barns, nine other buildings, supplies, and equipment were lost to fire at Pleasant Hill. "Records of the Church at Watervliet, N.Y. Vol. III," OClWHi V B 338, 25 Aug. 1876.

239. See Emlen, *Shaker Village Views*.

240. "A Journal Kept by the Deaconess of the Church Family at Watervliet Commencing Sept. 1, 1866," 9 Dec. 1866. One measure of the immense resources available for this period is the following: the Western Reserve Historical Society contains 416 manuscript letters from the 1860s alone, not counting correspondence that has been collected by the Believers and transcribed into copybooks. Likewise, this one repository has thousands of pages of diary and journal entries for that decade.

241. "A Summary Statement of the Observance of Certain Days Appointed to be Kept," DLC sec. 296; "Journal of Meetings Commencing Sept 17th 1851 and ending May 17th 1852," MWiW, 29 Feb. 1852; "Account of Removals and Reburials," N, 9–12 May 1835; "Diary by Wealthy Storer," 31 Aug. 1848; Evans, *Autobiography,* 54; "Mother Ann Lee, the Shaker," *The Phrenological Miscellany: Or, The Annuals of Phrenology and Physiognomy from 1865–1873* (New York: Fowler and Wells, 1882), 382–385; Lomas to L. A. Wells, 9 May 1871, cited in Eugene F. Kramer, "Identifying Mother Ann Lee's Picture," *New York Folklore* 16 (1960):226–227.

242. "Records Kept by Order of the Church. Volume III January 1856–August 1871," NOC, 22 Aug., 26 Oct., 31 Dec. 1870; "Ministerial Journal, Pleasant Hill, 1868–1880," KyLoF, 23 Apr. 1870.

243. "A Record Commenced Dec' 28th 1864. Groveland," N, 31 Dec. 1864, 31 Dec. 1872; "Ministerial Journal, Pleasant Hill, 1868–1880," 1 Jan. 1869, 1 Jan. 1876; Nordhoff, *Communistic Societies,* 195, 256; "Society Removed," *Shaker and Shakeress* 5 (1875):41.

244. Historians generally have divided the narrative of religion in America at the Civil War. See Sydney E. Ahlstrom, *A Religious History of the American People* (New Haven: Yale University Press, 1972), 633–729; Robert T. Handy, *A History of the Churches in the United States and Canada* (New York: Oxford University Press, 1976), 185–196, 227, 262–271; and Edwin S. Gaustad, ed., *A Documentary History of Religion in America,* 2 vols. (Grand Rapids, Mich.: William B. Eerdmans, 1982–1983).

245. For a time, the most serious competitor to the central ministry was Philemon Stewart. It is not insignificant that after he fell from favor, Stewart was sent to Sabbathday Lake, where he served in a leadership role at the Poland Hill Family. See Stewart's "A Brief Weekly Journal, 1870–1874," DeWint.

246. The move away from the rigor of the revival period is discussed briefly in Johnson, ed., "'Millennial Laws,'" 40–41.

247. For further reflections on the antistructural implications of the revival's rituals, see Victor Turner, *The Ritual Process: Structure and Anti-Structure* (Ithaca: Cornell University Press, 1977), 166–203.

248. See Turner, "Liminality and Communitas," ibid., 94–130.

249. White and Taylor, *Shakerism,* is an account of Shaker history from the progressive perspective.

250. The Shaker experience confirms the observations of Anthony F. C. Wallace in "Revitalization Movements."

251. See Part IV for a fuller discussion of the notion of decline within Shakerism.

Part Four

1. Lally Weymouth and Milton Glaser, *America in 1876: The Way We Were* (New York: Random House, 1976), 12–47; James W. Campbell, *America in Her Centennial Year 1876* (Washington, D.C.: University Press of America, 1980), 5–20. See also Ray Ginger, *Age of Excess: The United States from 1877 to 1914* (New York: Macmillan, 1965); Robert H. Wiebe, *The Search for Order, 1877–1920* (New York: Hill and Wang, 1967); and Charles Reagan Wilson, *Baptized in Blood: The Religion of the Lost Cause, 1865–1920* (Athens: University of Georgia Press, 1980).

2. Paul A. Carter, *The Spiritual Crisis of the Gilded Age* (DeKalb: Northern Illinois University Press, 1971); William R. Hutchison, *The Modernist Impulse in American Protestantism* (Cambridge: Harvard University Press, 1976); George M. Marsden, *Fundamentalism and American Culture: The Shaping of Twentieth-Century Evangelicalism, 1870–1925* (New York: Oxford University Press, 1980); R. Laurence Moore, *In Search of White Crows: Spiritualism, Parapsychology, and American Culture* (New York: Oxford University Press, 1977).

3. *Shaker* 6 (1876), 49, 59, 72.

4. *Shaker* 2 (1872):21; "Our Centennial," *Shaker and Shakeress* 4 (1874):77–78.

5. For an account of eastern Shakerism during the opening decades of this period, see Priscilla J. Brewer, *Shaker Communities, Shaker Lives* (Hanover, N.H.: University Press of New England, 1986), 178–202.

6. For a story of contrasting development during these years, see Thomas G. Alexander, *Mormonism in Transition: A History of the Latter-Day Saints, 1890–1930* (Urbana: University of Illinois Press, 1986).

7. The most instructive public statement from within the society during this period is Anna White and Leila S. Taylor, *Shakerism Its Meaning and Message Embracing An Historical Account, Statement of Belief and Spiritual Experience of the Church from Its Rise to the Present Day* (Columbus, Ohio: Fred J. Heer, 1904).

8. "A Family Journal, Second Family, Watervliet N.Y. 1885," MWiW, 19 Sept. 1886.

9. William Sims Bainbridge, "Shaker Demographics, 1840–1900: An Example of the Use of U.S. Census Enumeration Schedules," *Journal for the Scientific Study of Religion* 21 (1982):354–355. Bainbridge has identified the villages on the basis of census schedules. In other lists, Pittsfield is lumped with Hancock, Poland with Sabbathday Lake, and Canaan with New Lebanon. Bainbridge does not include the small group of blacks in Philadelphia in 1880. See Jean McMahon Humez, ed., *Gifts of Power: The Writings of Rebecca Jackson, Black Visionary, Shaker Eldress* (Amherst: University of Massachusetts Press, 1981), 358.

10. See J. P. MacLean, "Rise, Progress and Extinction of the Society at Cleveland, Ohio," in *Shakers of Ohio: Fugitive Papers concerning the Shakers of Ohio, with Unpublished Manuscripts* (Columbus, Ohio: F. J. Heer, 1907), 112–189; Caroline B. Piercy, *The Valley of God's Pleasure: A Saga of the North Union Shaker Community* (New York: Stratford House, 1951); and Mary Lou Conlin, *The North Union Story: A Shaker Society, 1822–1889* (Shaker Heights, Ohio: Shaker Historical Society, 1961).

11. "Account of the Rise and Progress of the Church at North Union," OClWHi V B 177, 19 Oct. 1877, 14 Oct. 1883; William Reynolds to Giles Avery, 29 June 1876, NOC; "Annual Report of Business Conditions, 1881," OClWHi II A 10. See MacLean, *Shakers of Ohio*, 175–178, for a short biography of Prescott.

12. "Account of the Church at North Union," 18 Feb. 1882, 27 June 1884, 4 July 1885, 5 July 1886; James Higgins to Matthew Carter, 18 Sept. 1884, OClWHi IV A 51. For more concerning the Shaker response to Hering, who had predicted President James Garfield's assassination, see Oliver C. Hampton to Lydia Cramer, 18 June 1882, OClWHi IV A 51. See also John E. Murray, "Tuberculosis in a Shaker Commune: North Union, Ohio, 1822–1889" (unpublished essay).

13. "Obituary," OClWHi III B 29; Matthew B. Carter to Benjamin Gates, 13 Sept. 1889, NOC; "Records at New Lebanon 1871–1905," NOC, 3 Nov. 1889; Conlin, *North Union Story,* 5; MacLean, *Shakers of Ohio,* 133; Paul T. Skove to Louis Baus, 21 Mar. 1932, OClWHi IV A 51. Giles Avery lists the sale price as $287,000 in Central Ministry Journal 1874–1890, 15 Oct. 1889.

14. Herbert A. Wisbey, Jr., *The Sodus Shaker Community* (Lyons, N.Y.: Wayne County Historical Society, 1982), 5–24; Proctor Sampson and Calvin Green to New Lebanon Ministry, 10 Mar. 1826, OClWHi IV A 35; "A Record of the Commencement and Progress of the Believers at Sodus and Portbay," OClWHi V B 21; Seth Wells to Jeremiah Tallcott, 5 Nov. 1828, N; "Account" of the financing of Portbay and Sodus, NOC no. 13,393.

15. Wisbey, *Sodus Shaker Community,* 25–26; Wisbey, "Stories of the Groveland Shakers: Lucius Southwick," *Shaker Messenger* 10 (Spring 1988): 9–11, 22.

16. Wisbey, *Sodus Shaker Community,* 27–28; Fran Kramer, *Simply Shaker: Groveland and the New York Communities* (Rochester, N.Y.: Rochester Museum and Science Center, 1991), 35–43.

17. Wisbey, *Sodus Shaker Community,* 26; "South Family Events, Kept by Anna Goepper 1912 and 1913," DeWint, 2, 5, 11, 16, 25, 29 Aug., 5 Sept. 1912, 3 May 1913.

18. "Church Records, Volume 1, 1872–1877," McSl, pp. 13, 27; Central Ministry Journal 1874–1890, 19 Nov. 1877; Alaric Faulkner and Gretchen Fearon Faulkner, "The Poland Hill Shaker Settlement," *Shaker Quarterly* 17 (1989): 11–27; "Notes about Home," *Manifesto* 29 (1899): 60.

19. "Annual Inventories for Lower Family, Canaan," NOC, 1878.

20. "Journal Commencing January 1st 1875. Canaan Upper Family," DeWint.

21. Alice Braisted to Mother Emily, 24 July 1881, NN. These statistics conflict with Brewer's observations on the limited supply of potential leaders. See *Shaker Communities,* 96.

22. "Records at New Lebanon 1871–1905," 29 Dec. 1895; Lawrence Foster, *Religion and Sexuality: Three American Communal Experiments of the Nineteenth Century* (New York: Oxford University Press, 1981), 55. As late as 1906 the society was negotiating with Laura Langford concerning the potential sale of the "Canaan Shaker Farm," which had been leased. They were asking $8,000 for it. See Daniel Offord to Laura Langford, 28 June 1906, DeWint.

23. Mount Lebanon Ministry to Watervliet Elders, 4 Apr. 1872, OClWHi IV A 44; Central Ministry Journal 1874–1890, 7 July 1877.

24. Central Ministry Journal 1874–1890, 8–9 Sept., 5 Oct. 1876. The situation at the West Family suggests exercising caution in generalizating about the racial attitudes of the Shakers.

25. Central Ministry Journal 1874–1890, 7 Sept. 1876, 16 June 1878.

26. Ibid., 14 Aug. 1877, 13 Apr. 1889; Offord to Langford, 28 June 1906; Brewer, *Shaker Communities,* 184–189.

27. Bainbridge, "Shaker Demographics," 354; Edward Deming Andrews, *The People Called Shakers: A Search for the Perfect Society* (New York: Oxford University Press, 1953), 290–291.

28. Central Ministry Journal 1874–1890, 23 Apr., 31 Aug., 30 Sept. 1889; "Records at New Lebanon 1871–1905," 30 Mar. 1883, and 3 Nov. 1889; "Travel Journal Kept by Harriet Bullard," OClWHi V B 172, 2, 5 Apr. 1889. A great deal of the business correspondence from this period relates to these concerns. See the various manuscript collections, especially the legal records at NOC.

29. Edward R. Horgan, *The Shaker Holy Land: A Community Portrait* (Harvard, Mass.: Harvard Common Press, 1982), 141–147; John Whiteley to Mount Lebanon Ministry, 10 Jan. 1886, John Whiteley to Benjamin Gates, 10 Feb. 1886, NOC; deed to Mark Holden farm, NOC no. 10,054; copy of Shirley sale agreement, 8 Dec. 1908, NOC no. 15,615-F.

30. Horgan, *Shaker Holy Land*, 151–153, 167; "Inventory of Things taken from the Society of Shakers, of Harvard Mass. June 1918 by Hattie May Whitney," NOC no. 15,606; "Release" signed by Mary Jane Maxwell, 15 June 1918, NOC no. 15,607; "Inventory of things taken from the Shaker Society of Harvard Mass. by Myra McLain May 1918," NOC no. 15,605; "Release" signed by Laura Beal, 4 May 1926, NOC no. 11,848; Fiske Warren to Arthur Bruce, 10 Aug. 1917, 8 Mar. 1918, NOC.

31. G. W. Berry, "The Last of the Shakers," *Ohio Magazine* 3 (July 1907):14, 18.

32. "Records, Book No. 2. Kept by Rufus Bishop," NN, 15 Oct. 1912; L. O. Miller to Arthur Bruce and Irving Greenwood, 1 Mar. 1917, 4 Mar. 1922, Miller to Bruce, 16 Oct., 30 Nov. 1918, 23 Aug. 1920, 18 Mar. 1922, Canterbury Shakers to J. A. Runyon, 29 Sept. 1917, Mary A. Wilson to Arthur Bruce, 7 Jan. 1919, NhCa.

33. Julia Neal, *By Their Fruits: The Story of Shakerism in South Union, Kentucky* (Chapel Hill: University of North Carolina Press, 1947), 265–268; "A Diary Kept for the Church, Center Family South Union, Ky.," NOC, 8 May 1920, 9 Nov. 1921, 15 Mar. 1922; T. W. and R. C. P. Thomas to Walter Shepherd, 4 Jan. 1922, Shepherd to T. W. and R. C. Thomas, 7 Jan. 1922, Walter Shepherd to Sarah Burger, 10 Mar. 1922, NOC; "Contract" with J. W. Wallace, 20 Apr. 1922, NOC no. 10,331.

34. Neal, *By Their Fruits*, 267; New Lebanon Ministry to Second Family, Watervliet, N.Y., 18 June 1875, OClWHi IV A 44.

35. For background on women's sphere, see Kathryn Kish Sklar, *Catharine Beecher: A Study in American Domesticity* (New Haven: Yale University Press, 1973); Nancy F. Cott, *The Bonds of Womanhood: "Woman's Sphere" in New England, 1780–1835* (New Haven: Yale University Press, 1977); Ann Douglas, *The Feminization of American Culture* (New York: Alfred A. Knopf, 1977); and Barbara Welter, *Dimity Convictions: The American Woman in the Nineteenth Century* (Athens: Ohio University Press, 1976), which includes her essay "The Cult of True Womanhood: 1820–1860," originally published in *American Quarterly* 18 (1966):151–174. For a general account of spiritual motherhood among the Shakers, see Rosemary Diane Gooden, "The Language of Devotion: Gospel Affection and Gospel Union in the Writings of Shaker Sisters" (Ph.D. diss., University of Michigan, 1987).

36. Bainbridge, "Shaker Demographics," 360.

37. Ibid., 361; "Diary of North Family, South Union, 1872–1878," MWiW, 21–37.

38. See also Mary Farrell Bednarowski, "Outside the Mainstream: Women's Religion and Women Religious Leaders in Nineteenth-Century America," *Journal of the American Academy of Religion* 48 (1980):207–231.

39. See Mary L. Richmond, *Shaker Literature: A Bibliography*, 2 vols. (Hanover, N.H.: University Press of New England, 1977), 1:138–142, for a history of the journal. The publication has received surprisingly little attention from scholars. Priscilla J. Brewer makes almost no use of it apart from a discussion of Philemon Stewart's opposition to it. She speaks of it as a "newspaper" (*Shaker Communities*, 193–195). "Salutatory," *Shaker* 1 (1871):1, 32; Rainer Baumgaertner, "The Shaker Manifesto: A Missionary Tool and Forum for Inner-Society Discussion" (unpublished essay).

40. *Shaker* 1 (1871):1–8.

41. Widely varying amounts of space were devoted to these different sections during the years of publication.

42. Jane Knight, "Religious Organization—Shaker Homes," *Shaker* 2 (1872):7–8.

43. *Shaker* 2 (1872):96; *Shaker and Shakeress* 3 (1873):1, 5. Despite the name changes, the numbering of the volumes was consecutive during the twenty-nine years of publication.

44. Nancy C. Danforth, "Our Christian Home," *Manifesto* 15 (1885):244–245. See Colleen McDannell, *The Christian Home in Victorian America, 1840–1900* (Bloomington: Indiana University Press, 1986).

45. Ruth Webster, "Is Woman Any Longer Responsible?" *Shaker* 6 (1876).65.

46. Aurelia Mace, *Manifesto* 15 (1885):62; Cora C. Vinneo, "A Tribute to the Memory of Mother Ann Lee," *Manifesto* 25 (1895):245–247; Martha J. Anderson, "Mother Ann Lee's Mission," *Manifesto* 25 (1895):275–277; Emma B. King, "Mother Ann Lee," *Manifesto* 29 (1899):138–139. Anderson's reputation is discussed in White and Taylor, *Shakerism*, 324. Hawthorne's epithet appears in a letter dated 19 Jan. 1855. *Letters of Hawthorne to William D. Ticknor, 1851–1864* (Newark, N.J.: Carteret Book Club, 1910), 75.

47. "Correspondence," *Shaker and Shakeress*, 3 (1873):77–79. Many similar letters testifying to the impact of the publication appeared in its pages.

48. *Shaker* 6 (1876):4. One reason for the return to Lomas as editor was the negative reaction among some Believers to Evans's articles. The central ministry had a "long labor with Elder Frederick about [a] matter published in 'Shaker & Shakeress,'" Letters were also received from South Union and Groveland protesting his views. See Central Ministry Journal 1874–1890, 2, 5, 7 Oct., 31 Dec. 1874, 1–2 January 1875.

49. *Shaker Manifesto* 9 (1879):86, 8 (1878):14–15; 11 (1881):183–184; *Manifesto* 15 (1885):109, 207–208; *Circular* (Canterbury, N.H.: Shaker Village, 1877). For broadsides relating to the financial problems of the publication, see Richmond, *Shaker Literature* 1:138–142.

50. See Mary P. Ryan, *Womanhood in America: From Colonial Times to the Present*, 2d ed. (New York: Franklin Watts, 1979), 118–150; Carroll Smith-Rosenberg, *Disorderly Conduct: Visions of Gender in Victorian America* (New York: Oxford University Press, 1986).

51. "Is There Mystery in Truth?" *Shaker and Shakeress* 3 (1873):77.

52. Letter from New Gloucester, 17 Nov. 1844, OClWHi IV A 5; Leonard Brooks, "Sister Aurelia Mace and Her Influence on the Ever-Growing Nature of Shakerism," *Shaker Quarterly* 16 (1988):47–60; Aurelia Mace, *The Aletheia: Spirit of Truth. A Series of Letters in which the Principles of the United Society Known as Shakers are Set Forth and Illustrated*, 2d ed. (Farmington, Maine: Knowlton and McLeary, 1907).

53. Mace, *Aletheia*, 46–47, 64, 84, 130–131. For more about Tolstoy's correspondence with several Shakers, including Frederick W. Evans and Alonzo G. Hollister, see Henri Desroche, *The American Shakers: From Neo-Christianity to Presocialism,* trans. John K. Savacool (Amherst: University of Massachusetts Press, 1971), 1:89, 243–244.

54. White and Taylor, *Shakerism,* 3, 14–16.

55. Ibid., 221, 259, 261–277. In their reflections on biblical prophecy, White and Taylor were echoing the views of Frederick W. Evans on the Book of Revelation. See his *Autobiography of a Shaker, and Revelation of the Apocalypse, with an Appendix* ([Albany, N.Y.]: Charles Van Benthuysen and Sons, 1869), 89–148.

56. Brewer, *Shaker Communities,* 200; White and Taylor, *Shakerism,* 3, 379, 385–387, 392–393. For an account of the writing of the last chapter of the volume, see Richmond, *Shaker Literature* 1:209.

57. *The Motherhood of God* ([Canaan, N.Y.: Press of the Berkshire Industrial Farm, 1903]), 7–13.

58. "Journal for 1891," DeWint, 12 May 1891. Family journals were less numerous and less detailed by the end of the century. Those extant generally portray the less glamorous side of the Shaker woman's world.

59. "South Family Events, Kept by Anna Goepper," 25 July, 3 Aug., 20 Oct., 20 Nov. 1912, 1, 21 Feb. 1913. Sixty years later one of the former children at South Family recalled, "Sister Johanna baked good bread and pies!" Edith M. LaFrance to Bertha Lindsay, 19 Sept. 1974, NhCa.

60. "South Family Events by Anna Goepper," 25 July, 6 Aug., 10–11 Dec. 1912, 8 May 1913; D. T. Cochran to Ella Benedict, 22 July 1906, OClWHi IV A 8; Ada S. Cummings to Laura Langford, 13 Aug. 1911, NOC; Lillian Phelps to Ministry, 2 Feb. 1919, Arthur Bruce to Wallace H. Cathcart, 20 Jan. 1917, 9 Jan. 1930, OClWHi IV A 8.

61. Theodore E. Johnson, *Ingenious and Useful: Shaker Sisters' Communal Industries, 1860–1960* (Sabbathday Lake, Maine: United Society of Shakers, 1986); "Catalog of Fancy Goods Made at Shaker Village Alfred York County Maine, Fannie C. Casey, Trustee and General Manager 1908" (Sabbathday Lake, Maine: United Society of Shakers, 1971); Beverly Gordon, *Shaker Textile Arts* (Hanover, N.H.: University Press of New England, 1980), 185–186, 204–252. Helen Deiss Irvin provides a helpful corrective to the notion that Shaker women were totally preoccupied with handcrafted products. She demonstrates their interest in various laborsaving technologies. See "The Machine in Utopia: Shaker Women and Technology," *Women's Studies International Quarterly* 4 (1981):313–319. Nicholas A. Briggs depicts Eldress Durgin as a calculating, capable, efficient businesswoman in "Forty Years a Shaker," *Granite Monthly: A Magazine of Literature, History and State Progress* 53 (1921):59–62.

62. "South Family Events by Anna Goepper," 12, 28 Oct. 1912, 1–2 Jan. 1913. The family journals and personal diaries kept by Shaker women make little or no mention of female sanitary or health concerns. One modest exception is Goepper's entry for 16 Jan. 1913: "It seems Florence went to see a doctor yesterday Dr. Swineburne & he found her in a bad fix of female troubles and she will have to go every week for some time for treatment."

63. Karen K. Nickless and Pamela J. Nickless, "Trustees, Deacons, and Deaconesses: The Temporal Role of the Shaker Sisters, 1820–1890," *Communal Societies* 7 (1987): 16–24; Briggs, "Forty Years a Shaker," 60.

64. Ryan, *Womanhood in America,* 118–119; Smith-Rosenberg, *Disorderly Conduct,* 245.

65. Nickless and Nickless, "Trustees, Deacons, and Deaconesses," 16–18; Theodore E. Johnson, ed., "The 'Millennial Laws' of 1821," *Shaker Quarterly* 7 (1967).50–51, Johnson, ed., "Rules and Orders for the Church of Christ's Second Appearing Established by the Ministry and Elders of the Church and Reestablished by the Same, New Lebanon, New York May 1860," *Shaker Quarterly* 11 (1971):145–147. Local variations in the use of *trustee* and *deacon* persisted late into the century.

66. For the complexity of the office of trustee, see the New York State Library's collection of business correspondence directed to Benjamin Gates, trustee at Mount Lebanon. During a two-year period, 1878 and 1879, Gates received hundreds of letters on a wide range of issues.

67. "Financial Journal Church Order Pleasant Hill 1839–1910," KyLoF; "Transcript of August Ludemann v Robert Valentine, Supreme Court, New York County, 20 May 1901," NOC, pp. 31–32; "Petition to New York State Legislature Asking for Annual Report," NOC no. 10,383; circular letter, 6 Aug. 1883, OClWHi IV A 44; "Union Village Minutes of Church Council Sept. 1874–April, 1885 Vol. 1. O. C. Hampton, Sec.," OClWHi V B 266, 6 Mar. 1885. Much work remains to be done on the economic history of the United Society.

68. During this period the Shakers became land-poor, according to Andrews, *People Called Shakers,* 226–228.

69. A. M. Eskridge to Hervey Eads, 24 Feb. 1891, NOC. See also John B. Wolford, "Shaker Business, Folklife, and Relations with the World," Ph.D. dissertation in progress, Indiana University.

70. Charles R. Muller and Timothy D. Rieman, *The Shaker Chair* (Winchester, Ohio: Canal Press, 1984), 169–216.

71. "Editorial Notes," *Shaker Manifesto* 8 (1878):233; "Contract between Aaron Woodman and David Parker," 4 July 1864, NOC no. 13,410; "An Act Concerning Communities and Corporations, Connecticut Legislature, May 1874," NOC no. 9605; "Contract with Lebanon Springs Rail Road Company," 28 Oct. 1852, NOC no. 10,259.4; Hancock tax receipts on woodlot in Stamford, Vermont, NOC no. 10,312.

72. "Account Book Kept by Giles B. Avery of Investments Made by the Ministry at Mt Lebanon, 1872–1890," OClWHi II B 41, 22 July, 23 Sept. 1872, 23 Mar. 1881, 22 May 1890; "List of Land Sales," NOC no. 9735; "Financial Report 1858," NOC no. 9569.

73. Alan Trachtenberg, *The Incorporation of America: Culture and Society in the Gilded Age* (New York: Hill and Wang, 1982); Robert Higgs, *The Transformation of the American Economy, 1865–1914: An Essay in Interpretation* (New York: John Wiley and Sons, 1971).

74. "Records at New Lebanon 1871–1905," 3 Jan. 1876; Central Ministry Journal 1874–1890, 3 Jan. 1876; "Deed between Joseph and Mary L. Jones and Frederick Evans and Levi Shaw, 22 July 1878," NOC no. 10,211; "Sale Document for 4000 acres in Pike county, 18 May 1881," NOC no. 10,236; Netta A. B. Weitz to Levi Shaw, 25 Sept. 1902, NOC; "Sale Document for 10,000 acres Pike county, 17 April 1903," NOC no. 10,236aa; Joseph Holden to Eldress Annie, 10 Oct. 1907, NOC no. 10,236jj; "Documents relating to Byrdsall Suit," NOC no. 10,328; "Signed Statement by Frederick W. Evans," 20 Feb. 1893, NOC no. 10,239.

75. "Hancock Financial Records," NOC nos. 10,367-A,B; "Deed from John Whiteley and Isaac Bailey to Stephen Davis," NOC no. 10,054; "Sale Contract for Shirley, 8 December 1908," NOC no. 15,615; Andrew Barrett and Mary Gass to Peter F. Sering, 29 Dec. 1910, NOC; "Sale Document between Frances Hall (trustee) and Leonard and Catharina Bol," NOC no. 11,825; "Contract between Joseph Holden and Josephine Jilson

(trustees) and Fiske Warren, 17 April 1918," NOC no. 15,572; Fiske Warren to Arthur Bruce, 10 Aug. 1917, NOC.

76. J. P. MacLean, *Shakers of Ohio: Fugitive Papers concerning the Shakers of Ohio, with Unpublished Manuscripts* (Columbus, Ohio: F. J. Heer, 1907), 107–108; "Records at New Lebanon 1871–1905," 22 Dec. 1887; Matthew Carter to Benjamin Gates, 4 Oct. 1889, NOC; Joseph Slingerland to Benjamin Gates, 30 Sept. 1889, NOC; "Financial Agreement with Mary & Louisa Gass," 7 Jan. 1890, NOC no. 9717.

77. Andrews, *People Called Shakers*, 109–110; Benjamin Gates, "A Day Book or Journal of Work and Various Things, 1827–1838," DeWint; "Records at New Lebanon 1871–1905," 23 Mar., 17 Oct. 1887, 3 Nov. 1889, 16 Jan. 1903; *Shaker Manifesto* 8 (1878):233; Richmond, *Shaker Literature* 1:5–8; *Shaker Almanac* (New York: A. J. White, 1883–1891); M. Stephen Miller, *A Century of Shaker Ephemera: Marketing Community Industries, 1830–1930* (New Britain, Conn.: Privately printed, 1988), 28–29; Herman Tappan to Benjamin Gates, 14 Sept. 1903, NOC; "Memorandum Concerning Seed Business," NOC no. 9556.

78. "North Familys Book of Records, Mount Lebanon, 1814–1890," NN, 5 Nov. 1894; Russell H. Anderson, "The Shaker Community in Florida," *Florida Historical Quarterly*, 38 (1959):29–44; Andrew Barrett to Joseph Holden, 30 Jan. 1896, OClWHi IV A 29; Calvin G. Reed to Henry Blinn, April 1895, in *Manifesto* 25 (1895): 127–128; "Journal-Florida 1895–1900," NOC; Abraham Perkins to Corinne Bishop, 20 Mar. 1896, OClWHi IV A 8. For the debate concerning Florida, see *Manifesto* 25 (1895):45–46, 88, 92–93, 211–212. The Shakers at Mount Lebanon were looking for a buyer for their Florida property as late as 1935. Emma J. Neale to William P. Tyson, 14 Feb. 1935, MPH.

79. E. Richard McKinstry, *The Edward Deming Andrews Memorial Shaker Collection* (New York: Garland, 1987), 95; "Report for the Ministry," South Union, 4 Nov. 1919, NOC no. 10,311; "Levi Shaw Account Records," NOC no. 10,217; "Levi Shaw and Others v Olive Hand Court Records 1906," NSyU; Miller, *Century of Shaker Ephemera*, 32, 39; "Contract between Levi Shaw and Timothy Rayson and Charles M. Comstock," 8 Mar. 1898, NOC no. 11,860; David Comstock to Levi Shaw, 25 Sept. 1898, H. A. Brewster to Levi Shaw, 5 Aug. 1896, NOC.

80. MacLean, *Shakers of Ohio*, 108–111; letter to Sister Martha, 16 Nov. 1905, DLC sec. 351b; "Scrapbook," NOC no. 14,889. See MacLean, *Shakers of Ohio*, 91, for a photograph of the renovated Office, later called Marble Hall. See also fig. 34.

81. Anderson, "Shaker Community in Florida," 29–44; Burnette Vanstory, "Shakerism and the Shakers in Georgia," *Georgia Historical Quarterly* 43 (1959):353–364; Russell H. Anderson, "The Shaker Communities in Southeast Georgia," *Georgia Historical Quarterly* 50 (1966):162–172.

82. Vanstory, "Shakerism in Georgia," 360–363; Anderson, "Shaker Communities in Georgia," 167–171; 11 June 1898 note, DLC sec. 351b. There is some question about the existence of another large block of land in Georgia, between 40,000 and 50,000 acres, possibly purchased by the Shakers. See Anderson, "Shaker Communities in Georgia," 171–172 n. 4.

83. James H. Fennessey to Emma Neale, [1902], NOC. Following the revelation of this financial debacle, Neale wrote to Union Village asking how Slingerland "was getting along with the Societys recent embarrassment" (Mary Kies to Emma Neale, 2 Nov. 1902, NOC). Stripped of both titles and authority, after spending a number of years at Narcoossee, Slingerland died among the Believers at South Union in 1920. "Diary Center Family South Union," 24 Sept. 1920.

84. Mark M. Pomeroy to Robert Valentine, 31 Dec. 1891, NOC, "Stock Certificate, 22 June 1896," NOC no. 9680; "August Ludemann v Robert Valentine, Supreme Court, New York County, 20 May 1901," NOC; Thomas S. Smith to Robert Valentine, 23 June 1893, 28 June, 7 Nov. 1894, 10, 28 May 1895, 31 Oct. 1904, DeWint. Smith had certain reservations about investing in real estate. He wrote, "I am afraid this world, or life is too short to handle real Estate in. [A]ll men connected with it seem to forget bargains, promises and everything else except to call for their interest." Smith to Valentine, 30 Dec. 1889, DeWint.

85. "Contract for Timber Sales, December 1901," NOC no. 10,222; "Deed to Lindell T. Bates, October 1918," NOC no. 10,067; Willis G. Emmerson to Daniel Offord, 1 Feb. 1898, W. H. Wolfard to Sarah Burger, 20 Sept. 1919, 1 Mar. 1920, NOC. Burger attempted to salvage some return from investments that Daniel Offord had made in Wyoming in 1898 after he "left" the society unexpectedly, only to return several years later.

86. These circumstances undercut any suggestion that the Believers practiced a form of primitive communism during these years.

87. "Stock Holdings for 1915, Hancock Business Records," DeWint; "Report for the Ministry, South Union," 4 Nov. 1919.

88. "Receipt signed by Frederick L. Weston, Agricultural National Bank of Pittsfield, 18 June 1935," Upton Papers, NOC; "Day Book," MeSl.

89. "Hancock Financial Records," NOC no. 10,368; "Journal of Events, Pleasant Hill, Oct 24, 1868–Sept 30, 1880," KyLoF, 12 Sept. 1878, Charles V. Vickrey to Emma J. Neale, 8 Jan. 1918, Upton Papers, NOC; "Scrapbook," NOC no. 14,889, item dated 8 Jan. 1927.

90. The revenues generated by fancy goods were not comparable to those from the sale of real estate in this period.

91. "Home Notes," *Manifesto* 20 (1890):236; Richard D. Brown, "Modernization: A Victorian Climax," in *Victorian America,* ed. Daniel Walker Howe (Philadelphia: University of Pennsylvania Press, 1976), 29–44.

92. See Higgs, *Transformation of the American Economy.*

93. "Travel Journal by Bullard," 22–26 Mar. 1889; "Notes About Home," *Manifesto* 20 (1890):234–235, and 29 (1899):188.

94. "Contract signed by Jonathan Wood and Peter H. Long, 28 October 1852," NOC no. 10,259.4; "Deed to New York, Boston, Albany & Schenectady Rail Road Company, August 4, 1881," NOC no. 11,861; "Deed, April 11, 1911," NOC no. 10,256-R; "Social Record," *Shaker* 6 (1876):7; Thomas D. Clark and F. Gerald Ham, *Pleasant Hill and Its Shakers* (Pleasant Hill, Ky.: Shakertown Press, 1968), 75.

95. "Journal of Events, Pleasant Hill, Oct 1, 1880–Dec 25, 1890," KyLoF, 27 Oct. 1880, 7 Oct. 1889; "Journal of Events Pleasant Hill 1868–1880," 7 Sept. 1880; "Diary Center Family South Union," 9 Oct. 1902; "Receipt signed by Frederick L. Weston, 18 June 1935."

96. Elsie A. McCool, ed., "Gleanings from Sabbathday Lake Church Journals, 1872–1884," *Shaker Quarterly* 6 (1966):106–107; "Society Record," *Shaker* 6 (1876):7; "Society Items," *Shaker Manifesto* 10 (1880):70; MacLean, *Shakers of Ohio,* 268; David R. Starbuck, "The Shaker Mills in Canterbury, New Hampshire," IA: The Journal of the Society for Industrial Archeology 12 (1986):11–38; "Journal of Events Pleasant Hill 1880–1890," 10 Apr. 1884; "Notes About Home," *Manifesto* 20 (1890):66, 233; "Business Records," NOC no. 10,212A, 12 Apr. 1899.

97. Neal, *By Their Fruits,* 258–259; Mount Lebanon Ministry to Elder Austin Buckingham, 3 Aug. 1883, OClWHi IV A 44; Starbuck, "Shaker Mills," 14; MacLean, *Shakers of Ohio,* 268; "Journal of Events Kept by James W. Shelton, 1894–1917," KyLoF, 22 Aug. 1901.

98. Frederick L. Weston to Emma J. Neale, 18 June 1935, Upton Papers, NOC; "Hancock Business Records, List of Stocks, 1915," DeWint.

99. Dynamo Electric Machines to Benjamin Gates, 21 Mar. 1881; N; "A Domestic Journal of Daily Occurances and Events Kept by David Gill Beginning January 1st 1878," NOC, 19 Nov. 1889; Starbuck, "Shaker Mills," 14–15; Neal, *By Their Fruits,* 259; Horgan, *Shaker Holy Land,* 139; "North Family Journal Mt Lebanon," NOC (hereafter cited as "North Family Journal"), 26 May 1919; "Newspaper Clipping in Scrapbook," NOC no. 14,889. See also David R. Starbuck, ed., *Canterbury Shaker Village: An Historical Survey* (Durham: University of New Hampshire, 1981): 108–112.

100. "North Family Journal," 29 Dec. 1921; "Diary Center Family South Union," 15 June, 26 Aug. 1920; Maria Witham, *Manifesto* 25 (1895): 43; "Stock Certificate for Electric Scenic Company to Robert Valentine, 22 June 1896," NOC no. 9680; bonds held with Public Service Electric & Gas Company, Pacific Gas & Electric Company, Commonwealth Edison Company, receipt for Emma J. Neale from Agricultural National Bank of Pittsfield, Upton Papers, NOC; stock in General Electric, New York State Electric & Gas Corporation, Upton Papers; Herman Tappan to Benjamin Gates, 14 Sept. 1903, NOC.

101. Horgan, *Shaker Holy Land,* 139; "Church Records, Vol. 6, Sabbathday Lake 1907–1919," MeSl, 11 Nov. 1909; Neal, *By Their Fruits,* 259–260; "North Family Journal," 7 Oct. 1918, 23 Aug. 1920; "Diary Center Family South Union," 24 May, 18 July 1921.

102. "North Family Journal," 10 Nov. 1921, 28 Dec. 1923; "Diary Center Family South Union," 27 Aug. 1920.

103. Bertha Lindsay, *Seasoned with Grace: My Generation of Shaker Cooking,* ed. Mary Rose Boswell (Woodstock, Vt.: Countryman Press, 1987), 59, 86; Elmer R. Pearson and Julia Neal, *The Shaker Image* (Boston: New York Graphic Society, 1974), 182–183; Amy Bess Miller, *Hancock Shaker Village/The City of Peace: An Effort to Restore a Vision, 1960–1985* (Hancock, Mass.: Hancock Shaker Village, 1984), 16–18; newspaper clipping, n.d., DeWint; Irving Greenwood to Wallace H. Cathcart, 6 Feb. 1939, OClWHi IV A 8.

104. "Scrapbook, newspaper clipping, May 27, no year," NOC no. 14,889; Aida M. Elam to Irving Greenwood, 21 Sept. 1933, NhCa.

105. "North Family Journal," 13 Dec. 1923; Lindsay, *Seasoned with Grace,* 12, 32; Frieda Sipple to Friends, 13 July 1942, Upton Papers, NOC; Dorothy M. Filley, *Recapturing Wisdom's Valley: The Watervliet Shaker Heritage, 1775–1975,* ed. Mary L. Richmond (Albany, N.Y.: Albany Institute of History and Art, 1975), 108. The receiver built by Greenwood is part of the collection of the Shaker Museum and Library, Old Chatham, N.Y.

106. Arthur Bruce to J. P. MacLean, 15 July 1905, OClWHi IV A 8. A few Shakers proposed radical applications of this principle of accommodation to the world. Louis J. Kern has described a "heretical spirit" that appeared after the Civil War, causing some to advocate "purified generation" for the Believers based on certain spiritualistic notions. He linked this unorthodox position with contacts between the Believers and the followers of John Humphrey Noyes in the Oneida Community. See *An Ordered Love: Sex Roles and Sexuality in Victorian Utopias—the Shakers, the Mormons, and the Oneida Commu-*

nity (Chapel Hill: University of North Carolina Press, 1981), 103–104, and Brewer, *Shaker Communities,* 160–161.

107. Dolores Hayden, *Seven American Utopias: The Architecture of Communitarian Socialism, 1790–1975* (Cambridge: MIT Press, 1976), 42; *Manifesto* 9 (1879):47; 20 (1890):92, 231–232; *Shaker* 6 (1876):7.

108. "Notes About Home," *Manifesto* 20 (1890):67, 92, 235; "North Family Journal," 14 Mar. 1914; "Receipt for $1628.14 from Prince & Walker Company, Pittsfield, Massachusetts, 1 August 1929," Upton Papers, NOC.

109. Gordon, *Shaker Textile Arts,* 170–188, 193–194; "Church Records Sabbathday Lake 1872–1877," 5 Dec. 1875; "Travel Journal by Bullard," 28 Apr. 1889; MacLean, *Shakers of Ohio,* 109. For opposing views on beards, see Elisha Blakeman, "The Propriety of Wearing a Beard," OClWHi VII B 113, and Hervey L. Eads, "Beards vs. Shaving," *Shaker Manifesto* 11 (1881):175–176. The most useful published collection of photographs is Pearson and Neal, *Shaker Image.*

110. "Notes About Home," *Manifesto* 20 (1890):18, 161, 234; 29 (1889):43.

111. Ibid., 20 (1890):19, 160, 232; 29 (1899):92, 123; "Excerpts from the Andrew D. Barrett Book," DLC sec. 328, 25 Apr. 1906; "Family Journal or Current Events, Compiled and Transcribed by Jessie Evans, et al. 1901–1931 Church Family East Canterbury NH," NhCa, 8 Mar. 1907; "Church Records Sabbathday Lake 1907–1919," 11 Aug. 1911.

112. "Journal by James W. Shelton," 24 June 1897; Anna White to Laura Langford, 5 May 1906, NOC.

113. "William Anderson's Notes," 21 June [1913], Upton Papers, NOC; letter with no addressee, 30 Oct. [1913], Upton Papers; William Anderson to A. H. Clark & Son, 26 Aug. 1913, Upton Papers; William Anderson to Joseph Holden, 24 Apr. 1913, Upton Papers; "Clipping in Scrapbook," NOC no. 14,889; William H. Perkins, Margaret Egelson, Susie P. McLaughlin, and Ida Lillian Barlow to Joseph Belden, Walter Shepherd, Ministry Sisters and Trustees, 9 Dec. 1918, Upton Papers. See Edward Deming Andrews and Faith Andrews, *Fruits of the Shaker Tree of Life: Memoirs of Fifty Years of Collecting and Research* (Stockbridge, Mass.: Berkshire Traveller Press, 1975), 42, for a photograph of Anderson sitting on the South Family steps.

114. Neal, *By Their Fruits,* 261; Pearson and Neal, *Shaker Image,* 185; "North Family Journal," 5 Oct. 1910, 30 Aug. 1922; "Journal of Events Pleasant Hill 1880–1890," 30 Aug., 19 Sept. 1882, 31 July 1883; MacLean, *Shakers of Ohio,* 223.

115. "Notes About Home," *Manifesto* 29 (1899):123; "Journal of Events Pleasant Hill 1868–1880," 4 July 1876.

116. Pearson and Neal, *Shaker Image,* 56–58; White and Taylor, *Shakerism,* 338–340; Daniel W. Patterson, *The Shaker Spiritual* (Princeton: Princton University Press, 1979), 450–454; Henry Blinn to Joseph Holden, 3 Sept. 1897, OClWHi IV A 8. See also Harold Vaughn Smith, "Oliver C. Hampton and Other Shaker Teacher-Musicians of Ohio and Kentucky" (D.A. diss., Ball State University, 1981), and Daniel W. Patterson, "Implications of Late Nineteenth Century Shaker Music," *Shaker Quarterly* 17 (1989): 214–235.

117. Patterson, *Shaker Spiritual,* 230–231; Andrews, *People Called Shakers,* 265–266; White and Taylor, *Shakerism,* 351–353; MacLean, *Shakers of Ohio,* 160–164; "Church Records Sabbathday Lake 1872–1877," 25 Dec. 1874, 25 Dec. 1876; "Church Records Sabbathday Lake 1898–1906," p. 486; "Church Records Sabbathday Lake 1907–1919," 26 Dec. 1908; "South Family Events by Anna Goepper," 25 Dec. 1912; Marian Bennett to Bertha Lindsay and Gertrude Soule, Thanksgiving 1986, NhCa.

118. "Church Records Sabbathday Lake 1872–1877," 17 Dec. 1876.

119. Calvin G. Reed to Henry Blinn, April 1895, *Manifesto* 25 (1895): 127–128; "Notes About Home," ibid., 88, 211–212.

120. "Notes About Home," *Manifesto* 29 (1899): 44; "Journal–Florida 1895–1900," NOC, 17 Mar. 1898; "Diary Center Family South Union," 1 Oct. 1901, 1 Apr. 1902; E. Ennis to Elder Egbert, 23 Mar. 1906, OClWHi V B 175.

121. "Notes About Home," *Manifesto* 20 (1890): 66–67.

122. Frederick W. Evans, "Editorial Change—Summary," *Shaker and Shakeress* 5 (1875): 89.

123. Ibid. See Carter, *Spiritual Crisis*.

124. Evans, "Editorial Change"; Evans, "Good Bread," *Manifesto* 16 (1886): 210; Daniel Fraser, "Manna," *Shaker Manifesto* 9 (1879): 48; Frederick W. Evans to G. A. Lomas, 2 Dec. 1877, ibid., 8 (1878): 10.

125. Evans, "Editorial Change"; Ernest Pick, "Vegetarianism and the Millennium," *Manifesto* 20 (1890): 175–176.

126. Anna White to Henry Blinn, 8 Dec. 1894, Daniel Offord to Henry Blinn, 9 Dec. 1894, in *Manifesto* 25 (1895): 6–8.

127. Evans, "Editorial Change"; "Life Insurance! Upon the Only True Plan," *Shaker Manifesto* 11 (1881), advertisements.

128. Evans, "Editorial Change"; Alonzo Hollister, "Resist Beginnings to Evil: Argument for Total Abstinence," *Manifesto* 16 (1886): 85–86; "Temperance Notes," in "Scrapbook of Clippings, kept by Alonzo Hollister," OClWHi XIII 16. See also Norman H. Clark, *Deliver Us from Evil: An Interpretation of American Prohibition* (New York: W. W. Norton, 1976).

129. "South Family Events by Anna Goepper," 3 Dec. 1912, 23 Mar. 4, 6, 29–30 Apr., 15, 22, 29–30 May 1913; "Events at Groveland, N.Y., 1873–1888, Kept by Abigail Crossman," DeWint, 4, 14, 17 Apr. 1874, 17 June 1887; "Diary Mt Lebanon Center Family 1894–1898," NOC, 30 Nov. 1894, 23 Jan. 1899; "Journal of Events Pleasant Hill 1868–1880," 5 Oct. 1877; "Journal of Events Pleasant Hill 1880–1890," 8, 23, 30 July 1887.

130. Catherine Allen, "Social Improvement Society," *Manifesto* 25 (1895): 155. See Richmond, *Shaker Literature* 1 : 4, concerning the variants of Allen's name.

131. Allen, "Social Improvement Society," 155–157.

132. Catherine Allen, "Democracy," *Manifesto* 25 (1895): 200–202.

133. Antoinette Doolittle, "A Shakeress on American Institutions," *Shaker Manifesto* 11 (1881): 250–252.

134. Catherine Allen, "Gaining Ground," *Manifesto* 25 (1895): 197–198.

135. Catherine Allen, "Speech at the National Council of Women, October 1907," OClWHi VII A 3.

136. "Memberships for Catherine Allen," OClWHi II A 9.

137. Daniel Offord, "Seven Travails of the Shaker Church," *Manifesto* 20 (1890): 5–9.

138. "Diary Mt Lebanon Center Family 1894–1898," 5 Dec. 1895, 6 Nov. 1898; "Records at New Lebanon 1871–1905," 5 Dec. 1895, 24 Mar. 1899; "Is Shakerism Advancing? An Article in a New York Paper Thinks So," newspaper clipping, 10 Jan. 1896, NOC.

139. Frederick W. Evans, "Proposed Additions to the Rochester Platform," *Shaker Manifesto* 8 (1878): 61–62; Frederick W. Evans, "Why Do Not Shakers Vote?" ibid., 10 (1880): 213–214; Evans, "Settled at Last," *Shaker and Shakeress* 3 (1873): 92; Offord, "Seven Travails of the Shaker Church."

140. Daniel Fraser, "The Labor Question: The Millionaire and the Republic," *Shaker Manifesto* 8 (1878): 217–219.

141. Hampton letter, June 1890, *Manifesto* 29 (1899): 110; "North Family Journal," 21 July 1914; *Manifesto* 29 (1899): 188. See Edward Bellamy, *Looking Backward, 2000–1887,* ed. John L. Thomas (Cambridge: Harvard University Press, 1967), and Edward K. Spann, *Brotherly Tomorrows: Movements for a Cooperative Society in America, 1820–1920* (New York: Columbia University Press, 1989), 180–209.

142. Richmond, *Shaker Literature* 1:87; *Shaker* 6 (1876): 80; Charles DeBenedetti, *The Peace Reform in American History* (Bloomington: Indiana University Press, 1980), 59–62; "Address of Antoinette Doolittle Before Peace Society, New York Feb 21, 1876," OClWHi XIII 10; "Broadside on Peace Convention at Salt Point, Dutchess Co., N.Y. 1881," reprint; Frederick W. Evans, "Salt Point Peace Convention," *Manifesto* 12 (1882): 234; White and Taylor, *Shakerism,* 216–217; Frederick W. Evans, *The Conditions of Peace* (Mount Lebanon, N.Y.: The Shakers, 1890).

143. "Announcement for Peace Convention, August 31, 1905," OClWHi VII A 3; "The Shakers of Mount Lebanon, N.Y. will Hold a Peace Conference this Month," *New-York Tribune,* 20 Aug. 1905, pt. 2, pp. 1, 5, 8.

144. Pearson and Neal, *Shaker Image,* 150 151; "Resolutions Adopted at the Peace Convention of the Shakers of Mount Lebanon Held at Mount Lebanon, N.Y., August 31, 1905," NOC.

145. *Manifesto* 29 (1899): 189; Reynolds, "Tobacco," *Shaker* 1 (1871): 45; "Twelve Reasons Why No Rational Being Should Use Tobacco," *Shaker and Shakeress* 3 (1873): 36; "Alonzo Hollister Clippings," OClWHi XIII 16.

146. Central Ministry Journal 1874–1890, 20 Jan. 1874; Frederick W. Evans, "Rational Funerals," *Shaker Manifesto* 8 (1878): 130–131; H. Bull, "Shaker Funeral," *Shaker and Shakeress* 3 (1873): 90; George Lomas, "Notes," *Shaker Manifesto* 9 (1879): 86; Otis Sawyer, "Shaker Cemeteries," *Shaker* 2 (1872): 47; "Society Record," *Shaker Manifesto* 10 (1880): 237; "Church Records Sabbathday Lake 1907–1919," 31 Mar., 1 Apr. 1910.

147. "Carpets," *Shaker and Shakeress* 3 (1873): 44.

148. "Self-Improvement Society," OClWHi XIII 5; *Shaker Manifesto* 15 (1885), advertisements; "A Journal of the Various Literary Attempts of the Church Family Beginning June 21 1880," DeWint.

149. See Charles H. Hopkins, *The Rise of the Social Gospel in American Protestantism, 1865–1915* (New Haven: Yale University Press, 1940); Norris Magnuson, *Salvation in the Slums: Evangelical Social Work, 1865–1920* (Metuchen, N.J.: Scarecrow, 1977); and Henry F. May, *Protestant Churches and Industrial America* (New York: Harper and Brothers, 1949).

150. Catherine Allen, "The Golden Age," OClWHi VII A 3. It would be a mistake to assume that all Shakers shared this progressive vision. They did not. The members of the North Family at Mount Lebanon and others of similar persuasion dominated the media during this period and were extremely effective in communicating their ideas to the outside world.

151. William James, *The Varieties of Religious Experience,* vol. 15 of *The Works of William James,* ed. Frederick H. Burkhardt, Fredson Bowers, and Ignas K. Skrupskelis (Cambridge: Harvard University Press, 1985); *Chicago Daily News,* 11 Sept. 1893; Carter, *Spiritual Crisis,* 209–217. An abstract of Offord's paper "The Doctrine and Life of the Shakers" appears in John Henry Barrows, ed., *The World's Parliament of Religions: An Illustrated and Popular Story of the World's First Parliament of Religions, Held in Chicago in Connection with the Columbian Exposition of 1893,* 2 vols. (Chicago: Parliament Publishing Company, 1893), 2:1380.

152. Barrows, ed., *World's Parliament of Religions* 2:1380.

153. Charlotte Byrdsall, "Who Are True Spiritualists?" *Shaker Manifesto* 11 (1881): 172–173; Antoinette Doolittle, "The Supernatural," ibid., 8 (1878): 127–128.

154. "Journal Commencing January 1st 1875. Canaan Upper Family," DeWint, 23 July 1876, 15–18 May 1878; Central Ministry Journal 1874–1890, 15 July 1876, 15 Feb. 1878; "Records by Anna White," 17–19 Aug. 1880; Cecelia Devyr, "Dawn of a New Era," *Shaker and Shakeress* 5 (1875):54. Kathleen Patricia Deignan speaks of Shakerism's "radical pneumatology," or doctrine of the Holy Spirit, in the period after the Civil War. See "The Eschatology of Shaker Christianity" (Ph.D. diss., Fordham University, 1986).

155. George Lomas, "Materializations by Spirits," *Shaker Manifesto* 8 (1878):167; Daniel Offord to Laura Langford, 15 Nov. 1908, NOC; Rebecca A. Hathaway to Catherine Allen, 18 Apr. 1920, OClWHi IV A 8; Delmer Wilson, "Dreams," 19 Jan. 1923, 4 Mar., 25 Nov. 1924, MeSl.

156. James M. Peebles, "As a Spiritualist, I Believe," *Shaker* 6 (1876):60; "Diary Mt Lebanon Center Family," 12 Apr. 1898; Central Ministry Journal 1874–1890, 28 Oct. 1877; Peebles, "Spiritualism," in White and Taylor, *Shakerism,* 250–252.

157. James M. Peebles, *Seers of the Ages: Embracing Spiritualism, Past and Present; Doctrines Stated and Moral Tendencies Defined* (Boston: W. White, 1869), 139–140, 182–184.

158. Anna White, "True Spiritualism," *Manifesto* 25 (1895):77–80. For more on the relation between spiritualism and social reforms, see Mary Farrell Bednarowski, "Women in Occult America," in *The Occult in America: New Historical Perspectives,* ed. Howard Kerr and Charles L. Crow (Urbana: University of Illinois Press, 1983), 177–195.

159. *Manifesto* 25 (1895):212–213; Barrows, ed., *World's Parliament of Religions* 2:972; Frances Ellen Burr to Anna White, 24 Feb. 1903, NOC; "William Anderson's Astrological Documents," Upton Papers, NOC; "North Family Journal," 3 Sept. 1918. For more on Vivekananda's career, see Steven F. Walker, "Vivekananda and American Occultism," in *Occult in America,* ed. Kerr and Crow, 162–176; and Carl T. Jackson, *Vedanta for the West: The Ramakrishna Movement in America* (Bloomington: Indiana University Press, forthcoming). On psychical research, see Moore, *In Search of White Crows,* 133–168.

160. Robert S. Fogarty, *Dictionary of American Communal and Utopian History* (Westport, Conn.: Greenwood, 1980), 110–111, 214–215; Howard D. Fine, "The Koreshan Unity: The Chicago Years of a Utopian Community," *Journal of the Illinois State Historical Society* 68 (1975):213–227; Cyrus R. Teed, *The Cellular Cosmogony or the Earth a Concave Sphere,* with a new introduction by Robert S. Fogarty (Philadelphia: Porcupine Press, 1975), [i–vi]; Frederick Evans, *Shakers and Koreshans Uniting* (Mount Lebanon, N.Y.: The Shakers, [1892]). For a comparative study of feminism

among the Shakers, the Koreshans, and the Sanctificationists (a single-sex community formed in Texas in 1890), see Sally L. Kitch, *Chaste Liberation: Celibacy and Female Cultural Status* (Urbana: University of Illinois Press, 1989).

161. J. W. Woodrow to Charles Clapp, 22 Mar. 1890, DLC sec. 352a; Andrews and Andrews, *Fruits*, 175–181; Laura Holloway, *The Ladies of the White House: of, In the Home of the Presidents: Being a Complete History of the Social and Domestic Lives of the Presidents from Washington to the Present Time, 1789–1881* (Philadelphia: Bradley, 1881); Holloway, *The Buddhist Diet-Book* (New York: Funk and Wagnalls, 1886). The largest body of Holloway (Langford) correspondence with the Shakers is part of the Shaker Papers at DeWint.

162. Anna White to Laura Langford, 30 May 1902, NOC.

163. "Records at New Lebanon 1871–1905," 20, 26 Dec. 1882, 17 Mar. 1884, 1 Aug. 1887, 14–15 Feb. 1890, 25 June 1897, 11 Aug. 1902, 11 June 1903, 4 Jan., 3 Apr. 1905. For background on changing attitudes toward death and dying, see Douglas, *Feminization of American Culture;* Stanley French, "The Cemetery as Cultural Institution: The Establishment of Mount Auburn and the 'Rural Cemetery' Movement," in *Death in America,* ed. David E. Stannard (Philadelphia: University of Pennsylvania Press, 1975), 69–91; and Martha V. Pike and Janice Gray Armstrong, eds., *A Time to Mourn: Expressions of Grief in Nineteenth-Century America* (Stony Brook, N.Y.: Museums at Stony Brook, 1980).

164. Catherine Allen, "Come to the Judgment," *Manifesto* 25 (1895):53–55; "Diary" 30 Oct. 1883, DLC sec. 327.

165. "North Family Journal," 30 Oct. 1910; "Diary Watervliet, Ohio," DLC sec. 297, 11, 22 July 1894; Leila S. Taylor, "A Remarkable Statement," *Christian Science Journal* 25 (December 1907):543–549; "Notes About Home," *Manifesto* 25 (1895):45–46; "South Family Events by Anna Goepper," 1 May 1913, "South Family, Watervliet, N.Y. Record of Events from Day to Day Kept by Anna B. Goepper Beginning Apr. 5th 1915 for Annie Case, Eldress and Trustee," N, 30 May 1915. For background on Eddy and Christian Science, see Robert Peel, *Mary Baker Eddy,* 3 vols. (New York: Holt, Rinehart and Winston, 1966–1977); Stephen Gottschalk, *The Emergence of Christian Science in American Life* (Berkeley: University of California Press, 1973); R. Laurence Moore, "The Occult Connection? Mormonism, Christian Science, and Spiritualism," in *Occult in America,* ed. Kerr and Crow, 135–161; and Rennie B. Schoepflin, "Christian Science Healing in America," in Norman Gevitz, ed., *Other Healers: Unorthodox Medicine in America* (Baltimore: Johns Hopkins University Press, 1988), 192–214.

166. "Sister Aurelia's Journal 1896–1908," MeSl, 9, 11, 12, 17 Jan. 1896, 13 Feb. 1897. See Alonzo Hollister, *Mission of Alethian Believers, Called Shakers* (Mount Lebanon, N.Y.: The Shakers, 1892).

167. "Diary Watervliet, Ohio," 24 July 1889. See Moore, *In Search of White Crows;* Robert S. Ellwood, Jr., *Alternative Altars: Unconventional and Eastern Spirituality in America* (Chicago: University of Chicago Press, 1979), 65–103, and Ann Braude, *Radical Spirits: Spiritualism and Women's Rights in Nineteenth-Century America* (Boston: Beacon, 1989).

168. James W. Mathews, "Howells and the Shakers," *Personalist: An International Review of Philosophy, Religion, and Literature* 44 (1963):212–219; Joel M. Jones, "A Shaker Village Revisited: The Fading of the Familial Ideal in the World of William Dean Howells," *Old Northwest: A Journal of Regional Life and Letters* 8 (1982):85–100; William Dean Howells, "A Shaker Village," *Atlantic Monthly* 37 (1876):699–710; Howells, *The Undiscovered Country* (Boston: Houghton, Mifflin, 1880); Howells, *A*

Parting and a Meeting. Story (New York: Harper and Brothers, 1896); Howells, *The Day of Their Wedding. A Novel* (New York: Harper and Brothers, [1896]); Howells, *The Vacation of the Kelwyns; An Idyl of the Middle Eighteen-seventies* (New York: Harper and Brothers, [1920]); "Book Notices," *Shaker Manifesto* 10 (1880):207.

169. For background on evangelicalism during this period, see Ernest Sandeen, *The Roots of Fundamentalism: British and American Millenarianism* (Chicago: University of Chicago Press, 1970), and Marsden, *Fundamentalism and American Culture*. For parallel developments in another religious tradition, see Thomas D. Hamm, *The Transformation of American Quakerism: Orthodox Friends, 1800–1907* (Bloomington: Indiana University Press, 1988).

170. Central Ministry Journal 1874–1890, 13 Feb., 5 Mar. 1876, 11 Nov. 1877, 27 Feb. 1878; "Journal of Events Pleasant Hill 1868–1880," 27 Feb. 1876, 24–25 May, 23 July 1879; "Journal of Events Pleasant Hill 1880–1890," 29 July 1883; Henry Blinn, "A Shaker on Moody and Sankey," *Shaker* 7 (1877):33; "Moody and Sankey," *Shaker Manifesto* 8 (1878):16.

171. "Journal of Events Pleasant Hill 1868–1880," 23 July 1879, 26 July 1880; "Journal of Events Pleasant Hill 1880–1890," 6 June, 1 Aug. 1885, 18 July 1886; "Records at New Lebanon 1871–1905," 24 Aug., 1 Sept. 1902; Pearson and Neal, *Shaker Image*, 148–149; "A Record of Events as they Transpire from Time to Time, Mt Lebanon Columbia County N.Y. Commencing January 22nd 1901 South Family," MWiW, 15, 31 Aug. 1903; "Church Records Sabbathday Lake 1907–1919," 13 Aug. 1907.

172. Anne M. Boylan, *Sunday School: The Formation of an American Institution, 1790–1880* (New Haven: Yale University Press, 1988), 166–170; "Journal Canaan Upper Family," 5 Mar. 1876; "Journal of Events Pleasant Hill 1880–1890," 27 Mar., 12 June 1887; "Travel Journal by Bullard," 21 Apr. 1889; "Church Records Sabbathday Lake 1890–1897," 23 Dec. 1894; "Records at New Lebanon 1871–1905," 23 Mar. 1902.

173. Flora Rothwell, "The New Love," *Manifesto* 29 (1899):80, Henry Blinn, "Search the Scriptures," ibid., 129; Blinn, "God's Promises," ibid., 97–98.

174. Diane Sasson, *The Shaker Spiritual Narrative* (Knoxville: University of Tennessee Press, 1983), 86; Alonzo G. Hollister to Delmer Wilson, 14 Apr. 1904, MeSl; "Records at New Lebanon 1871–1905," 9 Apr. 1887.

175. Elijah Myrick, "Christmas Musings," *Manifesto* 15 (1885):49–51; Abraham Perkins, "Are the Shakers Christians?" *Shaker Manifesto* 8 (1878):25–26.

176. "Society Record," *Shaker* 6 (1876):80; Richmond, *Shaker Literature* 1:72; Arthur W. Dowe, *The Day of Judgment as Taught by the Millennial Church (Shakers) with a Few Rays of Light Gathered from Scriptures and Other Sources* (San Francisco: Rembaugh, 1896), 5–6; "Journal by James W. Shelton," 20 Oct. 1896. Dowe visited Mount Lebanon in 1899. There had been several expressions of interest in a California colony in the 1890s. Cornelia R. Powers, who had once lived at Watervliet, New York, wrote from San Diego County in 1890: "I truly believe that the time has come, and that this is the place that Mother meant when she said; 'The next opening of the gospel will be in the south-west.'" See *Manifesto* 20 (1890):142; 25 (1895):137; and 29 (1899):188. On the Jehovah's Witnesses, see Herbert Hewitt Stroup, *The Jehovah's Witnesses* (New York: Columbia University Press, 1945).

177. "Travel Journal by Bullard," 28 Apr. 1889; "The Last of the Shakers—A Community Awaiting Death," *New York Times*, 23 July 1911, pt. 5, p. 7; Neal, *By Their Fruits*, 260–261; "South Family Events by Anna Goepper," 25 Aug. 1912; "Journal of Events Pleasant Hill 1880–1890," 25 Dec. 1885; Ministry at Harvard and Shirley to Ministry at Mount Lebanon, 7 Oct. 1889, in *Manifesto* 20 (1890):55–56; "Journal by James W.

Shelton," 14 Sept. 1894, 31 Oct. 1910; "Church Records Sabbathday Lake 1890–1897," 8 Oct. 1896; *In Memoriam: Sister Aurelia G. Mace, 1835–1910* ([Portland, Maine: George Loring, 1910]), 17. See *A Shaker Hymnal: A Facsimile Edition of the 1908 Hymnal of the Canterbury Shakers* (Woodstock, N.Y.: Overlook Press, 1990).

178. "Central Ministry Journal 1874–1890," 11 Nov. 1877, 31 Oct. 1880; Giles Avery, *Sketches of "Shakers and Shakerism": Synopsis of Theology of United Society of Believers in Christ's Second Appearing* (Albany, N.Y.: Weed, Parsons, 1884), 13–17. See Richard T. Hughes and C. Leonard Allen, *Illusions of Innocence: Protestant Primitivism in America, 1630–1875* (Chicago: University of Chicago Press, 1988), and Richard T. Hughes, ed., *The American Quest for the Primitive Church* (Urbana: University of Illinois Press, 1988), for background on the concept of restoration.

179. Henry Blinn, *The Life and Gospel Experience of Mother Ann Lee* (East Canterbury, N.H.: The Shakers, 1901), 9–10; *Testimonies of the Life, Character, Revelations and Doctrines of Mother Ann Lee, and the Elders with Her, Through whom the Word of Eternal Life was Opened in this Day, or Christ's Second Appearing, Collected from Living Witnesses, in Union with the Church*, 2d ed. (Albany, N.Y.: Weed, Parsons, 1888); Richmond, *Shaker Literature* 1:16; Thomas Swain, "The Evolving Expressions of the Religious and Theological Experiences of a Community: A Comparative Study of the Shaker *Testimonies* concerning the Sayings of Mother Ann Lee; An Exploration of the Development from Oral Traditions to Written Forms as Preserved in Four Documents," *Shaker Quarterly* 12 (1972):3–31, 43–67; Cora C. Vinneo, "A Tribute to the Memory of Mother Ann Lee," *Manifesto* 25 (1895):245–247; Emma B. King, "Mother Ann Lee," ibid., 29 (1899):138–139.

180. Charles Edson Robinson, *A Concise History of the United Society of Believers Called Shakers* (East Canterbury, N.H.: The Shakers, 1893), 69–74; Hervey L. Eads, *Shaker Sermons: Scripto-Rational. Containing the Substance of Shaker Theology. Together with Replies and Criticisms Logically and Clearly Set Forth* (Albany, N.Y.: The Shakers, 1879).

181. Eads, *Shaker Sermons*, [i], 151–166, 193–200, 211–222.

182. Ibid., 14–21.

183. Sasson, *Shaker Spiritual Narrative*, 84–99; Diane Sasson, "A Nineteenth Century Case Study: Alonzo Giles Hollister (1830–1911)," *Shaker Quarterly* 17 (1989): 154–172, 188–1903.

184. Alonzo G. Hollister, *Divine Judgment, Justice and Mercy. A Revelation of the Great White Throne, Judgment is an Influx of Higher Truths; Their Influence is an Efflux, and Their Effects are Purifying and Uplifting* (Mount Lebanon, N Y: The Shakers, 1895), 1; Hollister and Calvin Green, *Pearly Gate of the True Life and Doctrine for Believers in Christ* (Mount Lebanon, N.Y.: The Shakers, 1894), iii–iv, 21, 34–52; ibid., pt. 2 (Mount Lebanon, N.Y.: The Shakers, 1900), 1.

185. Joseph Smith, *The Doctrine and Covenants of the Church of Jesus Christ of Latter-day Saints*, sec. 49, verses 1–28; Andrews, *People Called Shakers*, 222–223; Louis Basting, "The Mormon Church," *Manifesto* 15 (1885):229–230; Abigail Crosman, "Events at Groveland, N.Y., 1873–1888," DeWint, 27 Dec. 1887. For a general history of Mormonism, see Leonard J. Arrington and Davis Bitton, *The Mormon Experience: A History of the Latter-day Saints* (New York: Alfred A. Knopf, 1979).

186. "Journal of Events Pleasant Hill 1868–1880," 26 Aug. 1876; William Hinds, *American Communities: Brief Sketches of Economy, Zoar, Bethel, Aurora, Amana, Icaria, the Shakers, Oneida, Wallingford, and the Brotherhood of the New Life* (Oneida, N.Y.: Office of the American Socialist, 1878); Richmond, *Shaker Literature* 2:57; "Our

Book Table," *Shaker* 6 (1876):40; "Notes," *Shaker Manifesto* 9 (1879):86–87. For more on the social arrangements at Oneida, see Foster, *Religion and Sexuality,* 72–122, and Kern, *Ordered Love,* 205–279.

187. See John Hick's useful discussion "Religious Pluralism," in Mircea Eliade, *The Encyclopedia of Religion,* 16 vols. (New York: Macmillan, 1987), 12:331–333. See also "Should All Be Shakers?" *Shaker Manifesto* 8 (1878):92–93.

188. Giles Avery, "Are the Shakers Dying Out?" *Shaker Manifesto* 9 (1879):123–125.

189. George Lomas, "Shakerism: The World's Spiritual Metre," *Shaker Manifesto* 8 (1878):67–69; "The Decay of Shakerism: A Letter from Elder Lomas," ibid., 274–275.

190. Oliver Prentiss, "Shakers Dying Out," *Shaker Manifesto* 9 (1879):132; "Maintenance of Shakerism," ibid., 10 (1880):62–63; Anna White, "The Good Time Coming," ibid., 11 (1881):171–172; Giles B. Avery, "The Shaker Problem," *Manifesto* 15 (1885):51–53; Giles Avery to Abraham Perkins, ibid., 86–88; White and Taylor, *Shakerism,* 389.

191. Bainbridge, "Shaker Demographics," 357–363; Martha J. Anderson, "Old Age," *Manifesto* 25 (1895):255. See David A. Karp and William C. Yoels, *Experiencing the Life Cycle: A Social Psychology of Aging* (Springfield, Ill.: Charles C. Thomas, 1982), and Robert C. Atchley, *Aging: Continuity and Change* (Belmont, Calif.: Wadsworth, 1983). For information on specific inquirers during this period, see E. M. Jerrold to Charles Clapp, February 1891, H. D. Medlock to Charles Clapp, 2, 4, 12 May 1891, DLC sect. 352a; and John Whiteley to Joseph Holden, 19 Aug. 1900, OClWHi IV A 59. Jerrold was a Presbyterian minister in Macomb, Illinois, Medlock a nineteen-year-old living in Hot Springs, Arkansas, and Whiteley described Jon Pine as a person who was "consciencious—Inclined to be a little Moody."

192. Julius Assman, "Old Age," *Shaker and Shakeress* 5 (1875):76; "Society Record," *Shaker Manifesto* 8 (1878):73; Sadie A. Neale, "The Dying Year," ibid., 9 (1879): 273–274.

193. "Society Record," *Shaker Manifesto* 11 (1881):115. See Aurelia Mace's "Tribute to Elder Giles B. Avery," in *Aletheia,* 82–83; *To Our Well Beloved Mother in Israel Elderess, Eliza Ann Taylor Whose Spirit Passed "Within the Vail" November 28, 1897, in the 87th Year of Her Age* (Mount Lebanon, N.Y.: The Shakers, 1897); and *In Memoriam.*

194. Katie Ambrose to Lida Speake, 27 Aug. 1886, NOC; "South Family Events by Anna Goepper," 10 Dec. 1912; "Notes About Home," *Manifesto* 29 (1899):43.

195. "North Family Journal," 13 Sept. 1911; Anderson, "Shaker Community in Florida," 39–43; *New York Times,* 14 Sept. 1911, p. 3, 15 Sept. 1911, p. 8, 16 Sept. 1911, p. 5, 17 Sept. 1911, pt. 4, p. 12, 19 Sept. 1911, p. 1, 21 Sept. 1911, p. 4, 22 Sept. 1911, p. 10. The last article ended, "Sympathy is not deserved by them. They [the Shakers] are criminals and should be treated as such."

196. *Manifesto* 29 (1899):187, 189–190, 231.

197. "A Church Record Including in Consecutive Order the Appointments to, and Removals from Office of Ministry, Elder Trustees & Deacons of the Church & Society of White Water from its Commencement in 1823," OClWHi V B 357, 18–19 Mar., 1, 7, 17 Apr., 2 May, 4 Oct. 1910.

198. "The Last of the Shakers—A Community Awaiting Death," *New York Times,* 23 July 1911, pt. 5, p. 7; Clifton Johnson, "The Passing of the Shakers," *Old-Time New England* 25 (1934):66.

199. Crosman, "Events at Groveland 1873–1888," 30 Nov. 1887; *Manifesto* 29 (1899): 43.

200. "Unidentified Newspaper Clipping," Albany, 29 Nov. 1937, DeWint.

201. Lindon W. Bates to Emma J. Neale, 9 Mar. 1916, NOC; Emma J. Neale to W. P. Tyson, 11 Feb. 1926, MPH; Fred M. Seiverd to Emma J. Neale, 9 June 1926, Nora to Emma J. Neale, [5 Oct. 1927], F. S. Stoepel & Co. to Emma J. Neale, 6 Oct. 1927, Seiverd to Neale, 12 Nov. 1928, Memorandum from Seiverd to Neale, 12 Nov. 1928, NOC; Emma J. Neale to George H. Cooper, Jr., 6 Oct. 1930, Upton Papers, NOC. The Church Family at Mount Lebanon spent $1,628 for paint, wallpaper, and labor in the summer of 1929. Receipt from Prince & Walker Co., Pittsfield, 1 Aug. 1929, Upton Papers.

202. "Records. Book No. 2. By Rufus Bishop," 25 July, 13 Aug. 1929.

203. Lillian Barlow to Mrs. John Roberts, 9 Jan. 1939, DeWint; "Receipts to Mrs. Roberts of Brooklyn," DeWint; Ella F. Winship to Hugh Strobel, 17 May 1940, NOC. See "Notice to Emma J. Neale" of AT & T dividends on 139 shares, 15 Apr. 1942, Upton Papers, NOC, and "Tax receipt for 636 acres in Osceola County, Florida, 1 November 1938," Upton Papers.

204. Sadie A. Neale to Edward D. Andrews, 27 June 1932, Neale to Faith Andrews, [1942], Neale to Edward D. and Faith Andrews, 5 Apr. 1945, DeWint. See also Andrews and Andrews, *Fruits*, 85–92.

205. Sarah Collins to Grace Reynolds, n.d., 1 Jan. 1934, NOC; *Berkshire Evening Eagle*, 13 Aug. 1933, quoted in Muller and Rieman, *Shaker Chair*, 228 (see also p. 215); Sarah Collins to Mrs. John S. Roberts, 24 Feb. 1934, 25 Jan. 1935, DeWint. See also Andrews and Andrews, *Fruits*, 81–84. For records of the chair factory during the 1920s and 1930s, see Upton Papers, NOC.

206. Martha Wetherell to Mrs. John S. Roberts, 21 Dec. 1935, 5, 16, 31 Jan., 8 Feb. 1942, DeWint.

207. Arthur Bruce to Wallace H. Cathcart, 23 Nov. 1912, OClWHi IV A 8; "Scrapbook," NOC no. 14,889.

208. Emma B. King to Grace Dahm, Jennie Wells, and Mary Dahm, [1947], NhCa.

209. Jennie Wells to John Schott, August 1947, NhCa; Berton Roueché, "A Small Family of Seven," *New Yorker*, 23 Aug. 1947, 47–57; Emma B. King to Jennie Wells, August 1947, 28 Sept. 1947, Parent Ministry to John Schott, 20 Oct. 1947, NhCa.

210. Frieda Sipple to Dear Friends, 25 Dec. 1938, Mary Dahm to Mrs. Rextrue, n.d., Mary Dahm to Dorothy, 23 May 1948, Upton Papers, NOC.

211. The biographies of these twentieth-century Shakers need to be written.

212. Arthur Bruce to Emma J. Neale, 10 June, 5 July 1937, Prudence Stickney to Emma J. Neale, 24, 26 Jan. 1936, 19 June 1937, Upton Papers, NOC; R. Mildred Barker, *Holy Land: A History of the Alfred Shakers* (Sabbathday, Maine: Shaker Press, 1986).

213. A. W. Levensaler to Emma B. King, 23 Apr. 1947, NhCa.

214. Charles C. Adams to Estella Weeks, 16 Dec. 1947, Upton Papers, NOC.

215. Marguerite Fellows Melcher, *The Shaker Adventure* (Princeton: Princeton University Press, 1941), 293; Andrews, *People Called Shakers*, 224–240.

216. Emma J. Neale to John Whitbeck, 8 Jan. 1938, NOC; Flo Morse, *The Shakers and the World's People* (New York: Dodd, Mead, 1980), 181–182. The ballet was first performed on 30 Oct. 1944.

217. The exceptions will be discussed in Part V.

218. The continued use of the spiritual names for the villages documents the perception of their importance to the Believers.

219. Karen H. Stephan and G. Edward Stephan, "Religion and the Survival of Utopian Communities," *Journal for the Scientific Study of Religion* 12 (1973): 89–100.

220. If Rosabeth Moss Kanter had examined twentieth-century Shakerism, the society would not have measured so high on commitment mechanisms. *Commitment and Community: Communes and Utopias in Sociological Perspective* (Cambridge: Harvard University Press, 1972).

221. These generalizations need to be tested against detailed demographic studies of particular families at specific sites. To date, little such research has been conducted. One exception is David R. Starbuck and Margaret Supplee Smith, eds., *Historical Survey of Canterbury Shaker Village* (Boston: Boston University, 1979).

222. Some striking developmental parallels exist between the Shakers and the Amana communities. See Diane L. Barthel, *Amana: From Pietist Sect to American Community* (Lincoln: University of Nebraska Press, 1984).

223. Andrews speaks of "pure Shakerism" in *People Called Shakers*, 235.

Part Five

1. Marshall McLuhan coined this phrase when he wrote, "The new electronic interdependence recreates the world in the image of a global village." See Marshall McLuhan and Quentin Fiore, *The Medium Is the Massage* (New York: Random House, 1967), 67.

2. David M. Potter, *People of Plenty: Economic Abundance and the American Character* (Chicago: University of Chicago Press, 1954).

3. Robert Wuthnow, *The Restructuring of American Religion: Society and Faith since World War II* (Princeton: Princeton University Press, 1988), 37; Sydney E. Ahlstrom, *A Religious History of the American People* (New Haven: Yale University Press, 1972), 953–954; Will Herberg, *Protestant, Catholic, Jew: An Essay in American Religious Sociology* (Garden City, N.Y.: Doubleday, 1955); *New York Times*, 23 Dec. 1952, p. 16.

4. Frances Hall and Emma B. King to John Schott, 19 Oct. 1948, NhCa.

5. Ibid. On the changing impact of aging on individuals, see Robert C. Atchley, *Aging: Continuity and Change* (Belmont, Calif.: Wadsworth, 1983), and Barry D. McPherson, *Aging as a Social Process: An Introduction to Individual and Population Aging* (Toronto: Butterworths, 1983).

6. Caroline B. Piercy, *The Valley of God's Pleasure: A Saga of the North Union Shaker Community* (New York: Stratford House, 1951), 241; Edward Deming Andrews, *The People Called Shakers: A Search for the Perfect Society* (New York: Oxford University Press, 1953), 240.

7. Cable, Samuel Clemens to Associated Press, 1897.

8. I have attempted to be fair and accurate in discussing the contemporary conflict among the Shakers. Limitations on access to materials makes the task difficult.

9. My Shaker friends and their partisans may find some of the following materials painful, if not offensive. I regret that. I hope that the discussion of these issues will promote greater understanding.

10. Emma B. King to John Schott, October 1947, NhCa.

11. Emma B. King to Iona Geckler, 3 Aug. 1947, 10 June 1948, Emma B. King to Agnes E. Tuttle, 21 Aug. 1954, NhCa.

12. "The Shakers: A Strict and Utopian Way of Life Has Almost Vanished," *Life*, 21 Mar. 1949, 142–148.

13. Charles C. Adams to Estella T. Weeks, 8 Feb. 1949, Upton Papers, NOC; F. D. to the Shakers, 23 Oct. 1949, M. B. to Emma B. King, 10 Apr. 1949, J. D. to Shaker Sisters, 20 Apr. 1949, P. P. to Emma B. King, 21 Mar. 1949, S. H. to Shaker Sisters, 14 Apr. 1949, B. F. to Believers, 7 May 1949, M. S. to Emma B. King, 29 June 1949, E. E. to Emma B. King, 24 May 1949, P. B. to Emma B. King, 1 June 1949, NhCa.

14. Emma B. King to H. Phelps Clawson, 4 Mar. 1949, 8 Dec. 1950, 3 Jan., 3 June, 12 Aug. 1951, NOC; Amy Bess Miller, *Hancock Shaker Village/The City of Peace: An Effort to Restore a Vision, 1960–1985* (Hancock, Mass.: Hancock Shaker Village, 1984), 19, Emma B. King to John S. Williams, 7 Feb. 1949, NOC.

15. Emma B. King to Mrs. Williams, 8 Nov. 1952, Ethel Peacock to H. Phelps Clawson, 1 Dec. 1952, Emma B. King to H. Phelps Clawson, 12 Mar. 1953, 5 June 1956, Mildred Barker to John S. Williams, 17 May 1955, NOC; Gerard C. Wertkin, *The Four Seasons of Shaker Life: An Intimate Portrait of the Community at Sabbathday Lake* (New York: Simon and Schuster, 1986), 137; Emma B. King to John S. Williams, 25 July 1955, NOC.

16. Mildred Barker to John S. Williams, 25 July 1955, Emma B. King to John S. Williams, 1 Nov. 1956, Emma B. King to H. Phelps Clawson, 18 Apr. 1954, NOC; Bertha Lindsay, *Seasoned with Grace: My Generation of Shaker Cooking,* ed. Mary Rose Boswell (Woodstock, Vt.: Countryman Press, 1987), 32.

17. King to Clawson, 18 Apr. 1954; Emma B. King to John Schott, 19 Oct. 1948, NhCa; Emma B. King to John S. Williams, 13 Jan. 1956, 22 Sept. 1957, Mildred Barker to Emma B. King, 24 Feb. 1957, NOC.

18. Emma B. King to John S. Williams, 9 Feb. 1957, NOC; Emma B. King, *A Shaker's Viewpoint* (Old Chatham, N.Y.: Shaker Museum Foundation, 1957), [1–3].

19. King, *Shaker's Viewpoint,* [3–5]; Emma B. King to John S. Williams, 16 Jan. 1957, NOC.

20. Miller, *Hancock Shaker Village,* 18–19; Charles Adams to Estella T. Weeks, 16 Dec. 1947, Upton Papers, NOC.

21. Emma B. King to Charles C. Adams, 20 Jan. 1949, Upton Papers, NOC; Parent Ministry to Vera Eikel, February 1948, NhCa; Richard Morse, telephone conversation with author, 6 Aug. 1990.

22. Miller, *Hancock Shaker Village,* 19–26; "A Record of Deaths Occurring in Lebanon, (Watervliet N.Y.) and Hancock. 1782–1960," NOC no. 13,420. In the fall of 1990 the ashes of Egbert B. Gillette, at one time an elder at the Narcoossee colony, were buried in the Hancock cemetery. Gillette left the society after the dissolution of the Florida site and married, and therefore he was not a Shaker at his death. See *Shaker Messenger* 13, no. 1 (1991): 16.

23. "In Memoriam Delmer Charles Wilson, 1873–1961," *Shaker Quarterly* 1 (1961): 135–137.

24. King to Adams, 20 Jan. 1949; Emma B. King to H. Phelps Clawson, 26 Mar. 1950, NOC; "Shakers," *Time,* 28 July 1961, 53; Mildred Barker to Helen Upton, 31 July 1961, Upton Papers, NOC.

25. The reluctance of the Believers in Maine to open their records to serious scholars is understandable, yet frustrating. For a spirited exchange on this issue, see Mildred Barker to Charles Upton, 10 Jan. 1974, Helen Upton to Mildred Barker, draft copy, n.d., and Mildred Barker to Helen Upton, 24 Jan. 1974, Upton Papers, NOC. Barker summarized crisply the Believers' position: "Our Library is, of course, a private one. . . . I do know, however, that the Trustees of the Society have every right to decide who may or who may not use what is ours. In addition, I find it strange that anyone outside of the Society would think he or she had the right to question the action the Society's Trustees have taken in a purely private decision." In response, Helen Upton stated eloquently the position of professional historians: "The Shaker area is such a significant part of Amer. social & religious history that we believe there should be every opportunity for its study."

26. Marguerite Frost, *About the Shakers* (Canterbury, N.H.: n.p. [1958]), [8].

27. "Talk to Shaker Historical Society, 30 October 1960," MeSl; Mildred Barker to Muriel Collins, 16 Nov. 1960, NOC; Mildred Barker to Harold Cook, 29 Aug. 1961, MPH; Prudence Stickney to Emma J. Neale, 19 June 1937, Upton Papers, NOC.

28. Emma B. King to Nellie, 10 May 1964, NhCa.

29. Andrews, *People Called Shakers.*

30. James W. Gilreath, "The Formation of the Western Reserve Historical Society's Shaker Collection," *Journal of Library History* 8 (1973): 133–142; Kermit J. Pike, "Shaker Manuscripts and How They Came to Be Preserved," *Manuscripts* 29 (1977): 226–236.

31. William Coyle, *Ohio Authors and Their Books* (Cleveland, Ohio: World, 1962), 418; Pike, "Shaker Manuscripts," 230–231; J. P. MacLean, *Shakers of Ohio: Fugitive Papers Concerning the Shakers of Ohio, with Unpublished Manuscripts* (Columbus, Ohio: F. J. Heer, 1907), and MacLean, *A Sketch of the Life and Labors of Richard McNemar* (Franklin, Ohio: Franklin Chronicle, 1905). Most of MacLean's essays appeared originally in the *Ohio Archaeological and Historical Quarterly*. "Receipts from Boston Public Library," 29 May 1903, 9 Feb. 1905, NOC no. 10,331 C–D. MacLean's catalogs are listed in Mary L. Richmond, *Shaker Literature: A Bibliography*, 2 vols. (Hanover, N.H.: University Press of New England, 1977), 2:77–78. See also Emilius O. Randal, "Shakers and the Historical Society," *Ohio Archaeological and Historical Quarterly* 13 (1904): 566–567. Randal reported that MacLean had been "made a member" of the Shaker families at several villages he visited.

32. MacLean, *Shakers of Ohio*, 9–18; Pike, "Shaker Manuscripts," 234–235. Anna White and Leila S. Taylor called MacLean a "valued friend of Shakers" who appreciated and understood the society. *Shakerism Its Meaning and Message Embracing An Historical Account, Statement of Belief and Spiritual Experience of the Church from its Rise to the Present Day* (Columbus, Ohio: Fred J. Heer, 1904), 325.

33. Gilreath, "Formation of the Collection," 136–138; Alonzo Hollister to John P. MacLean, 30 June 1903, OClWHi IV A 46.

34. Gilreath, "Formation of the Collection," 137–141. Wallace H. Cathcart, 1 Feb. 1912, Catherine Allen to Wallace H. Cathcart, 7 Aug. 1912, OClWHi IV A 48. See also Wallace H. Cathcart to Canterbury Sisters, 8 Jan. 1913, OClWHi IV A 8; Wallace H. Cathcart to Ed Bohoun, 23 June 1914, OClWHi IV A 55; and Arthur Bruce to Wallace H. Cathcart, 9 Jan. 1930, OClWHi IV A 8.

35. H. H. Ballard to Anna White, 1, 5 Nov. 1904, Richard T. Ely to Successor of F. W. Evans, 4 June 1903, Richard T. Ely to Daniel Offord, 13, 23 June 1903, NOC; Anna White to Laura Langford, 3 Oct. 1904, DeWint; Richmond, *Shaker Literature* 1: xxii–xxiii.

36. Edward Deming Andrews, *The Community Industries of the Shakers* (Albany: University of the State of New York, 1932), 37, 229, 266. *Community Industries* was reissued by Emporium Publications (Charlestown, Mass., 1971) and by Porcupine Press (Philadelphia, 1972). The same materials appeared also under a new title, *Work and Worship: The Economic Order of the Shakers* (Greenwich, Conn.: New York Graphic Society, 1974).

37. Biographical information on Edward Deming Andrews, DeWint; Edward Deming Andrews and Faith Andrews, *Fruits of the Shaker Tree of Life: Memoirs of Fifty Years of Collecting and Research* (Stockbridge, Mass.: Berkshire Traveller Press, 1975), 21–22, Andrews, *Community Industries*, 301–307. In 1931 Max Charleston, editor of the *Mercer County News*, wrote a 400-page manuscript entitled "The Shakers of Kentucky," which he was unable to get published. A representative from Macmillan called it a "very interesting book" (L. H. Titterton to Max Charleston, 23 Jan. 1932, KyLoF). Bobbs-Merrill rejected it because of limited sales possibilities during the Depression. Jessica B. Mannon to Max Charleston, 1 Aug. 1932, KyLoF.

38. "Sadie Neale Diary no. 1 1929," MPH, 26, 28 Mar., 2, 9 May, 13 June, 27 Aug., 21 Oct., 5 Nov. 1929; Emma J. Neale to Faith Andrews, 4 Feb. 1929, Josephine E. Wilson to Edward D. Andrews, 28 Apr. 1930, Sadie A. Neale to the Andrewses, 13 Oct. 1942, DeWint. On one occasion Mr. and Mrs. Andrews had to be reminded that they had not paid for their purchases for several years. See Alice Smith to Edward D. Andrews, 3 Mar. 1933, DeWint.

39. Walter Shepherd to Edward D. Andrews, 7 Mar. 1931, Prudence Stickney to Edward D. Andrews, 17 Sept. 1932, DeWint; Prudence Stickney to Charles Adams, 19 Feb. 1934, Upton Papers, NOC.

40. Edward Deming Andrews and Faith Andrews, *Shaker Furniture: The Craftsmanship of an American Communal Sect* (New Haven: Yale University Press, 1937), 23, 96. *Shaker Furniture* was reissued by Yale University Press (New Haven, 1939) and later by Dover (New York, 1950).

41. Milton Sherman, "Catalogue for the William F. Winter, Jr. Collection of Shaker Photographica, Books and Ephemera" (Armonk, N.Y.: n.p., n.d.); William F. Winter to Charles C. Adams, 28 June 1933, Upton Papers, NOC.

42. "Shaker Portfolio by William F. Winter," final typescript draft, p. 2, cited in Sherman, "Winter Collection"; Andrews and Andrews, *Shaker Furniture,* plates 3, 15, 39. See also Winter, "Shaker Portfolio: A Picture Record of an American Community," *U.S. Camera* 1 (1939): 22–25, 73.

43. Constance Rourke, "Authentic American Commune," *New York Herald Tribune,* 16 May 1937, p. 17, cited in Sherman, "Winter Collection"; Rourke, "The Shakers," in *The Roots of American Culture and Other Essays,* ed. Van Wyck Brooks (New York: Harcourt, Brace, 1942), 195–237.

44. Edward Deming Andrews, *The Gift to Be Simple: Songs, Dances and Rituals of the American Shakers* (New York: J. J. Augustin, 1940), 7–8, 39. This volume was reissued by Dover (New York, 1967). During the 1940s Estella T. Weeks spent a great deal of time studying the music of the Shakers in hopes of publishing a major study. She thought the Shakers "had a curious prescience that was more American than Shaker, at core, in the words they chose and the ideas they embodied" in their songs. She wrote, "Even that world they foreswore they nevertheless did endlessly mirror" (see Estella T. Weeks to Charles Adams, 26 Jan. 1949, Upton Papers, NOC). Weeks died before publishing her book. Her notes and papers are part of the Upton Papers.

45. Marguerite Fellows Melcher, *The Shaker Adventure* (Princeton: Princeton University Press, 1941); Julia Neal, *By Their Fruits: The Story of Shakerism in South Union, Kentucky* (Chapel Hill: University of North Carolina Press, 1947); Piercy, *Valley of God's Pleasure.* Each of these authors published other works related to Shakerism. Melcher wrote a play entitled "Rose in the Wilderness" (1949) depicting conflict within a Shaker community in 1846. Emma B. King commented on the play in a letter to Charles C. Adams (20 Jan. 1949, Upton Papers, NOC). Neal edited *The Journal of Eldress Nancy [Moore]* (Nashville, Tenn.: Parthenon, 1963); Moore was a leader at South Union during the Civil War. Piercy wrote *The Shaker Cook Book: Not by Bread Alone* (New York: Crown, [1943]).

46. Review of "Rose in the Wilderness," *New York Times,* 5 Jan. 1949; Estella T. Weeks to Charles C. Adams, 15 Jan. 1949, Upton Papers, NOC; Flo Morse, *The Shakers and the World's People* (New York: Dodd, Mead, 1980), 307.

47. John S. Williams to Emma B. King, 14 Oct. 1948, 1, 9 Feb. 1949, NhCa; King to Williams, 7 Feb. 1949, NOC; H. P. Clawson to Emma B. King, 8 June, 5 Sept. 1950, NhCa. See Robert F. W. Meader, "The Story of the Shaker Museum," *Curator* 3 (1960): 204–216.

48. Emma B. King to John S. Williams, 14 July 1952, 18 Oct. 1953, 4 Dec. 1955, Gertrude Soule to H. P. Clawson, 2 Nov. 1952, Emma B. King to Williams family, 25 June 1953, Gertrude Soule to Mr. and Mrs. Williams, 3 June 1956, NOC. Emma B. King had earlier refused to sell any more items to the Western Reserve Historical Society. She was resentful that the Historical Society was selling materials that had been

"given into their keeping." See Russell H. Anderson to Emma B. King, 23 Sept. 1947, King to Anderson, 28 Sept. 1947, NhCa; Emma B. King to John S. Williams, 9 Nov. 1952, NOC.

49. Andrews, *People Called Shakers*, 239–240.

50. Homer Eaton Keyes, preface to Andrews and Andrews, *Shaker Furniture*, vii.

51. Mildred Barker at Sabbathday Lake was critical of Andrews's scholarship. She wrote, "I am not surprised that Mr. Andrews has done a paper on the Spirit Drawings. That would be the only subject that he hasn't touched I guess. He seems to feel that he has a monopoly on everything Shaker and tries to scare everyone else away. I hear he is now trying to [do] something on Shaker music." Barker to Helen Upton, 24 Oct. 1961, Upton Papers, NOC. Earlier critics of Andrews include Charles Adams and Estella Weeks. See Charles Adams to Josephine Wilson, 2 Dec. 1943, and Estella Weeks to Charles Adams, 16 Dec. 1947, Upton Papers.

52. Andrews, *People Called Shakers*, 175, 237–239, 248; Andrews and Andrews, *Fruits*, ix.

53. John Cournos, "An Attempt at Utopia," *Commonweal*, 11 Sept. 1953, 567; Marguerite Frost to the Andrewses, 29 Aug. 1954, DeWint; Marguerite Frost to Charles C. Adams, 22 Apr. 1954, Upton Papers, NOC. More than twenty years later, Gertrude M. Soule wrote to Faith Andrews with a different judgment. "I love all your books," Soule declared, "and am proud in telling all that visit the gift shop that you and Mr Andrews were the first friends to bring to the public interest about the Shakers." See Soule to Faith Andrews, 22 Feb. 1976, DeWint.

54. Edward Deming Andrews and Faith Andrews, "The People Called Shakers," *Yale University Library Gazette* 31 (1957): 154–162; Edward D. Andrews, "The Shakers in a New World," *Antiques* 72 (1957): 340–343; "Yale University News Bureau release, 17 February 1957," DeWint; Richmond, *Shaker Literature* 2: 148–150; Andrews and Andrews, *Fruits*, 194–196.

55. Henri Desroche, *Les Shakers américains: D'un neo-Christianisme à un pre socialisme?* Ouvrage Publié avec le Concours du Centre National de la Recherche Scientifique ([Paris]: Les Editions de Minuit, 1955). It was translated in 1971 by John K. Savacool as *The American Shakers: From Neo-Christianity to Presocialism* (Amherst: University of Massachusetts Press, 1971).

56. Janice Holt Giles, *The Believers* (Boston: Houghton Mifflin, 1957), 301–302. This novel has been reissued by the University Press of Kentucky (Lexington, 1989). For more details surrounding Giles's intentions, see Dianne Watkins, "Janice Holt Giles and *The Believers*," *Shaker Messenger* 11 (Summer 1989): 5–7, 24–28.

57. *Charles Sheeler, Paintings, Drawings, Photographs: A Catalogue with an Introduction by William Carlos Williams* (New York: Museum of Modern Art, 1939); Constance Rourke, *Charles Sheeler: Artist in the American Tradition* (New York: Harcourt, Brace, 1938); Faith and Edward D. Andrews, "Sheeler and the Shakers," *Art in America* 53 (1965): 90–95.

58. Mary Johnston, "Union," *Manifesto* 20 (1890): 31.

59. Prudence A. Stickney to Emma J. Neale, 24 Jan. 1936, Upton Papers, NOC.

60. On Canterbury's history, see David R. Starbuck and Margaret Supplee Smith, eds., *Historical Survey of Canterbury Shaker Village* (Boston: Boston University, 1979), and Starbuck, ed., *Canterbury Shaker Village: An Historical Survey* (Durham: University of New Hampshire, 1981).

61. It is important to point out that amicable relations had existed between Canterbury and Sabbathday Lake throughout the first half of the twentieth century. Members from both villages, for example, frequently visited one another.

62. Tim Clark, "Shattering the Shaker Image," *Yankee,* 44, no. 1 (1980):131–133; Richard Morse, telephone conversation with author, 6 Aug. 1990.

63. Transcript of oral history interview with Frances A. Carr, 1985, MeSl.

64. Transcript of oral history interview with Theodore Johnson, 2 May 1985, MeSl; Amy Bliss to Stephen J. Stein, 30 July 1990, author's possession; Mildred E. Barker, "In Memoriam," *Shaker Quarterly* 15 (1987):5–6. The details of Johnson's biography have been inaccurately rendered several times. See, e.g., Barker, "In Memoriam"; Rebecca Sheble, "Shaker Revival at Sabbathday Lake," *Salt: Journal of New England Culture* (Winter 1984):21; Wertkin, *Four Seasons,* 174; Mildred Barker to Helen Upton, 11 Apr. 1962, Upton Papers, NOC; and Cynthia Bourgeault, "Hands to Work, Hearts to God," *Down East: The Magazine of Maine* (December 1984):37.

65. Oral history interview with Theodore Johnson; Barker, "In Memoriam."

66. "Home Notes," *Shaker Quarterly* 2 (1962):141; 8 (1968):112. See also Edward R. Horgan, *The Shaker Holy Land: A Community Portrait* (Harvard, Mass.: Harvard Common Press, 1982), 184. Horgan eliminated discussion of the controversy, pp. 181–186, from the paper edition (1987) of his book after receiving negative reactions to it.

67. "Maine's Shakers: Does It Have to Be Suicide?" *Portland Sunday Telegram,* 5 Aug. 1973, p. 18A.

68. Clark, "Shattering," 133–134. One source reports that some limited funds were restored in 1982. See Sheble, "Shaker Revival," 36.

69. Oral history interview with Theodore Johnson.

70. Ibid.

71. Clark, "Shattering," 134–135; Robert Meader to Gertrude Soule, 24 Aug., 14 Oct. 1983, NhCa.

72. "Maine's Shakers"; Clark, "Shattering," 132–133.

73. Frances A. Carr, "Open the Doors," *Portland Press Herald,* 8 Jan. 1979.

74. Clark, "Shattering"; Mildred Barker to Tim Clark, 6 Nov. 1979, Theodore E. Johnson to Tim Clark, 7 Nov. 1980, *Yankee* archives.

75. The Canterbury community has continued to receive inquiries about possible membership over the years. See, e.g., C. W. to Canterbury Sisters, 19 Nov. 1986, and J. W. to Shaker Brethren, 7 Nov. 1986, NhCa.

76. Transcript of "The Shakers: Hands to Work, Hearts to God" (New York: Non Fiction Television, 1984); Amy Stechler Burns, *The Shakers, Hands to Work Hearts to God: The History and Visions of the United Society of Believers in Christ's Second Appearing from 1774 to the Present* (Hong King; Aperture [1987]), 11, 125. See also Jane Holtz Kay, "Last of the Shakers," *Historic Preservation* 34 (March–April 1982):14–21.

77. Wertkin, *Four Seasons,* 8, 14, 47, 169; "Home Notes," *Shaker Quarterly* 10 (1970):90, and 12 (1972):35–36; videocassette, "I Don't Want to Be Remembered as a Chair" (Timewatch, British Broadcasting Corporation, 1990).

78. June Sprigg to Gertrude Soule, 17 July 1975, June Sprigg to Bertha Lindsay, 1 June 1986, NhCa; June Sprigg, *By Shaker Hands* (New York: Alfred A. Knopf, 1975); June Sprigg, *Shaker Design* (New York: Whitney Museum of American Art, 1986); "Home Notes," *Shaker Quarterly* 14 (1974):60; Michael Taylor, "From the Bookshelf," ibid., 15 (1987):65–67; Taylor, "The Flickering Flame: 20th Century Shaker Spirituality," ibid., 17 (1989):121–134.

79. In larger religious organizations, such differences usually result in the formation of separate denominations. Because the numbers are so small, it makes little sense to speak of the "denominationalization of Shakerism." Yet in fact that is what has taken place.

80. There is no existing history of the manifestations of Shakerism in American popular culture. Perhaps this sketch will encourage further research.

81. King to Williams, 7 Feb. 1949; King to Clawson, 4 Mar. 1949.

82. Helen M. Upton, "Collecting Shaker," *Shaker Quarterly* 2 (1962). 105–109; Williams to King, 1 Feb. 1949, 9 Dec. 1957.

83. Andrews and Andrews, *Fruits*, 21–23.

84. Ibid., 23, 59–65; Sadie Neale, "Diaries," vol. 13, 29 Nov., 19 Dec. 1943.

85. "Shaker Revival," *Newsweek*, 17 Apr. 1961, 99; "Home Notes," *Shaker Quarterly* 2 (1962):96; William Lawrence Lassiter, "Shakers and Their Furniture," *New York History* 27 (1946):369–371; Barbara Harrison, "The Background of Shaker Furniture," ibid., 29 (1948):319–326; Edward Deming Andrews and Faith Andrews, *Religion in Wood: A Book of Shaker Furniture* (Bloomington: Indiana University Press, 1966); Mary Lyn Ray, "Heaven Invalidated: Divergence from Orthodoxy in Shaker Persuasion and Furniture Form" (master's thesis, University of Delaware, 1970); John G. Shea, *The American Shakers and Their Furniture with Measured Drawings of Museum Classics* (New York: Van Nostrand Reinhold, 1971), Robert F. W. Meador, *Illustrated Guide to Shaker Furniture* (New York: Dover, 1972); John Kassay, *The Book of Shaker Furniture* (Amherst: University of Massachusetts Press, 1980); Charles R. Muller and Timothy D. Rieman, *The Shaker Chair* (Winchester, Ohio: Canal Press, 1984).

86. Beverly Gordon, *Shaker Textile Arts* (Hanover, N.H.: University Press of New England, 1980), William Lawrence Lassiter, *Shaker Architecture: Descriptions with Photographs and Drawings of Shaker Buildings at Mt. Lebanon, New York, Watervliet, New York, West Pittsfield, Massachusetts* (New York: Vintage, 1966); John Poppeliers, ed., *Shaker Built: A Catalog of Shaker Architectural Records from the Historic American Buildings Survey* (Washington, D.C.: National Park Service, 1974); Dolores Hayden, *Seven American Utopias: The Architecture of Communitarian Socialism, 1790–1975* (Cambridge: MIT Press, 1976), 63–103; Herbert Schiffer, *Shaker Architecture* (Exton, Pa.: Schiffer, 1979); Edward Andrews and Faith Andrews, *Shaker Herbs and Herbalists* (Stockbridge, Mass.: Berkshire Garden Center, n.d.); Amy Bess Miller, *Shaker Herbs: A History and a Compendium* (New York: Clarkson N. Potter, 1976); Frances A. Carr, *Shaker Your Plate: Of Shaker Cooks and Cooking* (Sabbathday Lake, Maine: United Society of Shakers, 1986), 41–47; "Home Notes," *Shaker Quarterly* 11 (1971):118.

87. *Mary Whitcher's Shaker House-Keeper* (Boston: Weeks and Potter, [1882]; Piercy, *Shaker Cook Book*, 13–15. Whitcher's book was reissued in facsimile under the sponsorship of Amy Bess Miller ([Hastings-on-Hudson, N.Y.: Morgan and Morgan, 1972]). See also Amy Bess Miller and Persis Wellington Fuller, *The Best of Shaker Cooking* (New York: Macmillan, 1970); Elizabeth C. Kremer, *We Make You Kindly Welcome* (Harrodsburg, Ky.: Pleasant Hill Press, 1970); *Old Shaker Recipes* (Nashville, Ind.: Bear Wallow, 1982); and Arthur Tolve and James Bissland III, *Sister Jennie's Shaker Desserts* (Bowling Green, Ohio: Gabriel's Horn, 1983).

88. Carr, *Shaker Your Plate*, 16, 93, 97; Lindsay, *Seasoned with Grace*, vii–viii, 131. Mary Rose Boswell identifies two earlier cookbooks by the Canterbury Shakers: *Shaker Tested Recipes* (Canterbury, N.H.: n.p., [1965]); and *Gourmet's Delight: Favorite Shaker Recipes* (Canterbury, N.H.: n.p., [1968]).

89. Clara Endicott Sears to Edward Andrews, 5 Dec. 1926, Prudence Stickney to the Andrewses, 13 Jan.[?], DeWint; "Home Notes," *Shaker Quarterly* 6 (1966):19, and 8 (1968):113. In 1989 Canterbury reported 44,500 visitors at Shaker Village. Charles A. DeGrandpre to Friends of the Village, 1 Dec. 1989.

90. Miller, *Hancock Shaker Village*, 25–31, 34–41, 43–53, 93–104; Andrews and Andrews, *Fruits*, 194–196.

91. Miller, *Hancock Shaker Village*, 157, 162–163. See also John Harlow Ott, *Hancock Shaker Village: A Guidebook and History*, 2d ed. (n.p.: Shaker Community, 1976).

92. "Note dated 15 December 1941," Upton Papers, NOC; Earl D. Wallace, *Shakertown at Pleasant Hill: The First Fifteen Years* (Harrodsburg, Ky.: Shakertown at Pleasant Hill, n.d.); Wallace, *The Story of Shakertown at Pleasant Hill, Kentucky, Inc.: From Inception in 1961 to 1984* (Harrodsburg, Ky.: Shakertown at Pleasant Hill, 1984); Wallace, *The Restoration of Pleasant Hill: Authenticity in the Purest Sense* (Harrodsburg, Ky.: Shakertown at Pleasant Hill, 1987). See also Thomas D. Clark and F. Gerald Ham, *Pleasant Hill and Its Shakers* (Pleasant Hill, Ky.: Shakertown Press, 1968), 81–87.

93. Wallace, *Shakertown at Pleasant Hill*, 2–7; "Kentuckians Restore Shaker Community," *History News* 19 (1964):141.

94. Wallace, *Shakertown at Pleasant Hill*, 7–16; Wallace, *Restoration of Pleasant Hill*, 5; "Pleasant Hill's Chairman Wallace Dies," *Shaker Messenger* 12, no. 3, (1990):27.

95. "The South Union Shakers," *World of Shaker* 1 (Fall 1971):4–5; "South Union Shaker Community: Preservation Assured!" ibid. (Winter 1971):5; John H. Danner, "National Passion and National Past," *Christian Century*, 11 May 1983, 445–446. The Shaker Heritage Society sponsors a small publication series and a quarterly newsletter, the *Watervliet Shaker Journal*. The Dana Robes Wood Craftsmen firm, specializing in the manufacture of handcrafted furniture "in the Shaker tradition," is located at Lower Shaker Village.

96. Robert F. W. Meader, *Catalogue of the Emma B. King Library of the Shaker Museum* (Old Chatham, N.Y.: Shaker Museum Foundation, 1970); Andrews and Andrews, *Fruits*, 199–201; E. Richard McKinstry, *The Edward Deming Andrews Memorial Shaker Collection* (New York: Garland, 1987). The Shaker Museum and Library publishes a newsletter, the *Shaker Museum and Library Report*.

97. "North Family Barn Destroyed by Fire," *World of Shaker* 2 (Fall 1972):1; Robert F. W. Meader, "Fire Destroys Barn at Canterbury," ibid., 3 (Fall 1973):1; Meader, "Mt. Lebanon North Family Dwelling Passes into History," ibid. (Summer 1973):3; "Whitewater Meetinghouse Sold at Sheriff's Sale," *Shaker Messenger* 5 (Spring 1983):12; Fran Kramer, "Battle Lost to Save Groveland Building," ibid., 6 (Summer 1984); 19; "Enfield, Conn., Bids Farewell to Shaker Sawmill," ibid., 10 (Winter 1988):13; Ernest Wiegand, "Archaeological Study Fills Missing Links," ibid., 7 (Summer 1985):25; "Mt. Lebanon Brethren's Workshop Update," ibid., 10 (Winter 1988):15; "Mt. Lebanon Preservation Funds Granted," ibid., 11 (Summer 1989):19; David Hewett, "The Darrow School Shakes the Money Tree Again," *Maine Antique Digest* (July 1990), 26A–27A; Fran Kramer, "Mt. Lebanon's Future Becoming Uncertain," *Shaker Messenger* 12, no. 3 (1990):7; Kramer, "Darrow Collection Preserved for Now," ibid., no. 4 (1990):8; "Businessman Buys Shaker Artifacts," ibid., 8, 20.

98. "A World of Welcome!" *World of Shaker* 1 (Fall 1971):1.

99. Ibid., 1–8.

100. K. J. Kammeraad to Subscriber, 11 Nov. 1977.

101. Diana Van Kolken, *Introducing the Shakers: An Explanation and Directory* (Bowling Green, Ohio: Gabriel's Horn, 1985), 57.

102. *Shaker Messenger* 12 (Winter 1990): 2, 6.

103. Prudence A. Stickney to Edward D. Andrews, 31 Aug. 1929, DeWint; *World of Shaker* 4 (Winter 1973): 1, 7; Fran Kramer, "Shaker Antiques in the Marketplace," *Shaker Messenger* 10 (Winter 1988): 18; 11 (Summer 1989): 20–21; 12 (Winter 1990): 20; "Antiques," *Boston Sunday Globe*, 12 Aug. 1990, p. B43; "I Don't Want to Be Remembered as a Chair."

104. Jim Betts, prospectus for *Shaker Spirit*.

105. "A Hot Market That's Not Cooling," *Shaker Spirit* 1 (May 1989): 8–9, 49–50; Jim Betts, "The Shakers as New Product Developers," ibid., 10–12; Betts, "Shaker Village of Pleasant Hill," ibid., 20–25; Russell Swinton Oatman, "Shaker House: The Simple Beauty and Functionalism of Shaker Design in a Home for the Present," *Shaker Spirit* 1 (July–August 1989): 25–28; "Shaker Showcase," ibid., 29–31. The *Shaker Spirit* stopped publication after two issues.

106. Linda Butler and June Sprigg, *Inner Light: The Shaker Legacy* (New York: Alfred A. Knopf, 1985); L. Edward Purcell, *The Shakers* (New York: Crescent, 1988); John T. Kirk and Jerry V. Grant, "Forty Untouched Masterpieces of Shaker Design," *Antiques* 135, no. 5 (May 1989): 1226–1237. See, e.g., *Country Living*, which regularly features Shaker artifacts. See also "Art Historian John Kirk Explains Intent," *Shaker Messenger* 10 (Spring 1988): 13. Photographs taken by the Shakers have also recently received new attention. See "Shaker Spirituality and Photographic Documentation," a special issue of *New Mexico Studies in the Fine Arts* 11 (1987), ed. Diana Emergy Hulick and Peter Walch.

107. Alice and Martin Provensen, *A Peaceable Kingdom: The Shaker ABECEDARIUS* (New York: Viking, 1978); *Cobblestone: The History Magazine for Young People* 4 (April 1983); Edmund V. Gillon, Jr., *A Cut and Assemble Shaker Village* (West Chester, Pa.: Schiffer, 1986); Nancy M. Thompson, *Learning about Shakers: For Young People* (n.p.: Pleasant Grove, 1988); Mary Lyn Ray, *Angel Baskets: A Little Story about the Shakers* (Sanborton, N.H.: Martha Wetherbee Books, 1987); Kathleen M. Moriarty, *A Shaker Sampler Coloring Book* (Old Chatham, N.Y.: Shaker Museum, 1981); Marjoram and Rosemary, *Shaker Paper Dolls: Believers on the Beaver Creek* (Kettering, Ohio: Kitchen Table Sisters, 1981). See Jean M. Burks, "Shaker Sweaters: The Real Story," *Shaker Messenger* 13 (June 1991): 6–9, 27.

108. Tim Lamb, "Shaker Store Opens in London," *Shaker Messenger* 12 (Winter 1990): 26; videocassette, "Build a Shaker Table," with Kelly Mehler (Newtown, Conn.: Taunton, 1989); Land's End catalog, January 1987, 26; Block's advertisement; Yield House catalog; Richard V. Nalley, "The Shaker Simple Style," *USAir Magazine* 5 (June 1983): 42–54, 58–60. In 1989 an international conference on Shakerism was held at Exeter University; see Geoffrey Gale, "England's Exeter University Holds Shaker Symposium," *Shaker Messenger* 11 (Spring 1989): 25.

109. Lindsay, *Seasoned with Grace*, 31–32; Ethel Frost to Catherine Allen, 17 Mar. 1919, OClWHi IV A 8.

110. "Home Notes," *Shaker Quarterly* 2 (1962): 143; Marlene Hall to Bertha Lindsay, December 1986, NhCa; Franklin Parker to the Shakers, 26 Dec. 1987, NhCa; "Village Notes," *Shaker Messenger* 7 (Summer 1985): 20; 8 (Summer 1986): 18; 9 (Winter 1987): 17.

111. "Home Notes," *Shaker Quarterly* 1 (1961): 165–166; 6 (1966): 19; 8 (1968): 64.

112. "Home Notes," *Shaker Quarterly* 2 (1962):77, 3 (1963):96; 4 (1964):13, 61; Marguerite Frost, "Our Faith," *Shaker Quarterly* 2 (1962):4.

113. Marguerite Frost, *The Shaker Story* (Canterbury, N.H.: n.p., [1963]), [1–6]. Frost was described as "an avid student of comparative religion and a continued seeker after truth." "In Memoriam Lily Marguerite Frost, 1892–1971," *Shaker Quarterly* 11 (1971):3–4.

114. Frost, *Shaker Story*, [17–21].

115. Paul Katzeff, "Shake-up in Paradise," *Boston Herald Sunday Magazine*, 18 May 1986, p. 17; Burns, *Shakers*, 10–11; Cable Neuhaus, "The Shakers Face Their Last Amen," *People Weekly*, 2 Mar. 1987, 78. See Donald Meyer, *The Positive Thinkers: Religion as Pop Psychology from Mary Baker Eddy to Oral Roberts*, new ed. (New York: Pantheon, 1980), and Robert H. Schuller, *Self Esteem: The New Reformation* (Waco, Texas: Word Books, 1982).

116. Stickney to Neale, 24 Jan. 1936; "Home Notes," *Shaker Quarterly* 3 (1963):62. Stephen A. Marini makes the case for Sabbathday Lake's religious conservatism. He argues that the Maine Believers "had maintained the original teachings and spirituality of Shakerism more completely than perhaps any other community, and the power of that faith was the invisible essence that animated their entire experience after the Civil War as it had before." The documentary evidence for his judgment, however, is unavailable. See his essay "Shaker Documentary Literature, Photography, and the Modern Age: The Literature, 1872–1918," *New Mexico Studies in the Fine Arts* 11 (1987):9.

117. "Our Still Small Voice," *Shaker Quarterly* 1 (1961):1.

118. "Home Notes," *Shaker Quarterly* 10 (1970):120–121; 13 (1973):62.

119. "Home Notes," *Shaker Quarterly* 4 (1964):14, 126; 7 (1967):10; 8 (1968):24; 11 (1971):7; "The Fellowship of the Spirit," *Shaker Quarterly* 7 (1967):114–115; 11 (1971):135–136; Theodore E. Johnson, sermon transcript, February 1986, MeSl.

120. This paragraph and the one following are based on the author's observations.

121. Theodore E. Johnson, ed., "The 'Millennial Laws' of 1821," *Shaker Quarterly* 7 (1967):35–58; Johnson, "Biographical Account of the Life, Character & Ministry of Father Joseph Meacham the Primary Leader in Establishing the United Order of Millennial Church by Calvin Green 1827," ibid., 10 (1970):20–32, 51–68, 92–102.

122. Theodore E. Johnson, "Shakerism for Today," *Shaker Quarterly* 3 (1963):3–6.

123. Theodore E. Johnson, "Life in the Christ Spirit: Observations on Shaker Theology," *Shaker Quarterly* 8 (1968):67–76.

124. Theodore E. Johnson, "Deo Soli Gloria," *Shaker Quarterly* 4 (1964):115–117.

125. John Morgan, "Radical Christianity: On Taking the Christ-Presence Seriously," *Shaker Quarterly* 14 (1974):75–83. See also Morgan, "Experience as Knowledge: A Study in Shaker Theology," *Shaker Quarterly* 14 (1974):43–55, and Morgan, "Communitarian Communism as a Religious Experience: Exemplified in the Development of Shaker Theology" (Ph.D. diss., Hartford Seminary Foundation, 1972). Other students influenced by Johnson were Thomas Swain, Robert P. Emlen, and Virginia Weis, all of whom developed close friendships with the Believers in Maine.

126. "Home Notes," *Shaker Quarterly* 15 (1987):19. See also ibid., 3 (1963):97; 4 (1964):62–63, 109; 5 (1965):103; 6 (1966):91; 10 (1970):49; and 14 (1974):64. The Canterbury Shakers also developed close friendships with members of monastic communities. See Father Thomas [Whittaker] to Canterbury Sisters, Christmas 1987, and Karlyn Cauley to Bertha Lindsay, 6 Jan. 1988, NhCa. Cauley, a member of the Sisters of

the Divine Savior in Milwaukee, draws "in the Shaker style" and runs a Shaker art studio. See Karlyn Cauley, "Spirit and Symbol through Drawing," *Shaker Messenger* 9 (Winter 1987):8–9.

127. "Home Notes," *Shaker Quarterly* 5 (1965):139; 6 (1966):49.

128. Della Haskell, "What Is Shakerism?" *Shaker Quarterly* 1 (1961):21–25; Haskell, "Faith and Courage," ibid., 2 (1962):102–104; Haskell, "Stewardship of Life," ibid., 4 (1964):103–104.

129. Lewis Hillier, "Sister Mildred Reflects on Her Life as a Shaker," *Lewiston Daily Sun*, 6 Aug. 1974; Linda Galway, "Spiritual Leader of Maine's Shakers Dies," *Lewiston Sun-Journal*, 26 Jan. 1990.

130. R. Mildred Barker, *Holy Land: A History of the Alfred Shakers* (Sabbathday Lake, Maine: Shaker Press, 1986); Barker, *The Sabbathday Lake Shakers. An Introduction to the Shaker Heritage* (Sabbathday Lake, Maine: Shaker Press, 1985); Barker, "A Shaker Viewpoint on the Authority of the Bible," *Shaker Quarterly* 1 (1961).140 1441 Barker, "We Have Kept the Faith: Sister Mildred's Speech to the Auburn Historical Society, March 23, 1965," *Shaker Quarterly* 18 (1990):21–31.

131. Daniel W. Patterson, *The Shaker Spiritual* (Princeton: Princeton University Press, 1979), xix; "Mother Has Come with Her Beautiful Song," *Shaker Quarterly* 4 (1964):128–129. Barker's approval of Patterson's scholarship is apparent in her letter to Harold E. Cook, 10 Sept. 1961, MPH.

132. "Home Notes," *Shaker Quarterly* 6 (1966):121. A few years earlier Edward Andrews had a hand in planning "a pageant or dance drama" at Smith College, which he thought "would undoubtedly serve to popularize Shaker music" (Andrews to Harold E. Cook, 28 Sept. 1962, MPH). Barker consistently spoke out against reenactments of Shaker worship.

133. For an outstanding example of the "Home Notes," see *Shaker Quarterly* 14 (1974):147–166.

134. "Home Notes," *Shaker Quarterly* 2 (1962):111–112; 7 (1967):137; 8 (1968):29; 11 (1971):119; 13 (1973):103; Robley Edward Whitson, "The United Institute: A Clarification," *Shaker Quarterly*, 8 (1968):30, Whitson, "The Why behind the What," *Good Work*, 28 (1965):115–128, Whitson, *The Shaker Vision: Centennial Celebration, 1774–1974* (N.p., 1974); Whitson, ed., *The Shakers: Two Centuries of Spiritual Reflection* (New York: Paulist Press, 1983), xiii–xiv.

135. Program for Symposium at Yale Divinity School, 28 Mar.–1 Apr. 1979. For a more recent appropriation of Shaker forms into the Christian worship setting, see J. G. Davies, P. van Zyl, and F. M. Young, *A Shaker Dance Service Reconstructed* (Birmingham: Institute for the Study of Worship and Religious Architecture, 1984).

136. The national computer network for the exchange of information about Shakerism was organized in 1990 by Professor Marc Rhorer of the University of Kentucky, Lexington. The information exchanged about the Shakers spans a broad range of topics, from bibliography to recipes, from the substantive to the trivial.

137. When lawyers for the Shaker Central Trust Fund challenged the use of the name Shaker Arts by a manufacturing firm, Lenore A. Howe wrote, "The growing interest in the Shakers is sure to bring increased difficulties for those of you trying to protect the Shaker name. I share your concern, but doubt that the New Hampshire Shakers can stop the world's people from using the word Shaker in a generic way to describe a style of art." See Richard A. Morse to Lenore A. Howe, 29 May 1980, and Howe to Morse, 9 June 1980, NhCa.

138. Sprigg, *Shaker Design,* 6–7, 19; Edward Frost, "In Time and Eternity: The Whitney Museum Has Major Retrospective," *Kennebec Journal,* 27 June 1986, p. 12; "Upton's Address Focuses on Fountain Stone," *Shaker Messenger* 7 (Spring 1985):20.

139. Marjorie Procter-Smith, "Artifact or Icon? Clues for a Theology of Shaker Design" (paper delivered at the Shaker Museum, Old Chatham, N.Y., September 1987).

140. Faith and Edward D. Andrews wrote, "The forms created by the Believers were an authentic expression of the forces animating their life and work. Time was required, however, before the nature of the forces could be realized. In our own case Shaker furniture and other artifacts were, at first, just interesting collectibles. Appreciation of their full meaning took time and study and insight. It was a matter of really knowing the people, their devotion to a cause, their search for rightness. It was a subtle alchemy, a process of absorption, of identification, and in the end a spiritual experience." "Sheeler and the Shakers," 95.

141. See, e.g., Irving I. Zaretsky and Mark P. Leone, eds., *Religious Movements in Contemporary America* (Princeton: Princeton University Press, 1974), and John T. Biermans, *The Odyssey of New Religious Movements: Persecution, Struggle, Legitimation: A Case Study of the Unification Church* (Lewiston, N.Y.: Edwin Mellen, 1986).

142. Ronald Berman, *America in the Sixties: An Intellectual History* (New York: Harper and Rowe, 1968); Peter Clecak, "The Movement of the 1960s and Its Cultural and Political Legacy," in *The Development of an American Culture,* ed. Stanley Coben and Lorman Ratner (New York: St. Martin's, 1983), 261–311; James M. Gustafson, ed., *The Sixties: Radical Change in American Religion, Annals of the American Academy of Political and Social Science* 387 (January 1970); David F. Wells and John D. Woodbridge, eds., *The Evangelicals: What They Believe, Who They Are, Where They Are Changing* (Nashville, Tenn.: Abingdon, 1975); Dean M. Kelley, *Why Conservative Churches Are Growing: A Study in Sociology of Religion* (New York: Harper and Row, 1977).

143. These projections are not totally hypothetical. I was once visited by the owner of a tool and die manufacturing firm who had successfully broken a strong union at her shop. She was interested in knowing more about the Shakers so that she could develop an alternative sense of community for her workers. She was disappointed to learn how central the concept of union was for the Believers.

144. The works mentioned in this paragraph are reproduced in Morse, *Shakers,* 37, 272, 317, 351, and on the cover of *Shaker Messenger* 9 (Winter 1987). See also ibid., 10 (Spring and Summer 1988). See Mary Jo Flanagan, "Shaker 'Practical Spirituality,'" *Catholic Herald* 12 (November 1987):5, for an analysis of Cauley's artistic interpretation of the Shakers.

145. Cathy Newman, "The Shakers' Brief Eternity," *National Geographic* 176 (September 1989):302–325; Cathy Newman to Bertha Lindsay, 21 Apr. 1987, NhCa.

146. Van Kolken, *Introducing the Shakers,* 1.

147. Sprigg, *Shaker Design,* 19.

148. Ahlstrom, *Religious History,* 493–494.

149. D. B. to Bertha Lindsay, 27 Jan. 1985, K. F. to Bertha Lindsay, 23 Aug. 1985, J. H. to Bertha Lindsay and Gertrude Soule, 8 Sept. 1977, NhCa.

150. See "Publications of Edward Deming Andrews and Faith Andrews: A Select Chronological List, Compiled by A. D. Emerich," in *Shaker Furniture and Objects from the Faith and Edward Deming Andrews Collections Commemorating the Bicentenary of the American Shakers* (Washington, D.C.: Smithsonian Institution Press, 1973), 41–46.

151. John Cornforth, "Creating the Cult of the Shakers," *Country Life*, 21 Mar. 1974, 634; "Remaining Twelve Shakers Keep Sect's Final Vigil," *Los Angeles Times*, 11 Dec. 1974, pt. IB, p. 4. Davenport's film was produced with funds from the National Endowment for the Humanities.

152. Robert Peters, *The Gift to Be Simple: A Garland for Ann Lee* (New York: Liveright, 1975); John Fowles, *A Maggot* (London: Jonathan Cape, 1985), 5–6, 455–456.

153. *Shaker Smalls Newsletter* (January 1986). See "Home Notes," *Shaker Quarterly* 9 (1969): 133; 14 (1974): 56; Marius B. Peladeau, "At Sabbathday Lake, Maine," *World of Shaker* 4 (Fall 1974): 3; album cover for "Early Shaker Spirituals" (Sabbathday Lake, Maine: United Society of Shakers, 1976). Others, too, were once listed in the "Home Notes," as "brothers," including Kenneth Hatcher and Steven Foster. See "Home Notes," *Shaker Quarterly* 13 (1973): 17, and 14 (1974): 147.

154. Charles Edson Robinson, *A Concise History of the United Society of Believers Called Shakers* (East Canterbury, N.H.: The Shakers, 1893), iv, 32–33. The original essays appeared under the pseudonym C. R. Edson in *Manufacturer and Builder* 23–24 (1891–1892).

155. Peladeau, "At Sabbathday Lake, Maine," 1, 3; "At Canterbury, N.H.," *World of Shaker* 4 (Fall 1974): 1–2; "The Shaker Bicentennial National Convention in Cleveland, Ohio," ibid. (Winter 1974): 4.

156. Newman, "Shakers' Brief Eternity," 304. Widespread ignorance about the contemporary situation still exists. A recent essay in a travel magazine described the Shakers as "an extinct communal religious society." See Carla Kallan, "Traveling through Time," *USAir Magazine* 12 (May 1991), 59.

157. Not even the most optimistic observers of the contemporary situation propose a future without immense problems. See Flo Morse's observations about contemporary Shakerism in *The Story of the Shakers* (Woodstock, Vt.: Countryman Press, 1986), 69–91.

158. Barker, "In Memoriam," *Shaker Quarterly* 15 (1987): 5–6; Michael Taylor to Arnold Hadd, 21 Apr. 1986, and Stephen Marini to Christian Friends, 23 Apr. 1986, in *Shaker Quarterly* 15 (1987): 7–9; Flo Morse, "Brother Theodore E. Johnson Dies," *Shaker Messenger* 8 (Spring 1986): 12; Katzeff, "Shake-up in Paradise," 6–7, 17–19. This last piece includes Robley Whitson's assessment of the relationship between the two villages following Johnson's death.

159. "Gertrude Soule, 93, of Shakers," *New York Times*, 13 June 1988, p. D12; "Gertrude Soule, 93; A N.H. Shaker Leader," *Boston Globe*, 13 June 1988, p. 25; Wendy Mitman, "A Death Leaves the Shaker Faith near Extinction," *USA Today*, 15 June 1988; Darryl Thompson, "Eldress Gertrude Soule: A Personal Remembrance," *Shaker Messenger* 10 (Summer 1988): 9, 22; "In Memoriam," *Shaker Quarterly* 16 (1988): 64.

160. "The Shakers: Serene Twilight of a Once-Sturdy Sect," *Life*, 17 Mar. 1967, 58–67; Hillier, "Sister Mildred Reflects on Her Life as a Shaker"; "Shaker Bicentennial: Is the End Near?" *Newsweek*, 21 Nov. 1983, 24; Mildred Barker to Harold Cook, 29 Aug. 1961, MPH; Galway, "Spiritual Leader of Maine's Shakers Dies," reprinted as "Sister Mildred Dies at Sabbathday Lake," *Shaker Messenger* 12 (Winter 1990): 8, 19; Elaine Disch to Friends of the Shakers, 3 Feb. 1990; "In Memoriam Sister R. Mildred Barker, 1897–1990," *Shaker Quarterly* 18 (1990): 3–5. Barker's picture was on the cover of *Smithsonian* 5 (September 1974). That photograph, in turn, appeared on billboards advertising the magazine.

161. Lindsay, *Seasoned with Grace*, 1–3; "Bertha Lindsay, Last of the Shaker Eldresses, Dies," *Shaker Messenger* 13, no. 1 (1991):9; Jane McLaughlin, "God Bless You, I Love You," ibid., 9–10; "In Memoriam, Eldress Bertha Lindsay (1897–1990)," *News* 5, no. 1 (1991); *Clarion* 16 (Winter 1991):2; "In Memoriam: Eldress Bertha Lindsay, 1897–1990," *Shaker Quarterly* 18 (1990):117–119. Through the years Lindsay received scores of letters from children who had visited Canterbury. One fourth grader summarized the excitement many have felt after meeting the Shakers. He wrote, "I heard that the Shakers had a barn almost as long as three football fields. That was the funnest field trip I've ever been on." Ryan Ouellette to Bertha Lindsay, 21 Oct. 1987, NhCa.

162. Galway, "Spiritual Leader of Maine's Shakers Dies"; M. Kathleen Wagner, "At Sabbathday Lake, Two Try to Revive the Past," *Kennebec Journal,* 27 June 1986, p. 12.

163. Newman, "Shakers' Brief Eternity," 316, 324.

164. Wayne Smith to Stephen J. Stein, 29 Jan. 1990, author's possession; "Home Notes," *Shaker Quarterly* 11 (1971):170–171.

165. Richard L. Williams, "The Shakers, Now Only Twelve, Observe Their Two Hundredth Year," *Smithsonian* 5 (September 1974):48. See Frances Carr, "A Letter to Jennifer, Written from Chosen Land, August 6, 1974," *Shaker Quarterly* 14 (1974):84–86; "She Labored for the Gift: Eldress Prudence Stickney," ibid., 17 (1989):135–153; and oral history interview with Frances Carr. See also Carr's public remarks concerning Bertha Lindsay in "A Tribute," *Shaker Quarterly* 18 (1990):119.

166. See Arnold Hadd, "And I Shall Make You a Fisher of Men: The Life and Testimony of Elder Elisha Pote," *Shaker Quarterly* 17 (1989):55–66, and Hadd, "To the Memory of Our Dear Fathers in the Gospel: Elder John Vance and Elder William Dumont," ibid., 194–213.

167. "Editor's Notes," *Shaker Quarterly* 17 (1989):70. For a glimpse into the family life of the Maine Believers, see Sheble, "Shaker Revival at Sabbathday Lake," 18–37, and Bourgeault, "Hands to Work, Hearts to God," 34–39, 62–63. The fullest account of life among the Maine Shakers is Wertkin, *Four Seasons*.

168. "Bud: Inspired by Shaker Ideals," *News* 3 (October 1989), [2]; "Home Notes," *Shaker Quarterly* 15 (1987):62. The *News* is a newsletter published by Shaker Village at Canterbury.

169. The Friends of the Shakers at Sabbathday Lake publish a newsletter entitled *Clarion*.

170. For some thoughtful reflections on the resurgence of the Americana movement in the 1950s and 1960s, see Thomas J. Schlereth, "Material Culture Studies in America, 1876–1976," in *Material Culture Studies in America,* ed. Schlereth (Nashville, Tenn.: American Association for State and Local History, 1982), 29–32.

171. Recent feminist studies of the Shakers include Sally L. Kitch, *Chaste Liberation: Celibacy and Female Cultural Status* (Urbana: University of Illinois Press, 1989); Linda A. Mercadante, *Gender Doctrine and God: The Shakers and Contemporary Theology* (Nashville, Tenn.: Abingdon Press, 1990); and Marjorie Procter-Smith, *Shakerism and Feminism: Reflections on Women's Religion and the Early Shakers* (Old Chatham, N.Y.: Shaker Museum and Library, 1991). The National Historic Communal Societies Association, the International Communal Studies Association, and the Shaker Seminar sponsored annually by Berkshire Community College are three of the primary organizations committed to continuing study. In addition, there are Shaker study groups scattered across the United States, from New England to California.

172. Melcher, *Shaker Adventure,* 244–245; Newman, "Shakers' Brief Eternity," 316; "All Things Anew," *Shaker Quarterly* 12 (1972):119–120; 17 (1989):70–71.

SUGGESTIONS

FOR

FURTHER

READING

There is a wealth of primary materials available to persons interested in Shaker studies, and readers should turn to these sources for further study. I have identified in the notes the principal scholarly publications that deal with the Believers. Access to both published and unpublished Shaker materials is possible through microfilm and microfiche collections, which interlibrary loan services put within the reach of everyone in the United States.

Few contemporary documents remain from the Age of the Founders. Those manuscripts that are extant deal principally with legal and financial affairs. The most significant publication bearing on the early years is the *Testimonies of the Life, Character, Revelations and Doctrines of Our Ever Blessed Mother Ann Lee, and the Elders with Her* (1816), edited by Rufus Bishop and Seth Y. Wells. Valuable information about the earliest Shakers also appears in the polemical literature directed against the society by apostates and outsiders, including tracts by Valentine, Reuben, and Daniel Rathbun, Benjamin West, and Amos Taylor.

Manuscript resources become abundant for the study of Shakerism after the turn of the nineteenth century. These include such religious documents as church covenants, personal testimonies, society regulations, and membership lists. Financial records provide detailed accounts of expenditures and sales for families as well as for individual shops and industries. The correspondence exchanged among the Believers is especially revelatory. The Western Reserve Historical Society's collection contains a large number of letters. Family journals and private diaries from these same years also abound.

During the Formative Period the society launched its initial publication efforts, beginning with Joseph Meacham's *Concise Statement of the Principles of the Only True Church* (1790), Richard McNemar's *Kentucky*

Revival (1807), and Benjamin S. Youngs's *Testimony of Christ's Second Appearing* (1808). Other major theological and historical works followed within the next two decades, including the *Testimonies,* John Dunlavy's *Manifesto* (1818), and the *Summary View of the Millennial Church* (1823), by Calvin Green and Seth Y. Wells. Nevertheless, outsiders continued to attack the United Society. Works by Thomas Brown, Eunice Chapman, and Mary Marshall Dyer gained wide audience.

The Middle Period of Shaker history is more fully documented in the manuscript record than any other age. Abundant family journals describe a range of phenomena, including daily weather patterns, the comings and goings of visitors, business transactions, religious observances, and innocent amusements—immense resources for study. The central ministry's journals for this period are available at the New York Public Library. Documents detailing the spiritualistic revivals and records of the inspired messages and other gifts constitute perhaps the largest single group of unpublished Shaker manuscripts. The revelations given to Philemon Stewart, the *Sacred and Divine Roll* (1843), and to Paulina Bates, the *Divine Book of Wisdom* (1849), are especially significant.

Apostates and outsiders, including Hervey Elkins, David Lamson, and Charles Nordhoff, offered commentary on the Shakers. In the Middle Period, Frederick W. Evans emerged as the leading public voice for the Believers, publishing scores of essays, broadsides, and tracts, including his *Autobiography* (1869). In 1870 the society launched its own periodical, *The Shaker,* which served as a means of intervillage communication as well as public representation to the outside world.

After 1876 the manuscript records thin out as the number of members declined. During this Time of Transformation the Shakers' monthly publication charts the changing patterns of thought and life. The society also issued a host of other publications, addressing religious and social issues, by such authors as Antoinette Doolittle, Aurelia Mace, Anna White, Alonzo Hollister, Hervey Eads, Henry Blinn, and Catherine Allen. Eads published a major theological statement in *Shaker Sermons: Scripto-Rational* (1879); Mace issued *The Aletheia* (1899).

In the twentieth century, the stream of documents produced by the Shakers, both published and unpublished, has shrunk. The most important early publication of the period was *Shakerism Its Meaning and Message* (1904) by Anna White and Leila S. Taylor. Family journals were kept irregularly; the central ministry journals, if any were kept, are unavailable. The preoccupation with family survival replaced regular record keeping.

Bertha Lindsay, *Seasoned with Grace* (1987), provides a view of life at Canterbury in the opening decades of the century.

Documents from the Believers dating from the second half of the twentieth century are relatively few. The correspondence of the Shakers is scattered among various repositories. The letters collected at Canterbury are especially instructive. No family journals from this period are available for scholars. After 1961 the *Shaker Quarterly* provides useful information about the Maine Believers, including essays by Theodore E. Johnson. Information concerning the Shakers at both Canterbury and Sabbathday Lake has been a regular feature of the *World of Shaker* and the *Shaker Messenger*. Magazine articles, newspaper accounts, documentary films, and photographic essays provide additional information. Gerard C. Wertkin, *Four Seasons of Shaker Life* (1986), offers an inside view of life at Sabbathday Lake in the mid-1980s.

The manuscript collection at the Western Reserve Historical Society is the largest and most comprehensive, containing materials from every Shaker settlement. Kermit J. Pike, *A Guide to Shaker Manuscripts* (1974), is an invaluable finding aid for this collection, which is available on microfilm. The Library of Congress and the Henry Francis du Pont Winterthur Museum possess large, diverse manuscript collections. The manuscripts at the Library of Congress are on microfilm; for materials at Winterthur, E. Richard McKinstry has compiled a useful guide, *The Edward Deming Andrews Memorial Shaker Collection* (1987). Diversified manuscript collections exist at the Emma B. King Library in Old Chatham, New York, the Williams College Library, the New York State Library, and the New York Public Library. Those who wish to examine materials bearing especially on the last three eastern villages should consult the collections at Hancock Shaker Village, Shaker Village at Canterbury, and the United Society of Shakers at Sabbathday Lake. Manuscript collections focusing on western Shakerism are located at the Ohio State Historical Society, the Filson Club in Louisville, the University of Kentucky, and Western Kentucky University.

INDEX

Willard, Francis, 319
Willard, Isaac, 23
Willard, Julian, 171
Willard, Nathan, 142
Williams, Esther, 167
Williams, J. William, 212
Williams, John S., 379
Williams College, 373
Willis Henry auction, 405–406
Wilson, Delmer: and automobile, 291; illness and death of, 367, 386, 387; mentioned, 398; photograph of, 362; as Santa Claus, 302; on spirit communication, 321; tasks of, 361
Wilson, Josephine E., 347, 374
"wind, fire, and earthquake," 169
Winfrey, Oprah, 406
Winnepesaukee, Lake, 299
Winship, Ella E., 345, 347
Winter, William F., Jr., 375 376, 377
"winter Shaker," 162, 257
Wise, Stephen S., 319
witchcraft, 15, 78, 129
Witham, Maria, 290
witnesses. See eye and ear witnesses; first witnesses; living witnesses
Woburn, Mass., 24
women: advice to, 197; in American culture, 53, 263, 272; central role in redemption, 195; clothing of, 265; criticized, 30, 31, 215, 230, 260; drive for rights, 205, 206, 207, 260, 261, 262, 310–312; elderly, 359, 367; excluded from theological writing, 76; among French Prophets, 6; among instruments, 187; and labor-saving devices, 492n.61; as leaders of the society, xvii, 132–133, 241, 256, 257–259, 349; love and affection among, 270; molested, 164; new Shaker women, 262–263, 272; opposition to leadership by, 48, 52–53, 129, 187; outnumber men, 256; and periodical, 258–260; sanitary concerns, 492n.62; as trustees, 270, 272, 285; at Upper Canaan, 248, 250; widows in society, 257; work of, 61, 99–100, 140, 152–154, 268–270, 272, 296–297, 398
Woodman, Aaron, 27
"Word of the Lord Against the Physical Sins of his Zion, The" (Stewart), 205
work ethic, 139, 161, 346

"world," the: accommodation to, xvi, 200, 205; Believers embraced by, 409; condemned by the society, xiii, 94–95, 210, 409; interaction with, 135, 142, 274; separation from, xvi, 12, 198–199, 333
world of Shaker, xvii, 358, 409, 441, 442
World of Shaker, 403–404, 405
World's Parliament of Religions, 320, 323
World War II, 345, 425
Worley, Malcolm, 58, 59, 60–61, 188
worship: changes in, 47–48, 101–105, 331; disappeared at sites, 298; ecstasy in, 3–4, 17, 105; foot washing in, 105; lithograph of, 102; music in, 331; praised, 221; ridiculed, 102, 175, 217, 220; at Sabbathday Lake, 387, 415–416, 421
Wright, Dorothy, 325
Wright, Eleazar. See McNemar, Richard
Wright, Lucy: as administrator, 45, 49, 50, 53, 54, 92, 95, 124; as associate of Ann Lee, 27, 43, 53; background of, 53, 79; charged with isolation from members, 55; conflict with Alfred, 129; death and burial of, 95, 107–108, 113, 232; as first in the ministry, xv, 43, 49, 53, 57, 78; introduces motioning, 104; mentioned, 65, 66, 122, 257; as "Mother," 49, 50, 51, 57, 84, 107, 117; opposition from men, 53, 92; place in Shaker history, 49, 57, 116–118, 466n.198; quoted, 144; recipient of gifts, 93, 95; relation to J. Meacham, 48; during revival, 170, 191, 195; sayings of, 104; on succession, 122–123; and western enterprise, 57, 60, 63, 73, 74, 90; and writing of theology, 67, 69, 73, 74, 83, 87
writing, 9, 67, 69
Wuthnow, Robert, 356
Wyoming, 495n.85

Yale Divinity School, 422
Yale University, 374, 382, 400
Yankee, 390, 407
Yankee zone, 11, 15
"yea and nay," 17, 432
yearly sacrifice, 232, 301, 302. See also annual fast
Yellow Springs, Ohio, 217
Yon, Christana, 162